Art, Word and Image

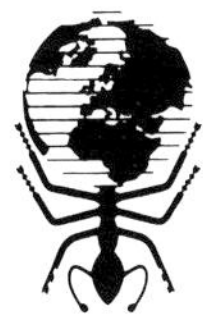

Art, Word and Image

Two Thousand Years of Visual/Textual Interaction

JOHN DIXON HUNT

DAVID LOMAS

MICHAEL CORRIS

with essays by Jeremy Adler, Stephen Barber, Rex Butler and Laurence Simmons, Joseph Viscomi, Hamza Walker, Barbara Weyandt, Michael White

REAKTION BOOKS

Published by Reaktion Books Ltd
33 Great Sutton Street
London EC1V 0DX, UK
www.reaktionbooks.co.uk

First published 2010

Designed by Finn Lewis

Printed and bound in China by C&C Offset Printing Co., Ltd

British Library Cataloguing in Publication Data

Hunt, John Dixon.
Art, word and image: 2000 years of visual/textual interaction.
1. Words in art.
I. Title II. Lomas, David. III. Corris, Michael.
701'.08-DC22

ISBN 978 1 86189 520 2

Contents

Preface *by* Michael R. Leaman 7

Introduction *by* John Dixon Hunt 15

I The Fabric and the Dance: Word and Image to 1900 35
JOHN DIXON HUNT

1 Blake's Illuminated Word *by* Joseph Viscomi 87

II 'New in art, they are already soaked in humanity': Word and Image 1900–1945
DAVID LOMAS 111

2 Paul Klee as 'Poet-Painter' *by* Jeremy Adler 178

3 Sense and Nonsense in Kurt Schwitters *by* Michael White 203

III Word and Image in Art since 1945
MICHAEL CORRIS 215

4 August Walla: Devil/God, Image/Text *by* Stephen Barber 317

5 'The Sound of Painting': Colin McCahon *by* Rex Butler and Laurence Simmons 329

6 Revelation in Image and Word: The Apocalypse according to Horst Haack *by* Barbara Weyandt 346

7 Raymond Pettibon: Words and Images *by* Hamza Walker 365

References 381
Contributors 397
Select Bibliography 399
Photo Acknowledgements 402
Index 406

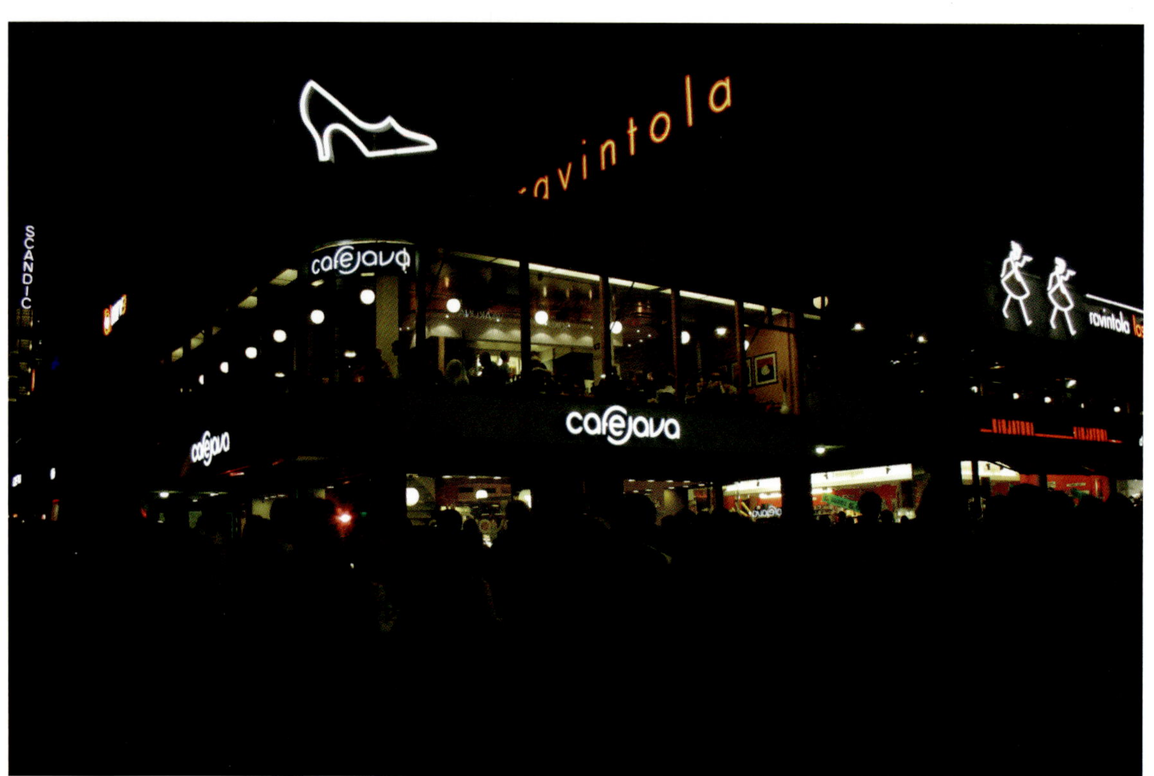
ravintola
cafejava
SCANDIC
cafejava
cafejava
ravintola

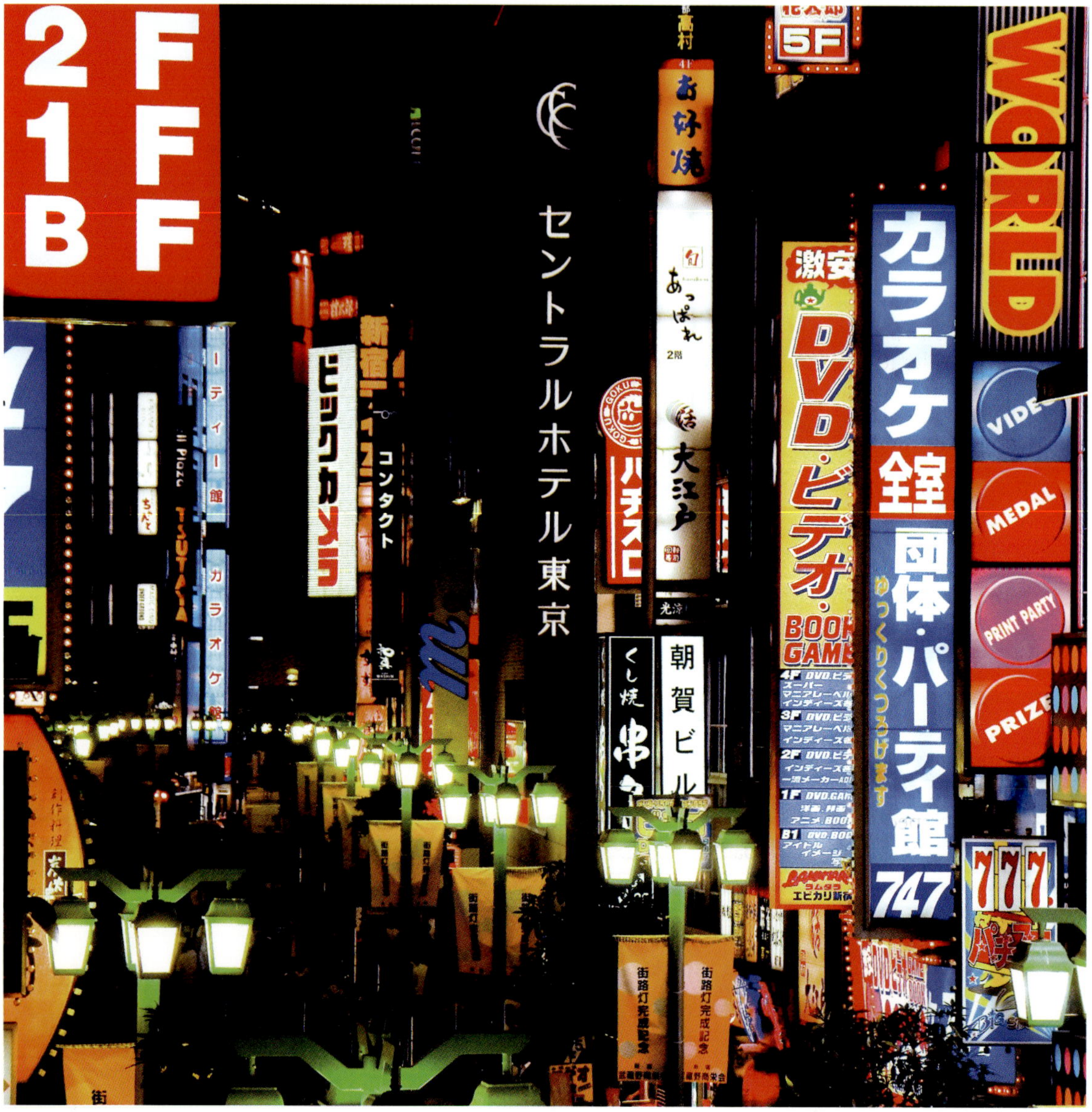

Preface

MICHAEL R. LEAMAN

Walking Helsinki's streets at night or in Shinjuku, Tokyo, a forest of neon signs flash, defying translation, street signs direct speeding vehicles, advertisement screens relay their messages, loud music from a passing car drowns out the engines' hum. Recorded in a photograph, a film – memories of a scene frozen in paint?

We live in a world saturated with word and image. Was it always so? At what points in history did word and image combine? How can such a history be constructed, particularly in relation to the visual arts?

Egyptian tombs were covered with paintings of scenes from everyday life and with hieroglyphic commentaries on both those scenes and the lives of those buried within the tombs. Most of those who painted the scenes were trained as scribes, and required to draw the hieroglyphic inscriptions as well. Roman buildings bore inscriptions on their facades celebrating the gods and the owners of those edifices. Babylonian and Etruscan haruspicy was solidified in clay and in bronze versions of animal livers respectively. Runes in Norway and Denmark in the Viking period were carved on stones, and rune stones acted as roadside memorials, with both magical and mundane messages. Vikings lived in Constantinople for long periods and visited Hagia Sophia, the greatest Christian cathedral of the Byzantine empire. Their presence is attested by runic inscriptions found there.

When writing was manual, from the eighth century onwards illuminated manuscripts teemed with images and letters which could metamorphize into beasts or human forms, and by the fifteenth century images often took over the background and foreground of letters in such manuscripts to create illusions of space. Books of the Italian Renaissance continued this tradition but with the addition of perspectival images which turned the book into a quasi-theatrical space of transforming scenes as pages turned, sometimes with *trompe l'œil* imagery which made them into multi-sided reflections of meaning. Lutheran images used words as propaganda; they were decorative as well as communicative and pedagogical. Images and prints of the Northern Renaissance contained such

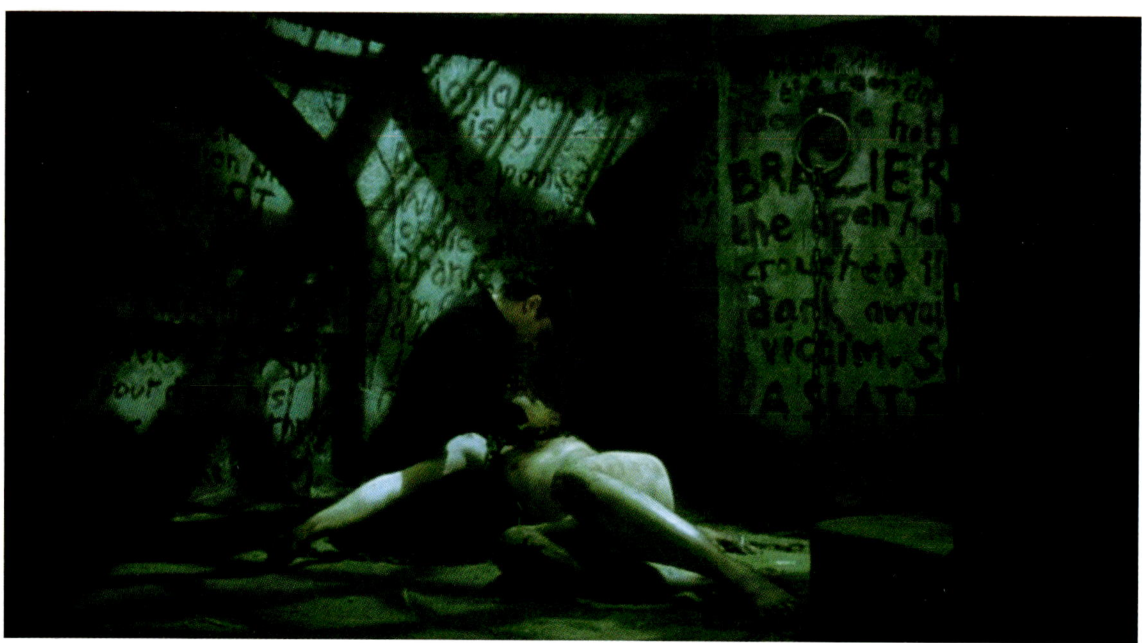

3 The Marquis de Sade, having had his writing materials and tongue removed, makes his prison walls his writing canvas in *Quills*, director Philip Kaufman, 2000.

messages in interesting and innovative combinations, occasionally including speech bubbles which look just like those in today's cartoons. Luther instructed parents to cover their houses with biblical quotations.[1]

With the advent of printing in its many forms – woodcuts, engravings, etchings and of course the Gutenberg press and later lithography – the sheer amount of images and texts disseminated knew no bounds. Thereafter both word and image had political as well as social and religious significance. As a result, both words and images became the objects of censorship. When either were restricted they found ways of transformation to escape their oppressors (illus. 3). The powerful images made for public display during the French Revolution (illus. 4), with analogous images produced across the Channel in Britain by artists such as James Gillray and later George Cruikshank, brought about radical new ways of grabbing the attention of the viewer and were the antecedents of the poster art of the nineteenth century, which in turn changed the face of the city and gave visual artists a radically new platform of expression. Modernism found ways of replicating the experiences of the modern city – letters and words began to cover the city's streets, hoardings and surfaces, and soon also inhabited the surfaces of painting, as in Cubism, or were stuck to their surfaces as collages. Futurism carried with it an aggressive barrage of typography and onomatopoeic utterances, Dada and Russian Suprematism could involve a wide range of manifestations including innovations in typography and references to the urban and rural (illus. 5). As David Lomas's essay in this book explains, Surrealism was also a highly significant moment – not surprisingly since it was both a literary and visual enterprise from the start with the influence of Freudian psychology at its origins. In automatism and the object/poem this dream quality is visible, as in the play of photographs and images in such works as *Nadja* by André Breton and *La Mort et les Statues* by Jean Cocteau and Pierre Jahan.

The story of the twentieth century and beyond involves an accelerating and intensifying engagement with the textual and verbal in the visual arts, complicated no doubt by the parallel development of photography, film and the video/digital arts. This should not be seen as one linear progression, but rather as a trajectory on a spiralling and giddy path with some highs and lows. The concrete and visual poetry word/image experiments of Guillaume Apollinaire, Blaise Cendrars and Sonia Delaunay, Stéphane Mallarmé, Augusto de Campos,

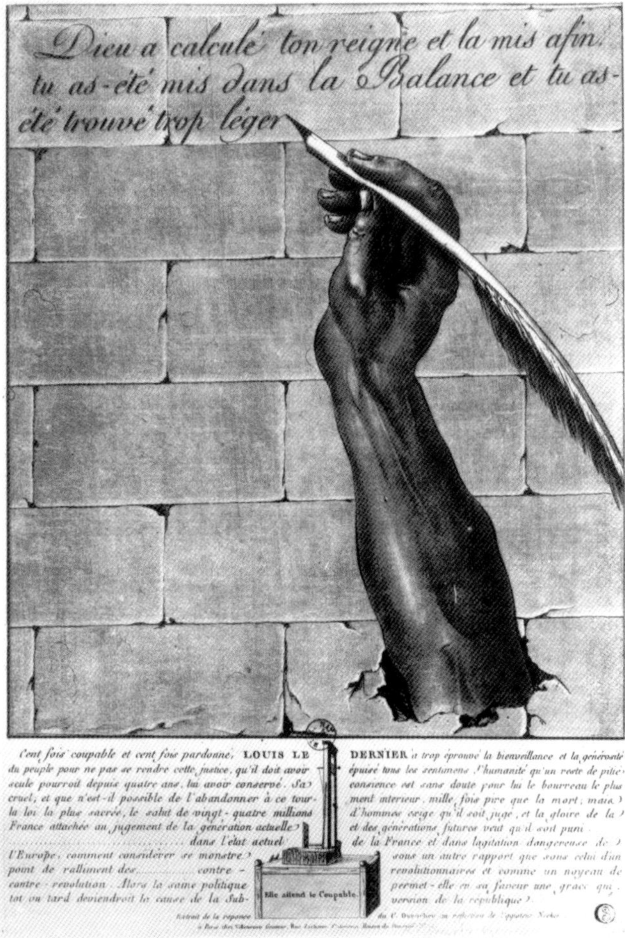

4 Villeneuve, *Traitor Louis XVI Read Your Sentence*, 1793, etching and aquatint.

'In Roman law the word *manus* has the meaning of "power" and its derivations imply either juridicial gestures having the function of transmitting, raising or recognizing a power, or the power itself': J. C. Schmitt, *La Raison des Gestes dans l'Occident Medievale* (Paris, 1990), pp. 100–101.

Eugen Gomringer, Francisco Pino and Ian Hamilton Finlay are significant historical moments (with historical antecedents), but they seem far from the concerns of many contemporary practitioners of conceptual art, where self-reflective meaning is imbued in a short (sometimes seemingly banal) statement on a gallery wall (Lawrence Weiner).

Tachism from the 1940s onwards involved the spontaneous marking of the canvas and was a link with both the automatism of the Surrealists and the calligraphy of China and Japan. This was investigated in different ways by artists such as Henri Michaux, Mark Tobey, Cy Twombly and Jackson Pollock. The body became the main instrument of writing, the hand or arm its slave or executioner, exemplified in its most extreme form by the naked body of a woman imprinted on a canvas (Yves Klein). The Nouveaux Réalistes and Situationists both wanted to subvert the world of the mass media and reorder information and this found its form in a renewed interest in collage and decollage (Raymond Hains, Jacques Villeglé) and printed materials, reassembled fragments and processes of tearing in which meaningful words disappeared. Once we enter the realm of contemporary art one can see strands of influences from the conceptual art of the 1960s and '70s as well as Pop art and the world of commercial advertising. A new freedom from the constraints of language or the literary world is demonstrated by artists who benefited from earlier practitioners and who subverted the act of reading, as Michael Corris describes in his essay in this book, as well as those artists today working in a 'postmedia of culture'. There is no doubt that 'Word and Image' has taken its place at the centre stage of contemporary artistic practice.

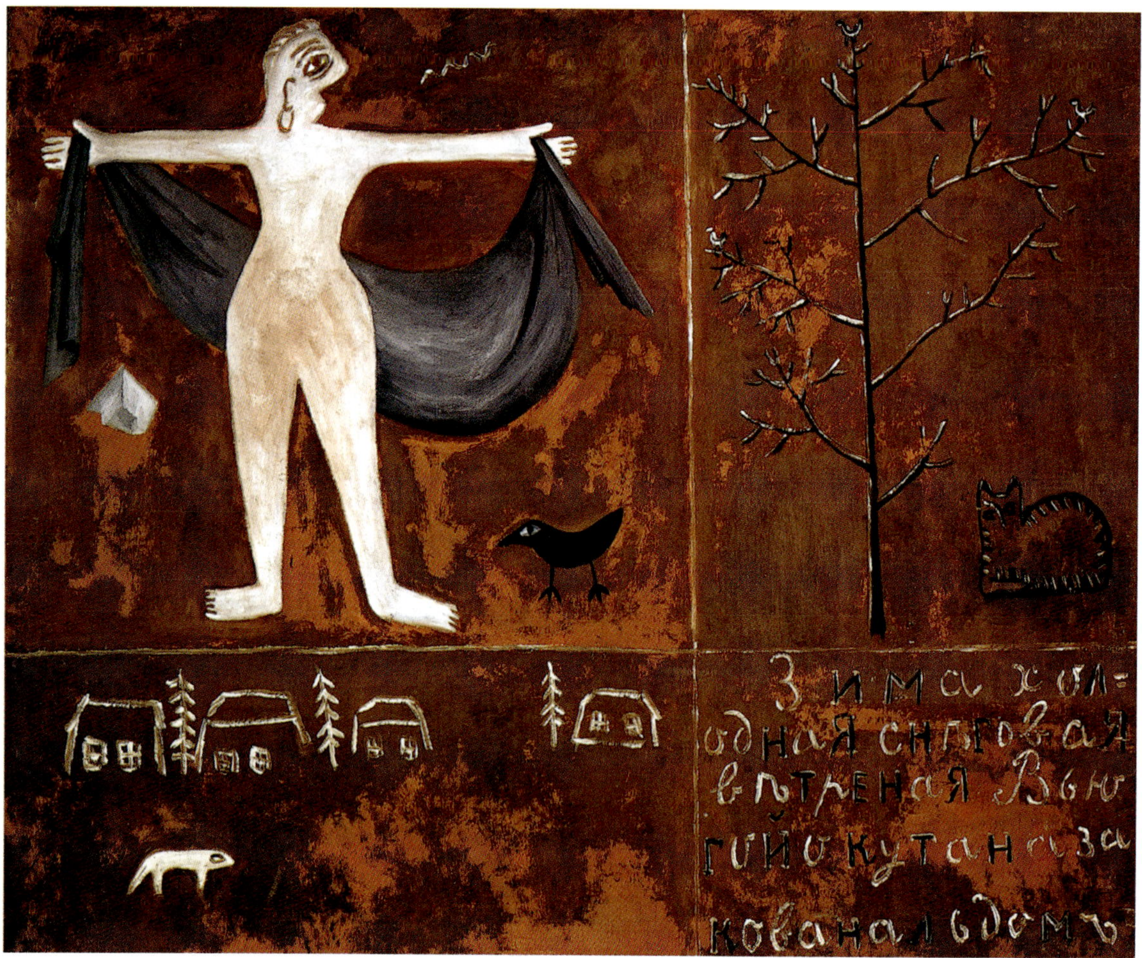

5 Mikhail Larionov, 'Winter', from *The Seasons Series*, 1912, oil on canvas: 'Winter cold, snowy, windy, of storms armour-clad in ice'.

The idea of a dialectic of word and image can be taken further to a trilectic combination of art, word and music or indeed to the *Gesamtkunstwerk* which became a feature of modernism in the nineteenth century. Many forms of experimental film could be taken as *Gesamtkunstwerken*. Let us not forget that the cinema or computer screen is rectangular, like a typical canvas, and that sounds, words and images appear on it in an array of combinations. Sound texts accompanying images fall conceptually within the scope of this book.

These are merely bite-sized observations about what follows in this book and the reader will need to read and look further to get a sense of the complexity and diversity of imagery entailed in the multi-faceted subject of word and image.

There are histories of painting from antiquity to the present and there are histories of writing and language. This book attempts to construct in the reader's mind connections between different ways of using words (or language) in art – most often painting. What does it mean when a painting is invaded by another medium, another powerful form of communication? How do the two forms interact, combine; and what messages are intended for the viewer? For when language appears in painting or art, we can be sure that the reason for this is beyond the merely aesthetic – for otherwise, why not just stick to painting or pure language? Whether the picture frame is invaded by doodlings, as with Adolf Wölfli's seemingly irrational scribbles, or a plea to spirituality is blazened across a vast canvas, as in the moving images of Colin McCahon, we can be sure that words here have a special meaning – one beyond normal language and communication.

Writing involves language systems and communication. In reality, painting contains and is constrained by many similar systems to language. Painting and writing are in many ways analagous. The languages of painting rely, like language itself, on precedent and imagination; in every age they rely on conventions – and it is only (seemingly) so in our own age that there are no constraints on such conventions. So both these modes of communication are effective in their own ways – early cave paintings told a story, as did hieroglyphs and similar writing systems like the Sumerian. (Egyptian hieroglyphs generated the Arabic, Mongol and Manchu scripts and were the indirect inspiration for Sanskrit.[2]) The word has never been just a means of communication and the word *as* image has historically taken on symbolic as well as magical and mystical properties, whether alchemical, kabbalistic, runic or astrological, not to mention what we now consider mainstream religious symbolism. Mapping is another example of communication with an aesthetic and imaginistic dimension.

Let us not forget that the process of writing is not so different from painting: we write with the artistic medium of ink; the Chinese and Japanese write traditionally with a brush (illus. 7 and 8); and in Islamic lands the scribe's pen can lead to woven incantations (illus. 6). When we write we search our imagination and set down thoughts in language. The piece of paper we mark is our canvas, a blank infinity which can be filled like a painting by Roman Opalka or minimally inscribed with a haiku or one-word poem. A canvas is similarly an infinite and blank space to which textures and colour can be added. In one sense, the written word (or character in Chinese) is already an inscription with both meaning and artistry. Even with the advent of printing the printed word carried and continued the historical

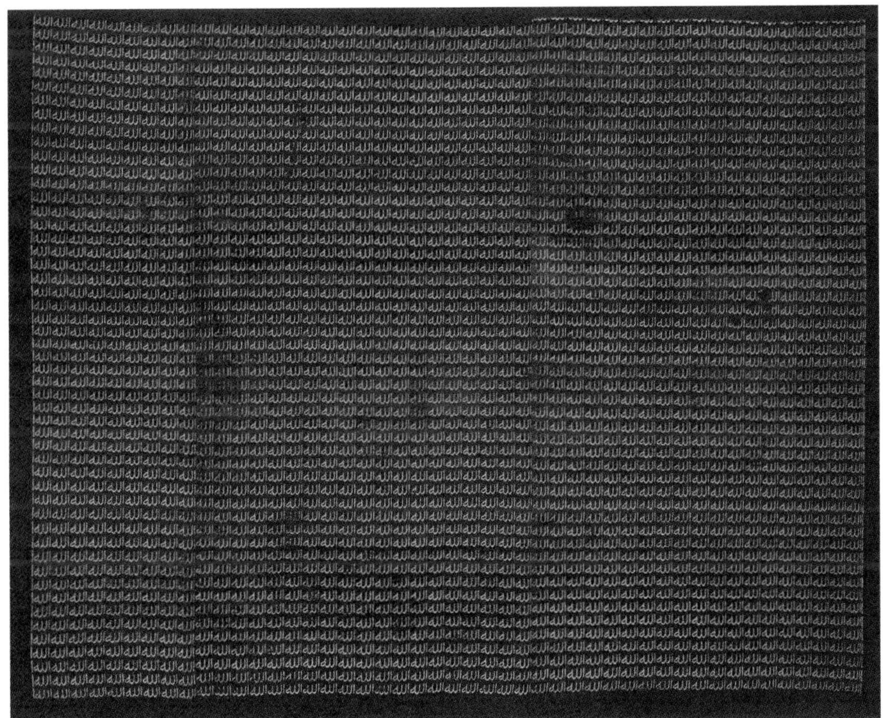

6 An 18th-century North African plain weave silk panel with a single word, *Allah*, repeated.

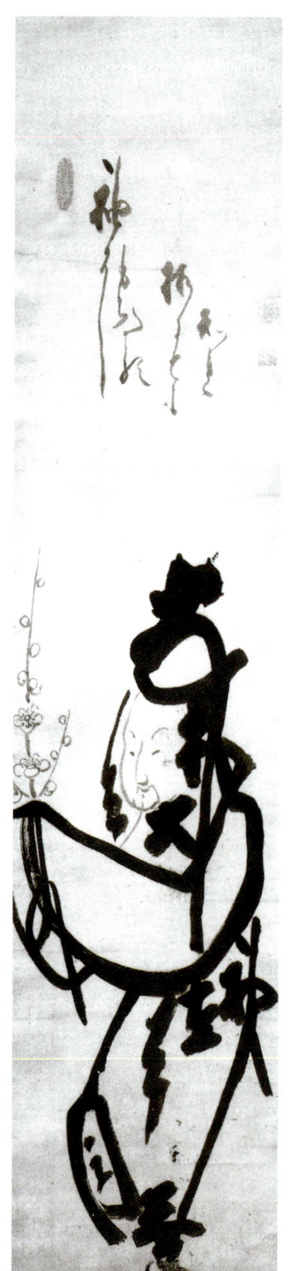

7 Ekaku Hakuin (1685–1769), *Tenjin*, sumi on paper. Tenjin is the deified form of a 9th-century scholar. His body is constructed out of the incantation 'Hail to Tenjin, God of Great Freedom at Temman Shrine'.

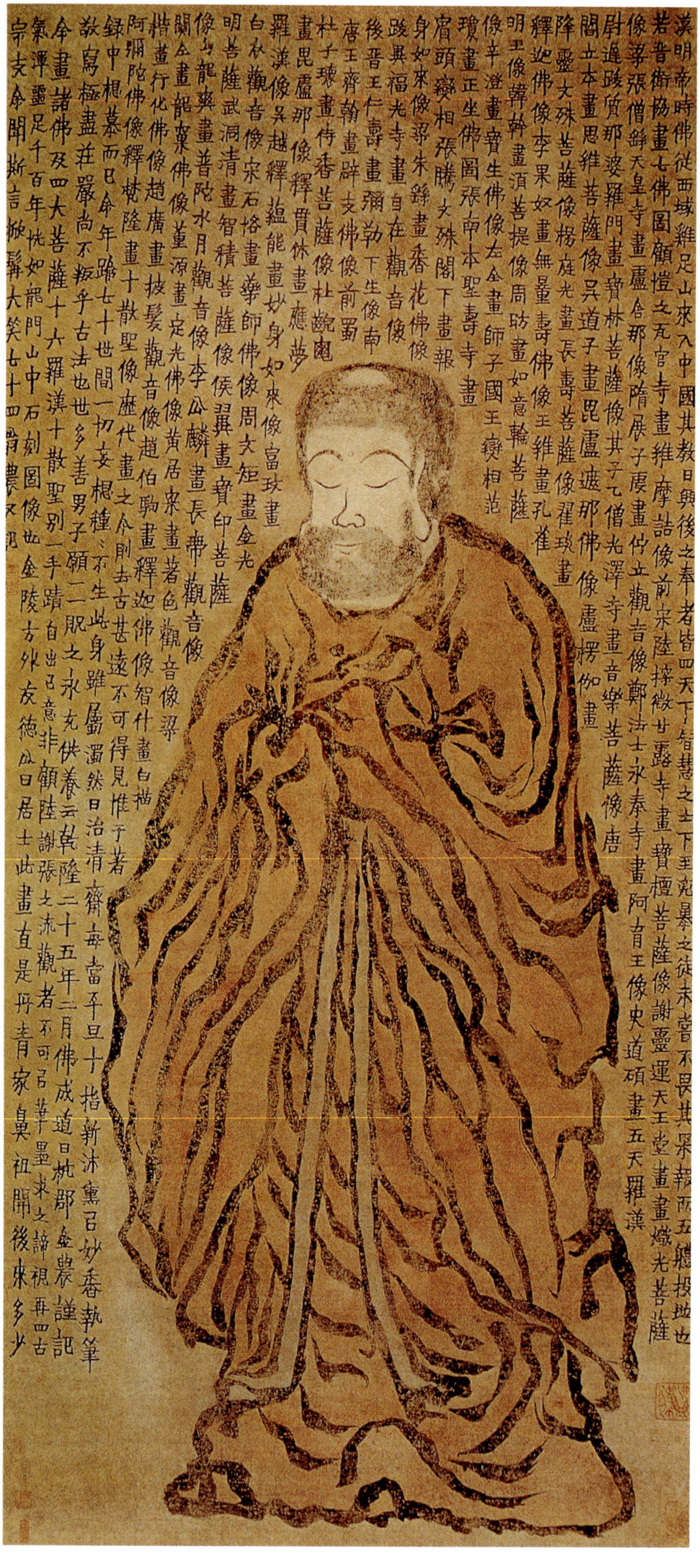

8 Jin Nong, *Shakyamuni Buddha*, 1760, hanging scroll, ink and colour on paper. An extraordinary image of a standing Buddha, archaic in its effect, entirely surrounded by writing like certain stone reliefs from pre-Tang times.

trajectory of its written ancestors (since typography in wood and later metal developed from handwriting), just as all painting retains a consciousness of the history of painting.

This book looks at many kinds of art in relationship to word and image and tries to analyse different forms and historical developments across a huge time span. Art must here be interpreted in the broadest sense, and the authors of the essays in this book try to stretch the conventional notions of what is constituted in word/image relationships by providing many new and thought-provoking ways of conceptualizing word and image in reference to developments in art and other artistic spheres. Not only is the formal relationship of word and image discussed, but also the 'naming' of the image, either its titling (surprisingly, artists have only given their own titles to their paintings within the last 150 years or so), inscriptions within or without paintings, and the stories conveyed by paintings whose narratives are meant to be 'read' by the viewer. We now come to a paradoxical situation in contemporary art where a phrase, word or title can become the key to the very *raison d'être* of a work of art (as in the work of Marcel Duchamp or Jimmie Durham). This book also deals with collaborations between writers and artists such as Blaise Cendrars and Sonia Delaunay, and the literary ambitions of visual artists, such as Paul Klee and William Blake. As artists became interested in words, so poets and writers became fascinated by the visuality and form of language. It also touches on the book as a medium for interplay between text and image (this crops up at several historical junctures, but the reader should not look here for a consequential history of the book as art, whether in the form of illuminated manuscripts, emblem books, *livres illustrés* or the artist's book of the last 40 years or so).

The three major historical essays in this book provide itineraries through the terrain I have outlined here, while the spotlight essays on major artists whose work entails a consequential engagement with word and image show in more depth how such issues impinge on the artistic process.

The story of word and image also involves the story of a jostling for position and prestige among the arts – and it is said that art as we know it has only existed for about two centuries.[3] No longer were images subordinate to words. There are various levels at which visual art can become verbal or textual – the stories which images tell or even the resonances in the eye of the beholder through criticism of the artwork. We do not come to art in a state of innocence. Prisms of meanings are added to these readings when words inhabit the surface of paintings.

Despite formalist claims by those who claim that the arts are separate and who would wish to constrain and categorize them, this book celebrates the 'dance', as elegantly expressed by John Dixon Hunt, between the word and the image, a dance which has intensified in frenzy and which disrupts neat categories but opens up words of spiralling correspondences – a reflection of a world in motion.

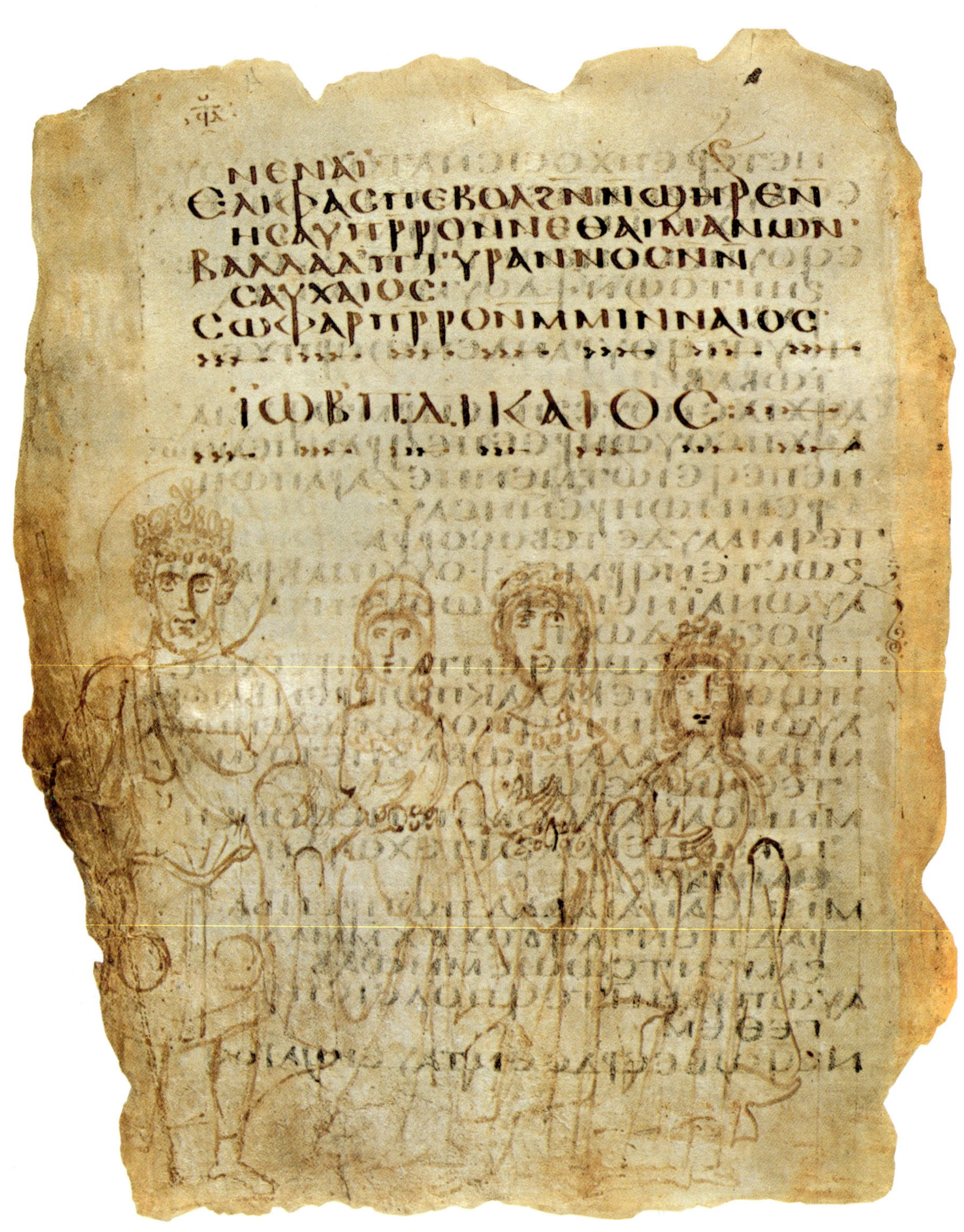

1 Job and his Daughters, with text in Coptic-Sahidic, the dialect of Southern Egypt in the early Christian era. One of 8 leaves comprising an Old Testament MS, now in Naples.

Introduction

JOHN DIXON HUNT

I

The human brain, we now know, has two main capabilities – to review and respond to visual stimuli (images) in the right hemisphere and a parallel ability in the left hemisphere for verbal information (illus. 2).[1] Persons who have suffered brain damage to one side or the other reveal their incapacity to manage both kinds, privileging only the side and skill not affected by the accident. It is also clear – a matter of everyday observation, perhaps – that some people have a greater aptitude for words over images, while others enjoy the reverse situation. There are also variables in different cultures and in different eras. The Chinese written character, for example, combines both 'verbal' and 'visual' signifiers: the form of the character for 'garden' (illus. 3) suggests an enclosed space with lakes, hills and pavilions. A thoroughly visual, modern, Western culture – fed on TV and other photographic media – can be less agile with verbal skills. There are also situations in which people presented with, say, an aerial view of a place otherwise familiar to them, cannot quickly 'read' it, because they are unused to the formal language of that kind of imagery. Some people, similarly, have difficulty understanding architectural plans or elaborate mappings for the same reason.

In their turn artists have opted to perform in one medium or the other, their reasons for the 'choice' (if choice at all) being as various as unconscious recognition of inherent aptitude, social or educational conditioning, or professional opportunity; but the result has often been that graphic artists celebrate visual skills and visual achievements at the expense of the verbal, while writers who perform well in words denigrate visual performances. This seems to be especially true of those who comment upon artistic matters – critics – rather than those engaged in making art. Hence there has arisen a kind of puritanical formalism, of which Lessing's separation of the aptitudes of painting and poetry in his *Laocoön* (1766) may be a major expression:

> Painting, by virtue of its symbols or means of imitation, which it can combine in space only, must renounce the element of time entirely, progressive actions ... cannot be considered to belong among its subjects. Painting must be content with coexistent actions or with mere bodies which, by their position, permit us to conjecture an action [i.e., imply a narrative]. Poetry, on the other hand ...[2]

There have been times, too, when for one reason or another emphasis was placed exclusively on one medium. The period of iconoclasm in the Eastern church during the eighth and ninth centuries necessarily saw a privileging of verbal over visual representations of sacred narratives, as does a continuing Jewish and Islamic prohibition of

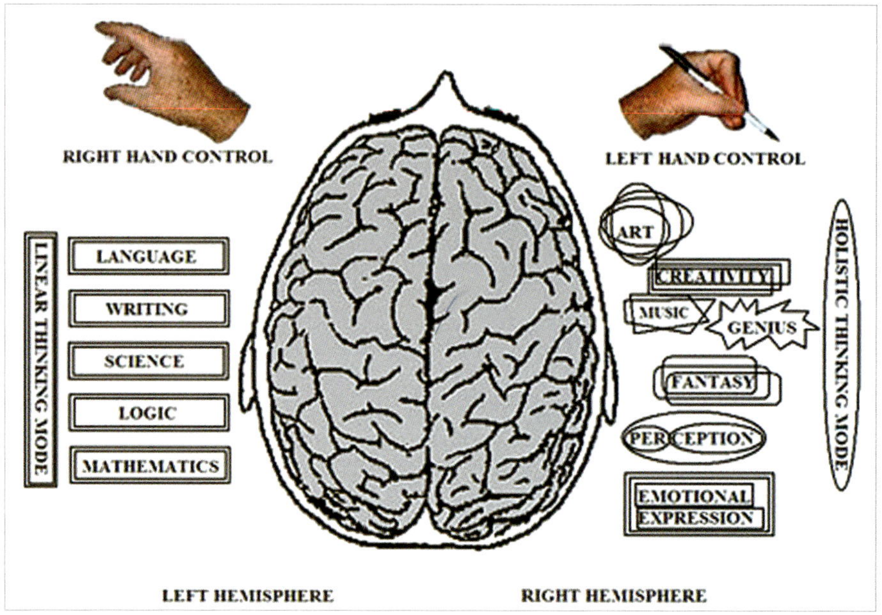

2 The way the brain is organized.

images; there were other periods, too, when iconophobia banished or severely reduced the incidence of religious images.[3] And one effect of these bursts of antagonism was to give greater authority to the efficacy of words in performing narrative or explanatory functions, which in its turn bolstered their authority as a resource within images when these were allowed or returned to favour. Rare, if any, are the times when the reverse was true: when words were denigrated at the expense of images throughout a whole culture.

Twentieth-century modernism also made itself conspicuous, for a while at least, by a partisan and austere determination to make each art abide by the materials deemed endemic to it: thus, paintings observed the flat surface of the canvas and the deployment of pigments, eschewing any reference (by way of narrative or representation) to items and events outside itself.[4] Likewise, the art film wished to free itself from literary models. Writers, though less proscriptively, applied themselves to narrative – words in time – and even to matters as various as sound or *mise en page*, that is to say, manipulations of the formal properties and functions of words and their inscription and printing; though here, with the fascination for how words were presented on the page, in concrete poetry for example, the visual impact was as crucial as the denotative or connotative value of the language. And there is also to be noted the phenomenon of words used as graphic shapes and forms, or the practice of one art via another, as in Robert Morris's sequence of *Memory Drawings* (1963), or in what is termed figure poetry, where the configuration of the words also tries to represent the object about which they speak.[5]

But it is also necessary to remember that, just as most people enjoy an adequate skill in both verbal and visual aptitudes, so there have been artists who found both media equally attractive and eloquent and seized upon both opportunities to advance their own particular concerns. Sometimes they simply worked in both media on different occasions or – Blake and Klee suggest themselves – relied on both simultaneously within the same

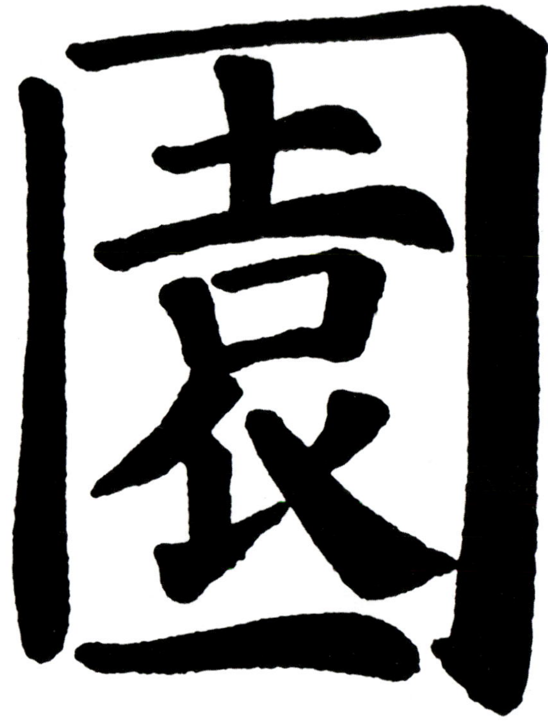

3 Chinese character *yuan* – originally suggesting an open park, later connoting a 'garden' that encloses lakes, artificial hills and pavilions.

piece of work. A partial list of this otherwise infinitely miscellaneous group would include Michelangelo, William Blake, Dante Gabriel Rossetti, Théophile Gautier, Victor Hugo, Eugène Fromentin, Wyndham Lewis, Henri Michaux, Paul Klee and Kurt Schwitters, as well as most emblematists, graphic designers and advertisers.

II

The theme of this book is the use of *words* in visual arts. It is not, therefore, about its converse: literary descriptions of visual things, or any such ekphrastic endeavours. Fascinating as those are, they confront the duality of verbal/visual from the opposite direction from that pursued here. However, it must be said that the scholarship and criticism of ekphrasis and other literary invocations of the visual seem to be more profuse and more sophisticated than considerations of the word in visual arts.[6] Therefore, in order to provide something of an entry into this rather daunting and certainly vast territory (if not exactly *terra incognita*), and at the same time in an attempt to map its scope, it may be worth discriminating four ways in which visual artists have used words. Very schematically, these are:

1. *Explicitly*: when words, decipherable and meaningful by their own account outside the graphic medium, are included in or on the visual artwork. This is *the* main focus and stimulus for enquiry in this book, since without the example of visual art actually employing and inscribing words, the other possibilities of association and use of the verbal would be far less compelling and would indeed have little *raison d'être*. It is only when we recognize that words are deliberately inscribed within visual artworks that we can become aware of and appreciate their other, less direct presences. However, it is also clear that the explicit presence of actual words is most evident in two distinct periods of visual art: during very early periods, prior to the invention of printing, and in the postmodern era, when (perhaps *en ravanche* from doctrinaire modernism) visual artists sought to involve verbal elements. Or perhaps they sought to subdue words' habitual role of denotation and connotation in order better to promote their merely physical shape and formal presence.

Between those two, there is evidence, nonetheless, for a strong commitment of many artists to the implicit reliance upon words. It is as if the expected and explicit alliance of word with image has gone undercover, though the physical absence of words from images did not mean that their role in the full experience of visual art was negligible. At least two particularly rich periods for visual art – the late Middle Ages and the Renaissance – suggest how this was so. Much medieval art addressed the history and traditions of Christianity, where the word assumed a central position: not only was the 'Word made flesh and dwelt among us', but the verbal became the medium of spreading that word, its sacred texts and commentaries upon them, like the gospels or Paul's epistles. Consequently, when artists chose to image a Christian event or idea, the presence of the word was either explicitly entered upon the surface of the artwork or emphatically assumed as sustaining its visual performances.

Similarly, a wholly new opportunity existed for painters in the Renaissance to consult verbal narratives circulating in printed books for the first time; these certainly now included the written and oral traditions of the Christian faith, but also, more importantly, all the texts of classical authors, with their rich repertoire of mythical events and historical narratives. Paintings were inevitably nourished on this new verbal repertoire. It is therefore undeniable that, at least in these two instances, the word did not have to appear within the image to be an ineluctable part of the experience of that image.

Those visual occasions of strong and explicit reliance upon the verbal must be distinguished from those many occasions in which almost any verbal image can elicit some verbal response, often sentimental and redundant to the formal work. Beyond, therefore, explicit appearances of words, there are three further ways in which a role for the verbal can be identified: it can be implicit (with good reason or with less), it can work in a supplementary fashion, or, in the richest sense, its role can be collaborative. These provide three further categories, which (somewhat paradoxically) will detain us more than the 'explicit' mode.

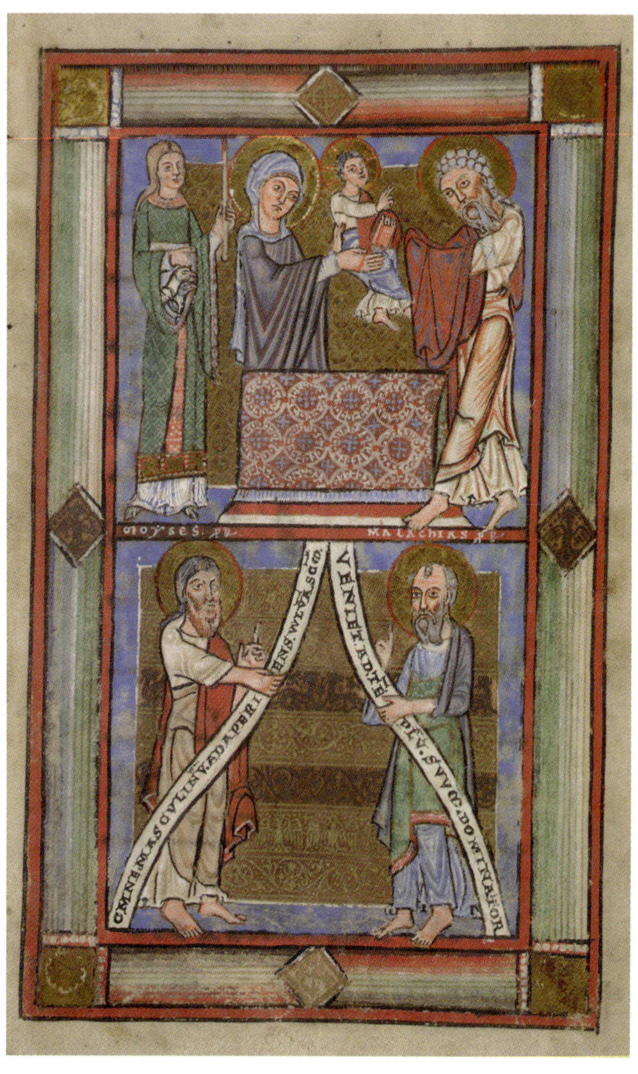

4 The Presentation of Christ with Moses and Malachi holding descriptive texts, from the Psalter of Henry the Lion, produced in Germany, *c.* 1168–89.

2. *Implicitly*: when visual art invokes, relies on or indeed even seems to depend upon words that do not exist either on or adjacent to the specific work, but are summoned into its magnetic field by the viewer's recognition of some trigger within the visual field that prompts him/her to need and use them. The most obvious example is when a viewer of some painting recites the story or narrative that it either visualizes or suggests and names the participants depicted. This implicit verbalizing can also be materialized in some critical or museological context, in which case it properly constitutes or overlaps with the third mode.

3. *Additively or supplementarily*: when actual, discernible and legible words are added by way of supplement to the visual work of art. One major form that this supplementary act can take involves the adducing of titles for pictorial works, either as 'handles' by which to refer to them or even inscribed on a frame. But titling extends itself into the catalogue entry or wall label in a museum, and – by generous extension – into critical commentary on a specific visual artwork that expands and extends its significance. By that point, we are usually a long way physically from the actual image that has provoked the additional wordage and there is obviously a different overlap with the second, implicit category.

4. *Collaboratively:* when it would be difficult to adjudicate which of the three categories so far listed applies, for example, to such items as medieval manuscripts, graphic design, emblems and certain kinds of advertising, because word and image are so interdependent. This fourth mode is therefore useful: when, as in those genres, the verbal and visual emphatically rely upon the other's presence, even perhaps ape or affect the other's strategies to the extent that the removal of one from the whole ensures a loss, as when watching certain TV programmes with the sound turned off (though it must be confessed that on many occasions this offers a merciful release from banal verbal redundancy).

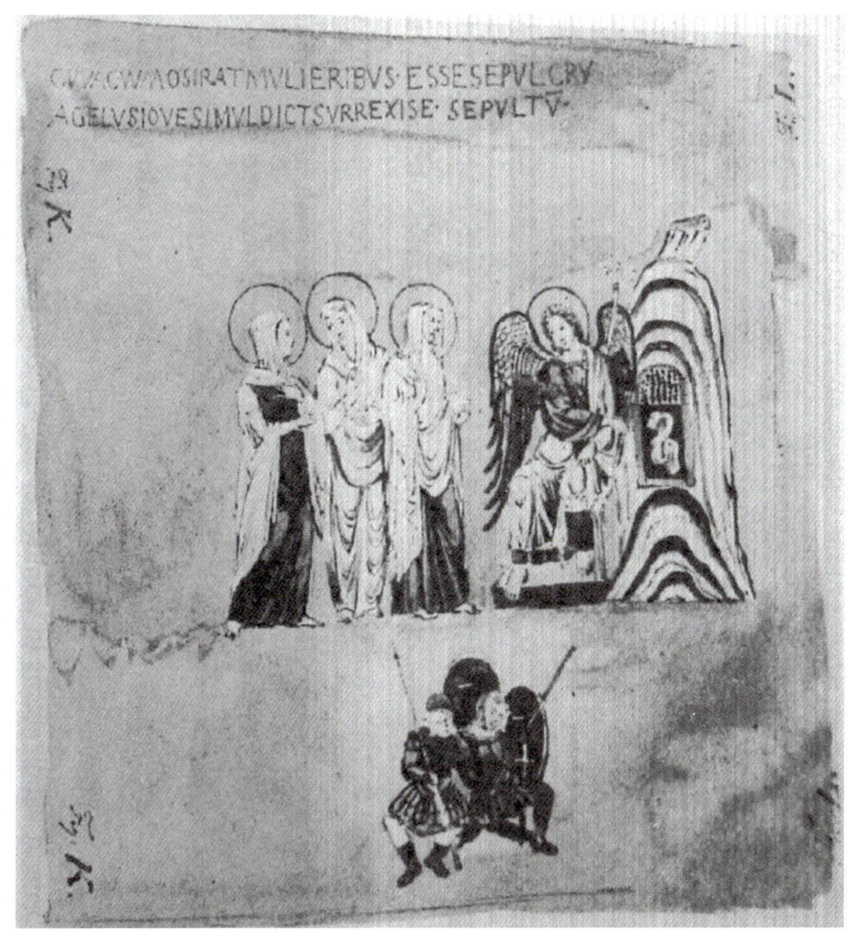

5 Gustaf Wilhelm Palm, *The Women at the Tomb,* watercolour rendering of a mosaic in San Marco, Venice, 1840.

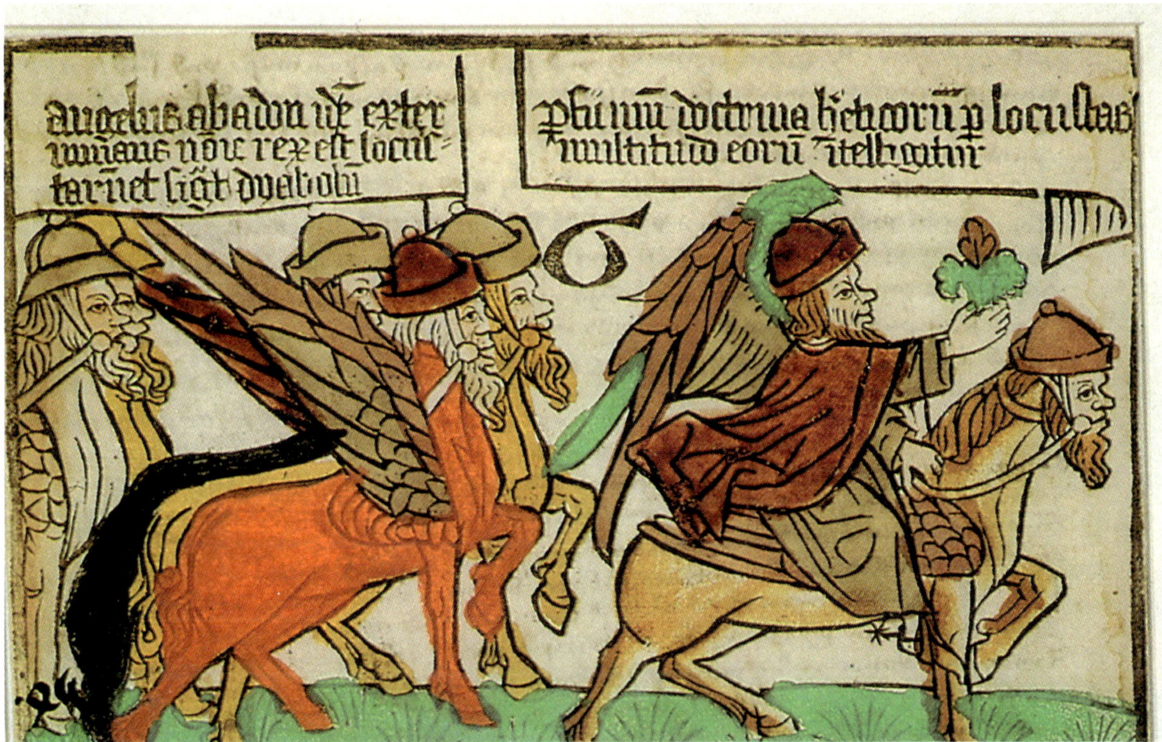

6 Anonymous, *Horsemen of the Apocalypse*, coloured woodcut, *c.* 1465.

The relative simplicity of this fourfold taxonomy conceals myriad ways in which any of the modes can be employed, and above all it conceals the range of repercussions that result in responding to or experiencing the visual art that relies on them. So some examples of these varieties of verbal relationship with the visual will help define some of the strategies of association between words and images that have been practised by creative artists; in turn this will illuminate the kinds of critical responses that such bifocal manoeuvres have elicited, and provide some interpretational structure for the more historical surveys that follows.

III

The *explicit word* is easily recognized in visual art and generally readily understood. Its effect, intended or unintended, can be more complex. In John Foxe's *Actes and Monuments* of 1563 (the popular 'Book of Martyrs') the historical figures are identified in the woodcuts with scrolls bearing their names.

A mosaic in the church of San Marco at Venice shows the women at the sepulchre where Christ was buried after the Crucifixion, and in recording it in 1840 the visiting northern artist Gustaf Wilhelm Palm also transcribed the accompanying words which constituted an identifying caption (illus. 5). The horsemen of the Apocalypse are depicted in an anonymous German woodcut of 1465 alongside a text that recalls the relevant text about them (illus. 6). In representations of saints their figures may be identified, labelled by writing on scrolls or banderols they carry or have wrapped around them, on the hems of their garments or by some such device (illus. 4). We do not assume that they actually wore such name tags or carried the scrolls – they are not, after all, either participants in some modern international symposium or walking in a political parade. But the device orientates us, and perhaps triggers our discovery of some further, implicit wordage in the imagery, like recalling the biography of a given saint and relating it to some symbol he or she is carrying. Similar and more extensive wordage can appear in the form of scrolls that articulate statements or sayings uttered by the persons represented and which might be familiar from listening to biblical narratives. Later artists cottoned onto this device (illus. 7), and the modern cartoon has made it a perfectly unproblematic device in our reading of older images. What is a fairly routine mode of identification in medieval and Renaissance paintings is also used on public statues of eminent men and women, where the inscriptions both identify them and suggest how we might recall their lives and contacts.

IV

Implicit words are a more evasive as well as a much more extensive phenomenon. They are also more problematic than the other kinds in that they need either more explanation or even special pleading. Some paintings clearly demand – or respond to a human desire – that its viewers formulate in words what is depicted; some paintings get this treatment, however, even when their demand is far less insistent. The obvious example of the former (illus. 8) is a painting where figures are engaged (or conspicuous by their refusal to engage) in some action, the articulation of which will take the form of a verbal narrative that the visual medium can only suggest or imply, leaving it to our imaginations – the verbal part supplementing the visual – to fill out the story. This verbal mode is termed 'implicit' here, because it is *neither* something on or in the painting or artwork itself, *nor* is it something that along the way during the life of the artwork has been attached to the work by the artist or the critic/curator whose title or commentary we somehow accept as inherent to the painting. Clearly, there are some works of art which encourage, notably through their titles or configuration of their imagery, this particular temptation to elaborate one's own words about an image; it is therefore crucial to assess the aptness or usefulness of such a response. There is a strong sentimental streak in humans that is drawn towards finding something to say about just about any image, whether or not it is justified by the viewing. Friedrich's figures on the chalk cliffs (illus. 9) manage to impose their presence visually long before we may be tempted to ask what they are up to, whereas Andrew Wyeth (illus. 8) seems to impose or require a verbal contribution to the visual, as

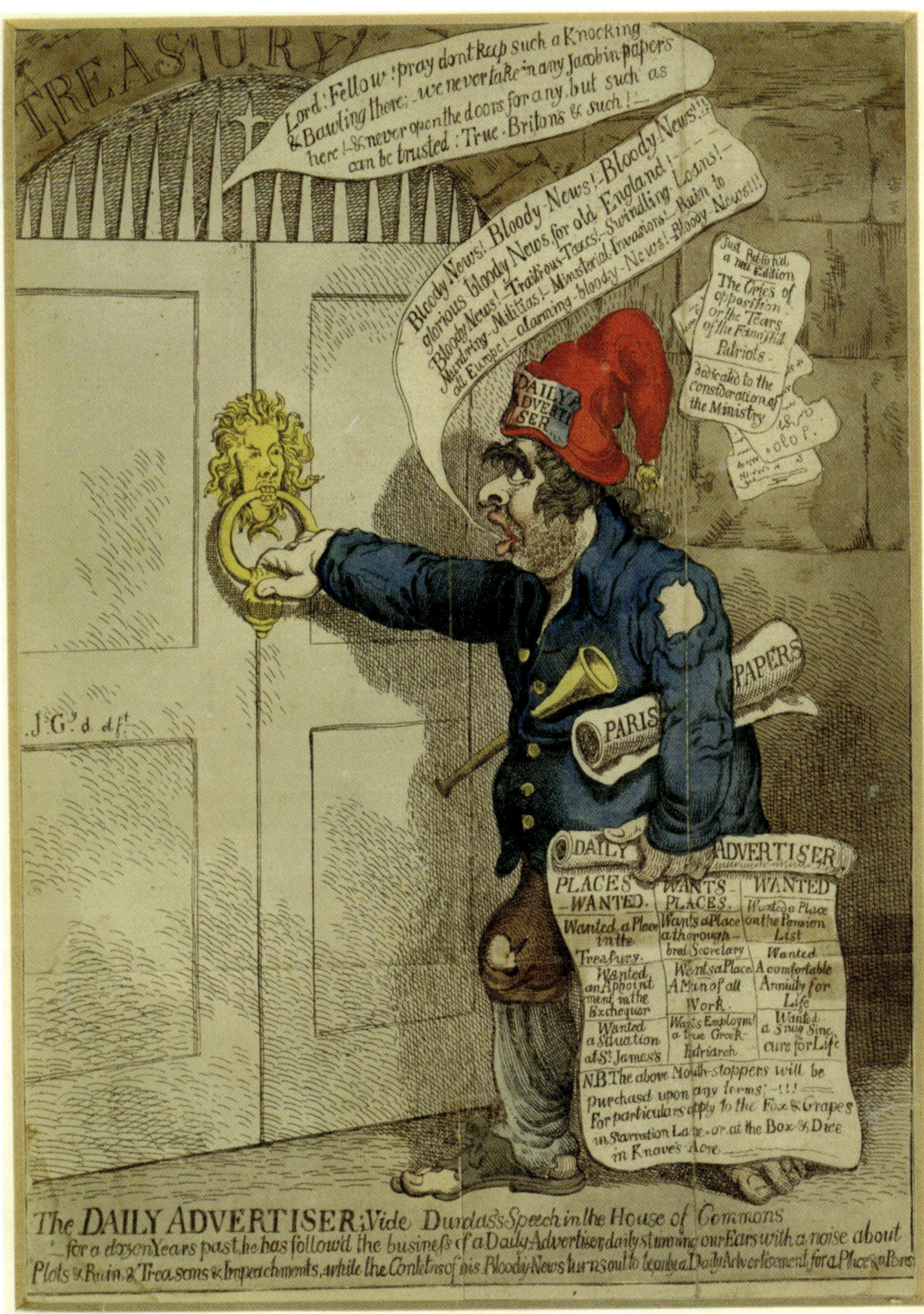

7 James Gillray, *The Daily Advertiser*, 1780, engraving.

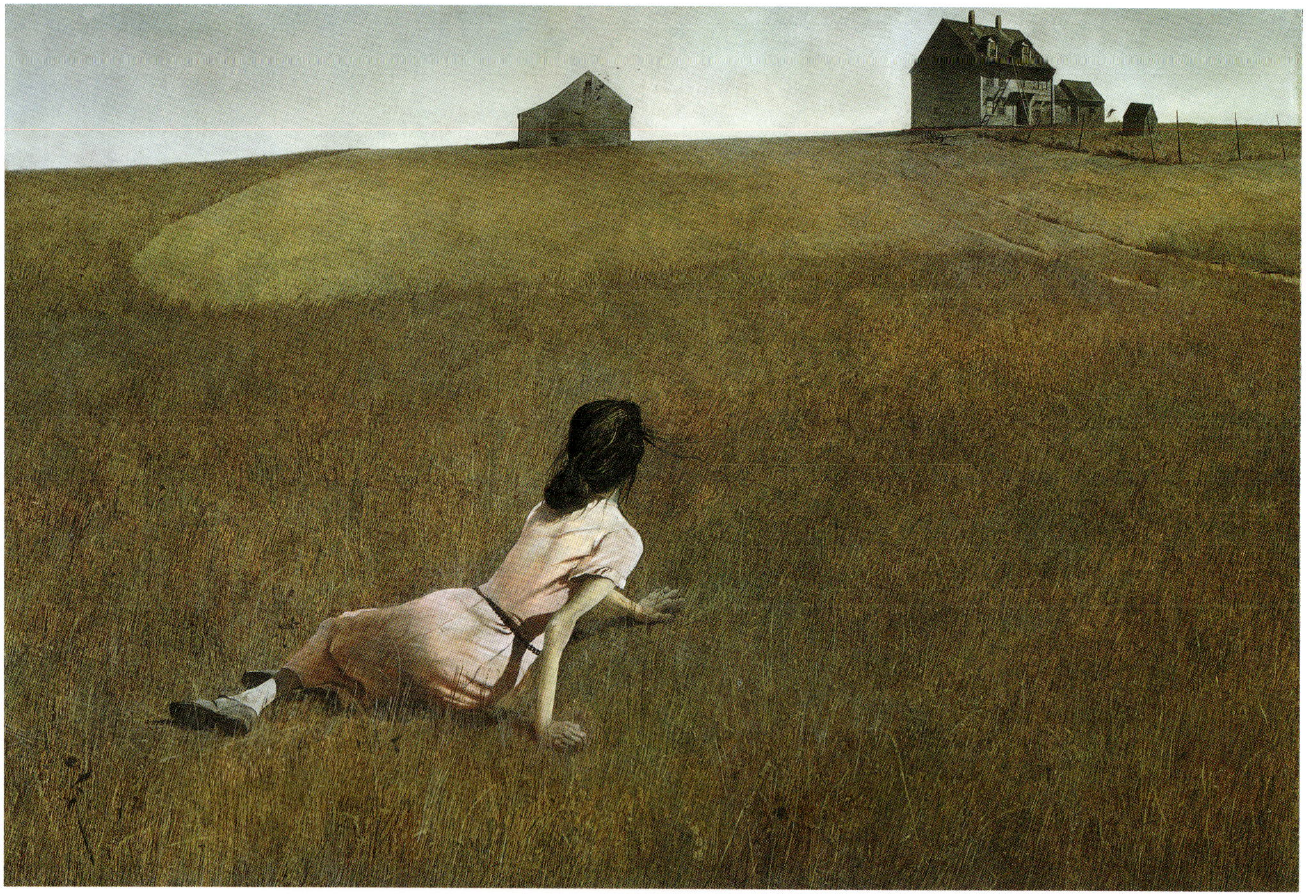

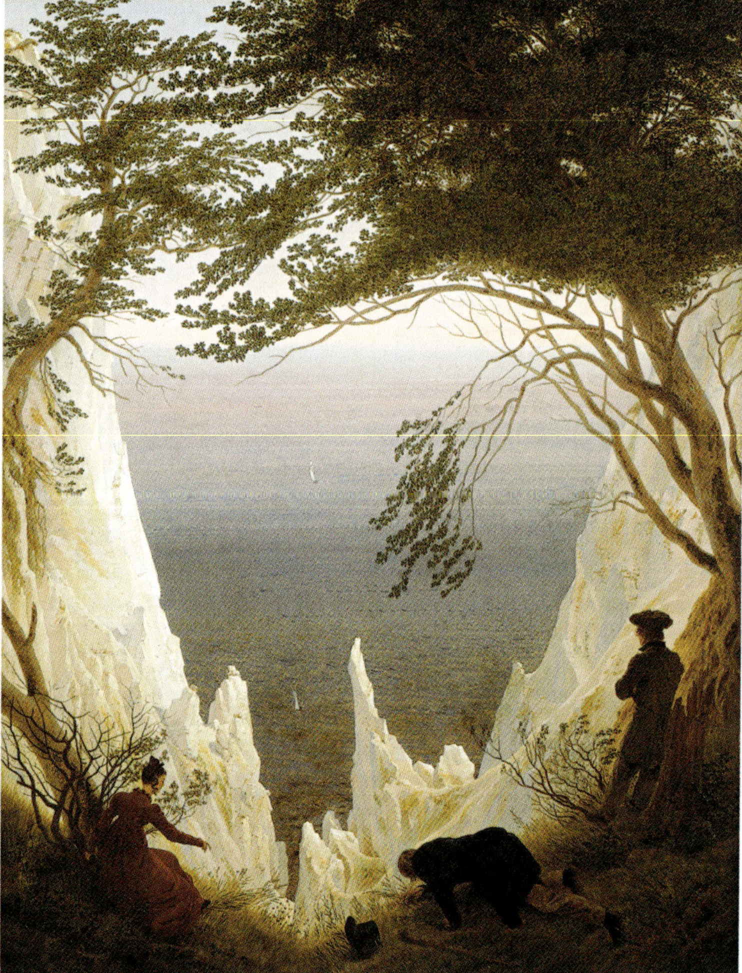

8 Andrew Wyeth, *Christina's World*, 1948, tempera.

9 Caspar David Friedrich, *Chalk Cliffs on Rügen*, 1818–19, oil on canvas.

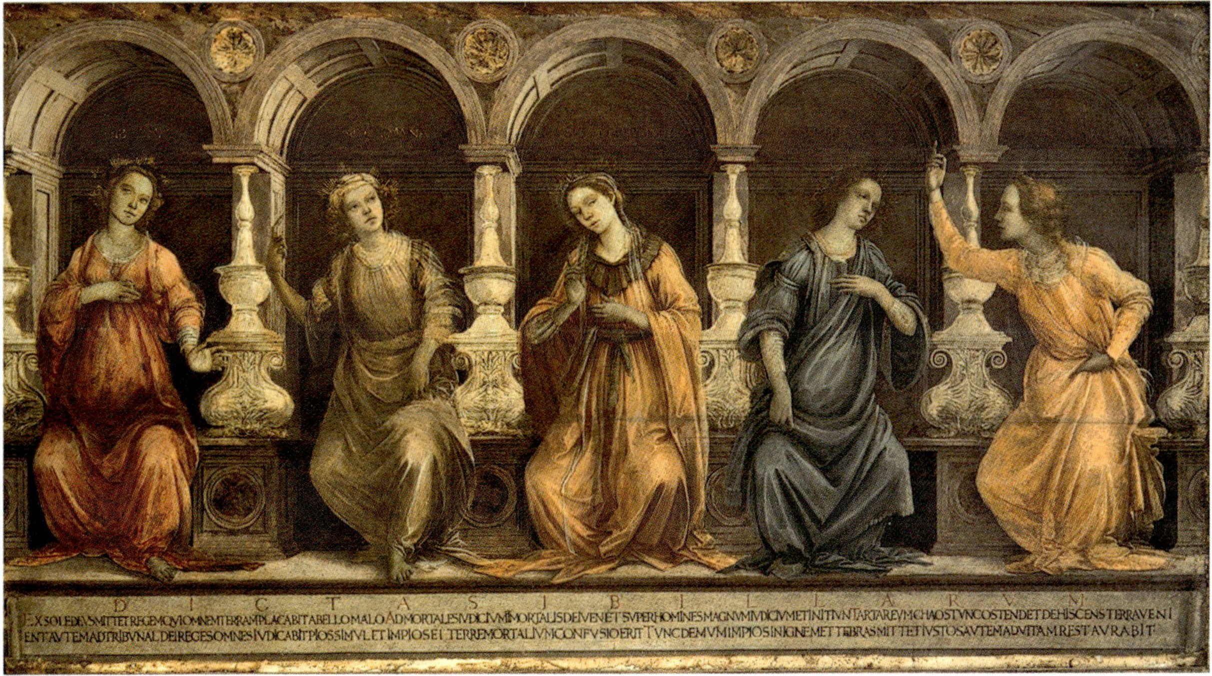

10 Filippino Lippi (*c.* 1457–1504), *Five Sybils*, oil on panel.

did earlier Victorian genre scenes, which can seem to outweigh the pictorial impact.[7] Such invitations to expand the image verbally are not easily tolerated by many artists and critics; the recourse to some implied wordage bespeaks a refusal to rest content with what is seen, an irrelevant and a sentimental, literary weakness in either the commentator or the artist who opens him/herself to such responses.

V

The *additive word* is readily identified, even if its role is unclear in relation to the visual object. We are used to paintings being given titles by wall labels in modern museums or in captions of illustrated books like this one; we are probably lost without them. But early artists could also provide what is essentially a title, even an ancillary 'label'. For example, a panel by Filippino Lippi (*c.* 1457–1504) depicts a line of classically garbed women seated beneath the canopies of five stalls (not unlike where clergy might sit in a church choir) and appearing to talk and to gesture among themselves (illus. 10). Across the bottom, presented in the form of an ancient inscription, is the Latin 'DICTA SIBILLARUM' (Sayings of the Sibyls), which performs the task of titling Lippi's image: consequently we know that we are looking at sibyls and that they are speaking. An additional pleasure of the panel is perhaps that, because we recall that sibyls were famous for speaking gnomically and because their utterances needed to be deciphered, the panel's viewers recognize that this silent communication has to be articulated for them; so they either put their own words into play or, more likely, draw upon a further text, which is run together in imitation of antique inscriptions and also stretches across the bottom of the panel. Deciphering this unbroken sequence of letters may amplify what their 'Dicta' might be. But this second part of the added words seems more usefully considered an example of implied narrative or speech.

Chinese art has traditionally been so closely allied with calligraphy and the making of poetry that we accept that its paintings will include written information. This has a variety of functions (though most Western viewers, this one included, cannot readily respond to them without interpretative aids). The words may simply record a subject or the ownership of a scroll or drawing (though ownership itself can be a vital ingredient in the overall meaning of a Chinese image); but more usefully for our purposes is the practice of inscribing on, say, a landscape painting some poem or other literary reflection that is intended to guide the receptive viewer into a fuller experience of the visual image. When Wang Hui (late seventeenth century) painted a view of 'countless peaks and vales' he inscribed the hanging scroll with an acknowledgement of his inspiration by a poem about a Taoist monastery and of his working in the style of two other artists, all of which would help to shape a viewer's appreciation of the image (illus. 11). Modern Chinese artists continue this practice, so much more ingrained is it than in Western art: Liu Maoshan (b. 1942) writes down the side of an

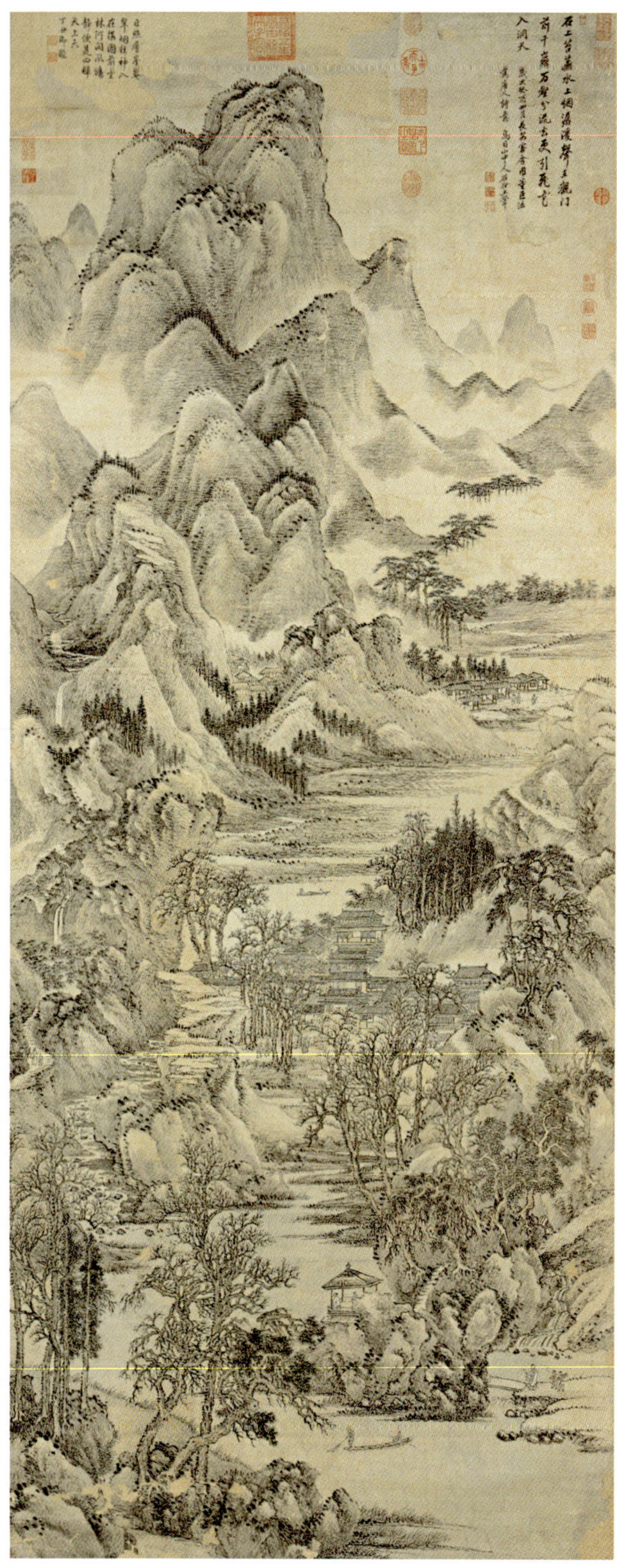

11 Wang Hui, *Countless Woods and Vales,* 1693, hanging scroll in ink and light colours.

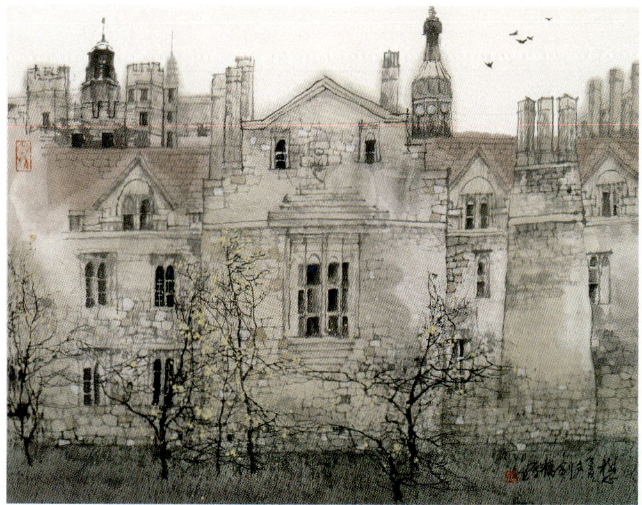

12 Liu Maoshan, *A View of Oxford*, ink and wash on an album leaf.

image that he drew this impression of Oxford 'in London at the end of the year' (illus. 12).

The practice of giving titles to works of art is essentially modern. Or, more accurately, what is modern is rather the stabilization of a title, a process that has benefited from the work of established art history during and after the late nineteenth century in cataloguing early works.[8] However, even in modern times, the formulation and attachment of a title to a painting is not necessarily straightforward. Joan Miró objected when the Guggenheim exhibited what is now called *Personnage* under the title 'Painting' or 'Composition'; Marc Chagall protested to the same museum when his *The Flying Carriage* (its current title) was given the generic label of 'Landscape' or the much more specific 'Burning House'. In both cases the artists clearly wished to shape a beholder's share in their art; the curators seemingly wished to withdraw from any role that seemed to relate the image to something beyond itself.

In earlier times, when printed catalogue or museum displays were not in place to define what titles were, titles enjoyed or suffered a more precarious existence. Nicolas Poussin's painting, the accepted title of which is now *Landscape with a Man Killed by a Snake* (illus. 13), was viewed by two French contemporaries – Félibien and Fénelon – as being a representation of the effects of terror; this latter description-cum-title makes more explicit how a viewer might understand and respond to the events depicted by offering what is in fact an interpretation of the scene (the three different responses to the serpent's attack: that of the terrified victim, the horrified observer escaping the scene and the third party who only sees and reacts to the observer running towards her but not to the serpent's attack itself). Emerging out of art historical scholarship, the modern title simply isolates the genre of this painting – landscape – and then identifies a subject in it as a means of distinguishing it from other Poussin landscapes that display different incidents. Yet the very blandness of the 'Landscape …' formula, with its avoidance of any interpretative element, has spawned a whole series of proposals for some literary text that, it is argued, must be what Poussin is illustrating (as distinct – another whole corpus of writing again – from the critical explications of the image that invoke a whole congeries of learned literary sources that Poussin might or might not have known).[9] In all these cases, both the scholarly assumption that seventeenth-century paintings of such landscapes depended upon texts and the universal human instinct to discover a tale in such imagery drive the formulation of implicit and additive wordage.

As we gather from the history of the Poussin, as of many other early works, an owner may adduce titles for items in his collection: Browning's famous poem about a princely Renaissance connoisseur has him gesturing verbally as well as with his arms – 'That's my last duchess on the wall …' or 'Notice Neptune, taming a sea-horse … Which Claus of Innsbruck cast in bronze for me'. The verbal commentary that devolves in the process of presenting an image collection to a group of visitors can be assimilated with and used to augment whatever title is announced.

What happens today in many an art history class gathered before a canvas or during a guided museum visit evolved in classical times: the *Imagines* of the third-century BC Philostratus purports to tell of a visit to a Neapolitan art collection (maybe a real one or perhaps simply imagined for the purposes of the writing), where a teacher lectures his pupil on the paintings. While the text is valuable for its ekphrastic skills, our interest must be in the tradition in which any visual work was deemed incomplete or ill-understood without a detailed *verbal* version, first, of its subject (telling exactly what it is you think you see), then expanding the still images into some temporal narrative, and finally adjudicating both the painterly skills exhibited and the beholder's ability in viewing. Paintings, then and always, are able to 'nourish the flow of thought'[10] and it is inevitable that words spell out those responses.

Most people need, even love, to know what a painting is called, because it will (they assume) guide them in their response to it; it will tell them what it is 'about'. Hence museums add to an adjacent wall some plaque that gives a title along with

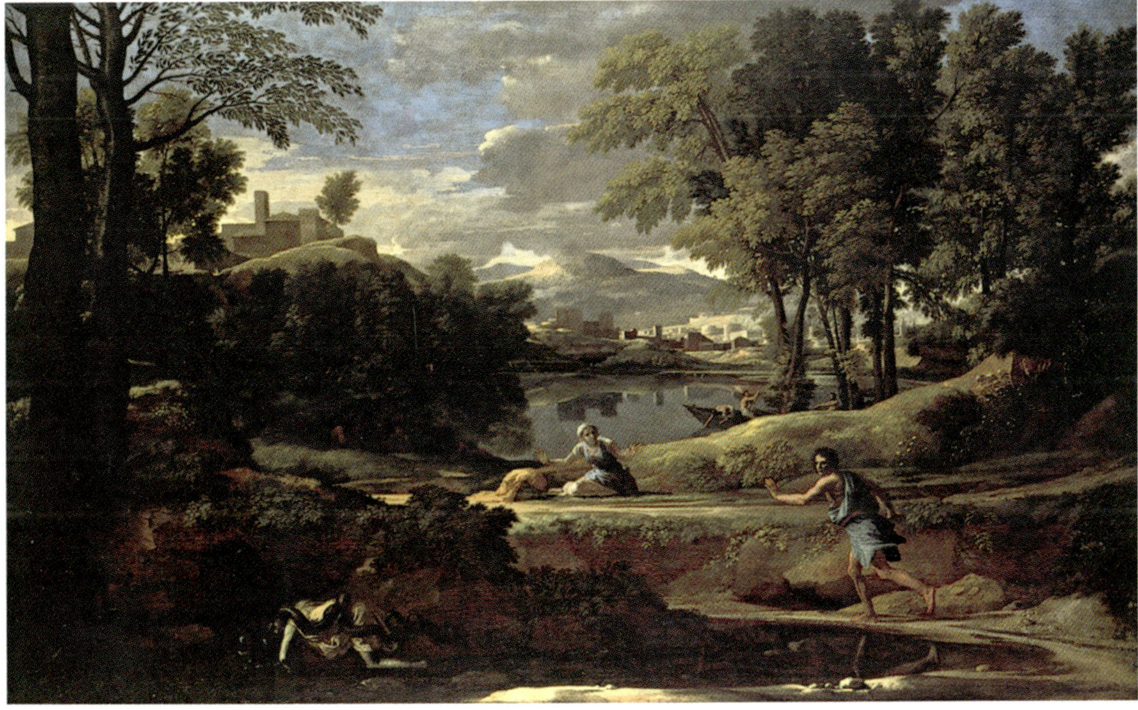

13 Nicolas Poussin, *Landscape with* a *Man Killed by a Snake*, *c.* 1648, oil on canvas.

other details deemed pertinent to the painting on display, occasionally even beginning to offer a critical exegesis of the item on display (the necessary brevity of these often renders them a trifle absurd). However, some institutions or older, private collections neglect this. In the famous exhibition held in Manchester in 1857, *Art Treasures of the United Kingdom*, there were no wall captions at all; instead, a catalogue listed titles and artists' names, while the show itself simply arranged works chronologically (on the advice of Prince Albert, the patron of the exhibition).[11] And it is still possible, even in these days of advanced and interpretative museology, to stumble upon a small, usually provincial, museum in Europe where the paintings in the collection are simply identified by a number, which presumably signals some catalogue elsewhere containing the extra verbal information. The Barnes Foundation in Philadelphia still does not display titles (the artist's name alone being attached in most cases to the frame), reserving the other information to be communicated in other ways and elsewhere than in the gallery; nowadays an audio tape that the viewer listens to in front of the painting brings that commentary directly before the image, but originally visitors at the Barnes were expected to respond to the formal imagery regardless of what a title might say it 'was about'.

In certain circumstances – one thinks readily of the Pre-Raphaelites here – a title is inscribed on the frame of the painting that was specifically designed for it by the artist. Further, and again Pre-Raphelitism offers many examples, the frame will also accommodate verses that gloss the image in some way (gloss is a useful word in this context, since it derives etymologically from the Greek for tongue, without which we cannot speak). William Holman Hunt's painting of *The Scapegoat* (illus. 14) will serve as an example: on the frame are quotations from Isaiah (53.4) and Leviticus (16.22) that provide words by which to explain what we are looking at: respectively, 'Surely he hath borne our griefs and carried our sorrows, Yet we did esteem him stricken, smitten of God, and afflicted', and 'And the goat shall bear upon him all their iniquities unto a land not inhabited'. The words direct our thinking beyond the dominant and (for many original Victorian viewers) unappealing goat, imaged in sometimes repellent colour, to its religious symbolism, which involves both Old Testament sin and sacrifice and its typological reenactment in the life and death of Christ. Without the words, which direct us to specific stories outside the painting, the image would be at best puzzling, if not simply an animal painting. It requires the added sentences to fulfill Hunt's intentions or, at the very least, to point his viewers towards a relevant commentary on what they see.[12] Other paintings in the symbolist vein make certain that their titles or other verbal supplements help the beholder to move beyond what Stephen Dedalus called the 'ineluctable modality of the visible'.[13]

While it extends the additive mode to possible excess and with little direct physical relationship with the image, there is also the commentary that an art critic or historian offers (as already noted with regard to Poussin's landscape). At their most economical, these can be included on museum wall plaques, though it sometimes beggars belief that a curator actually thinks that in those circumstances you need to be told what you can see with your own eyes! (Presumably, this is an unconscious affirmation of the painting's independence of any literary gloss or explanation, since it states what is visually obvious and therefore notionally redundant). Exhibition catalogues are a means of expanding the wall notices into longer essays. This practice may have sprung into life after 1798, in which year the Royal Academy in London allowed the inclusion in exhibition catalogues of explanatory or supplementary written materials, and artists like J.M.W. Turner seized the chance to direct their viewers' reception with narrative titles and long, presumably apposite and usually poetic, quotations. A slightly earlier, related format and perhaps even precedent – though not offered specifically in a catalogue accompanying an exhibition – is the elaborate exegeses that Denis Diderot developed in his famous series of *Salons*.[14] Here he imagined what a beholder might experience if he were able to walk into one of the painted landscapes displayed in public exhibition: Diderot's words rehearse the graphic invitations of the painting and could be read while standing

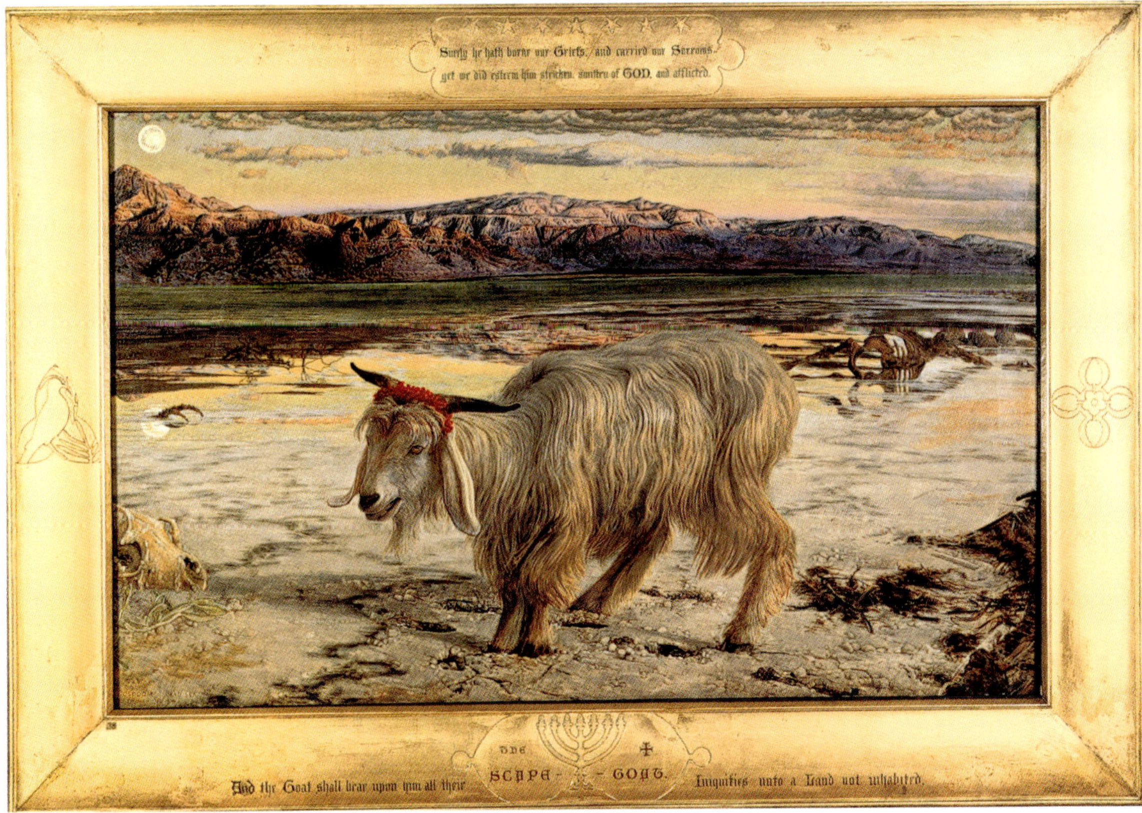

14 William Holman Hunt, *The Scapegoat*, 1854–5, oil on canvas.

before it, opening up a whole imaginative field of associations and thoughts.

Especially with particularly famous paintings – the *Mona Lisa* by Leonardo da Vinci, or exceptionally mysterious ones, Giorgione's *Tempestà* (illus. 15) – it is doubtful if many people can now view them either without being aware of the commentary and the explicatory criticism that has been generated in the hope of explaining them, or without investing the image with their own, often sentimental gloss that provides a narrative or psychological profile for the depicted characters. The titles of these two paintings are themselves the first step in that expository direction, which in almost all cases involves a narrative exposition: we ask who was the woman called Mona Lisa, and what did she 'mean' to Leonardo? And what are those figures, separated from each other, doing as the storm gathers in that redolent Venetian landscape? The *Mona Lisa* and the *Tempestà* contain no words whatsoever; even the titles conventionally given to these paintings are inauthentic to the extent that the artists did not provide them. Yet a verbal commentary hangs about them as an irreducible element of our experience of their images and their current titles – it would probably be wholly otherwise if they were known only as 'Portrait of a Woman' or 'Figures in a Landscape'. The considerable commentary that has developed on and around such images can never be communicated by a wall label or even a catalogue entry, but many viewers will be aware of such additive wordage and will not be able to ignore its burden entirely. It is no surprise that whole books have gathered invented titles and captions for the *Mona Lisa* and discussed the endless wordage that the painting has invoked.[15]

VI

In all cases so far examined there is, of course, an element of collaboration – sometimes willed, sometimes reluctant, sometimes required, sometimes forced – between the visual work and its invocation of words. Yet we need also to make clear that there is some visual art that requires no verbal adjuncts whatsoever, however much some, including titles, are foisted upon them. The best one can say of such examples as illustration 16 is that the titles they have been landed with do no more than identify them for purposes of curatorial and art historical reference. Sometimes, perhaps, modern artists have even teased what they imagine is their audience's unnecessary dependence upon verbal direction: for example, Wassily Kandinsky's *No. 160b (Improvisation 28 [?])* in the New York Guggenheim Museum, where the doubly parenthetical question mark wittily undermines even the artist's certainty about how many improvisations he has thus far executed and its usefulness for our viewing of this particular one.

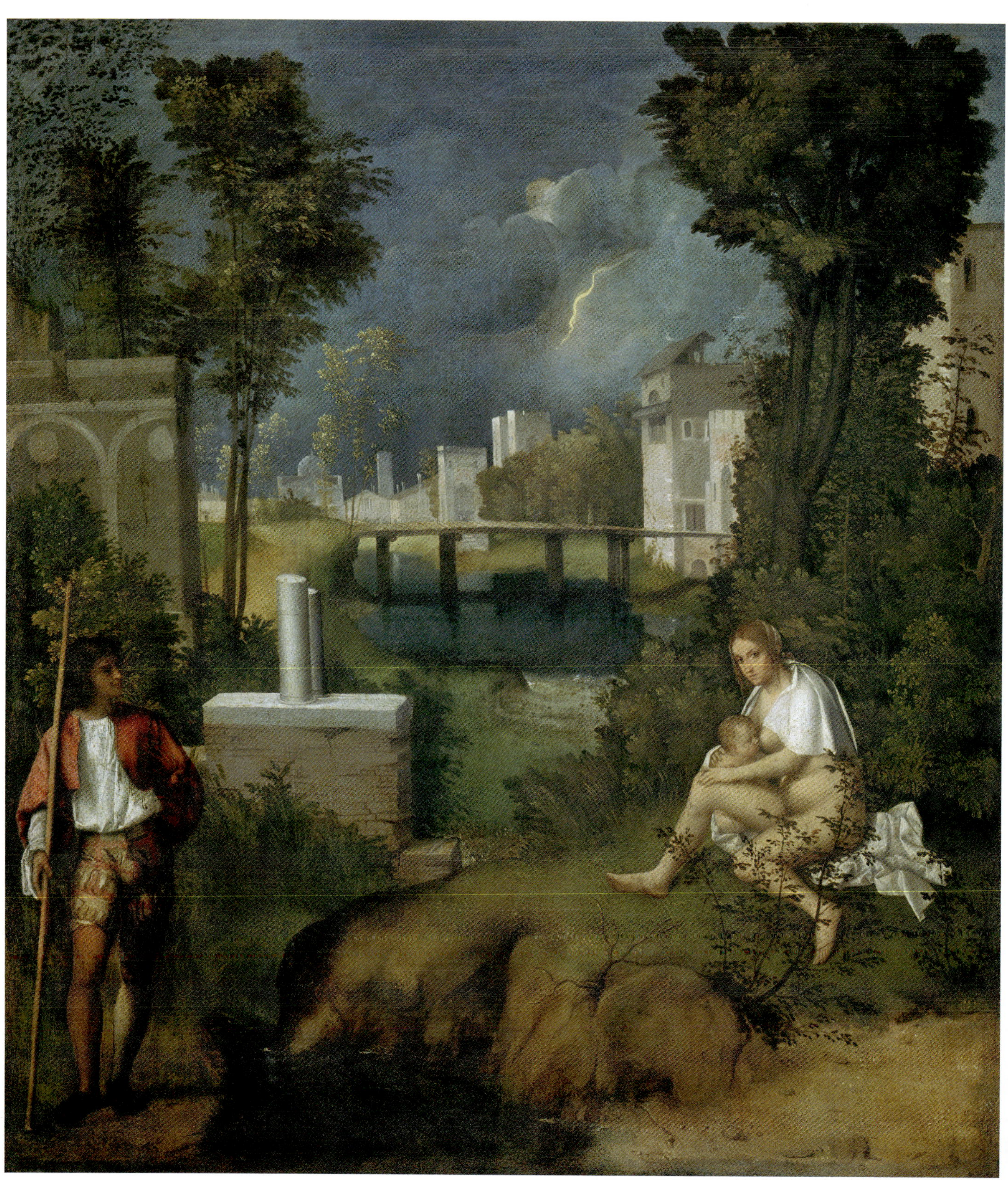

15 Giorgione, *La Tempestà*, 1507–8, oil on canvas.

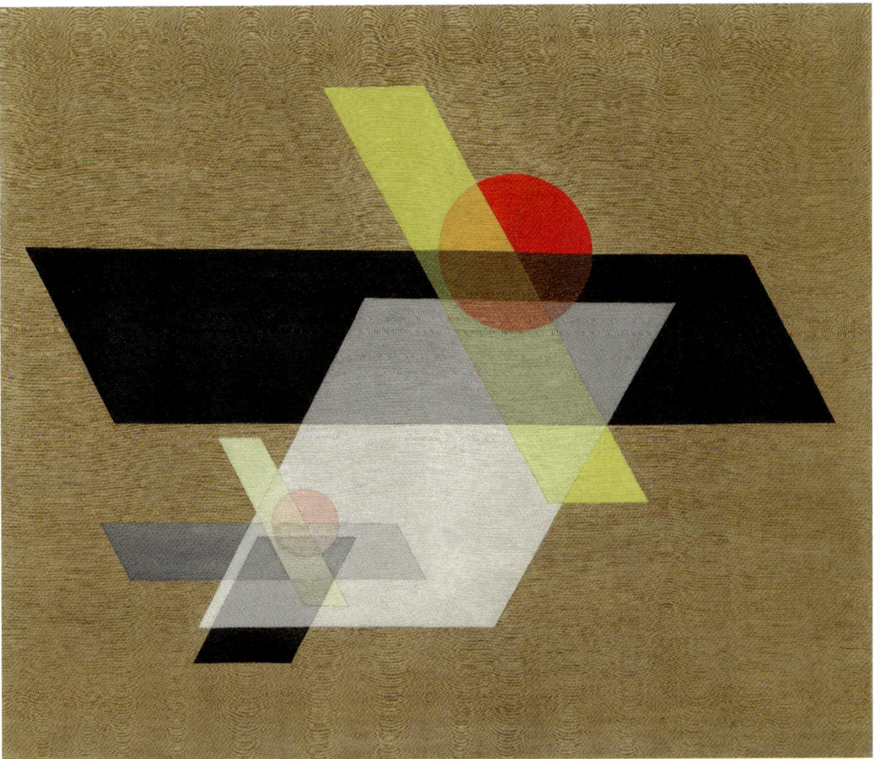

16 László Moholy-Nagy, *A II*, 1924, oil on canvas.

But there are many examples of graphic work where a special mode of collaboration needs to be identified, a mode which makes the reliance of image upon word so far discussed seem casual and indeed inessential. This mode involves a necessary and obligatory reliance of the beholder on both visual and verbal languages and of each medium on the other. Maps, concrete poetry, illuminated manuscripts, emblems, art deco book design, advertising, film and video, and all manner of contemporary digital formats like websites – these modes rely upon words so involved within the graphic medium and its message that, in the first place, words may seem to be transfigured as graphic imagery and, second, the graphic imagery itself aspires to the condition of linguistic denotation.

Maps without words are almost unthinkable. The famous 1933 'map' of the London Underground system is useless without *both* the coloured lines and the naming of stations. Modern in-car navigation systems equally require verbal augmentations of the graphic codes in order that the driver may relate the screen to the real world through which s/he drives. Some maps, certainly, may rely largely upon graphic codes for routes or coastal outlines or on colours for a variety of purposes (administrative, topographical, geological and so on); but detailed maps like the Ordnance Survey supplement their visual codes with glosses that provide verbal equivalents to ensure distinct legibility. The collaboration of word with image in these cases is vital. And sometimes words have been invoked for geographical experiences that the map maker cannot yet define ('here be savages'). Equally visual explanation enlarges and authorizes verbal accounts: the map of the landscape of Winnie the Pooh gives immediate credence to the story because it *shows* where places are that otherwise we only know by words. This authority that the collaborative effect of words and images in maps enjoys has been used at different times for political and legal ends: a survey map defines property and ownership, or it may declare – even claim – sovereignty; the 1993 *State of Religion Atlas* charts the spread or range of a given sect or faith; but the word must always work with the diagrammatical vocabulary to provide the information.

Illuminated manuscripts, to be discussed more fully in the following historical narrative, are a key example of an art form that relies upon the simultaneity of its graphic and its scriptural markings. What is less sure of interpretation and analysis are the ways – the seemingly innumerable ways – in which a user of these items made (and in modern exegesis continues to make) connections between those two elements. Even when we know – it was anyway a usual practice – that a scribe wrote out the words on sheets where the spaces for the images, to be added by a different craftsman, had been previously marked out, this dual and not always co-ordinated activity often produced objects to

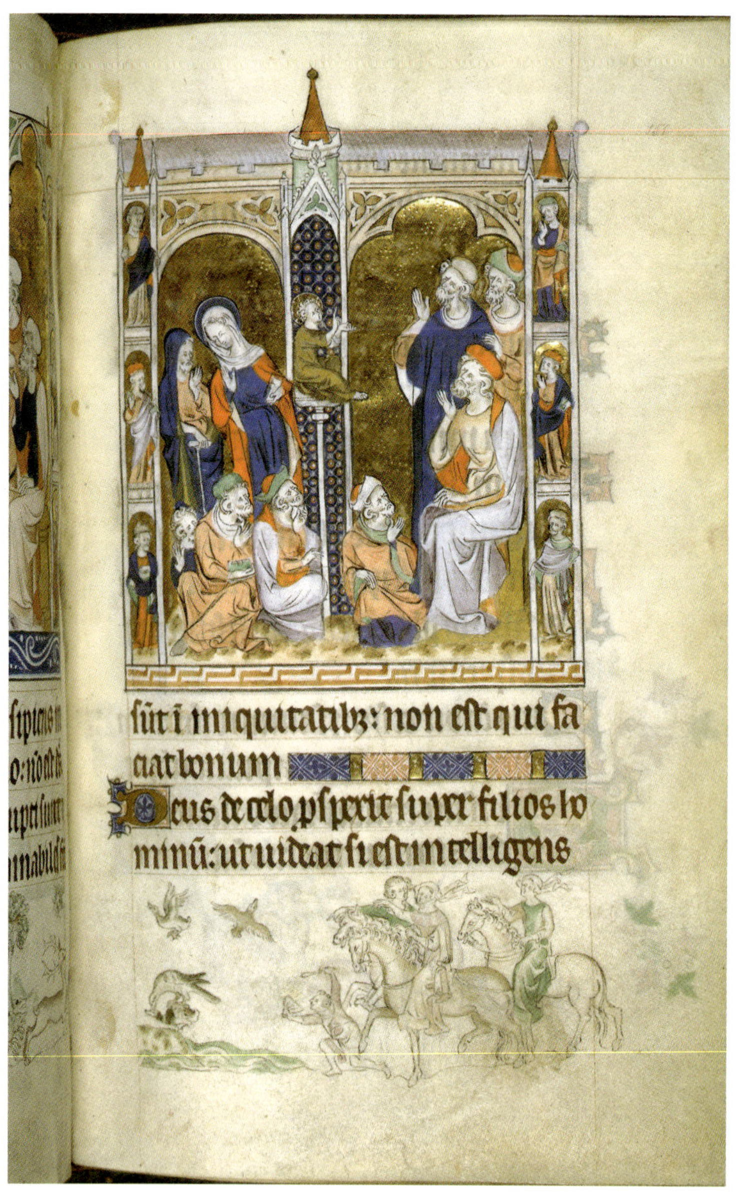

17 The Queen Mary Psalter, *Christ in the Temple*, *c.* 1310–20, vellum.

whose unified field we need to respond, even if our doing so poses some interpretative problems.

For example, in the Queen Mary Psalter there is a page on which the dominant image is of the young Christ debating with the scribes in the Temple, below which we read a text and a further, less elaborate, but still attractive, drawing of a hunting party at the foot of the page (illus. 17).[16] The text is from Psalm 52, one of the main breaks or divisions in medieval psalters and usually therefore given a major illustration. Yet how do the psalmist's words 'work with' the images? The text we read has begun on the previous sheet:

> [*Corrupti sunt, et abominabiles facti*] *sunt in inquitatibus; non est qui faciat bonum. Deus de caelo prospexit super filios hominum; ut videat si est intelligens …*

> [They are corrupted and become abominable] in iniquities; there is none that does good. God looked down from heaven on the children of men: to see if there were any that did understand …

The thoughtful reader can make many connections: perhaps Christ and the six figures down either side of the main image (of prophets or apostles, like statues on a church facade) may well be those sent by God into a world to cure its iniquities. Hunting with raptors can also suggest some plausible analogies, or be an instance of the world's corrupt pastimes, or be a suitable but innocent if courtly interlude at this point in the manuscript, or simply introduce a diverting sketch. The 'reading' of the page, in short, is neither straightforward nor prescribed; the intelligent and devout reader has her options open.

16

MISSING

Then I looked up, and lo, a man there came
From midst the trees and stood regarding me
Until my tears were dried for very shame;
Then he cried out: O mourner where is she
Whom I have sought o'er every land and sea?
I love her, and she loveth me, and still
We meet no more than green hill meeteth hill.

With that he passed on sadly, and I knew,
That these had met, and missed in the dark night
Blinded by blindness of the world untrue
That hideth love, and maketh wrong of right.
Then midst my pity for their lost delight
Yet more with barren longing I grew weak
Yet more I mourned that I had none to seek.

18 William Morris, *A Book of Verse*, 1870. Writing and decoration by William Morris, with watercolour miniatures of Morris and his wife by Fairfax Murray.

The tradition of manuscript production was carried over into early book production, to the extent that a printed page may well evince the same kind of collaboration as an illuminated manuscript. However, the assumptions of such collaboration cannot always be what they were in the production of illuminated manuscripts, and the practical exigencies of book-making (the availability and expense of artists' involvement, the lazy and/or cost-cutting repetition of woodblock images, the greater clout of the author's writing) gradually loosened the interconnections between printed words and engraved imagery. That we nowadays refer to 'book illustrations' usually betrays our acceptance that the book's imagery is there to aid and abet the author's words, rather than ensure or encourage a unified and seamless (if complex) communication. It took an artist like William Blake to recover the opportunities of the integrated page where words and images not only come from the same hand but, as a result, contributed equally or mutually to the final reading. And we may track this nostalgia for a truly collaborative enterprise between word and image that the medieval manuscript could achieve beyond Blake to craftsmen in the late nineteenth and early twentieth centuries: works produced by William Morris in connection with his Kelmscott Press (illus. 18),

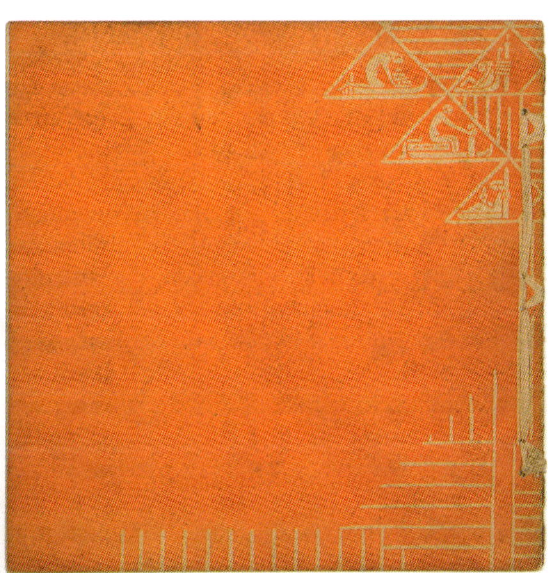

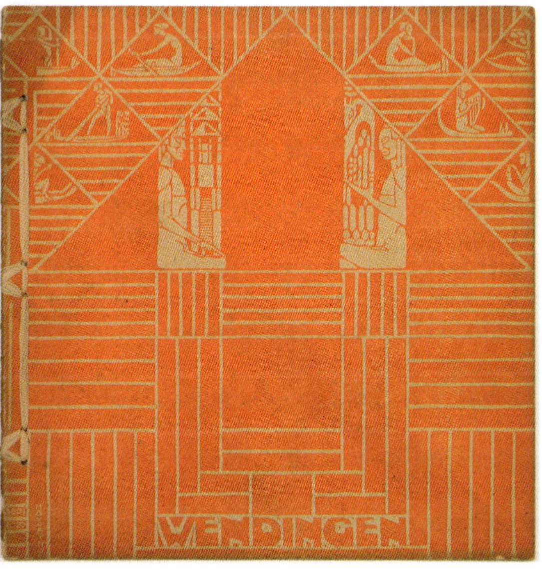

19 Cover of *Wendingen*, a woodcut design by H. A. van den Eijnde after Josef Hoffmann, volume 3, issue 8/9, November/December 1920.

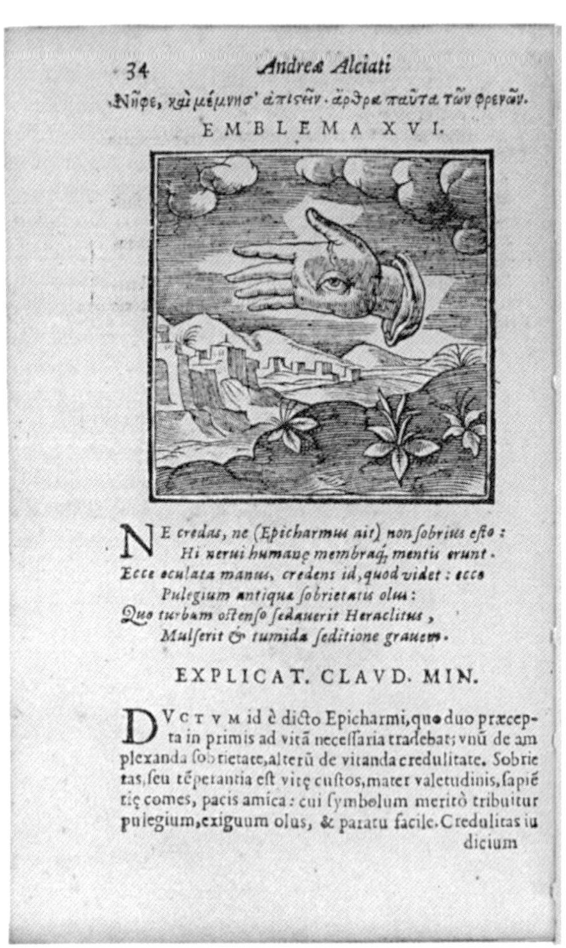

34 Andreæ Alciati

Νῆφε, καὶ μέμνησ' ἀπιστεῖν· ἄρθρα ταῦτα τῶν φρενῶν.

EMBLEMA XVI.

NE credas, ne (Epicharmus ait) non sobrius esto:
Hi nerui humanæ membraq; mentis erunt.
Ecce oculata manus, credens id, quod videt: ecce
Pulegium antiquæ sobrietatis olus:
Quo turbam ostenso sedauerit Heraclitus,
Mulserit & tumida seditione grauem.

EXPLICAT. CLAVD. MIN.

DVCTVM id è dicto Epicharmi, quo duo præcepta in primis ad vitā necessaria tradebat; vnū de amplexanda sobrietate, alterū de vitanda credulitate. Sobrietas, seu tēperantia est vitę custos, mater valetudinis, sapiētię comes, pacis amica: cui symbolum meritò tribuitur pulegium, exiguum olus, & paratu facile. Credulitas iu

dicium

20 Andrea Alciato, *Emblem XVI*, from Tozzi's 1618 edition.

the creation of artist's books or other such integrated productions as the Dutch journal *Wendingen*, which between 1918 and 1932 achieved an astonishing sequence of covers where the words of the journal title inhabit and hold their own while contributing to a rich, inventive and unified graphic field (illus. 19).[17] In these, the balance between word and its graphic context is maintained: textual elements do not wholly 'give up their identities and become pictorial',[18] yet their mutual work is crucial.

However, there have been some book forms even after the invention and development of the printing press that still contrived to hold word and image in something like a collaborative balance. Emblem books need to be considered in this category (illus. 20), and their production often harkened back to manuscript production.[19] The visual part depends upon its verbal commentary, and even those publications with an overwhelming text lean and enlarge upon the accompanying graphic component. It is true that in some early emblem books, the image was the supplement, being introduced to clarify or reify the verbally articulated idea or concept involved, but eventually the picture came to earn its place in the whole to the extent that our use of the term 'emblematic' can now sometimes refer less to a verbal/visual complex than to a visual sign to which we bring some verbal explanation; indeed, many discussions of emblem books illustrate only the graphic element. Ideally, the equality between an emblem's image and words is maintained and they perform together. The emblem book certainly lay behind Blake's composite works; indeed in the children's book *The Gates of Paradise* (1793) he had produced work in a format more obviously emblematic than his later illuminated books, where text and image blend seamlessly.

The late twentieth century has seen a considerably increased interest in and production of emblem books. The emblem's ambition to communicate verbally and visually was the attraction for an artist like Ian Hamilton Finlay (1926–2006), one of its most devoted and accomplished modern exponents. His reliance upon its dual languages, sustained by his instinct for the terse, gnomic and bare formulations of concrete poetry, has revived the emblem's reputation and extended its scope. Especially when collected in a gathering of related emblems, as in his *Heroic Emblems* (1977) with Ron Costley and Stephen Bann, or *A Wartime Garden* (illus. 21),

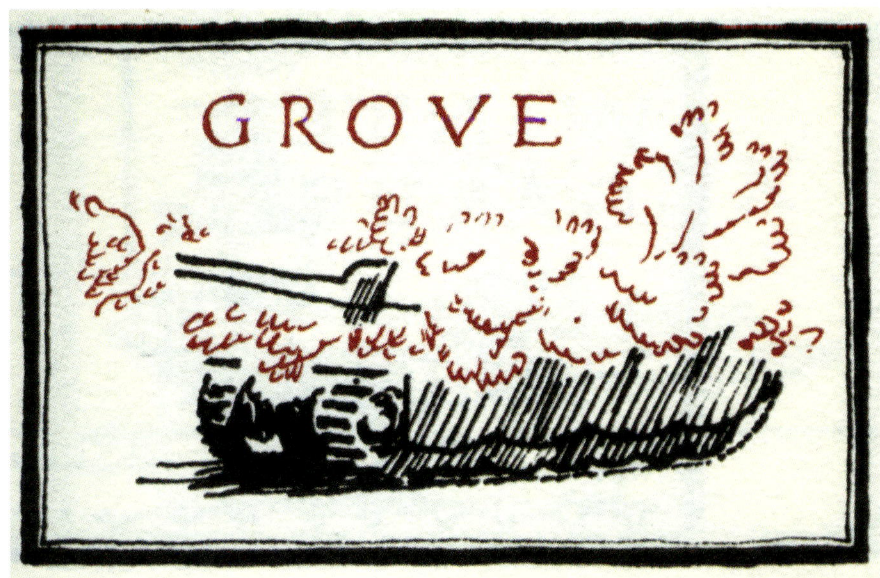

21 Ian Hamilton Finlay, with Ron Costley and John Andrew, *Grove* from *A Wartime Garden*, 1990.

Finlay can exploit both the affiliations and the tensions between word and image to renew the emblematic duality with fresh vigour, and even to carry this bifocal collaboration beyond the printed page into a variety of other formats, including gardens and parks.[20]

Modern technology has exponentially increased the creative opportunities for words and images to cohabit the same space. Advances in printing technology have ensured that the more intricate combination of word and image (more complex than just laying in woodcut blocks beside movable type) became increasingly feasible and exploited. If Walter Benjamin in the 1920s and '30s could envisage authorship radically altered by the 'precision of typographic forms' and the defeat of the pen by the typewriter (with 'variable typefaces' – eventually the IBM golfball),[21] computer and digital technology developed since have so much further encouraged the collaborations between graphic imagery and verbal texts that the term 'collaboration' even seems a somewhat old-fashioned notion.

These four modes by which visual art and imagery have annexed and relied upon words – the explicit, the implied, the additive and the collaborative – are not clearly self-contained. They can merge and can even usurp each other's function, as when a title like *Mona Lisa* or *Tempestà* has so identified itself with the image we see that it might as well be inscribed on the surface, or when scholarly and journalistic commentary has so coloured the public's assessment of a painting – Picasso's *Guernica*, perhaps – that it is impossible to confront it 'innocently', that is to say, without verbal presuppositions and supplements. Bearing in mind, then, the fluidity of our four modes of understanding how words work in and with visual arts, some sketches of a historical narrative that traces the fortunes of these collaborations will chart different cultural resolutions of the role words can play.

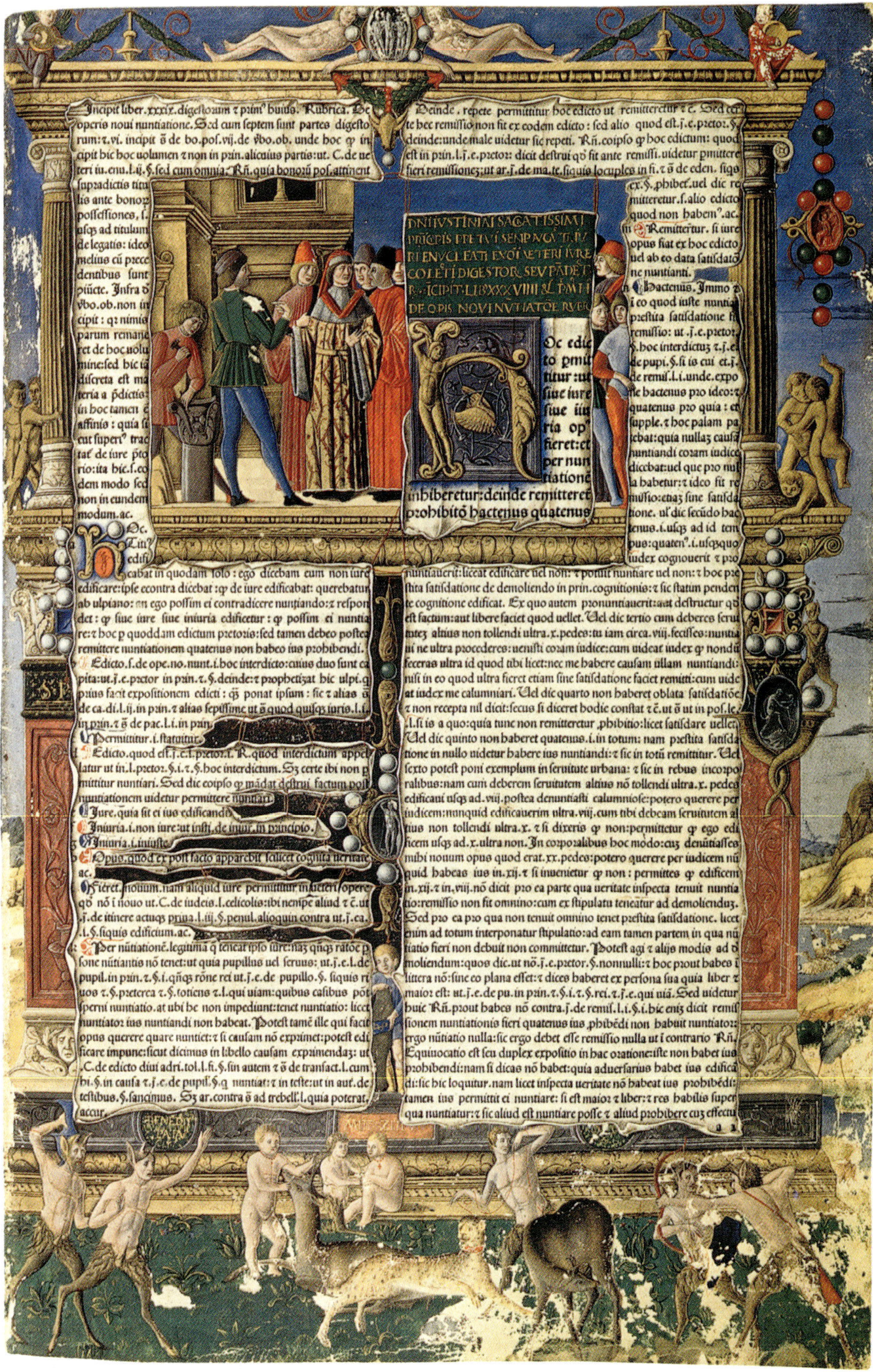

1 Justinian's *Digest* with the *Commentary* of Accursius of Florence, printed by Nicolaus Jenson, Venice, 1477, and ornamented with minatures.

I

The Fabric and the Dance: Word and Image to 1900

JOHN DIXON HUNT

I

In *Image, Text, Ideology* W.J.T. Mitchell observes that the verbal and the visual seem forever locked in a 'dialectic' exchange, weaving a fabric of signs that draws differently in different cultures upon the warp and the woof of word and image (or maybe image is the warp and word, the woof): it is, he writes, 'a protracted struggle for dominance between pictorial and linguistic signs, each claiming proprietary rights on a 'nature' to which only it has access'.[1] Elegant as this formulation is, it adopts, surely, a very modernist perspective, insisting on the 'struggle', the power game ('dominance'), between the two sign systems. Indeed, he goes on to stress that the critic's task is not to 'heal' this 'split' but to adjudicate 'what interests and powers' are served by the contest, which is not necessarily what the scrutiny of a woven cloth is all about.

To look at some early historical examples of this 'fabric' is to apprehend far more co-operation, even collaboration, between word and image. Especially if our focus is upon visual work that invokes the verbal and on how the visual is influenced or conditioned by its use of the verbal (and these are the concerns here), many early works of art reveal ample indications of a 'unity', as Michel Foucault puts it (nicely blurring the competing terms in his formulation of it), 'between what is depicted by language and what is uttered by plastic form'.[2] Indeed, Mitchell's metaphor of a woven cloth more readily suggests that, however dominant the *separate* colours of warp and woof may be, it is the overall texture that catches the eye; we may specifically track, say, the coloured warp through the cloth, but it succumbs in the end to the fabric's overall, if discernibly mottled, hue. My own metaphor for what this liaison of depicting language and plastic utterance can achieve would be the dance, where again the effect of a certain totality or ensemble is crucial: it takes two to tango, or, in the words of W. B. Yeats, 'who can tell the dancer from the dance?'

This cohesion or unity that blends without obliterating distinct differences between word and image is more striking in the work that concerns this volume – the image's use of the word – than if we were to focus on literary evocations, emulations and presentations of the visual – the work generally called ekphrastic.[3] When the verbal mimes or tries to replicate effects of the visual, there is more truth to Mitchell's emphasis on power struggles: the verbal has always yearned to be on a par with what the painter or sculptor can do. The *Imagines* of Philostratus, the descriptions of paintings in early fictions, the famous account of Achilles' shield in Homer's *Iliad*, all betray an envy of the visual that does indeed imply a creative determination to use the verbal means at a writer's disposal to compete with, even outdo, his visual colleagues. Mitchell himself largely approaches his materials

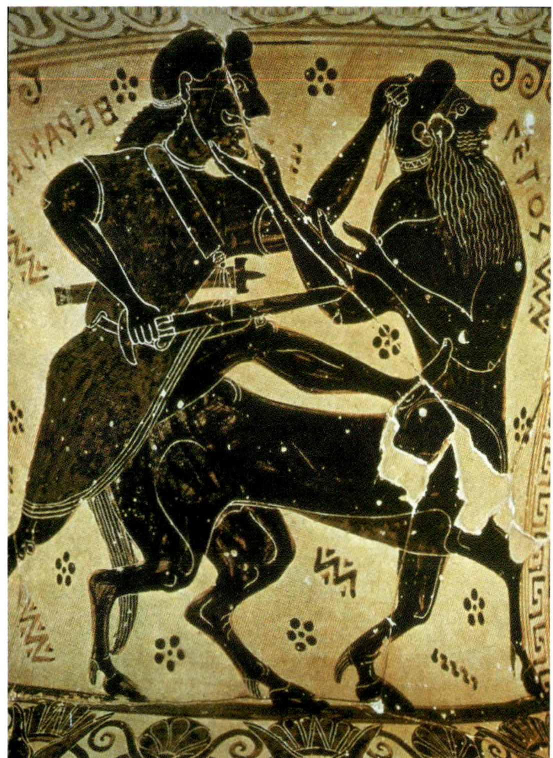

2 *The Nessos Amphora*, detail of Herakles fighting Nessos, both of whom are identified by name, 7th century BC.

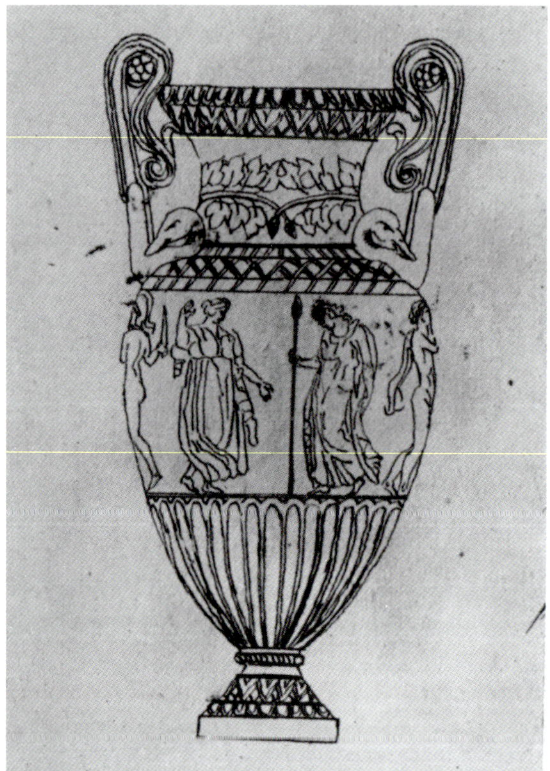

3 Keats's own traced drawing, *c.* 1819, of an engraving of the *Sosibios Vase* in the Louvre.

with that literary bias and of course he does it in words, both of which encourage a fascination with the power plays of inter-art rivalry; he writes, furthermore, from within a university system still much compartmentalized between different and sometimes rival disciplines.

II

Early examples of words invoked by image-makers suggest a much more relaxed recognition that either each needs each other or, at the very least, each tolerates the other's intrusions. It seems that any culture with a written or scripted language found it useful to add words to its visual imagery. Examples are many, if scattered. But they suggest that explanatory *text* was never deemed hostile to or incompatible with graphic imagery, which could be allowed extra scope and impact by its addition. If Greek vases inscribed names alongside the persons represented (an innovation of the seventh century BC[4]), this was to provide quick access to beholders' recollections or even provoke their recitations of the stories depicted (illus. 2). The same is true of a mosaic in the Beth-Alpha Synagogue, Israel, of the sacrifice of Abraham, where the players in this important Jewish drama are identified (illus. 4). When otherwise generic illustrations (without visual attributes that identified them) were verbally identified, it allowed the viewer to recall an event and then project a recollection of it upon the visual scene; in the moment of reading the words that identify the participants, their story springs to life.

Needless to say, literacy ensured an elite and educated audience for such art, though one can imagine situations in which those who could read both deciphered the lettering for those who could not and thereby 'released' the narratives from their iconic forms for a wider audience. This is, of course, the activity that sustains John Keats's famous ekphrastic 'Ode on a Grecian Urn': except that the Romantic poet not only, we must assume, supposes that he is confronted with a vase that contains no explanatory verbal inscriptions (illus. 3), but is also obliged in his belatedness, because of his distance from classical Greece, to struggle over interpreting its imagery; he must ask 'Who are these coming to the sacrifice?', because the vase

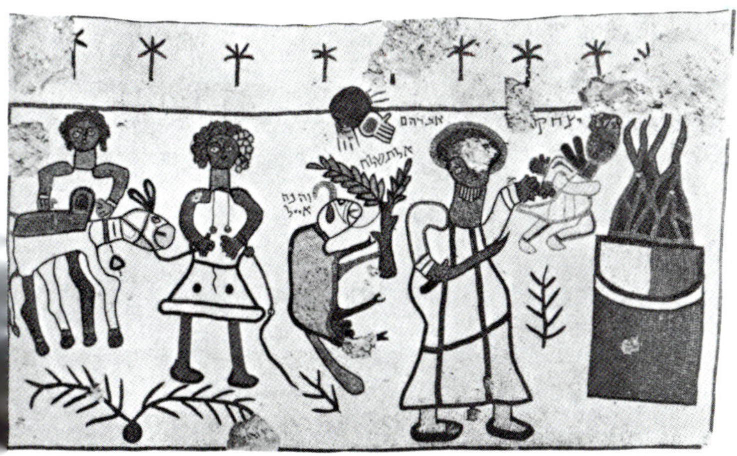

4 Beth-Alpha Synagogue, Israel: mosaic showing the sacrifice of Isaac by Abraham, 6th century.

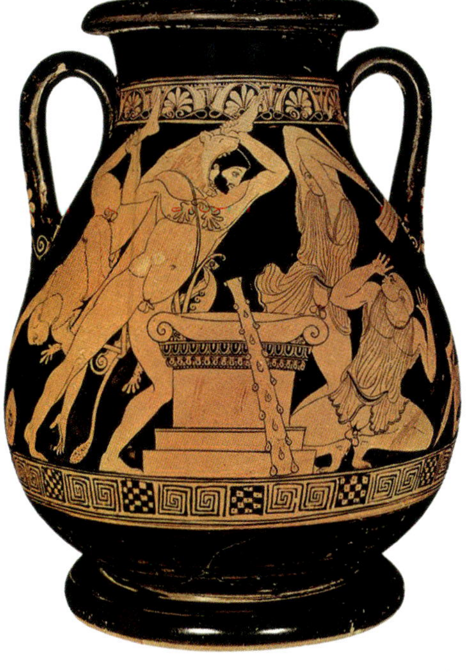

5 Red-figure pelike, with a depiction of Herakles killing Busiris, neither of whom are identified; the story came from Herodotus. *c.* 430 BC.

does not display any labels or verbal identifications, and he does not have a secure way of identifying a story that he knows is there before his eyes. That Greek vases were able to neglect or abandon inscriptions (illus. 5) suggests, nonetheless, that their imagery was familiar enough to contemporaries without verbal adjuncts and could still promote verbal recitations or commentaries on the events depicted on them; it is their much later audience who will lament, like Keats, that 'not a soul . . . can e'er return' to 'tell' their story.

In Assyrian sculpture, texts were included in reliefs as a mode of exegesis.[5] Some panels from *c.* 825 BC show the Assyrian king (illus. 6) receiving tributes from Jehu, the king of Israel – the cuneiform caption above the depicted scene lists the items carried as 'silver, gold, a golden vase, a golden dish, golden goblets, golden buckets, a load of tin, a staff for the hand of the king, wooden hunting spears', presumably because the sculpture cannot differentiate the different materials and therefore adequately celebrate their value. On other scenes (illus. 7) of conquest and triumph (now *c.* 645 BC) the cuneiform captions make clear, for example, the prestige of the Babylonian booty that Ashurbanipal is inspecting, adding its expository gloss to the visual scene where the status of the conqueror is communicated graphically – he is simply represented at an obviously larger scale.

Not unlike Chinese characters, briefly cited in the Introduction, Egyptian hieroglyphs function both visually (they are pictures of items in the world) and verbally (they are orally translated), until their repression by Christian decree in the fourth century AD. In a tomb wall from *c.* 1900 BC (illus. 8) we see different hunting scenes that feature Khnumhotep, his wife, his concubine and one of his sons. One inscription tells their names and many titles, and describes Khnumhotep himself as 'great in fish, rich in wild-fowl, loving the goddess of the chase'; another rehearses the pleasures of the various scenes, but essentially tells the viewer what is clearly depicted: 'Canoeing in the papyrus beds, the pools of wild-fowl, the marches and the streams, spearing with the two-pronged spear, he transfixes thirty fish; how delightful is the day of hunting the hippopotamus'.[6] We may tend to see such verbal additions as no more than identifying captions to the imagery, but the incidence of this usage and above all the visual impact of the 'writing' itself make them a very early merger of the two modes.[7]

One of the most ubiquitous remains of ancient Roman civilization is the inscribed tablet or stonework; not aesthetically as satisfying as their sculptural figures of gods and emperors, the carved words nevertheless often have an iconic force of their own beyond whatever they denote (that this recognition is forced on many people because they cannot read Latin does not under-

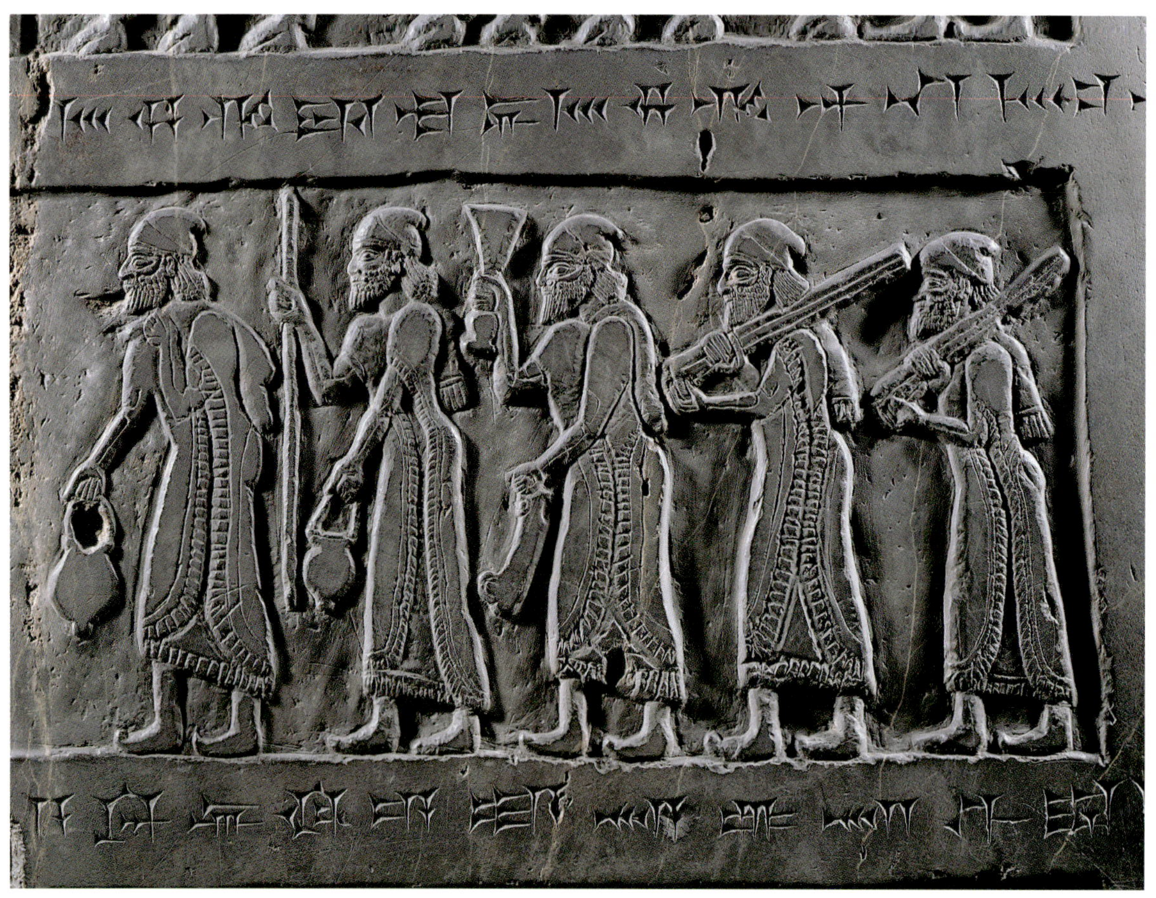

6 Panel from the *Black Obelisk of Shalmaneser III*, from Nimrod, *c.* 825 BC.

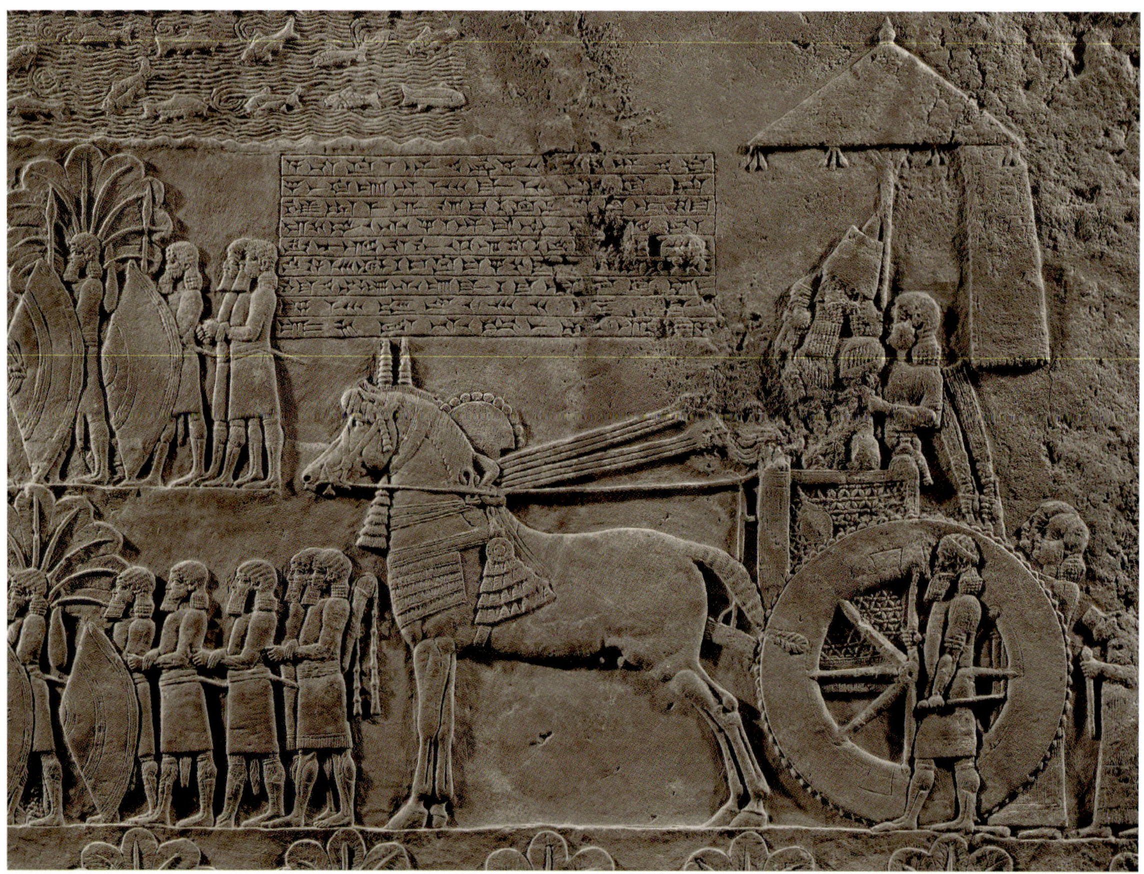

7 Ashurbanipal inspecting the booty of Babylon, *c.* 645 BC.

mine the point for those who also understand them). The visual effect of many classical inscriptions is part of their appeal (illus. 9),[8] something that was recognized by many subsequent carvers who for various reasons needed to recall *romanitas*: distinctive calligraphy like the V (for the U), the careful shaping of other capital letters, the use of Roman numerals, even the running together of words (see Introduction, illus. 10) and the prominent display of such inscriptions on buildings constitute a distinctly visual inheritance that gives a *color romanus* or classical aura even when the language used is modern and vernacular. Ian Hamilton Finlay, in particular, has invoked the visual emphases of non-Latin inscriptions, but carved in imitation of Roman work, in his explorations of the neo-classical imagination. For him the word can have added meaning by virtue of its visual performance (illus. 10).

III

These early traditions whereby visual art relied upon written notations to clarify and enlarge the attention and understanding of its viewers did not, obviously, get displaced in later centuries. Given that the church building was a focal point of cultural performance, it is not surprising that in all of its decorative elements the word was invoked, not least in its various stained glass.[9] The recourse to texts was wide-ranging: donors and saints are identified by name, especially needed perhaps for those saints with lesser name recognition, who continued to need identifying in the windows of the chapel at All Souls College, Oxford (illus. 11). The acts and associations of saints could be rendered best by the accompaniment of words – St Anne, known to have taught the Virgin to read, is shown with a book on which the alphabet is inscribed. Texts drawn into the ensemble of a window included such obvious ones as the Bible (the great east window of York Minster displays 81

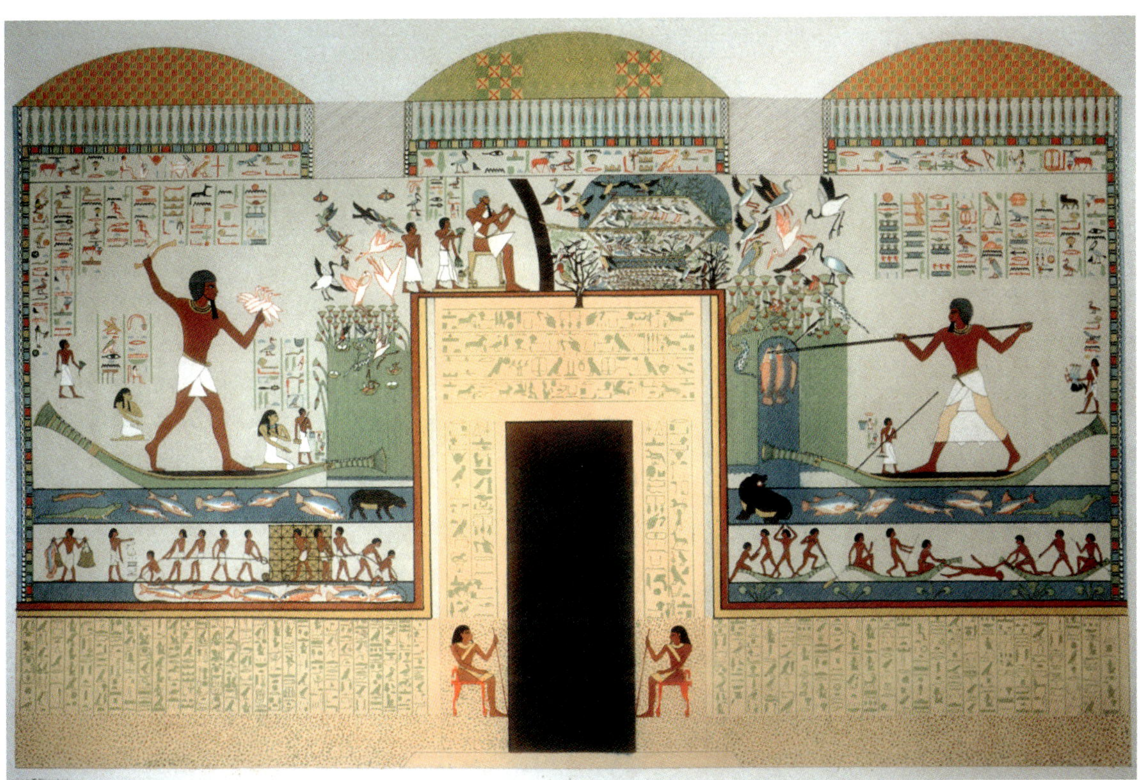

8 Wall from the tomb of Khnumhotep near Beni Hassam, *c.* 1900 BC.

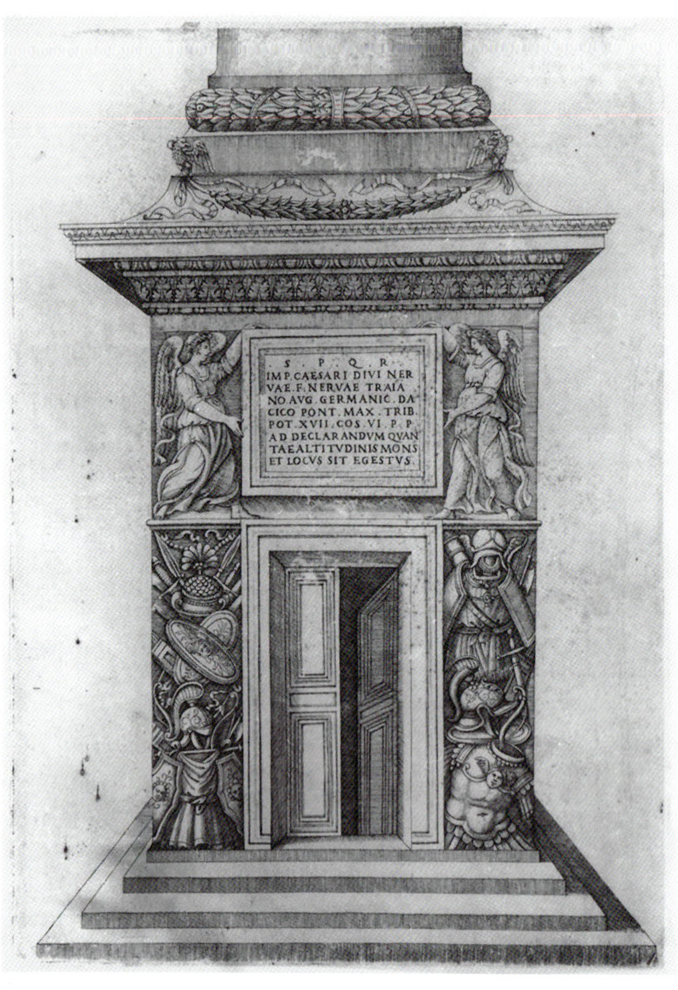

9 A 16th-century engraving of Trajan's Column, Rome.

10 The Temple of Apollo, Little Sparta, Stonypath, near Dunsyre, Scotland.

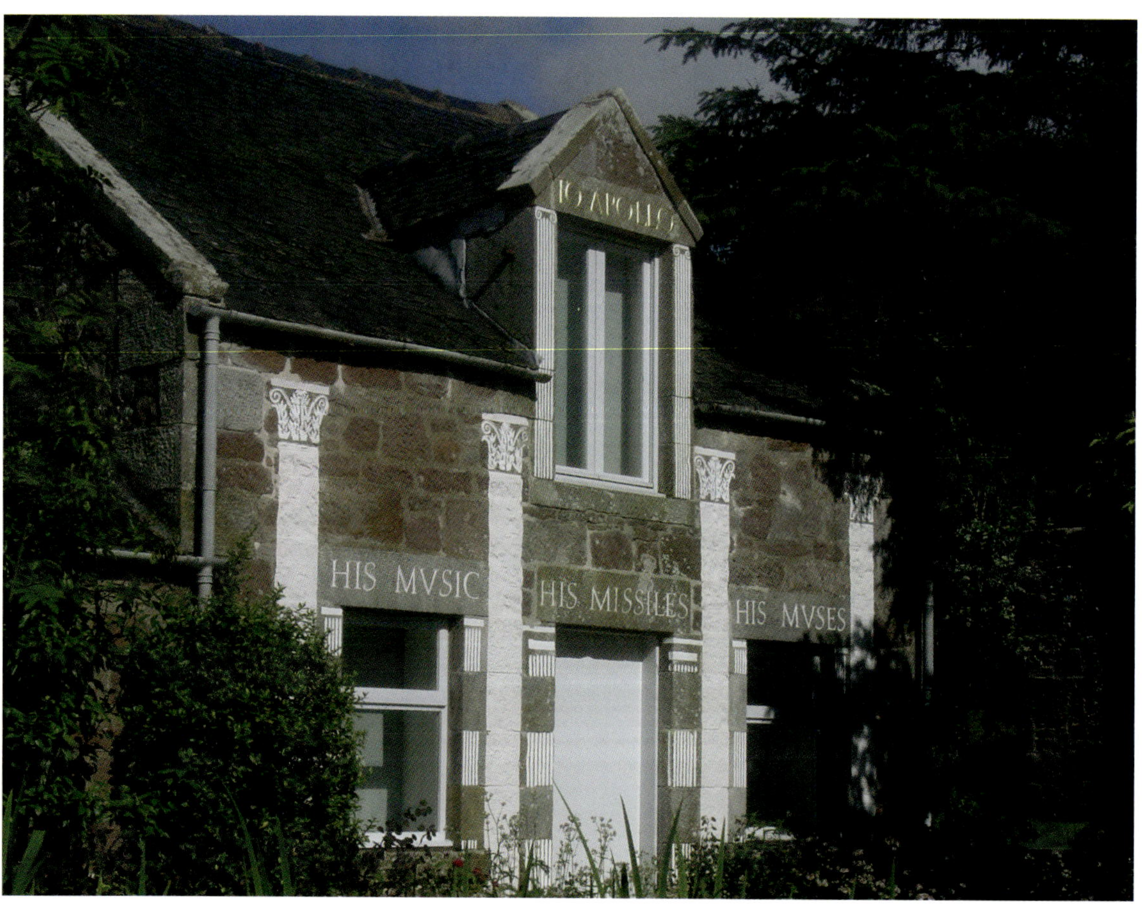

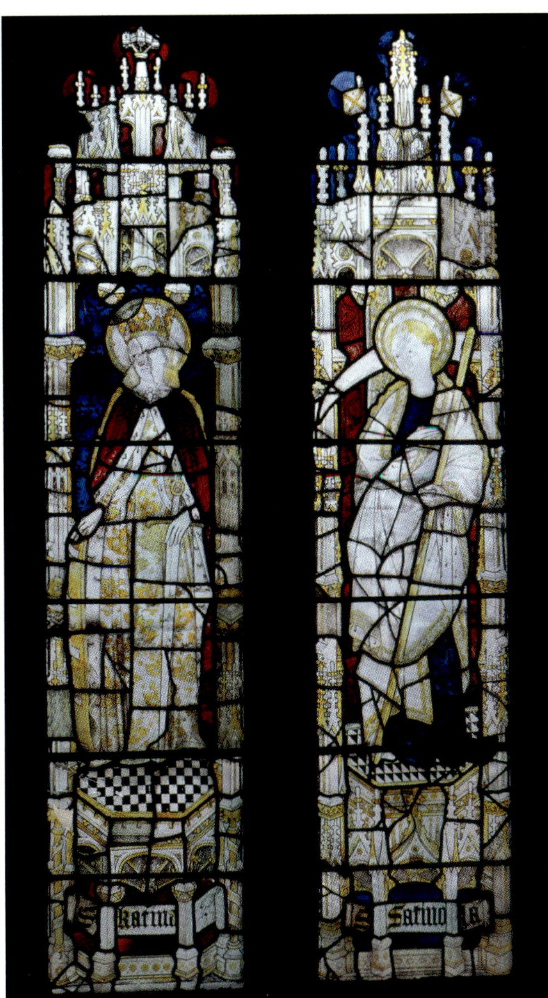

11 Saints Catherine and Sativola, 1400–50, stained-glass window, All Souls Chapel, Oxford.

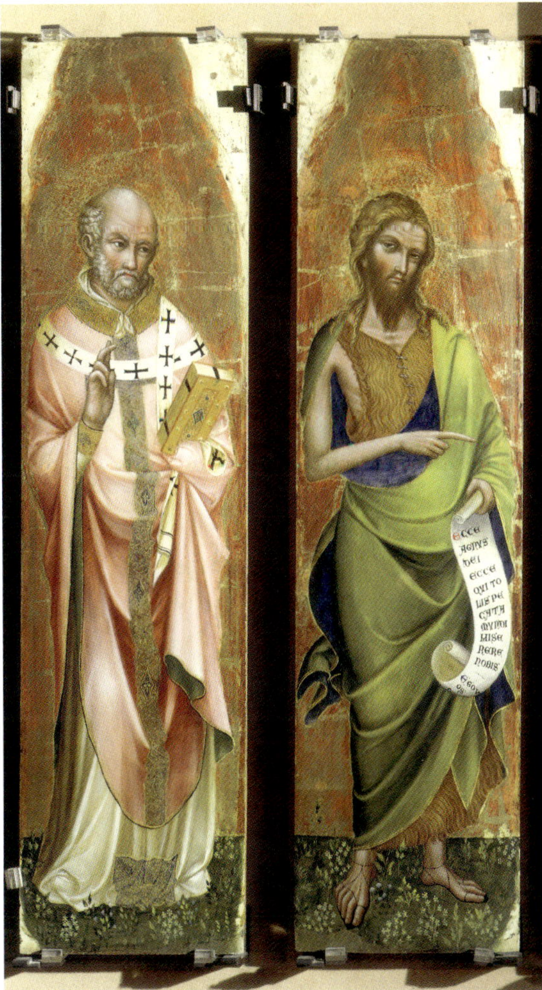

12 Lorenzo Veneziano, *St Gregory and John the Baptist*, detail from polyptych of the *Annunciation and Saints*, 1371.

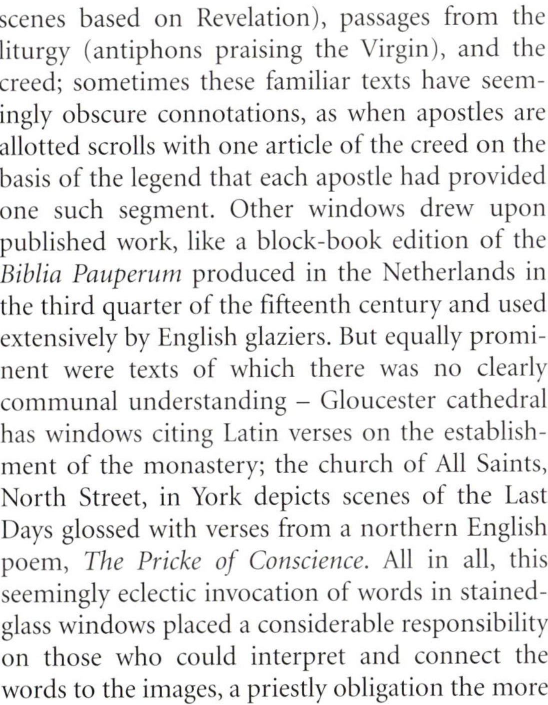

scenes based on Revelation), passages from the liturgy (antiphons praising the Virgin), and the creed; sometimes these familiar texts have seemingly obscure connotations, as when apostles are allotted scrolls with one article of the creed on the basis of the legend that each apostle had provided one such segment. Other windows drew upon published work, like a block-book edition of the *Biblia Pauperum* produced in the Netherlands in the third quarter of the fifteenth century and used extensively by English glaziers. But equally prominent were texts of which there was no clearly communal understanding – Gloucester cathedral has windows citing Latin verses on the establishment of the monastery; the church of All Saints, North Street, in York depicts scenes of the Last Days glossed with verses from a northern English poem, *The Pricke of Conscience*. All in all, this seemingly eclectic invocation of words in stained-glass windows placed a considerable responsibility on those who could interpret and connect the words to the images, a priestly obligation the more needed in that 'only rarely did churches present a coherent iconographical programme'[10] the narrative of which was either self-evident or familiar. And in many other incidents the total absence of words from the glazing means that the exegesis had to be derived via priestly commentary or, somewhat unusually, by the provision of actual scrolls (crib sheets, so to speak) within the body of the church.[11]

The centrality of stained glass in the Christian church did not exempt other media from the same reliance upon verbal glasses. Even John the Baptist, alone of the four saints in Lorenzo Veneziano's *Annunciation and Saints* (illus. 12), is 'identified' by the scroll upon which his announcement of the saviour's coming is set out (in Latin), though his pointing to the Annunciation scene on his left should perhaps have made clear who he was.[12] And the insertion of words written on scrolls within a painting came to serve other purposes than simply the identification of a subject or the provision of some clue for a possible reception: artists

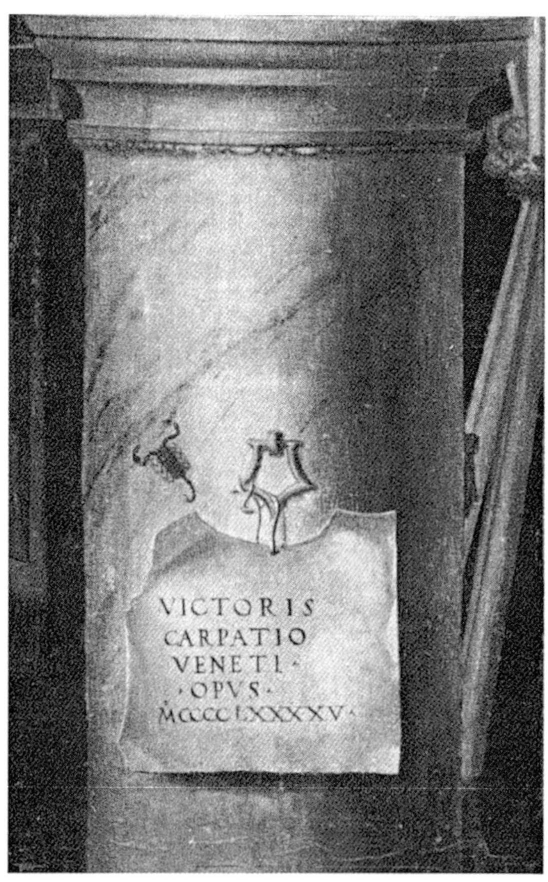

13 Vittore Carpaccio, A detail of the *Meeting of St Orsola and Ereo and the Departure of the Pilgrims*, 1495.

14 Vittore Carpaccio, *Portrait of a Knight*, 1510, oil on canvas.

announced their 'authorship', sometimes with illusionistic labels plausibly discovered (and sometimes hard to find) within the depicted territory of the narrative (illus. 13). Another Carpaccio, the handsome but anonymous knight in shining armour (illus. 14), contains a visible piece of paper caught in the plants at its bottom left corner; on the sheet we can read MALO MORI QVAM FOEDARI ('I would rather die than foul/ disgrace myself') which functions as the man's credo, impresa or personal motto (something we shall also find in later portraiture, where heraldic or other signs declare what the silent image cannot do). Similarly, but now with more panache and deliberation, Mantegna not only labels the fleeing vices on their headbands in bottom right (illus. 15), but paints a long scroll wrapped around the figure of Daphne in the process of changing into a laurel tree on which are written the Latin words that explain the scenario that is performed by the painting.

Words added within the picture surface may have various plausible justifications: a scrap of paper dropped in the undergrowth or tacked to a wall on which a scorpion crawls; scrolls or rolls containing written messages were familiar enough, so their possession by figures who might be reading from them is credible; a scroll wrapped around a morphing tree has less claim to 'realism' but serves, along with the other words, to steer the viewer directly to the moralizing allegory. Clothes, too, might be embroidered, as in an extraordinary painting by Jan van Eyck where letters are embroidered on the hem of the Virgin's dress (illus. 16). The Virgin herself needed no identification, but her size (disproportionate to the church where she stands) and the odd fact that the sun is shown striking the floor from the *north* (by a painter noted for his fidelity to representing space and light) might have needed explanation. It is provided obliquely by the Latin verses embroidered on her red robe, a text that connects the Madonna with mystical symbolism; the words were for the canonical hour of Lauds on the Feast of her Assumption and were taken from a devotional text used in northern churches and drawn from the *Book of Wisdom*: they read in translation:

> It [that is, Divine Wisdom embodied in the Virgin and the Church] is more beautiful than the sun and above the whole order of the stars. Being compared with [natural] light, she is found its superior. She is the brightness of eternal light, and the flawless mirror of God's majesty.[13]

For those who could spot and then read the Latin, a whole larger significance was thus opened up and the painting's strange dislocations of reality made symbolically meaningful. Even before such a clue was unearthed and applied, the original frame for the panel would have been inscribed with the words of a hymn that contained the lines, 'as the sunbeam through the glass,/ Passeth but not

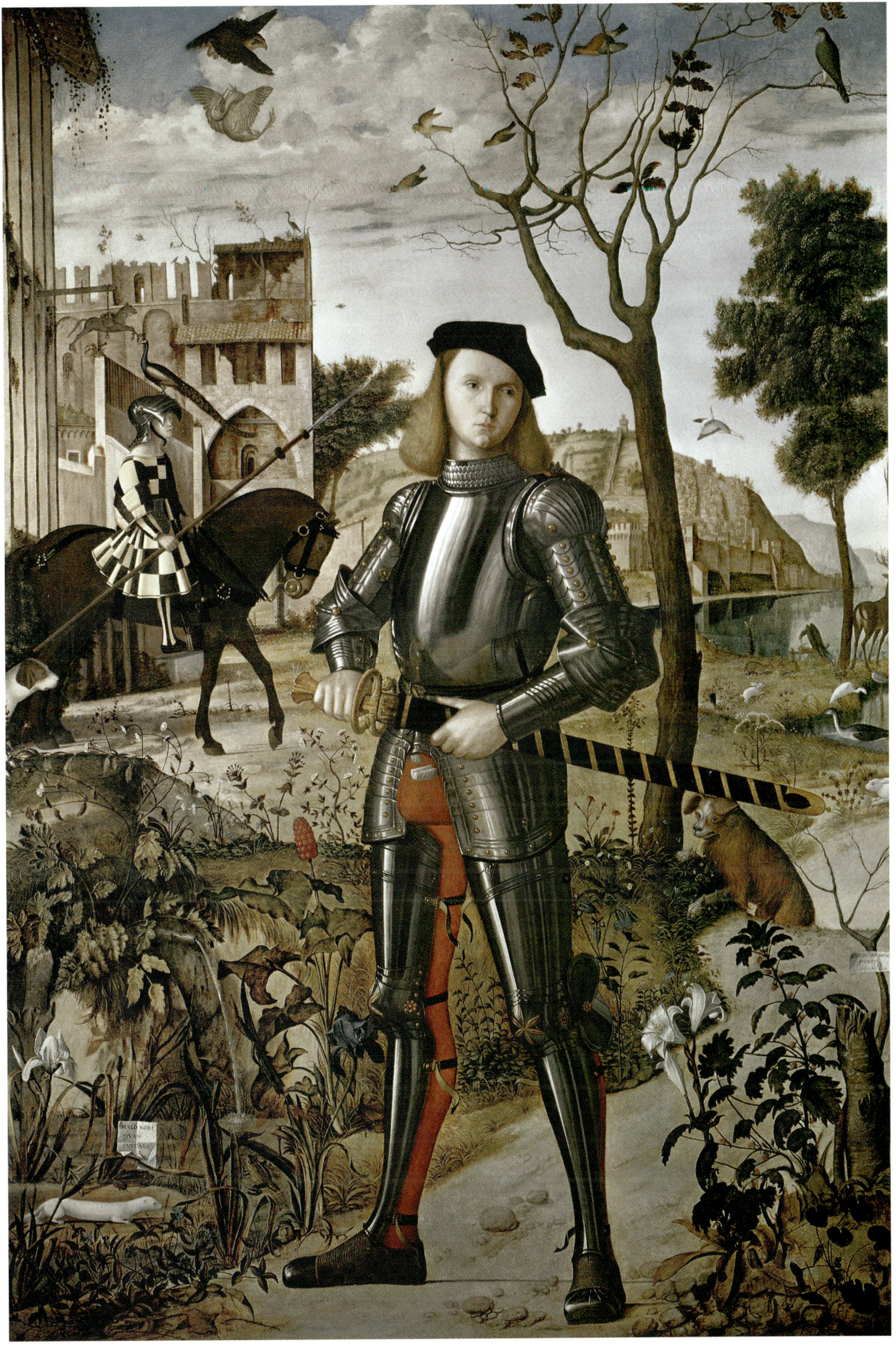
MALO MORI
QVAM

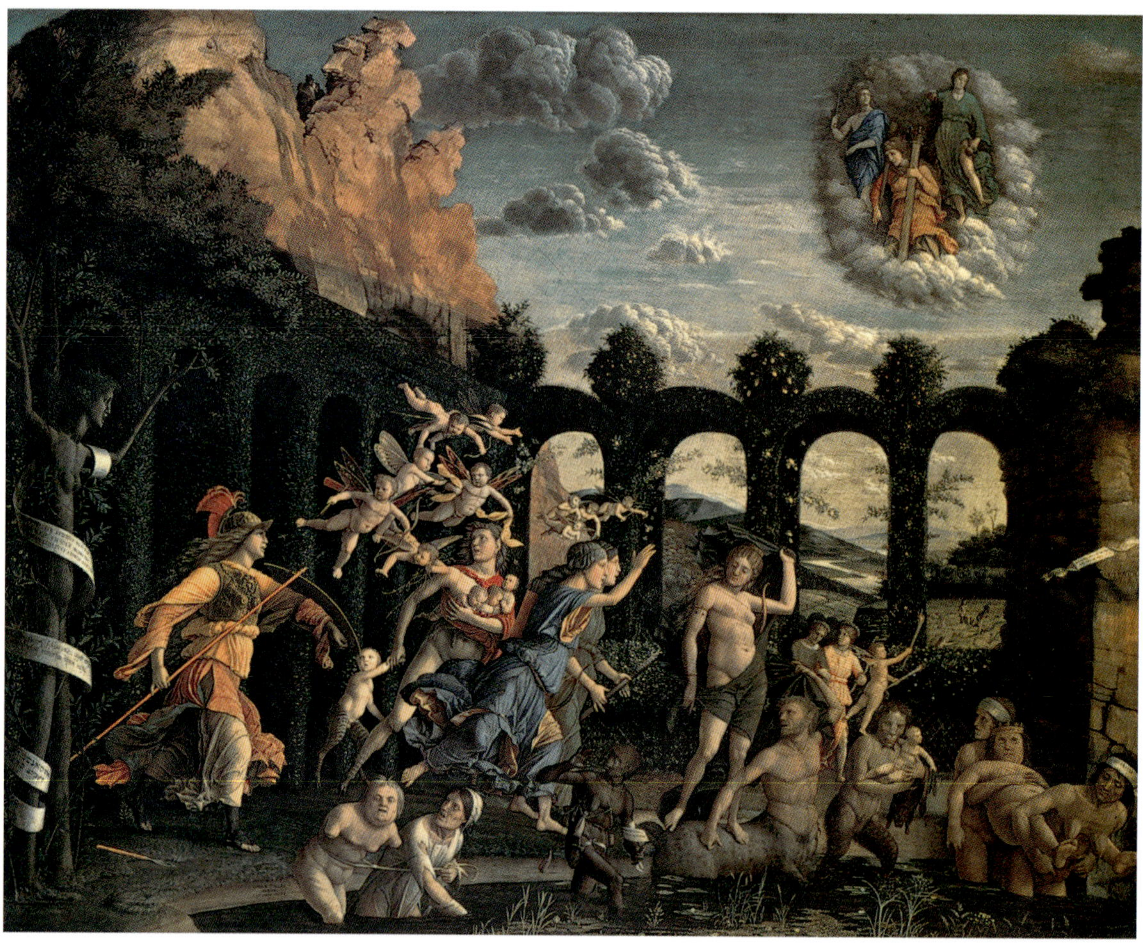

15 Andrea Mantegna, *Minerva Chasing Away the Vices from the Garden of Virtue*, 1502, tempera on canvas.

breaketh', lines that would perhaps have initiated for the faithful a more strenuous scrutiny of what the painter had presented to them.

The human love and even need of sustaining and/or entertaining narratives were undiminished.[14] The requirement to extend the visual into verbal gloss and exegesis did not lose any of its force. Indeed, Western Christianity relied heavily upon the alliances that it could forge between word and image in the interests of education and faith. If the ancient worlds imaged their conquests, heroes and symbolic events familiar in oral literature, the new Christian religion had its own wealth of admonitory and sustaining verbal narratives, which, given widespread illiteracy, needed to be communicated in images (as well as through oral recitation). There were the stories of characters and events in both Old and New Testaments, then increasingly there were the lives of saints and church fathers to be told, and elaborate, even arcane, notions of theology, religious behaviour and belief to be demonstrated visually as well as elaborately expounded in verbal commentary. Some of these visualizations must have been self-explanatory, at least within the context of priestly commentary and daily liturgies: three crosses, 13 persons seated at a supper table, a man and a woman taking an apple off a serpent entwined in a tree, a figure pouring water over the head of another haloed man, even a beautiful woman seated in a walled garden beside a fountain, or other familiar images from the *Psalms* or *Song of Songs*: most of these presumably needed no verbal gloss. But nonetheless artists still added identifying

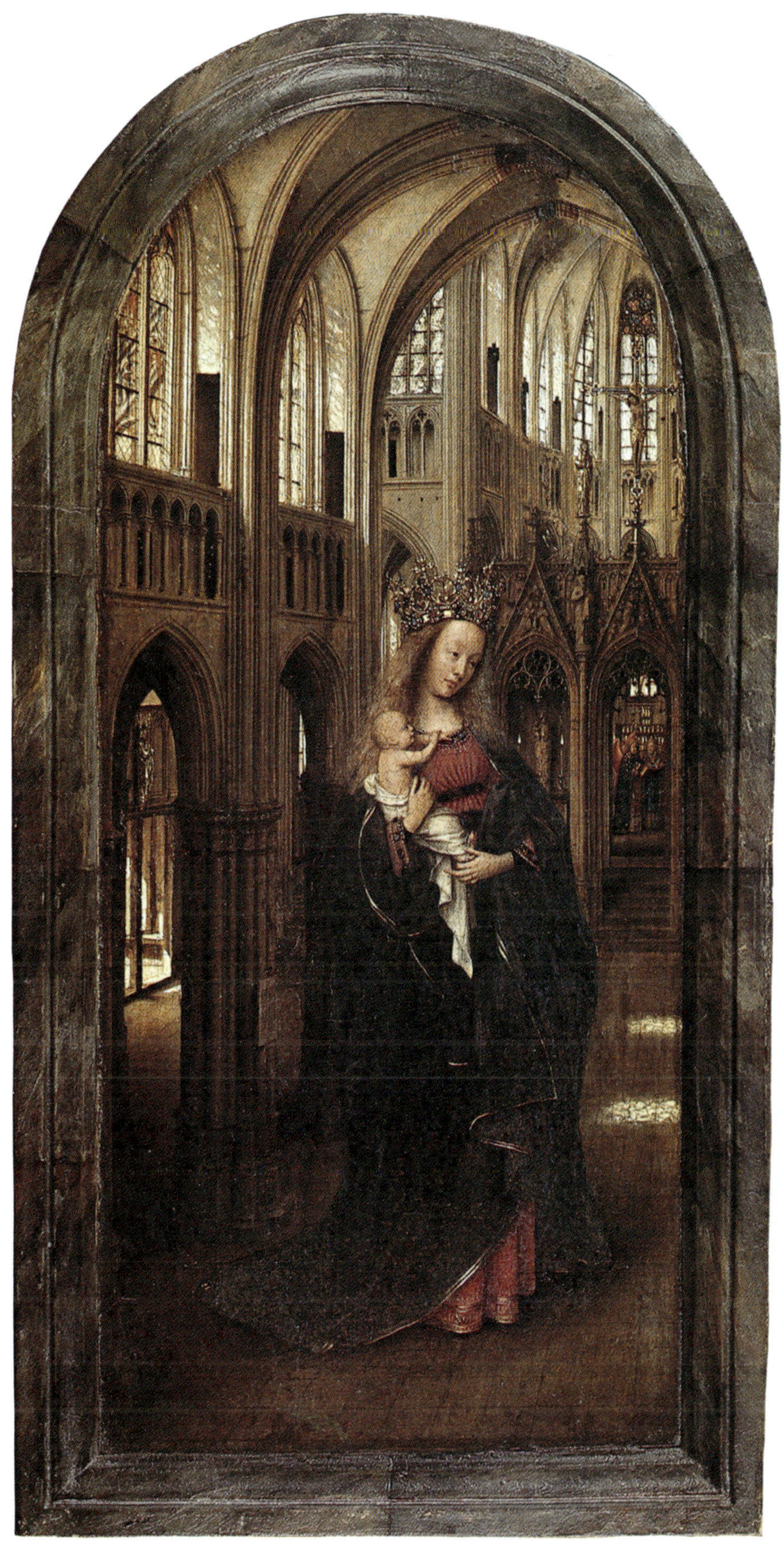

16 Jan van Eyck, *Madonna in the Church*, 1437–9, oil on wood.

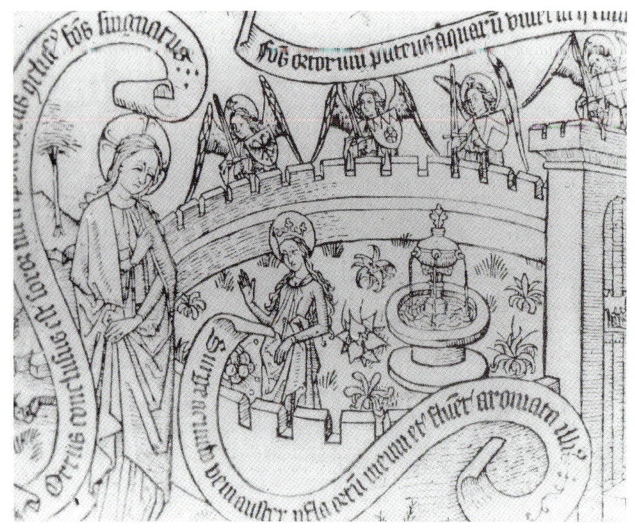

17 Woodcut detail illustrating the *Song of Songs*.

captions, just as the modern museum would add labels, and even invented titles, presumably to make doubly sure the incident was understood or to make its literary 'source' available (illus. 17), or to lead meditation off in any number of appropriate, even if recondite, directions. Many medieval examples in different media suggest that the simple captioning of an image would quickly identify the pictorial scene: the crowning of David is announced in Latin in the Glazier Psalter presumably because the crowning of a monarch was routine and the biblical typological event needed to be distinguished for its own associations (illus. 18). One might imagine that Cain's murder of his brother Abel would be visually accessible: but in English art the murder weapon was conspicuously represented as the jawbone of an ass, which the Biblical text does not mention (that weapon features in stories of Samson, not Cain),[15] so the annotation of a drawing with the victim's name makes sense (illus. 19).

But as the Christian centuries acquired more and more narratives of saints and martyrs, and hymns, volumes of scriptural exegesis and literary directions for spiritual conduct were composed, so there grew in equal measure the necessity to signal even on clear visual imagery what the originating verbal text had been. Saints' biographies became a major pictorial subject and in the Eastern church by the thirteenth century these developed a sophisticated format in which a central icon of the saint was surrounded by smaller scenes of his life's crucial actions or encounters (illus. 20); these incidents are often labelled, and even in Latin, not Greek, if the icon was destined for a community where that was the habitual language.[16]

But in large part because of the challenge to visual representations during the iconoclastic period (roughly 726–843), the relationships of word to image in Byzantine art became considerably complex, as did the relationship of their ensemble to the beings represented.[17] The Virgin, Christ and saints, along with the donors who wished to honour and pray to them, are not only usually identified but more frequently may hold scrolls or open volumes which script a dialogue or direct a prayer. Given the complicated culture of icons, those words could function as a means of interacting with the image rather than (for instance) being taken as the utterance of the divine figures represented; thus reading the texts of such icons (or having them read for one by the literate) established a direct involvement between the worshipper and the saint or divinity. In many Orthodox churches, what may seem like a bombardment of images combined with carefully selected and annexed words that totally surround, envelop and presumably wholly absorb the worshippers is a means of directing their understanding of both the icons themselves and their own relationship to them.[18] We even know of Eastern clergy being

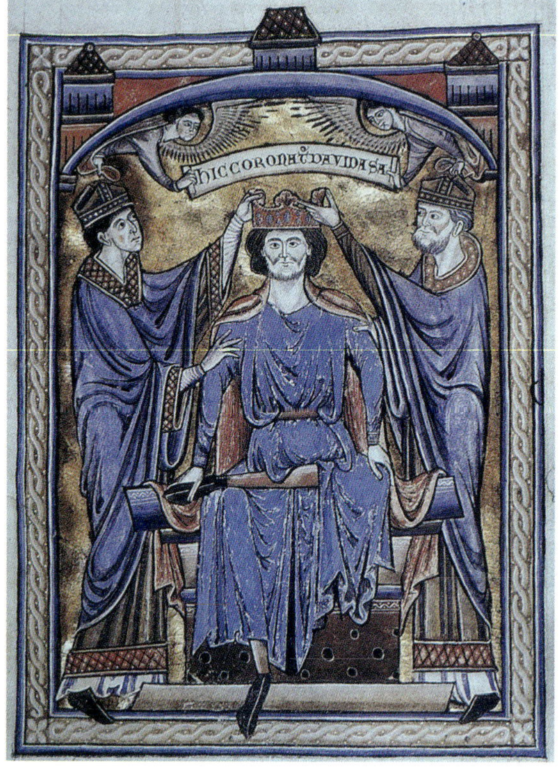

18 The Crowning of David, from the Glazier Psalter *c.* 1230.

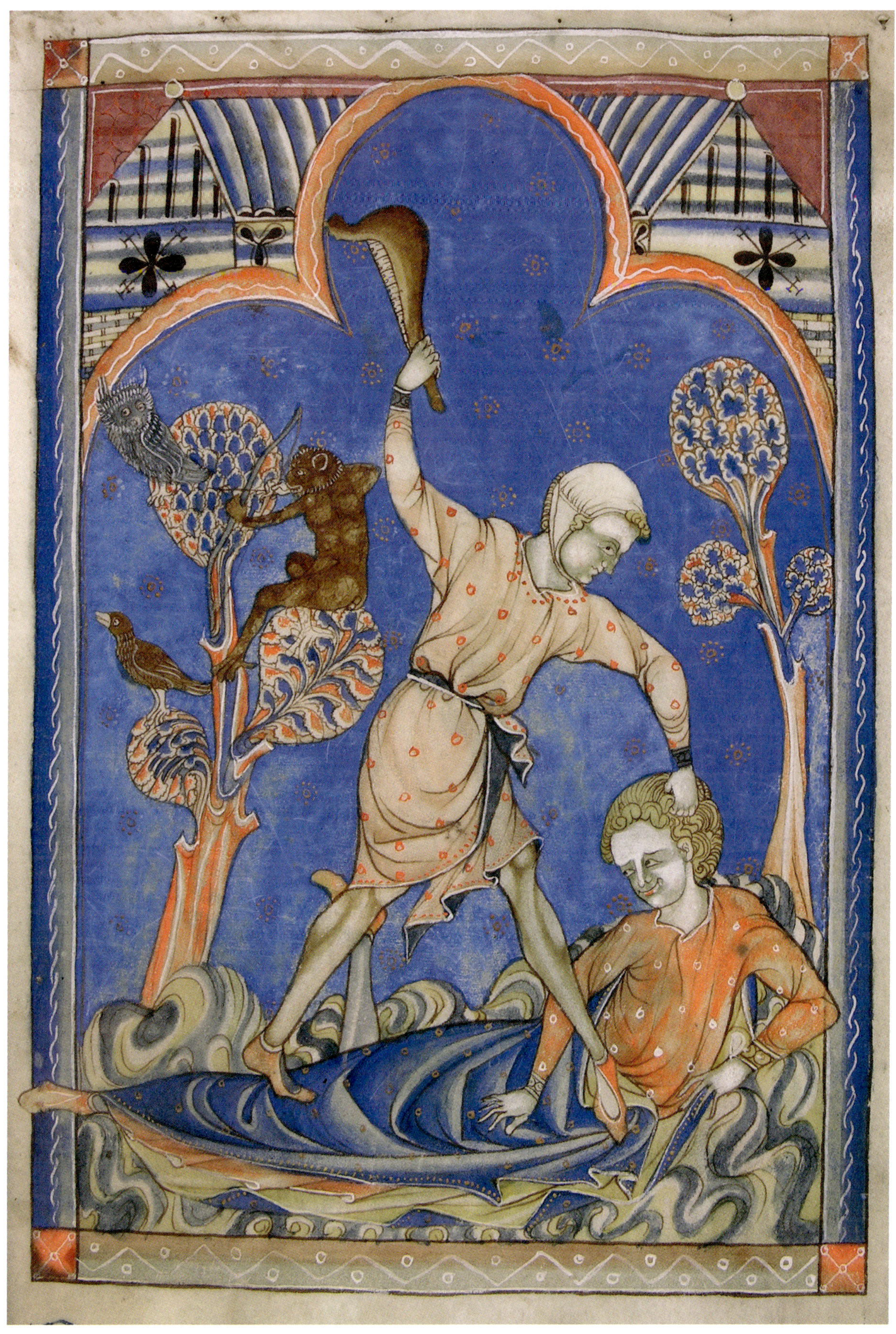

19 Cain killing Abel, in a late 13th-century Psalter.

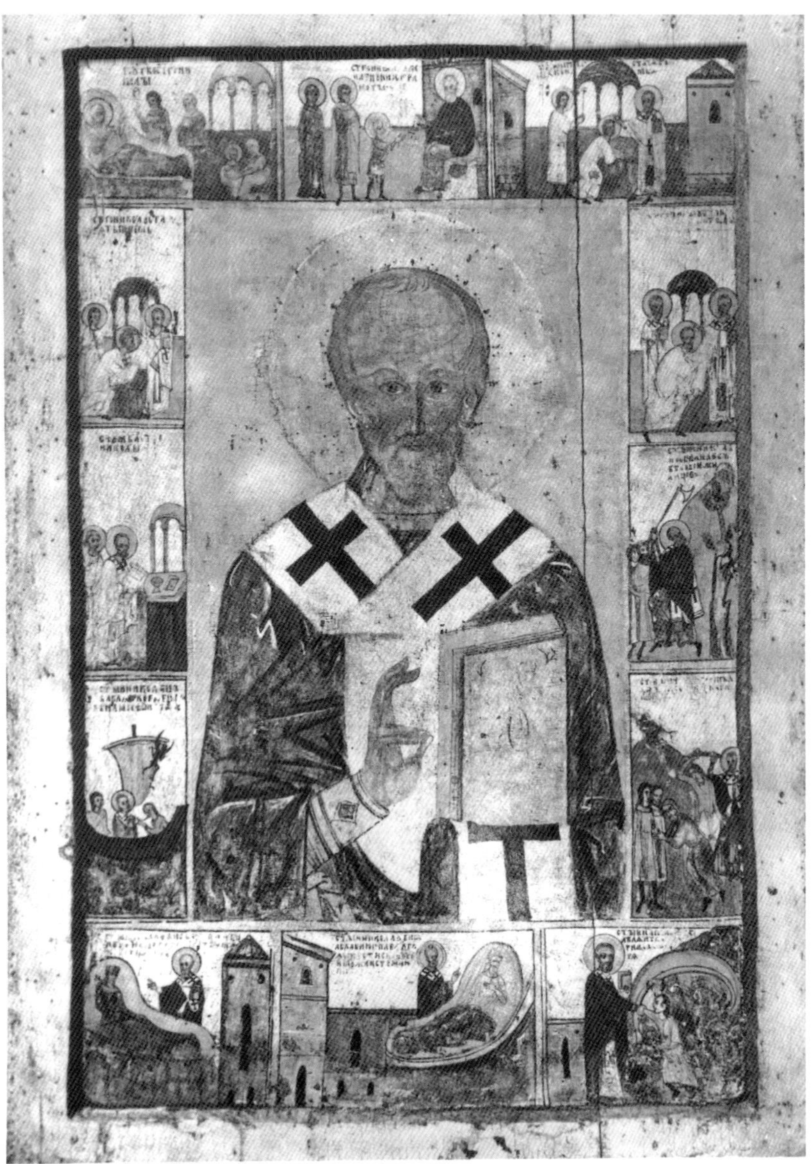

20 Icon of the Life of St Nicholas.

unable to respond to Western church imagery, where the absence of inscriptions frustrated apt religious response and veneration.[19]

There are frequent examples of religious imagery containing verbal adjuncts that are surprisingly complex and raise issues of the interpretative skills of their original beholders (even when those who could read the texts – priests, specifically – were available to guide this activity). A key example might be the famous seventh-century Ruthwell Cross, which is inscribed in runic characters on its side with verses from the Anglo-Saxon poem *The Dream of the Rood* (i.e., *Cross*). It seems appropriate that the stone cross would 'speak' about itself, as it does in the poem, but the 'detailed images carved into its sides do not pertain directly to the art', and one carving of Christ trampling on the beasts is framed within a Latin inscription that has nothing *prime facie* to do with the Cross (illus. 21).[20] It is hard to see how early visitors and beholders of this cross would connect what they could see with the verbal supplements (if they could read them) and accordingly either enhance their apprehension of the cross itself or elucidate the images carved upon it (themselves not perhaps immediately identifiable – like the hermit Saints Paul and Anthony dividing bread brought to them by a raven). The question of literacy aside, if the range of reference that modern scholars have invoked to situate the Cross in a complex web of significance was actually available, then the exegesis of a visual work in the light not only of its own imagery but its specific inscriptions reveals how far the imagination and mind must have needed to travel from the immediate objects of their visual scrutiny.

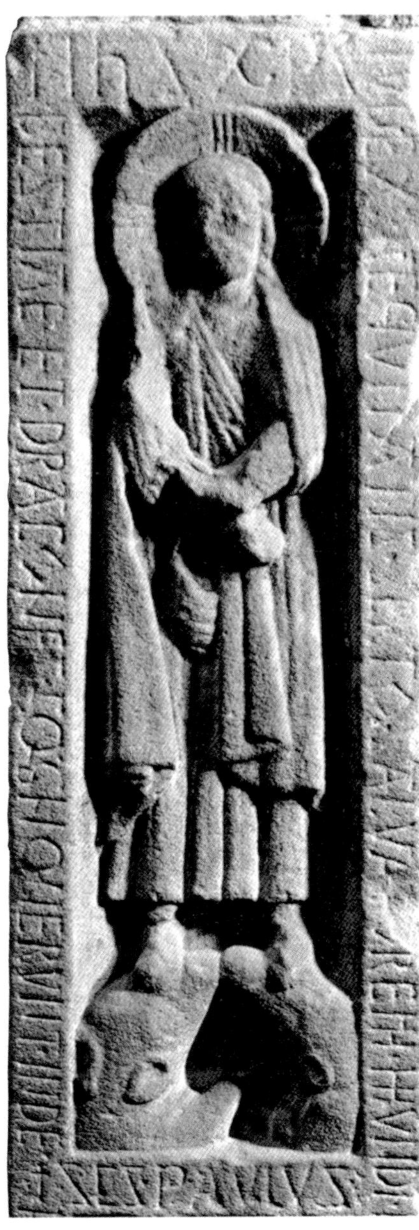

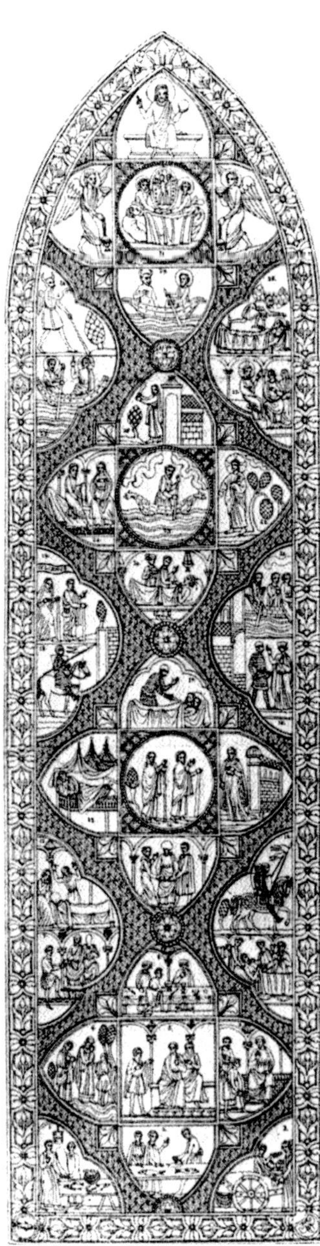

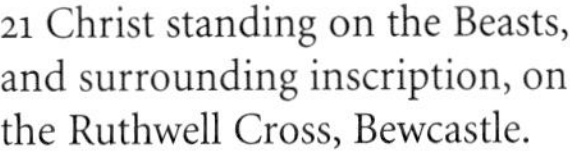

21 Christ standing on the Beasts, and surrounding inscription, on the Ruthwell Cross, Bewcastle.

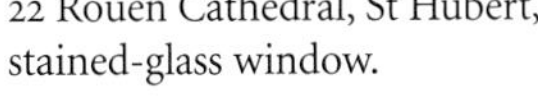

22 Rouen Cathedral, St Hubert, stained-glass window.

But the readability of imagery that presented far less canonical items than the Cross or less mainstream ideas than Christ's trampling of the serpent could be infinitely more of a challenge. There is a stained glass window in Rouen cathedral created in the early thirteenth century (illus. 22), made famous by Gustave Flaubert's story 'La Legende de St Julien l'Hospitalier', published in 1877.[21] However, it is not the novelist's ekphrasis that is relevant here, but the story that Flaubert and others like him derived from or pinned upon the window's imagery: in other words, its implicit wordage. The visual repertoire is rich, complicated and composed of over 30 separate episodes; these do seem to require that we attribute to it or devise for it a narrative, reading from bottom to top and also (because of the way the figures are moving) across the window from right to left. Yet to articulate this story we need to maintain some real discipline and diligence in following that sequence and to be alert to such details as the change in Julien's appearance, which tells us that time has passed between different episodes, or to see the parallel between the two scenes where Julien first helps Christ across a turbulent river and is forgiven for his past sin of murder, already depicted in the glass narrative, and then himself offers the same service to a notorious thief who kills him. However, it is apparently the case that what the window represents visually has no exact counterpart in any 'written source know today';[22] furthermore, the narrative was hardly a major and familiar one (at least before Flaubert). Consequently, the story that the window obviously tells and any interpretative

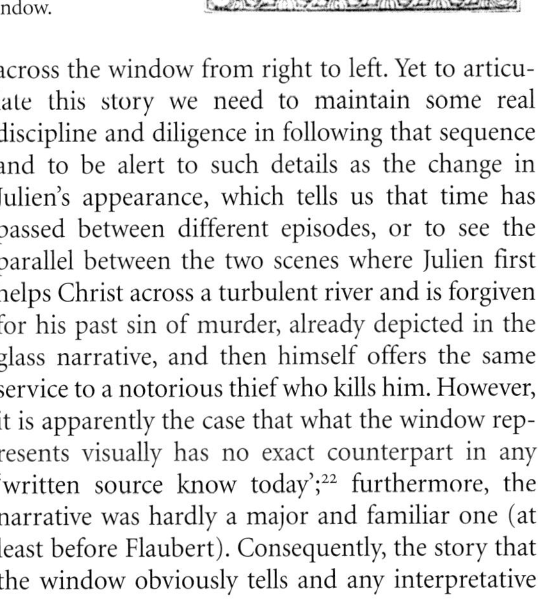

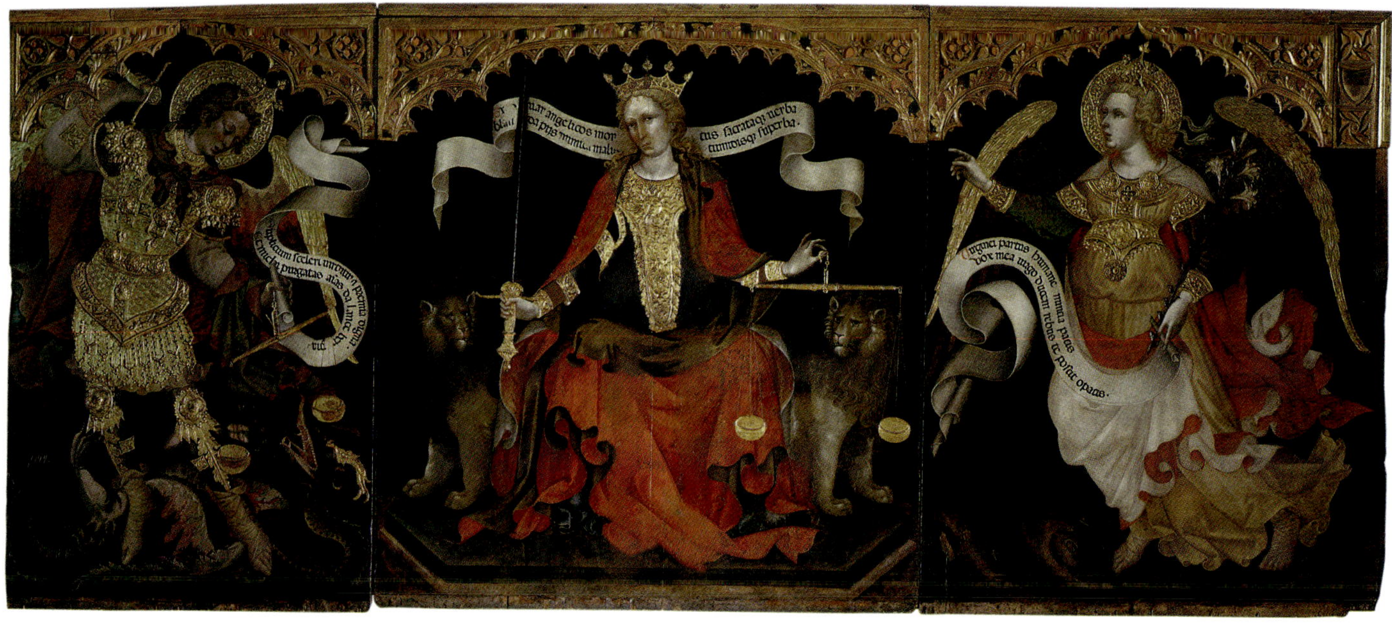

23 Jacobello del Fiore, *Justice between the Archangels Michael and Gabriel, c.* 1421, tempera on panel.

response to it will be determined by a viewer's prior knowledge of the St Julien legend, enshrined in various manuscript accounts and, of course, articulated by priests in the cathedral who might (or might not) have known those same narratives or who even invented one. Even so, some skill and patience in 'reading' the glass images were required. Indeed, it seems very doubtful whether a truly coherent tale could be deduced from the images, even when read carefully in sequence, without guidance from some text or other, written or oral, where *sequence*, endemic to writing and speech, places one event after another and explains their connection.[23] Either contemporaries were led through the window's story by an informed exegete or they worked out the storyline and its internal links and logic over many sessions through trial and error in front of the window (during services, for example). What is important here, however, is that for such a narrative to be articulated a sequence of words must be devised for it, whatever their source and whatever their 'accuracy' (Flaubert, who apparently never saw the window for himself, amplified and altered the tale in his own telling).

The medieval religious imagination and experience seem extremely complex, and modern scholarly adjudications of their formal productions have demonstrated an immense range of ways in which image used word, or word relied on image, and how both elicited a habit of mind that could move or drift from one image and/or text to others suggested by it. Much medieval religious imagery obviously required slow and thoughtful scrutiny by its original beholders, especially those fortunate or wealthy enough to have commissioned their own missal, book of hours or other devotional manuscript. Perhaps we are too accustomed to instant recognition and understanding of images – modern advertising could not work without such habits, neither could cinematographic montage – to appreciate the pleasures and the challenges of such sustained 'reading'. But long hours of contemplation, many repeated opportunities to find oneself in front of imagery that often suffused the walls and windows of churches, plus the pedagogic commentary of priests eager to elucidate what St Gregory called the 'Bible of the poor', produced an audience more competent than we can imagine to find appropriate words with which to enunciate the stories and meanings of visual art. For the illiterate and indeed for those who could read, but in an age before printed books were yet available, visual imagery was a ubiquitous and unique vehicle for narrative and instruction. Indeed, we might reverse one of Wittgenstein's aphorisms ('What really comes before our mind when we *understand* a word? Isn't it something like a picture? Can't it *be* a picture[?]'[24]) and ask whether in a medieval, Christian world, where the devout believed that the word had been made flesh and dwelt among them, all the religious imagery around them was but a fleshing out, a reifying, of words and so necessarily and readily translatable back again into the language of human inhabitation.

Or take another, later example, the *Justice Triptych* (*c.* 1421) by Jacobello del Fiore, now in the Accademia Galleries in Venice (illus. 23). On the three panels are images that are readily recognizable by the manner in which the three figures are visually presented; but each of the segments also features a lettered scroll, held by or entwined around the particular figure. The visual information is clear: on the right, the Archangel Gabriel, carrying the lily and with a hand raised in a familiar gesture that shows he is speaking about the Son who will come to bring justice to the world; on the left, St Michael trampling the dragon, symbol of Satan, yet holding the scales of justice that dip towards the writhing body of the almost conquered monster; and the Virgin herself, enthroned between the two other figures as Mother Church, and holding the scales of justice, which are now perfectly balanced; she raises the sword of justice aloft, unlike Michael, who lifts it only to strike off the serpent's head. Much is communicated visually about the different modes of justice that rule the world: the Virgin's, being accompanied by (two!) Lions of St Mark, one of whom's head appears between the hanging scales, affirms the judiciary power and integrity of the Venetian Republic as the greatest of all contemporary justicers (the painting was probably executed for the Magistrato del Proprio in the Doge's Palace). But no beholder can ignore the whirling lettered scrolls that are associated with each person. The Latin inscribed there (for those who could read it or for those who needed it translated for them) gives to Gabriel a plea to the Virgin to guide men and women, while Michael begs her to distribute '*premi e castighi* (rewards and punishments) according to merit'. On the Virgin's scroll the words 'EXEQUAR ANGELICOS MONITUS SACRATAQUE VERBA/ BLANDA PIIS INIMICA MALIS TUMIDISQUE SUPERBA' announce her determination to heed both the angel's entreaty and the Holy Word, to deal gently with the pious and harshly with the wicked and proud so as to overcome them. The words would have augmented what is seen, but do little more than emphasize what the physical postures, gestures and the ensemble of figures do visually; they are, so to speak, the script for a dialogue between the Virgin and her two companions that another commentator might use to expatiate further on the idea of Christian justice.

IV

The illuminated or illustrated manuscript presents a special case of word and image. Is it 'visual' art with added words, or the reverse (where images augment the text), or a genuinely mutual endeavour by the two media? Most serious scholarship would point to the latter, but the rather ambiguous entity that resulted both from the production methods of codex creation and from the variety of receptions accorded to the finished product puts it into a rather special category among the rest of the materials considered here. It was rarely a question of a text's being accompanied by images that illustrated or somehow commented upon its subject matter; codices could have illuminated initials, and a whole host of marginal pictures and decorations (as well as further words) that augmented or bounced their own purposes off the central text and its visualization.[25] For instance, in even a small and otherwise unremarkable twelfth-century Byzantine psalter there are illuminated capitals at the start of each psalm (the only 'illustrations'); yet it seems that the scribe sought to make them a visual commentary on the words rather than a decorative entry into each psalm, just as some of its written marginal comments reverse the process and set the words out on the page in shapes that are indicative of their content. Both moves would require the reader to connect their visual scanning of the codex and their reading of its texts, but the cross-references are not always explicit: thus, a psalm introduced by an initial representing a naked boy climbing a palm tree (a rough version of the capital letter 'A') could be read as referring, via its verbal echo, to the shouts that greeted Christ's entry into Jerusalem, when palm leaves were strewn across his path.[26]

Manuscripts performed most of the tasks we now expect to be achieved by printed books, but the very conditions of their manual production, even in 'factories' of scribes and artists who may well have often worked independently, ensured a wide range of agreement between image and word: sometimes interconnected and complex, because of genuine collaboration between the different craftsmen and the mindset of those for whom they worked, sometimes parallel and even idiosyncratic in following their own ideas and the specific

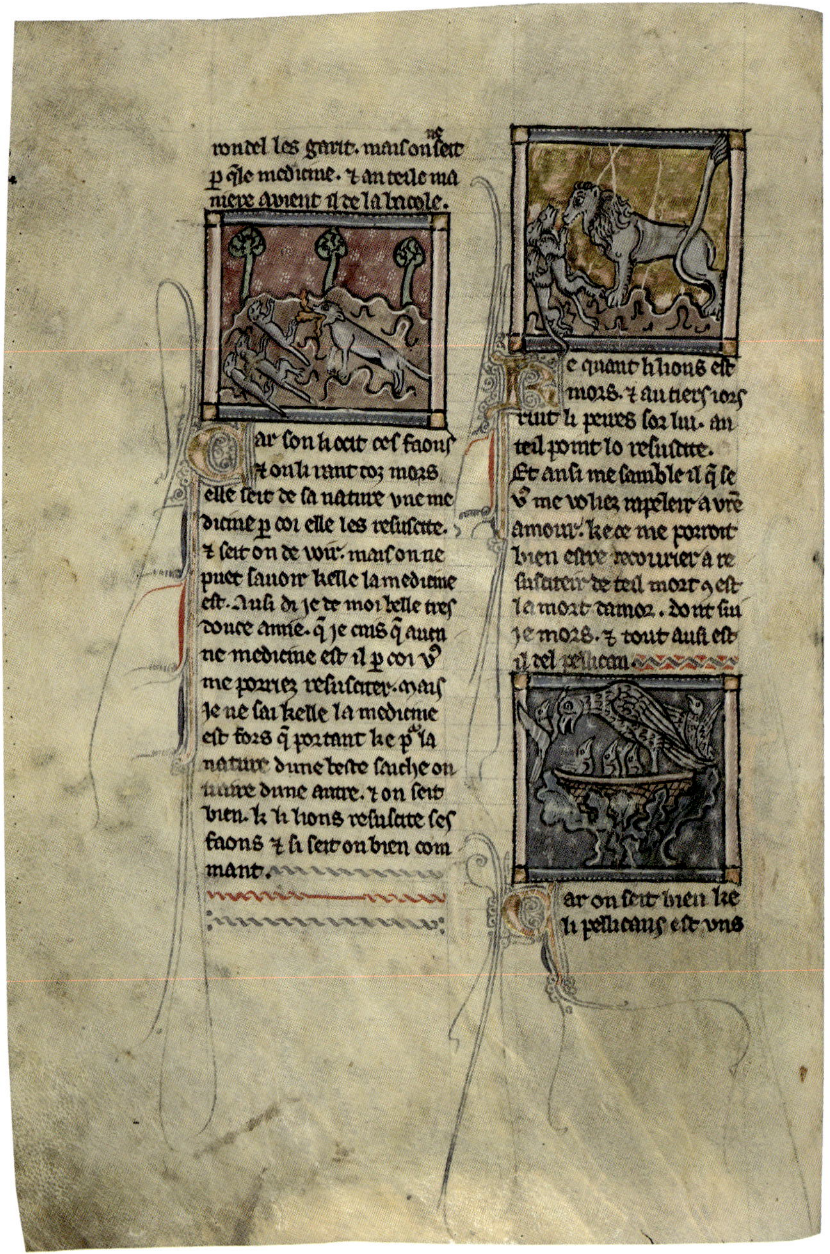

24 Weasel, Lion and Pelican, from Richard of Fournival, Bestiary d'Amour, early 14th century.

opportunities of their own medium.[27] Where we would today turn to illustrated encyclopedias like animal or bird identification handbooks, medieval persons had bestiaries (illus. 24), herbals and botanical (often medical or pharmaceutical) compilations. In these the words offered their own descriptions plus information on an object's properties, symbolism and uses, while the image worked to provide a visual identikit (with some bizarre results, when a beast had not been seen by the artist who was probably working only from an eccentric verbal description anyway).[28] And many bestiaries were devoted more to mythical or fabulous creatures, which – not being in the real world at all – could hardly be drawn from the life! Too often, in modern texts these wonderful creations are illustrated without their accompanying wordage, but for the medieval viewer the dialogue between verbal and visual definitions could be essential. The curiosities of the natural world – like two bunches of grapes fused together and sprouting a red beard (illus. 25) – needed both to be depicted and to have their circumstances explained, in this instance the where and how of its discovery, before any credence could be given to their authenticity.[29]

The kind of illuminated manuscripts where modern scholars have identified truly intricate and arcane collaborations between the words and images were those which treated of ideas. To track how a medieval man or woman, faced with a succession of especially rich folios of text and imagery, might read some devotional volume has elicited a commentary that ranges far and wide in its exegetical endeavours. This is not the occasion on which to adjudicate any examples.[30] But we do need to recognize that the physical assemblage of words and images on a succession of folios needed and also encouraged a 'reading' for which an agility of mind, memory and education, combined with the opportunities of priestly or other specialist instruction, were required. A prayer book, a psalter or a book of hours by its very nature had a prescribed sequence and format, which certainly directed its perusal – the user knew the structures of services and the canonical hours, or the sequence of biblical texts – but the reader's response was not limited to a 'single thing or a particular event', and neither would he or she

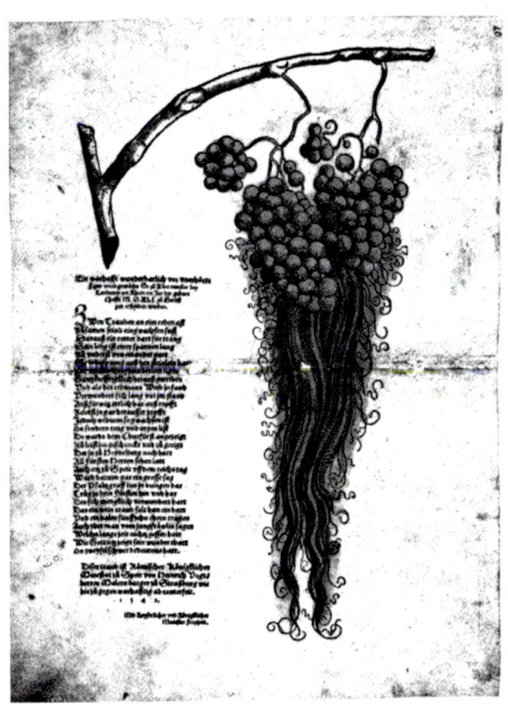

25 Heinrich Vogtherr, *Miraculous Grapes*, 1542, hand-coloured woodcut broadsheet.

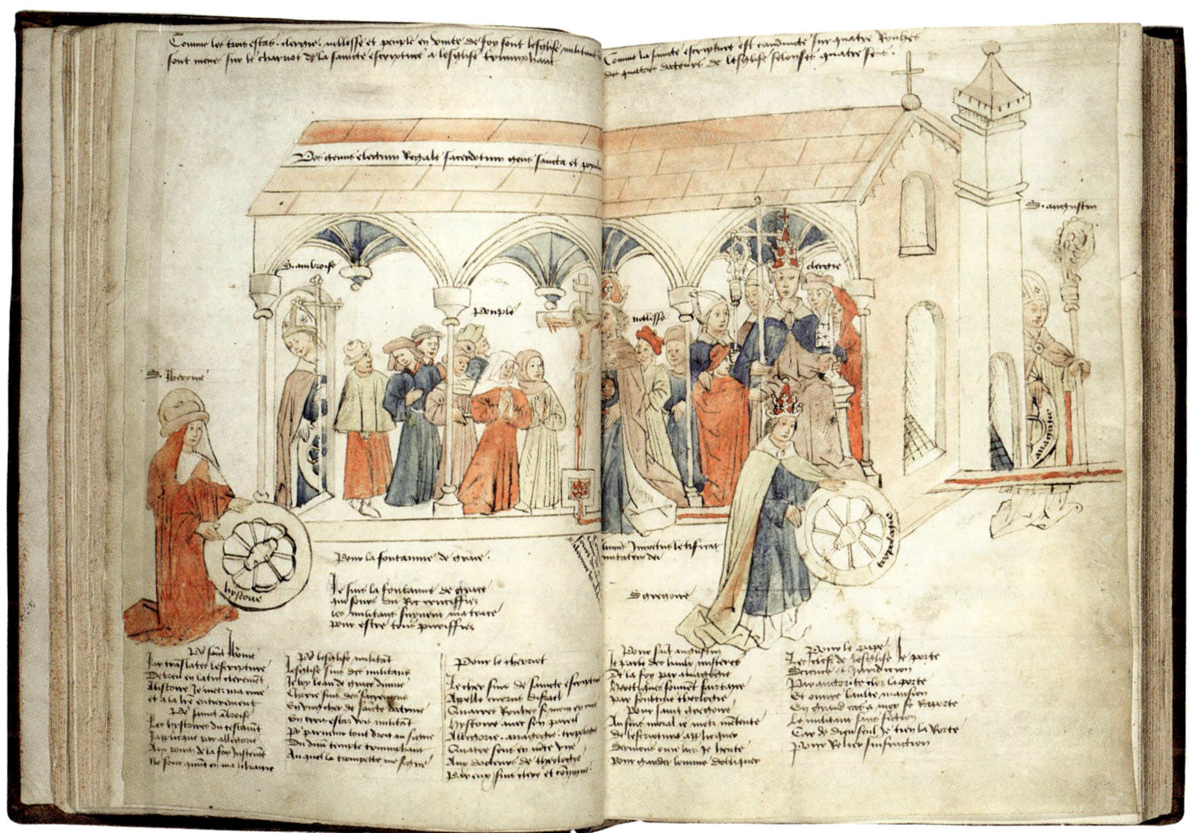

26 The Carriage of Christian Triumph in Jean Germain's *Le Chemin de Paradis c.* 1473.

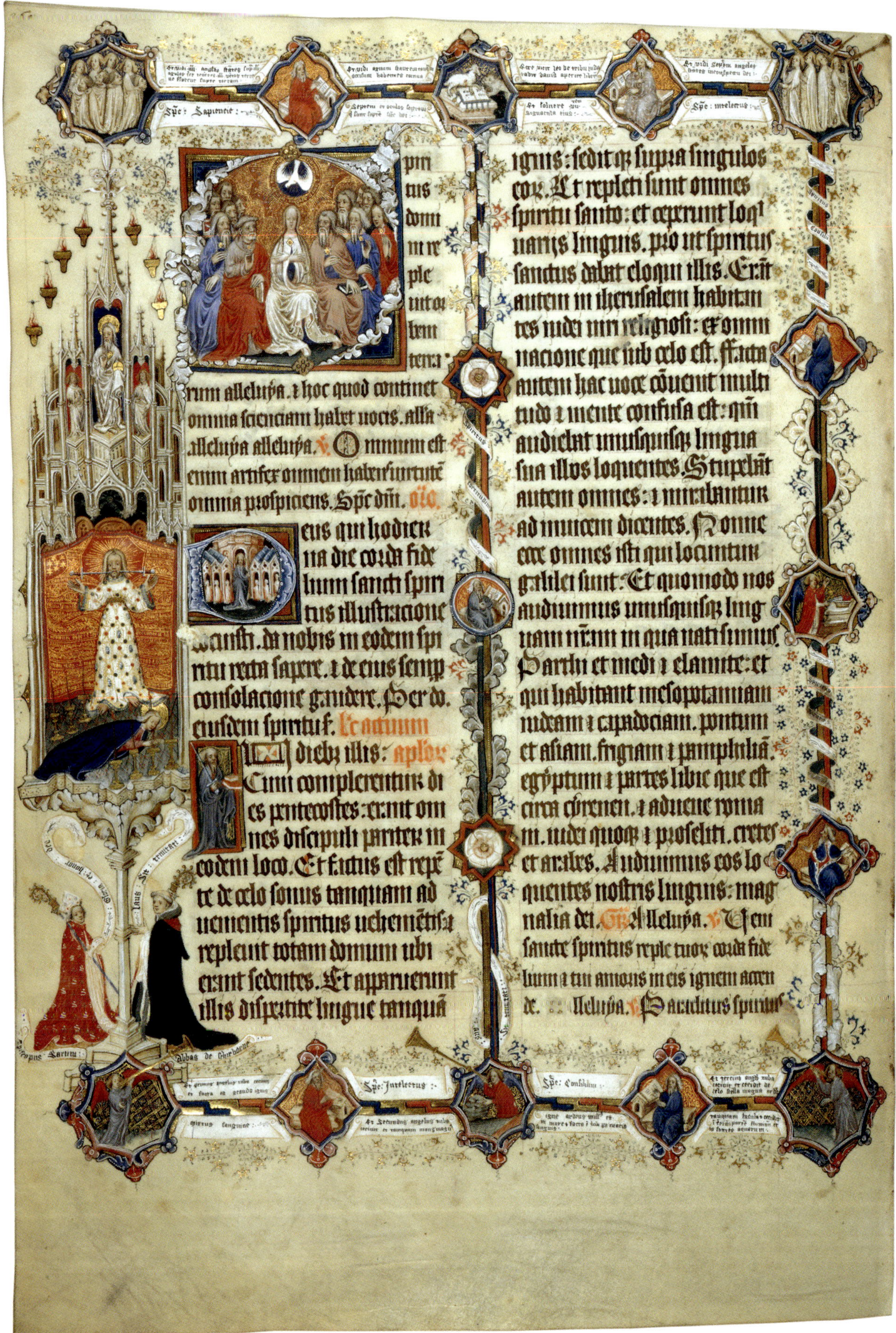

27 The Sherborne Missal, begun *c.* 1404.

necessarily adduce the relevant words for that single visual motif or message, but could discover 'as many references as are consistent with accepted belief'.[31] Further, the 'interpictorial exchange', by which one image (or text) is permeated with others to the extent that beholding (or reading) involves 'a constant effort to encompass these relations',[32] makes the identification of implicit or additive wordage extremely difficult.

Jean Germain's *Le Chemin de Paradis* (*c.* 1473), as its title indicates, offers instruction on the road to a happy afterlife, so presumably it is likely to be instructive, if not simple.[33] Its image in a manuscript in Brussels (illus. 26) accompanies and illustrates a didactic treatise, but it is also meant to work by and for itself, both as a readable image and as a programme or cartoon for a tapestry, where it would be effectively separated from that treatise and need to rely upon whatever words were woven into the piece. The whole drawing is a perfect example of give and take between what is depicted and the words inscribed on the image, but also between every verbal/visual thing we have before us on the sheet (or later the tapestry) and our recollections of Holy Scripture and commentaries thereon, to which we are also directed by inscriptions. The four Fathers of the Church are identified by name above each head (Augustine, Gregory, Jerome and Ambrose). They are in the process of pushing a church on wheels (along the road to Paradise, no doubt), inside which are worshippers and clergy. On the rim of each wheel is further written the word that defines the four modes of scriptural reading that each father was known to have promoted: analogy for Augustine, tropology for Gregory, 'Ystoire' (narrative) for Jerome and allegory for Ambrose. Words at top of the whole image tell us that the Church is driven by the four wheels of the four doctors of the Church and the different exegetical accounts of Scripture that each had advanced. The whole visual/verbal ensemble, whether as a page in a treatise or (if manufactured) as a piece of tapestry, would have been and continues to be an exercise in connecting the dots between words and images and between both and the four interpretations of scriptural writings that the church fathers had authorized.

Even the reading of what seems explicit wordage (given its incorporation within the pictorial frame) can enlarge the possibility of the viewed object to quite complicated ends, and in practice blurring or at least blending the explicit words and their message with a whole hinterland of implicit or additive commentary. Indeed, it proves quite difficult to know when the medieval viewer of an image inscribed with words would stop in their verbal exegesis that takes its cues and then its flight from a visual representation. Sometimes the words are simply labels that steer our responses to already familiar images by injecting into our minds a biblical passage heard on other occasions, perhaps, or some often cited observation by a church father. The complexities or densities that could be achieved are astonishing: perhaps an extreme example, but nonetheless typical of the intricate dialogues set up between words and images, and between the page and events beyond its immediate reading, is contained in the Sherborne Missal (illus. 27). The page is dedicated to Whit Sunday, and within the opening visual initial 'S[piritus domini . . .]' words on the dove's halo recall the Pentecostal hymn invoking the coming of the Holy Spirit; but around the central text are elaborate marginal images and scrolled texts that represent the Apocalypse. The relation between this and the texts of Pentecost can be understood only subsequently by reading passages inserted six pages later from a commentary on the significance of the Apocalypse, attributed to St Ambrose.[34]

Between the original exponents of religious imagery as the bible of the illiterate poor, and the modern iconographers who can adduce often logical – or at least plausible – verbal but usually learned sources that gloss the pictures, there is less distance than we might imagine. Whoever painted church frescoes or altarpieces was either given a specific scenario or devised one out of his own head from whatever resources he could draw upon. Either way, there was an implicit, verbalized meaning or tale that the artist sought to fix in images from which that meaning could be deduced.

V

During the long Middle Ages and continuing into the early Renaissance, visual art relied heavily upon

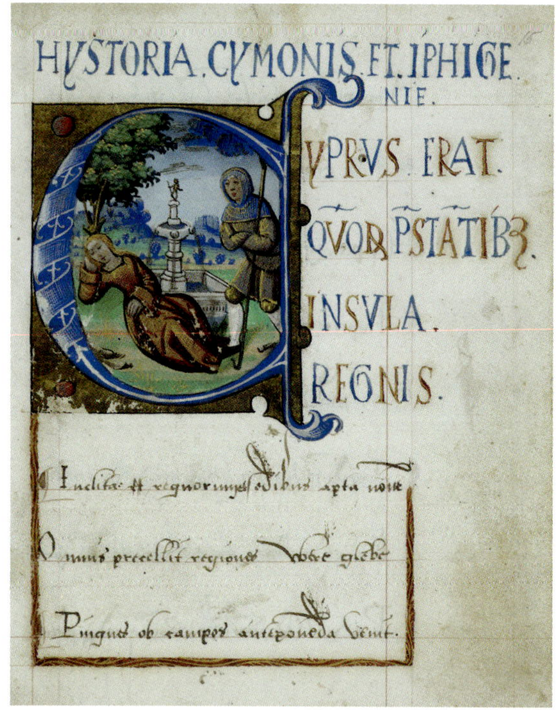

28 The Cimone and Efigenia episode in the *Decameron*, here in a manuscript collection miniature.

written materials for its subject matter.[35] But the invention of printing in the late fifteenth century increased enormously the number, availability and range of texts upon which painters could draw for their subjects. This explosion of available verbal sources for painted subjects involved Greek and Latin works, but equally vernacular writers like Dante, Boccaccio, Tasso and Ariosto (to stay within Italy for the moment). Indeed, it seems as if the very success of a painting, sculpture or stained-glass window depended upon its invocation of or reliance on some anterior set of words. We know, too, that patrons commissioning works of art would often prescribe some narrative or (as it is called) 'programme' for the artist to follow (though not all did, at least to the letter); artists themselves would also acknowledge texts from which they were drawing their subjects. And eventually, printed books in their turn would be the forum in which learned commentary on executed works of art would be expounded and circulated, in the process usually citing literary 'sources' or precedents. Given our own very visual culture and its frequent separation from the verbal, we perhaps neglect the astonishing appeal of printed works as resources and prompts for painters and sculptors in the Renaissance.

However, it is also clear that the explicit appearance of the word in visual art diminished considerably during and after the Renaissance: no doubt the increased and very flourishing world of printing ensured that the word was available and acknowledged as an adjacent resource without now having to be inscribed within a painting. It would be clear, even without the learned instruction of mod-

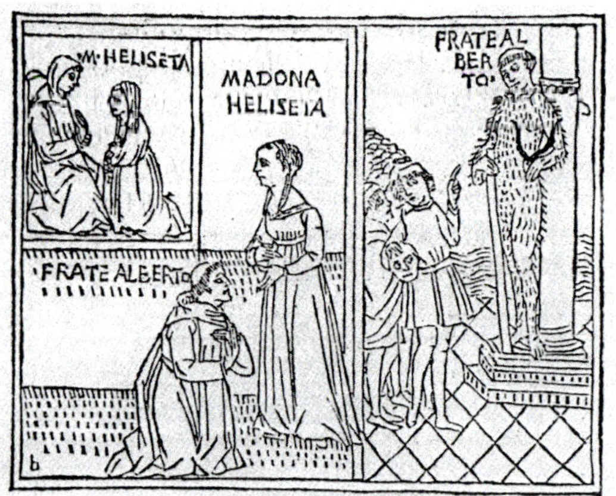

29 A woodcut illustrating the 1492 Venetian edition of the *Decameron* published by Giovanni and Gregorio de Gregori.

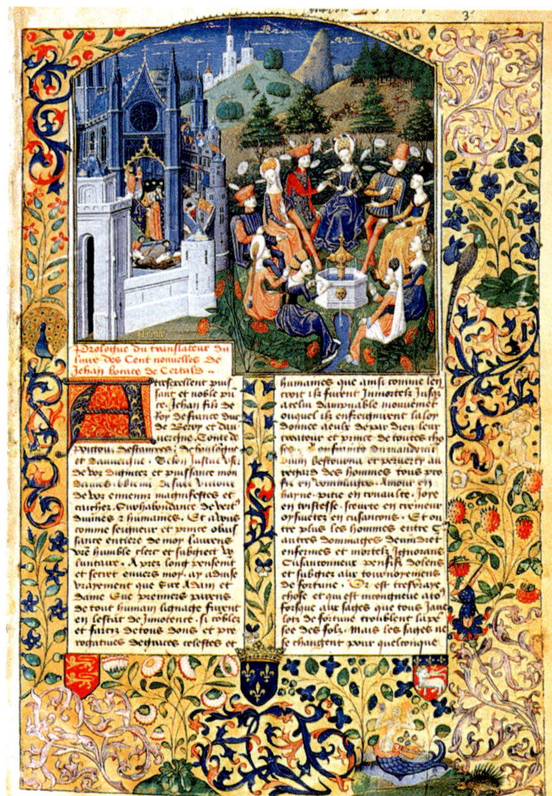

30 An audience gathered in a garden to hear the text of the *Decameron* that is here written out.

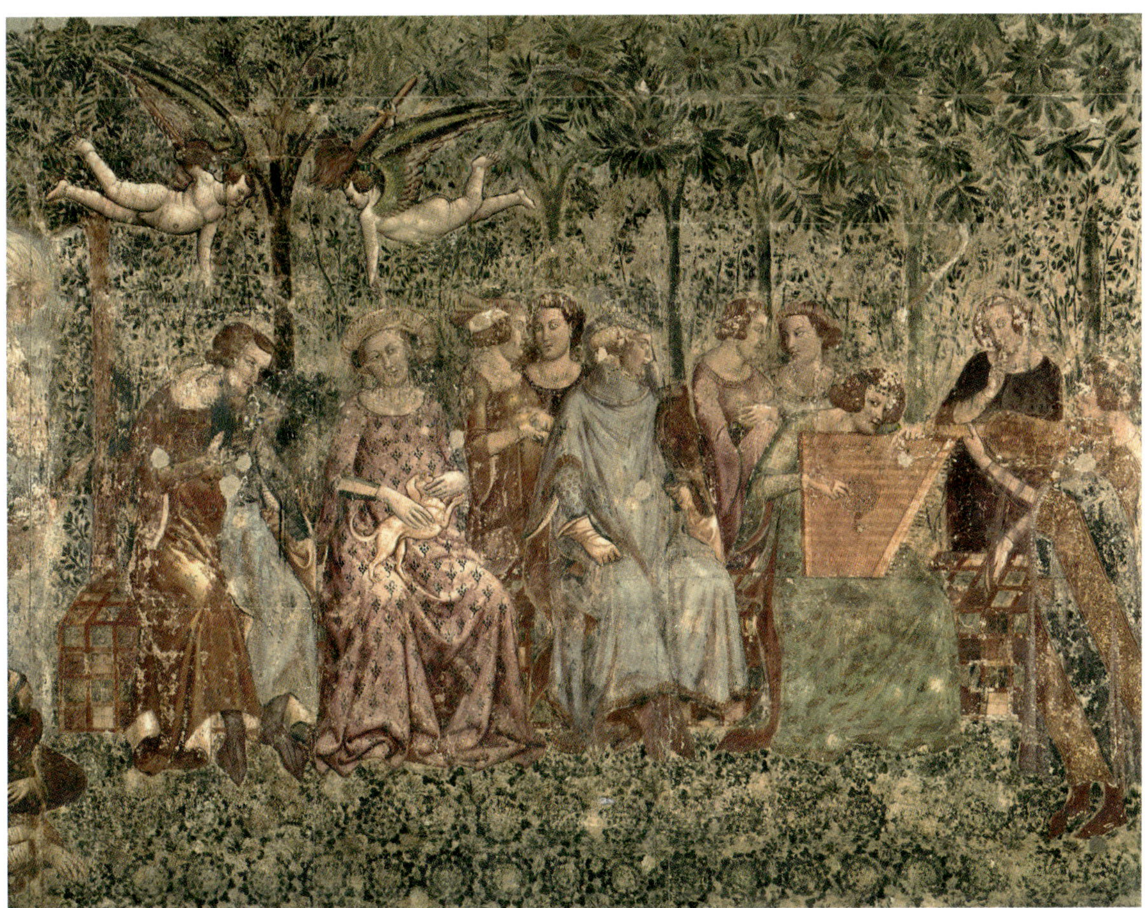

31 Anonymous master, *Triumph of Death*, first half of the 14th century, fresco.

ern art historians, that paintings from Bellini to Poussin and beyond told stories from classical literature and religious history and that it was anticipated that viewers would bring those narratives into play when contemplating the paintings. Such a confident assumption of the implicit wordage to be invoked in both the making and the viewing of visual art lasted a very long time: many images of Victorian painters like Burne-Jones or George Frederick Watts seem to solicit a narrative gloss, though in fact the artists may not have had any specifically in mind before providing the finished work with its title.

Yet modern art history has worked strenuously to disclose often elaborate scenarios in Renaissance and seventeenth-century paintings, and this iconography of course requires verbal expression and has accordingly come to be linked inextricably with the meaning of the paintings concerned. We may perhaps detect a reaction against this: an essay in the catalogue of a 2008 exhibition of Poussin landscapes at the Metropolitan Museum in New York 'wonders if the hidden secrets of these paintings were really invented by the artist or are rather the creation of all-too-erudite art historians'. Nonetheless, the curators still acknowledge Poussin's learning and – while sensibly marginalizing 'erudite' commentary and reminding us that Poussin's contemporaries thought his landscape paintings in particular were 'without obscurity' – insist that we look at his work in relation to his favourite texts, such as Virgil, Ovid and the Bible.[36] Such a necessary and undeniable emphasis, therefore, requires an intimate connection between the image and the 'implicit' word. That words are indeed only implied does not lessen their considerable, if invisible, impact: we might indeed adapt Keats's famous aphorism and say that 'seen words are sweet, but those unseen are sweeter'.

The case of painterly versions of stories derived from Boccaccio can be a useful demonstration of the various interrelationships of image and word that were at stake.[37] Artists drew on his various works, notably the collection of tales in the *Decameron*, even before printing took off and made them more accessible, and in such illustrated codices it was generally very straightforward for a reader to grasp the relation of the two media (illus. 28). In some early printed books characters had their names attached to their images (illus. 29). Even so, a reader could well be taken or puzzled by the fashion in which an artist had chosen to visual-

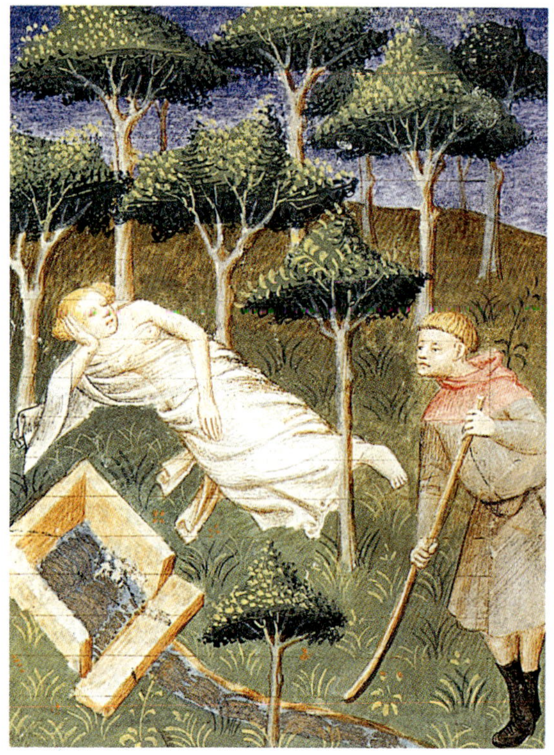

32 The story of Cimon in a miniature from a *Decameron* of *c.* 1415.

ize either an action or its dramatis personae, but the basic connection of image to relevant wordage was given: there are instances when an illustrator of Dante's *Divine Comedy*, for example, would choose for some reason to 'mis-'interpret a bit of text visually, even though the very words were there to guide him in the first place and subsequently to confront readers trying to 'read' the accompanying images.[38] But when a written or printed text of the *Decamaron* images a group of young people gathered in a garden or a flowery place (illus. 30), its purpose in illustrating the adjacent narrative framework of Boccaccio's work is clear – here are the people fleeing from the plague and assembling to tell each other stories which we are about to read. It is when a similar scene has no such contingency, indeed is on its own and entirely divorced from any verbal context, like the fresco in the *Triumph of Death* in the Camposanto at Pisa (illus. 30), that art historians at least are forced to find a subject matter for it and plausibly enough choose to connect it to the same event in Boccaccio. On the other hand, there are many paintings that look as if they are clearly pictorial versions of a story that existed in words or in oral transmission, but for which there is no identifiable pre-text. This is an

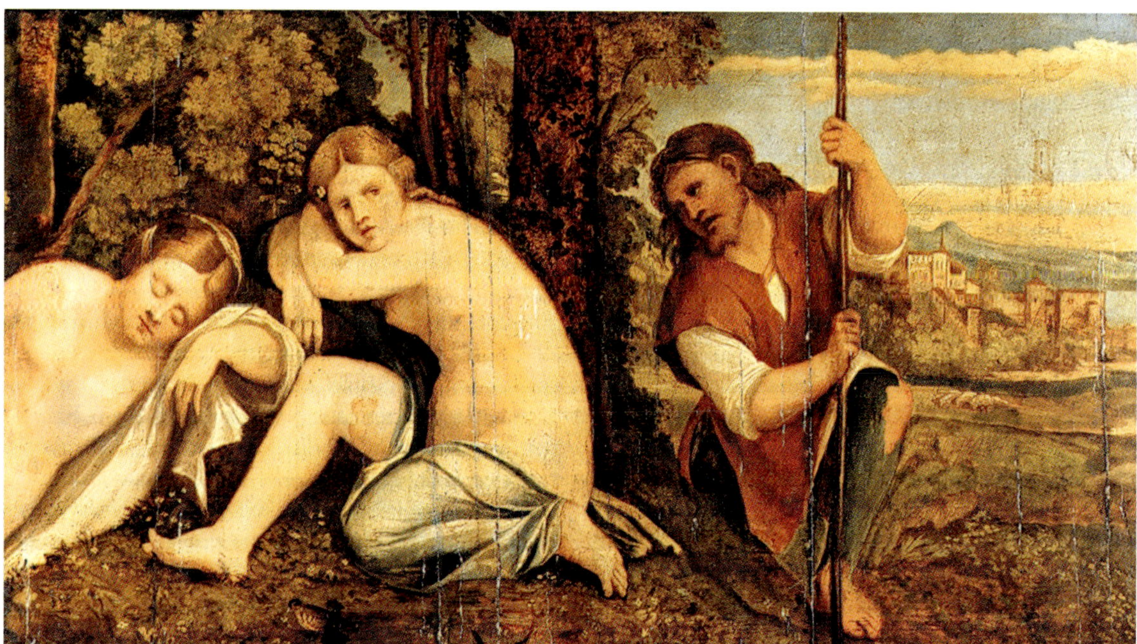

33 Circle of Palma il Vecchio, *The Story of Cimon and Efigenia*, 16th century, oil on wood.

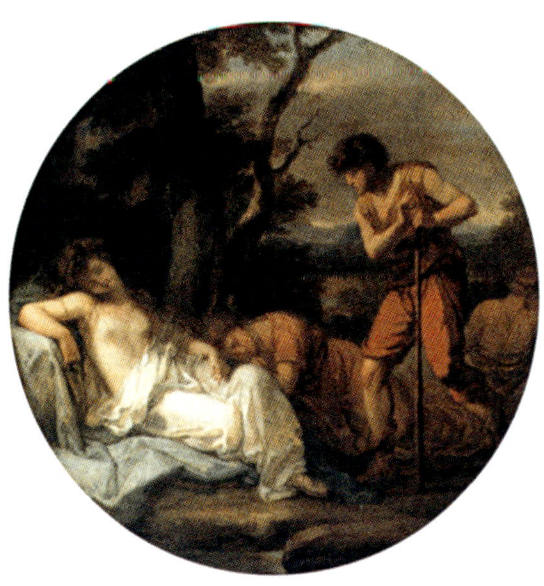

34 Angelica Kauffman, *Cymon and Iphigenia c.* 1780, oil on canvas.

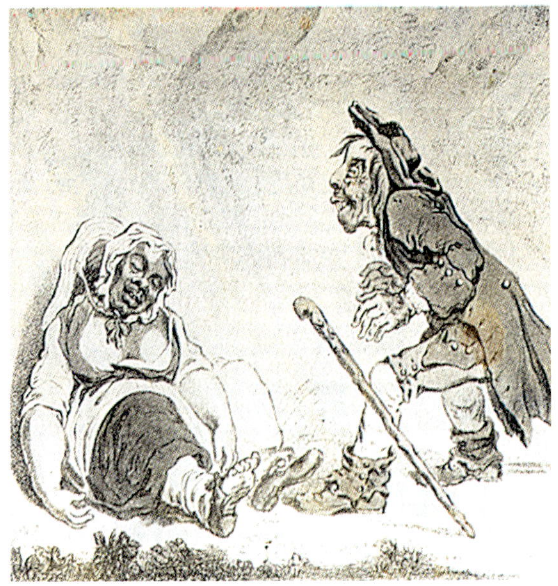

35 James Gillray, *Cymon and Iphigenia*, 1796, detail from an etching with watercolour.

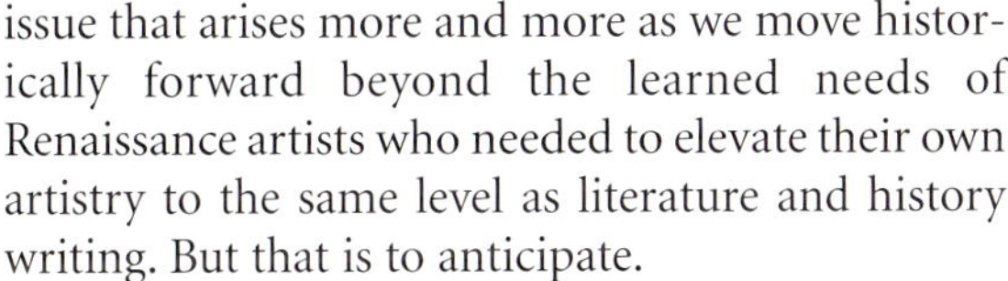

issue that arises more and more as we move historically forward beyond the learned needs of Renaissance artists who needed to elevate their own artistry to the same level as literature and history writing. But that is to anticipate.

What becomes interesting is when artists took their subjects from a specific literary source – say Boccaccio's stories – but in circumstances when their painting provided no explicit acknowledgement of this connection by either context (an illustration alongside a text) or inscription. For instance, the tale of the rough shepherd Cimone discovering the sleeping nymph Efigenia (*Decameron*, V.1) was an immensely popular theme,[39] no doubt because it gave the artist a chance to show off his painting of the nude and allowed the representation of a beautiful scenery (*locus amoenus*), and it doubtless pleased patrons or collectors for less artistic reasons! (A version of the erotic episode seems to be illustrated in the famous printed book of 1499, the *Hypnerotomachia Poliphili*, but without any connection to Boccaccio's text; the cross-reference from the book's woodcut to the story, if such it is, might have been a subtle manoeuvre on the part of anonymous author and illustrator.[40]) In a manuscript like Vatican Pal. Lat. 1989 (folio 150v, illus. 32) or any other illustrated codex or book of the *Decameron* (see illus. 28), at least those who could read – its likely possessors or those with access to it – could know what the image depicted because of its adjacency to the text. But a host of painters took up the same theme – Palma il Vecchio (illus. 33), Veronese, Titian, Bernardino Luini, Abraham Bloemaert, Peter Paul Rubens, Claude Lorrain, Nicolas Poussin, Angelica Kauffman (illus. 34), Joshua Reynolds, James Gillray and John Everett Millais. By the time we reach Gillray's coarse rustic pair (illus. 35) we have probably left behind any reference to Boccaccio for the majority of those who saw or purchased the print; maybe there was an extra frisson or smile for those who recognized how Renaissance pastoral had been diminished or naturalized. But generally, Boccaccio's contribution to the viewer's enjoyment of a painting has slipped slowly away over the years, as artists found the motif of the vulgar voyeur and the naked nymph a worthwhile theme in itself without an implicit literary handle. It is, in fact, only the presence of a title (whether contributed by the artist, connoisseurs or critics) that maintains the Boccaccian connection, which in the absence of any brief commentary on a museum wall can easily lose its value.

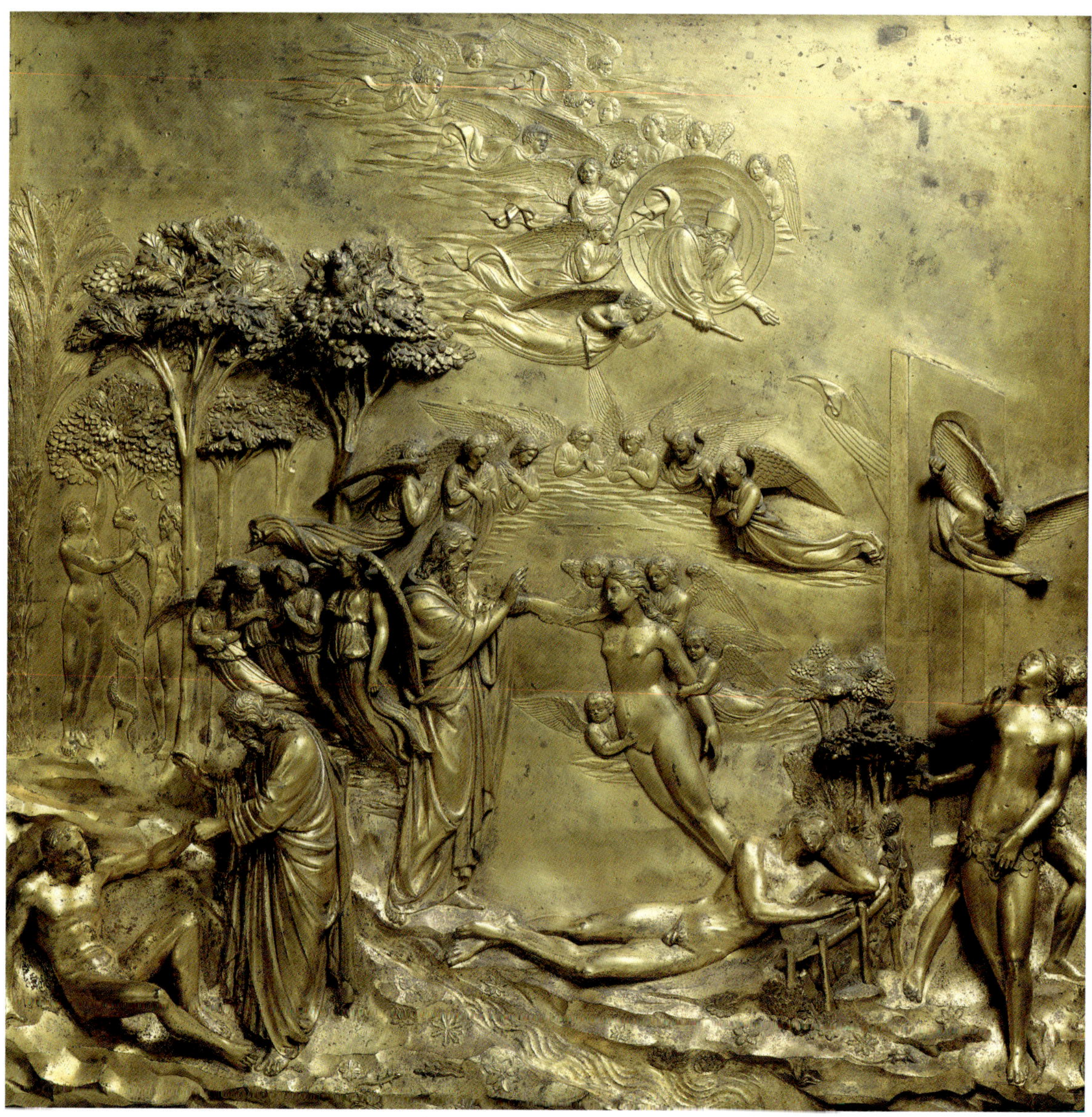

36 Lorenzo Ghiberti, *Creation of Eve* from the *Gates of Paradise*, 1525–52, bronze panel.

How much an artist was in practice controlled by the literary sources chosen by him or to which he was directed by his patron, as opposed to using them as stimulus, seems debatable. When modern scholars and commentators interpret visual art by reference to 'pre-texts' and literary contexts, they benefit from an even greater abundance of published information than was accessible for the Renaissance artist or patron. Yet this does not always make their task easier, and sometimes blurs the line of their exegesis between an artist's intentions, some original receptions of a visual image and what our own enhanced range of reference permits us to make of it now. We know, for example, that Lorenzo Ghiberti, in being commissioned to make bronze doors for the Florentine Baptistry, was instructed as to what scenes and themes to depict, and that this programme was not only delivered verbally but also referred him to verbal sources for which he would have to find visual

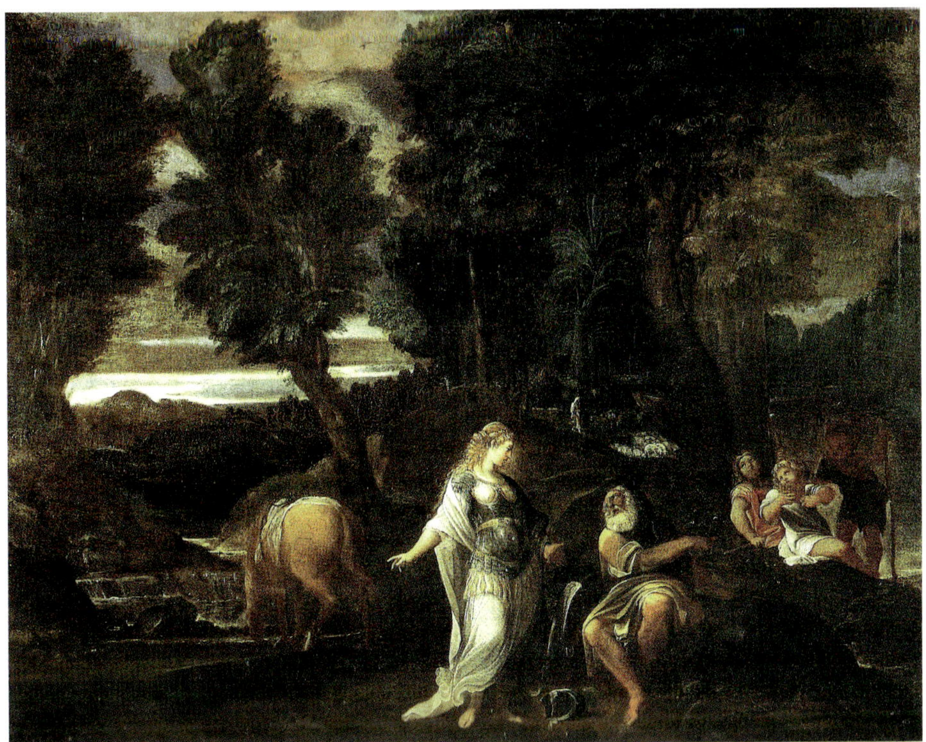

37 Ludovico Carracci (1555–1619), *Erminia and the Shepherds.*

equivalents in his panels. Modern research has shown that for one particular panel (illus. 36) he was apparently confronted with a vexing theological (and so verbal) ambiguity about the actual role of angels, as opposed to the Creator, in the extraction of Eve from Adam's body: did God do the work by himself, or was he assisted by angels? Yet how much the considerable literature potentially available to him on this apparently crucial (if to us arcane) topic actually determined the imagery of his door, and, if it did, whether it was also available to those who sought to understand the bronze scene in front of them, remains unclear.[41]

How imagery was connected to words by artists and their audiences, an intriguing element of different medieval arts, becomes even more complex with Renaissance imagery. A new self-consciousness in inventing and discussing subjects for paintings and sculpture by the artists themselves or their early commentators such as Vasari may provide us with more guidance in knowing how to connect words and images. Even so, as with medieval art, those connections could also alter and depend upon our access to 'sources' that may now be arcane or even lost, and upon the particular situation – social, intellectual, political – in which an image was created and originally viewed. Indeed, if the painter, sometimes in conjunction with his patron, could draw upon a larger and larger library for both subject matter and the special 'take' upon it that they desired, then the viewer's reception of the work was also conditioned by his or her dependence upon and knowledge of an equally large body of reference, which, given the absence of direct verbal direction in or attached to the painting itself, permitted, even perhaps encouraged, a particularly rich – not to say various – pattern of response. What was true for some of the original receptions of Renaissance artwork is even more so for the modern scholarly exegesis of them, which rides a neap tide or *mare maggiore*[42] of texts to gloss visual work.

One consequence of the hugely enlarged and enhanced field of collaboration between the visual artist and his written sources during the Renaissance was the beginnings of rivalry between

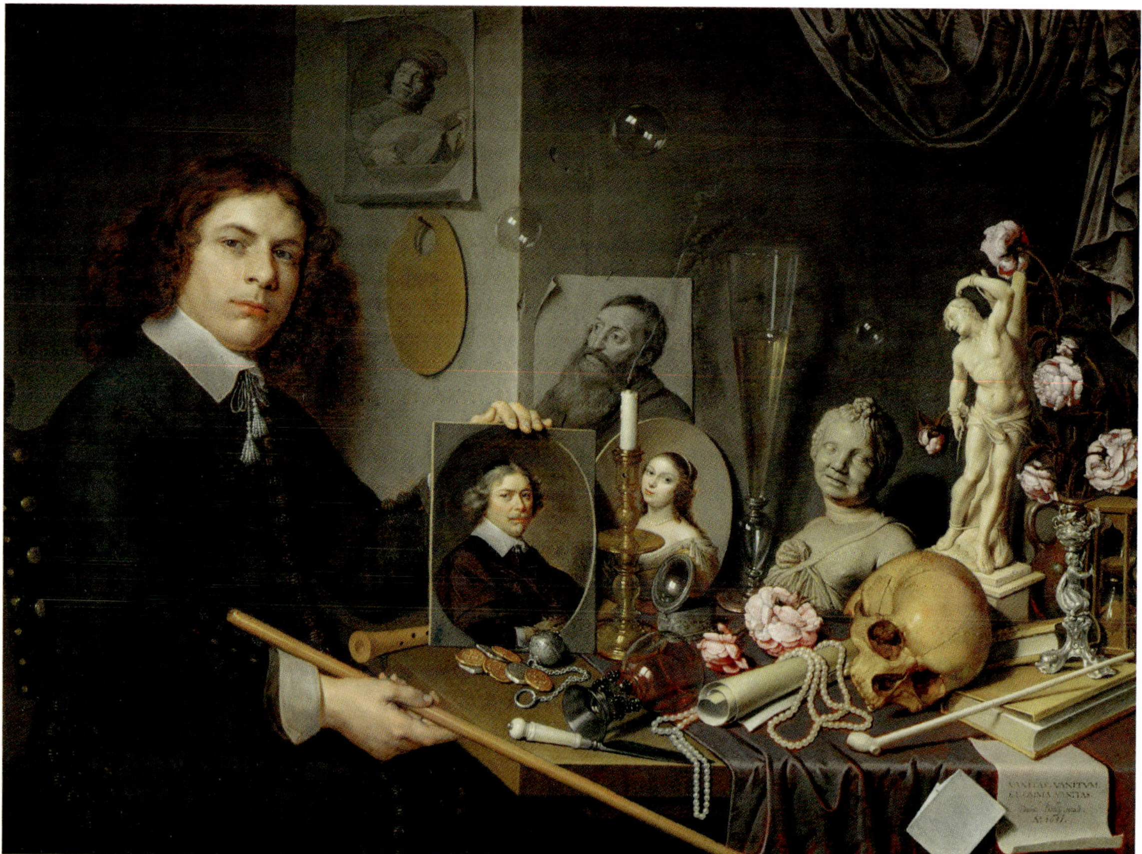

38 David Bailly, *Still-life with Vanitas Symbols*, 1651, oil on panel.

word and image. Classical criticism had seemed to champion their collaborative existence, in phrases like Horace's 'ut pictura poesis' (as in a picture, so in a poem), or Simonides' celebration of 'silent poetry' (painting) and 'speaking pictures' (poetry/rhetoric).[43] But the Renaissance saw an emerging cult of the *paragone*, a competition between the visual arts of sculpture and painting in the first instance and then between the visual and the verbal (and even musical) arts as to which could perform more effectively and efficiently in any one particular task.[44] Those were the seeds of Lessing's later separation of the capabilities of words and images and, later still, of the competitive power-struggles to which Mitchell directs our attention.

It is hard to think of any Renaissance painting that cannot be found to have either originated in a literary text or to have been the subject of commentary that invoked one. One of the provoking aspects for art historians of the Giorgione painting discussed in the Introduction, the so-called *Tempestà*, is that it will not abide our question as to what 'it is about'; we are tempted into extraordinary flights of invention, like a proposal that its subject is Adam and Eve banished from the garden (with a baby)! Without any original title, without any history of being specifically commissioned to illustrate some literary text, and without having been saddled with any more explicatory title than *La Tempestà*, Giorgione's wonderful panel survives in a verbal limbo. Other paintings are more lucky (if that is indeed the word): one (illus. 37) that shows a female in warrior's garb talking to shepherds in a vaguely pastoral setting had been commissioned as a specific scene from Tasso, so either knowledge of that commission and/or a naming of the subject as *Erminia and the Shepherds* gave it a title along the way, enough to recall for viewers a particular episode in Tasso's epic romance, *Gerusalemme Liberata*.[45] Now the painting seems to be anchored by its verbal association for those who recall their Tasso.

It does not, however, really help *Erminia and the Shepherds* or any number of even finer Renaissance paintings to class them as 'literary illustration'. The painterly skills, the organization of spaces, colours, lights and shades and the very posturing of the figures are to be appreciated for themselves; one suspects, indeed, that both originally and now in a modern museum many people responded in precisely that way to its formal rather than its anecdotal scope, of which they might probably be ignorant. Viewers can be drawn into a painting by many features besides (or before) its narrative programme; they can, for example,

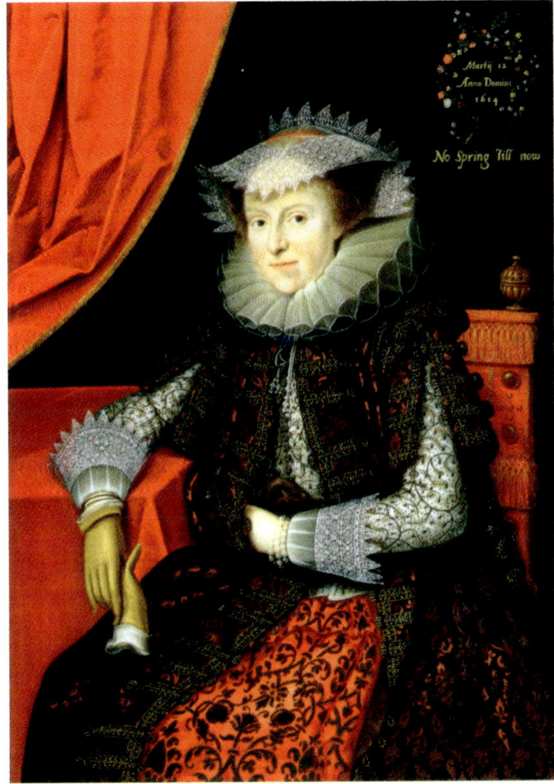

39 Marcus Gheeraerts the Younger, *Mary Throckmorton, Lady Scudamore*, 1615, oil on panel.

respond to a goodly number of visual codes, many of which have an ancient provenance: a raised, vertically pointing finger almost always signifies that the person is supposed to be speaking, while the further repertoire of gestures used formulaically by actors and orators and circulating in engraved, illustrated manuals was a useful resource in examining a painting.[46]

In and long after the Renaissance, landscape, still-life (illus. 38) and portraiture were esteemed less than history painting, which drew upon classical or biblical narratives for its subjects and in one way or another involved the word with its images. During the sixteenth and seventeenth centuries, however, artists working in these 'minor' genres frequently sought to enhance their reputation by adopting practices that deliberately involved a contribution by words. Still-life became emblematic, inviting its viewers to translate its various visual items into moral aphorism and ethical injunction; portraits sported heraldic as well as emblematic signs, the verbalization of which was inherent in understanding the sitter's person or status; landscape became the site either of mythological or biblical events or of incidents that, in the manner of still-life, prompted socio-moral commentary. The word still lingers about such images.[47]

Portraits, it would be sensible to suppose, represent or describe their sitters without verbal adjuncts other than their names. Yet – as in the allegorical 'portrait' by Carpaccio (see illus. 14) – words can extend the physical presence into ethical or moral territory which in its turn requires us to articulate its significance vis-à-vis the sitter. During the flourishing period of portraiture in Tudor and Stuart England, these verbal additions became a vital component, along with the more expected heraldic arms and shields. These range from the merely practical identification of name, age and position, or some tag (often Latin) that was either a family motto or a personal impresa, to moralizing inscriptions (especially when a funeral portrait is involved, but sometimes being the implied utterance of the sitter), inscriptions that announce the occasion of the portrait, and occasionally whole poems (a sonnet is inscribed on Marcus Gheeraerts the Younger's *Queen Elizabeth*).[48] While many such inscriptions place the sitter without ambiguity in time and society (a residual narrative instinct), others can be teasing and gnomic: Gheeraerts's *Lady Scudamore* (illus. 39) contains an elegant wreath of spring flowers within which is her given name and the date of the portrait; below this is the phrase 'No spring till now'. It has been assumed that the words are hers – or articulate her thoughts – upon the marriage of her son that year, perhaps signifying that the family line may now hope to blossom.

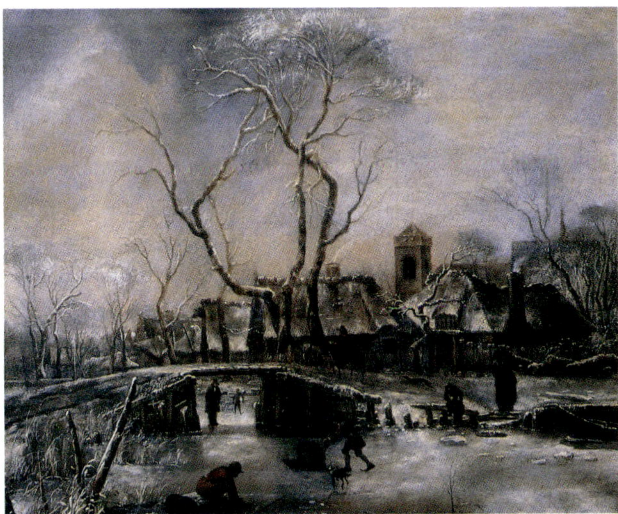

40 Jan van de Cappelle, *Winter Landscape*, 1653, oil on canvas.

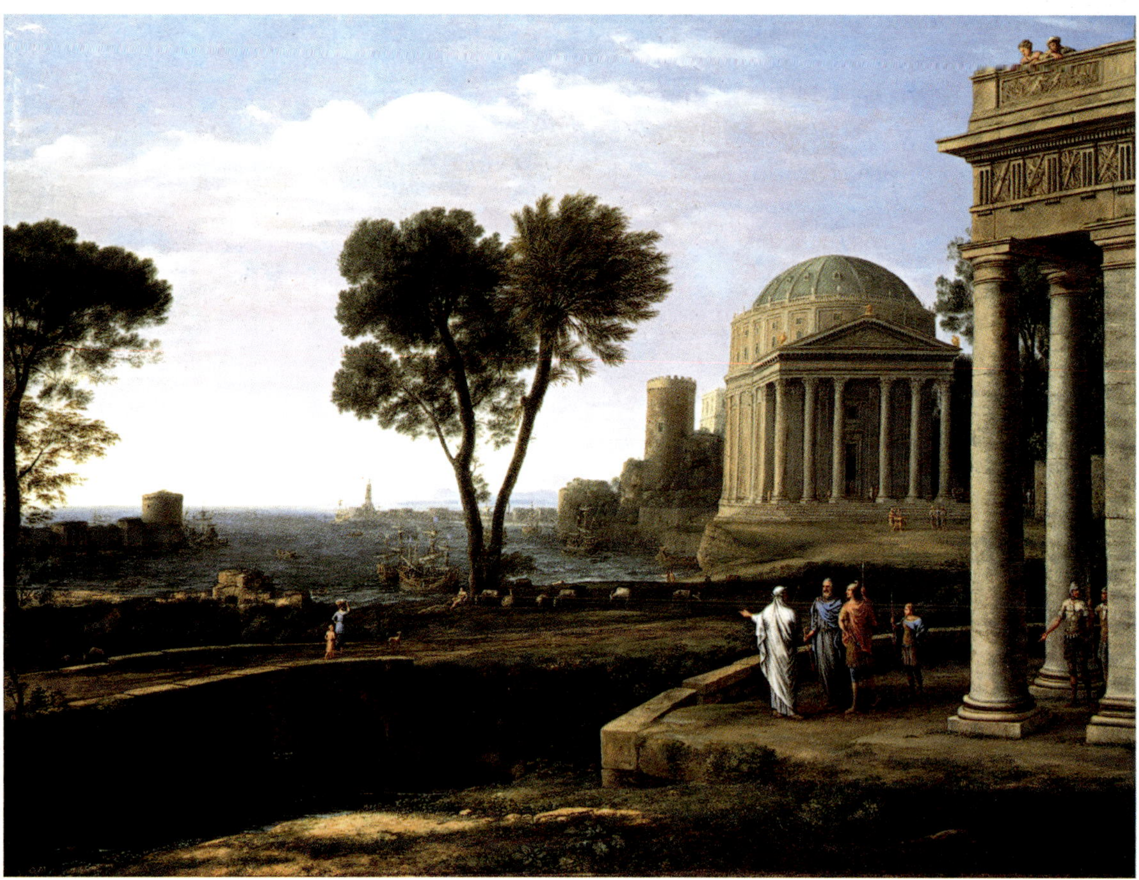

41 Claude Lorrain, *Aeneas on the Coast of Delos*, 1672, oil on canvas.

Dutch and Flemish genre painters, dedicated to depicting the ordinary circumstances of their daily lives and landscapes, would insert episodes that seemed to demand a narrative (and so verbal) commentary that responded to such questions as: what are those people doing? Where is that group going? What is happening as those boats approach each other? What are all those skaters up to? And the titles such paintings have received at one time or another are in effect answers to such demands: they are hunters in the snow returning to their village; one ship is going about to avoid colliding with the other; it is simply a winter landscape (illus. 40) with perfectly familiar and identifiable activities such as pushing a pram across the ice. We still tend to respond to such images by extending its still moment into narrative or anecdote.

Another favourite subject of Dutch and Flemish painters was the person reading a letter, or contemplating a book or other printed matter. Whether or not the texts of such items was readable, our curiosity is aroused as to what significance the words being read have to our appreciation of the scene. These silent verbal appendages continue to haunt genre painting, often influenced by the Dutch, well into the eighteenth and nineteenth centuries, as we shall see.[49] And the theme of a person reading offers the same opportunities for some verbal improvization by the beholder, as when we are shown a figure writing. Dürer's 1526 portrait of Erasmus shows the humanist holding a pot of ink and writing, maybe a letter (another is half-opened beside him), while an opened book, its print facing away from us and toward the scholar, lies conspicuously at the front of the engraving. Many other works by Dürer display both opened books – in St Jerome's study, or held by the Godhead at the Apocalypse – and books in the process of composition (by St Ambrose); in most cases the printed or manuscript words are decipherable.

Landscape painting, whether focused on genre subjects or representing scenes from classical and biblical literature, flourished in the seventeenth and eighteenth centuries. Titles might direct the viewer's memory to some antecedent narrative or just the verbal formulation of some moral apophthegm; but for many viewers, one suspects, that extra dimension was not needed and not called upon for their experience of the painting. Claude Lorrain and Breughel – landscapists in wholly different modes and cultures – both provide wonderful sceneries, where light, colour, different zones of interest (foreground, middle ground,

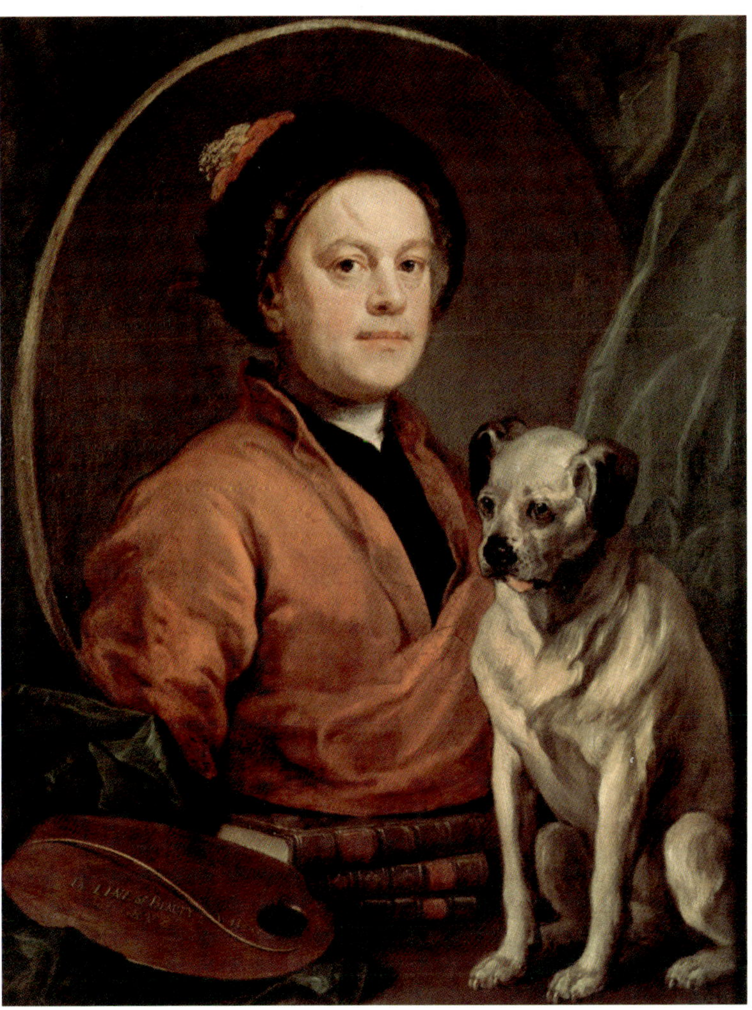

42 William Hogarth, *Self-portrait: The Artist with his Pug*, 1745, oil on canvas.

background) and 'staffage' all contribute to an essentially painterly enjoyment. Indeed, 'staffage', the technical term for the insertion into a painting of people and activities that give a bit of business for the eye, is our art-historical way of discouraging any instinct to translate the depicted events into narrative; we can just see these folk and their activities as part of the landscape. Yet working within a moralistic culture, Breughel delighted in story beyond his painterly versions of the natural world; or rather, he apprehends stories as an integral part of that world and so involves them – Christian events, the fall of Icarus, children's games and popular aphorisms – in his pictorial depictions with the further option of their being the vehicles of non-visual commentary. Claude, we know, like Poussin, pillaged the Bible, Virgil and Ovid for subject-matter, and the proper recognition of those subjects (to which modern titles usually point) extends our appreciation of how his landscapes have been made apt sceneries for those very stories.[50] In the case of illus. 41 Claude not only signed the canvas but himself inscribed its subject – 'ANIVS ROY. SACER[D]OTE [DI] APOLLO. ANCHISE-ENEA' – alluding to the Ovidian (not Virgilian) story of the Apollonian priest Anius showing the city of Delos to Aeneas, Anchises and Ascanius.

VI

The reliance by painters on a 'source' anterior to and formally independent of their own work was a tradition that would die hard, if indeed it has completely expired. It was considerably strengthened and extended by the spread of literacy and the consumption of all sorts of reading matter by the middle classes. From Renaissance mythological and biblical subjects to Victorian genre scenes leads a well beaten track of words. Whether drawing extensively on the plays of Shakespeare, Milton's *Paradise Lost*, or pillaging Tennyson or Dickens for subject matter, artists have followed the ambition of early and late Renaissance artists to translate into powerful shapes and colours some event that has an earlier life in words but that now finds its own *modus operandi*. Such painting does not necessarily deny a source, and may even proclaim it explicitly; but it still offers its own visual version, the fullest beholding of which may draw

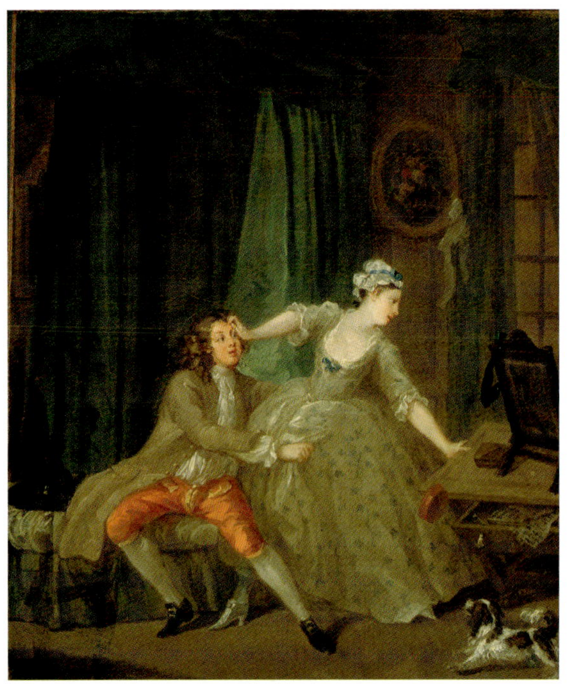

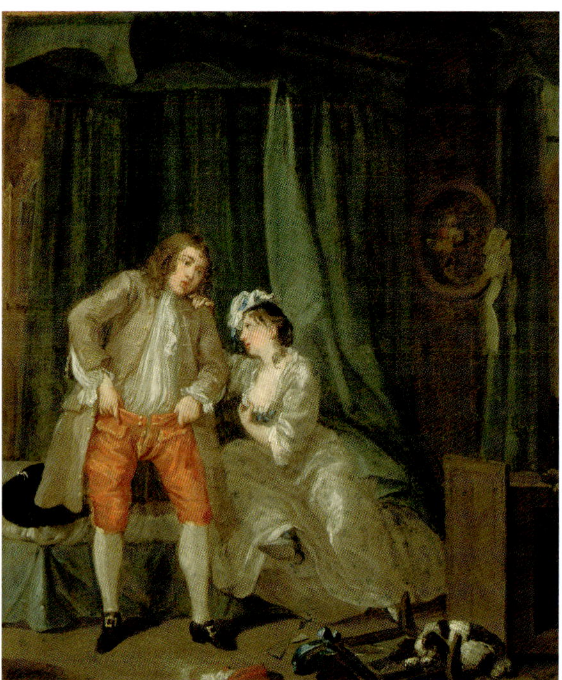

43, 44 William Hogarth, *Before* and *After*, 1730–31, oil on canvas.

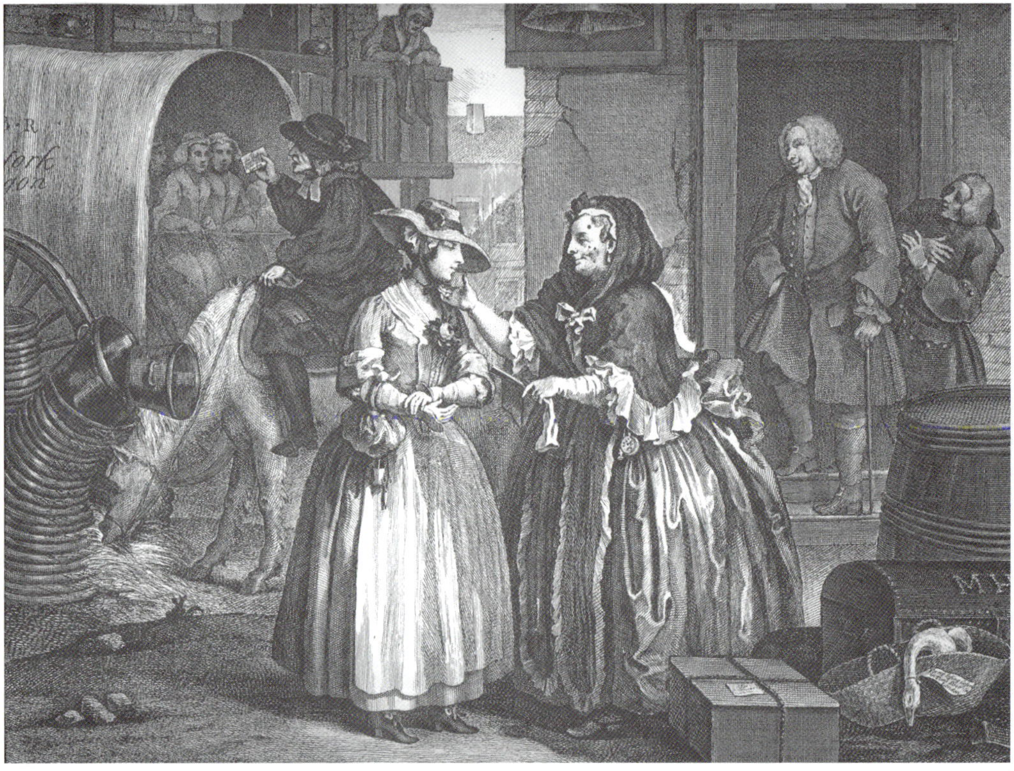

45 William Hogarth, *A Harlot's Progress*, Plate 1, 1732, engraving.

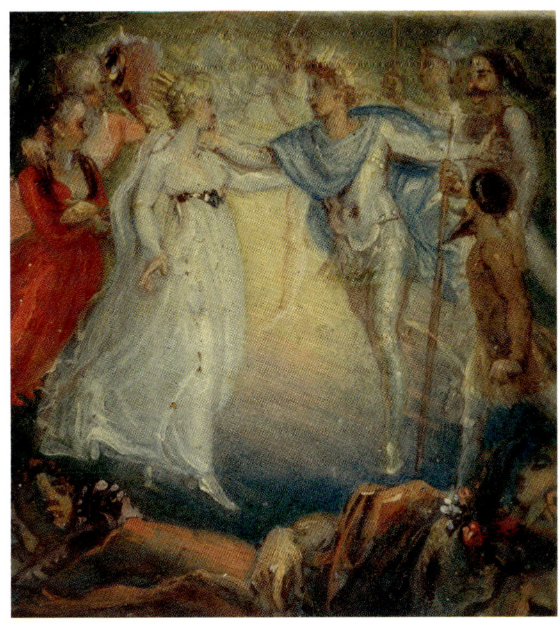

46 Thomas Stothard, *Oberon and Titania, from 'A Midsummer Night's Dream'*, 1806, oil on paper mounted on board.

upon an anterior narrative or idea but will aim to exceed those verbal capabilities. Whether those implied or referenced words are called into play rather depends on how an individual viewer wishes to respond to a given picture.

However, with the best-known works of William Hogarth a story was thoroughly intertwined, and words played a fundamental role in the overall meaning of his paintings and engravings. Even his self-portrait (illus. 42) manages to include his own celebrated 'Line of Beauty' from *The Anatomy of Beauty*, now etched onto the painter's palette. When he paints scenes from John Gay's *The Beggar's Opera*, they necessarily draw upon the pregnant moments that he has chosen to depict. His pair of canvases showing lovers *Before* and *After* the man has had his pleasure with the girl invite its spectators to rehearse for themselves the obvious plot that has intervened between the two images. A single engraving like *A Midnight Modern Conversation* may be less interested in duration, but insists with forensic elaboration upon the different modes of drunkenness which we spell out as we scan the image. But above all it is with his 'progresses' – those of the Harlot, the two Apprentices, the Rake – that Hogarth most fully exploits the verbal even while extending his own visual skills as painter (some were first produced as a series of paintings) and engraver. As their name implies, we need to follow the progress of their characters' stories, observing in the studied sequence of settings and dramatic personae how the stories unfold; the narrative is made wonderfully clear via these succeeding frames, but it is subtly aided and abetted by Hogarth's scattering of clues, both visual (paintings on the walls) and verbal. A second version of *Before* and *After* (illus. 43, 44), for instance, is set indoors and the lady's dressing table contains both a volume on *The Practice of Piety* and the poems of the licentious Earl of Rochester. Readable playbills litter the floor in *Strolling Actresses in a Barn*. The coach that brings the future harlot into the sinful city of London is marked as coming from York (illus. 45); the label around the neck of the dead goose, also presumably sent up from the country, anticipates a fateful conclusion (not least by encouraging viewers to pass judgement on the 'poor goose' of a country girl). From the coach at left to the goose at right the harlot's progress is epitomized. Words may never be required to follow Hogarth – he is too skilled graphically to need them; however, they enhance and play their various commentaries upon the ongoing theme.

If Hogarth is the great narrative painter of the eighteenth century, one other major activity must be accorded equal importance in this survey. This is the ambitious range of paintings that drew on literary sources like Dante, Chaucer, Shakespeare and Milton, by Blake, Henry Fuseli, James Barry and Francesco Zuccarelli, among others.[51] Two such enterprises were John Boydell's 'Shakespeare Gallery', realized during the final decade of the century, and Fuseli's less successful venture for a 'Milton Gallery'. Both had their origins in illustrated books, commercial enterprises in which major artists were asked by Boydell to paint scenes from Shakespeare's plays; Fuseli took on the Herculean task of depicting Milton's poetry all by himself. In both cases the projected book publications never materialized, which gave an independent existence to the paintings that were produced (Boydell obtained 89 large and 84 small paintings, Fuseli

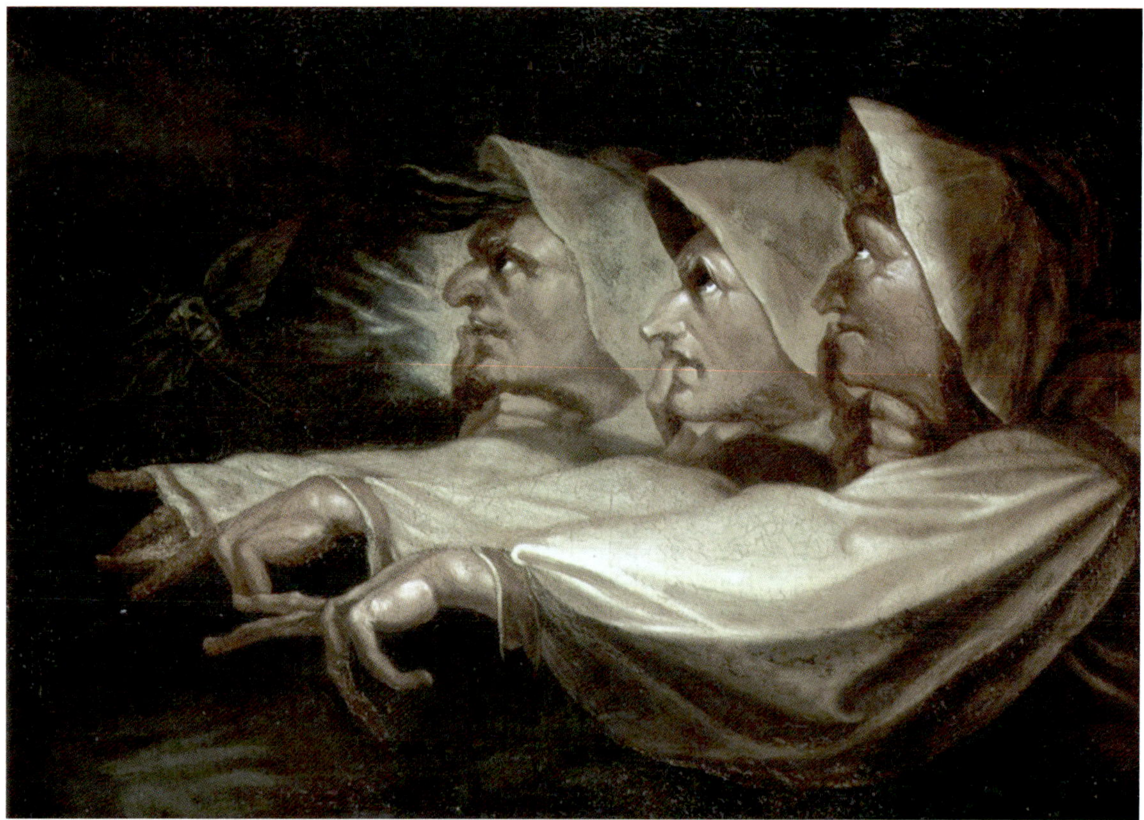

47 Henry Fuseli, *The Three Witches*, after 1783, oil on canvas.

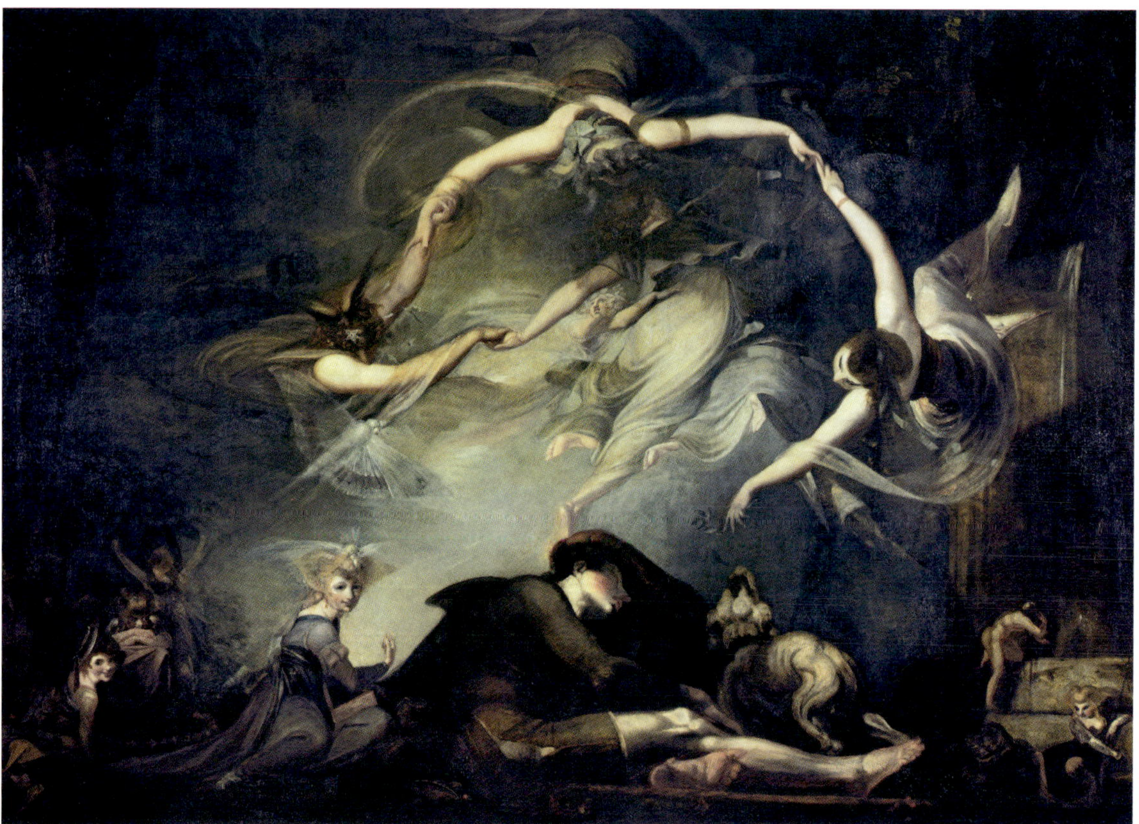

48 Henry Fuseli, *The Shepherd's Dream, from 'Paradise Lost'*, 1793, oil on canvas.

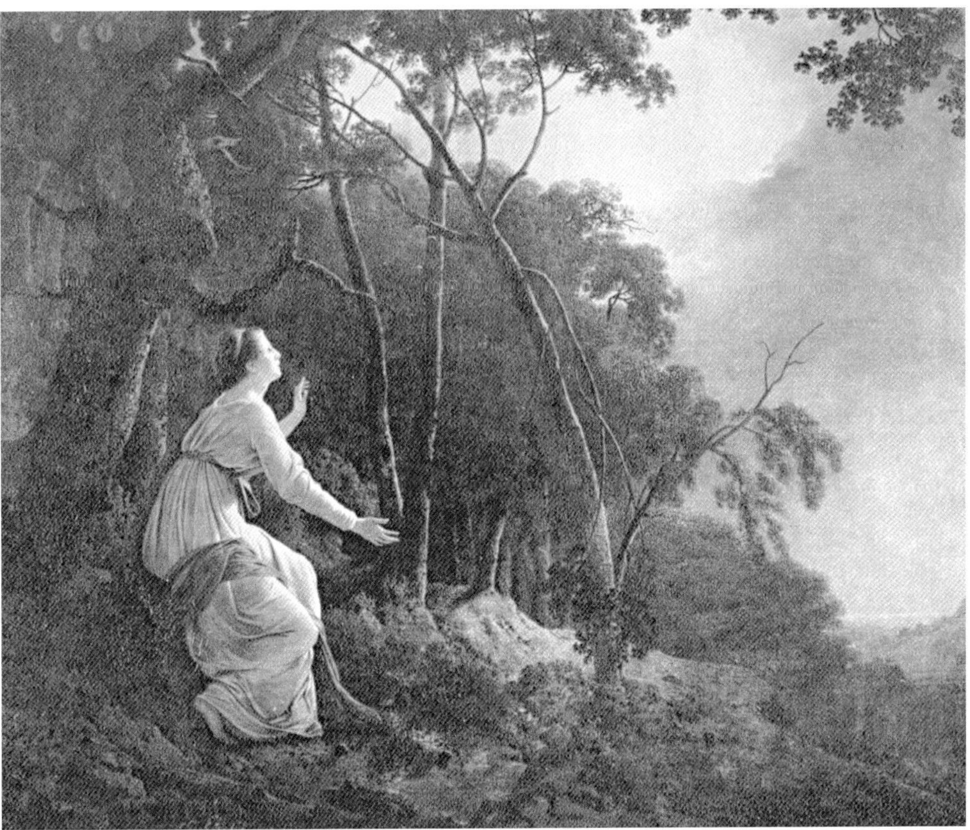

49 Joseph Wright of Derby, *The Lady from 'Comus'*, 1785, oil on canvas.

alone produced 47). These works generally go beyond illustration, primarily because they were designed to stand alone – that is, even if eventually engraved, the paintings were not set alongside texts – and secondarily because the artists involved by Boydell (including William Hamilton, Francis Wheatley and Robert Smirke) as well as Fuseli himself were as much concerned with exploiting their own skills as with paying mere homage to Shakespeare or Milton. For those who knew their plays (and many did), clearly there was a direct way into understanding the picture, while in its turn the pictures helped to visualize some of the dramatic highpoints of specific plays like *A Midsummer Night's Dream* or *Macbeth* (illus. 46 and 47); presumably patrons of the Gallery would be enticed via the images to return and find the contexts of their selected moments in the plays themselves either in Boydell's publications or on London's stages. But many of the paintings retained their own compelling focus.

The search for sublime subjects led many eighteenth-century artists back to Dante's journey through hell, purgatory and paradise, or to Milton's epic of the loss of paradise. The two-way communication of these paintings or drawings with their 'sources' is hard to define precisely: but the paintings gained a certain prestige by the literary provenance of their subjects, while the selection of subjects offered painters both the occasion to display their own imaginations on the same themes (another *paragone*) or provide them with opportunities to rescue and re-inhabit the sublime, a zone somewhat occluded by more sentimental, middle-class genres. Significantly, Fuseli chose for one painting, not an incident from *Paradise Lost*, but an image, a simile comparing the lower ranks of fallen angels to faeries bewitching a sleeping shepherd (illus. 48). His version, sometimes titled *The Shepherd's Dream,* pits the artist's invention specifically against Milton's own linguistic one: each is imaging one state by invoking another, each within his own medium. Joseph Wright of Derby seizes upon a moment from *Comus*, duly acknowledged in his title (illus. 49), but exploits his own fascination with the dramatic conflicts of dark and light – admittedly, at the same time, opening up one of the masque's themes ('glimpses into the nature of grace'[52]) through his representation of both the dazzle of light and the Lady's gestures towards it. But other artists, from Hogarth's *Satan, Sin and Death* to Fuseli's *Sin, Pursued by Death* and John Martin's visions of the architecture of Hell (illus. 50), explore the frissons, the terror and awe that the Miltonic epic inspired; their paintings try to honour both their source and their own explicit ambition to equal it by translating seventeenth-century poetry into a new visual

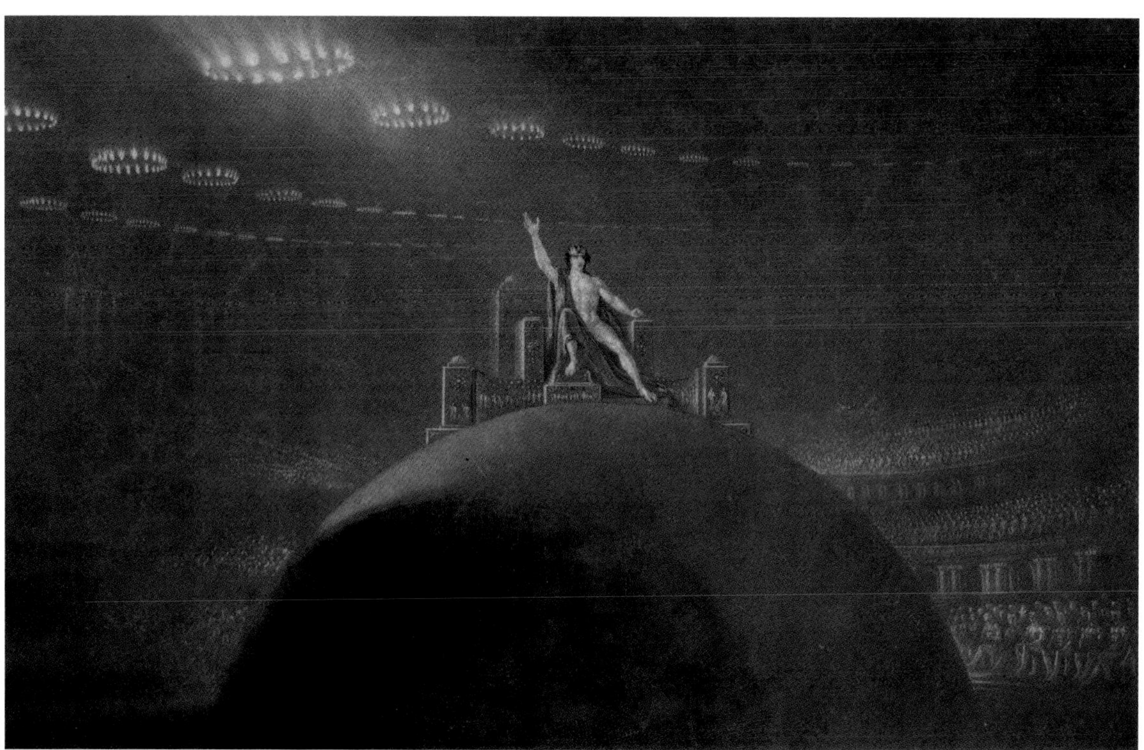

50 John Martin, *Satan Presiding at the Infernal Council*, a painting later engraved and re-titled 'Satan in Council', as here for the 1827 edition of *Paradise Lost*, Book II.

language (Martin seems to draw upon the architectural projects of Claude-Nicolas Ledoux, for instance).

The increased attention to landscape painting in the eighteenth century certainly suggests a flight from the requirement of finding a literary 'source' or bolstering a painted image with narrative or poetic meaning; the artist's delight in devising adequate forms of representation for the land around him became an exciting end in itself. True, it responded to a general excitement about the natural world that was expressed in both poetry and scientific treatise, but few artists found such written materials necessary grist for their mill. The popularity of genre subjects was partly that they implied anecdotal possibilities, yet without burdening the viewer with precise and perhaps mandatory references. George Morland's *Laetitia* series (1789) clearly looked to Hogarth for his six-part narrative of the country girl's progress from *Domestic Happiness,* through *The Elopement* to *The Tavern Door* and *The Fair Penitent* and used the sequence to sustain the narrative. But in single paintings his rural subjects are also imbued with some anecdotal context, if not imbued with larger narratives (illus. 51).[53]

But generally the pleasures of land as opportunities for the pencil or the brush eclipsed any anxiety to ensure the prestige of artwork by grounding it in *a priori* texts. We know how much Thomas Gainsborough loved to compose landscapes from bits and pieces of stone, coal or wood on his table top, and how he envisaged brushwork as providing a little 'business for the eye' rather than any vehicle for story or moral. Yet we have nonetheless to note that while the same fascination with the often wonderfully messy materials of the natural scene or its changeful cloudscapes drove John Constable, there was for him an underlying impulse to draw out some large significances for the scenery, whether sympathetic understanding of social mores and commercial practices, or the symbolisms of the Salisbury spire and the ruins of Hadleigh castle.

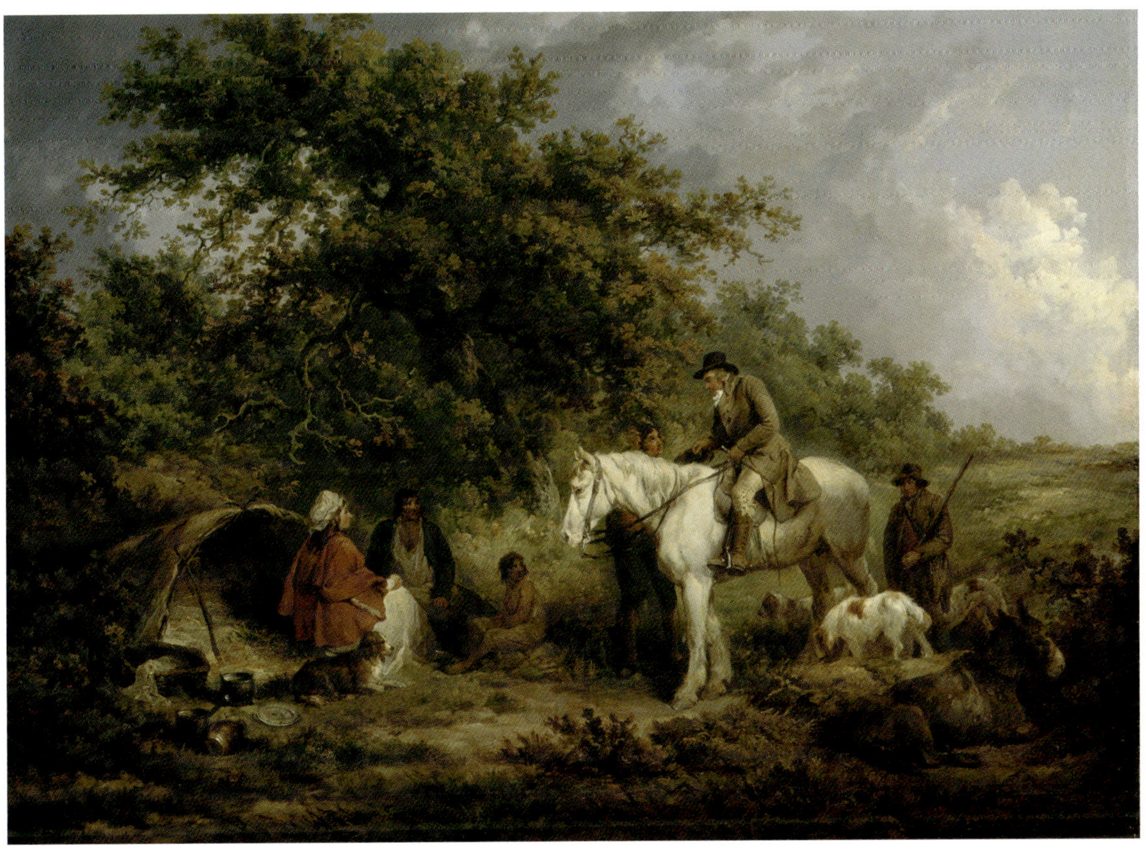

51 George Morland, *The Benevolent Sportsman*, 1792, oil on canvas.

In fact, the word clings suggestively to landscape painting through its fundamental role in picturesque practice and theory. We tend to think of this fad around the turn of the nineteenth century as a sometimes uncritical dedication to form and shape, colour and light, and to the static 'taking' of a scene (as in a modern snapshot); but it was also a mode of thinking about and responding to place and to the element of time or duration within which a place was experienced. The poet Robert Southey considered the picturesque 'a new language',[54] and, in this, words supplemented what the artful image could produce by articulating associations, moods, emotions and feelings that attended the optical observation of a site. Picturesque amateurs were encouraged to bring words in aid of their paintings; 'pen and pencil united', was the typical encomium heaped upon its major practitioner, William Gilpin (1724–1804), whose much-appreciated travel books encouraged travellers and amateur draughtsmen and -women to apply both their graphic skills and their literary talents to recording their landscape adventures.[55] Publications of picturesque scenery that preceded Gilpin's series of *Observations* were also presented as distinctly composite endeavours: the engraved view identified the site, gave its lineaments, while the text drew out the associations or historical circumstances for which that particular place was noted (illus. 52). While text and image did not necessarily cohabit on a single page, their ensemble mattered: sometimes they faced each other (depending on how the whole was bound), or, as in the example used here, the reader must be actively engaged in turning the page between the two and drawing upon both.[56]

We can track this linking of supplementary words to carefully contrived imagery in many ways in the years around 1800 when the picturesque 'language' was in vogue. The German poet Johann

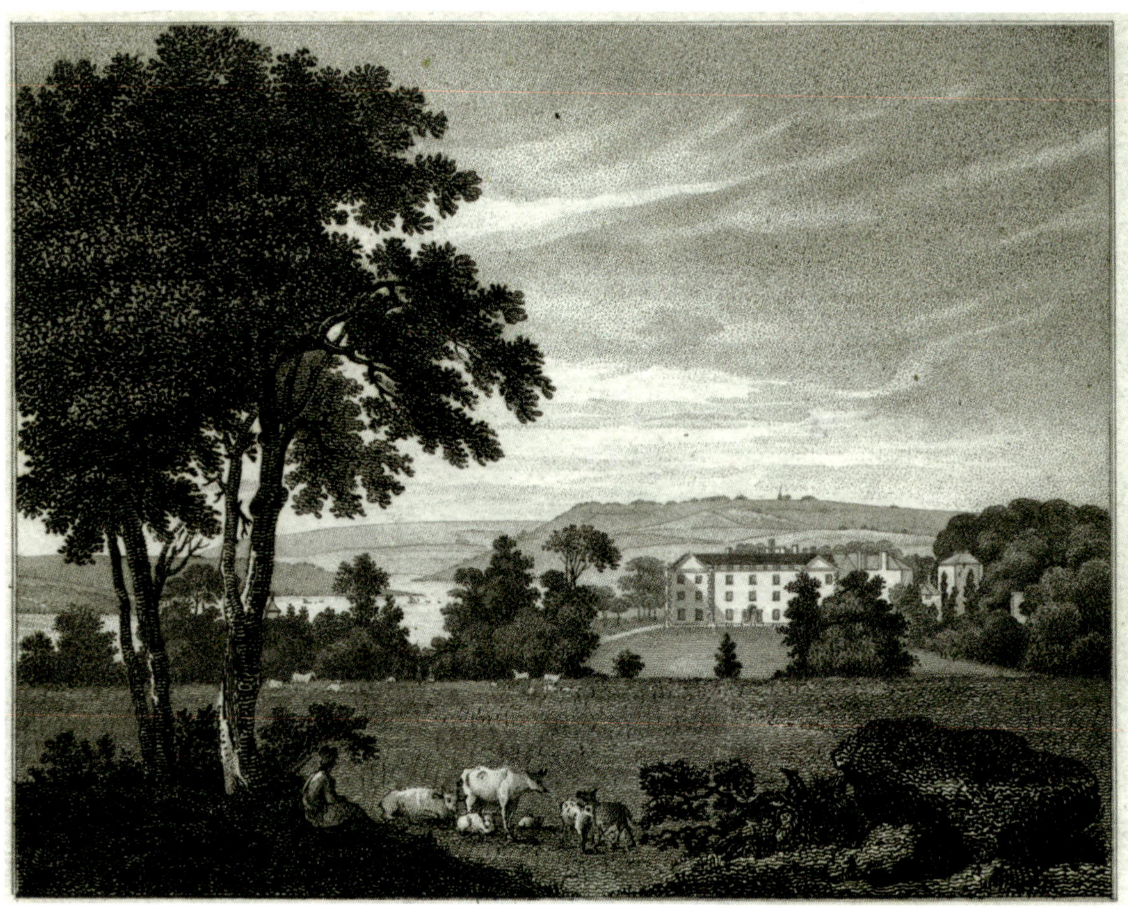

Saltram, Devonſhire,

THE ſeat of the Right Honourable Lord Borington, now a minor; was rebuilt by his late father: it is a grand and extenſive building, delightfully ſituated; the principal front is towards the ſouth, commanding a beautiful view of the Sound, Plymouth, Mount Pleaſant, Mount Edgecumb, and the water meandering in various directions through wood and lawn. Their Majeſties made this their reſidence for a fortnight, in the courſe of their late tour.

This view from the North was taken by Mr. Cowper, during their Majeſties ſtay at Saltram, in the Autumn of 1789.

52 Engraved view and letterpress (printed on a separate page) describing Saltram in Devon, from *Les Délices de la Grande Bretagne*, engraved and published by William Birch, London, 1791.

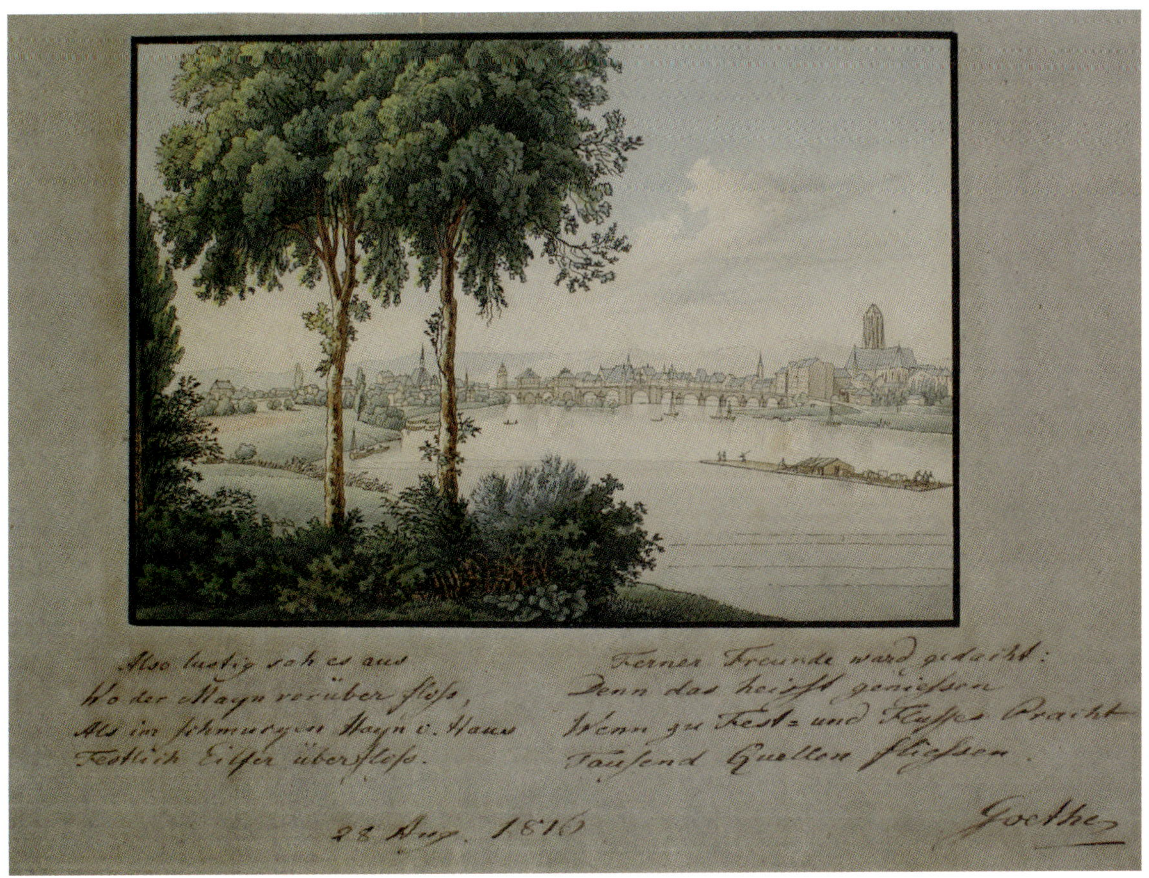

53 Johann Wolfgang von Goethe, verses attached to an etching of Frankfurt, 1816.

Wolfgang von Goethe drew as well as wrote, but on at least one occasion (illus. 53) he took a coloured engraving by Rosette Stadel of his birth town, Frankfurt am Main, and added to it verses that drew out of the pictured scene associations that it held but could not express. In his memory, he says, the overflowing River Main is compared to the 'festive joy' in a friend's house and thus the 'essence of pleasure' is 'when a thousand springs flow together/ To splendid celebrations and rivers'.[57] Innumerable sketchbooks rely upon a similar deployment of words, sometimes simply to annotate the time, place and conditions under which a sketch was taken, or more fully to flesh out elements of the scene for which words were better suited (illus. 54) and thus 'complete' the experience and the memory of it. So familiar and perhaps expected was this collaboration of word and image – either on the same sheet or in adjacent pages – that the landscape designer Humphry Repton very shrewdly adopted it as a prime marketing ploy during his quite extensive career.[58] In making his proposals for estate improvements to individual clients he gave them a small volume (sometimes called 'red books' from their Moroccan binding) where both his own drawings and descriptions made intriguingly clear the opportunities his 'improvements' would bring to the given property (illus. 55).

The greatest of English landscape painters in the late eighteenth and early nineteenth centuries may have had roots in picturesque practice, as they certainly grew up as artists within its magical field. That they transcended those beginnings and the simple appeals and formulae of the picturesque does not always mean they abandoned its significant strategies. Turner's fondness for infusing landscapes with both historical or even topographical events, with attaching verses and other

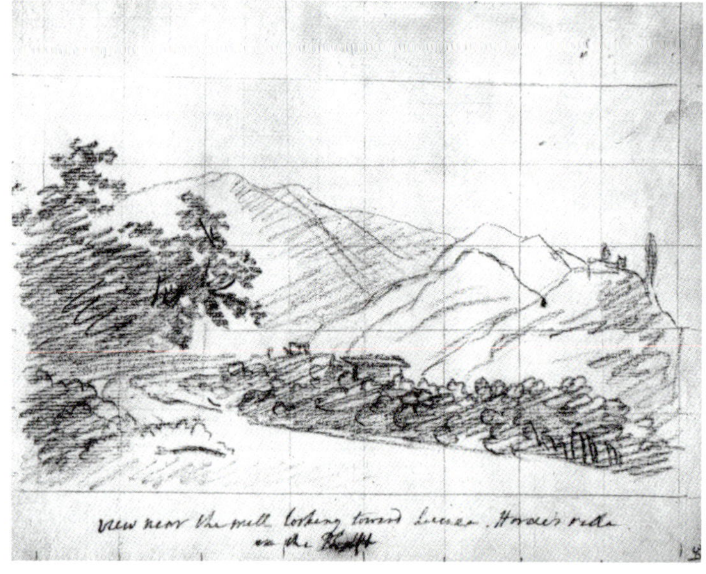

54 Allan Ramsay, pencil sketch and annotation of *View near the mill looking toward Licenza. Horace's villa on the left*, 1755, sketchbook.

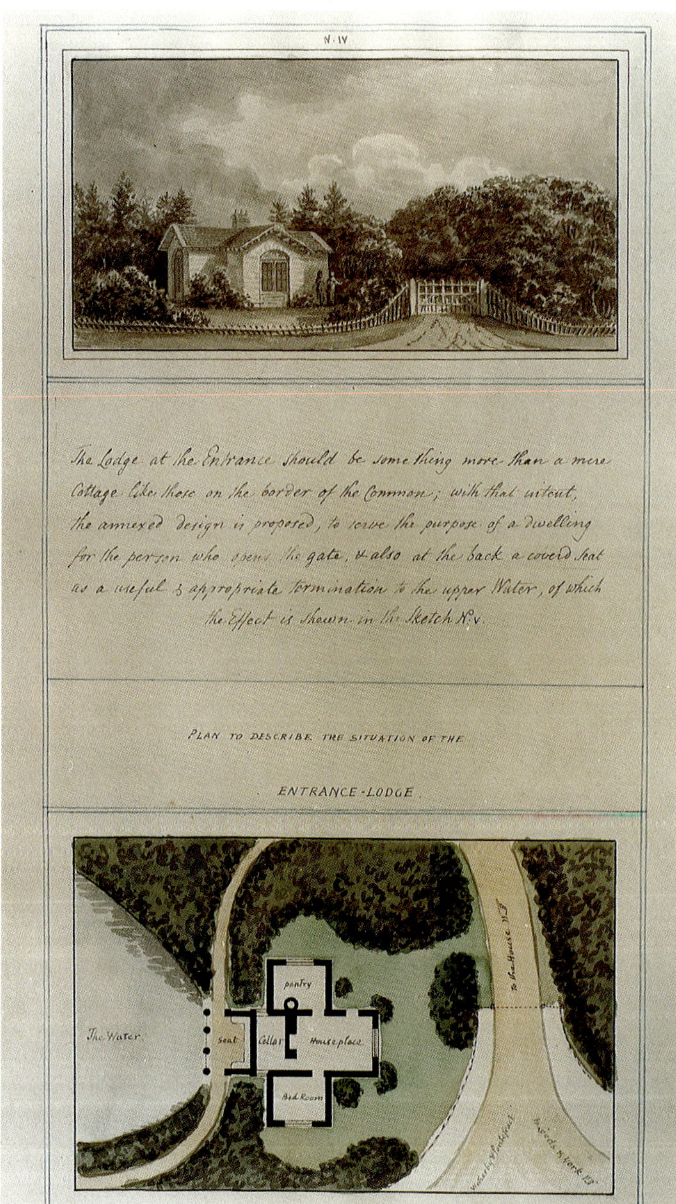

55 Humphry Repton, Folio 9 of the 'Red Book for Oulton near Leeds in Yorkshire', with remarks and images of the Entrance Lodge, 1810, ink and watercolour.

verbal glosses to his paintings, with crafting titles that deliberately added an interpretative or even narrative dimension to the imagery, all link his best work with the deliberate reliance upon the opportunities of word and image during the picturesque vogue (which itself, of course, is relying upon long traditions of such liaisons – he himself referenced Claude and Hogarth) as well as upon the bifocal ability of the human brain to cope with both verbal and visual stimuli in responses to the outer world).[59]

In 1798, when the Royal Academy first allowed verses to be printed in their catalogues, Turner added some lines scrambled from James Thomson's *The Seasons* to his picture of *Buttermere Water*: what is interesting is that the lines speak to the sublime effects of light – the 'effulgent' sun, the 'grand ethereal' rainbow and the yellow mist – and their contribution seems to draw our wondering attention to how the painter handles these things better than a poet. The instruction 'Vide Ovid' included in the actual title of *Apullia in Search of Apullus* may again play with the painter's own invention, since in the *Metamophoses* Book 14 there is no Apullia (he might better have asked us to 'Vide Claude', since that is where the really interesting dialogue is taking place). Likewise a painting of 1828 that references Boccaccio (*Boccaccio Relating the Tale of the Birdcage*) is not designed to send its beholders off to the *Decameron* once again – there is no birdcage in it! – but for the added resonance given by the title.

But Turner was relentless with his attachment of verses, many of which continue to

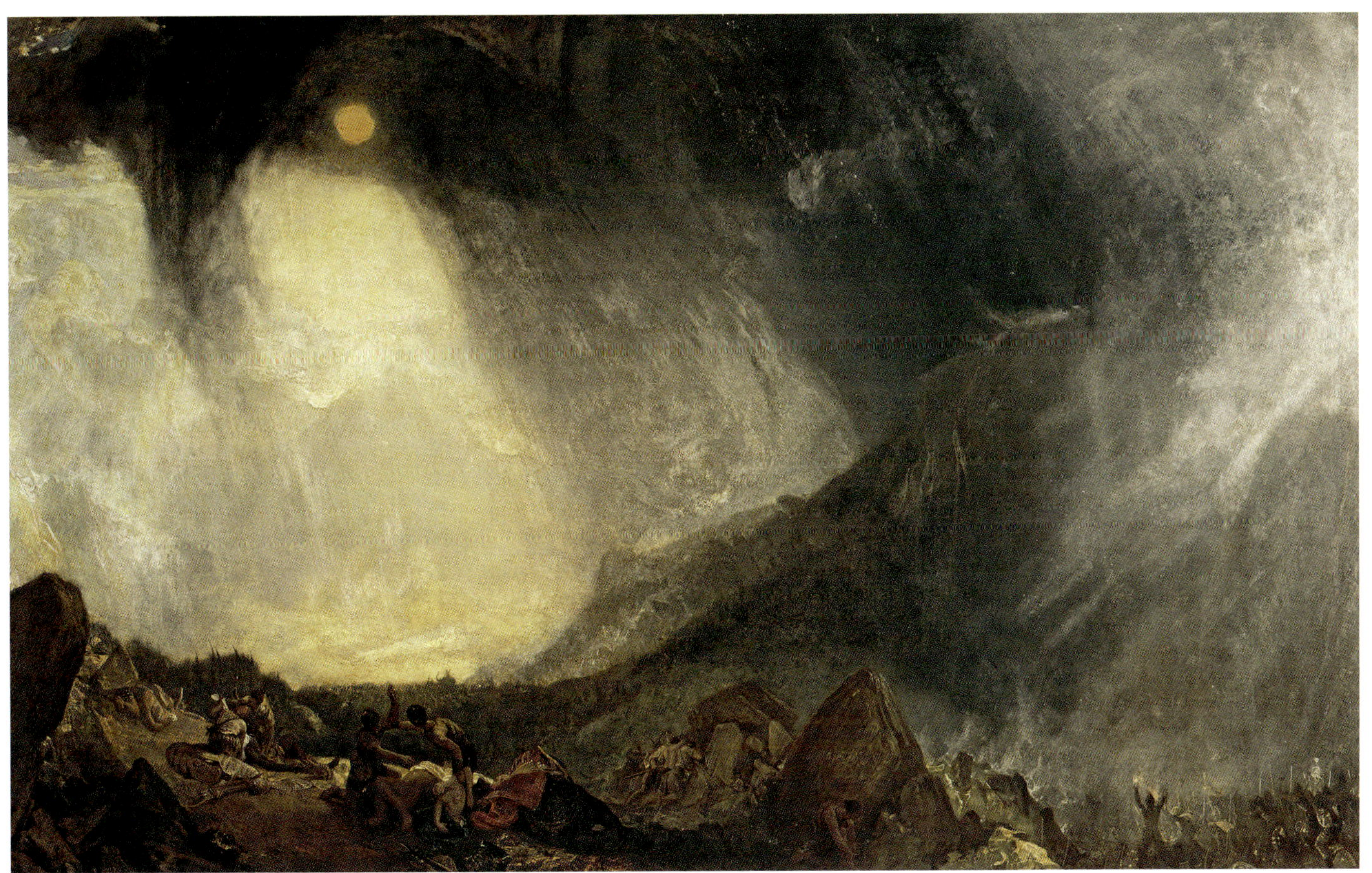

56 J.M.W. Turner, *Snow Storm: Hannibal and his Army Crossing the Alps*, 1812, oil on canvas.

function in a kind of rivalry or *paragone* with the paint; even though they were increasingly drawn from his own ambitious writing project, entitled the 'fallacies of Hope', as for the 1812 *Snow Storm: Hannibal and his Army Crossing the Alps* (illus. 56), the effect seems somehow merely rhetorical, even bombastic, when considered alongside the painting's achievements. However, his carefully worded titles are often a different matter: very deliberate, especially when attached to marine paintings, they direct the landlubber's understanding of what was shown: *Boats Carrying our Anchors and Cables to Dutch Men of War in 1665*, or *Snow Storm – Steam Boat off a Harbour's Mouth Making Signals in Shallow Water, and Going by the Lead. The Author* [sic] *was in this Storm on the Night the 'Ariel' left Harwich* (illus. 57). This last contains a very picturesque move in its identification of time, place and the occasion of the painter's observation. Turner's colossal skills as a colourist and observer of topography, his extraordinary range and his appetite for so many and various subjects, tend rightly to marginalize the rare agility he showed in steering or manipulating his viewers via titles, literary allusions and quotations. But that talent – notwithstanding the often miserable quality of his own verses – adds a rare chapter to this history of words in or about visual art.

The continuities between Renaissance painters and these early modern painters with their reliance upon verbal adjuncts and supplements may get obscured by our art-historical concern to distinguish different periods and styles of art: but we need only recall John Ruskin's otherwise odd claim that Tintoretto's *Annunciation* was a 'sublime Hogarth'[60] and this same critic's apprehension of a wholly discursive art in both Turner's landscapes and Pre-Raphaelite paintings to see affinities between artworks where image absorbed the word. Turner's *The 'Sun of Venice' Going to Sea* (illus. 58) is not on the face of it anything more than what its title purports to tell us, a boat putting out to sea. Even the words 'Sol de VENEZIA' inscribed on the sail do not necessarily do more than give its Italian name. But the Royal Academy 1843 catalogue contained verses by the artist himself (changed slightly in different copies):

> Fair shines the morn, and soft the zephyrs
>   blow,
> Venezia's fisher spreads his painted sail so gay,
> Nor heeds the demon that in grim repose
> Expects his evening prey.

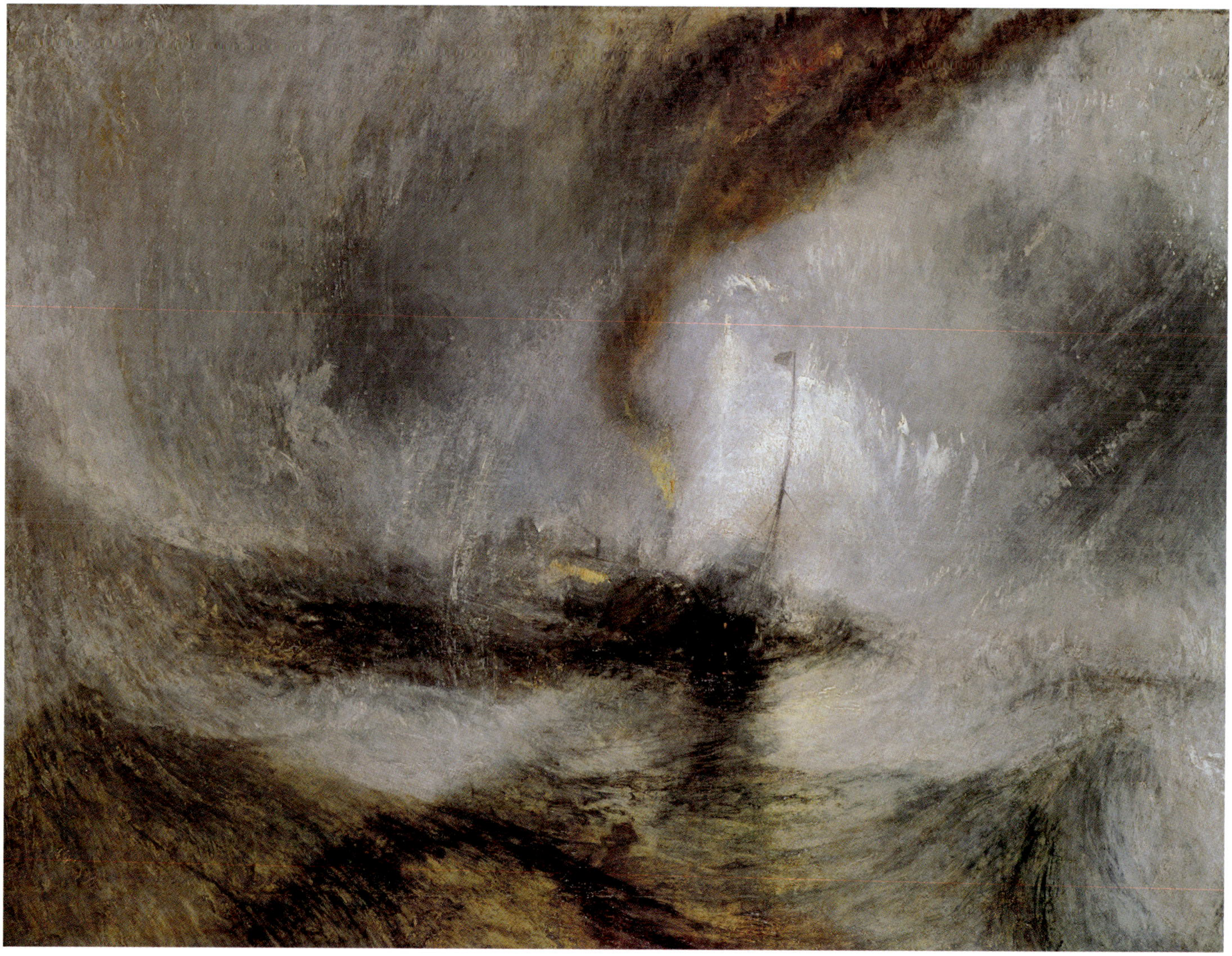

57 J.M.W. Turner, *Snow Storm: Steam Boat off a Harbour's Mouth Making Signals in Shallow Water, and Going by the Lead. The Author was in this Storm on the Night the 'Ariel' left Harwich*, 1842, oil on canvas.

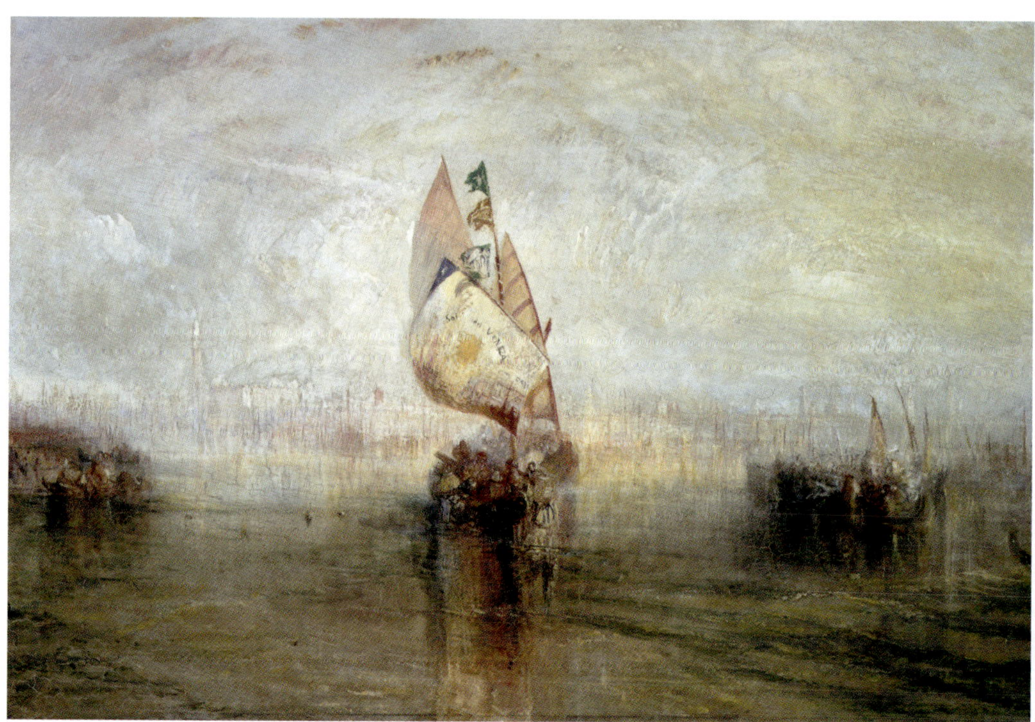

58 J.M.W. Turner, *The 'Sun of Venice' Going to Sea*, 1843, oil on canvas.

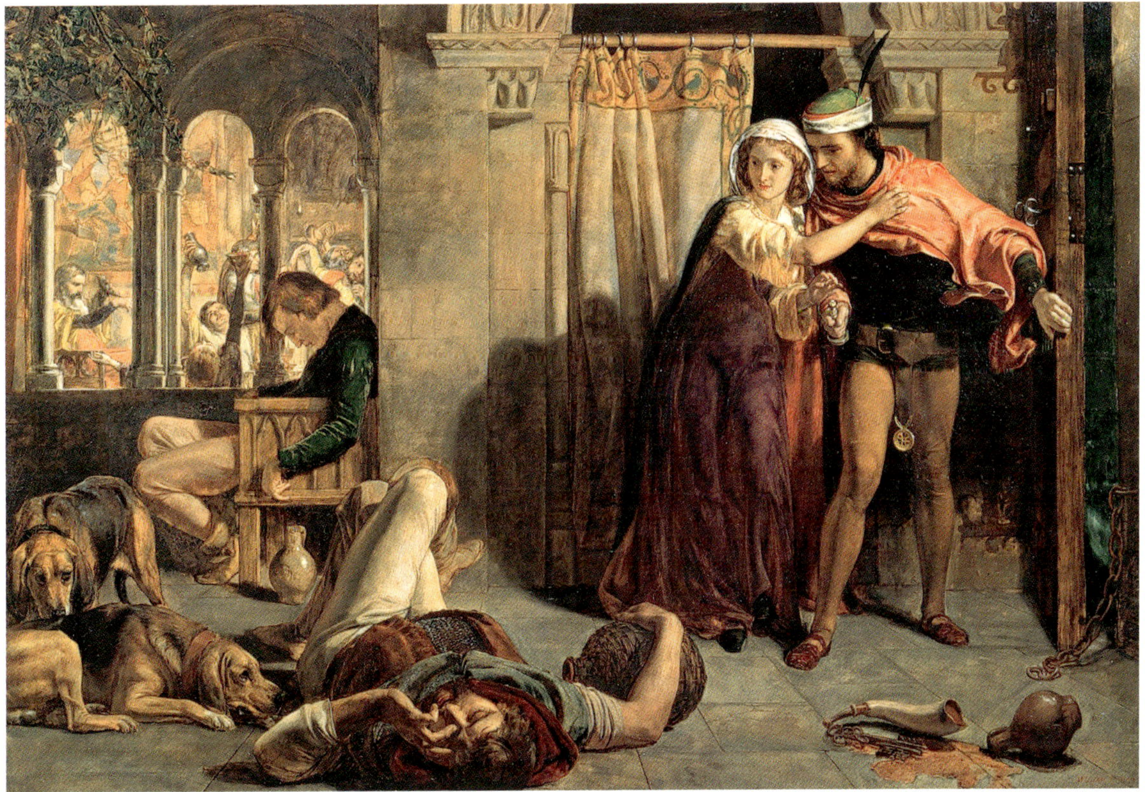

59 William Holman Hunt, *The Flight of Madeline and Porphyro during the Drunkenness attending the Revelry (The Eve of St Agnes)*, 1848, oil on canvas.

Yet this 'demon' lurks only in the indifferent verses and nowhere appears in the picture itself; indeed, some original viewers were put off by its gloomy and seemingly gratuitous addition (the *Athenaeum* of 17 June thought his 'dealing with quotations' was 'unscrupulous'). To see the painting today at Tate Britain and to be oblivious of that original verbal gloss makes for a wholly different experience, in which the Venetian sun shines brightly without being loaded with any fatalistic aura; to then learn how words originally entered into the picture is to be required to contextualize the image both within Turner's own political-philosophical mentality and in contemporary attitudes to a doomed and ruined Venice.

VII

The long tradition of artists looking to or being directed by a patron to literary works for both subject-matter and for some 'handle' on it did not show any signs of decline. Indeed, the traditions of genre painting from seventeenth-century Dutch through the British landscape modes during the following century seemed to gather extra strength in the Victorian period.[61] More and more potential patrons wanted their paintings to tell stories, to have some extra-pictorial potential, perhaps something to be talked about beyond technical discussions of painterly performance; more and more, even established, artists were called upon to provide illustrations for books,[62] which new technologies of reproduction and an eager reading public made a lucrative and flourishing trade. Furthermore, the mildly conventional depictions of familiar, quotidian scenes and events, long since a staple of the artistic culture, was given an extraordinary boost by the Pre-Raphaelite movement from the mid-point of the century with its deliberate references to early literary work. The chance, furthermore, of printing some quotation in the catalogues of the Royal Academy and other exhibitions, as we've seen with Turner, proved almost irresistible to many artists.

It was partly the Pre-Raphaelite resolve to return to painting techniques and formal devices of Italian painting before Raphael that led them to find subjects in early literature or literature about earlier historical eras, which they saw as an essential practice among those early painters. Many of the paintings from the early days of the Pre-Raphaelite Brotherhood, founded in 1848, relied upon the titles being able to alert people to an already established and even well-known incident. Holman Hunt's *The Flight of Madeline and Porphyro during the Drunkenness Attending the Revelry* (illus. 59) counted upon its allusion to Keats's 'Eve of Saint Agnes', the name of which poem was later added parenthetically to the title;

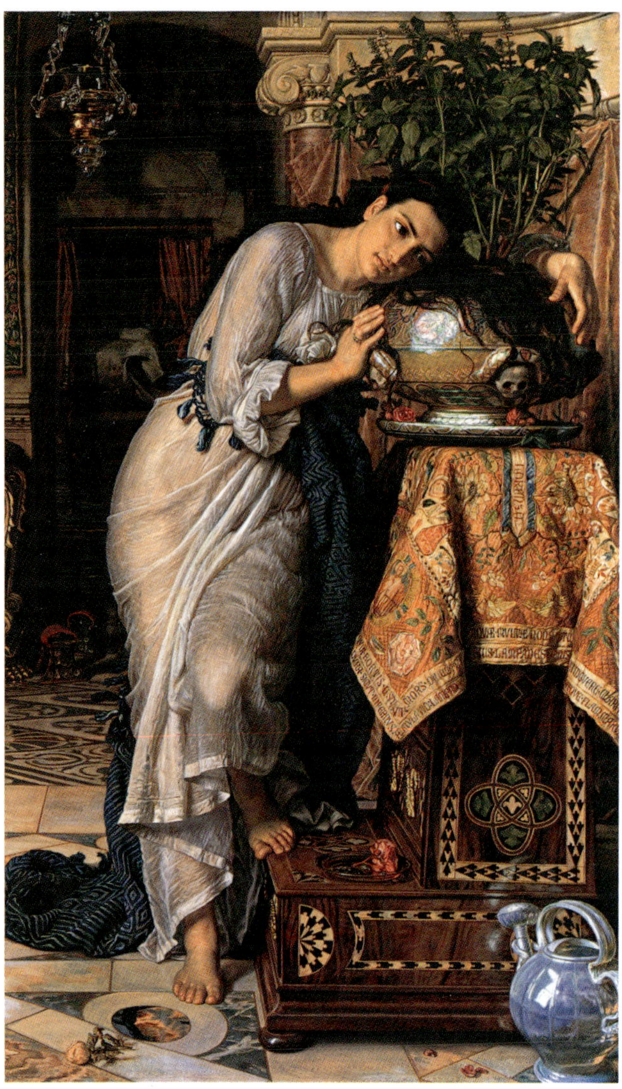

60 William Holman Hunt, *Isabella and the Pot of Basil*, 1867, oil on canvas.

the wordy title stimulated recollections of the poem's story and, when exhibited at the Royal Academy, the catalogue also printed nine lines from the poem. Both Hunt and Millais returned to Boccaccio, as retold by Keats, for *Isabella and the Pot of Basil* (illus. 60) and *Isabella* (illus. 61) respectively (Millais also did a painting in 1848 of the Cimone and Efigenia story from the *Decameron*, noted earlier). In all cases the catalogue of the exhibitions where they appeared provided some relevant lines to anchor the viewer's attention, should it have wandered from or been wholly captured by the often striking painterly forms. None of these paintings contain any conspicuous words, and the cloth embroidered with Lorenzo's name in Hunt's is their only intrusion; the verbal nudge or even shove was delivered in the title. But its effect was not always the same: a knowledge of Keats's poem would 'explain' why the two figures were fleeing and thus perhaps provide a necessary gloss; the pot of basil might intrigue viewers and make them enquire why the lady was so amorous of a flower pot; but the dining table scene needs less literary push than the others, and there is enough in its presentation of the various characters and their behaviour to satisfy the anecdotal curiosity of a viewer. But the narrative thrust of almost all the Pre-Raphaelite paintings – whether from literary texts, historical events, or even contemporary issues like immigration – was strong and, to judge from reviews of their work, proved satisfying to many who needed to find ulterior or anterior meanings.[63] Even portraiture could perhaps be raised from its conventional purposes and lesser artistic evaluation by the addition of words: Millais persuaded William Michael Rossetti to pen a sonnet for his portrait of *James Wyatt and his Granddaughter* when it was submitted to the British Institution in 1849 (portraits were inadmissible, but the ruse did not work, and the sonnet has not survived). A later recruit to the Pre-Raphaelite movement, Edward Burne-Jones, whose painterly skills were considerable and whose paintings did not rely usually on more verbal adjuncts than their titles, manages to infuse such paintings as *Laus Veneris* (illus. 62) with an atmosphere that evokes a hinterland of suggestive meanings, perhaps because we see the music book open and even legible. Maybe Swinburne's poem 'Laus Veneris' lurks behind the painting, though exactly how it informs it is difficult to adjudicate; yet it may well be a reverse 'influence' of artist upon poet. However, Burne-Jones's implicit reliance upon the verbal is made wholly explicit in many of his fine designs for stained glass, which revived the formal combination of image with words in mediaeval church ensembles, naming the saints or allegorical figure (SPES – Hope) depicted, added moralizing glosses to the Egyptians drowning in the Red Sea,

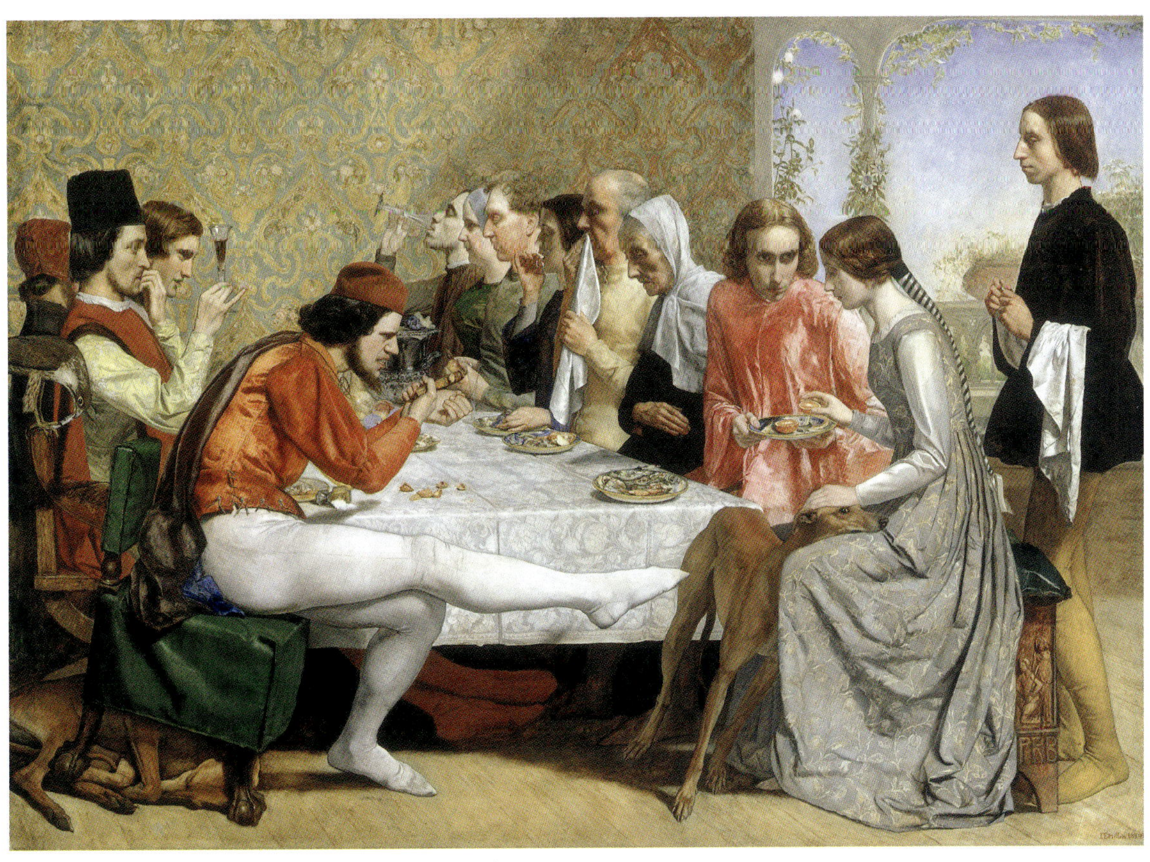

61 John Everett Millais, *Isabella and Lorenzo*, 1848–9, oil on canvas.

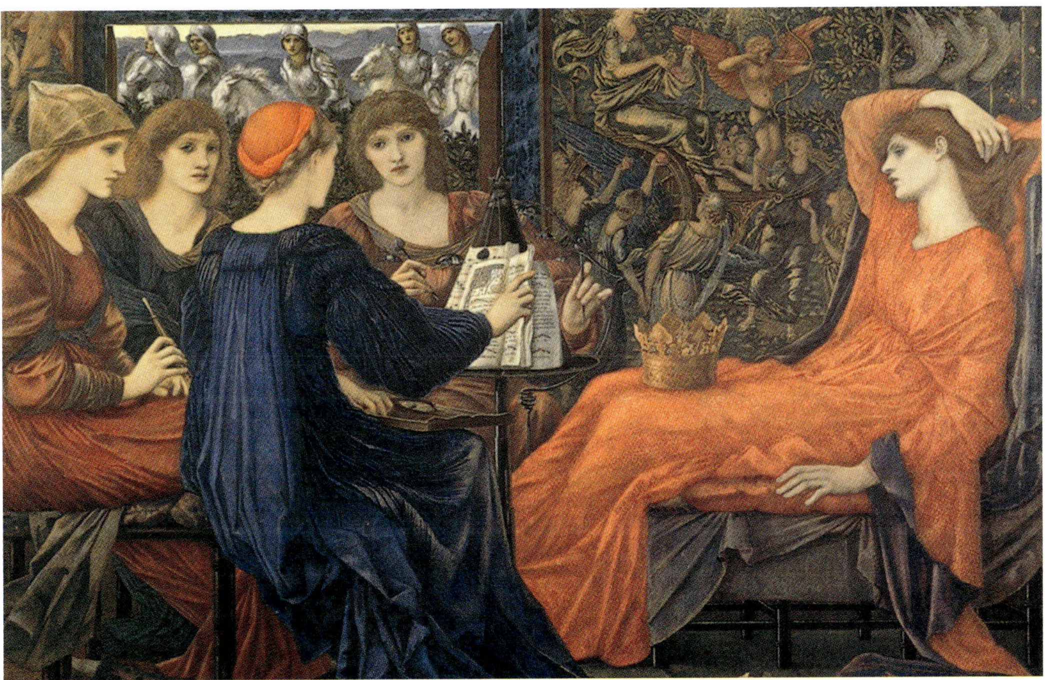

62 Edward Burne-Jones, *Laus Veneris*, 1873–8, oil on canvas.

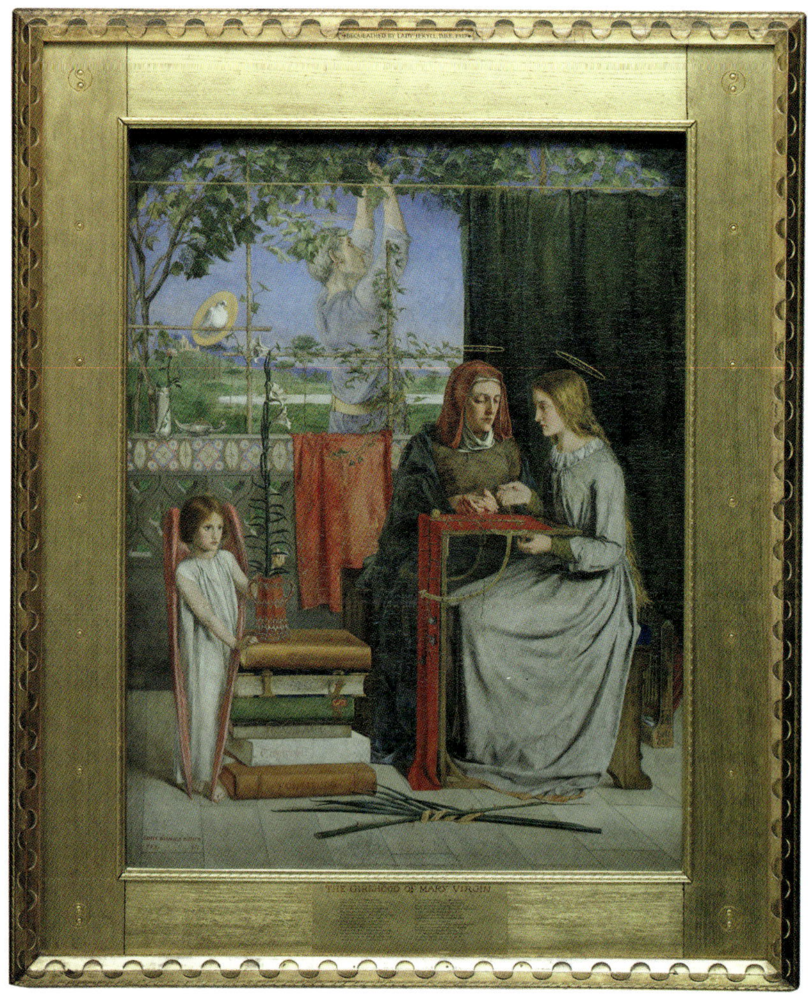

63 Dante Gabriel Rossetti, *The Girlhood of Mary Virgin*, 1848–9, oil on canvas.

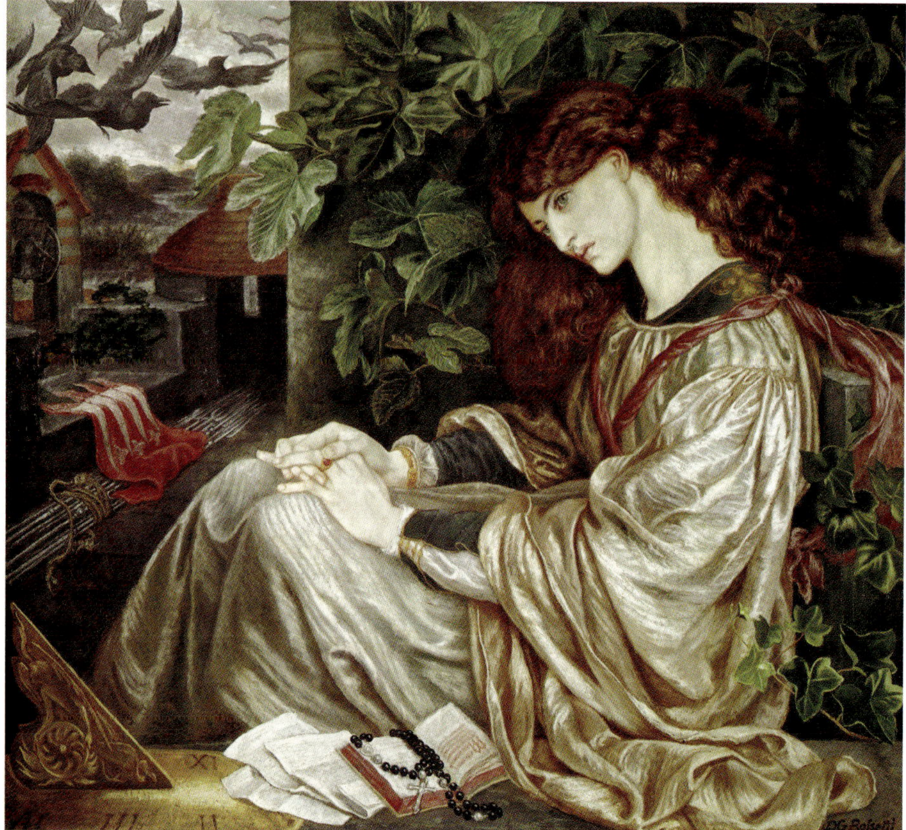

64 Dante Gabriel Rossetti, *La Pia de' Tolomei*, 1868–80, oil on canvas.

and narrating in Latin such Biblical episodes as the lamentation of David or Malory's English incidents from Arthurian legend.[64]

That Dante Gabriel Rossetti was himself a poet as well as becoming a painter (seeking out Hunt for instruction after seeing the *Madeline and Porphyro*) can explain his own instinct for discovering subjects for paintings in literary texts and broadcasting that inspiration, along with commentary on the visual symbolism, in verses attached to his frames or catalogue. The original frames for both *The Girlhood of Mary Virgin* (illus. 63) and his Annunciation painting, *Ecce Ancilla Domini!*, were inscribed, the first with a sonnet (another sonnet was offered in the catalogue, and eventually both were put upon a subsequent frame) and the second with Latin mottoes that gave it a more Popish flavour. Rossetti never abandoned either his poetry or his painting's reliance upon literary plots or ideas, writing ekphrastic poems about his own images (as well as those of other artists), and in the case of his own paintings seeking some close connection between them and his sonnets. These literary resonances – especially when drawn from Dante's *La Vita Nuova*, which Rossetti translated in 1848 – are difficult to hold at bay when his titles direct us (*La Donna della Fiamma*, *Beata Beatrix*, *La Pia de' Tolomei* (illus. 64), *Dante's Vision of Rachel and Leah*) so clearly to literary sources.

Victorian genre painting, as much as the work of the Pre-Raphaelites, enjoyed the opportunities to invoke literary stories or events. Provided the title or catalogue was explicit enough, viewers could be released by a painted image into a whole narrative world from a wide range of literature. And periodicals like *The Art Journal* even encouraged artists to turn to such works as Tennyson's 'Enoch Arden': 'here, then, is a rare gallery for the

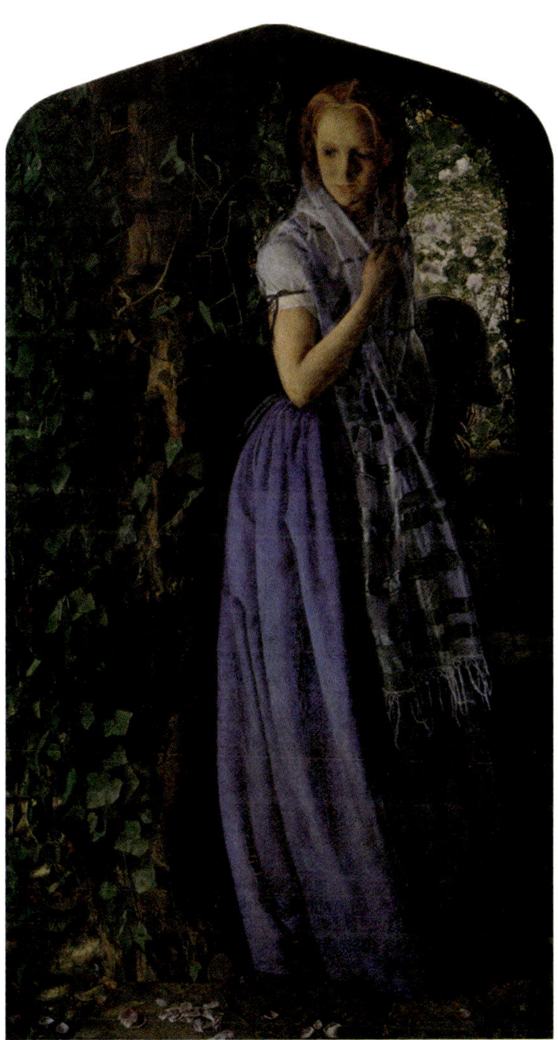

65 Arthur Hughes, *April Love*, 1855, oil on canvas.

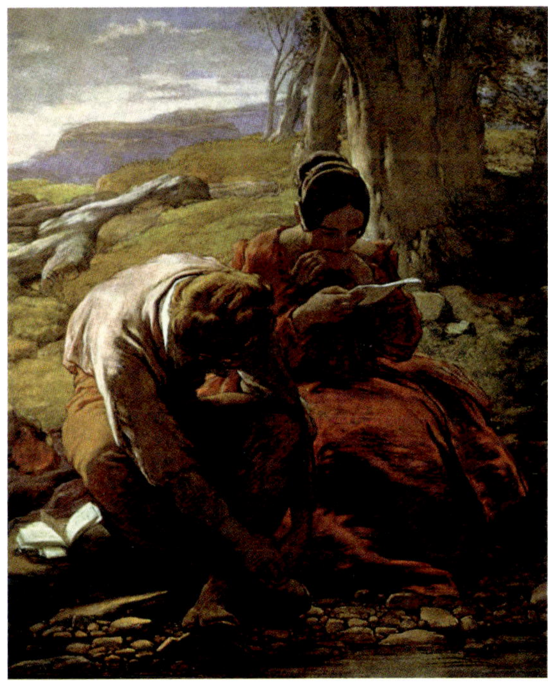

66 William Mulready, *The Sonnet*, 1838, oil on canvas.

painter: every page supplies a subject – nay, subjects more than one – for the pencil; and, no doubt, "the exhibitions" will be full of evidence that the Poet has conferred an incalculable boon on Art'.[65] Arthur Hughes had already in *April Love* (illus. 65) drawn on lines from Tennyson's 'The Miller's Daughter', which the catalogue dutifully recorded, even though their relevance to the canvas's scene is extremely slim. What transpired in a viewer's mind while looking at such paintings or drawings and accepting their literary subject matter is, almost inevitably, a mystery: did the literary handle promote and sustain the beholder's (as reader's) share? Did the mere fact of a literary basis help to make the artwork more authoritative because of its appeal to an established author? Did the viewers actually grapple with what the visual was now telling them about the text, perhaps noticing subtle reformulations of an original narrative emphasis? Maybe even learning how much the painted 'version' had found its own inestimable independence?

But an interesting sub-genre of Victorian narrative paintings is where the picture shows a person or persons reading a book, letter, newspaper or other words; it is a subject that dates back at least to Dutch painting, with Jan Vermeer's *Woman Reading a Letter* being a famous example.[66] Yet Victorian explorations of the same episode drew a certain energy from the current culture of paintings that relied explicitly upon literature in one form or another. Unlike W. H. Deverell's *The Grey Parrot* (illus. 67), William Mulready's *The Sonnet* (illus. 66) doesn't actually show us any words, but the evident absorption in reading (or recalling former reading) opens up for our imaginations what those words might be. The depiction of any paper or book, visually inscribed and with decipherable words, or even with these only implied, becomes an invitation to project a narrative or some emotional intensity of our own devising onto the image. What is perhaps the decisive Victorian contribution is the assumption by an artist and often by his viewers that we will make that further move: we seem to be required to wonder what the woman is reading in John Callcott Horsley's *A Pleasant Corner*, what news is contained in Thomas Webster's *A Letter from Abroad*, or what book the young *Schoolmaster's Daughter* is showing the young pupil in James Sant's picture (both Royal Academy). There is the somewhat wicked temptation to think that in James Archer's *La Mort d'Arthur*, the open book on the lap of one of the mourning women must be (*avant la lettre*) Malory's famous story!

Victorian painting was largely anecdotal (to the point sometimes of outright sentimentality), and the Pre-Raphaelites benefited, while also contributing their own sharp-edged forms to, this fashion. Even when Holman Hunt did not invoke biblical texts (as he did conspicuously for *The Scapegoat* – see Introduction illus. 14), or select titles that directed viewers immediately towards a discursive commentary, his art nonetheless elicited them: a case in point is his painting first exhibited in 1852 with the title *Our English Coasts* (illus. 68). The title apart, there are no words in the painting, which was initially commissioned simply as 'a picture with *sheep*', as Hunt told Rossetti;[67] its frame apparently was inscribed with 'The Lost Sheep'. The painting was taken originally to be a commentary upon the undefended coast and the current fears of a French invasion; but by 1855 such a theme had lost its urgency and Hunt renamed it *Strayed Sheep*. Yet it is only when we have found the 'right' words, the words that Hunt implied in the conception and organization of the work, that its fuller meaning becomes clear: we must notice the significant absence of a shepherd caring for and guarding the flock, one of which has already 'fallen' to the left (itself the 'sinister' side), to sense that the otherwise unremarkable pastoral scene is a parable of unreligious Victorian culture. It was precisely this kind of silent appeal to narrative or moralizing wordage, the overwhelmingly literary inclination of so much nineteenth-century painting and sculpture, that explains the 'backlash' of modernity, the determination of twentieth-century visual artists to tear away from any dependence on discursive explanations or justifications. It was not simply, if at all, a rejection of the moral sentimentality of Hunt's sheep piece, but of an aesthetic 'sentimentality' that needs to attach a message verbally and portentously to such a slight visual occasion. But even Ruskin, whose oddly entitled 1851 pamphlet on the divisions within

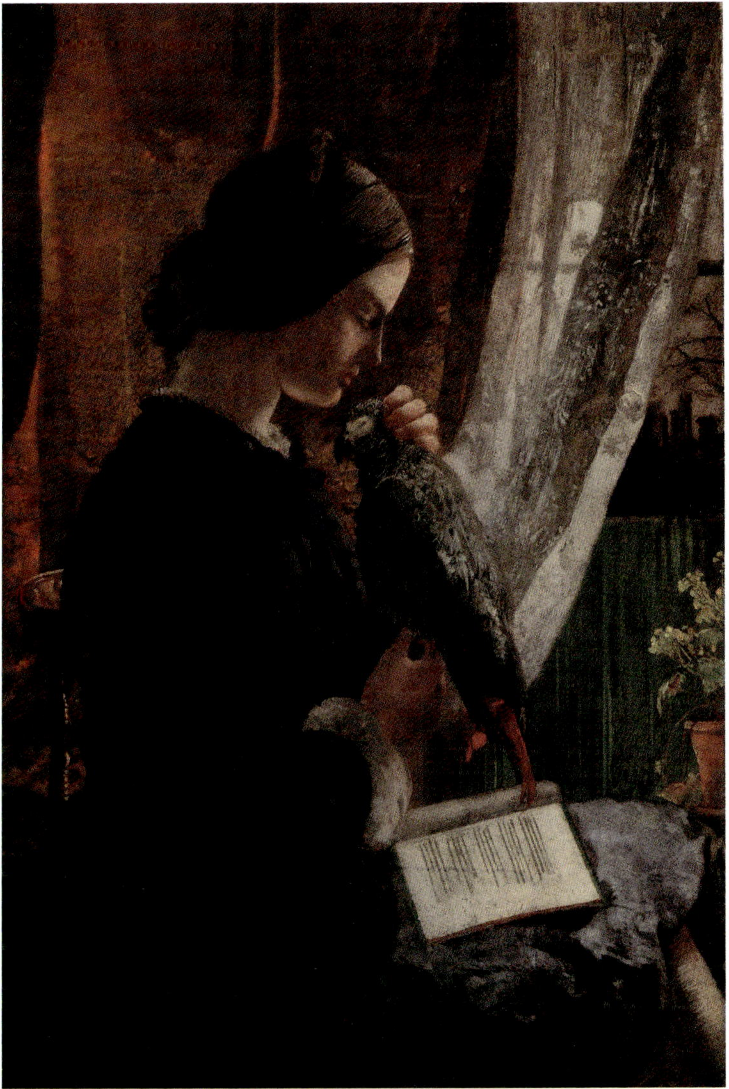

67 Walter Howell Deverell, *The Grey Parrot*, 1852–3, oil on canvas.

Protestantism, *Notes on the Construction of Sheepfolds,* may have been a text originally in Hunt's mind, had come by 1883 to see the work in largely painterly terms: on its appearance in the Parisian Exposition Universelle, Ruskin could write that 'for the first time in the history of art, the absolutely faithful balances of colour and shade by which actual sunshine might be transposed into a key in which the harmonies possible with material pigments should yet produce the same impressions upon the mind which were caused by the light itself'.[68]

It was in Victorian painting that the reliance by painters on subjects already published and available to a reading audience assumed a major importance: words may not often have appeared within a picture frame, but they hovered about its frame or its receptions by the general public. Aubrey Beardsley pinpointed this activity with his phrase 'story painters and picture writers',[69] and the incidence of painters telling stories, usually those with which their viewers were already familiar, is extraordinary and has been well researched and published. Henry James noted (with perhaps

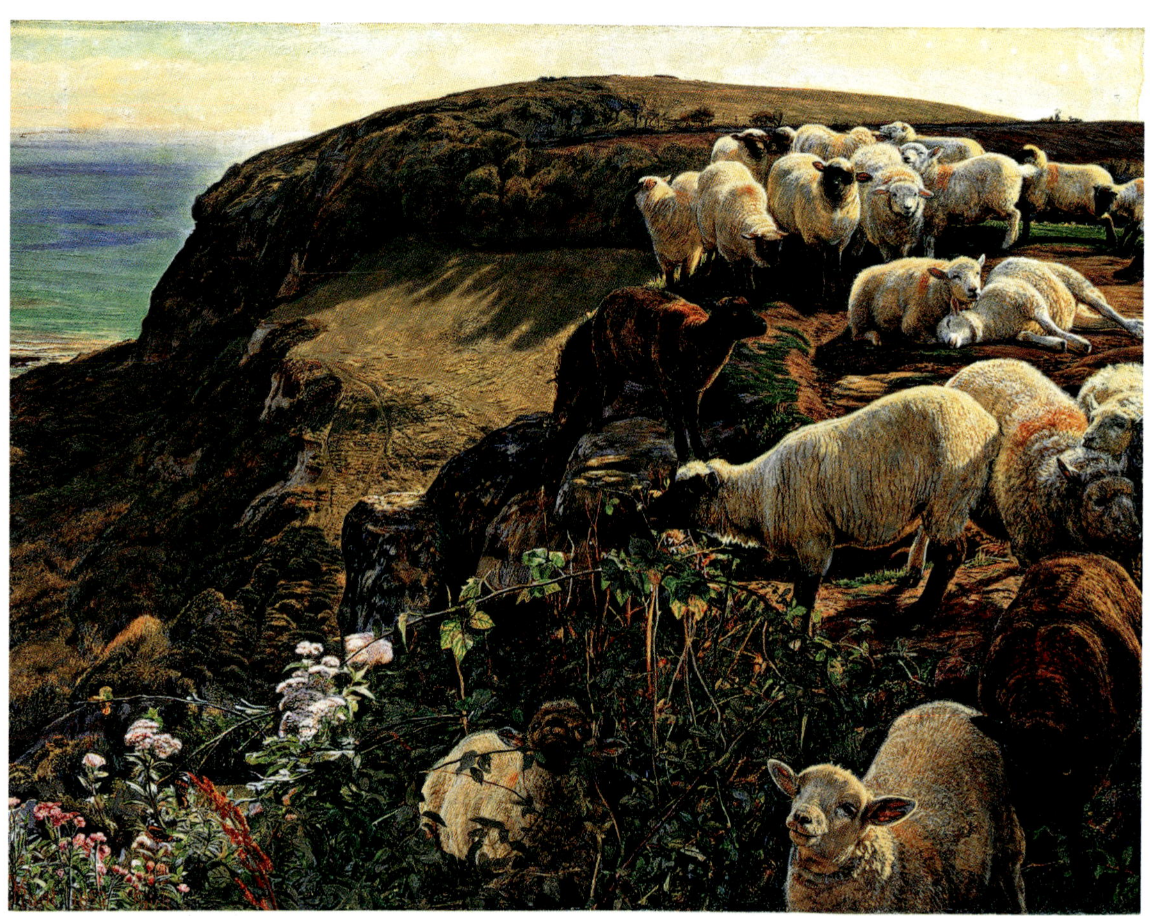

68 William Holman Hunt, *Strayed Sheep* (originally *Our English Coasts*), 1852, oil on canvas.

his own mild disapproval of the phenomenon) that the French referred to such paintings as belonging to 'the anecdotical class', that they usually required 'a taking title, like a three-volume novel', and that their 'picturesque' subject needed to 'be substantiated by a long explanatory extract in the catalogue'.[70]

By the end of the nineteenth century, painting had surely run through the gamut of its possible relations with and reliance upon words. The deliberately miscellaneous or eclectic selection of illustrations through this essay and the Introduction has been designed to reveal an inherent richness as well as instability in image/word relationships. By 1900 it must have seemed that everything had been tried, and visual artists as well as their critics had to regroup and rethink.

On the one hand, nineteenth-century paintings had relied so much upon *a priori* texts (with a blithe openness about this debt unmatched even by Renaissance painters) that a modernist backlash against 'literary paintings' was inevitable. The fear of narrative in the twentieth-century art world became almost paranoid. But the converse, too, had happened: though Impressionism played still with genre subjects that might invite a narrative response, its formal experiments inaugurated a fresh concern with painterly achievements *per se* that, in its turn, prompted a reaction by artists who would seek to re-incorporate words into their formal manoeuvres. Anything was now possible, and the reinvention of old treaties between image and word (speech balloons, titles and other identifications inscribed within a picture frame) could always be presented as experimental, not atavistic.

Given the inexhaustibly verbal agility of art criticism to redraw the contemporary map of the gallery scene, it is no surprise to encounter such explanations as the 'interface' of word and image, or celebrations of single art works where 'legibility and visualization coincide'.

The long-standing *paragone* or rivalry between media has often had the inherent effect of breeding new confidence in both the visual and the verbal; if speech balloons in part declare the inability of paint to 'say' what the words now do, and if words and images are inherently contrary in the functions they perform, why not explore painting that celebrates that inherent antagonism? And then there is always the question of address – to whom are painting's words actually directed? – which finds ever new answers: from the medieval confidence in the church's painting and stained glass being a Bible for the poor (coached by the priest), via the Renaissance humanist reliance upon a wealth of classical lore recently made available in print for the cognoscenti, to a Victorian middle-class public that found the interconnections of media to their taste, we have reached a culture where the artist relies much upon the hermeneutic and verbal skills of commentators to awe what it takes to be (and maybe is) a less skilful visual spectatorship. Generic boundaries have been transgressed or called in question, above all in collage, video or installation art. In the final resort, though, everybody brings to bear the brain's multiple resources, where word and image jostle and cohabit. And we are still far from understanding exactly how that works.

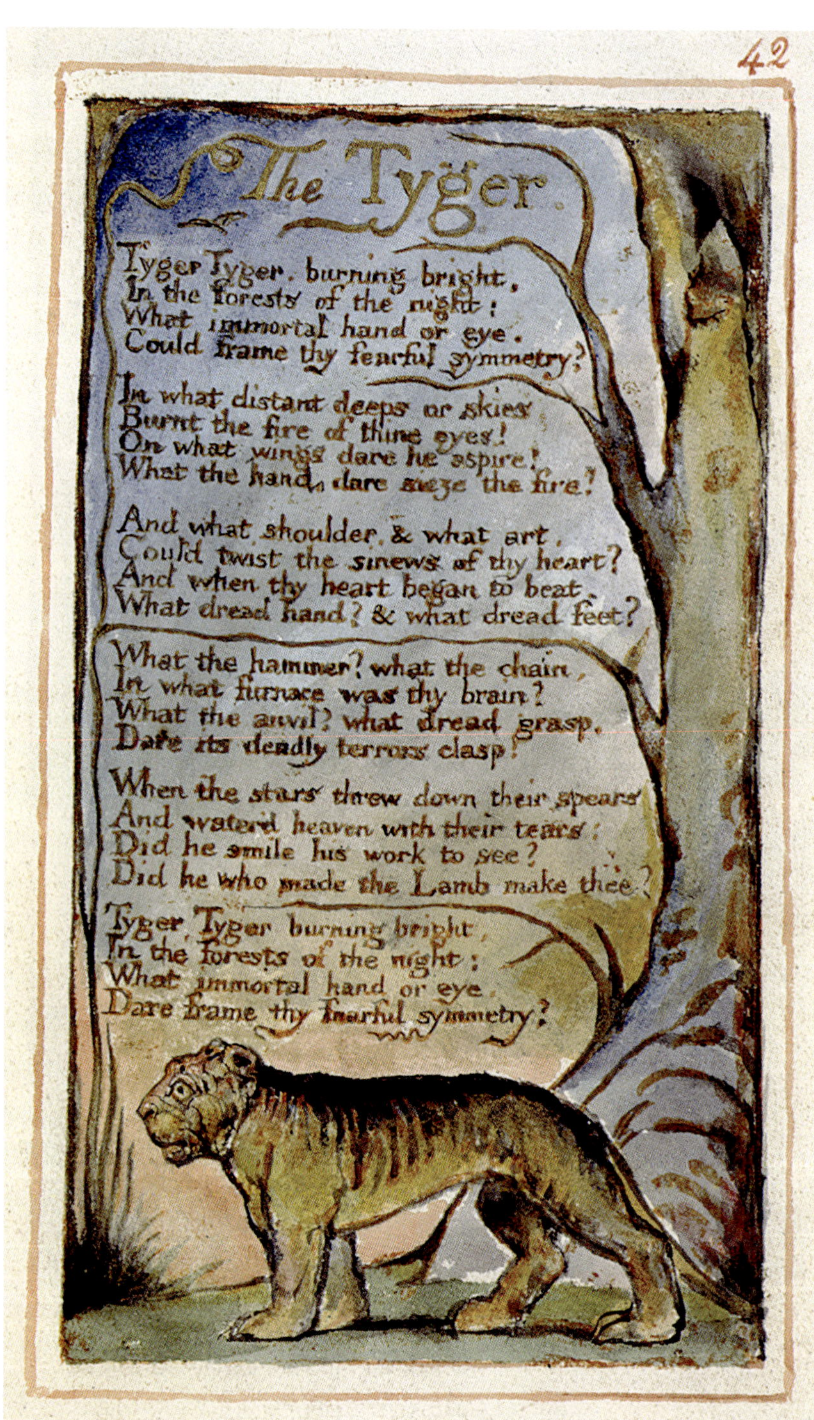

1 William Blake, *Songs of Innocence and of Experience*, copy Z, plate 42 ('The Tyger').

1

Blake's Illuminated Word

JOSEPH VISCOMI

Tyger Tyger, burning bright,
In the forest of the night;
What immortal hand or eye,
Could frame thy fearful symmetry?

I

William Blake, the British Romantic poet who penned the immortal lines above, was also a professional engraver, an original printmaker and a painter of great visionary power. He was born in London in 1757 to Catherine and James Blake, a hosier who kept a shop at 28 Broad Street. Except for the three years spent in Felpham, Sussex, under the patronage of William Hayley (1800–3), he lived his entire life in London, where he died in 1827. His parents, recognizing his artistic ability early, enrolled him at the age of ten in Henry Pars's drawing school, where he learned to draw the human figure by copying from plaster casts of ancient statues. At fourteen, he began his seven-year apprenticeship under James Basire, engraver to the Society of Antiquaries and the Royal Society. Basire's style of engraving emphasized line over tone and was by then already considered old-fashioned, yet it fitted well with – or helped to shape – Blake's lifelong preference for firm outline, which he associated with his heroes, artists like Michelangelo and engravers like Albrecht Dürer.[1]

Engraving, the period's primary means for reproducing images – from paintings to book illustrations – had long been a commercial business, particularly in England, where engravers were perceived more as craftsmen than artists. Blake found this hierarchy – and his second-class status – deeply annoying. To him, 'Painting is Drawing on Canvas & Engraving is Drawing on Copper & Nothing Else & he who pretends to be either Painter or Engraver without being a Master of Drawing is an Impostor' (E 574). The technique itself had undergone major changes since its origin in the Renaissance, when the first, or 'ancient', engravers, like Dürer, transferred designs (often their own) and cut them directly into the metal plates with their burins, hatching lines for shading as in pen and ink drawings. In Blake's day, to save time and labour, this 'pure engraving' was entirely replaced with a 'mixed method', which combined etching and engraving. 'Modern' engravers polished, cleaned and covered the copper plate's surface with an acid-resistant ground, onto which the composition's outline was transferred and traced with a needle to expose the underlying copper to acid, which etched the design into the copper. Engravers used their burins to deepen these lines and to fill in the forms in an elaborate 'dot and lozenge' pattern (dots incised in the interstices of crosshatched lines, characteristic of bank-note engraving) that enabled them to represent mass and tone more convincingly than the more linear style of Blake's heroes, whose works were often dismissed as 'Hard Stiff & Dry Unfinishd Works of Art' (E 639). As an apprentice, then, Blake learned the graphic fashions of the day as he learned to both etch and engrave and to work in various styles with needles, grounds and acid, as well as with burins, scrapers and burnishers. He would also have learned to ink and wipe the resulting intaglio plates and to print them on a rolling press, the machine that forces the dampened paper into the incised lines to pick up the ink.

Upon completing his apprenticeship in 1779, at the age of 21, Blake became a journeyman copy engraver, making his living by working on projects for London book and print publishers like Thomas Macklin, Harrison and Co. and Joseph Johnson. Throughout the 1780s, Blake was one of several engravers who helped to popularize the work of Thomas Stothard, a versatile commercial artist and a prolific book illustrator whose delicate designs influenced Blake's own for *Songs of Innocence* (1789). In 1779 he had also begun studying seriously to be a painter, enrolling in the Royal Academy of Art's School of Design. Founded ten years earlier and led by Sir Joshua Reynolds, the Royal Academy provided formal training and annual exhibitions. Blake began exhibiting there in 1780, with *The Death of Earl Goodwin*, one of a series of watercolour drawings on the early history of England that also included such subjects as *The Landing of Brutus*, *The Making of Magna Carta* and *The Penance of Jane Shore*. In 1784 Blake exhibited a pair of thematically related works, *A Breach in a City the Morning after the Battle* and *War Unchaind by an Angel; Fire, Pestilence, and Famine Following*, depicting the ravages of war. The following year, he exhibited four works: *The Bard, from Gray* and three drawings illustrating the biblical story of Joseph and his brothers, the latter reflecting Blake's increasing interest in Old Testament subjects. In all these drawings, Blake adheres to the prevailing neoclassical style as interpreted by such contemporary artists as James Barry.

During these formative years, Blake, with no formal education, was also writing poetry. His *Poetical Sketches*, a collection of poems he had written as a teenager, was privately printed for him as a 72-page pamphlet in 1783. Blake had been attending the literary salons of Ms. Mathew, singing his songs to the delight of other artists and writers in attendance, a few of whom took note and raised the money to have a selection of his poems set in type. Blake was given the unbound sheets but apparently made no concerted effort to sell them, for most were still in his studio when he died. The prefatory 'Advertisement' (p. ii) may have given him pause:

> The following Sketches were the production of untutored youth, commenced in his twelfth, and occasionally resumed by the author till his twentieth year; since which time, his talents having been wholly directed to the attainment of excellence in his profession, he has been deprived of the leisure requisite to such a revisal of these sheets, as might have rendered them less unfit to meet the public eye.
>
> Conscious of the irregularities and defects to be found in almost every

page, his friends have still believed that they possessed a poetic originality, which merited some respite from oblivion. These their opinions remain, however, to be now reproved or confirmed by a less partial public. (E 846)

Blake's early poems echo English precursors from Spenser to the mid-eighteenth century, not unexpectedly for juvenilia of the period, but they also demonstrate a keen willingness to experiment with form and language and to explore politically daring themes like tyranny, revolution and liberty, themes at the heart of his mature poetry and mythology.

Blake's companion throughout these eventful years was Catherine Boucher (1762–1831), the daughter of a market gardener, whom he had married in 1782. Their marriage was by all accounts happy and she became a perfect helpmate for the artist. Blake taught her to read and write as well as to draw and operate the rolling press – to be, in effect, his perfect assistant, known in the printing trade as a 'devil'. In 1784 the Blakes set up a printing and publishing partnership with James Parker, another former Basire apprentice, at 27 Broad Street, next to the family's hosier shop, now run by his older brother James. In *An Island in the Moon*, a satire of the Mathew set that he wrote around this time, Blake depicts himself as 'Quid', a publisher planning an outrageously expensive and impractical project 'in three Volumes folio', with 'all the writing Engraved instead of Printed & at every other leaf a high finishd print'. He would 'Print off two thousand' and 'sell them a hundred pounds a piece'. Though described as 'Illuminating the Manuscript', the project was poking fun at those connoisseurs who would spend such great sums on the fancy illustrated books of the day – more than most working men made in a year – because they feared 'whoever will not have them will be' seen as 'ignorant fools & will not deserve to live' (E 465). His real publishing business, however, was far more modest; after producing only two 'finished prints' on mythological themes, both engraved by Blake after Stothard, it had broken up, apparently by the end of 1785.

Three years later, in their new home at 28 Poland Street, the engraver, painter and poet invented relief etching, a printmaking technique that enabled him to combine his three arts in unprecedented ways. He announced it 'To the Public' in his Prospectus (1793) as 'illuminated printing' and defined it explicitly as a 'method of Printing which combines the Painter and the Poet' and as a 'means to propagate' the 'Labours of the Artist, the Poet, the Musician' without the added costs of publishers, typesetters, illustrators and engravers. Indeed, 'even Milton and Shakespeare could not publish their own works', he says, a 'difficulty' solved by his 'method of Printing both Letter-press and Engraving in a style more ornamental, uniform, and grand, than any before discovered' (E 692).

In eighteenth-century book production, word and image – letterpress and engraving – were executed separately, in different media and by different hands. Technically, integration of word and image was possible in conventional (intaglio) etching, as Blake himself demonstrated in 1793 with a small emblem book, but the economics of publishing had long defined intaglio printmaking as image reproduction and letterpress as text reproduction, making all illustrated books the product of much divided labour. Even Quid, who envisioned a deluxe set of volumes in which words and images were in the

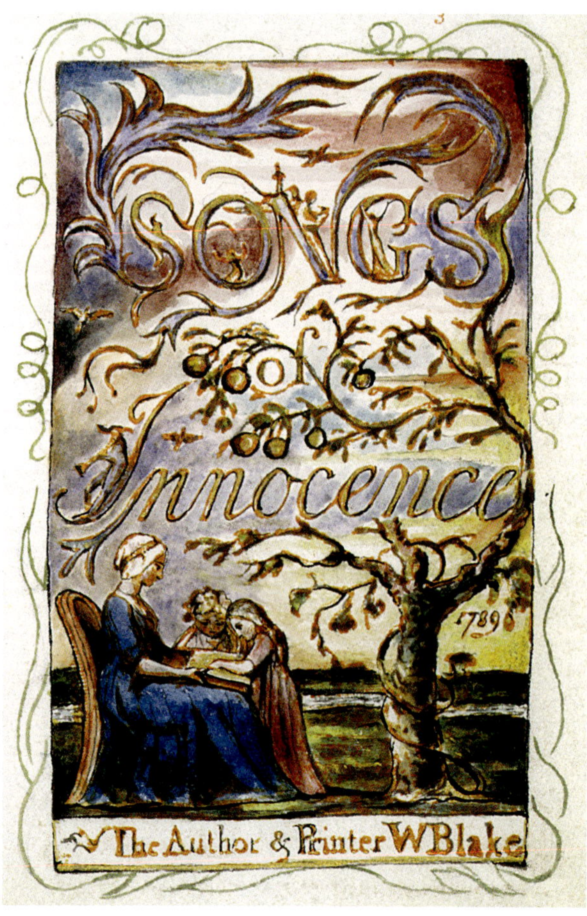

same medium – both engraved – and the text, with 'a high finishd print . . . at every other leaf', excessively illustrated, assumed that images would be separate – and presumably executed by different people. Setting type with wood blocks placed word and image on the same leaf, but they remained unintegrated and production remained divided. But in illuminated printing, text and image were executed together, on the same surface, with the same tools, by the same artist. Instead of needles, burins and the other metal tools of the graphic artist, Blake worked on copper plates with quill pens, small brushes and an ink impervious to acid (probably the standard stop-out varnish used in etching). He wrote text backward (a skill he would have practised as a trained copy engraver), illustrated it and etched the uncovered metal below the surface in nitric acid to leave the integrated design of text and image standing in relief. Blake and his wife printed the plates in coloured inks on a rolling press and tinted most impressions in watercolours.

2 *Songs of Innocence and of Experience* copy Y, plate 3 (*Innocence* title-page).

II

To appreciate just how radical Blake's invention is, we need only compare an illuminated poem as conventionally printed with its original form. 'The Tyger', for example, one of the most anthologized poems in the English language, is known to most readers in its letterpress form, as in the epigraph to this essay:

> Tyger Tyger, burning bright,
> In the forest of the night;
> What immortal hand or eye,
> Could frame thy fearful symmetry? (E 24)

While these lines may evoke the image of an illuminated beast no matter what the font or its size, their being set in type translates Blake's original (illus. 1) into another medium and distorts his intentions. Immediately, we see that Blake's text is calligraphic, finished in watercolours and strengthened in pen and ink, features that contribute to the meaning of the whole. Not only is text pictorial, but it is also integrated into a design, unfolding down the page, structured and underscored by tree branches and culminating in a surprisingly inscrutable but tame-looking tiger that further complicates the reading. The typographic translation clearly misrepresents the original artefact, a hand-coloured impression of words and images printed from a relief-etched plate of about 11 x 6.3 cm onto thick wove paper. The small design, with its 9-point roman text,

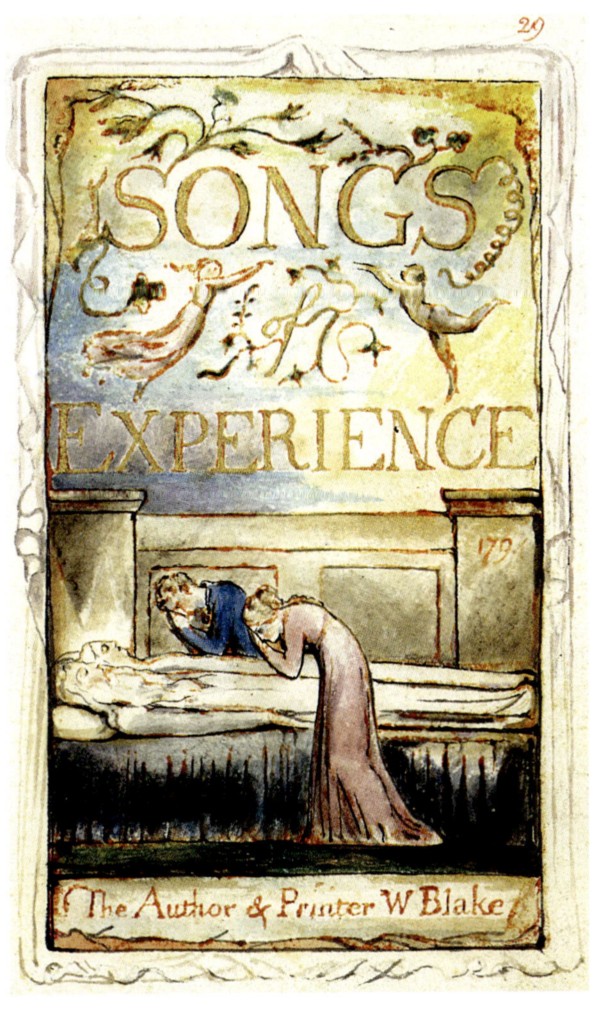

3 William Blake, *Songs of Innocence and of Experience*: copy Y, plate 29 (*Experience* title-page).

requires the reader to hold the book close, creating an intimate and sensual reading experience impossible to duplicate except with the finest facsimiles.

Though he never explained the technique, Blake did describe his 'infernal method' in *The Marriage of Heaven and Hell* as 'melting apparent surfaces away, and displaying the infinite which was hid' (E 39). He claimed to have learned it in 'a Printing house in Hell', where he 'saw the method in which knowledge is transmitted from generation to generation' (E 40) and discerned its major (much allegorized) stages, from cleaning the copper to writing and illustrating the text, etching the design, printing the plates and binding the prints into books. According to John Thomas Smith, however, it was his recently deceased brother Robert, in a vision, who directed Blake toward this discovery. Robert, whom Blake was teaching to be an artist, died in February 1787; Blake, who had remained constantly at his bedside for two weeks, collapsed into a continuous sleep that lasted three days and nights after his death (G 1: 59). The following year, Robert appeared to him in a vision and instructed him in a new method of printing his works without 'the expense of letter-press' (BR 460). Appropriately, one of Blake's first experiments in this medium was *The Approach of Doom,* a print in imitation of one of Robert's wash drawings. While the combination of word and image is a prominent feature of illuminated printing, it appears not to have been the impetus for the invention. Rather, illuminated poetry evolved out of relief etching, which appears to have been motivated by Blake's desire to reproduce the appearance of wash drawing. The very tools of pens and ink that enabled Blake to produce original drawings in metal probably inspired him to use the new technique to write and print words as well.

The first relief etchings to incorporate text were the ten very small plates of *All Religions are One* and the equally small twenty plates of *There is No Natural Religion*, philosophical tractates executed in 1788 on perception and the imagination, or what Blake called the 'Poetic Genius'. The following year he used the technique to publish poetry, beginning with the 31 plates of *Songs of Innocence* and eight plates of *The Book of Thel*, demonstrating in both works a mastery of his new medium missing in the earlier tractates. The italic letters forming 'Songs of Innocence' are alive, bursting into flame-like vegetation (illus. 2). They support children playing, an angel reading and Blake, as the piper from the 'Introduction', 'piping songs of pleasant glee' (E 7). Blake returned to a

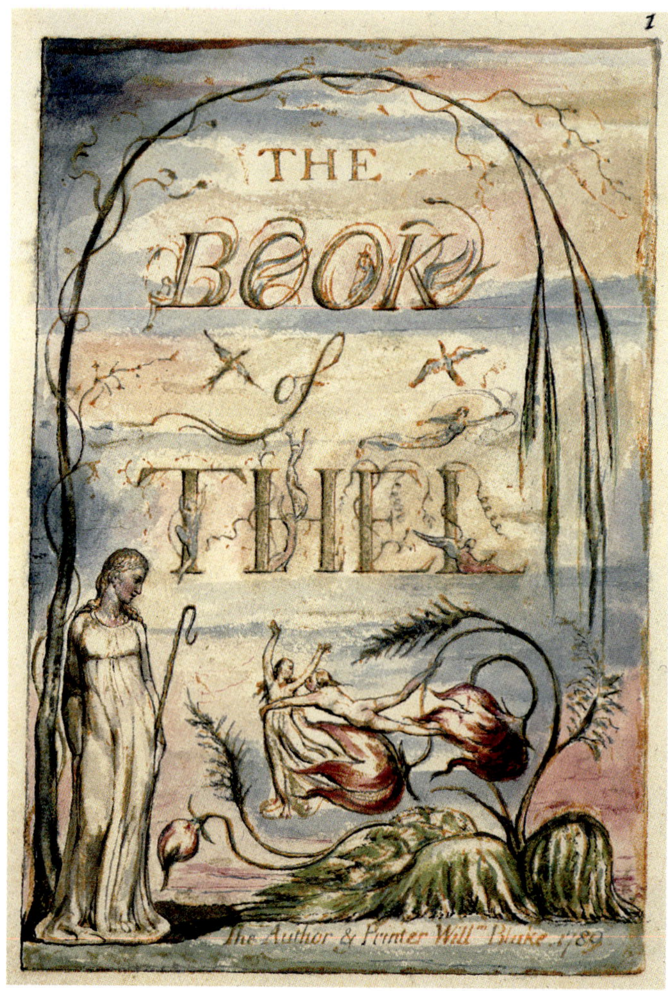

4 William Blake, *The Book of Thel*, copy O, plate 2 (title page).

similar iconic use of lettering five years later in the title page to *Songs of Experience* (illus. 3), which is designed as a counterpart to *Innocence* (also paired visually are the frontispieces and, thematically, numerous poems). The space where grown children are brought together by the death that also separates them appears especially dark and enclosed compared to the open and lively space where children, in the security of a guardian, are brought together by a book. That death is equated with experience is indicated by the bare roman capitals of the word 'Experience' mirroring the shape of the dead bodies, much as innocence is equated with life by the word 'Innocence' being filled with energy as it stems from a fruit-filled tree.

Blake expresses a similar playfulness in the mix of italic and roman lettering in the title page of *The Book of Thel* (illus. 4), which also serves as the book's frontispiece, in that it is a full-page illustration introducing key ideas or events in the narrative. Thel, a young shepherdess on a quest, receives advice from a personified Lily, Cloud and Clod of Clay; in the end, she flees from a 'voice of sorrow' that rises from 'her own grave plot' (E 6). The slender tree arches protectively while also suggesting a tombstone, anticipating Thel's descent in the netherworld to her own gravesite in the final plate. The letters support a piper with crook, an angel reading, a figure writing and a naked male figure climbing the T of 'Thel', whose name refers to 'wish' or 'desire' and whose book is about the awakening of – and retreat from – desire. Wearing a long gown and holding a shepherd's crook, Thel gazes at a nude man embracing a woman around the waist, figures who suggest the 'raptures' of the Cloud and the 'fair eyed dew' (E 5) during their courtship.

In 1790 Blake moved to 13 Hercules Buildings, Lambeth, then a London suburb, where he wrote, designed, etched, printed and coloured his next ten illuminated books, starting with the 27 plates of *The Marriage of Heaven and Hell*. Through the voice of the 'Devil', Blake parodies and attacks the theology of Emanuel Swedenborg and biblical history and morality as constructed by the 'Angels' of the established church and state. Energy and passion are positively valorized; reason and temperance are characterized as restraints on spiritual insight and self-expression. Blake pictures himself in plate 10 recording the Devil's voice, writing the 'Proverbs of Hell', ten of 70 of which are shown above him, with pictograms and other interlinear decorations. Blake writes from infernal inspiration, eyes firmly focused on the scroll across his lap (illus. 5). The image mirrors the acts in plate 12 of Isaiah and Ezekiel, who, recognizing 'the voice of honest indignation' as 'the voice of God', 'cared not for consequences but wrote' (E 38). Blake's contrary, sitting on the other side of the Devil, straining to copy his texts instead of going to the origin himself, represents imitation. He prefers the outward form or the letter of the law to its spirit or origin. These were Swedenborg's failings, according to Blake, who had become disillusioned with the Swedish mystic after a year or more of reading his works.

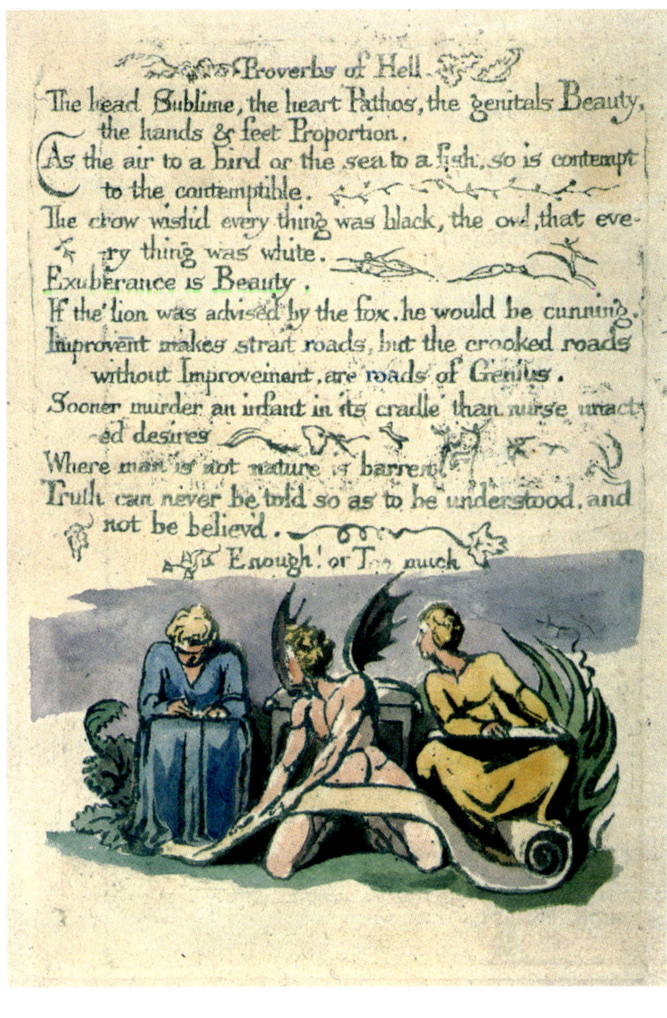

5 William Blake, *The Marriage of Heaven and Hell*, copy C, plate 10.

Over the next three years Blake executed 80 engravings for the publishers. He returned to illuminated printing in 1793 with the eleven plates of *Visions of the Daughters of Albion*, producing at least eleven copies in its first print run. Oothoon, *Visions*'s victimized heroine, can be seen as Thel's contrary, in that she seeks to fulfil desire, but is raped on her way to her lover. She adds her eloquent lament on the themes of slavery and the rights of women, themes prominently addressed by authors published by the radical Joseph Johnson, for whom Blake often worked as an illustrator and engraver and who displayed copies of Blake's illuminated books in his shop. In plate 7, Bromion, Oothoon's lover, sits tightly enclosed within himself, disconnected and self-pitying, rejecting Oothoon, who hovers within a wave, shackled and restricted like a slave, pleading that he open his mind and heart and recognize that she remains pure and that he need not be ruled by patriarchal codes (illus. 6).

For Children: The Gates of Paradise, an emblem book comprising eighteen small intaglio etchings accompanied by brief inscriptions on the human condition, also appeared in 1793. The imprint on plate 2, the title page, reads 'Published by W Blake No 13 Hercules Buildings Lambeth and J. Johnson St. Pauls' Church Yard.' Blake later revised the work as *For the Sexes* (*c.* 1820). Also produced in 1793 were the eighteen plates of *America a Prophecy*, which, at approximately 24 x 17 cm each, form Blake's the largest illuminated book to date, the texts of which appear more organically integrated with illustrations and interlinear decoration (illus. 7) and less blocked out above or below a vignette than the texts in *Thel*, *Marriage* and *Visions*. Like *Gates*, the first copies of *America* were purposely printed in dark inks and left uncoloured because pages were designed in terms of strong black and white forms. The first of Blake's 'Continental Prophecies', *America* treats the American Revolution as an event with mythological as well as historical dimensions. Thomas Paine makes an appearance here, as do Washington, Franklin and other American luminaries, but so do new figures from Blake's personal mythology: Urizen, representing

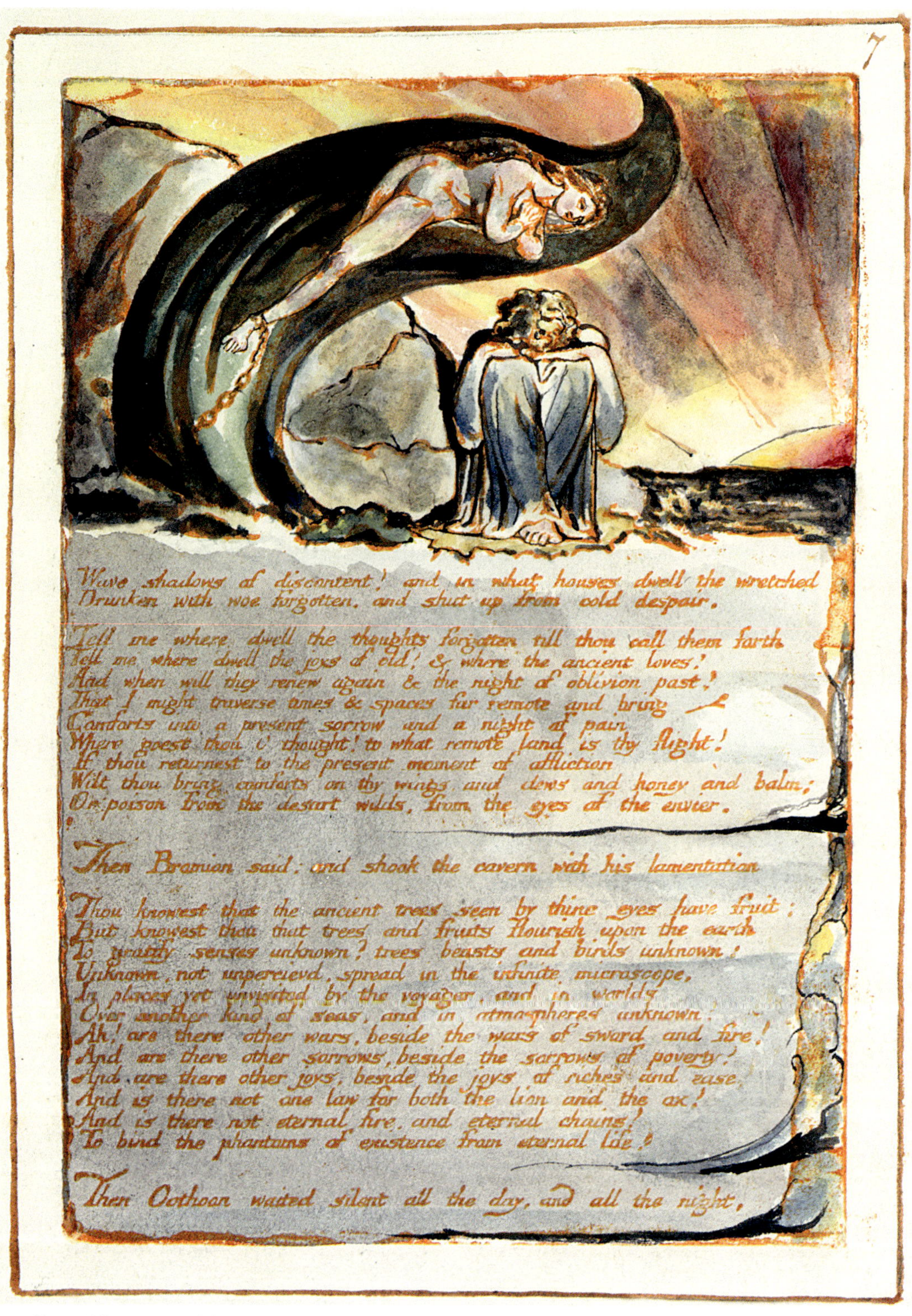
7

Wave shadows of discontent? and in what houses dwell the wretched
Drunken with woe forgotten. and shut up from cold despair.

Tell me where dwell the thoughts forgotten till thou call them forth
Tell me where dwell the joys of old! & where the ancient loves?
And when will they renew again & the night of oblivion past?
That I might traverse times & spaces far remote and bring
Comforts into a present sorrow and a night of pain
Where goest thou O thought? to what remote land is thy flight?
If thou returnest to the present moment of affliction
Wilt thou bring comforts on thy wings. and dews and honey and balm;
Or poison from the desart wilds, from the eyes of the envier.

Then Bromion said: and shook the cavern with his lamentation

Thou knowest that the ancient trees seen by thine eyes have fruit;
But knowest thou that trees and fruits flourish upon the earth
To gratify senses unknown? trees beasts and birds unknown:
Unknown, not unpercievd, spread in the infinite microscope,
In places yet unvisited by the voyager. and in worlds
Over another kind of seas, and in atmospheres unknown:
Ah! are there other wars, beside the wars of sword and fire!
And are there other sorrows, beside the sorrows of poverty!
And are there other joys, beside the joys of riches and ease?
And is there not one law for both the lion and the ox?
And is there not eternal fire, and eternal chains?
To bind the phantoms of existence from eternal life?

Then Oothoon waited silent all the day, and all the night,

6 William Blake, *Visions of the Daughters of Albion*, copy O, plate 7.

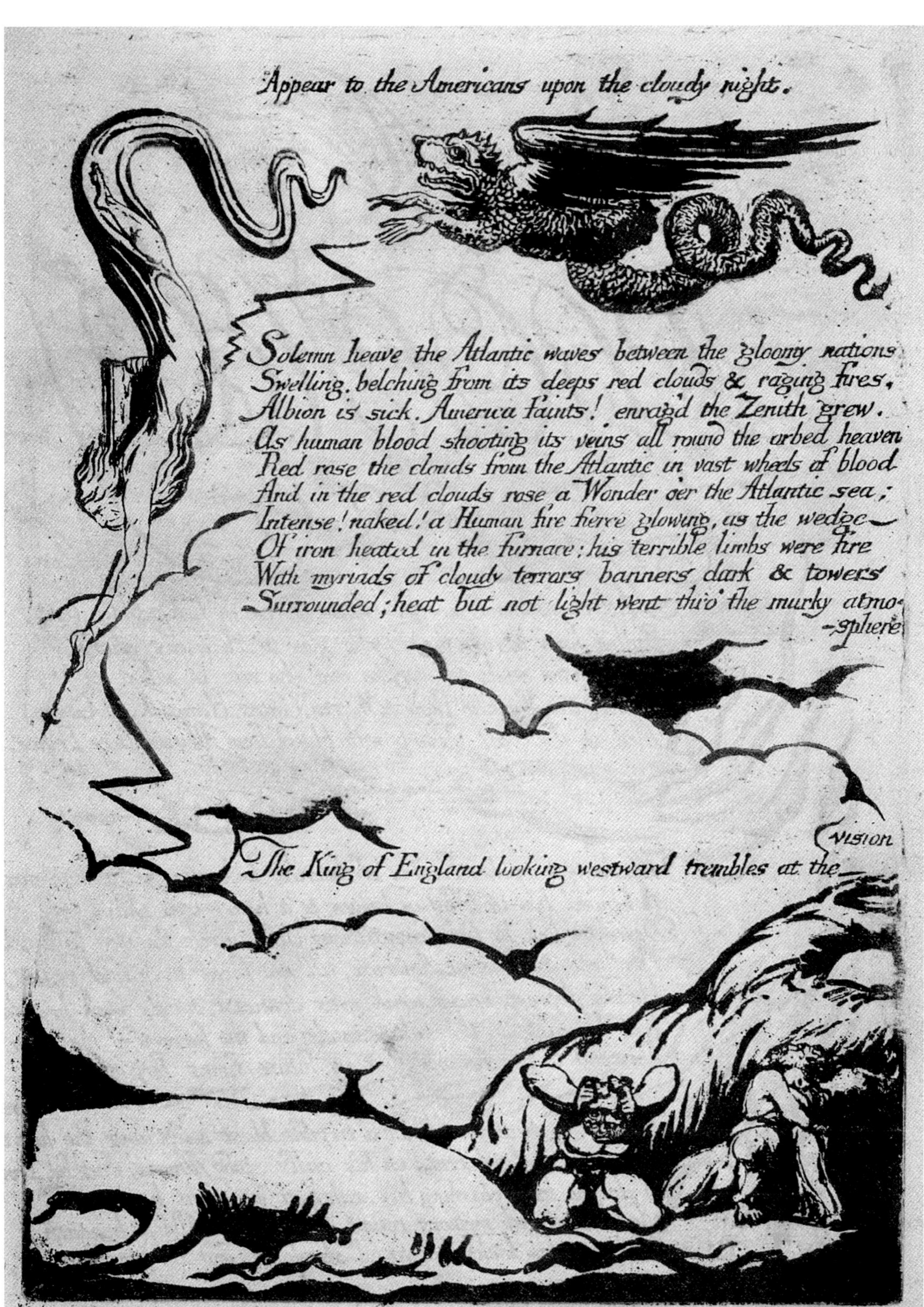
Appear to the Americans upon the cloudy night.

Solemn heave the Atlantic waves between the gloomy nations
Swelling, belching from its deeps red clouds & raging fires;
Albion is sick. America faints! enrag'd the Zenith grew.
As human blood shooting its veins all round the orbed heaven
Red rose the clouds from the Atlantic in vast wheels of blood
And in the red clouds rose a Wonder o'er the Atlantic sea;
Intense! naked! a Human fire fierce glowing, as the wedge
Of iron heated in the furnace; his terrible limbs were fire
With myriads of cloudy terrors banners dark & towers
Surrounded; heat but not light went thro' the murky atmo-
-sphere

The King of England looking westward trembles at the vision

7 William Blake, *America a Prophecy*, copy E, plate 6.

reason as restriction, first mentioned in *Visions* but first pictured in *America*, and Orc, the fiery revolutionary, who act out the conflict on a cosmic scale.

For these early books, Blake printed the plates as book pages, wiping the plate's borders of ink to conceal the rectangular shape that signals copper plate and 'machine' (that is, the press); he printed on both sides of the leaf so there would be facing pages, as in conventional books, and, except for *Gates* and *America*, coloured the illustration lightly, leaving the text uncoloured. Plate 10 from *Marriage* copy C (illus. 5) exemplifies this style. The visual result, as Robert N. Essick has noted, is an oxymoronic 'printed manuscript'.[2] Indeed, no two impressions from the same relief-etched plate are exactly alike, because each impression was printed and coloured by hand. However, impressions printed in the same press run are materially and stylistically alike, sharing inks, papers, palette and placement of colours. Impressions pulled in different press runs and periods differ extensively because they were printed and coloured in different styles (for example, illus. 1 and 5). Consequently, each copy of each book is assigned a letter to designate its uniqueness. Clearly, for Blake, the print was not an exactly repeatable image.

By the autumn of 1793, having printed his books in small press runs, sometimes changing the ink and the size of paper during the run to diversify stock, Blake and his wife offered the books for 'sale at a fair price'. He advertised them along with original engravings in his Prospectus:

> 1. Job, a Historical Engraving. Size 1 ft. 7½ in. by 1 ft. 2 in.: price 12*s*.
>
> 2. Edward and Elinor, a Historical Engraving. Size 1 ft. 6½ in. by 1 ft.: price 10*s*. 6*d*.
>
> 3. America, a Prophecy, in Illuminated Printing. Folio, with 18 designs: price 10*s*. 6*d*.
>
> 4. Visions of the Daughters of Albion, in Illuminated Printing. Folio, with 8 designs, price 7*s*. 6*d*.
>
> 5. The Book of Thel, a Poem in Illuminated Printing. Quarto, with 6 designs, price 3*s*.
>
> 6. The Marriage of Heaven and Hell, in Illuminated Printing. Quarto, with 14 designs, price 7*s*. 6*d*.
>
> 7. Songs of Innocence, in Illuminated Printing. Octavo, with 25 designs, price 5*s*.
>
> 8. Songs of Experience, in Illuminated Printing. Octavo, with 25 designs, price 5*s*.
>
> 9. The History of England, a small book of Engravings. Price 3*s*.
>
> 10. The Gates of Paradise, a small book of Engravings. Price 3*s*.
>
> The Illuminated Books are Printed in Colours, and on the most beautiful wove paper that could be procured.
> No Subscriptions for the numerous great works now in hand are asked, for none are wanted; but the Author will produce his works, and offer them to sale at a fair price. (E 693)

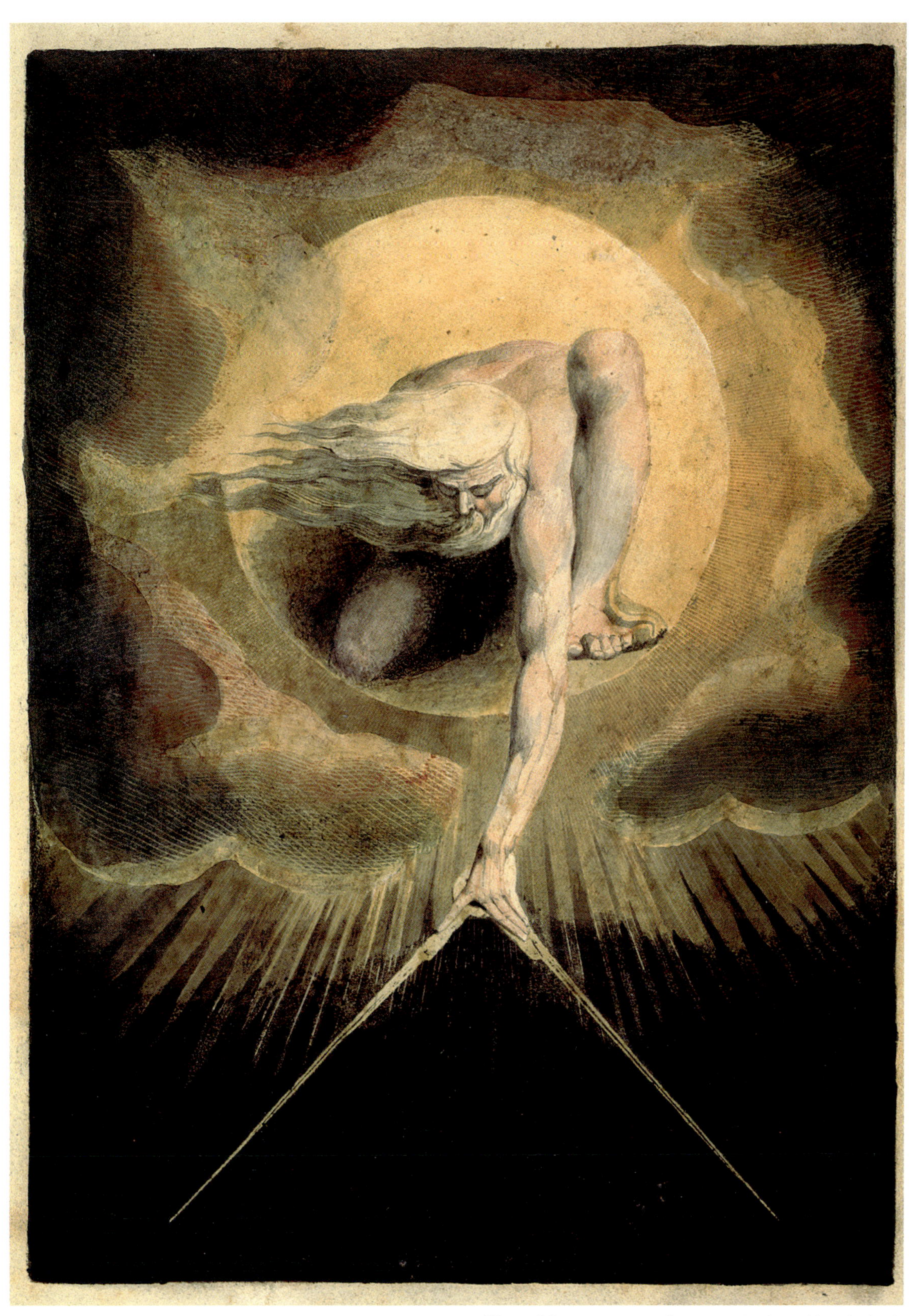

8 William Blake, *Europe a Prophecy*, copy E, plate 1 (frontispiece).

Though Blake advertised the *Songs of Experience* in 1793, the book was still in progress and was not completed until 1794, the date on the title page (illus. 3), though no date appears on the general title page joining the two works as *Songs of Innocence and of Experience*, with the subtitle of 'Shewing the Two Contrary States of the Human Soul'. Most of the *Experience* plates were etched on the versos of the *Innocence* plates, which saved Blake the cost of copper and allowed him to make back his initial investment with fewer copies per press run. He did the same with *Europe a Prophecy*, also 1794, continuing his 'Continental Prophecies' by using the versos of the *America* plates, ensuring that the two books were the same size. The *Europe* designs were executed in the same style as those in *America*. However, in 1794, Blake also began to colour-print his plates: that is, he began to add colours to the relief and shallow areas of the etched design and to print ink and colours together to produce images with opaque and thick colours, like oil sketches, rather than lightly washed manuscript pages. These he would finish in watercolours and pen and ink. Blake colour-printed the first eight copies of *Experience*, joining four with copies of *Innocence* printed in 1789 to form the first copies of the combined *Songs*, and he returned to *Marriage* and *Visions* to print two copies of each in this manner. Although Blake designed *Europe* to be printed in monochrome, he colour-printed all six copies of its first press run; its magnificent frontispiece, known as 'The Ancient of Days' (illus. 8), is one of Blake's most iconic images. It is also one of his most ironic, in that the Jehovah-like figure creating the world is Urizen and his seemingly creative act symbolizes man's fall from eternity and into the world of materialism, represented by the coiling serpent on the facing title page (illus. 9).

Blake etched his next book, also in 1794, mostly on the versos of the *Marriage* plates. To facilitate colour-printing, he etched in shallow relief the 28 plates of *The First Book of Urizen*, although only two of eight extant copies contain them all, and he sequenced the ten full-page illustrations differently in each copy. With its double columns of text and divisions into chapters and verses, the format of *Urizen* indicates its close relationship to the Bible. The poem is in many respects a heterodox rewriting of Genesis, one in which the creation of the universe is seen as a fall into materiality and its abstract laws. In the title page, which also functions as a frontispiece, Urizen writes his laws blindly and mechanically with both hands on both sides of an open book, the enrooting pages of which double as graves and echo the tablets/tombstones behind him (illus. 10). In copy G, the last copy, produced *c.* 1818, he erased 'First' from the title and covered it up with a tree branch. The text of Urizen's book, open and displayed to the reader in plate 5, comprises unreadable characters signifying chaos and meaningless confusion (illus. 11). (Blake used the same motif in the frontispiece of *The Song of Los*, showing Urizen kneeling under a globe that is inscribed with strange illegible markings.) Two related poems, telling the story of Urizen from other perspectives, are *The Book of Ahania* and *The Book of Los*, which followed in 1795. These are briefer and less lavishly illustrated than *Urizen*, and their texts are etched in intaglio rather than relief, with colour-printed frontispieces, title pages and tailpieces.

Later that year, Blake returned to his 'Continental Prophecies', producing the eight plates of *The Song of Los*, which is divided into sections entitled 'Africa' and 'Asia'. All six extant copies (A–F) were colour-printed in a single press run. While

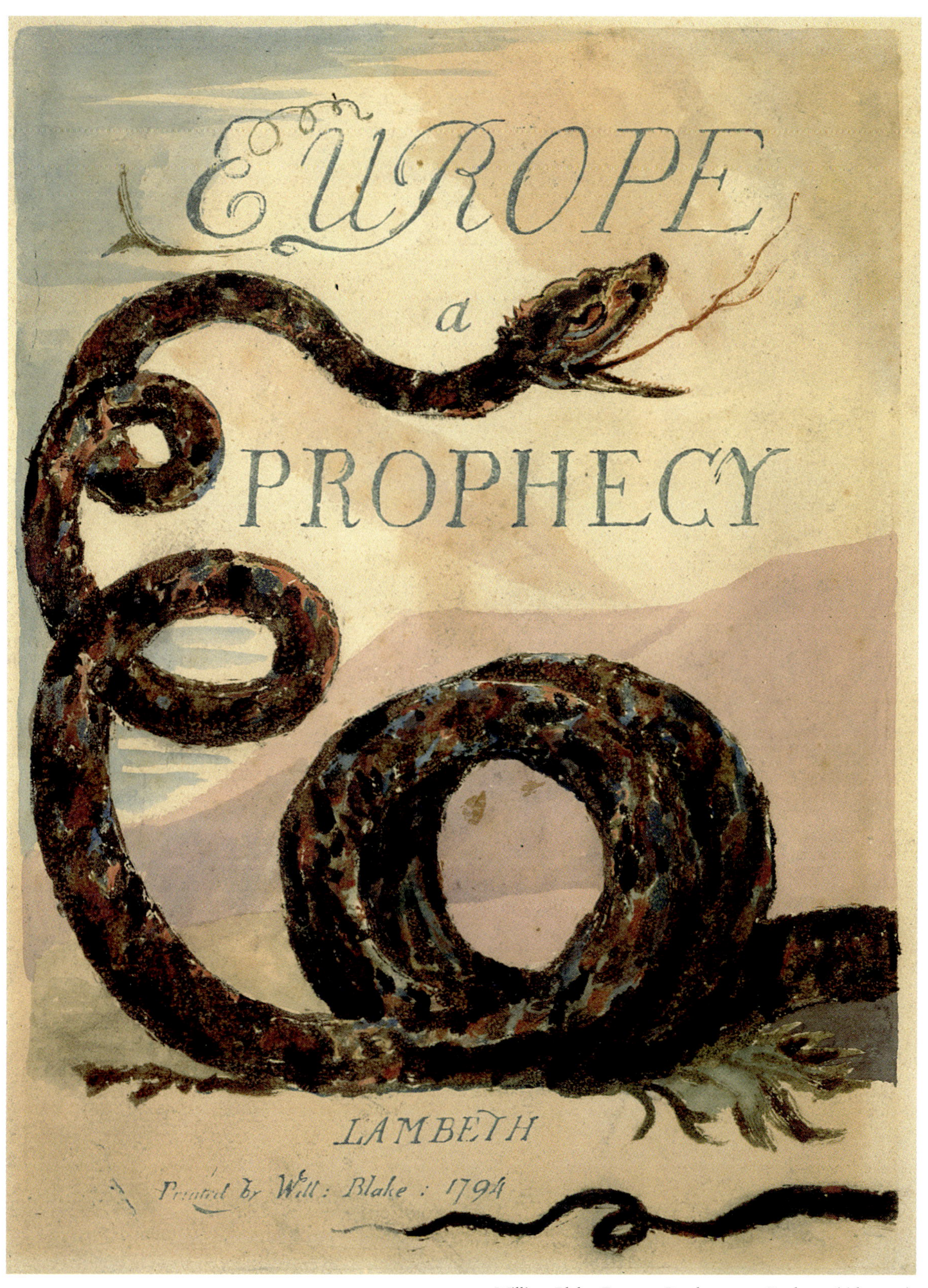

9 William Blake, *Europe a Prophecy*, copy E, plate 2 (title-page).

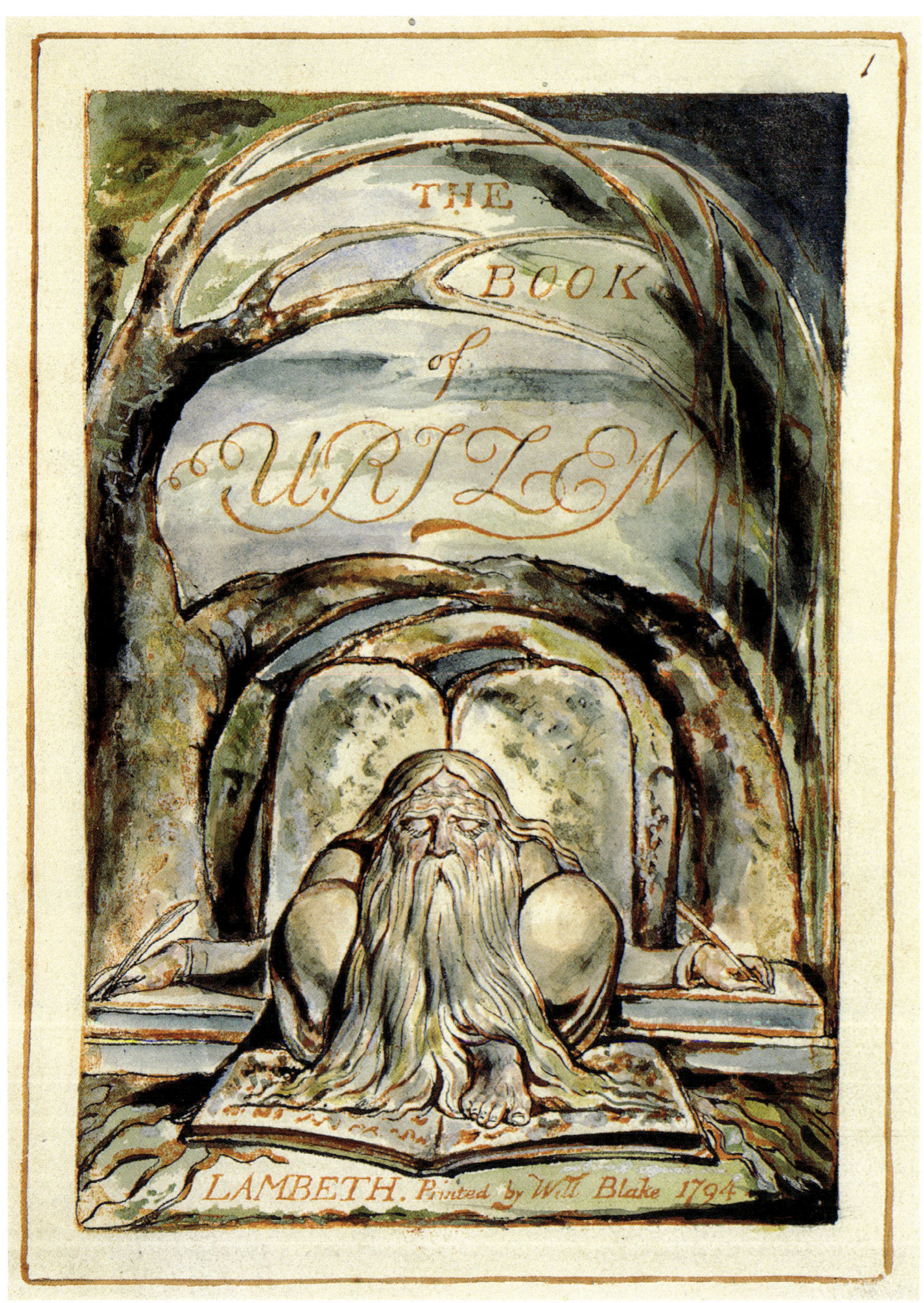

10 William Blake, *The First Book of Urizen*, copy G, plate 1 (title-plate).

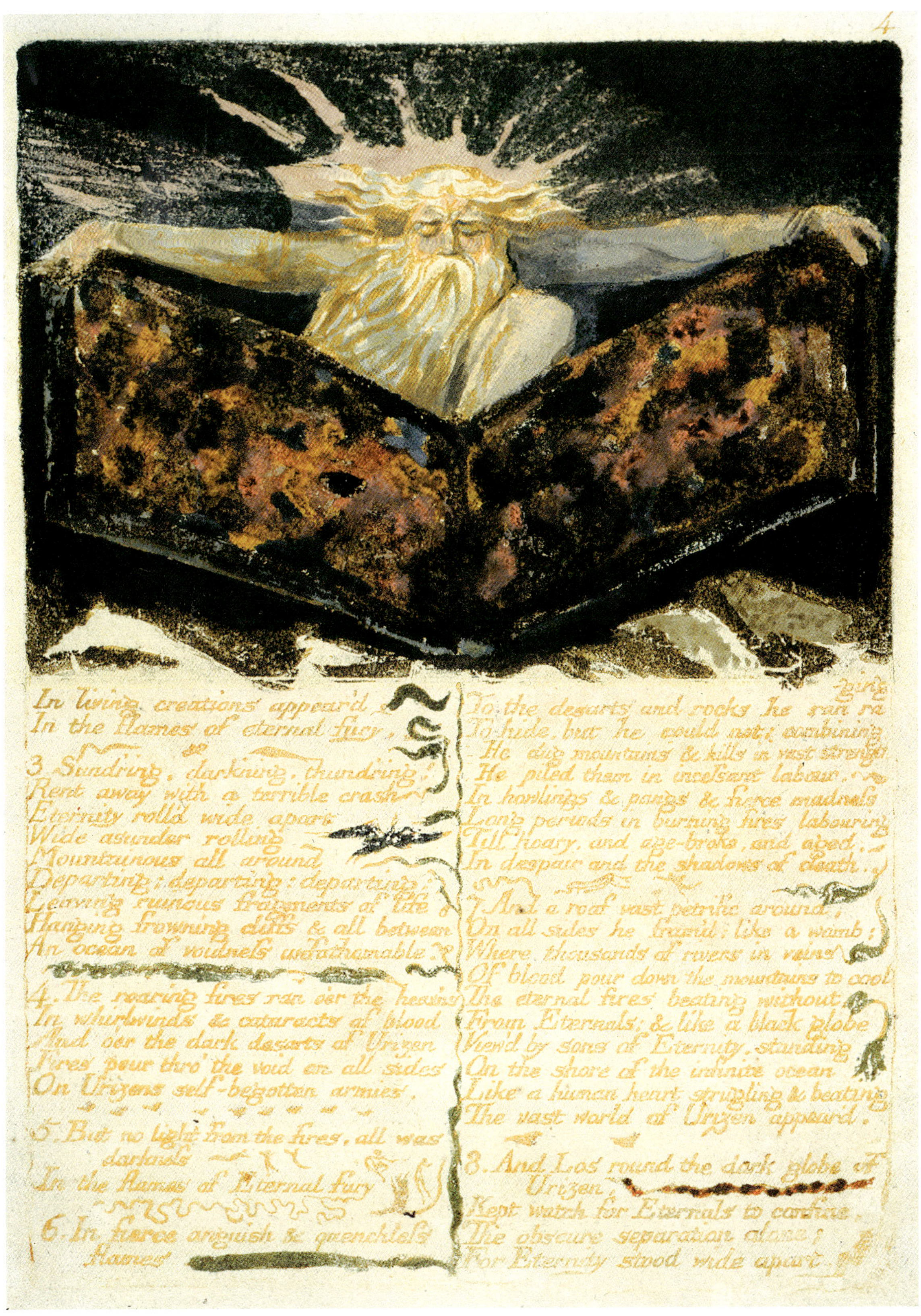

4
In living creations appear'd
In the flames of eternal fury.
3 Sundring, darkning, thundring!
Rent away with a terrible crash
Eternity roll'd wide apart
Wide asunder rolling
Mountainous all around
Departing; departing; departing:
Leaving ruinous fragments of life
Hanging frowning cliffs & all between
An ocean of voidness unfathomable.
4. The roaring fires ran o'er the heav'ns
In whirlwinds & cataracts of blood
And o'er the dark desarts of Urizen
Fires pour thro' the void on all sides
On Urizens self-begotten armies.
5. But no light from the fires, all was
darkness
In the flames of Eternal fury
6. In fierce anguish & quenchless
flames
To the desarts and rocks he ran raging
To hide, but he could not; combining
He dug mountains & hills in vast strength
He piled them in incessant labour,
In howlings & pangs & fierce madness
Long periods in burning fires labouring
Till hoary, and age-broke, and aged,
In despair and the shadows of death.
7. And a roof vast petrific around,
On all sides he fram'd: like a womb;
Where thousands of rivers in veins
Of blood pour down the mountains to cool
The eternal fires beating without
From Eternals; & like a black globe
View'd by sons of Eternity, standing
On the shore of the infinite ocean
Like a human heart strugling & beating
The vast world of Urizen appear'd.
8. And Los round the dark globe of
Urizen,
Kept watch for Eternals to confine,
The obscure separation alone;
For Eternity stood wide apart,

11 William Blake, *The Book of Urizen*, copy D, plate 5.

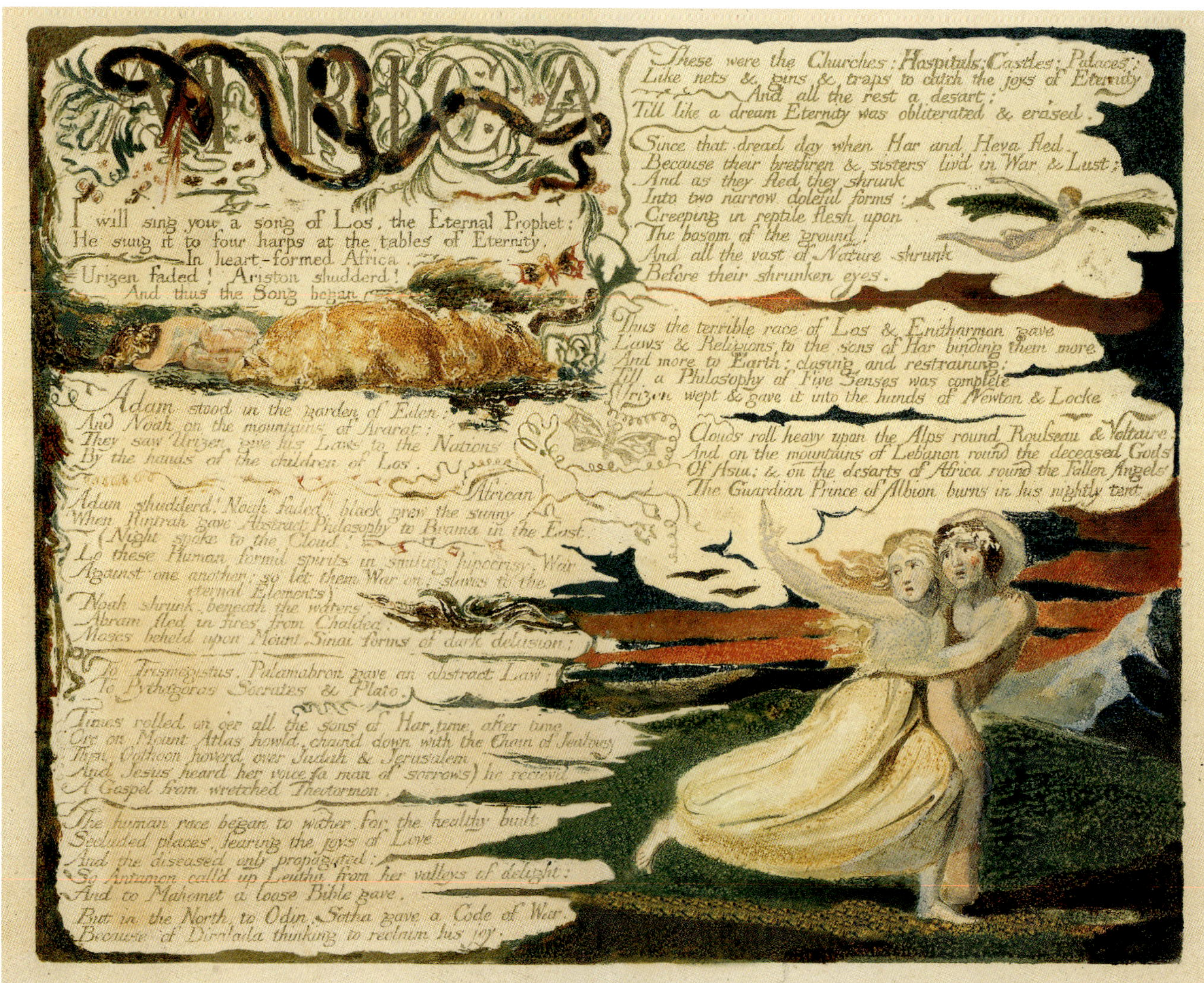

AFRICA

I will sing you a song of Los, the Eternal Prophet:
He sung it to four harps at the tables of Eternity.
In heart-formed Africa.
Urizen faded! Ariston shudderd!
And thus the Song began

Adam stood in the garden of Eden:
And Noah on the mountains of Ararat;
They saw Urizen give his Laws to the Nations
By the hands of the children of Los.

Adam shudderd! Noah faded! black grew the sunny African
When Rintrah gave Abstract Philosophy to Brama in the East:
(Night spoke to the Cloud!
Lo these Human formd spirits in smiling hypocrisy. War
Against one another; so let them War on; slaves to the eternal Elements)
Noah shrunk, beneath the waters;
Abram fled in fires from Chaldea;
Moses beheld upon Mount Sinai forms of dark delusion:

To Trismegistus. Palamabron gave an abstract Law:
To Pythagoras Socrates & Plato.

Times rolled on oer all the sons of Har, time after time
Orc on Mount Atlas howld, chaind down with the Chain of Jealousy
Then Oothoon hoverd over Judah & Jerusalem
And Jesus heard her voice (a man of sorrows) he recievd
A Gospel from wretched Theotormon.

The human race began to wither, for the healthy built
Secluded places, fearing the joys of Love
And the diseased only propagated:
So Antamon call'd up Leutha from her valleys of delight:
And to Mahomet a loose Bible gave.
But in the North, to Odin, Sotha gave a Code of War.
Because of Diralada thinking to reclaim his joy.

These were the Churches: Hospitals: Castles: Palaces:
Like nets & gins & traps to catch the joys of Eternity
And all the rest a desart;
Till like a dream Eternity was obliterated & erased.

Since that dread day when Har and Heva fled.
Because their brethren & sisters livd in War & Lust;
And as they fled they shrunk
Into two narrow doleful forms:
Creeping in reptile flesh upon
The bosom of the ground:
And all the vast of Nature shrunk
Before their shrunken eyes.

Thus the terrible race of Los & Enitharmon gave
Laws & Religions to the sons of Har binding them more
And more to Earth: closing and restraining:
Till a Philosophy of Five Senses was complete
Urizen wept & gave it into the hands of Newton & Locke

Clouds roll heavy upon the Alps round Rousseau & Voltaire:
And on the mountains of Lebanon round the deceased Gods
Of Asia; & on the desarts of Africa round the Fallen Angels
The Guardian Prince of Albion burns in his nightly tent

12 William Blake, *The Song of Los*, recreated design for plates 3–4 based on copy B.

working on this book Blake was also experimenting with colour-printing techniques that would enable him to print paintings from gessoed millboards onto thick wove paper, which he then finished in watercolours and pen and ink. The resulting twelve large colour-printed drawings (monotypes, approximately 54 x 42 cm), all executed in 1795, are among Blake's greatest achievements as an artist. Though certainly influenced by his earlier experiments in colour-printing illuminated books, they also influenced the conception and execution of *The Song of Los*. Plates 1, 2, 5 and 8 are full-page monotypes, printed in colours from both sides of two gessoed millboards, where the designs were outlined probably in pen and ink, filled in with colours and printed – the same technique used for the large colour-printed drawings. These beautiful illustrations were an afterthought, however, added to the text plates comprising 'Africa' and 'Asia', which Blake had initially conceived and executed on two oblong pieces of copper as autonomous but related designs. Blake initially divided his text for each section into two columns within a horizontal – or 'landscape' – format, a format used for paintings and prints but not in his time for the text of books (illus. 12).

'Africa' and 'Asia', as originally executed, fuse poetry, painting and printmaking in ways even more radical than in the other illuminated books. They function autonomously as painted poems or written paintings, with text superimposed on a landscape design. Each design could have been matted, framed, viewed and read

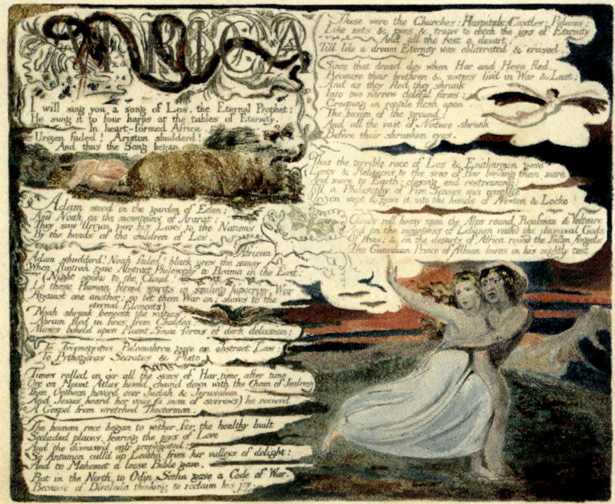
I will sing you a song of Los, the Eternal Prophet:

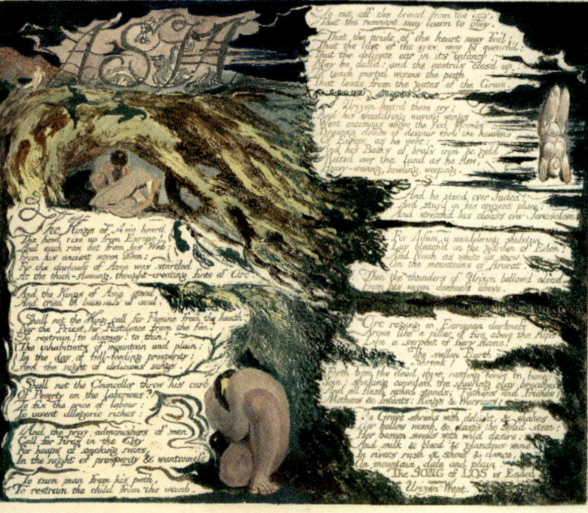
The SONG of LOS is Ended.
Urizen Wept.

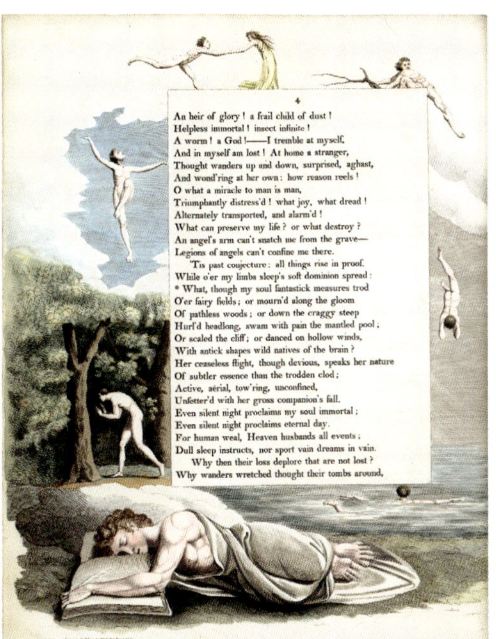
4
An heir of glory ! a frail child of dust !
Helpless immortal ! insect infinite !
A worm ! a God !——I tremble at myself,
And in myself am lost ! At home a stranger,
Thought wanders up and down, surprised, aghast,
And wond'ring at her own : how reason reels !
O what a miracle to man is man,
Triumphantly distress'd ! what joy, what dread !
Alternately transported, and alarm'd !
What can preserve my life ? or what destroy ?
An angel's arm can't snatch me from the grave—
Legions of angels can't confine me there.
'Tis past conjecture ; all things rise in proof.
While o'er my limbs sleep's soft dominion spread :
* What, though my soul fantastick measures trod
O'er fairy fields ; or mourn'd along the gloom
Of pathless woods ; or down the craggy steep
Hurl'd headlong, swam with pain the mantled pool ;
Or scaled the cliff ; or danced on hollow winds,
With antick shapes wild natives of the brain ?
Her ceaseless flight, though devious, speaks her nature
Of subtler essence than the trodden clod ;
Active, aërial, tow'ring, unconfined,
Unfetter'd with her gross companion's fall.
Even silent night proclaims my soul immortal ;
Even silent night proclaims eternal day.
For human weal, Heaven husbands all events ;
Dull sleep instructs, nor sport vain dreams in vain.
Why then their loss deplore that are not lost ?
Why wanders wretched thought their tombs around,

13 William Blake, *The Song of Los*, digitally recreated design for plates 3–4 and 6–7 as pages stitched together to form a diptych; based on copy E.

14 William Blake, *The Complaint, and the Consolation; or, Night Thoughts*, plate 3.

like a separate colour print or painting. Together, they suggest an ancient scroll (illus. 13), the predecessor of the printed codex, and thus a fitting medium for the Eternal Prophet. They did not, however, function so well as book pages. By masking one side of the design, probably with a sheet of paper, Blake was able to print each text column separately. Hence, he transformed a coherent horizontal design 27.2 cm wide into two seemingly independent vertical designs or pages approximately 13.6 cm wide.

By 1795, with a stock of illuminated books, Blake began to redirect his considerable energies toward other projects. Over the next five years he executed 537 watercolour illustrations to Edward Young's *Night Thoughts*, each surrounding – or seemingly lying behind – an off-centred text, engraving 43 of them for the only volume printed of the projected four. At least 27 copies of this volume were hand coloured (illus. 14). Using the same format, Blake executed 116 illustrations to Thomas Gray's *Poems*, which were commissioned in 1797 by his friend, the sculptor John Flaxman, as a gift for his wife Ann. The *Night Thoughts* project also influenced Blake's subsequent writings, as is most directly reflected by his dividing his long manuscript poem, *Vala*, into nine 'Nights', the same number and type of divisions in Young's poem. Blake's epic, which evolved into *The Four Zoas*, an exploration of the fourfold division of fallen consciousness, remained in manuscript, heavily revised and accompanied by designs that, like his *Night Thoughts* illustrations, surround the text. Blake eventually abandoned the poem, probably around 1807, but used material from it in his last two illuminated books, *Milton a Poem* and *Jerusalem*.

Throughout *Milton*, Blake experimented with new etching techniques that emulate the appearance of white-line wood engraving and black-line woodcut and which give the book a rough, primitive appearance. The lines in the title page (illus. 15), for example, were drawn with a needle through an acid-resistant

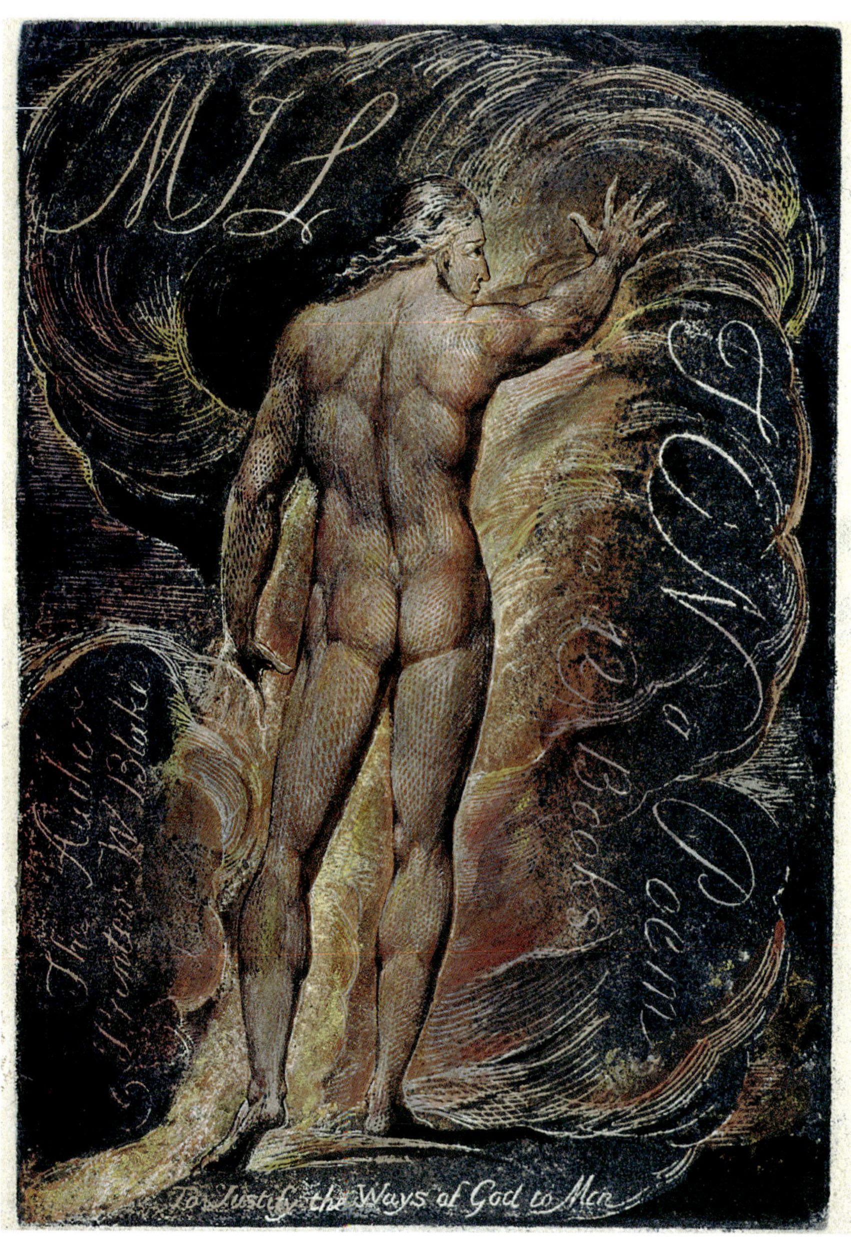

15 William Blake, *Milton a Poem*, copy D, plate 1 (title-plate).

ground and etched into the plate, as in intaglio etching, but because the plate was printed in relief, that is, from the surface, the uninked incised lines printed white, as in a negative. Delineated in a combination of white and black lines, the naked poet as muscular youth walks into a vortex of clouds or smoke, splitting his name and the book's title in half, forcing the reader to turn the plate in the circular motion of the vortex. The title page is dated 1804, but it was not until around 1811 that Blake produced the first three of its four extant copies, and he continued working on the fourth until around 1818. The three-directional text of the title page announces 'a Poem in 12 Books', a clear reference to Milton's *Paradise Lost*, as is the inscription along the bottom of the plate, 'To Justify the Ways of God to Man'. The poem, however, is divided into two parts: in the first, Milton, inspired by a bard's song, descends from heaven and returns to earth in order to correct the errors he had left behind; in the second, Milton's female 'emanation', Ololon, also returns to earth, and the poem culminates in their apocalyptic union.

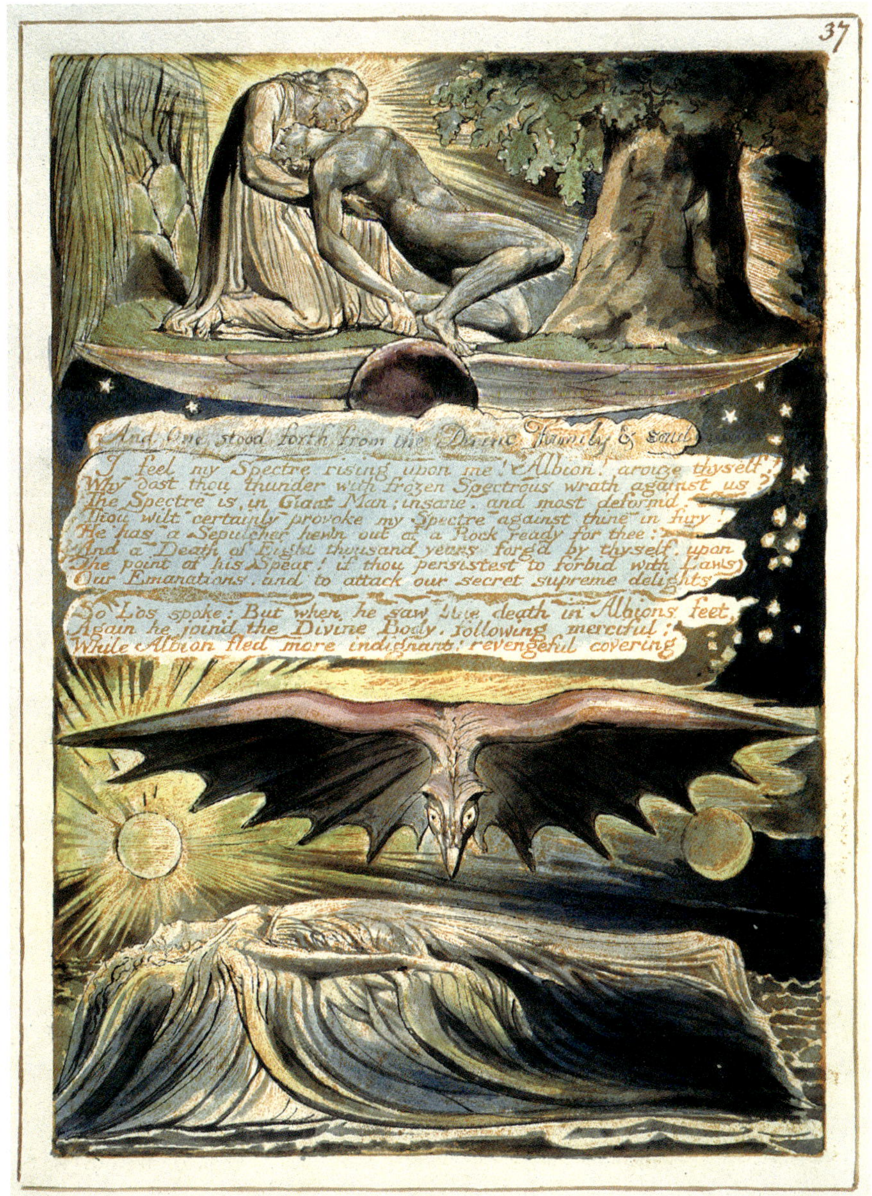

16 William Blake, *Jersusalem: The Emanation of the Giant Albion*, copy E, plate 37.

Jerusalem: The Emanation of the Giant Albion, at 100 plates Blake's longest illuminated book, is also dated 1804 on its title page, but was not printed in its entirety until about 1820. The plates were etched in relief, with many designs in white-line etching, 60 of which may have been completed by 1807; a few examples were exhibited in 1812. The poem tells of efforts to awaken the self-divided and sleeping giant Albion and reunite him with his female 'emanation', Jerusalem, the two separated at the fall from Eternity into the material world. Albion's cruel sons and daughters and the nature goddess Vala impose obstacles and temptations, but Los (the artist's imagination and Blake's alter ego and builder of the City of Art) eventually triumphs, with the help of Jesus, who is more prominent here than in any of Blake's other illuminated books. In plate 37, a white-line etching transformed in copy E into black line by its elaborate colouring, Jesus assists Albion, who faints as – or because – the bat-winged Spectre hides the sleeping, butterfly-winged Jerusalem (illus. 16).

III

On 12 April 1827, around four months before he died, Blake wrote to his lifelong friend George Cumberland to thank him for trying to sell copies of his recently published engraved illustrations to the Book of Job. The 22 Job engravings are 'pure engravings', executed entirely with burins and without preliminary etching, with tone subordinate to line and texture, with lines amassed in parallel strokes rather than in the conventional 'dot and lozenge' pattern, and with biblical texts engraved throughout the border designs (illus. 17). Blake's emulation of the ancient engravers produced his greatest work as an intaglio printmaker, but it was a masterpiece few were willing to buy. Cumberland thought the illuminated books would sell better, but the prospect of printing new copies did not excite their maker:

> . . . having none remaining of all that I had Printed I cannot Print more Except at a great loss for at the time I printed those things I had a whole House to range in now I am shut up in a Corner therefore am forced to ask a Price for them that I scarce expect to get from a Stranger. I am now Printing a Set of the Songs of Innocence & Experience for a Friend at Ten Guineas which I cannot do under Six Months consistent with my other Work, so that I have little hope of doing any more of such things. (E 783–84)

Blake's 'Corner' was two fair-sized rooms in the Strand – much less space than the 'eight or ten rooms' (BR 560) in Lambeth, or the first-floor apartment in South Molton Street which he moved to upon returning from Felpham and produced *Milton* and *Jerusalem*. He was working on his Dante watercolour illustrations and engravings, among other things, and was not set up for printing the illuminated plates. The steep increase in the cost of his books is due to the style in which he was then producing them, which required more labour and time. Blake printed the plate borders, printed on only one side of the leaf, and elaborately coloured the impression, strengthening lines in pen and ink, often adding gold leaf and emphasizing the rectangular printed shape with frame lines or border designs drawn around the plate (illus. 1, 2, 3, 4, 6, 16). The impressions now looked more like miniature paintings than 'printed manuscripts'.

Though dubious about their prospects, Blake listed six books he was willing to reprint: *America*, *Europe* and *Urizen* for £6 6s., *Visions* for £5 5s., *Thel* for £3 3s., and *Songs* for £10 10s. In a letter to Dawson Turner in 1818, he lists these books for one to two pounds less, and *Songs* for £6 6s., the price he charged his patron Thomas Butts for copy E in 1806. These prices are many times those advertised in the Prospectus (E 693). Such high prices, Blake's control over all stages of production, and even Quid's name and desires, have led some critics to assume an economic motivation behind the invention of illuminated printing. Alexander Gilchrist, Blake's first biographer, assumed that illuminated printing was a financial turning point, providing the 'principle means of support through his future life' (1:69). According to Northrop Frye, Blake wanted to 'make him[self] independent of publishers as well as of patrons, so that he could achieve personal independence as both poet and painter at a single blow.' W.J.T. Mitchell adds that 'Blake clearly had high hopes that "Illuminated printing" would make his fortune.'[3]

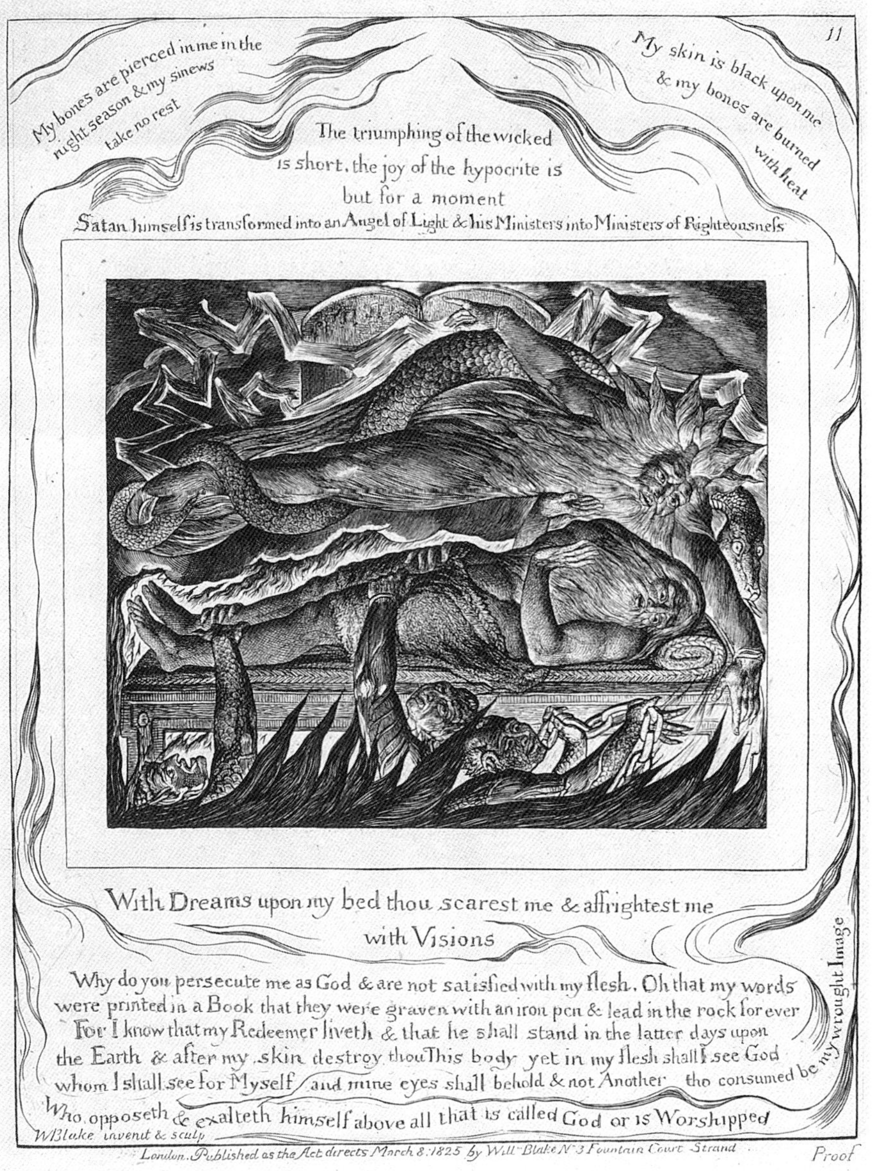

17 William Blake, *The Book of Job*, plate 12 ('Job's Evil Dreams').

This assumption, however, ignores the fact that approximately 75 per cent of Blake's stock, or 125 illuminated books (including copies of *Innocence* and *Experience* that were initially produced or issued separately) of 168 extant copies of illuminated books (excluding the late works of one plate, *On Homers Poetry* and *Laocoön*, and two plates, *The Ghost of Abel*), were produced between 1789 and 1795 and almost certainly sold at the prices nearer those listed in the prospectus of 1793 than the much higher prices recorded in 1818 and 1827. Indeed, in 1789, when he first began using relief etching to publish poetry, Blake had produced 22 copies of *Innocence*, presumably selling them for the Prospectus price of five shillings a copy, which would have grossed £5 10s., minus the approximately £1 1s the book probably cost to produce.[4] The income from the 40 or so copies of the other five books advertised in the Prospectus would have realized under seventeen pounds. The total value of his stock of books produced through 1793, in other words, was the equivalent of the labour required to engrave just one medium-sized separate plate for the publishers – which was the equivalent of about three months' income.[5] Of the 111 engravings of various sizes that Blake had produced between 1789 and 1795, he had executed 80 between 1790 and 1793, which suggests that he concentrated on illuminated printing during 1789–90 and 1793–5, intervals that correspond exactly with the books' printed dates; and, more importantly, suggests that he underwrote the cost of his original productions with his commercial work and that his new, original work could not free him financially from commercial engraving or patrons.

The huge increase in the 1818 and 1827 prices relative to those of 1793 reflect a change in Blake's idea of the book, from books of poems to series of hand-coloured prints, from prints as pages to prints as paintings. For example, the £3 3s. for *Innocence* in 1818 translates as approximately 2s. 5d. per print, which was the average price for an octavo-sized hand-coloured print, according to print catalogues of Boydell, Macklin and other print dealers. We do not know when Blake began charging the higher prices; the earliest known example is 1806, when Blake assembled *Songs* copy E from impressions printed in 1789, 1794 and 1795 because his stock of copies was already depleted. Most of these remaining impressions were poorly printed and forced Blake to rewrite texts carefully in pen and ink and to recolour the designs. This extra labour transformed *Songs* copy E into a series of splendid miniature paintings and no doubt accounts for its higher price. It influenced the printing and colouring styles of late copies of the books, the print-runs of which were limited to just two or three copies.

From the perspective of the writer, Blake's ability to publish himself is extraordinary; from the perspective of a painter and an original printmaker accustomed to controlling all stages in the production of an image, it is a matter of course, less about wanting such control for its own sake than about wanting to control form, more a matter of aesthetics than economics or ideology. With that aesthetic freedom, however, came the personal freedom from publishing conventions, class structures and other variety of institutional control. The tools of writing, drawing and sketching encouraged him to improvise, to integrate invention and execution in ways defeated by conventional printing and publishing. They enabled him to take a poem and maybe a vignette and to design the page directly on the copper plate as though he were drawing on paper. Blake's twenty years of drawing experience made this possible and the exigencies of the technique made it necessary, because the methods used by engravers to transfer designs did not technically work in relief etching. Moreover, except for a few full-page white-line etchings, Blake had no technical need to transfer a page design or any of its parts, since he was engaged neither in cutting it into the plate nor in translating it into different kinds of lines.

Blake realized very early that his new medium's autographic nature made the poem the only prerequisite for executing plates, that *rewriting texts* was also an act of visual invention, and thus that the medium could be used for production rather than reproduction. With no page designs to transfer or reproduce, the placement and extent of text, letter size and line spacing, as well as placement and extent of illustration, were invented only during execution. For single-plate work, like most of the *Songs*, Blake usually started with text and illustrated around it, visually composing the page design while executing it. For units of plates within a narrative, like *Marriage*, he could begin with a vignette, knowing he had enough room for the text to spill over to subsequent plates, and end with a vignette if there was room, as he did with *Marriage* plate 10 (illus. 5). This method of designing meant that Blake did not know what lines or stanzas would go on what plate, or how many plates a poem, section or book would need. Working without models allowed each illuminated print and book to evolve through its production in ways impossible in conventional book-making. As in sketching and drawing, illuminated printing allowed execution to generate invention, as well as enabling Blake to begin etching plates for a book or series before it was completely written, as he surely did with *Urizen*, *Milton* and *Jerusalem*.

The idea that an artist's first and spontaneous thoughts are most valuable because they are closest to the original creative spark, often obliterated by high finishing, had become very popular in the late eighteenth century, creating a taste for drawings and sketches and motivating printmakers to invent intaglio techniques, such as stipple, chalk engraving and aquatint, to reproduce them in facsimile and to simulate their various media and their visual characteristics and textures (for example, chalk, crayon and pen and wash). Such prints, however, were meticulously executed with needles, roulettes (a textured wheel used to roughen the plate's surface to produce tonalities), and other metal tools, their spontaneity a carefully crafted illusion. Blake, on the other hand, by actually using the tools and techniques of writing and drawing, had solved the technical problem of reproducing autographic pen and brush marks in metal. He was, quite literally, producing, not reproducing, 'printed manuscripts' and 'printed drawings'. In doing so, he created a multimedia site where poetry, painting and printmaking came together in ways that were both original and characteristic of Romanticism's fascination with spontaneity and the idea of the sketch.

Blake's illuminated books were produced as fine limited editions. They were not invented to secure financial independence, and they didn't. On the other hand, they did provide the means for Blake to express and publish himself without interference from the tastes of others. And though Blake stated in his Prospectus that his method cut production costs, the savings lay primarily in the author providing the manuscript, design and labour gratis. The method itself, while autographic in nature, was still labour intensive and not a cost-effective means of production. And while printing relief-etched plates was not difficult, it was slow compared to printing books in the standard way, because unlike type or stereotype, the relief-etched plate could not be inked on the bed of the press. Considering how few copies Blake produced during his early press runs, one can see why he told Turner that he was 'never . . . able to produce a Sufficient number for a general Sale', and why the books proved 'unprofitable enough to [him] tho Expensive to the Buyer' (E 771). But from the perspective of an artist accustomed to producing unique works, such as paintings and watercolour drawings, the books provided aesthetic freedom as well as wider audiences and greater opportunities to make his reputation, which he acknowledged to Turner: 'The Few I have Printed and Sold are sufficient to have gained me great reputation as an Artist which was the chief thing Intended.' He also insisted, though, that printing illuminated plates 'without the Writing' was at 'the Loss of some of the best things For they when Printed perfect accompany Poetical Personifications & Acts without which Poems they never could have been Executed' (E 771).

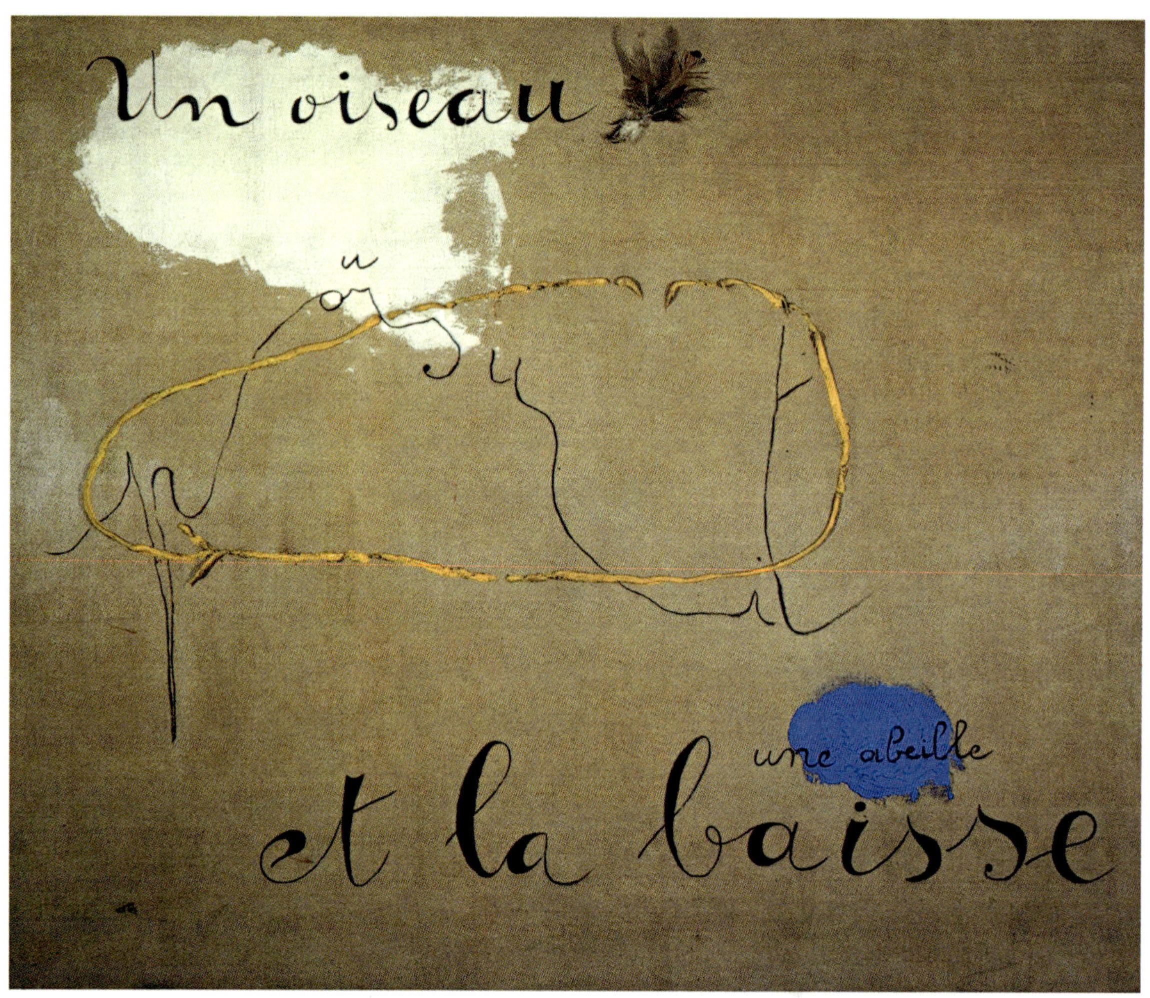

1 Joan Miró, *Un Oiseau poursuit une abeille et la baisse*, 1927, oil, aqueous medium, and feathers on glue-sized canvas.

11

'New in art, they are already soaked in humanity': Word and Image, 1900–1945

DAVID LOMAS

The introduction of words into the visual field is one of the dramatic ways that artistic production is transformed in the twentieth century, and among the most far-reaching in its consequences. Words participate in the interrogation of the nature of pictorial representation and contribute to the wholesale revision of the concept of art. Not coincidentally, words are first systematically incorporated in Cubist pictures, a movement which dismantled an idea of what a painting is that had prevailed since the Renaissance. Words also played a role in the anti-artistic stance of the historical avant-gardes, as well as reflecting and contributing to their wider social and political ambitions.

Delimiting our topic to a question of words in images, as a number of scholars who have treated the theme previously have done, is to overly restrict the matter and leads moreover to an undue emphasis upon the separateness of the historical (Dada-Surrealist) avant-garde.[1] Mine will be a more expansive conception that will attend, among other things, to collaborations of writers and artists, and the illustration of literary texts. The essay will highlight the conditions favourable to such interactions. I will foreground a common culture of artists and writers that characterizes the major art movements in this period. An objective will be to interrogate a modernist teleology according to which the aim of each of the arts is to pursue a path of self-definition. Instead, I will postulate more of a synergy between verbal and visual modes of expression that is a function, in part, of the make-up of avant-gardes in the period as well as a by-product of the introduction of new media, notably film, which subsumed the talents of both.

The proximity of painters and poets within avant-garde milieux contributed to a fruitful contamination of the visual field by verbal forms of expression, and vice versa. Henri Rousseau's beguiling portrait of Guillaume Apollinaire (illus. 2), pictured with his muse, the painter Marie Laurencin, pays homage to a poet who both inspired and championed the cause of the pre-war artistic avant-garde.[2] *Les Soirées de Paris*, the review edited by Apollinaire, afforded the first exposure to advanced art for a young poet, André Breton, who would play a similarly catalytic role for artists after the First World War. Not only did each poet write about the artists who congregated around them, the poetry of Apollinaire and Breton is imbued with a strong visual sensibility. Apollinaire was the inventor of the *calligramme*, a form of concrete poetry in which words assume the visual form of what they describe (illus. 3); Breton of the *objet-poème*, another hybrid of the verbal and visual in which words come to occupy the same level playing field as real objects. Filippo Tommaso Marinetti – redoubtable impresario, advocate and go-between – fulfilled an equivalent role among the bellicose Italian Futurists. The

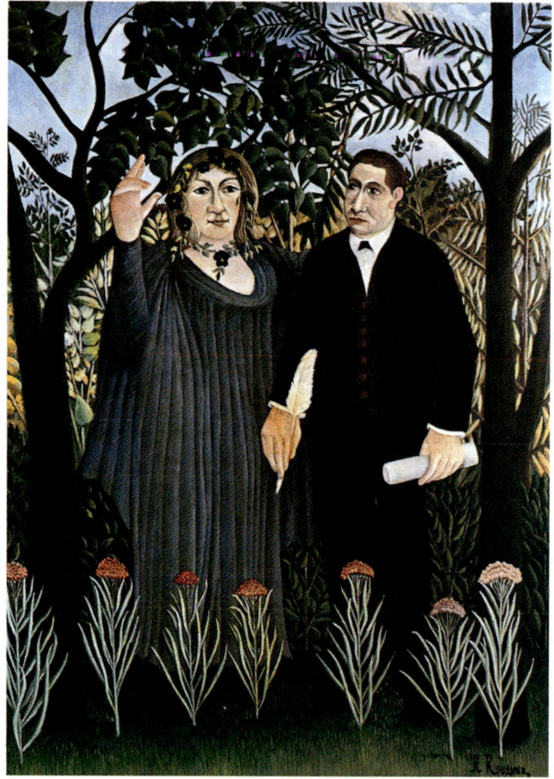

2 Henri Rousseau, *The Muse Inspiring the Poet*, 1909, oil on canvas.

painters, poets and dramatists of the Russian avant-garde comprise yet another rich case study in the social networks facilitating exchanges between visual art and literature, as Alexander Rodchenko's intimate portrait photographs of the poet Vladimir Mayakovsky well testify.

Words were crucial in explaining the new art to an uncomprehending public, with the genre of art criticism expanding to fill this mediating role. Even hostile critics had a necessary part to play in helping to define the embattled, adversarial stance of successive avant-gardes. Raoul Hausmann's thuggish *Art Critic* (illus. 5), who wields a pen like a sharpened rapier and thinks only of sinking a boot into the target of his criticism, encapsulates the stereotypical philistine art critic. Hausmann had the temerity to pose the critic against the background of one of his nonsensical phonetic poems. Rodchenko (illus. 6) more gently caricatures the writer and literary critic, Osip Brik, one of the founders of the magazine *LEF*. The reflection artfully caught by the camera on the critic's spectacles causes us to think about whether writing conduces to clear vision, or the reverse.

Deprived of access to official cultural institutions and forums for validating their art, the avant-garde had to invent their own channels of communication. The manifesto and the avant-garde magazine responded to this need. The latter were as short-lived as the movements whose rapid evolution they plot. Often distinctive in typography and design, avant-garde reviews combine words and images in carefully orchestrated layouts. In one of numerous Futurist manifestos, a literary genre they perfected, Marinetti proposed the idea of words-in-freedom. Contemptuous of symbolist ultra-refinement – 'the decorative, precious aesthetic of Mallarmé and his search for the rare word, the one indispensable, elegant, suggestive, exquisite adjective' – Marinetti advocates instead a jarring onomatopoeia in which sounds impact directly upon the nerve endings of the reader. Futurism also instigated a revolution in typography:

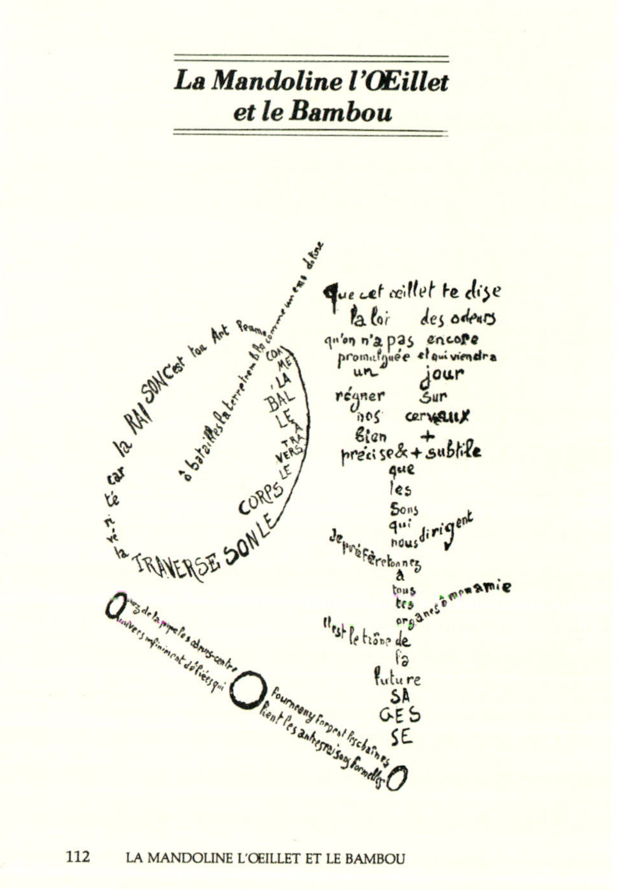

La Mandoline l'Œillet et le Bambou

Que cet œillet te dise
la loi des odeurs
qu'on n'a pas encore
promulguée et qui viendra
un jour
régner sur
nos cerveaux
bien +
précise & + subtile
que
les
sons
qui
nous dirigent
Je préfère tonnez
à
tous
tes
organes ô mon amie
Il est le trône de
la
future
SA
GES
SE
la RAISON c'est ton Art
COM
ME
LA
BAL
LE
TRA
VERS
LE
CORPS
TRAVERSE SON LE

112 LA MANDOLINE L'OEILLET ET LE BAMBOU

3 Guillaume Apollinaire, 'Mandolin, Carnation and Pipe', from *Calligrammes: poèmes de la paix et de la guerre, 1913–1916* (Paris, 1918).

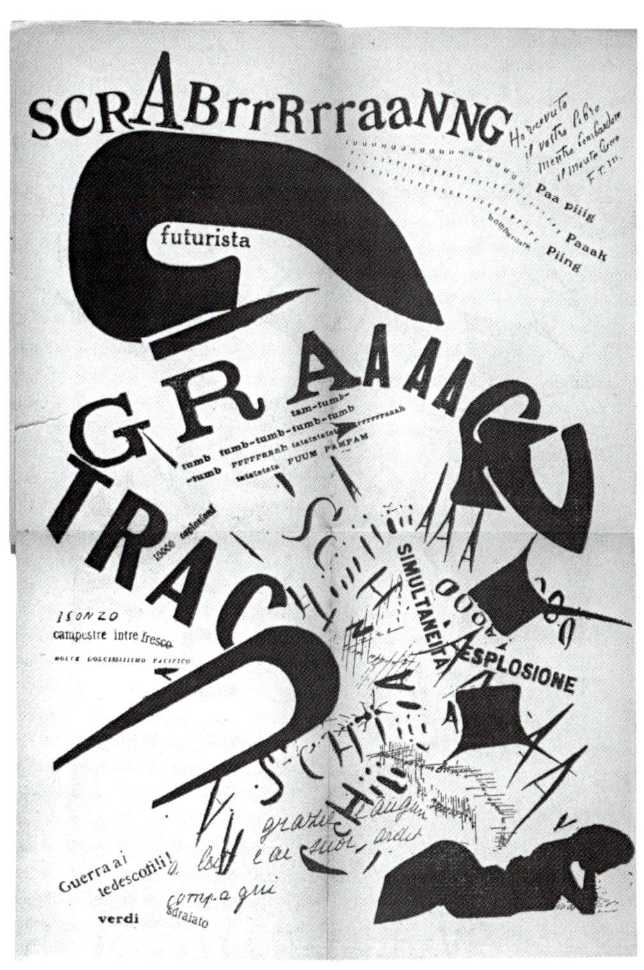

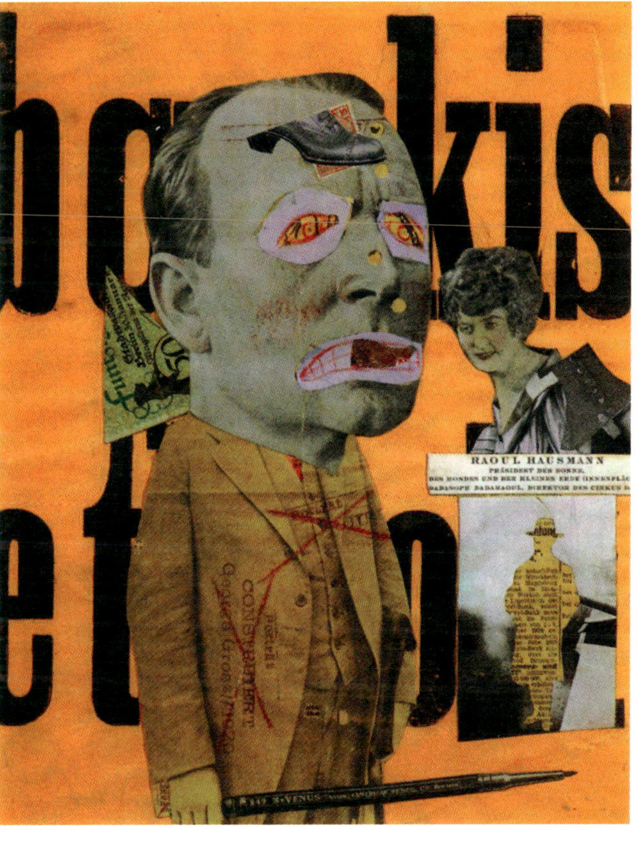

4 F. T. Marinetti, '*At night, lying in bed, she re-read the letter from her gunner at the Front*'.

5 Raoul Hausmann, *The Art Critic*, 1919–20, collage on printed poster poem.

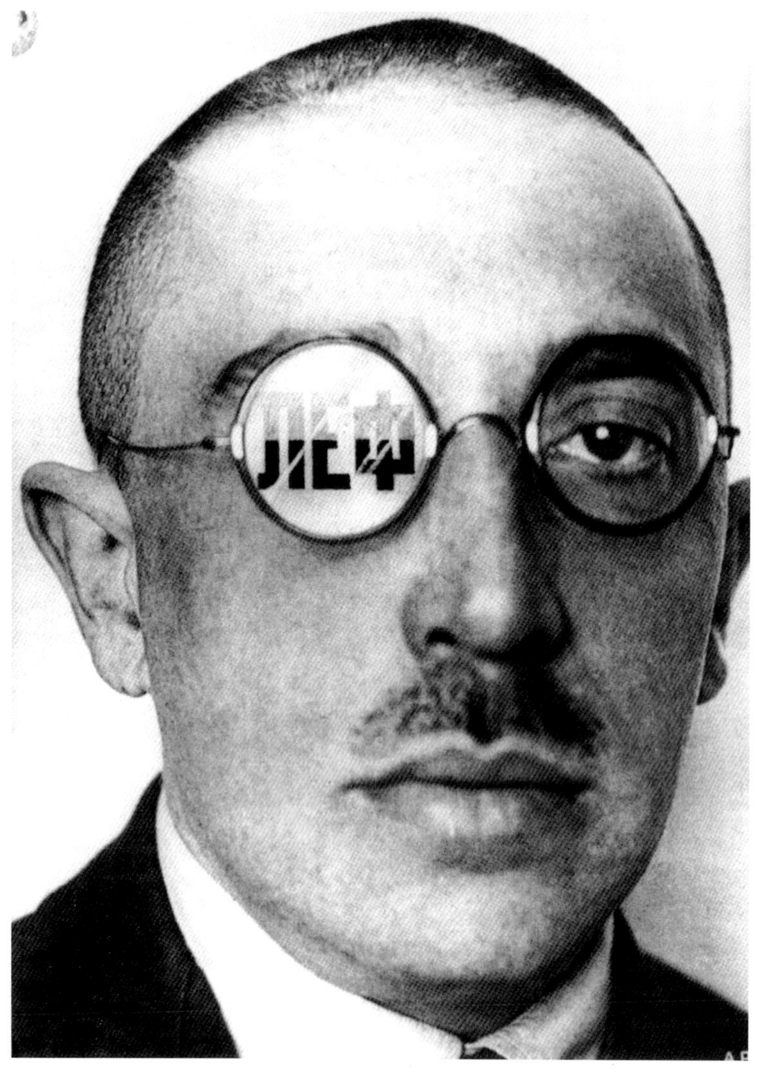

6 Alexander Rodchenko, *Osip Brik*, 1924, photograph.

Futurism and turned it against 'Art' with a capital A. The Futurist look became nigh ubiquitous in avant-garde manifestos, poetry and graphic design.[4] A residual debt to Futurism is even discernible in Breton's inclusion of a collage poem in the *Manifesto of Surrealism* that dutifully preserves the heterogeneous typography of the original source material.

The word-image compound also raises more theoretical issues: How is the relation construed by aesthetic discourse? To what extent are aesthetic stances informed by theories of language and vision? How far is it reasonable to regard art as a communicative language? For Gotthold Ephraim Lessing, writing in the 1760s, a major distinction between literature and visual art lay in the fact that in the former signs are organized consecutively in time whereas in painting (or sculpture) they are arrayed spatially, and hence are experienced as static and simultaneous.[5] For a number of modern artists, it was imperative to overcome this allegedly inherent limitation of the visual medium. The concept of simultaneity, which related to the experience of speed and collapse of distance owing to new forms of travel and communication, demanded new forms of expression. Blaise Cendrars' and Sonia Delaunay's *Prose du transsiberien* (1913) was an ambitious attempt to synthesize the axes of time and space, of poetry and abstract painting. The static and simultaneous nature of the visual sign was likewise raised as a major obstacle to painting by the Surrealists in the wake of Breton's *Manifesto of Surrealism*. In order for a form of artistic expression to qualify as Surrealist it was necessary that it was able to express the continual flux of thought, which automatic writing and drawing both endeavour to do.

> My revolution is aimed at the so-called typographical harmony of the page, which is contrary to the flux and reflux, the leaps and bursts of style that run through the page. On the same page, therefore, we will use *three or four colors of ink*, or even twenty different typefaces if necessary. For example: italics for a series of similar or swift sensations, boldface for the violent onomatopoeias, and so on. With this typographical revolution and this multicolored variety in the letters I mean to redouble the expressive force of words.[3]

Marinetti maybe protests too loudly about Mallarmé, whose poem *Un coup de dès* was surely a key influence on his thinking. He envisages a destruction of syntax and punctuation matching the urgency and economy of the telegraph – in practice, a kind of lexical and typographical anarchy (illus. 4) that would be hugely influential on the Dadaists who took up the destructive urge of

Other writers have tried to assimilate the image to language. It is in writing on the semiotics of Cubist collage that the language-like character of the visual has been most frequently asserted. The dealer Daniel-Henri Kahnweiler, whose enlightened patronage made possible the invention of

Cubism, was prescient in proposing a notion of Cubism as a sign system. 'These painters', he remarked, 'turned away from imitation because they had discovered that the true character of painting and sculpture is that of a *script*. The products of these arts are signs, emblems, for the external world, not mirrors reflecting the external world in a more of less distorting manner.'[6] Once this was recognized, the plastic arts were freed from the slavery inherent in illusionistic styles. More recent commentators have drawn upon the semiotic theories of Ferdinand de Saussure in accounting for the arbitrariness of the visual signs employed by Picasso and a play of presence and absence in Cubist collage. These authors do not generally claim that the Cubist painters knew anything of Saussure, however.[7]

Rather different in terms of the relation of art practice to theory was the situation in the Russian avant-garde. Roman Jakobson, one of the founders of structural linguistics, was in direct contact with the poets and painters responsible for the development of Cubo-Futurism, Kazimir Malevich chief among them. The encounter of art and linguistic theory was consequential for both sides. As early as 1919, Jakobson cited Futurism as demonstrating a metonymical turn in painting, and in a later essay on Cubism and Surrealism these movements are seen as epitomizing the two fundamental poles of metonymy and metaphor that Jakobson believed governed every semiotic system.[8]

In the case of Surrealism, theories of inner language, the Freudian model of the dream, studies of the origins of languages and pictographic signs, and the medical study of art of the insane, all bear upon the issue of how the relationship between verbal and visual modes of expression was construed. Breton was an eclectic who borrowed from whatever served his needs. *Inner language* or *inner speech*, terms that enjoyed a short-lived vogue in the 1880s and '90s, vindicated his natural disposition as a poet by affirming language, if not as the actual substrate of thought, then as its most faithful companion.[9] Victor Egger, a proponent of the concept of inner language, contended that all our thoughts are accompanied by a faint inward voice or echo. For Breton, who owned a first edition of Egger's book, inner speech was synonymous in his way of thinking with the discourse of the unconscious. No less important was the manner in which Egger defined subjectivity in relation to an experience of temporality, as this conditioned Breton's view of the relative merits of visual and verbal means of expression. The uninterrupted murmur of inner speech is the concomitant of a subjectivity that Egger defines, pre-Bergson, as '*durational and without spatial extension*'. This concurred with Breton's reading elsewhere in psychology and philosophy, reinforcing his belief in an intimate connection of time to interiority and lent support to the view that language is the natural counterpart to a durational idea of the self. Both strands of thinking are crucial ingredients in the doctrine of 'pure psychic automatism' set forth in the *Manifesto of Surrealism*.

This essay will examine in turn Cubism, Futurism and its offshoots, Dada in its variant forms, Russian Constructivism and Surrealism. Collage is a fundamental technical innovation in the period covered by the essay that was of incalculable importance in transforming conceptions of art as well as literature. Collage as a formal principle crosses over the verbal and visual and has equivalents in each. Fragments of text can now be imported with the same ease as images into the space of the picture. Collage demotes the role of talent and skill, one consequence of which is that poets can more easily create images while artists, by the same token, are freer to manipulate textual fragments. With the invention of collage, one moves a step nearer the famed 'death of the author' and a conception of the work as, to quote Roland Barthes, 'a tissue of quotations drawn from the innumerable centres of culture'.[10] In addition to two-dimensional media, my essay will take cognisance of film, which comes into its own as an artistic medium in the interwar period. Certain proponents of art film echoed formalist criticism in seeking to free the medium from dependence on literary models. This even included calls to eliminate the use of inter-titles, which in silent film define temporal relations between sequences and organize them into a coherent narrative. The examples of 1920s avant-garde film that I will examine all buck this trend by making conspicuous use of on-screen language in various permutations of word and image.

CUBISM: A LANGUAGE OF MODERNITY

To describe a picture that has been constructed according to a perspectival system, one resorts to the metaphor of a window looking onto the world. By contrast, the flat, coloured planes of a Cubist collage are resolutely visually opaque. Indeed, faced with a Cubist painting, metaphors of reading rather than seeing often seem more apposite. Not infrequently, newspaper cuttings or other textual fragments are there to be read quite literally. But the great liberties Cubism takes with the visual world, its quite arbitrary reference to external reality, means that in order to 'read' the image its visual language, or conventions of representation, must be understood as well.

Symbolist theories of language were crucial to the emergence of Cubist painting. A neo-symbolist revival was responsible for the persistence of symbolist attitudes within a French cultural milieu well into the first decade of the twentieth century. Symbolism arose in the context of a late-nineteenth-century reaction against positivism. Abandoning the naturalist faith that images simply register external reality, Symbolism stressed the independence of artistic and mental representations: a polemical statement of this position was J. K. Huysmans' novel *Against Nature* (1884). Idealist theories of perception indebted to the German physiologist Hermann von Helmholtz bolstered this view. Thus, according to Théodule Ribot, a French psychologist, 'sense data can only be considered as *symbols that we interpret*; there is no conceivable analogy between a perception and the object that it represents; the first is simply the spiritual *sign* of the second.'[11] The claim that there is no inevitable, or natural, link between a perception (or symbol) and the object in the external world paves the way for the notion of a 'conventional sign' which lies at the core of symbolist theories of language. The neo-symbolist writer and theorist Mecislas Golberg published a book called *La Morale des lignes* in 1908 that has been linked to Cubism. However, the very pervasiveness of symbolist aesthetics, of which Golberg offers a standard formulation, makes it hardly necessary to invoke his name.

A Cubist picture begins typically with a simple linear scaffold that is then elaborated to achieve a more crystalline pattern of fragmentation (drawings and etchings reveal this process more clearly). A shorthand system of signs is added to the scaffold to indicate musical instruments, still-life objects, and anatomical details or appurtenances – Picasso's unerring eye as a caricaturist is here exploited to the full. These visual signs are summary and polysemantic: the artists discovered to their evident satisfaction that less sometimes means more. And the resultant ambiguity meant that a penchant for punning rhymes, which Apollinaire also shared, could now be indulged to the full – between a guitar, female torso or face was a favourite example. Cubist pictures are consequently prone to amusing misreadings: a detail to the left of the *Portrait of Kahnweiler* (1911), for example, was long believed to be the neck of a bottle in a still-life. In fact, a studio photograph discloses that it belonged to a priapic African carving that hung on the wall. It is a misconception that Cubist images present a more objective or complete view of the world by surveying objects from several different angles at once. Picasso cautioned that the realism of Cubist painting is more elusive and impalpable, like a perfume. There is an irreducible element of mystery and enigma, doubtless another vestige of a symbolist heritage, which the term 'analytic Cubism' does not do justice to. André Breton, always unqualified in his support for Picasso, was attuned to this poetic (metaphoric?) side of Cubism, writing in 1961 of Picasso that: 'In his case, the rigid scaffolding of so-called "analytical" Cubism was very soon seen to be rocked by high winds, to be *haunted*. In this period of his work which I consider to be the most fascinating of all, the power of incantation shows no sign whatsoever of diminishing.'[12]

Apollinaire, in *The Cubist Painters* (1913), declared that 'it is perfectly legitimate to include numbers and printed letters as pictorial elements: new in art, they are already soaked with humanity.'[13] Depicted in careful imitation of commercial typography, the use of lettering by Picasso and Braque expanded the potential of Cubist painting to signify in a non-illusionistic manner. One of the first pictures to include stencilled letters was Picasso's *Ma Jolie* (illus. 7) from the autumn of 1911, the title of which references a song popular in music halls. An example of high analytic Cubism at its most austerely recondite, this work depicts a seated woman. At the bottom, stencilled letters appear in the usual place for a caption. A pet name for Picasso's new lover, Eva (Marcelle Humbert), they attribute an identity to the otherwise unrecognizable figure. The name originates from the refrain of 'Dernière chanson', which became an instant hit after it was performed at the Alhambra in October 1911:

O Manon ma jolie
Mon coeur te dit bonjour
Pour nous les Tziganes jouent m'amie
La chanson d'amour.

Oh Manon, my pretty one
My heart greets you
For us the gypsies play, my friend
The song of love.[14]

The boldness of *Ma Jolie* can be measured from the gap that it spans between, on the one hand, the refinement and esotericism of the painting style and, on the other, the utter triteness of the popular cultural reference. The café-concert and music hall offering variety entertainment underwent a growth in popularity in London and Paris in this period, attracting audiences across a wide class range. At the time, Picasso and his circle were habituées of the Cabaret de l'Hermitage on the Boulevard de Clichy; Fernande Olivier's memoir confirmed that Picasso 'loved risqué cabarets and music halls.' The words *ma jolie* recur like a musical refrain in a number of pictures after this date, up to 1914. A sequence of collages by Picasso from autumn 1912 again reference music hall songs. Georges Braque, it seems, had more refined tastes. He pays homage to the classical composer J. S. Bach (illus. 8), playing on their similar sounding names (Bach-Braque) and aligning him with the values of classicism – order, lucidity – to which he, more so than Picasso, was temperamentally disposed. Braque's Cubism possesses something of the structural clarity and lucidity of Bach's music.[15] In a similar vein, Picasso's *Violin 'Mozart / Kubelick'* cunningly alludes via the name of the performer Kubelik to the term Cubism. One can observe a dialogue between the two artists at this moment, their work constituting a kind of medley, evolving and transforming as each responds to the other. Their constant repartee was recalled by the poet André Salmon, who wrote: 'We invented an artificial world with countless jokes, rites and expressions that were unintelligible to others.'

The words and heteroclite materials, soaked with humanity, that infiltrate the hermetic space of Cubism are so many fragments of modern urban life. But beyond the self-evident contemporaneity of these source materials, Cubism as a style also appears resolutely modern. It is primarily a visual language of geometry and is not unlike technical drawing in its way of depicting objects in plan and elevation, and its use of projection. In 1883, as part of the reforms of education under the Third Republic, a system of drawing instruction for French school children was introduced. The generation of Cubist painters, Braque, Léger and so on, were subjected to a curriculum that was meant to inculcate the rudiments of geometric and technical drawing. The aim was to equip children with a modern visual language, a language of industry, as part of a concerted attempt to redress the relative backwardness of France compared with Germany. This language, it is persuasively argued, resurfaces in Cubist painting.[16]

The first Cubist collage is Picasso's *Still-life with Chair Caning* (illus. 9) of May 1912. The shaped canvas is covered with a strip of canvas imitation chair caning that was widely used as a cheap covering for tabletops. The equivalence of table and tableau is reiterated by the rope border: a makeshift frame, obviously, but a material widely used as table edging.[17] Resting on the tabletop is a newspaper, as indicated by the painted letters JOU[RNAL], which denote it without exactly corresponding to it. This word fragment, or synecdoche, puns on *jeu* (game) or *jouer* (to play). And clearly what Picasso contrives in *still-life with Chair Caning* is a *jeu d'ésprit* of surpassing elegance and complexity. There are numerous examples of such witty wordplays. One of the cleverest is *Still-life with Skull* (illus. 10) of 1913, in which a segment of *Le Journal* is partly concealed by the skull, a traditional motif in still-life painting. The art historian Robert Rosenblum explains the joke: 'The vowels, OU, of

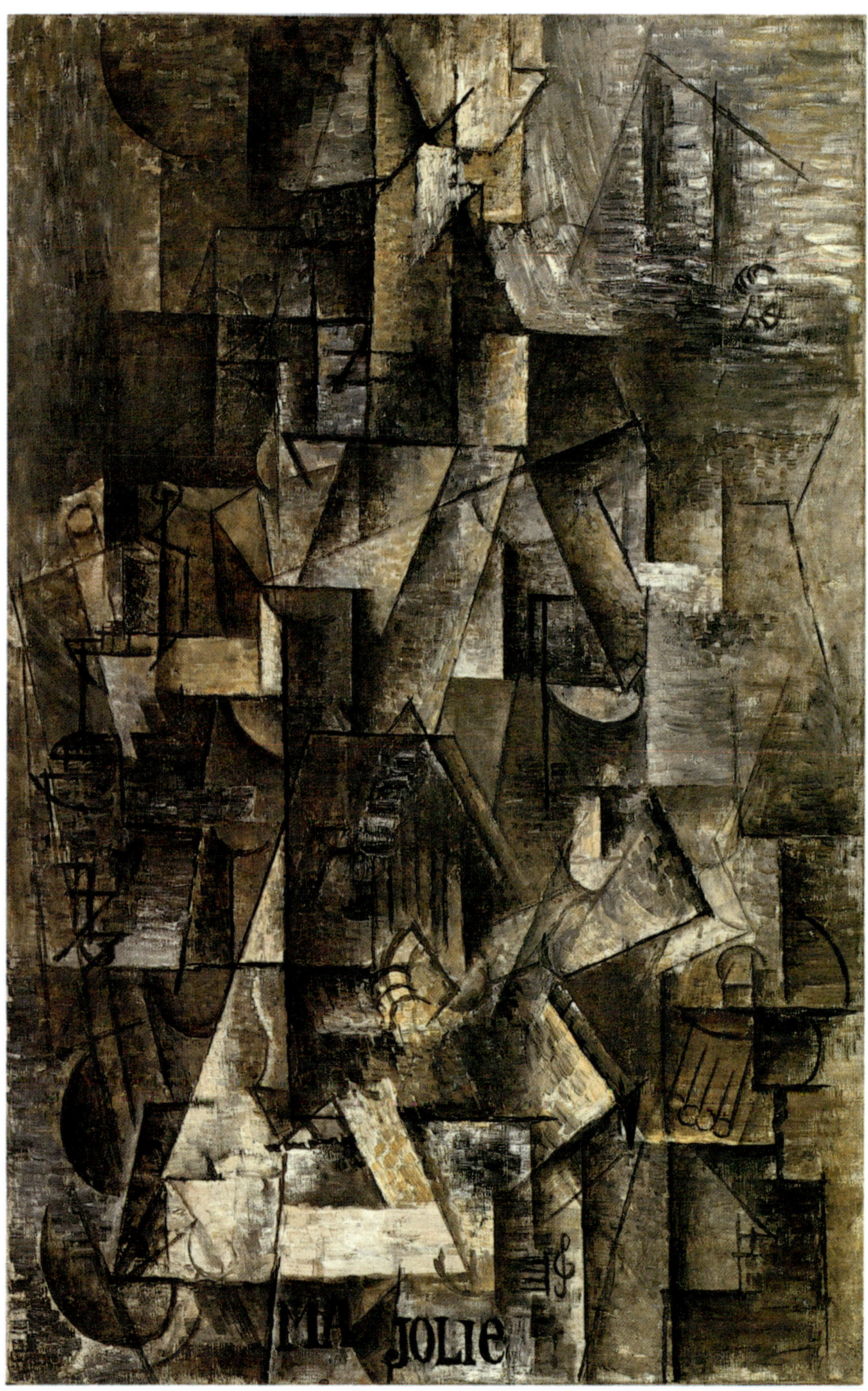

7 Pablo Picasso, *Woman with Guitar* (‘*Ma Jolie*’), Winter 1911–12, oil on canvas.

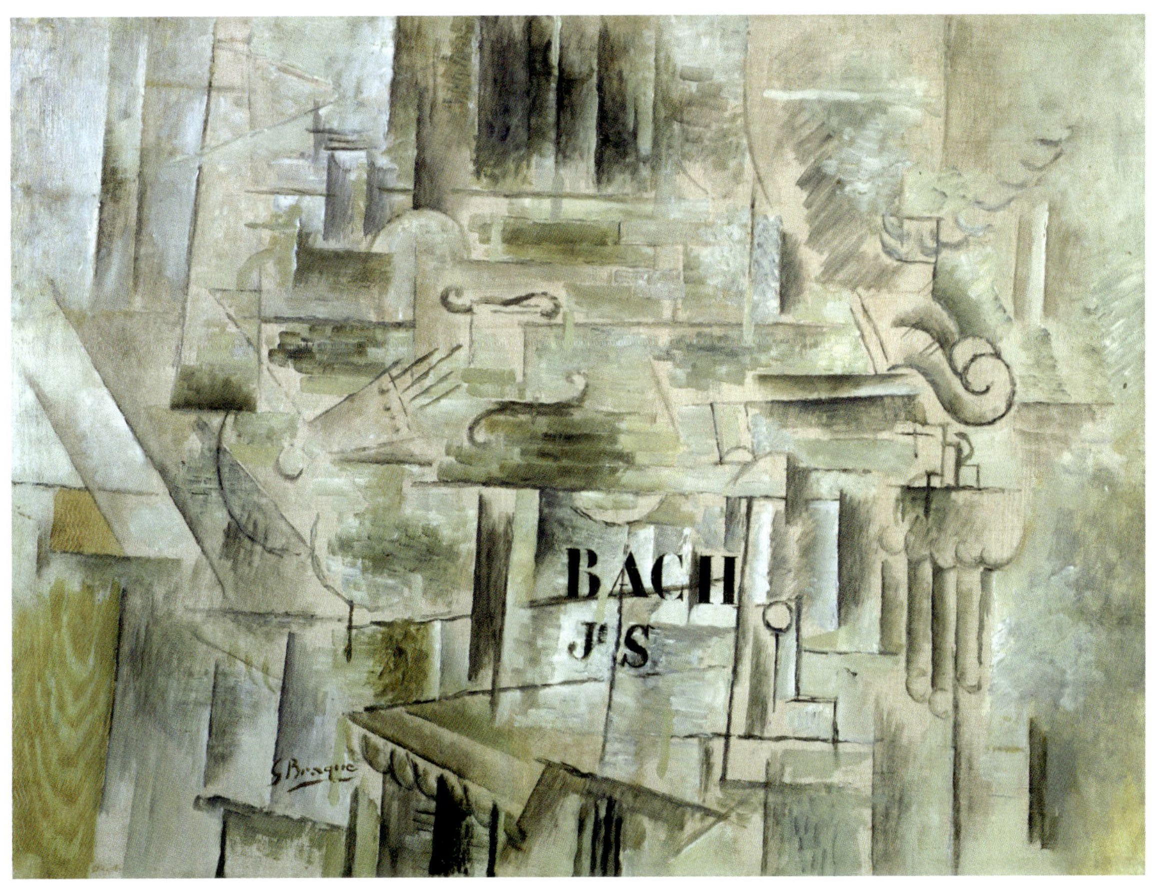

8 Georges Braque, *Homage to J. S. Bach*, 1911–12, oil on canvas.

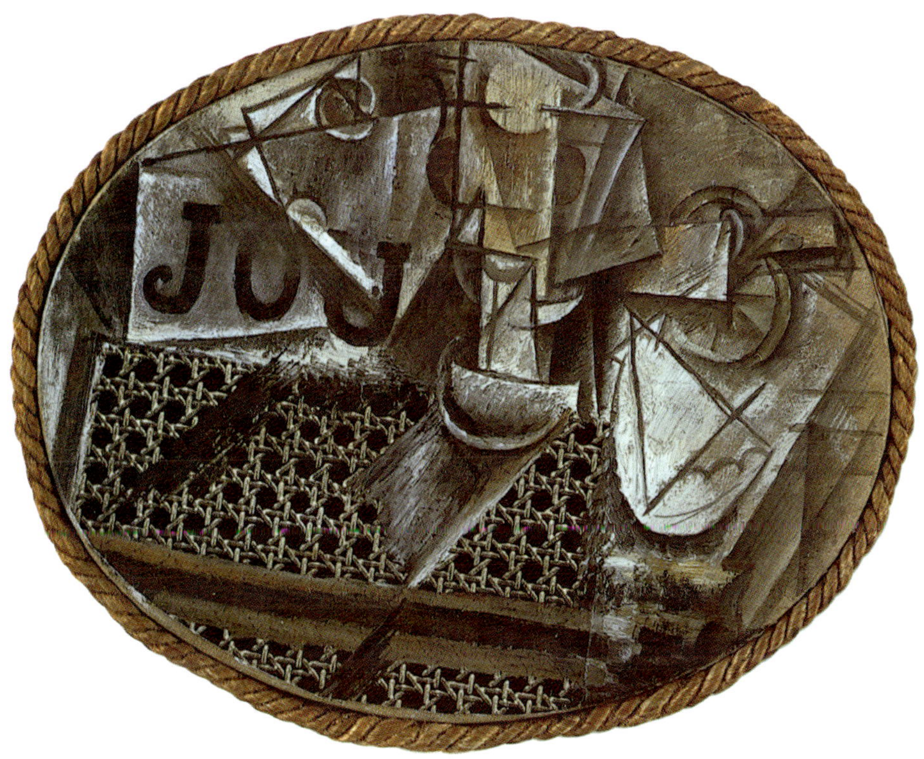

9 Pablo Picasso, *Still-life with Chair Caning*, May 1912, oil and oilcloth on canvas, with rope frame.

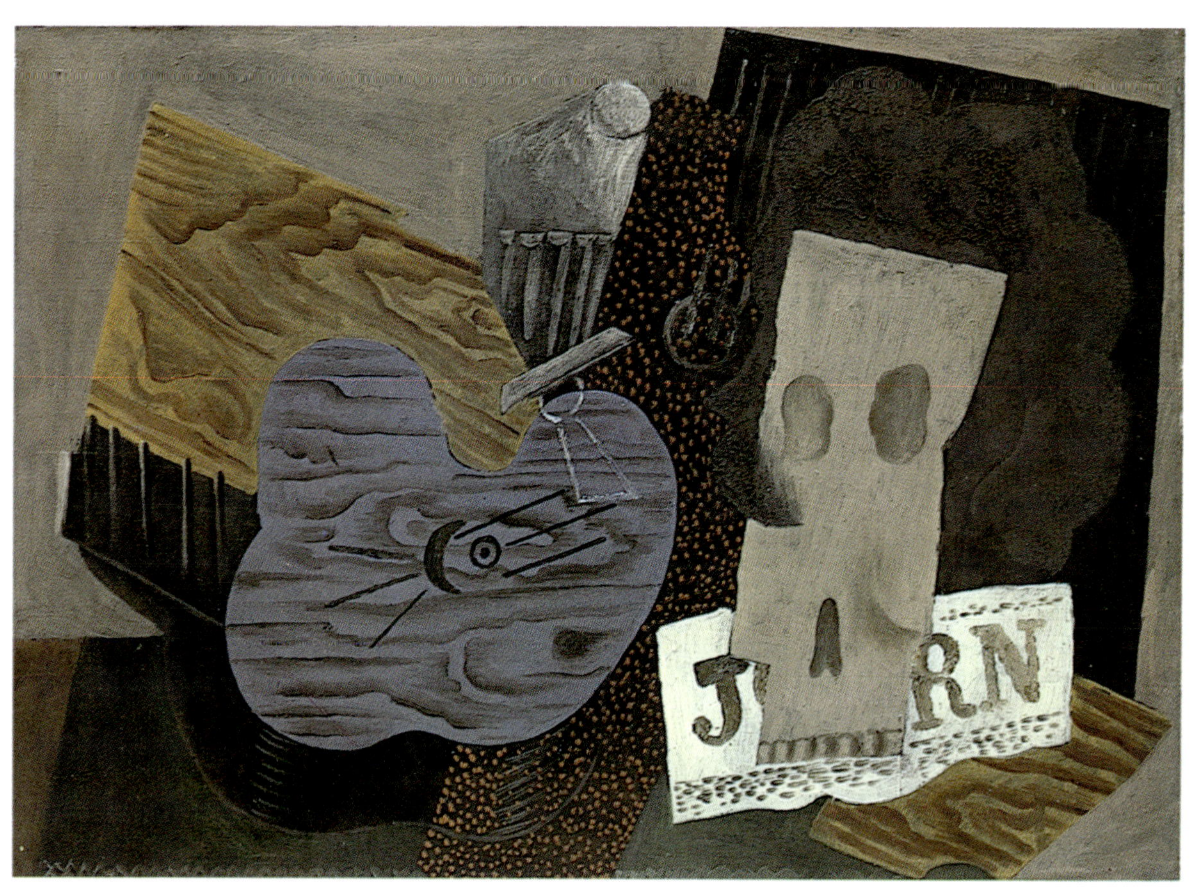
J
RN

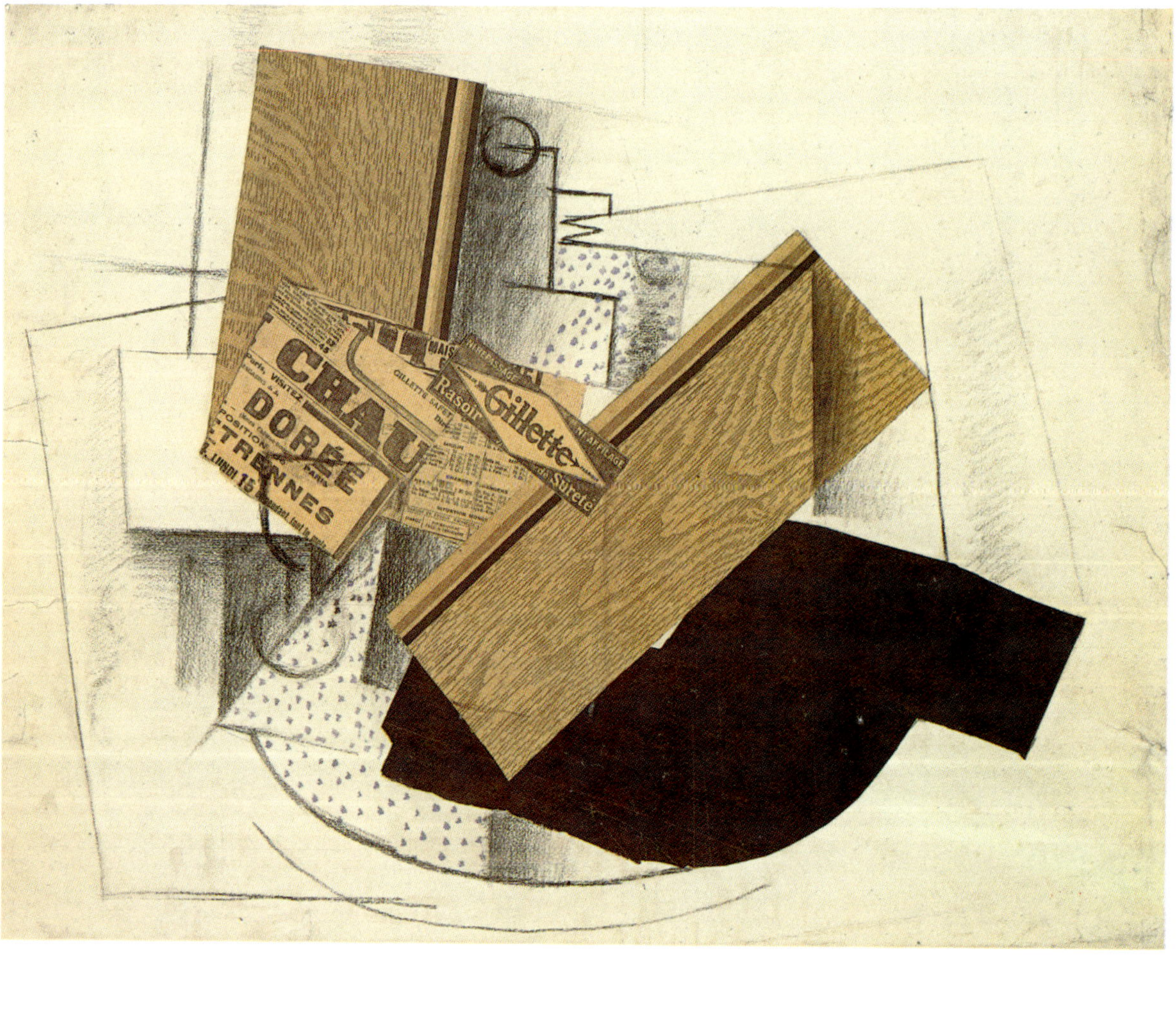

CHAU
DORÉE
TRENNES
LUNDI 15
Rasoir
Gillette
Sûreté

10 Pablo Picasso, *Still-life with Skull*, 1913–14, oil on canvas.

11 Georges Braque, *Still-life on a Table: 'Gillette'*, 1914, charcoal, pasted papers and gouache.

JOURNAL, are obscured by the lower part of the skull, whose nasal cavity suggests a carat, which points upward to the eye cavities, whose rounded hollows fulfil, as it were, the visual and verbal expectation of the concealed words.'[18] The subtle interplay of words and images in such pictures is not dissimilar to the calligram in which, as Rosenblum observes, the 'disposition of letters creates an image of the subject described'. Contemporary advertising also utilized similar oblique relations between images and texts to tantalize the public, arousing their desires for the commodities on sale in the department stores of Paris. In Braque's *Still-life on a Table: 'Gillette'* (illus. 11), the wrapper from a razor blade that may have been used to slice up the wood-grained wallpaper, incorporated in the work seemingly as an afterthought, reflexively denotes the process by which the image was made.

A great deal of recent Cubist scholarship has focused on collage and the various ways that it incorporates and responds to the worlds of advertising, popular entertainment and mass culture. All these scholarly approaches can be contrasted with the formalist reading of Clement Greenberg, for whom words in Cubist painting served merely to emphasize the flatness and autonomy of the picture plane. The driving force in the evolution of modernism, according to Greenberg, was its phobic avoidance of a commoditized mass culture. Recent studies suggest otherwise. As noted above, references to the music hall and popular entertainment abound in Cubist painting and collage. Jokes and puns – low forms of humour – bring things down and democratize the high art image. The collage elements often contain printed words: such things as adverts, brand labels, *cartes de visite*, sheet music and newspaper articles. Picasso's *Still-life: 'Au Bon Marché'* (illus. 12) incorporates adverts for two famous Paris department stores, La Samaritaine and Au Bon Marché. Molly Nesbit has demonstrated how the configurations of word and image in Cubist collage, soldered together by sexual innuendoes, parallel the strategies employed by advertisements. In a manner familiar to us from adverts, Picasso connects the disparate components of his image with a thread of erotic fantasy: at the top is a picture of a woman, beneath which are the words 'Au Bon Marché' and a reference to lingerie, and then beneath the reference is a gap with the words 'trou ici [hole here]'! This salacious schoolboy humour coincides with a shift to a more iconoclastic attitude toward picture-making in general.

Newspapers were yet another everyday item contributing to a new visual apprehension of reality. With the growth of literacy, newspapers increasingly came to mediate access to the outside world; Marinetti extolled 'the great newspaper (synthesis of a day in the world's life)'. The philosopher Walter Benjamin pointed to the disjunctive manner in which unrelated news items are presented side by side on the pages of newspapers by way of illustrating the shock principle that he saw as the essence of modern experience.[19] The arch-symbolist Mallarmé despised the newspaper as a debased, commodity form of literature; Apollinaire, on the other hand, regarded newspapers as the prose of his day. In common with innumerable other modern writers, Apollinaire found inspiration in the *fait divers*, brief newspaper stories of crimes and misfortunes that achieved the status of reportage on account of their lurid or sensational character – a source of endless fascination for the Surrealists too.[20] Artists were quick to depict the everyday activity of reading newspapers: Cézanne's portrait of his father reading a newspaper was one of the sources of inspiration for André Derain's enigmatic *Man Reading a Newspaper* (illus. 13). Depicting an unknown sitter, it was baptized '*Chevalier X*' by Apollinaire, who reproduced it in *Soirées de Paris* in February 1914. At that point, it evidently had a real newspaper doubled over and tacked onto the canvas, which Derain later removed prior to its purchase by the Muscovite collector, Schukine. Breton cherished the magic of this image, to which he referred on a number of occasions, reproducing it in the first instalment of his essay 'Surrealism and Painting' (1926). In 1928 Rodchenko photographed a fellow

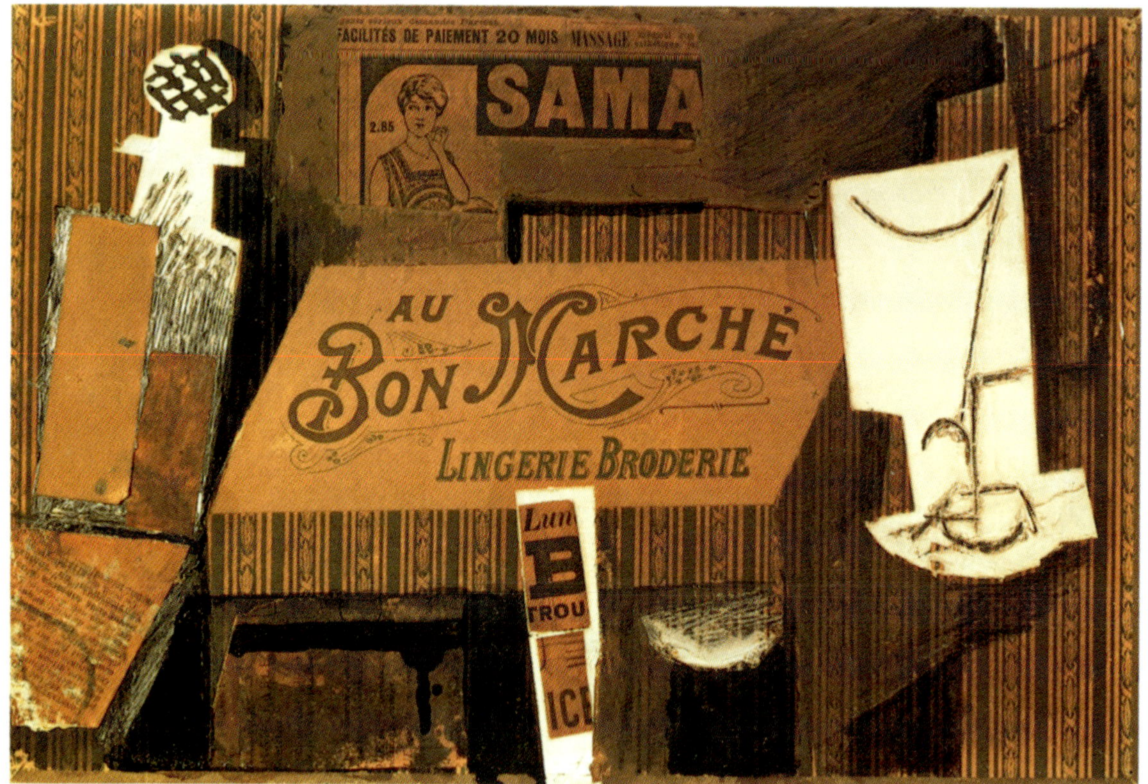

12 Pablo Picasso, *Still-life: 'Au Bon Marché'*, 1913, oil and pasted paper on cardboard.

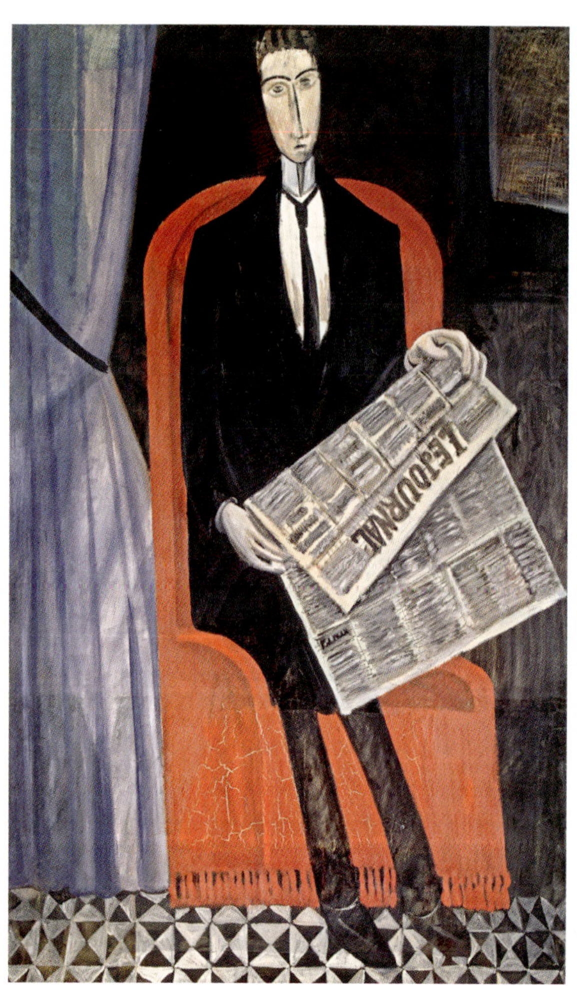

13 André Derain, *Man Reading a Newspaper (Chevalier X)*, 1911–14, oil on canvas.

artist, Varvara Stepanova, reading a newspaper while taking her breakfast, a nigh universal ritual, for a photo-documentary. John Heartfield's famous montage of a head wrapped up in newspapers, unable to see or hear, gives a sardonic, left-wing take on the insidious propensity of newspapers to distort and mislead.

Guitar, Sheet Music and Glass, executed in November 1912, is considered the first *papier collé* to have included newspaper cuttings. 'La bataille s'est engagé', it impatiently declares. Following soon afterwards are a cluster of collages by Picasso that make insistent references to the Balkan wars, anti-war demonstrations by pacifists and police reprisals. However, these topical political referents intrude into an aesthetic world of Mallarméan purity and refinement: the caption 'Un coup de thé[âtre]' evokes Mallarmé's famous poem 'Un coup de dès' (illus. 14 and 15). Mallarmé defined his poetic practice partly in opposition to the newspaper, which he regarded as a debased form of literature (this is said to account for his experimentation with alternatives to writing in regular columns). It seems that Picasso has deliberately imported newsprint, the depreciated mass cultural literary coinage, and placed it in tension with the rarefied, Mallarméan aesthetic.[21] It has been

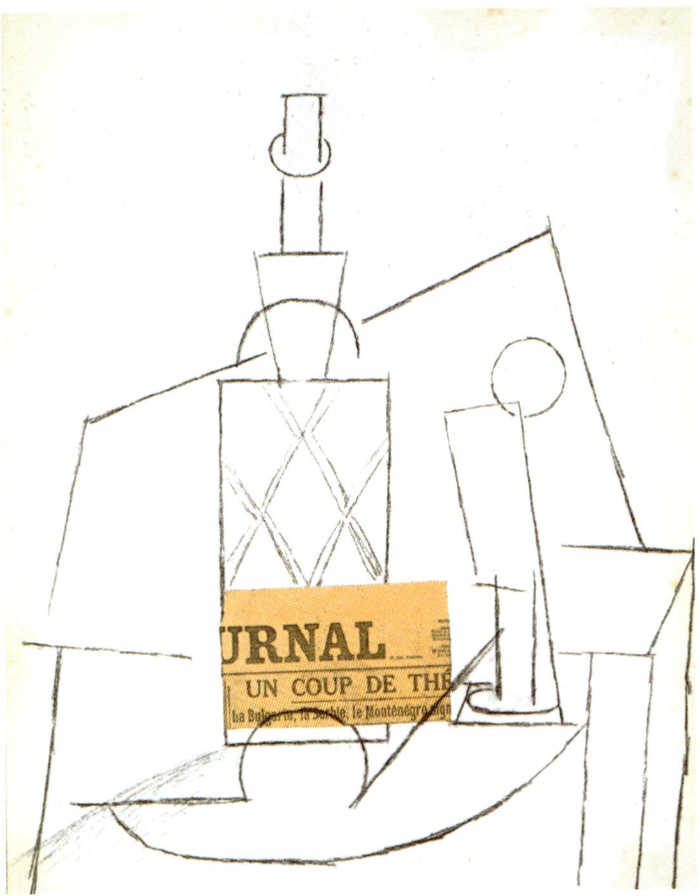

14 Pablo Picasso, *Table with Bottle, Wine-glass and Newspaper*, after 4 December 1912, newspaper, charcoal and gouache on paper.

15 Stéphane Mallarmé, '*Un Coup de dès*', original version, 1897.

claimed that the political references buried in the news cuttings instance Picasso's left-leaning anarchist politics.[22] However, this interpretation fails to take account of the fact that the newspaper fragments are sometimes pasted upside down or pushed to the background of works that flaunt the accoutrements of a bohemian lifestyle. The headlines are not infrequently diverted from their original signification: what *is* the battle that has been joined? Could it be the art world rivalry with the Futurists? It is the conflicted yet dependent relation between art and the dominant social order, between high art and low culture, that Picasso stages.[23] It is clear, I think, that Cubism does not simply jettison the symbolist ideology of artistic purity, which arose in response to the encroachments of mass culture. But where symbolism disavows this historical relation with false claims of artistic autonomy, in Cubism one witnesses the 'return of the repressed'.

While collage undermines the notion of art as an enclosed autonomous activity, it preserves and extends the symbolist belief in the conventional

c'était
issu stellaire
le nombre
EXISTÂT-IL
autrement qu'hallucination éparse d'agonie
COMMENÇAT-IL ET CESSÂT-IL
sourdant que nié et clos quand apparu
enfin
par quelque profusion répandue en rareté
SE CHIFFRÂT-IL
évidence de la somme pour peu qu'une
ILLUMINÂT-IL
ce serait
pire
non
davantage ni moins
mais autant indifféremment
LE HASARD
(Choit
la plume

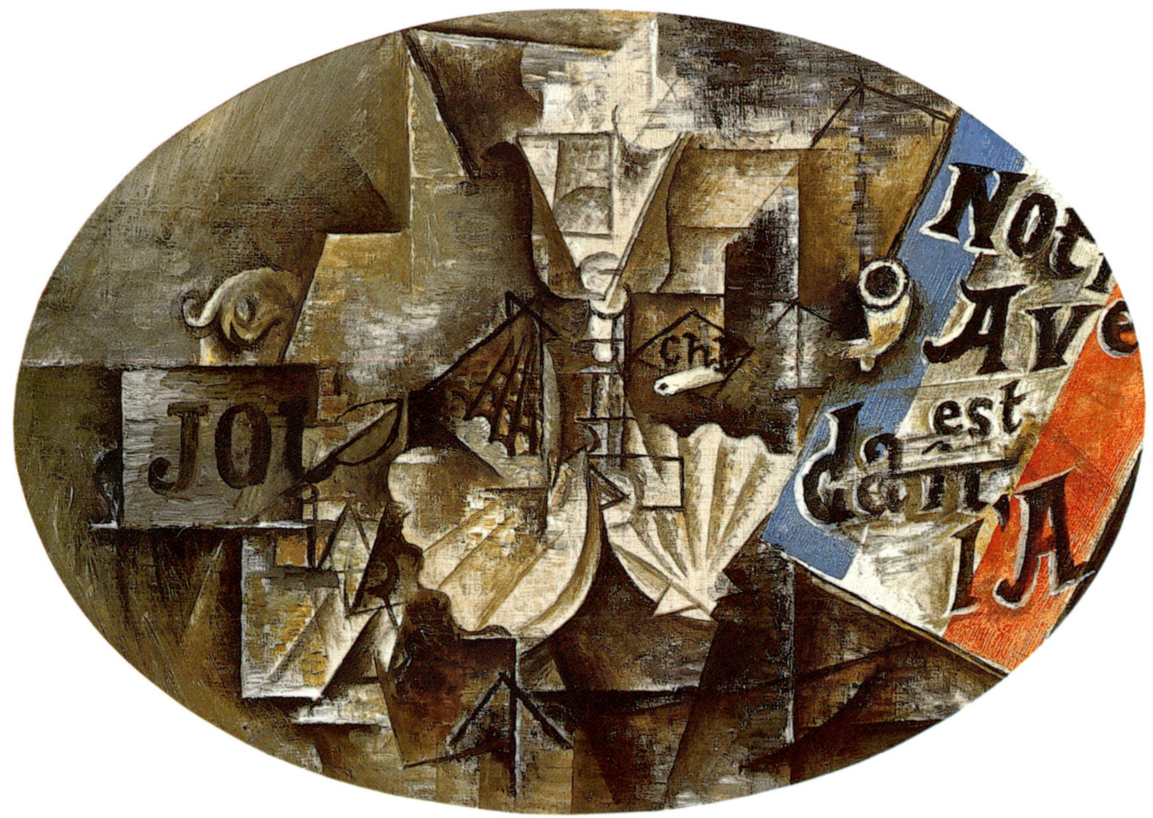

16 Pablo Picasso, *The Scallop Shell: Notre avenir est dans l'air*, 1912, oil on canvas.

nature of visual signs. In the winter of 1912 Picasso employed a projecting wooden cylinder to signify the sound hole of a sheet metal guitar, borrowing this device from a Grebo mask that used projecting wooden cylinders for eyes. What impressed Picasso was the arbitrary nature of the signs used by the primitive artist where a recessed hollow could be denoted by a positive mass. While this potential was already implicit in the positive/negative reversals, and multivalent signs of analytic Cubism, the Grebo mask experience prompted Picasso to exploit in a more systematic manner this newly discovered arbitrariness of the visual sign.[24]

ALLEGORIES OF THE MODERN

Charles Baudelaire, as a writer of Salon art criticism, drew the attention of artists to the heroism of modern life subjects. Contemporary Parisian life, he opined, 'is rich in poetic and marvellous subjects'; 'the true painter will be the one who can seize the life of today for its epic quality, and make us feel how great and poetic we are in our cravats and patent leather boots. Next year let's hope that the true seekers may grant us the extraordinary delight of celebrating the advent of the new!'[25] Against the grain of Academic art's piety to timeless tradition, Baudelaire reoriented artists towards the evanescent face of modernity, to what he termed: 'the ephemeral, the fugitive, the contingent.'[26] In so doing, Baudelaire defines an agenda for much of what is called modernist art.

While it is clear that neither Braque nor Picasso set out to depict modern life in its epic or heroic dimension – their work was small-scale, experimental – there are plenty of instances of modern life subject-matter in Cubist painting. Picasso richly exploits the novelty of aviation, which he employs as a metaphor for the new space of Cubism. A still-life composition of May 1912 (illus. 16) contains the phrase 'Notre avenir est dans l'air [Our future is in the air]'. It is one of three works that reference the cover of a popular book patriotically emblazoned with the colours of the French flag. In the run-up to the First World War, with nationalism rampant, the potential applications of manned flight were being widely touted. Picasso may have been prompted by Futurism's enthusiasm for the machine age to engage with this topical subject. Scallop shells opened like wings are a lofty metaphor for the artist as a modern Icarus. (Apollinaire would later write: 'As long as airplanes did not people the sky, the fate of Icarus was merely a supposed truth. Today, it is no longer a fable.') Around this time, Picasso gave Braque the nickname 'Wilbourg' after one of the Wright brothers, and it is evident that they saw themselves as inven-

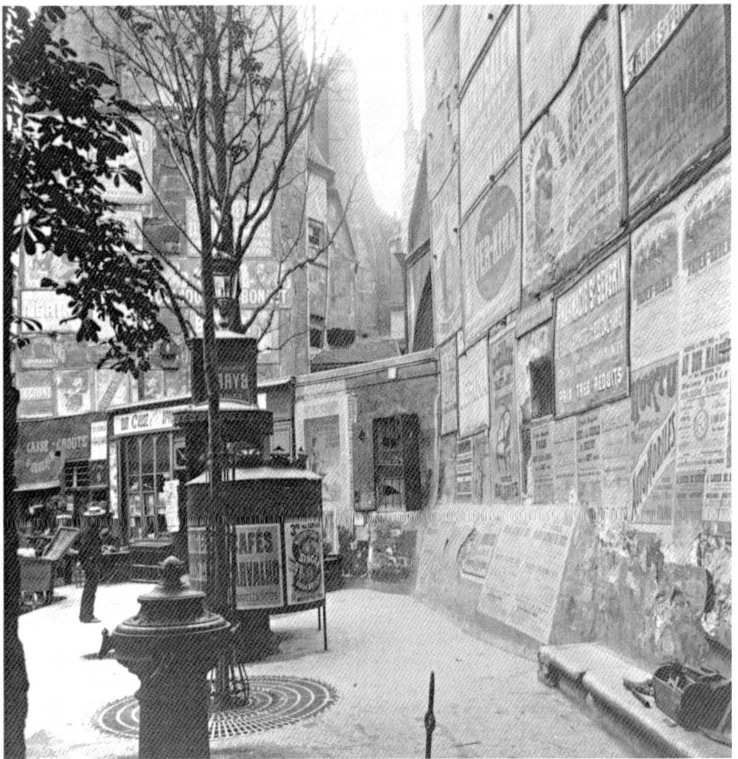

17 Eugène Atget, *Rue St Jacques, Paris*, 1906, albumen print.

tors whose audacity was on a par with the headline-grabbing exploits of these aviatory pioneers. Rodchenko, one of the architects of Russian Constructivism, designed a costume for himself like that of an aviator, another illustration of the potency of an analogy that placed the avant-garde artist in the driving seat, at the controls of technological modernity, so to speak.

The shift to collage expanded the repertoire of modern life subject-matter, coinciding with profound changes in the poetry of Apollinaire. No longer straining after mystic obscurity, the poet nearest to Picasso turns to a self-consciously prosaic imagery in which he records the raw vitality of modern experience and the overload of discordant perceptions bombarding the urban dweller. The poem 'Zone', exemplifying this new trend in Apollinaire's poetry, provides an inventory of the exciting new typography that also found its way into Cubist painting and collage:

You read the handbills the catalogues the singing posters
So much for poetry this morning and the prose is in the papers
Special editions full of crimes
Celebrities and other attractions for 25 centimes
... The inscriptions on walls and signs
The notices and plates screech parrot-wise
I love the grace of this industrial street.[27]

The evocation of the city as a dense forest of signs to be read and interpreted indicates that the symbolist belief that sense data are symbols that we interpret was in the process of acquiring an experiential reality. Artists and poets registered the rapidly changing urban environment (illus. 17), newly colonized by words and images in the form of billboards and posters that are celebrated by Apollinaire in Whitmanesque fashion. A view across rooftops by Picasso (illus. 18) is dominated in the foreground by billboards advertising Pernod, a liqueur, and the bouillon 'Kub', a popular beverage that puns on the recently coined term 'cubisme'. Reproduced in *Cahiers d'art* in 1932, this work was titled *Still-life with Bottle of Pernod* – an excusable error! On 26 April 1914 the newspaper *Matin-Paris* printed before and after photographs of the base of a monument showing the effects of a new law designed to curb the indiscriminate pasting of electoral posters. Soon after Juan Gris chose to include this amusing cutout in a still-life with newsprint collage. Fernand Léger's *The City* (illus. 19) utilizes a montage technique, shuffling urban vistas to convey an impression of fragmentation and discontinuity. Signs and advertising hoardings are the by now standard props of this affirmative vision of modernity. Stuart Davis, who in the 1920s belonged to an expatriate American artistic community in Paris where he came under the sway of Léger, produced works that in their frank emulation of advertisements for consumer wares such as cigarettes strikingly anticipate Pop art (illus. 20).

In a succession of manifestos written in bombastic and combative language the Italian Futurists declared their total commitment to the modern. Despising the 'fanatical worship of all that is old and worm-eaten', they vowed to unburden Italy of the museums that cover her like so many cemeteries. Led by the poet F. T. Marinetti, the Futurists declared themselves the primitives of a new, completely renovated sensibility and proclaimed a racing car to be more beautiful than the *Victory of Samothrace*. The aim in painting was to express their sense of universal dynamism. They differed from Picasso and Braque not only in their objective of rendering motion but also in their conspicuous attraction

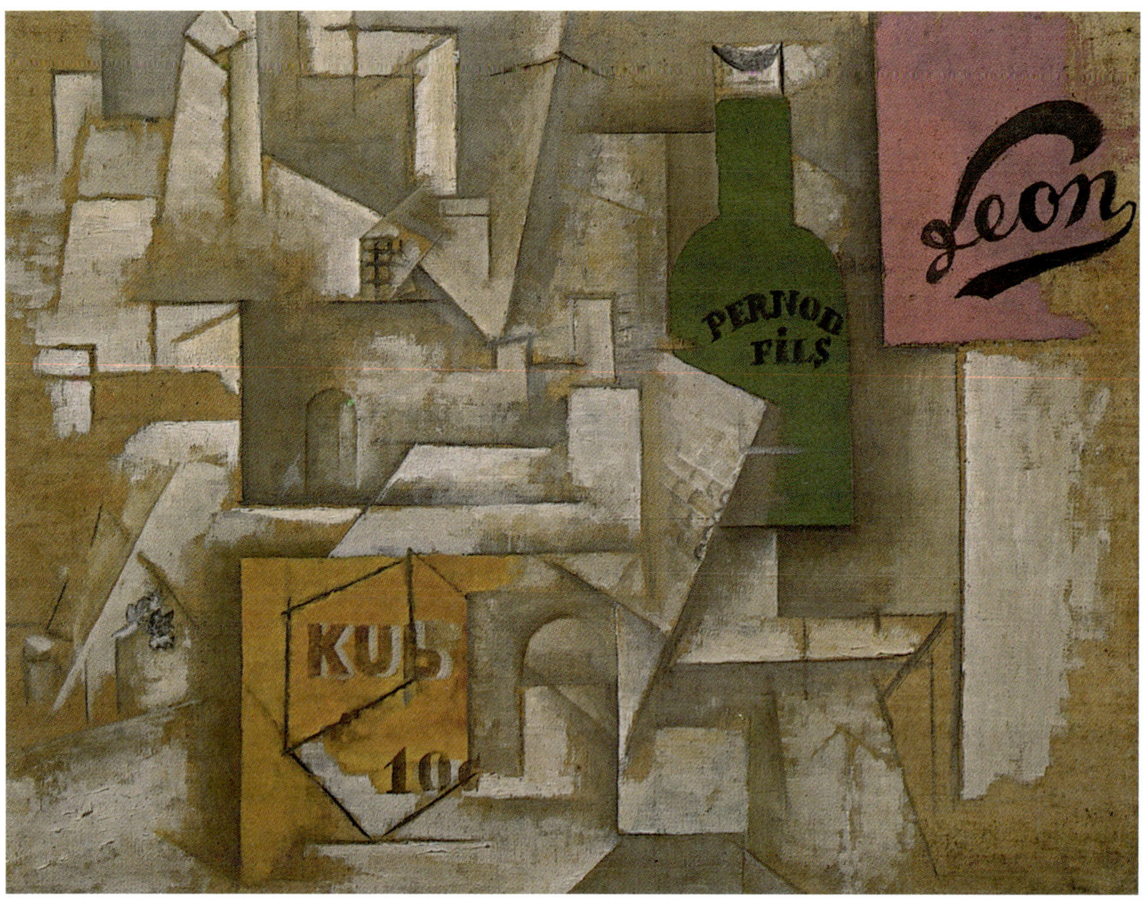

18 Pablo Picasso, *Landscape with Posters*, 1912, oil on canvas.

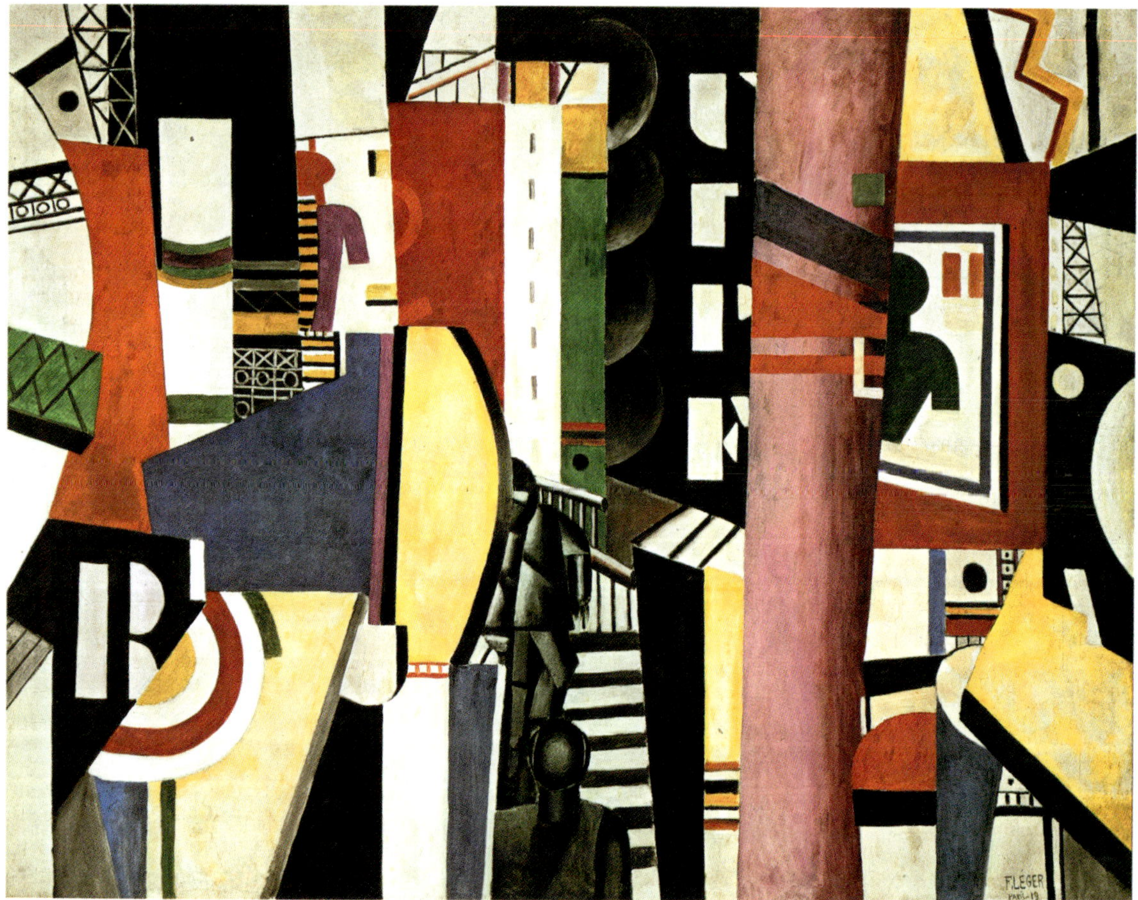

19 Fernand Léger, *The City*, 1919, oil on canvas.

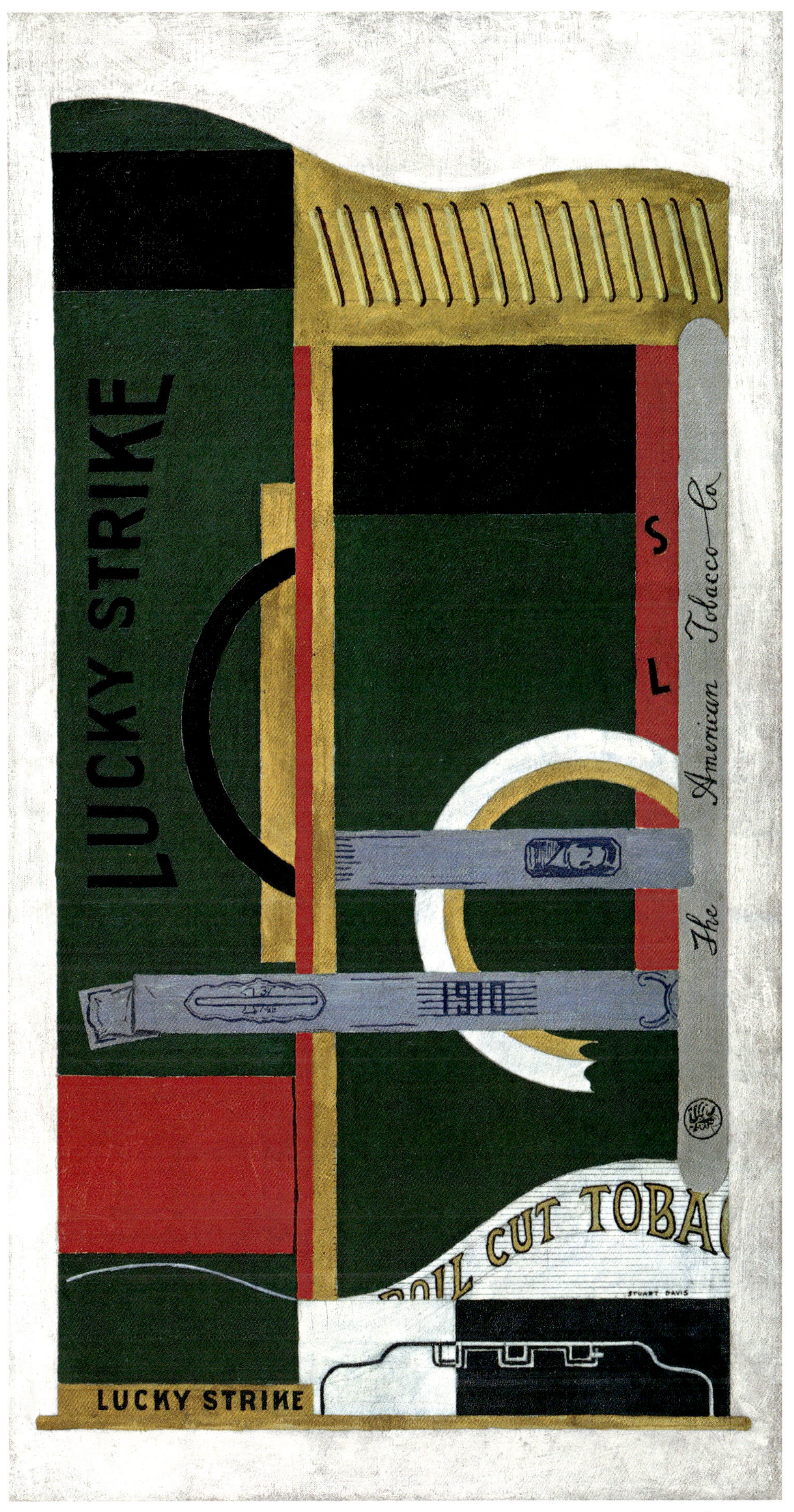

20 Stuart Davis, *Lucky Strike*, 1921, oil on canvas.

to modern life themes, above all, the city and the crowd. In this they were influenced by a movement in poetry known as Unanimism. Jules Romains, the instigator of Unanimism, celebrated the dynamism of modern life and sought to evoke circumstances in which the city dweller is caught up in vast collective rhythms. Romains recounts a kind of epiphany in 1903 that occurred on a crowded street in Paris when he became aware of 'a vast and elemental being, of which the streets, the carriages and pedestrians formed the body and of which he was the consciousness.'[28] Umberto Boccioni, the greatest of the Futurist painters, tries to recreate these rhythms in paintings such as *The City Rises* and *The Laugh*. His aim was to capture on canvas complex states of mind that synthesize memories and sensations, 'what one remembers and what one sees.'

'The simultaneousness of states of mind in the work of art: that is the intoxicating aim of our art', Boccioni declares, giving as an example his painting *The Noise of the Street Penetrates the House* (1911).[29] The scene is an archetypal modern one: the encounter of a subject with the noisy chaotic city street. Boccioni uses the contrivance of a window to suggest the interpenetration of inner and outer spaces, a fusion of subjective or psychical space with the objective world. The individual fuses with the collective rhythms of the urban spectacle. In a state of simultanist consciousness, the disparate sensations that continually assail the city dweller are meant to be somehow integrated and the fragmentariness of experience transcended. Robert Delaunay and Fernand Léger, the two French artists most receptive to Futurist ideas, both adapt this window motif to convey a notion of simultaneity, as we shall see. The poet Cendrars, likewise, would declare that the 'windows' of his poetry were wide open to the boulevards.

The concept of simultaneity, promoted by the Futurists, had major implications for artistic and literary production, not least by posing the problem of temporality and the image. Arguably, it was only after their encounter with Cubism that the Futurists found the means to adequately represent simultaneity. One of the first telltale signs of their response to Cubism was lettering that creeps into the space of the image, as in the second version of Boccioni's *States of Mind* (illus. 21). Gino Severini, an Italian artist who lived in Paris, was an intermediary joining the Italian and French avant-gardes. *Nord-Sud* (illus. 22) of 1912 is a simultanist picture taking as its theme the new metro linking Paris from north to south, Montmartre to Montparnasse. The poet Pierre Reverdy would later use the title *Nord-Sud* for his avant-garde periodical, alluding to the fact that the two main groupings of artists and poets in Paris were located at each end of the metro line. However, the main impact of Futurism did not occur until after the first exhibition of their painting in Paris in February 1912 at the Bernheim-Jeune Gallery. Inspired in part by the example of Futurism, Delaunay and Léger took up Cubist techniques to paint modern life subjects. Endeavouring to register the essence of modern experience, both artists were led for a short while to a non-figurative, basically abstract, 'pure' painting. And both of them were linked by a friendship with the poet Blaise Cendrars, whose attraction to the dynamic and the modern they shared.

Delaunay first explores an overtly modern life subject in a series of images of the Eiffel Tower – the 'great symbol of simultaneity', according to Stephen Kern.[30] An eminently useless structure, with no practical use, Roland Barthes speaks of its 'vocation of an infinite cipher ... the symbol of Paris, of modernity, of communication, of science or the nineteenth century, rocket, stem, derrick, phallus, lightning rod or insect.'[31] The Futurist presence in Paris appears to have been a direct impetus for Delaunay's *La Ville de Paris* of 1912, a mural scale picture organized according to a tripartite structure. The central section represents the Three Graces, a reference to the Judgement of Paris. This is flanked on the one side by the Eiffel Tower and, on the other, by a scene of old Paris. Apollinaire employed a similar discordant mix of classical mythology and modern life imagery in his poetry at this time. *La Ville de Paris* conveys through its allegorical subject matter a sense of Paris past, present and future. The ensuing *Fenêtres* series (illus. 23) would attempt to evoke simultaneity by purely pictorial means. Recalling the symbolist ideal of *l'art pour l'art*, Delaunay spoke of 'colour for colour's sake'; some of his titles gesture to musical composition, an analogy also employed by Frantisek Kupka in his contemporaneous abstractions.[32] Apollinaire, an advocate of the impulse towards pure painting, which he dubbed Orphism, was inspired by the latest works of Delaunay to write a poem in the summer of 1912, 'Les Fenêtres', that evokes in words the effects of pure colour. It opens with the line: 'Du rouge au vert tout le jaune se meurt'. Under the sway of Cendrars, Delaunay reverted to a figurative idiom in *The Cardiff Team* of 1912–13 (illus. 24), crammed with a stock iconography of modern life: a poster, a ferris-wheel, a tower, a biplane, sportsmen. The conjunction of place names 'New York–Paris' recalls the effects of simultaneity being explored by Cendrars in his poetry.

Energetic and infectious in proselytizing their cause, the Futurists contributed to the spread of Cubist techniques to other countries, notably Russia, where, since the turn of the century, a nidus of artists and literati that included the dramatist Meyerhold, who were outward-looking and receptive to modernist idioms emanating from France, had congregated around Diaghilev's Ballets Russes. Owing to the outstanding collections of Sergei Schukin and Ivan Morozov, Russian artists had ready access to the most up-to-date French art. The greater acceptance of female artists in the Russian avant-garde was a notable feature of it. This contrasts with the Italian Futurists, who were scathing of feminine weakness and sentimentality, and extolled the pursuit of war (praised as the great hygiene of the world) and violent action. Marinetti only grudgingly admitted as one of the defining features of the new era the 'semi-equality of man and woman and a lessening of the disproportion in their social rights'. Alexandra Exter, who regularly shuttled back and forth to Paris, and exhibited at the Salon des Indépendants and the 1914 Futurist Painting and Sculpture Exhibition in

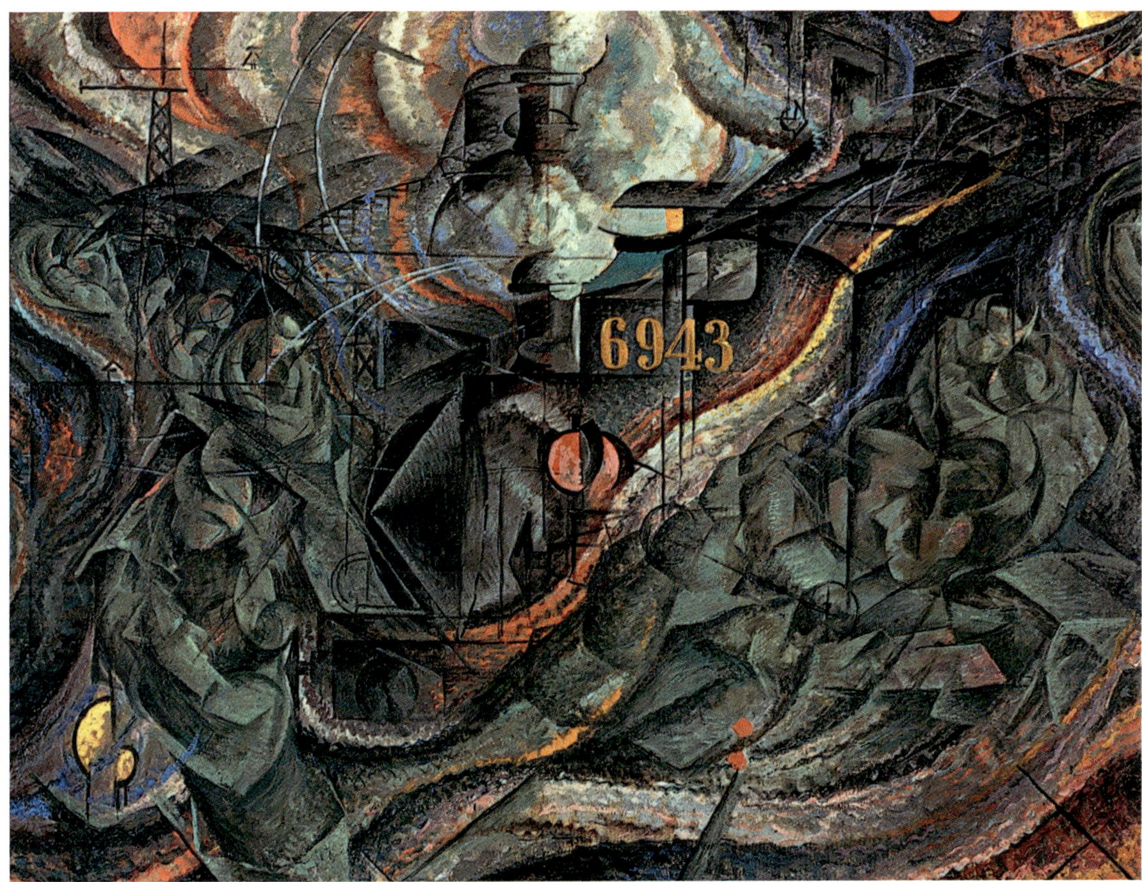

21 Umberto Boccioni, *States of Mind 1: The Farewells*, 1911, oil on canvas.

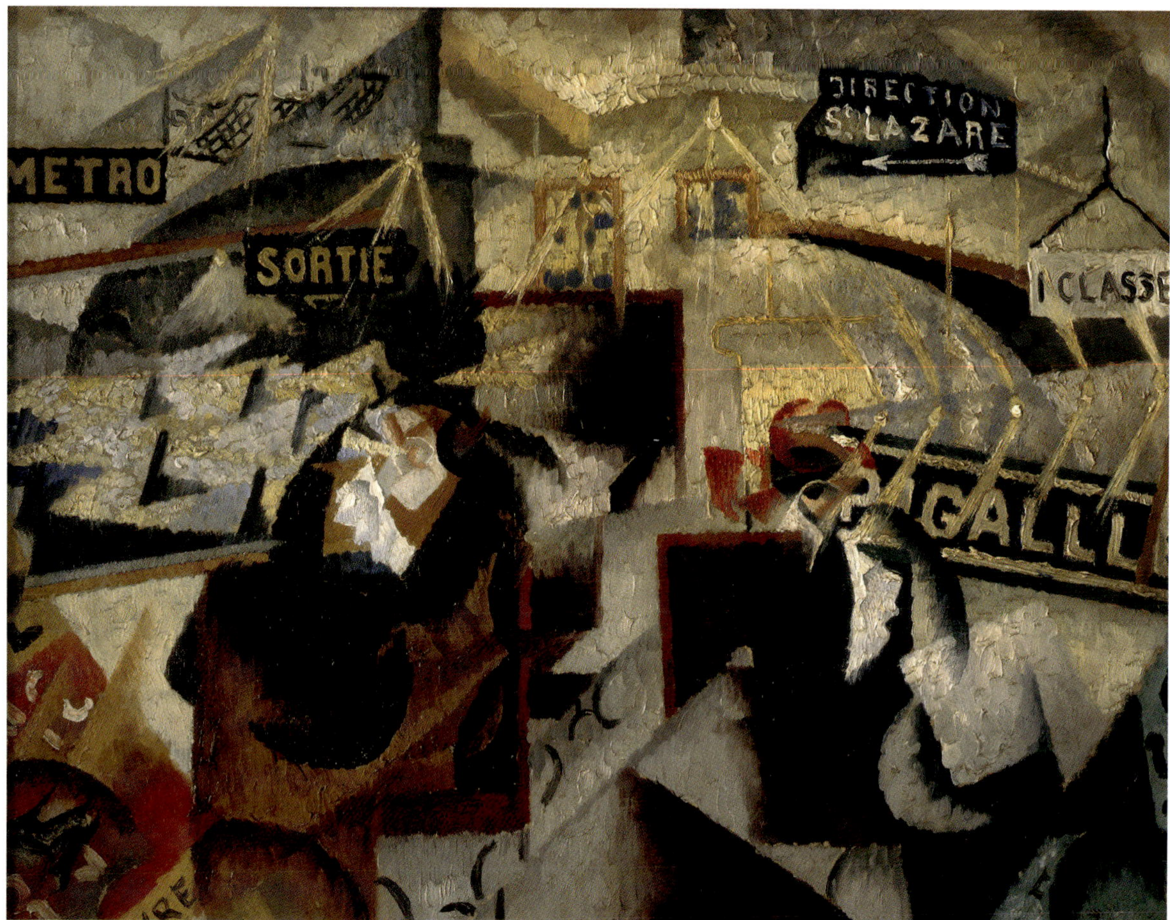

22 Gino Severini, *Nord-Sud*, 1912, oil on canvas.

Rome, expresses a feminine sensibility through the inclusion of an advert for the French perfume 4711 among the collage elements in *Still-life* of 1915. Olga Rozanova, an exhibitor at the *First Futurist Tramway V* exhibition in St Petersburg, created with *The Metronome* (illus. 26) a classic simultanist composition: appended in bold capitals are the words FRANCE AMERIQUE BELGIQUE ANGLETERRE HOLANDE. Artists inspired by Futurism sought to register a global connectedness brought about by new technologies of transport and communication. In 1913, Sonia Delaunay-Turk, Robert Delaunay's Russian wife, collaborated with Blaise Cendrars on his simultanist poem 'La Prose du Transsibérien et de la Petite Jehanne de France' (illus. 25).[33] Billed as 'le premier livre simultané', the narrative prose poem was inspired by Cendrars' travels across Russia in 1904–7. The text, which is coloured, and adjacent abstract designs were meant to be perceived together and to mutually reinforce one another. It was printed as a single long sheet that concertinas; joined end-to-end, the originally envisaged edition of 150 copies would have equalled the height of Delaunay's beloved Eiffel Tower. The folded-up sheet vividly conveys the notion that space-time was in the process of contracting. As Paul Valéry observed: 'For the past twenty years neither matter nor space nor time has been what it was from time immemorial.'[34]

DADA ANTI-ART

Word and image can operate in synergy to reinforce one another. At other times, the configuration may be calculated to produce disjuncture for the purpose of challenging or disrupting ideological representations of reality, as well as constructions of meaning and intelligiblity. Central to most definitions of the historical (Dada-Surrealist) avant-garde is a critique of art and its capitalist support system.[35] Francis Picabia, a prime mover in Paris Dada, and a disabused commentator on the Parisian art world, declared: 'Me, I would like to found a "paternal" School to discourage young people from what our snobs call Art with a capital A. Art is everywhere *except* among the Art dealers and the temples of Art.' This section will concentrate on Marcel Duchamp and Picabia, analysing the role of language and the readymade in the assaults they launched on painting.

Picabia boasted that 'the Dada spirit did not really exist except during three or four years: it was

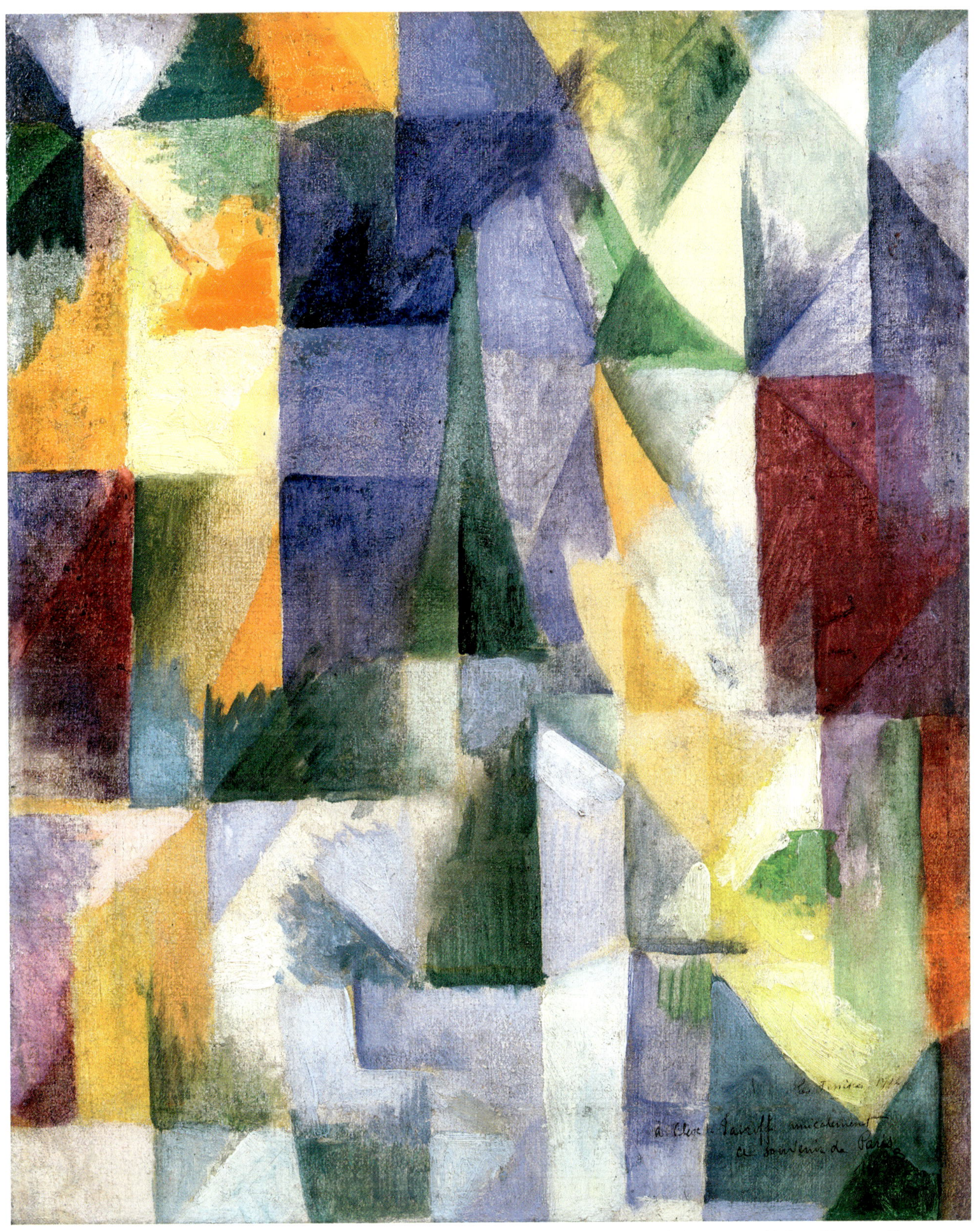

23 Robert Delaunay, *Windows Open Simultaneously (First Part, Third Motif)*, 1912, oil on canvas.

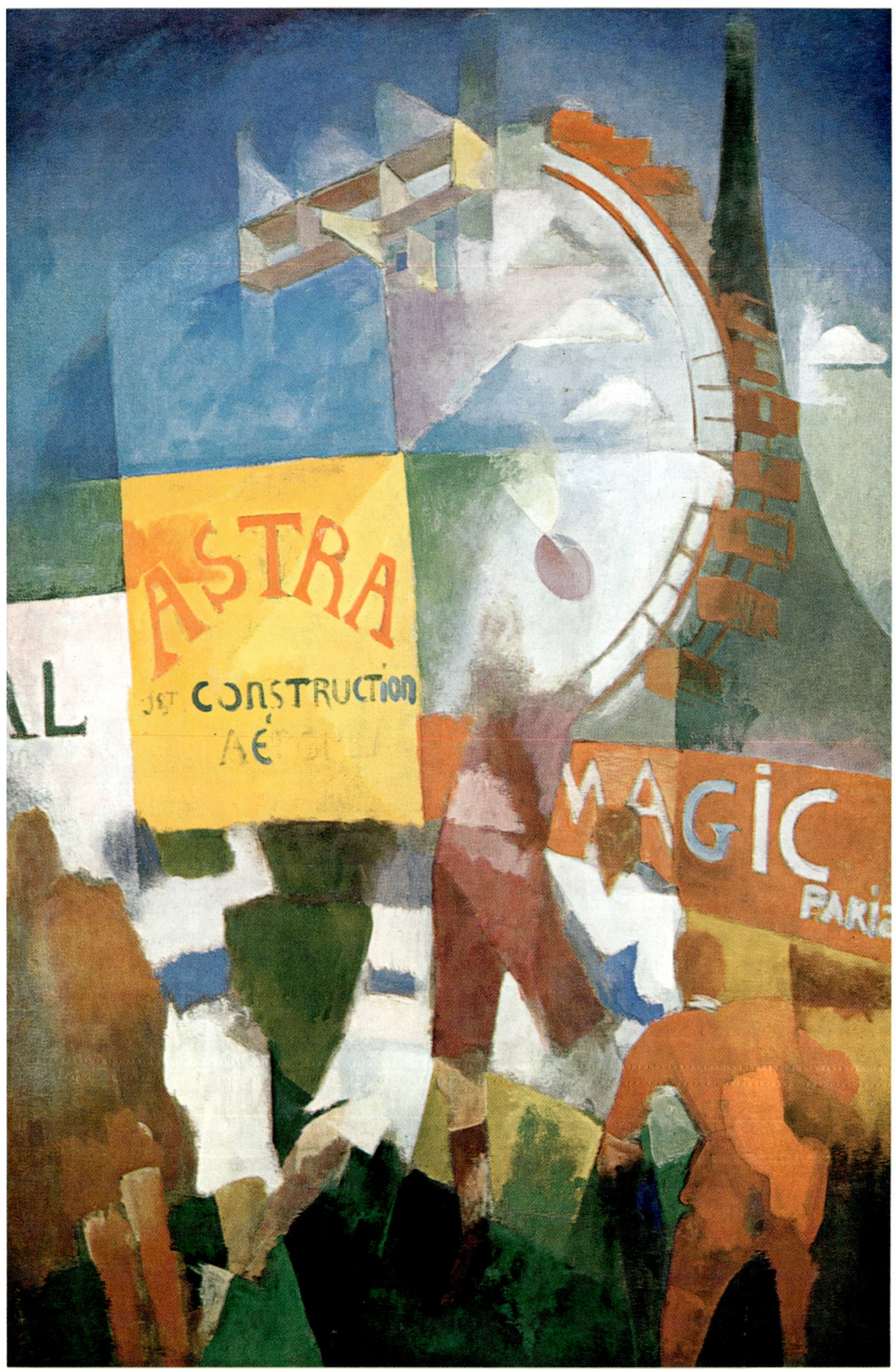

24 Robert Delaunay, *Third Representation: The Cardiff Team*, 1912–13, oil on canvas.

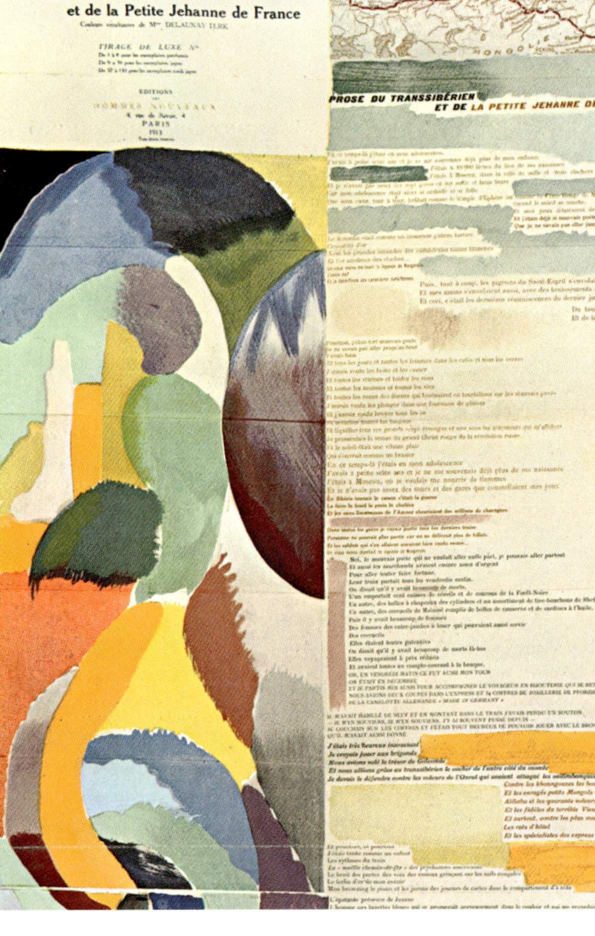
BLAISE CENDRARS
La Prose du Transsibérien
et de la Petite Jehanne de France
PROSE DU TRANSSIBÉRIEN
ET DE LA PETITE JEHANNE DE FRANCE

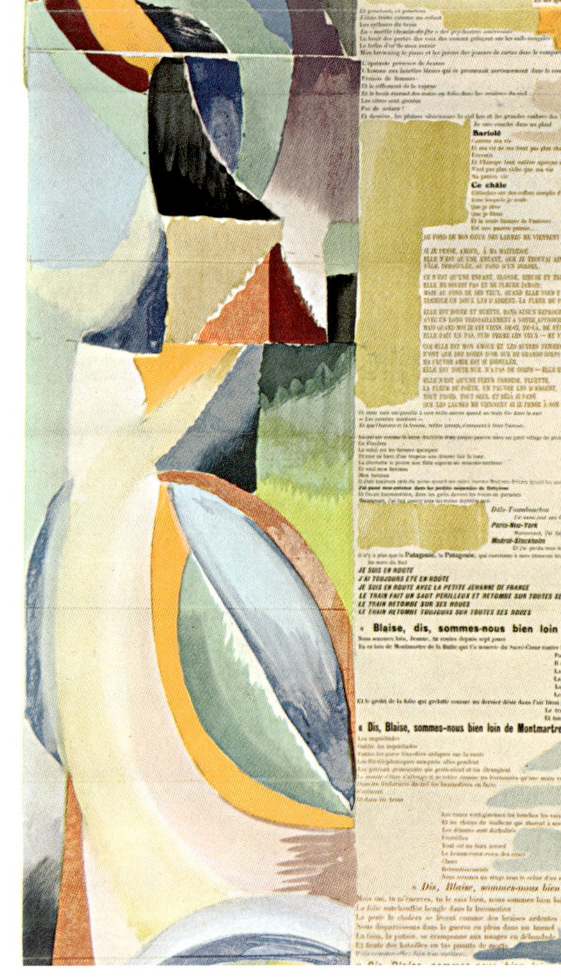
« Blaise, dis, sommes-nous bien loin de Montmartre? »
« Dis, Blaise, sommes-nous bien loin de Montmartre? »

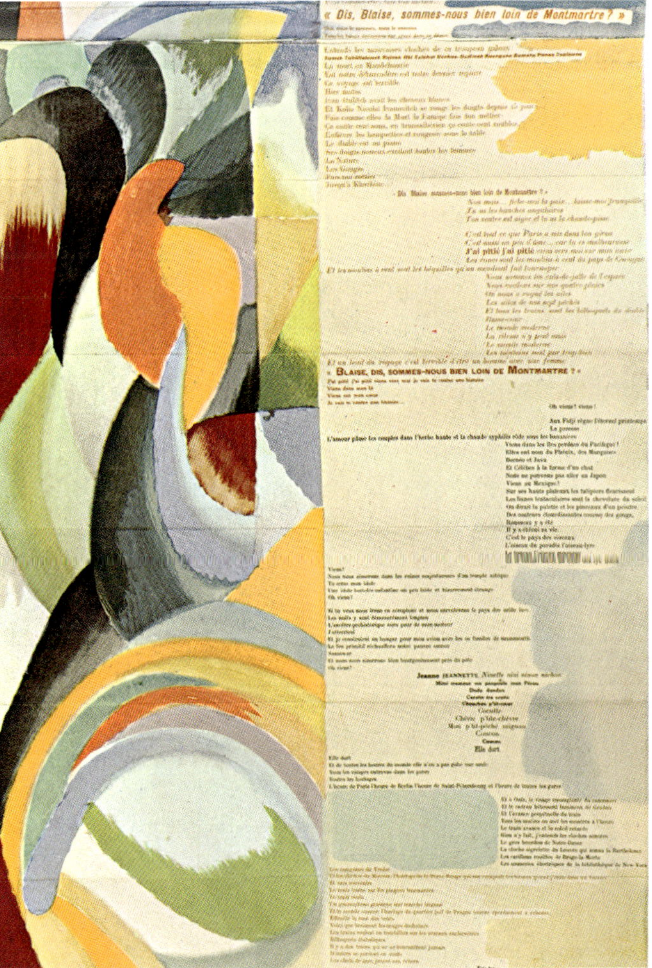
« Dis, Blaise, sommes-nous bien loin de Montmartre? »

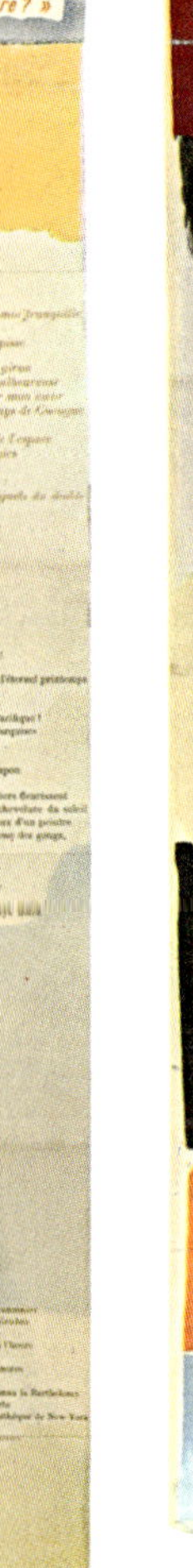

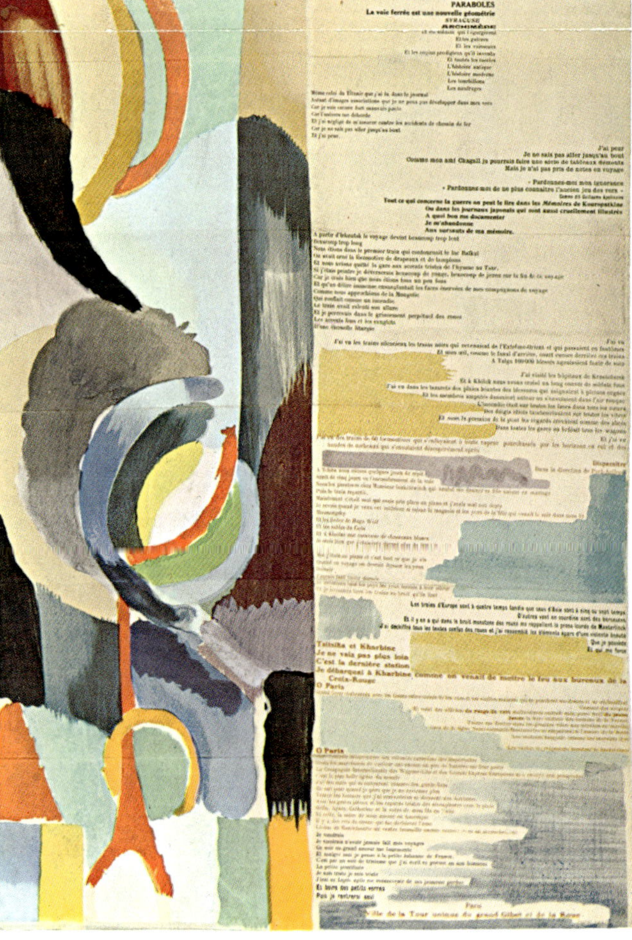
PARABOLES

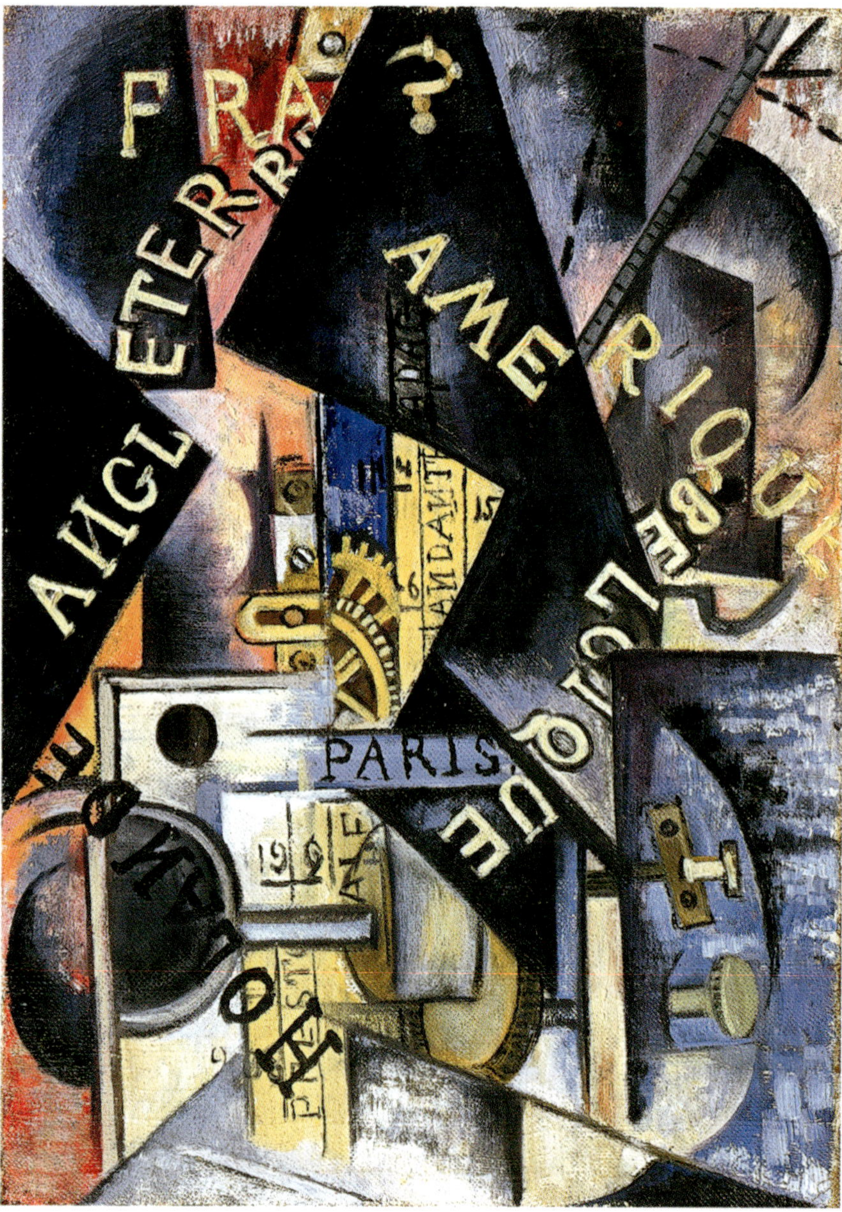

previous page: 25 Blaise Cendrars and Sonia Delaunay, *Prose on the Trans-Siberian Railway and of Little Jehanne of France*, 1913, watercolour and relief print on paper.

26 Olga Rozanova, *The Metronome*, 1915, oil on canvas.

expressed by Duchamp and myself at the end of 1912.' In May of that year, Apollinaire took Duchamp and Picabia to a performance of Raymond Roussel's anarchic play, *Impressions of Africa*, which, together with the work of Alfred Jarry, contributed vitally to forming a Dada mindset. What they derived from these authors was not so much an influence as an attitude, a deadpan humour and taste for the absurd. It has been pointed out that the *blague*, a glib form of humour reliant on *double entendre*, allusion and innuendo, was a stock in trade of music hall entertainment in the period. This has been linked with the punning tendency in Cubism. The word fragment 'jou', already noted, has meanings that are both innocent and obscene: *jouer* (to play) or *jouir* (to come). Duchamp hones the *blague* as a high cultural style.[36] Another factor adding to the indefatigable wordplay of this circle may have been Apollinaire's prescient interest in writing and art of the insane. Marcel Réja, author of *L'Art chez les fous* (1907), observed of the eccentric Jean-Pierre Brisset, another discovery of this avant-garde generation, that: 'Puns are used as pivotal symbols … The author has treated metaphysics, has explained the origins of man, his destiny … everything by means of word games'.[37]

Of the years that narrowly preceded the First World War, Duchamp stated that: 'The machine, motion and eros were things that touched me in a poetic way.' These interests coalesce in the Cubist-inspired *Nude Descending a Staircase* (illus. 27) of 1912, which references the motion photography of Jules-Etienne Marey. When he attempted to exhibit the picture at the Salon des Indépendants, Duchamp was forced to remove it by a committee made up of Cubist painters; this may have been on account of its perceived proximity to their arch rivals, the Italian Futurists. The rebuff set Duchamp on a path that would lead him away from the Cubists, whom he derided for their purely 'retinal' disposition. The title, prominently stencilled on the canvas, is indicative of the role that language would play as inseparable from a highly intellectualized art practice. Whether or not it was deliberately planned, this incident also set a pattern for numerous Dada provocations that followed, including Duchamp's most notorious hoax: a urinal titled *Fountain* (illus. 28) and signed by 'R. Mutt', his submission to the New York Society of Independent Artists in April 1917. An obsession with the machine and eroticism culminated in the monumental work on glass, *The Bride Stripped Bare by Her Bachelors, Even* … of 1916–21, a complex desiring machine in which physiological functions are analogized to mechanistic principles of hydraulics. Reluctant to explain the work, Duchamp declared the title to be simply: 'the bringing together of words to which I added a comma and "even", an adverb which makes no sense, since it relates to nothing in the picture or title.' Buried in the words of the title, MARié (bride) and CELibataires (bachelors), we can discern the letters of his first name. Duchamp also produced copious notes and drawings of a proto-conceptual character that were later collected in facsimile as the *Green Box* (1934). These comprise a textual supplement that makes it impossible to delimit what exactly constitutes the work, which Duchamp regarded as unfinished until it was accidentally shattered during transport, a freak occurrence that paradoxically 'completed' it.

Picabia pursues a roughly parallel itinerary. *Edtaonisl* (illus. 29) and *I See Again in Memory My Beloved Udnie* (1914), works in a post-Cubist idiom, combine the machine with the erotic in a similar fashion to Duchamp. Picabia had complex ambitions for these works, which synthesize personal memories and fugitive subjective impressions. The strange titles incorporate wordplays. *Edtaonisl* is a composite of the letters making up the words 'étoil[e]' and 'dans[e]', an obscure private reference to the star dancer whom Picabia had observed rehearsing on the boat that took him to New York. Picabia's fascination with the multiple meanings of words led him to the *Petit Larousse* dictionary listing of Latin and foreign phrases, which he plundered regularly during the period 1914–18.[38] Apollinaire had been using the 'pink pages' of the *Larousse* well before Picabia and may have introduced him to this source. *I See Again in Memory My Beloved Udnie,* a strange picture title from 1914, derives from an expression used by Virgil in the *Aeneid*: 'Dulces moriens reminiscitur Argos' (Dying, he sees again in memory his beloved Argos). Picabia is deliberately obfuscatory, withholding any clues from the viewer, lacking which the titles and inscriptions are merely baffling.

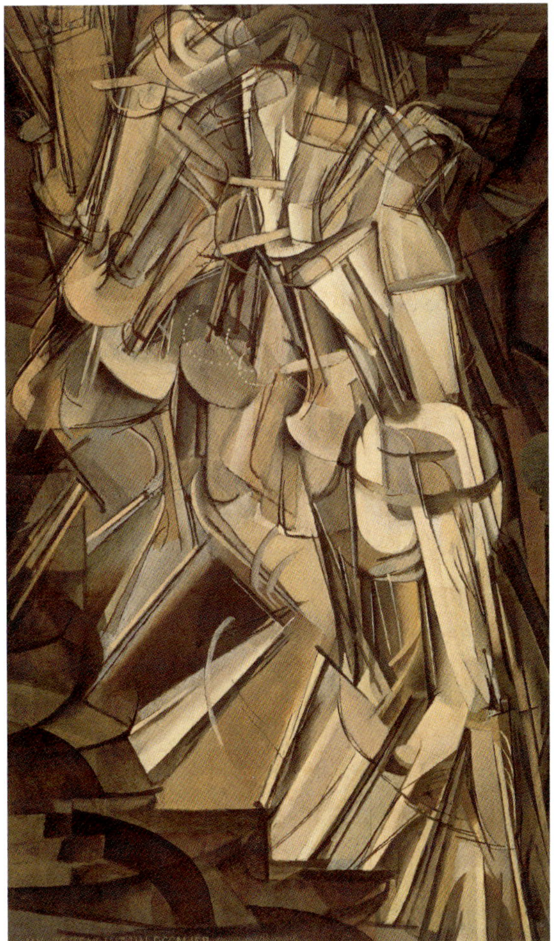

27 Marcel Duchamp, *Nude Descending a Staircase* no. 2, 1912, oil on canvas.

The emergence of a mechanomorphic style while Picabia was in New York was a result of his association with Alfred Stieglitz's '291' Gallery. Stieglitz was a photographer who founded a gallery and a journal, also called *291*, with the aim of promoting the artistic value of photography and only later became involved with modern art. Paralleling

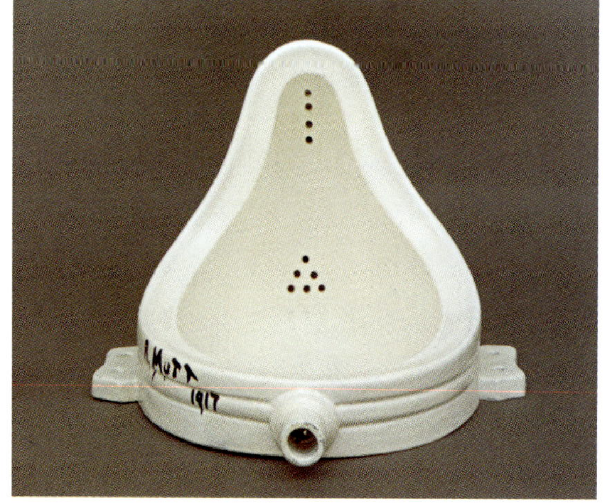

28 Marcel Duchamp, *Fountain*, 1917, porcelain.

Duchamp's rejection of traditional oil painting, Picabia undertook a series of portraits using found machine images in an attempt to bypass aesthetic decision-making. Mechanical attributes serve to denote the subject of the portrait. Depicted with 'the precision and relief of mail order catalogues', in the words of Picabia's partner, Gabrielle Buffet, they are only minimally transformed in comparison with their sources in industrial catalogues. Poetic inscriptions set up a tension between the languages of culture and engineering and operate as a counterpoint to the found machine image, diverting and subverting its rational imperatives. Just as Duchamp turned to glass as a support to avoid the noble materials of oil and canvas, Picabia used cardboard and introduced metallic gold and silver paint into his work. The mechanical was thus a weapon in a campaign against art: the painterly is eschewed in favour of an impersonal, diagrammatic layout. *Here, This is Stieglitz* (illus. 30) and *Guillaume Apollinaire* of 1918 are examples of Picabia's machine portraits. Stieglitz is straightforwardly portrayed by means of a camera. In the second case, the diagram may have suggested to Picabia the poet's corpulent figure. The phrases in both images are filched from the *Petit Larousse*. 'Je ne mourrais pas tout entier', on the second image, is part of a passage from Horace asserting the immortality of a poet through his verse. In 1924, reminiscing about their meeting, Picabia affirmed: 'Apollinaire would certainly have been a Dada, like Duchamp and me, had he not died prematurely.'

The Duchamp readymade was a Trojan horse whose incursion into the institutional spaces of art was pivotal to Dada's nihilistic project. Signing a found industrial object and thereby designating it as a work of art was an act that initiated a far-reaching philosophical questioning of the cultural categories of art and authorship. Consistent with Duchamp's whimsical pursuit of 'anti-sense', the labels are as deadpan and inscrutable as the found industrial objects to which they are applied: a snow shovel is titled *In Advance of a Broken Arm*; a birdcage containing marble sugar cubes is inscribed *Why Not Sneeze Rrose Sélavy?* The assisted readymade *Apolinere Enameled* (illus. 31) of 1917, made by altering the wording of an advertisement for Sapolin enamel, pokes fun at painting, as well as paying homage, once again, to Apollinaire. *L.H.O.O.Q* (illus. 32), a postcard reproduction of the Mona Lisa to which Duchamp added a moustache and goatee, has become a *locus classicus* for Dada's anti-art spirit. Spoken aloud, the letters of the hand-printed caption sound like 'Elle a chaud au cul' (She has a hot butt), a bawdy joke at the

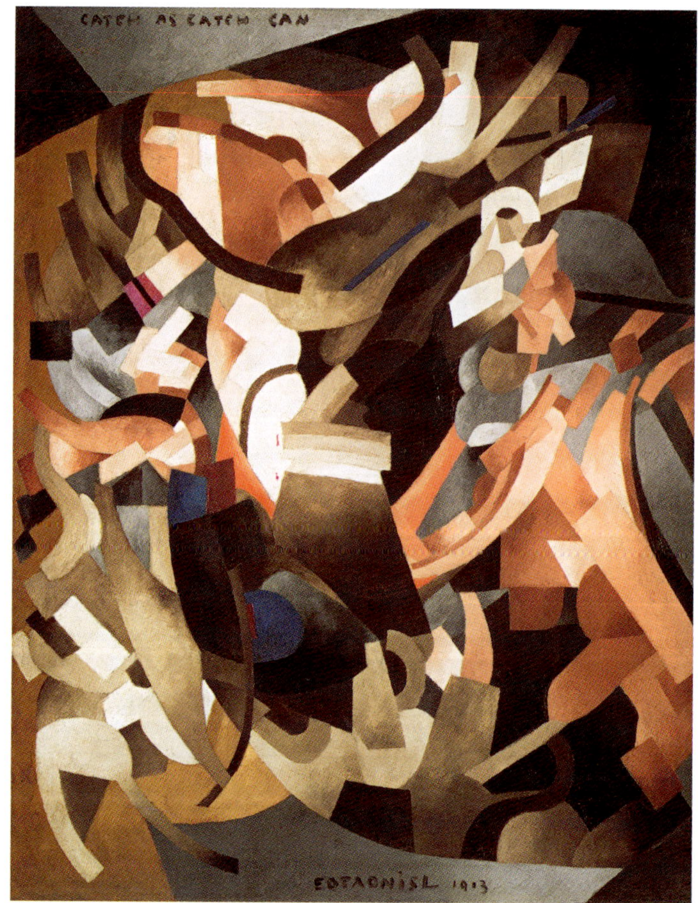

29 Francis Picabia, *Catch as Catch Can ('Edtaonisl')*, 1913, oil on canvas.

expense of one of art's most revered icons. This economical gesture has cast a long shadow across twentieth-century art. Dalí, who had himself photographed as the Mona Lisa with a real moustache, in a bid to outdo Duchamp quite possibly, stated that L.H.O.O.Q 'can be taken quite adequately as the death of modern painting'.[39] In cahoots with the cast object, the lowly pun would keep up its playfully subversive job, as in the vaguely repellent *Objet-dard (Dart-Object)* of 1951. A plaster cast of the side of the artist's face was titled, predictably, *With My Tongue in Cheek* (1959). Rising to the challenge, the American artist Bruce Nauman made a work, *From Hand to Mouth*, that is a literal cast of the respective parts of his own body.

Fresh Widow (1920), a work premised on a casual slip of the tongue (widow-window), was the occasion for the public début of Rose Sélavy, upon whom Duchamp bestows artistic copyright for the piece. Reputedly, Duchamp had considered adopting a Jewish name before settling upon a female alter ego. Some have seen a reference to this initial idea in the combination of *sel* (from 'Marcel') and *lavy* (as in the Jewish family name 'Levy'). Her name, modified to Rrose Sélavy, becomes a pun on 'Eros, c'est la vie' (Love is life). In 1923 Duchamp adopted the format of a comic wanted poster to announce Rrose Sélavy as an alias for the wanted man, himself, who is represented on the poster by two mugshot photographs. As a kind of readymade, or 'ready maid', Rrose is a conceit through which Duchamp places at a distance his own authorship and identity. Her existence has also been seen as interrogating the masculine gendered character of artistic creativity, but whether that was the intended purpose or whether it allowed him to usurp female otherness is a more open question. The relentless, laddish punning and banter of Duchamp and Picabia is, from a present-day vantage point, decidedly un-politically correct. Picabia's *Portrait d'une jeune fille Americaine dans l'état de nudité* (1915), an image of a spark plug, typifies the wholly uncritical sexism of their brand of humour, in which a woman as virgin, bride or widow is the inevitable butt of a joke.[40] Man Ray, who was introduced to Duchamp and Picabia at Stieglitz's gallery, became a willing co-conspirator. In *Violon d'Ingres* (illus. 33) of 1924, two sound

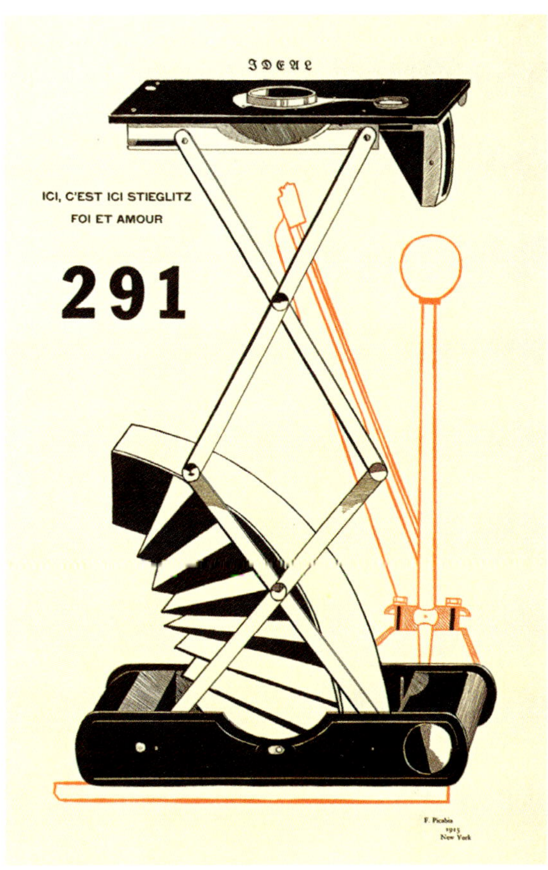

30 Francis Picabia, *Here, This is Stieglitz / Faith and Love*, 1915, cover for the journal *291*, nos. 5–6 (July–August 1915).

holes are tattooed on the back of a woman posed in the manner of one of Ingres' Orientalist nudes. Exploiting a visual rhyme of the female body with musical instrument, Man Ray portrays the female subject as a plaything or instrument of male desire. The title plays on the expression 'violon d'Ingres', which means a hobby. Notwithstanding the subtle play between verbal and visual registers, the work epitomises a problematic tendency to objectification in Surrealist images of the female body. An earlier work by Man Ray (who was born Emmanuel Radnitsky, the son of Russian Jewish immigrants) more innocently forms a landscape out of the letters of his adopted name.

As a protagonist of Paris Dada, Picabia utilized painting as a contingent weapon in a war of provocation against the art establishment. His two submissions to the Salon des Indépendants, *Danse de Saint-Guy* (illus. 34) of 1919–20 and *La veuve joyeuse* of 1921, were calculated to produce a scandal. Founded as an alternative to the official Salon, the Indépendants prided itself on having no jury, but Picabia's submissions tested the limits of the organizers' tolerance. The first work consisted of an empty frame containing a signature, title, and a description on strips of paper connected by string – the bare essentials of a painting! His other work

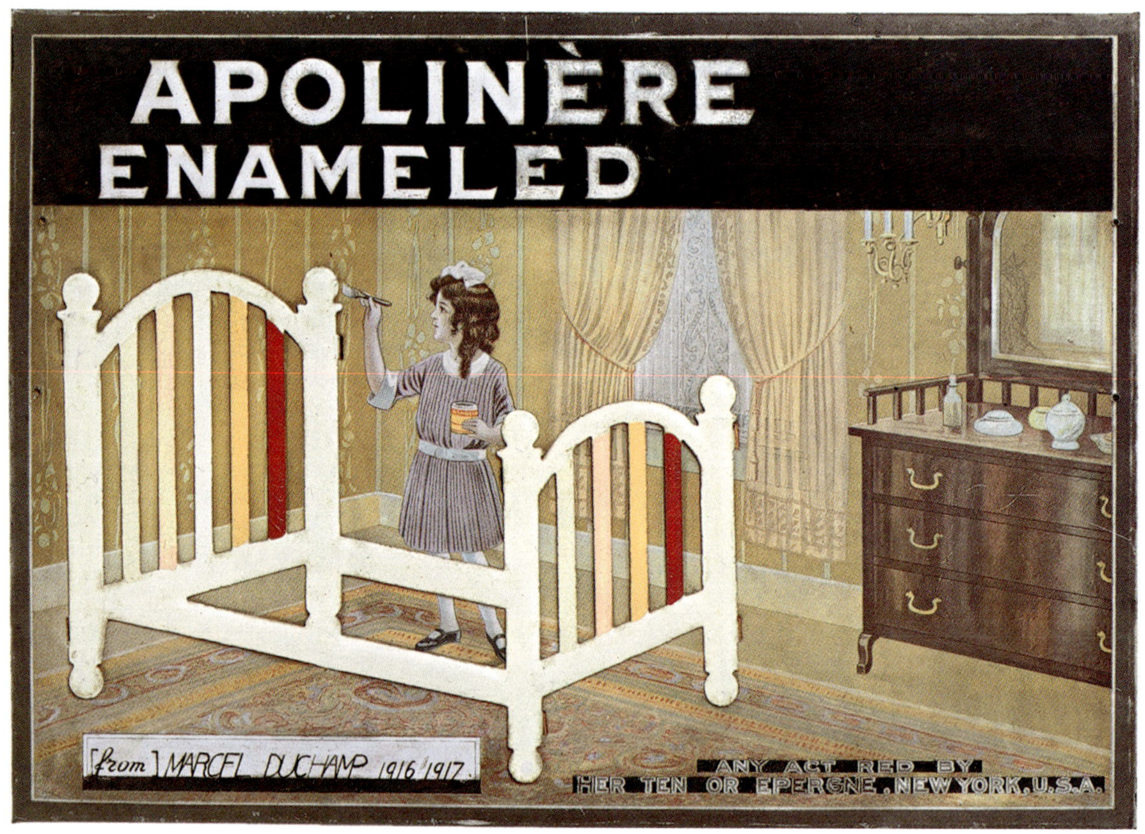

31 Marcel Duchamp, *Apolinère Enameled*, 1917, gouache and pencil on painted tin (advertising sign for Sapolin Enamel) mounted on board.

fell foul of the ruling that photography was excluded. In a similar vein, *Cacodylic Eye* (illus. 35) of 1921, dispatched to the Autumn Salon, mocks the idea that the value of a work of art depends upon a signature. Picabia, an inveterate socialite, collected all the signatures of his friends. The strange title refers to treatment he was receiving for an eye complaint. Louis Aragon reports that Picabia made a picture on a blackboard that was meant to be publicly erased as an attack on the values of permanence associated with high culture. It has disappeared without trace. Another of Picabia's targets was the resurgence of artistic tradition in the aftermath of the First World War. *The Vine-leaf* of 1922, a satirical pastiche of Ingres' *Oedipus and the Sphinx*, was over-painted on another picture to serve a polemical purpose of lampooning the vogue for French classicism, of which Picasso was the most high profile convert. An inscription on this work referring to 'le dessin française' spells out the target of his satire. In a similar mocking spirit, literature is made the butt of a lewd joke ('Lits et ratures') in one of Picabia's cover designs for the journal that provided a platform for the Paris Dadaists. Spelt backwards as 'Erutarettil', it is a

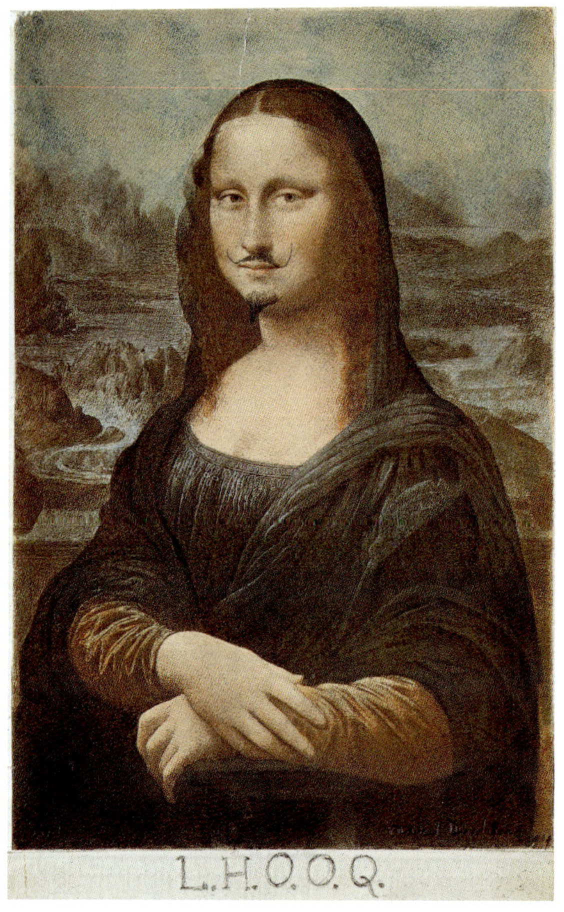

32 Marcel Duchamp, *L.H.O.O.Q.*, 1919, pencil on a reproduction of the *Mona Lisa*.

banner under which a proto-Surrealist canon of writers (de Sade, Rimbaud, Lautréamont, Jarry) is arrayed, their names in different sizes and typography to assert a hierarchy of proximity or distance. Max Ernst would later personalize the genealogical format of this table in order to present his favourite poets and painters of the past.

Echoes of Duchamp and Picabia abound in Max Ernst's use of language during his Cologne Dada phase.[41] An anti-art impulse is attested by the ironic title of a sequence of lithographs, *Fiat Modes – pereat ars* (*Let There Be Fashion. Down With Art*) of 1919 that mimic Picabia's use of Latin. He also produced object assemblages that evince an iconoclastic intent, one of which was cheekily titled *Objet dad'art* (*c.* 1920). Also in the context of Cologne Dada, Ernst produced machinist images with absurd titles and captions that have a clear derivation from works by Picabia that appeared in the *Anthologie Dada* of 1918 or in the issue of Picabia's *391* published in Zurich in February 1919. A picture of an army tank, incongruously titled in French, *Farewell My Beautiful Land of* MARIE LAURENCIN (1919), references Picabia's portrait of the same individual. *Little Machine Constructed by Minimax Dadamax* (illus. 36) of 1919 consists of two tottering figures, one male and one female, composed of stencilled letters. The humorous combination of the mechanical and the erotic is once again reminiscent of Picabia. There are insistent allusions to the recent war in such works as *The Roaring of Ferocious Soldiers*, *Hypertrophic Trophy*, *The Assimilative Threads' Attack Plans Found Out in Time on the Stronghold of Dada 1: 300,000*, 1920. These titles are flippant rather than respectful in tone and provocatively mix French with German words in a way that could be construed as unpatriotic. It is a truism that Dada arose in part as a reaction to the horrors and insanity of war. Ernst, who served in the German trenches, later stated that he died in 1914 only to be resurrected in 1919. The impact of this experience and its role in determining his artistic vocation ought not be underestimated. Stencilled roulette wheels appear in a several of these works, alluding to a Dada preference for chance over logic or reason. Whereas Picabia invariably opts for the one-liner joke, Ernst's humour is more whimsical, indirect.

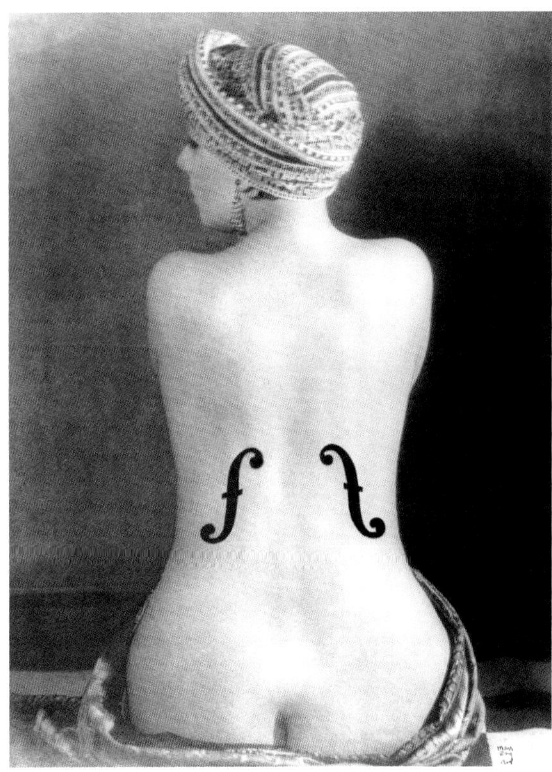

33 Man Ray, *Le Violon d'Ingres*, 1924, gelatin silver print.

He takes medical and scientific plates from encyclopedias, adding complex mixtures of collage and overpainting that transform the source image and subvert their pedagogic intent. Adopting a similar format to Paul Klee, Ernst accompanies the image with a lengthy handwritten poetic caption – Kurt Schwitters had proposed that a title might be a poem about a picture.[42] A number of these evocatively poetic images were exhibited in Paris at the gallery *Au sans pareil* in May 1920. An invitation card declared the works 'beyond painting'; in retrospect, Breton would designate them as the first Surrealist images. Subsequently, while still living in Germany, Ernst collaborated at a distance with the Surrealist poet Paul Eluard to produce two illustrated books, *Repetitions* and *Misfortunes of the Immortals*, that combine his collages with automatic poetry, one drawing inspiration from the other. This was an obvious prelude to his move to Paris where he joined the Surrealist group. At the end of the 1920s, Ernst reverted to making collages once again, inventing an entirely new format, the collage novel, consisting of sequences of images that employ Victorian illustrated 'trash' novels as source material.[43] In *Femme 100 têtes* (1929), a punning title meaning 'woman with a hundred (*cent*) heads' or 'woman without (*sans*) a head', the images are arranged in chapters with the sequence comprising a loose, dream-like narrative reflecting Ernst's interests in Freud and hysteria. Relating to the theme of a split or multiple self, Ernst's self-

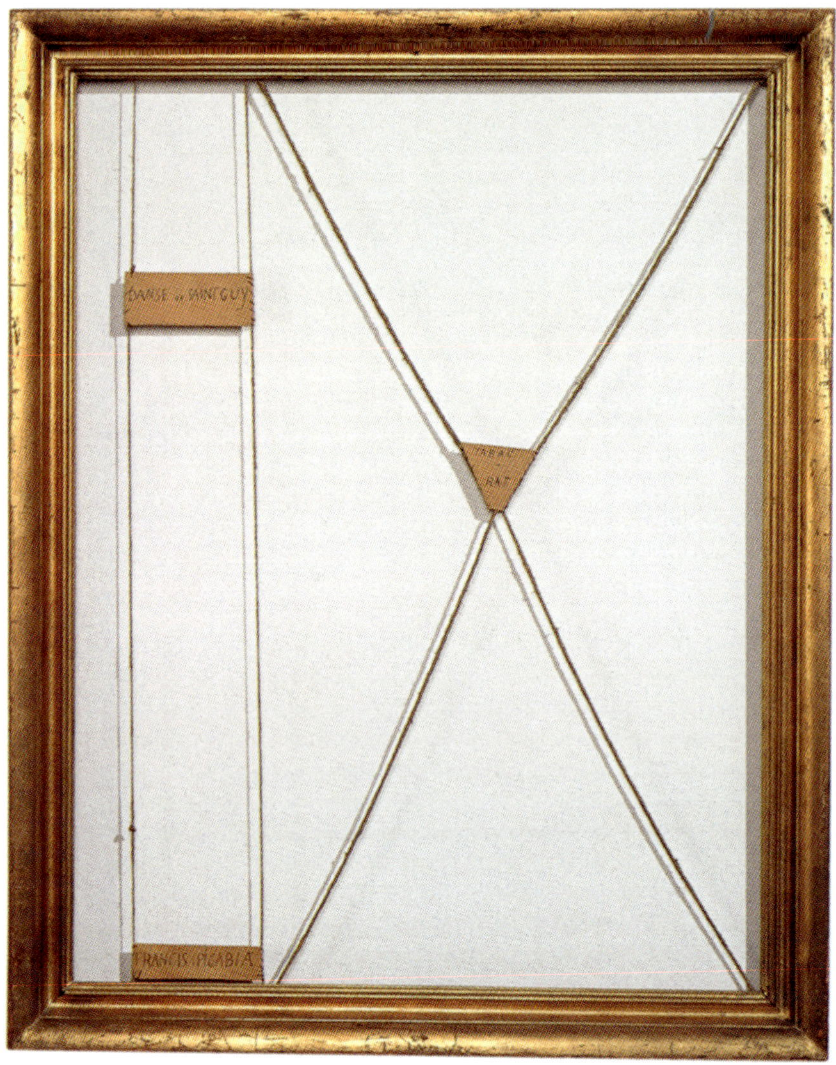

34 Francis Picabia, *Tabac-Rat*, or *Danse de Saint-Guy*, 1919–49, cardboard, ink, string, and wood frame.

conscious play with his own identity also suggests links with the foregoing group of artists. An early self-portrait photomontage (1920) is inscribed with the invented sobriquet of DadaMax. In the picture *Oedipus Rex* (1923), one of a number of works based on psychoanalytic themes, Ernst significantly reverses the usual positions of signature and title, inferring that he is an Oedipal son. Later on, around 1930, Ernst adopted as an alter-ego a bird persona called 'Loplop' – the repeated consonants of this made-up name recall the word Dada. He also plays upon his own initials, M. E.

Anemic Cinema (illus. 37–40) of 1926, a film signed by Rrose Sélavy, arises out of Dada experiments with language. Duchamp's fascination with optical illusions, and his bent for intricate wordplay ('anemic' is an anagram of 'cinema'), are both in evidence. Spiralling lines that pulsate inward and outward alternate with similar spiral lines of text that rotate as one attempts to read them: the eye is put in pursuit of a meaning that constantly eludes it. *Anemic Cinema* references the textual elements that are ubiquitous in silent film but eschews their narrative, explanatory function. The rhythmic alternation of word and image, the resultant pattern of interferences, exemplifies the role of language in Dada for disrupting the self-sufficiency and plenitude of the visual image. It also bears comparison with other abstract experimental films being produced in a French avant-garde context at this juncture. Léger and Dudley Murphy's *Ballet mécanique* (1924) incorporates typographic elements in the form of a newspaper story about the theft of a pearl necklace worth 5,000,000 francs. The camera close-ups of a string of zeros results in a punning visual rhyme with the lost pearls. Man Ray's *Etoile de mer* (1929) intercalates lines of poetry by Robert Desnos with filmic imagery to set up a complex, indirect relation of image and text. All these films, while

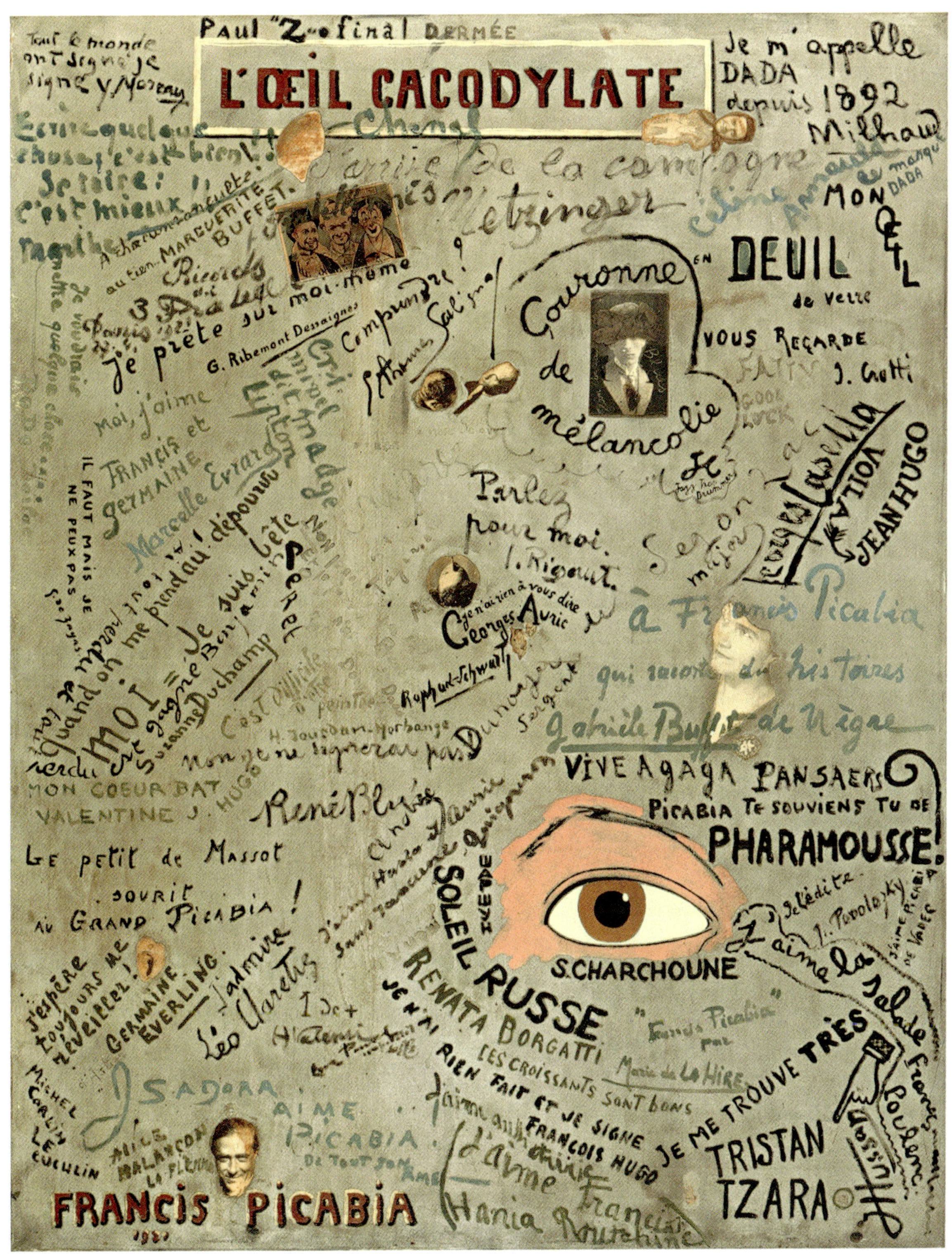

35 Francis Picabia, *Cacodylic Eye*, 1921, oil with collage on canvas.

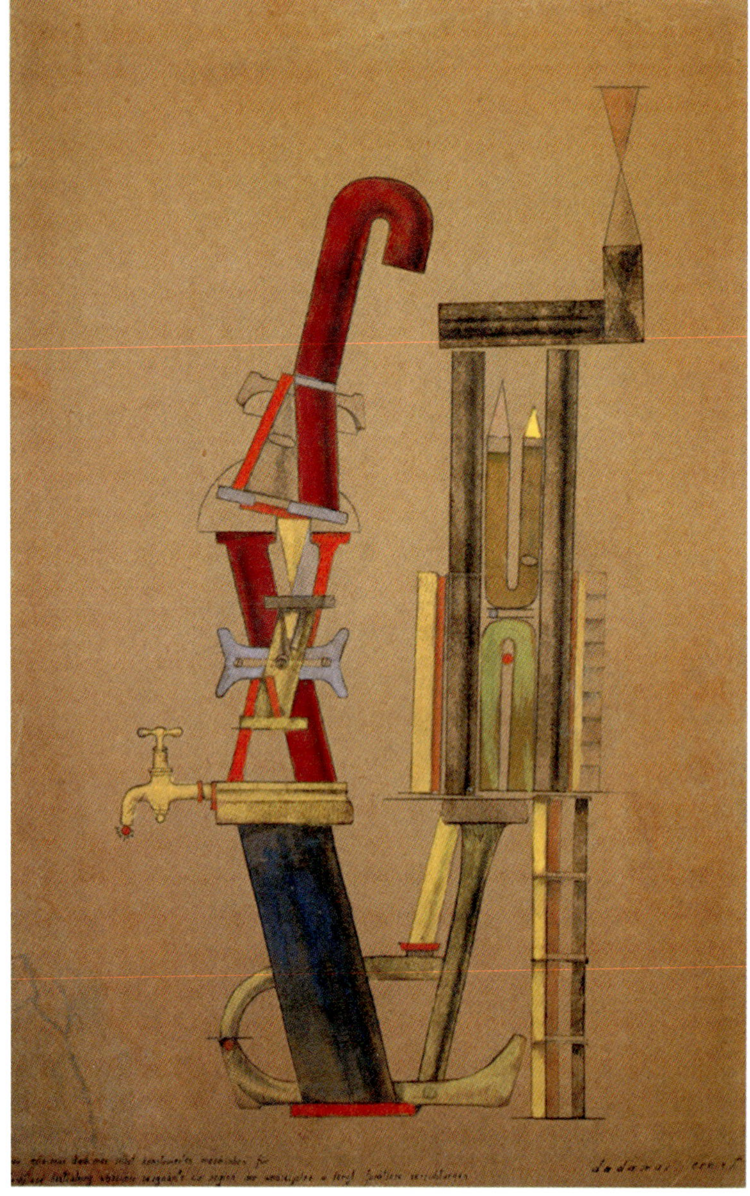

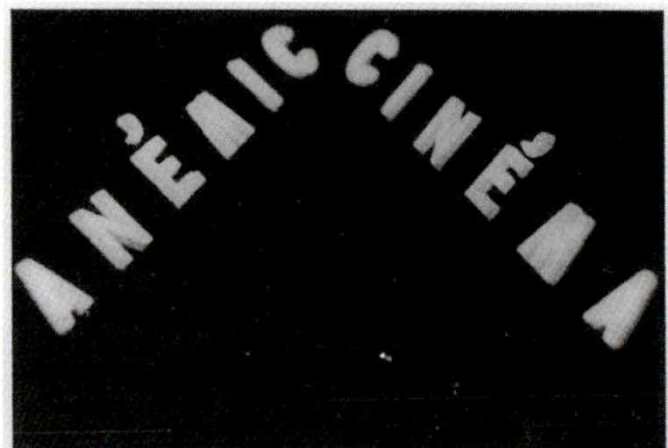

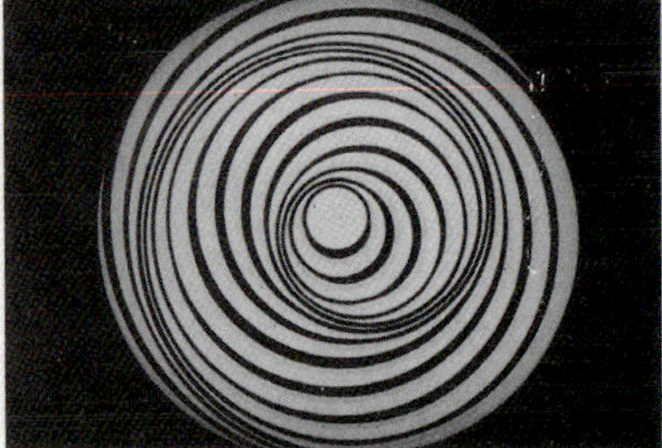

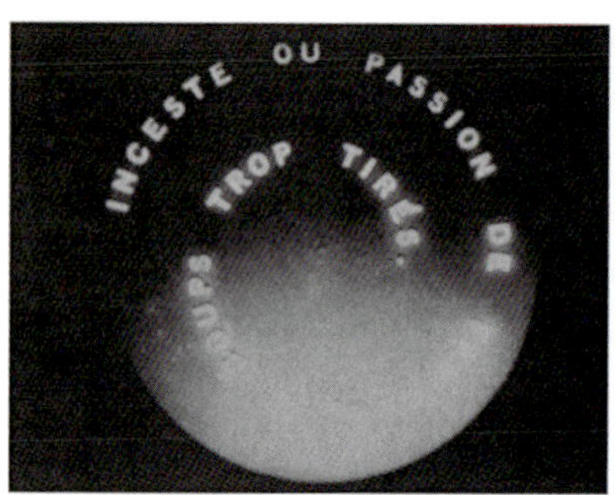

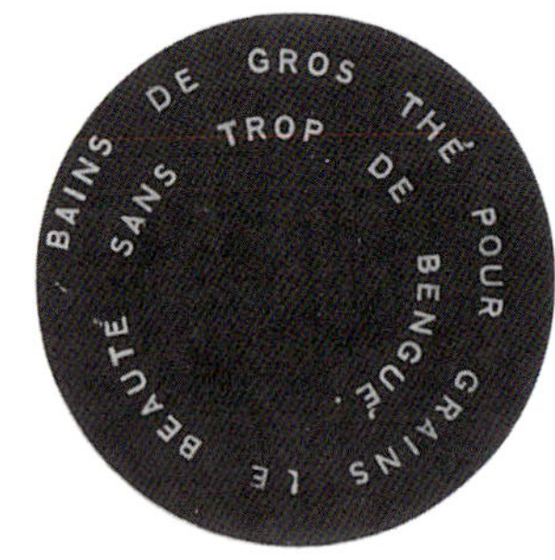

36 Max Ernst, *Little Machine Constructed by Minimax Dadamax in Person*, 1919–20, pencil rubbing of printer's blocks, ink, watercolour and gouache on paper.

37–40 Marcel Duchamp, Film stills from *Anemic Cinema*, 1926.

emphatically anti-narrative, contradict calls by formalist proponents of art film, notably Germaine Dulac, for the medium to be purged of all literary and textual elements.

MONTAGE AND POLITICS

Dada arose as a multifocal phenomenon, having a distinctive character in each of the widely separated metropolitan locations where it sprang up more or less simultaneously. Apart from a spirit of negation that all its manifestations shared, it is not easily generalizable in consequence of lacking a core programme, unlike Surrealism, which followed it. The circumstances of war and defeat and resultant political turmoil conditioned the character of Berlin Dada, which was more virulent in its political and social critique than Dada in either Paris or New York. George Grosz's mordantly pessimistic wartime caricatures (illus. 41, 42) epitomize the mood of Dada in Germany.

Believing that painting had been rendered defunct, a number of artists associated with Berlin Dada turned to photomontage, a technique they developed from Cubist collage. Raoul Hausmann, one of the claimants to the invention of photomontage, explained: 'This term translates our aversion to playing the artist, and thinking of ourselves as engineers (hence our preference for workmen's overalls) we meant to construct, to assemble [*montieren*] our works.'[44] The actual practice of photomontage antedates the use of the term, which apparently was not accepted coinage at the time of the Berlin Dada Fair in 1920. On the other hand, the radically subversive critical and communicative potential of the new medium, which combined the technology of the photograph with typographic elements inspired by Futurism, was quickly realized. Hausmann again: 'the idea of photomontage was as revolutionary as its content, its form as subversive as the application of the photograph and printed texts which, together, are transformed into a static film.' A photograph of Raoul Hausmann and Hannah Höch at the Berlin Dada Fair shows them flanked on the one side by Höch's complex allegorical photomontage *Cut with the Dada Kitchen Knife through the Last Weimar Beer-Belly Cultural Epoch in Germany*, 1919–20 (illus. 46) and on the other by the wall slogan 'Art is Dead! Long live the machine art of Tatlin!' The work by Hausmann placed immediately above it, *Dada Wins*! (illus. 43), which incorporates mechanical apparatus as well as mechanically reproduced imagery, confidently proclaims Dada victorious over art, a revealing example of how avant-garde exhibition installations orchestrated images with texts.

Walter Benjamin, writing amidst the ominous conditions in Nazi Germany in 1936, concluded that fascism's aestheticizing of politics left no option for the Left but to politicize art.[45] He had in mind no doubt photomontages by the likes of John Heartfield. *Adolf – The Superman – Who Swallows Gold and Spouts Junk* and *Millions Stand Behind Me*, icons of anti-fascism in the 1930s, were produced by Heartfield as covers for the Communist daily AIZ (*Arbeiter-Illustrierte Zeitung*). The X-Ray source in the former implies an ability to penetrate beneath the surface, in order to reveal a concealed truth, indicative for Heartfield of the nature of photomontage. When Heartfield shows us the meaning of the Hitler salute, as the subtitle states, it is the capitalist backers of Hitler's adventurism who are exposed. Heartfield's montages are meant to be read rather than consumed as aesthetic objects, according to

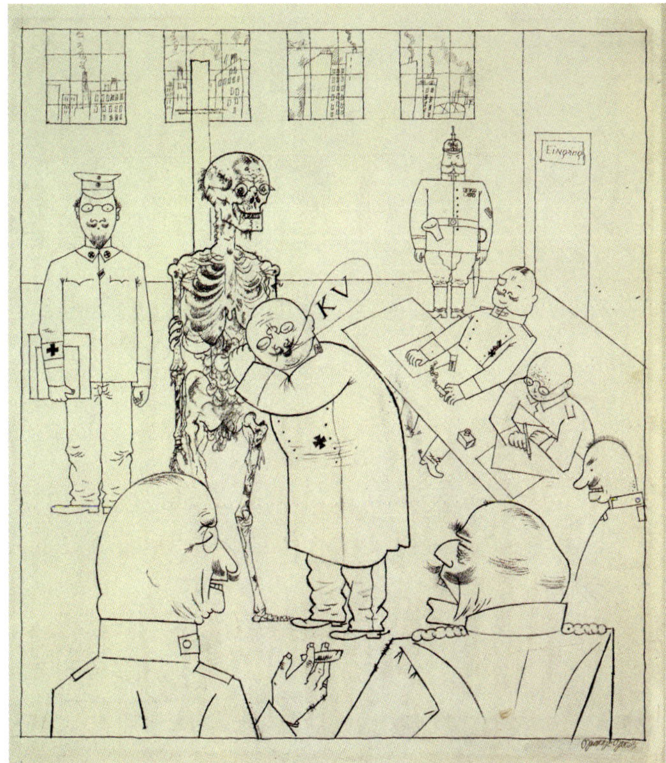

41 George Grosz, *The Faith Healers*, 1918, india ink on paper.

Peter Bürger, who argues that Heartfield reverted to the archaic form of the emblem: 'bring[ing] together an image and two different texts, an (often coded) title (*inscriptio*) and a lengthier explanation (*subscriptio*).'[46] Hannah Höch similarly deploys word and image in the service of politics, but underpinned by a very different notion of the political: mainstream Leftist politics in his case versus proto-feminist in hers. *Da-Dandy* (illus. 45) engages the interwar phenomenon of the emancipated New Woman, in part a journalistic and advertising stereotype; she also deals with the relatively novel phenomenon of stardom and celebrity, and media advertising, through which normative gender ideals are relayed to a mass audience.[47] *The Beautiful Girl* (illus. 47) of 1919–20 appears to replicate the tropes of the advertising industry, combining BMW insignia with the female body as objects of desire. The artist at top right peers out from behind this crowded layer of imagery that intervenes like a screen between herself and the viewer, bracketing it off and producing an ironic distance. Though her work is not devoid of humour, one has to imagine Höch as altogether more sceptical about the glib conflation of woman and machine than Picabia in his machine portraits. Hausmann salutes the machine art of Tatlin, but unlike their Soviet counterparts, the machine images in the montages of the Berlin Dadaists

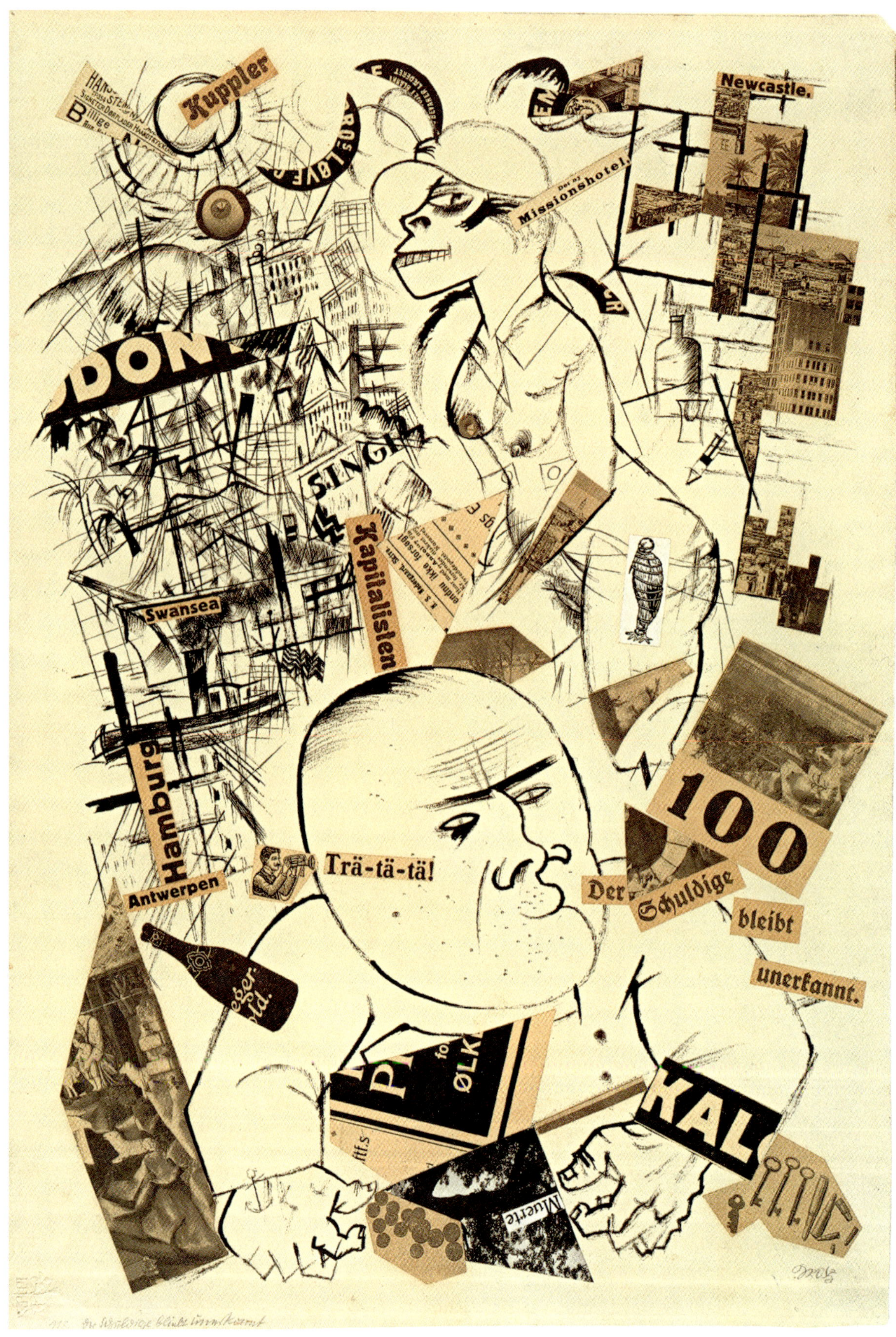

42 George Grosz, *The Guilty One Remains Unknown*, 1919.

express little sense of optimism about technological modernity; rather, the inclusion of machine images in such works as *Dada Wins!* or *Tatlin at Home*, both 1920, seems to be for their absurd incongruity and anti-artistic connotations. In the same period, Höch also produced a series of collages collectively titled *From an Ethnographic Museum* that superficially resemble the Die Brücke artist's incorporation of primitive art references, but that extend her deconstruction of gender to an interrogation of ethnic identity and difference.

Kurt Schwitters, in Hanover, broke the mould of German Dada. Committed to the preservation of a concept of art, he soon fell foul of his more politicized compatriots. Schwitters blended Dada with elements of expressionism, which the Berlin Dadaists viscerally opposed. The overt sentimentality of his poem Anna Blume, and its co-option of the term Dada, attracted the ire of Richard Heulsenbeck and the other Dadaists. In 1920 he announced the founding of Merz as a breakaway movement: 'Huelsendadaismus is politically orien-

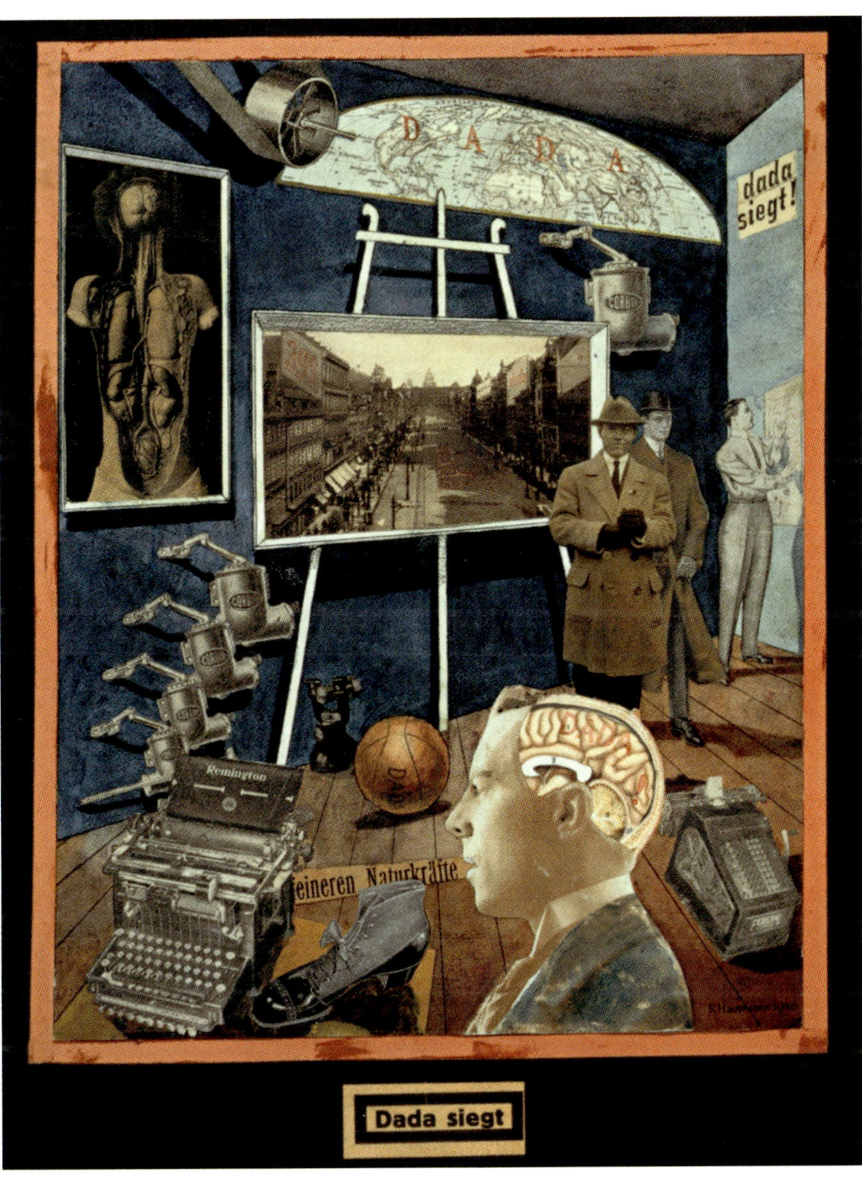

43 Raoul Hausmann, *Dada Wins!*, 1920, photomontage and collage with watercolour on paper.

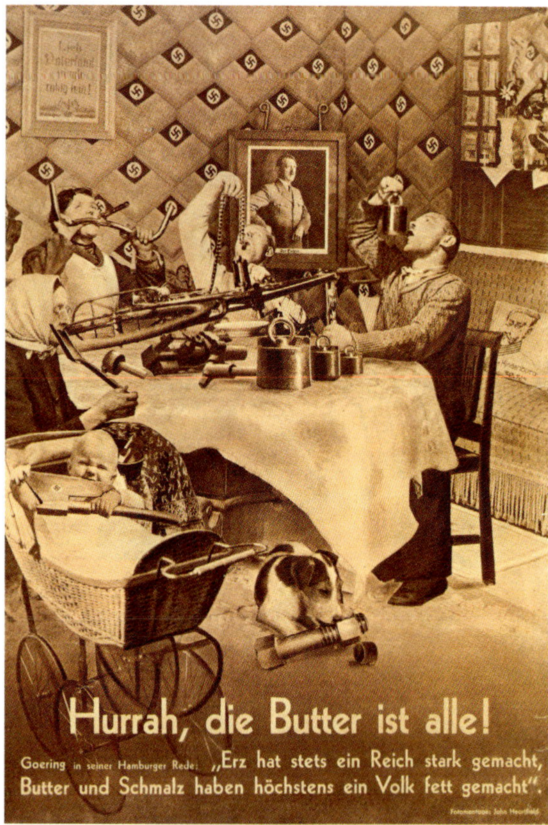

44 John Heartfield, *Hurrah, the Butter is all Gone!*, 1935, photomontage.

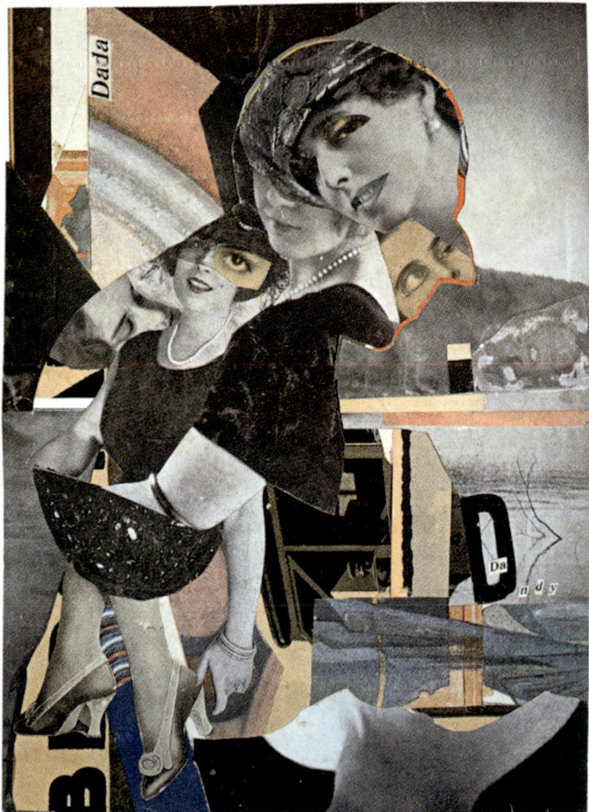

45 Hannah Höch, *Da-Dandy*, 1919, photomontage and collage.

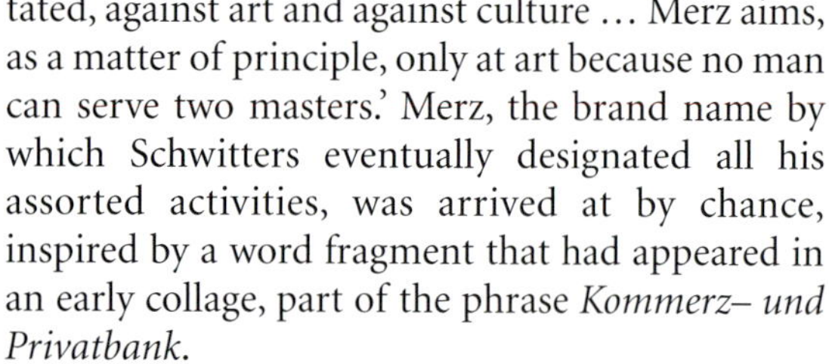

tated, against art and against culture ... Merz aims, as a matter of principle, only at art because no man can serve two masters.' Merz, the brand name by which Schwitters eventually designated all his assorted activities, was arrived at by chance, inspired by a word fragment that had appeared in an early collage, part of the phrase *Kommerz– und Privatbank*.

> The word Merz denotes essentially the combination, for artistic purposes, of all conceivable materials, and, technically, the principle of the equal evaluation of the individual materials ... A perambulator wheel, wire-netting, string and cotton wool are factors having equal rights with paint ... [48]

Schwitters produced collages that recycle worthless detritus, the flotsam and jetsam of a broken and destroyed postwar Germany. Ultimately, Schwitters' works have more in common with Cubist collages, which are likewise composed from ephemeral, disposable materials, than they do with Dada photomontage. His i-drawings and rubber-stamp drawings that utilize reject printers' material and office equipment to create images are comparable to works by Ernst. Schwitters nurtured an idea of a synthesis of the arts, harkening back to the romantic conception of the *Gesamtkunstwerk*: 'I have formed Merz, above all as the sum of individual art forms. Merz painting, Merz poetry.' From the start, his practice straddled literature as well as visual art. He used the collage technique to produce poetry: 'I have pasted together poems from words and sentences so as to produce a rhythmic design. I have on the other hand pasted up pictures and drawings so that sentences can be read in them. I did this so as to efface the boundaries between the arts.' The poem 'Anna Blume' incorporates phrases found in newspapers as well as snatches of overheard conversations. 'Ursonate' is an incantatory abstract poem using combinations of meaningless sounds. Owing to his links with El Lissitsky and Theo van Doesburg, Schwitters was simultaneously exposed to the influence of De Stijl and Constructivism, as witnessed in the increasing geometricism of his collage and design work (illus. 48), though his allegiance to these utopian rationalist trends was not at the expense of an anarchic Dada sensibility. An issue of the magazine *Merz* no. 8–9, co-edited with El Lissitzky in 1924, acclaimed the New Typography emanating from the Soviet Union. The same year, Schwitters set up an advertising agency, the Merz-Werbenzentrale, which won contracts with companies that included Wagner,

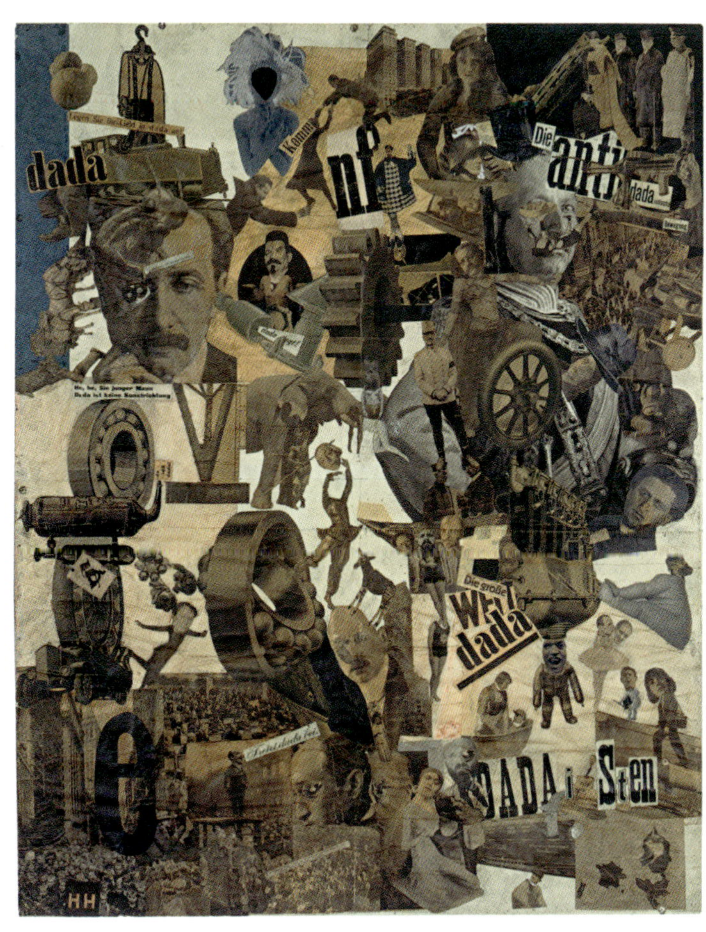

46 Hannah Höch, *Cut with the Dada Kitchen Knife through the Last Weimar Beer-Belly Cultural Epoch in Germany*, 1919–20, photomontage and collage.

47 Hannah Höch, *The Beautiful Girl*, 1919–20, photomontage and collage.

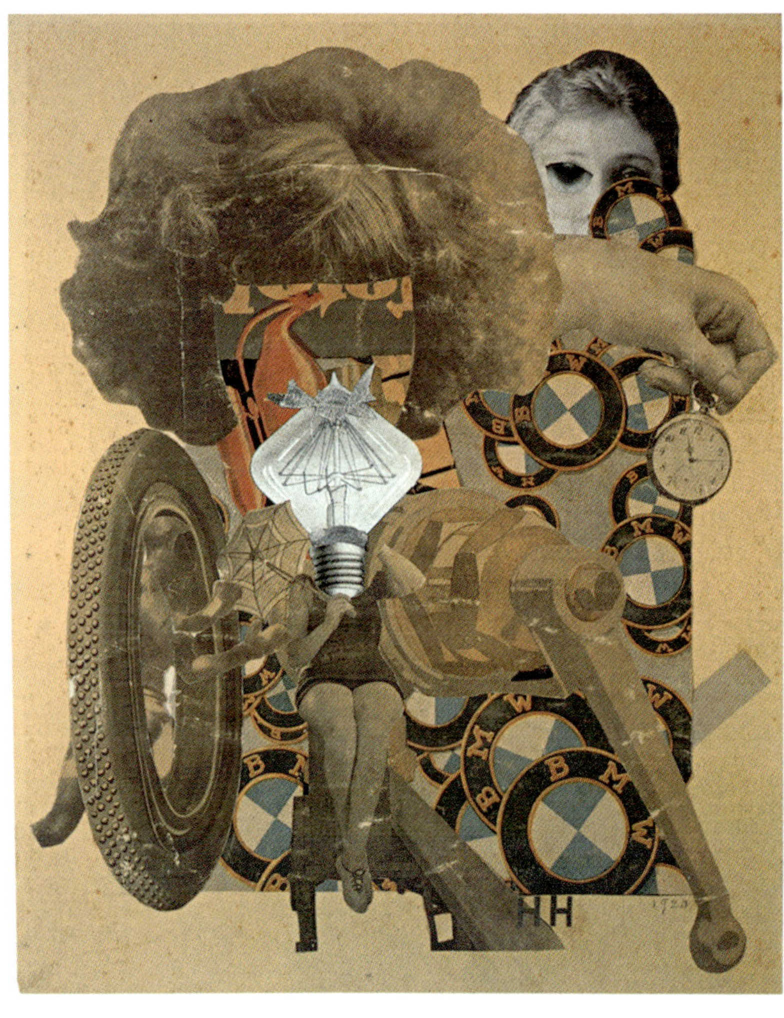

the maker of Pelikan inks. Constructivism also supplied the impetus for the extension of his collage practice into the creation of the *merzbau* environments, where accumulation as a technical procedure is carried over to the rebuilding of domestic space. These peculiar structures have been a source of inspiration for more contemporary artists wanting to situate their practice outside the institutional circuits of a commercial art world.

In the wake of the Soviet Revolution, photomontage was a technique of choice for avant-garde artists seeking to represent a new world in the process of being formed from the existing one. The chief practitioners of photomontage were all adherents of Constructivism: Gustav Klutsis, El Lissitzky and Alexander Rodchenko. As with Dada, the obsolescence of art as a bourgeois cultural form was central to the credo of Constructivism. Photography as a mass reproductive mechanical process signalled an allegiance with the revolutionary proletariat and also reflected the Constructivists' commitment to technological modernity. Photomontage was thus in tune with the objectives of the Soviet state faced with the task of modernizing a vast, industrially backward country and educating its populace. Constructivism in its initial utopian phase was abstract. The incorporation of the photograph has been seen as an accommodation to the growing preference of officialdom for realist art forms in the 1920s.[49] The establishment in 1920 of VKhUTEMAS, a new education institution for artistic and technical training, reflecting the wish of the state that art should play a role in improving the quality of industrial manufacture, included a faculty for graphic design. It was in the areas of graphic design and publicity (posters, kiosks and such like) that Constructivist artists found the most ready opportunities to implement their ideas. Whether Soviet photomontage was derivative of Berlin Dada or whether it arose independently, as Klutsis later claimed, is a moot point. The blockade of Russia that lasted until 1921 would certainly have inhibited the flow of information about art in Western Europe. Klutsis identified two tendencies in photomontage, one originating from American advertising, which he claims influenced the development of Dada, and a

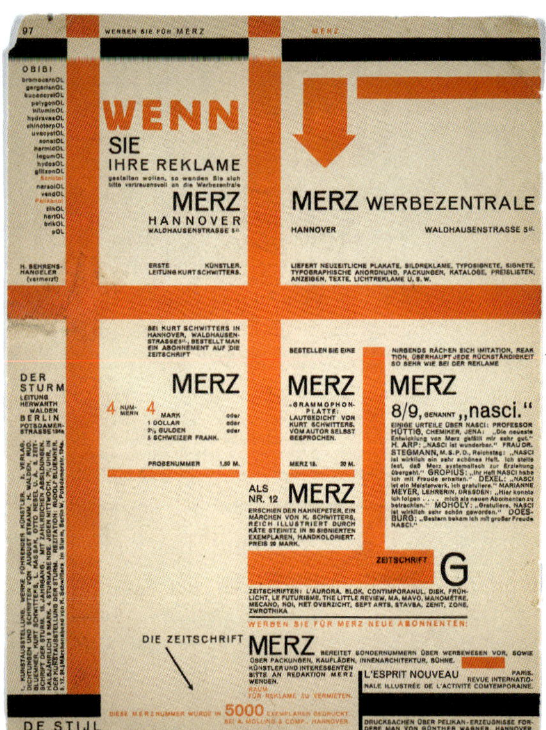

48 Kurt Schwitters, Cover for *Merz 11 Typoreklame (Pelikannummer), Hannover*, 1924.

second line of development, the 'agitational-political' photomontage, which he states appeared in the USSR in 1919–20. Soviet agitation propaganda and commercial advertising appear to us politically and ideologically as extreme, polar opposites, exemplifying the divergent aptitudes and applications of photomontage. Given the desire of the rulers of the new Soviet Union, including Lenin, to emulate the model of US industrial capitalism (montage images of New York skyscrapers reflect this adulation), they may however have more in common than is generally suspected.

Soviet photomontage combined the dynamic abstract forms of Suprematist and Constructivist compositions with the concrete legibility of the photograph in such a way that the utopian connotations of the former are brought into a dialectical relation with objective reality by the latter. As with Dada montages, text performs a critical function in the instrumentalization of the image, pinning down its propagandistic meaning. Gustav Klutsis was the inventor of a simple but effective formula for political posters in the 1930s, consisting of a dynamic axial composition, sans serif lettering, and blocks of red, white and black (illus. 50). El Lissitsky's photogram *Self-portrait: The Constructor* (illus. 49) of 1924 is analogous to a montage in its additive technical process. His innovative designs for exhibition halls, such as Pressa exhibition at Cologne in 1928 or the International Hygiene exhibition at Dresden in

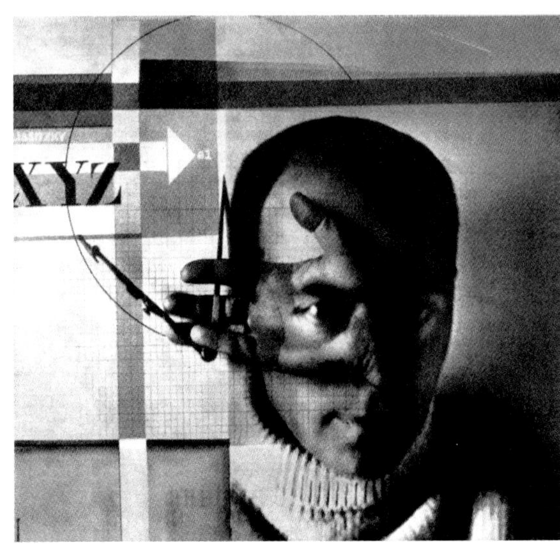

49 El Lissitzky, *Self-portrait: The Constructor*, 1924, photomontage.

1930 were hugely influential. Alexander Rodchenko's turn to photomontage in 1923 coincides with his collaboration with Vladimir Mayakovsky, whose poem 'About This' he illustrated with a series of photomontages, employing material from advertisements, magazines, newspapers and personal photographs of Mayakovsky and Lili Brik (illus. 51), and his participation with the avant-garde journal *LEF*, for which he produced the eye-catching covers. One of the animators of Soviet Constructivism, Rodchenko adhered to a conception of art as an experimental activity; the camera not only registers changing modes of perception, he believed, but also educates the masses in new ways of seeing. As Bertolt Brecht famously remarked: 'Reality changes; in order to represent it, modes of representation must also change.'[50] By the 1930s, social realism had become the only officially sanctioned art form, restricting the outlets for artists of an avant-garde persuasion. At that point, Rodchenko turned to photo-documentary work for magazines and newspapers, in which he presents a stock iconography of sportsmen and women, mass rallies, dynamic electricity pylons, that with the benefit of historical hindsight appears more as a wish-fulfilment dream than an objective record of Soviet life.

Constructivist design has been much copied. In the throes of a bitter Civil War, the organizers of the Spanish Pavilion at the Paris World's Fair in 1937 employed Agitprop techniques to broadcast their desperate plight to the rest of the world. Photo-documentary panels (illus. 52) combining images and explanatory text adorned the exterior and interior of the modernist building designed by Josep Lluis Sert. The whole ensemble, including Picasso's *Guernica*, which was displayed on the ground floor, together with works by Joan Miró and Alexander Calder, and an exhibition from Valencia of works in a social realist vein, was orchestrated in such a way as to subordinate art to urgent political exigencies. Miró designed a poster with the simple message 'Aidez Espagne' that was on sale for one franc. Proof of the efficacy of the propaganda techniques developed by the avant-garde was their hijack by the Nazis for the 'Degenerate Art' exhibition in Munich in 1937. In a ghastly reversal of avant-garde installation strategies, works by Ernst, Nolde and others were displayed alongside child art and the drawings of the insane together with mocking inscriptions scrawled on the walls.[51]

SURREALISM'S VISUAL POETICS

An invitation card (illus. 53) for an exhibition of his work in 1935 was an occasion for Ernst to interrogate our most entrenched beliefs about the self and self-portraiture. The collagist has taken to his own face with a pair of scissors, portraying himself as if seen in a mirror, but one that has been shattered. Writing, consisting of the titles of Ernst's pictures, fills the spaces amongst the broken shards of this reflected self. Where physiognomic theories of character would have us read the lines of the face, here we are required to read between the lines if we are to know the truth about the subject. Is it not the realm of the unconscious, this 'between the lines' which is structured like a language? It was in the hope of accessing this elusive realm that the Surrealists' creative efforts, both visual and verbal, were directed.

André Breton contended that by the time the *Manifesto of Surrealism* (1924) had been published, five years of experimental activity already lay behind Surrealism. He was referring, of course, to the publication in 1919 of *Les Champs magnétiques* (Magnetic Fields), a series of automatic texts written by himself and Philippe Soupault that laid the foundation of Surrealism, though the movement would not be officially launched until several years after. A first instalment, published in *Littérature* in October 1919, was titled 'La Glace sans tain' (A mirror without backing), the title of a picture by Henri Matisse that Breton had seen reproduced in

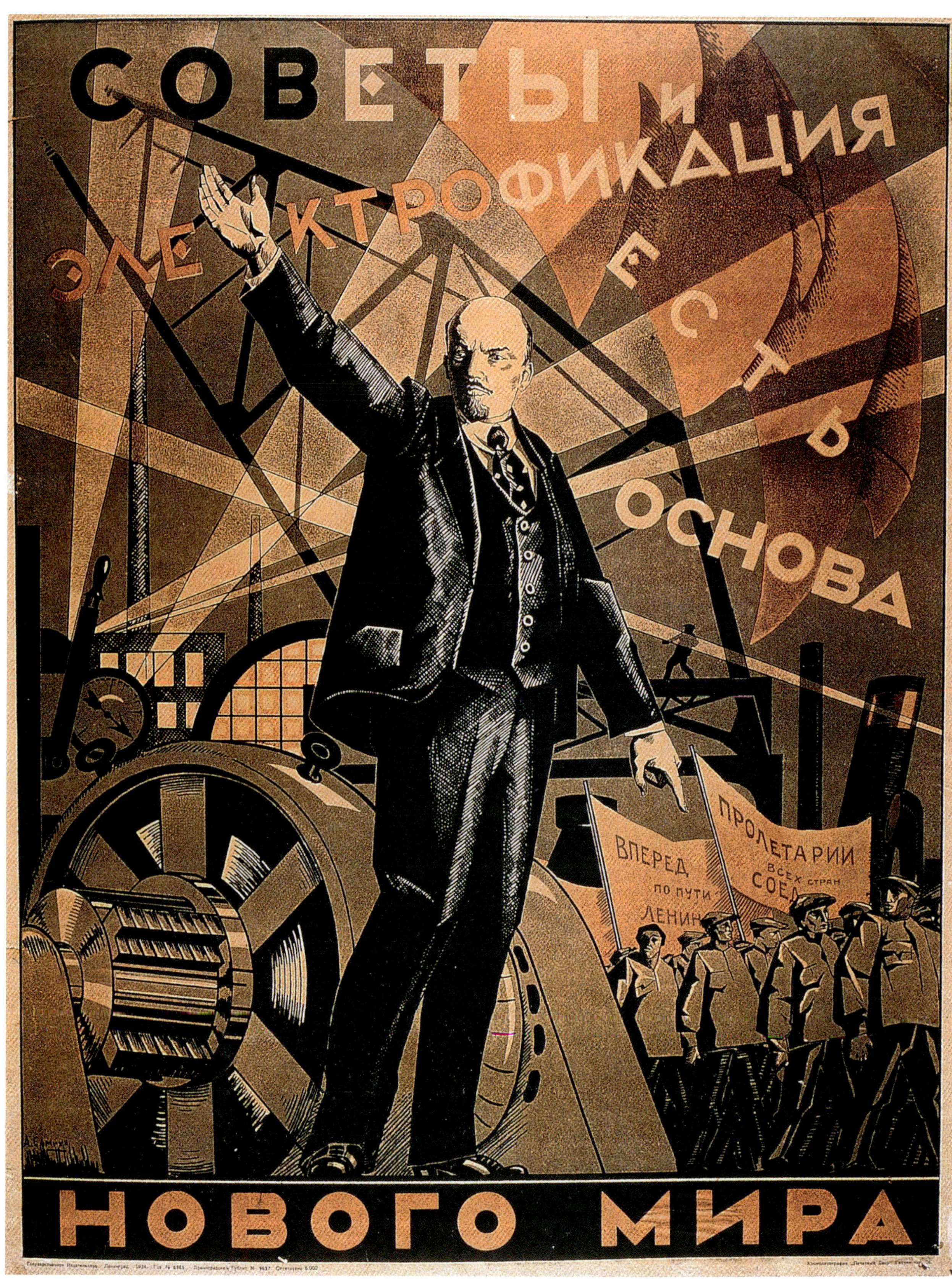

50 Alexander Samokhvalov, *'Soviets and Electrication – This is the Foundation of the New World'*, 1924, poster.

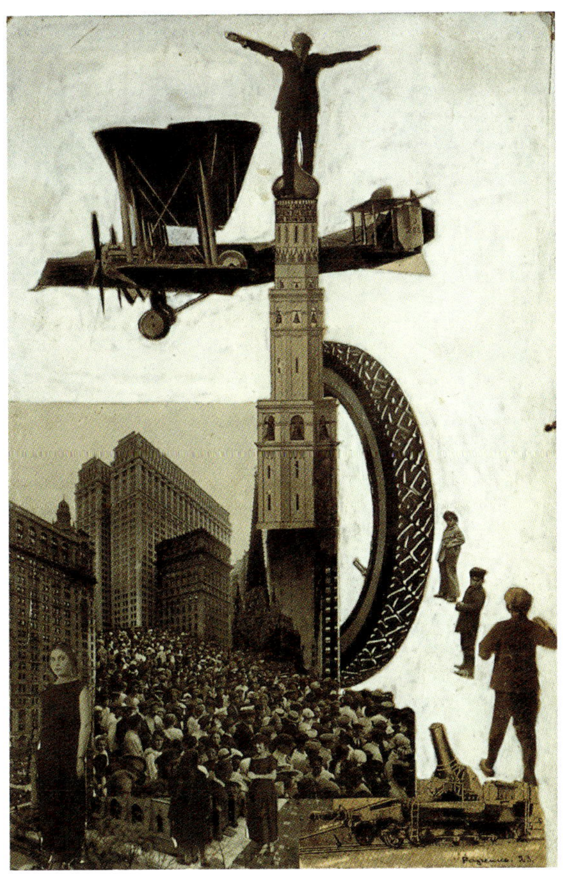

51 Alexander Rodchenko, Illustration for Vladimir Mayakovsky's *About This*, 1923, photomontage.

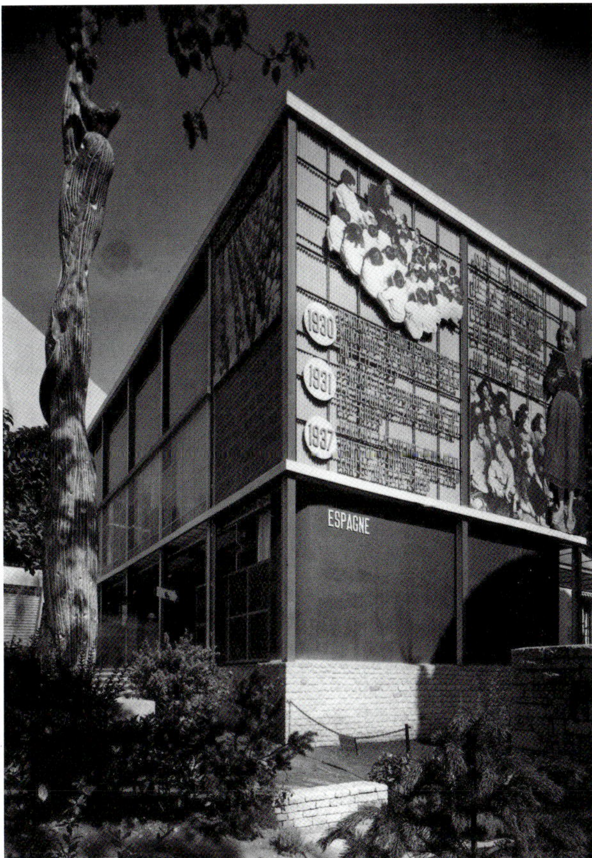

52 Photodocumentary murals on the exterior of the Spanish Republican Pavilion at the Paris World's Fair, 1937.

Apollinaire's *Soirées de Paris*. It confirms not only the revelatory character of Breton's exposure to that magazine but also the enduring value of experimental art for him, and the extent to which art and poetry stimulate each other in his thought. The *Manifesto* set an agenda for all those who sought to affiliate themselves with the new movement by proposing an inflexible dictionary-style definition of Surrealism as 'psychic automatism in its pure state, by which one proposes to express – verbally, by means of the written word, or in any other manner – the actual functioning of thought.'[52]

Joan Miró responded to the clarion call of the *Manifesto* in a body of works, the so-called dream paintings, which won him a slightly ambiguous accolade from Breton:

> Joan Miró cherishes perhaps one single desire – to give himself up utterly to painting and to painting alone (which, for him involves limiting himself to the one field in which we are confident that he has substantial means at his disposal), to that pure automatism which, for my part, I have never ceased to invoke ... It is true that that may be the very reason why he could perhaps pass for the most 'surrealist' of us all.[53]

As he was lured into the Surrealist milieu, Miró evinces a progressive evolution away from the painstaking realism of *The Farm* of 1921–2, a picture bought by Ernest Hemingway. The turn towards more whimsical, fantastical subjects reflects the influence of Apollinaire and Jarry. Apollinaire's 'L'Enchanteur pourrissant', a reworking of the medieval legend of Merlin the wizard, is considered a chief inspiration for the lizard that wears a cone-shaped cap while reading a newspaper in the foreground of *The Tilled Field* of 1923, a picture that also borrows from Catalan Romanesque sources.[54] The inclusion of word fragments stems from Cubism, as in the rolled-up newspaper with the word 'jour' in *The Tilled Field* or the letters 'sard' in the lower right-hand corner of *The Hunter (Catalan Landscape)* (illus. 54). Commentators have tried to guess at the meaning of the latter word fragment, which may denote the first syllable of *sardana*, a folk-dance performed in rural

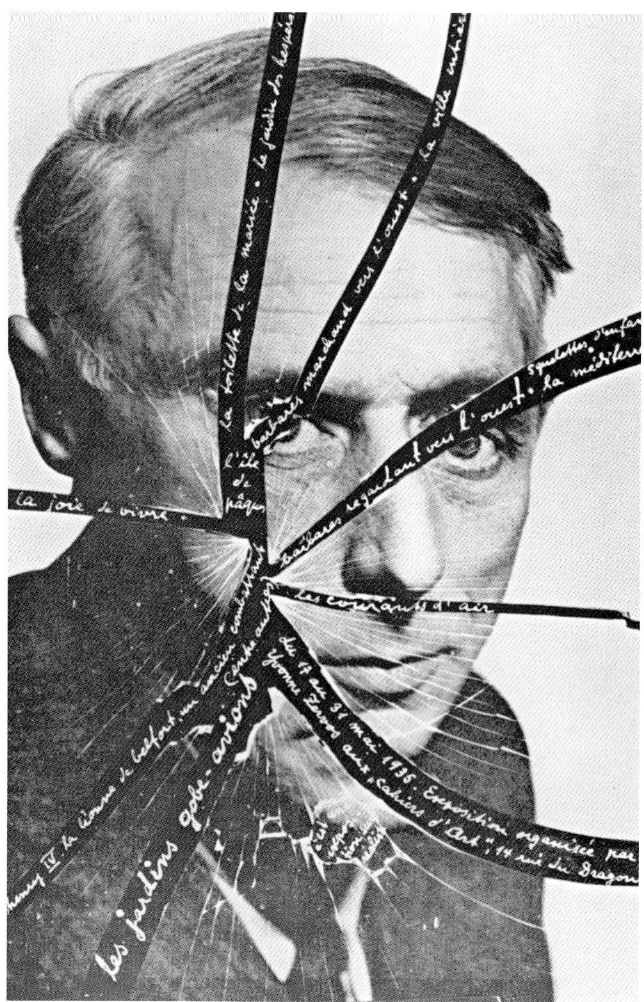

53 Max Ernst, *Invitation to a Max Ernst Exhibition*, 1935, photocollage.

Catalonia, or the word *sardine*, though the animal concealed in the foreground looks more like a rabbit. The simultaneous adoption of a vocabulary of rudimentary pictorial signs allows for the proliferation of rhymes across the picture (sun = spider = sex = heart). Miró's aesthetic of 'peinture-poésie' is premised on the equivalence of verbal and visual signs.[55] Recalling Picasso's *Ma Jolie*, *Sourire de ma blonde* of 1924 references a French popular song, 'Auprès de ma blonde', a source of inspiration likewise for *Le Corps de ma brune* of the following year. Body parts are treated like individual words in a poem describing the beloved metaphorically. These lexical elements are arrayed like a bouquet of flowers with the golden yellow of the tempera background evoking her blonde hair. A number of these works contain schematic indications of a perspectival space, and an emphatic horizon line, conjuring a space in which objects and written inscriptions cohabit. Especially marked in the more narrative works, such features may derive from the pictures that Robert Desnos, a close friend, had produced during the surrealist experiments in 1922 with trance states and hypnosis (illus. 55).

The culminating point of Miró's pictorial evolution is the series of highly abstracted, so-called dream paintings. Typically, these works combine a deep, atmospheric visual space with a flat surface plane, of language and the visual sign. Miró claimed that this body of works was produced in a state of hallucination brought on by fasting. In 1976, however, a cache of previously unsuspected sketchbooks came to light that contained exact preparatory drawings for every one of the pictures. These show the artist working in a highly improvisational manner, making use of tracings and imprints produced by the drawing above, and incorporating chance stains. An enigmatic list of numbers in *Peinture* ('*L'Addition*') of 1925, turns out to have originated in a shopping list of canvas sizes casually jotted down by the artist at the back of one of the sketchbooks! The prominence of arrows and numbers, mutely enigmatic symbols, bespeaks an affinity with Paul Klee, several of whose pictures are reproduced in early issues of the Surrealist magazine, *La Révolution surréaliste* (illus. 56). *Etoiles en des sexes d'escargots* (*Stars like the genitals of snails*) (illus. 57) and *Un Oiseau poursuit une abeille et la baisse* (*A bird pursues a bee and kisses it*) illustrate Miró's frequent use of assonance and repeated phonemes in titles and inscriptions. Michel Leiris, who was conducting similar experiments in the use of poetic language, remarked: 'We discover the most hidden virtues and secret ramifications which propagate in every language, channelled by associations of sound, of form and ideas.'[56] An example of this is a poem by Leiris where intersecting axes spawn the words *moi-mourir-miroi* but do not dictate their order. The palindromic 'sexes' of *Etoiles en des sexes d'escargots* may relate to the fact that snails are hermaphroditic, and their sex is reversible.

Perhaps the most celebrated of Miró's dream paintings is *Photo: Ceci est la couleur de mes rêves* (illus. 58). The spare disposition of typographic ele-

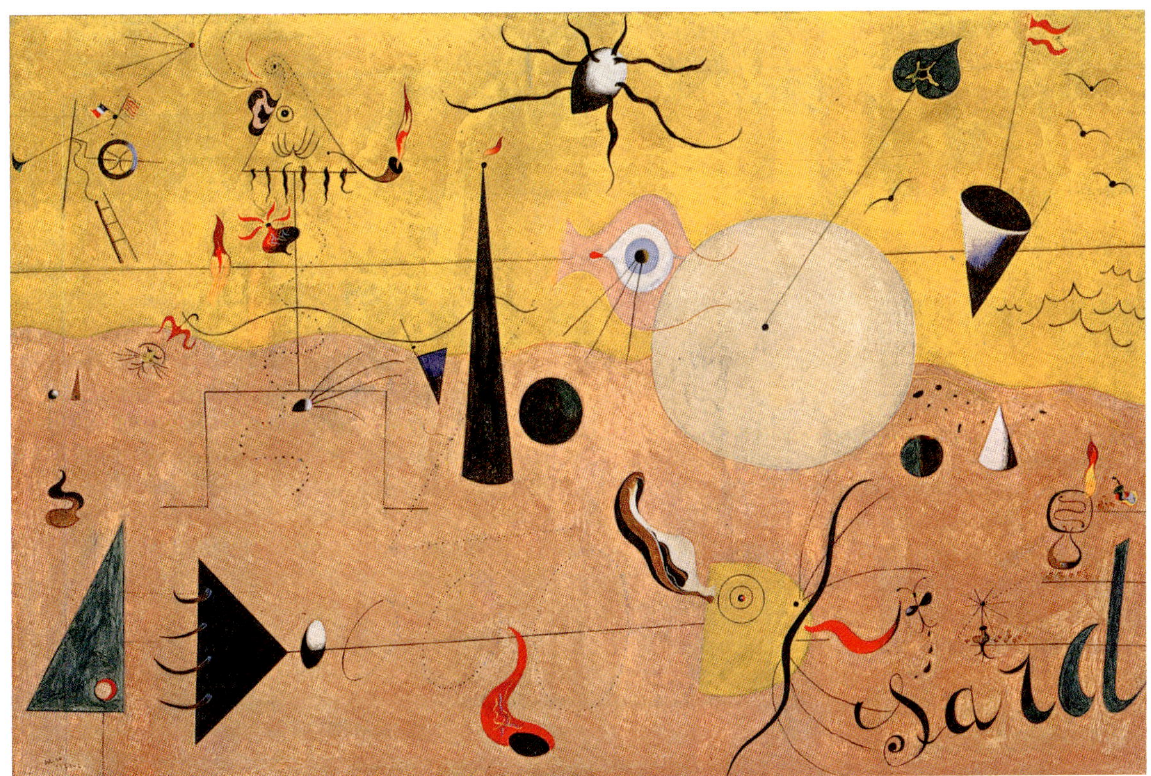

54 Joan Miró, *The Hunter (Catalan Landscape)*, 1923–4, oil on canvas.

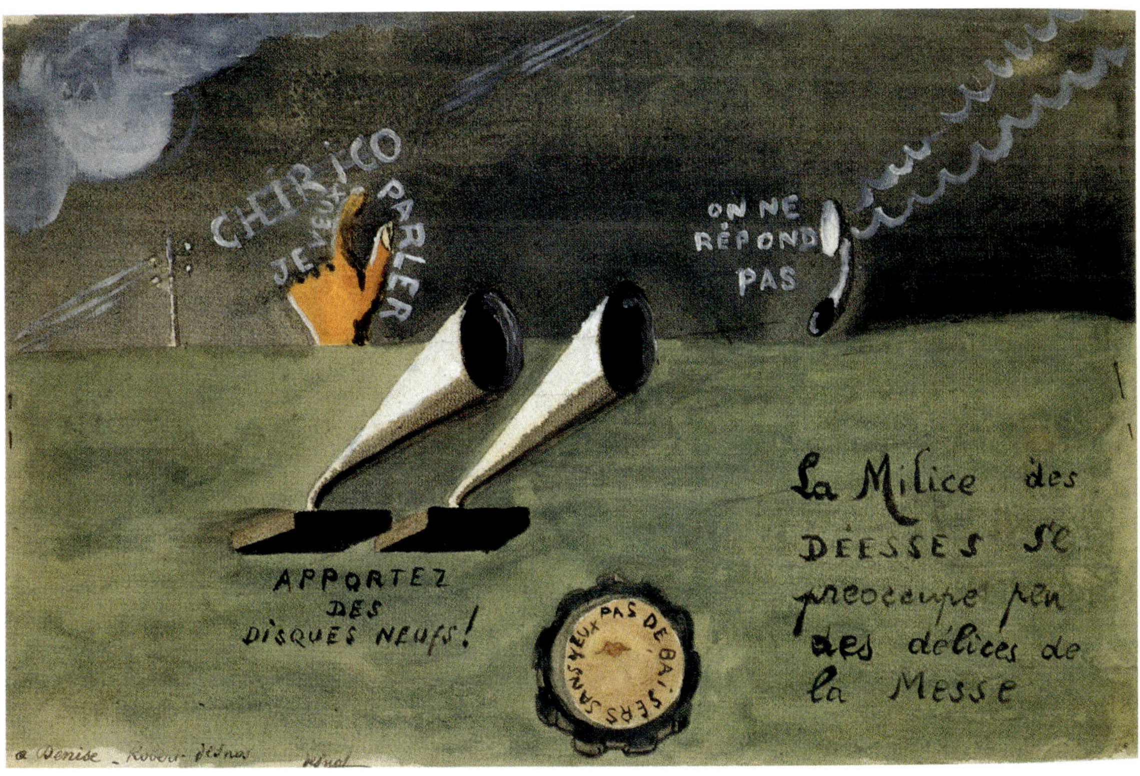

55 Robert Desnos, *Dream – Poetry*, 1922, ink and watercolour.

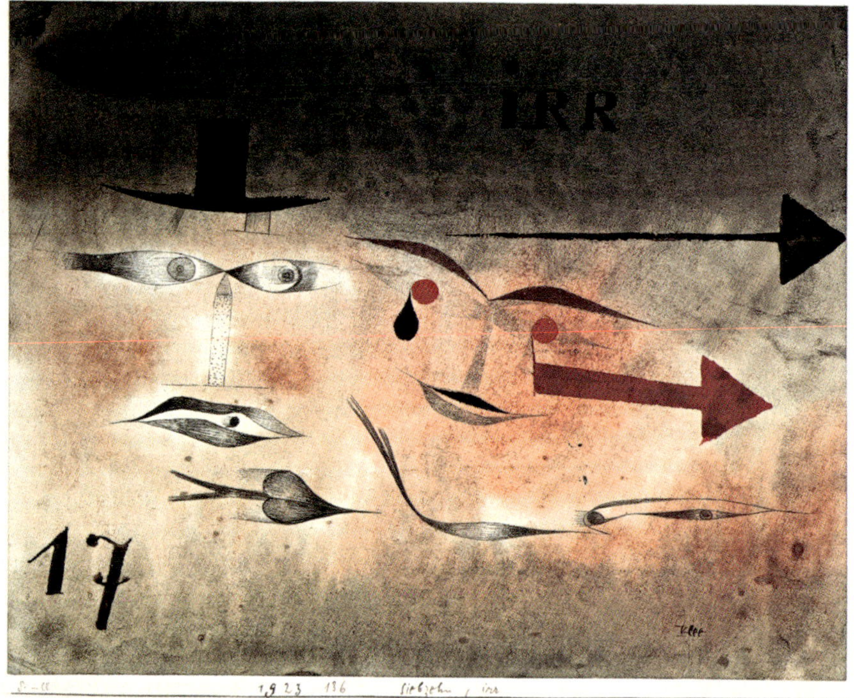

56 Paul Klee, *17 Astray*, 1923, ink and watercolour on paper mounted on cardboard.

ments and splotch of blue on an otherwise daringly bare canvas is reminiscent of Mallarmé, one of Miró's favourite poets, for whom the colour blue was also deeply symbolic. The title 'Photo', together with the inscription 'this is the colour of my dreams', brings to mind Breton's catalogue preface to the 1920 Max Ernst exhibition, where he wrote that: 'The invention of photography has dealt a mortal blow to the old modes of expression, in painting as well as in poetry, where automatic writing, which appeared at the end of the nineteenth century, is *a true photography of thought*.'[57] In the *Manifesto of Surrealism*, Breton insisted the Surrealist poet should as far as possible be a 'simple recording instrument'; elsewhere, he terms automatic writing 'écriture mécanique'. Later, in 1938, Breton reasserted the parallel of automatism with a quasi-scientific process of investigation when he appended the handwritten title 'Écriture automatique' beneath a self-portrait photocollage (illus. 59) in which his face is collaged onto the shoulders of a laboratory scientist or doctor. The microscope in the image affords another mechanical instrumental analogy for automatic writing. The entirely desultory character of *Photo: Ceci est la couleur de mes rêves* offers a foretaste of what would crystallize in the late 1920s as a neo-Dada ambition to assassinate painting. At that time, Miró announced: 'The only thing that's clear to me is that I intend to destroy, destroy everything that exists in painting.'[58] The typographic elements,

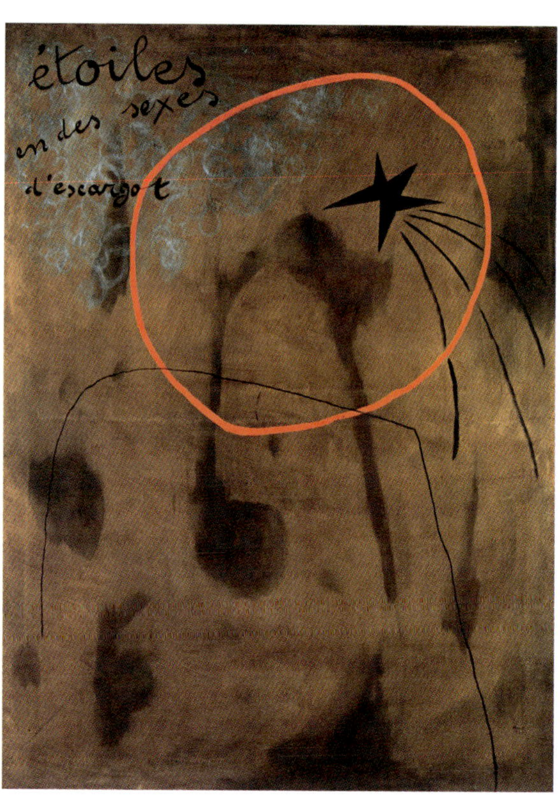

57 Joan Miró, *Painting-Poem* ('*Etoiles en des sexes d'escargots*'), 1925, oil on canvas.

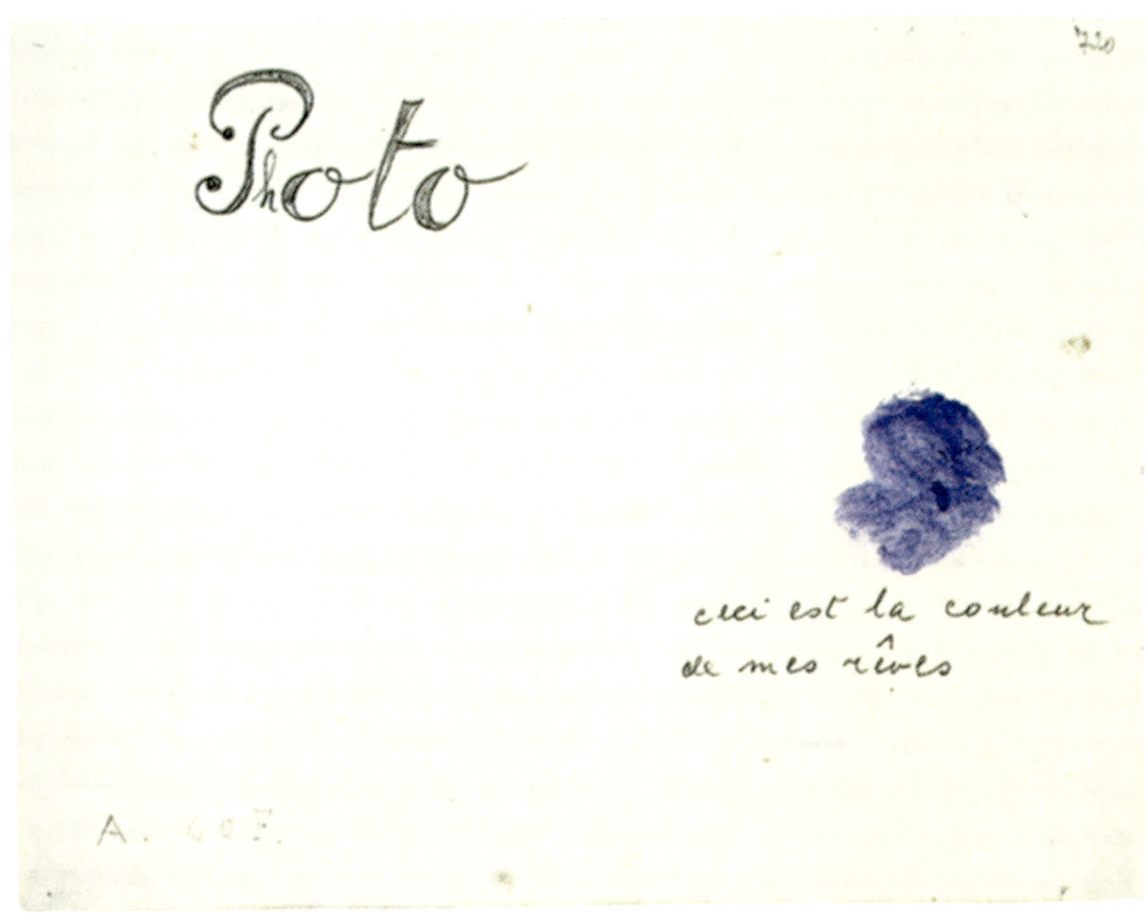

58 Joan Miró, *Painting-Poem* (*Photo: Ceci est la couleur de mes rêves*), July–September 1925, oil on canvas.

along with collage and assemblage, were weapons in a campaign against painting as conventionally understood.

A burgeoning literature about child and primitive art, as well as primitive sign languages and theories about the origins of written language, condition appreciations of Miró's work in the 1930s.[59] Henri Michaux, best known for his interest in Eastern philosophies and use of mescaline in the 1950s, began experimenting with automatic techniques in the late 1920s. His calligraphic writings (illus. 61), rooted in a phenomenology of gesture, reference Eastern pictographic scripts. Poised at the boundary of verbal and graphic forms of representation, they testify to an impulse to break violently with language as a conventional code. In an essay on pictures by André Masson from after the Second World War that combine the gesturalism of Surrealist automatism with a newfound interest in Chinese calligraphy, Roland Barthes characterizes the work as an *inter-text* circulating between the arts of painting and writing. Detaching writing from the purely instrumental function of transmitting a message, Masson's semiographs are traces or inscriptions of a living, pulsating body, '*le corps qui bat* (qui jouit).'[60] In order that such writing be manifested in its truth, it must be literally unreadable. Antonin Artaud belongs naturally with this company. The drawings and writings produced by Artaud whilst incarcerated in a mental asylum at Rodez (illus. 62) reflect his literal alienation from language. Charting his psychological breakdown and distress, they are poignant documents attesting to a pain that is as unbearable as it is inexpressible. Seen as a victim, a man 'suicided' by society, Artaud became a cult figure for the Beat generation poets Alan Ginsberg and William S. Burroughs. The American feminist artist Nancy Spero, who also drew inspiration from Artaud, stated that: 'I identified with Artaud's sense of victimage – using his language to exemplify my loss of tongue – fracturing his already fractured texts, because I felt a victim as regards both being a woman and an artist.' *Codex Artaud* (1971–2), consisting of scrolls made up of sheets of paper pasted end to end, juxtaposes statements by Artaud, printed in the style of telegraphic messages to convey a desperate urgency, with Spero's own painted cutout images, in order 'to exemplify the artist (myself) rejected in bourgeois society'.

Yves Tanguy's enigmatic titles are yet another

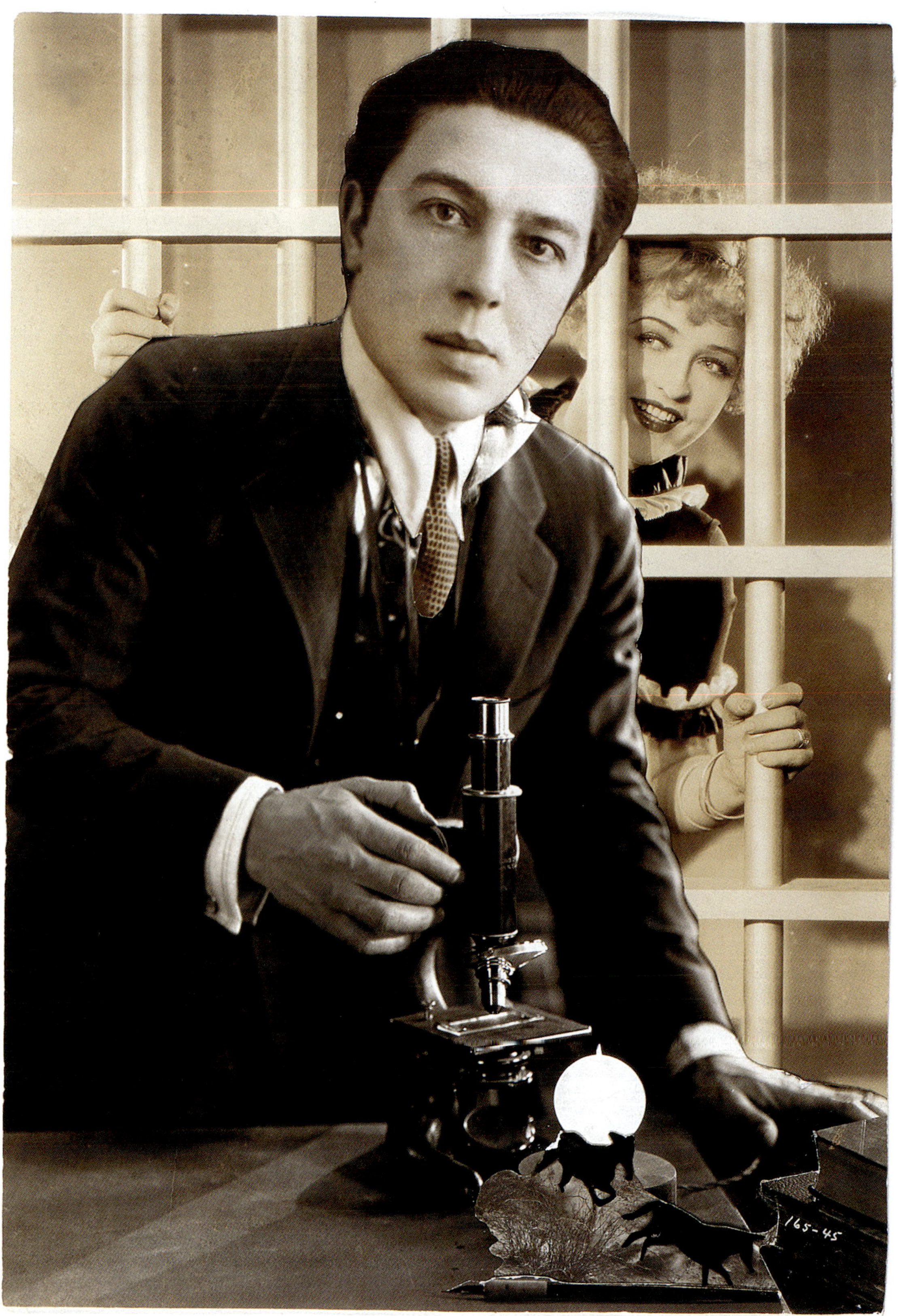

59 André Breton, *Self-portrait: Automatic Writing*, 1938, photomontage.

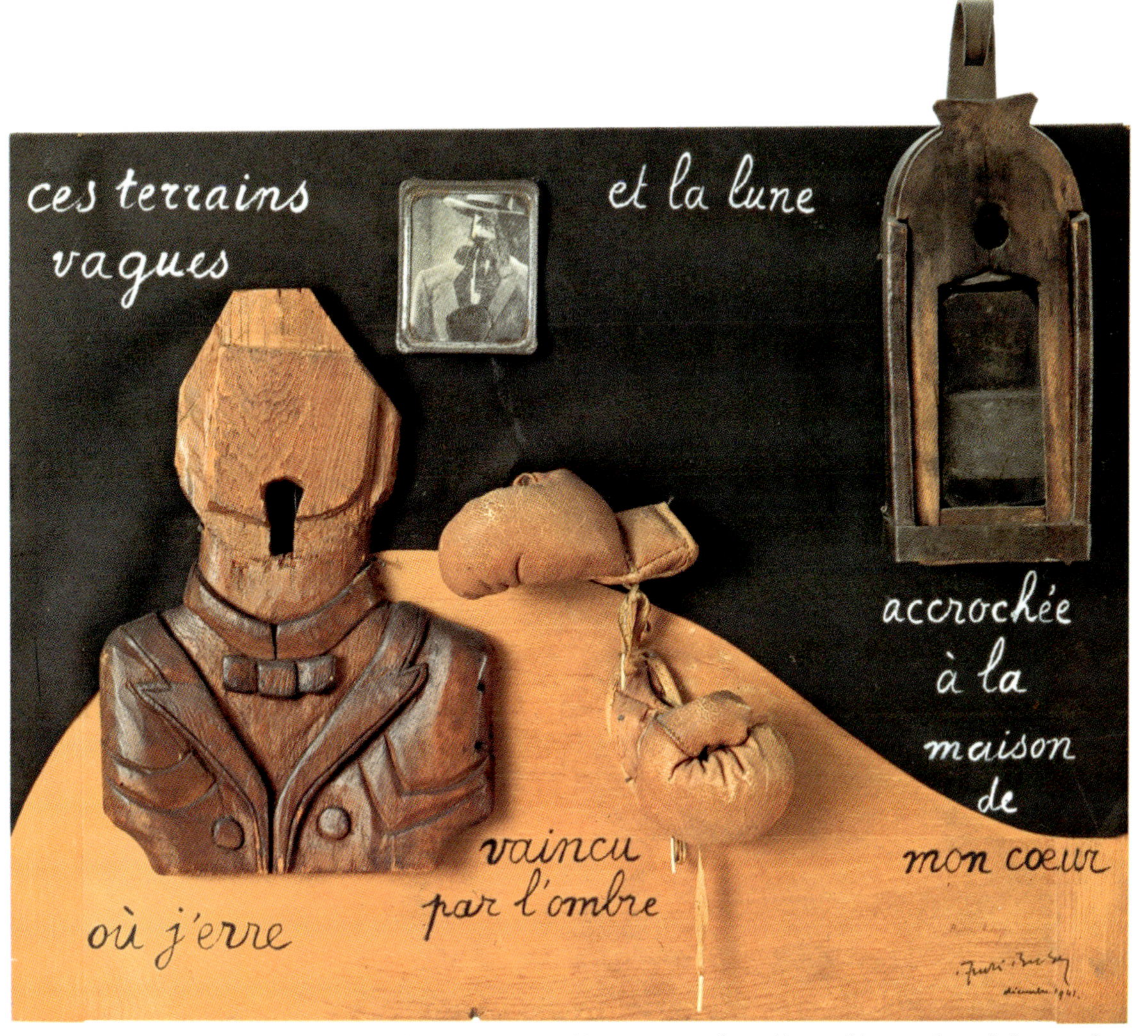

60 André Breton, *Poem-Object*, 1941, carved wood bust, oil lantern, framed photograph, toy boxing-gloves, and paper mounted on drawing board.

example of the pivotal role of language for an exponent of Surrealist visual automatism. Tanguy remembered an afternoon spent with Breton selecting the titles for his first one-man exhibition at the Galerie surréaliste in 1927. He recalls 'searching through texts of psychiatry for statements of patients which we could use as titles for the paintings'. In fact, the volume from which the titles were pilfered turns out to have been Charles Richet's *Treatise on Metapsychics* (1922).[61] Richet, a Nobel Prize-winning physiologist, advocated the scientific investigation of spiritualist phenomena. Dating from the *époque des sommeils*, Breton had evinced an ambiguous fascination with spiritualism, which underwent a well-documented revival in popularity after the war. While disputing the spiritualist belief in the immortality of the soul, Breton was on the other hand more disposed to accept the evidence of yet unknown forces in the mind and in the physical universe for which spiritist experiments with cryptaesthesia and materialization supposedly gave evidence. A number of the titles of Tanguy's pictures were excerpted from a section of Richet's book containing reports of premonitions. That Tanguy may have subscribed to such beliefs himself is shown by a decoration painted in 1925 for the bedroom door of Jacques Prévert, with whom he shared an apartment, a macabre dream image that includes a black-bordered invitation to Prevert's funeral. The allusive titles contribute to specifying a reading of his ambiguously aquatic landscapes as metaphors for the unconscious whose fathomless depths Surrealism sought to explore. For exponents of psychic research, the subconscious was conceived metaphorically as an ocean (one is also put in mind of Arthur Rimbaud's poetic image of 'un salon au fond du lac'). Letters are strewn wantonly across *He Did As He Wanted* (1927); the *Letter to Paul Eluard* (illus. 63), dated 1933, weaves a marvellous carpet of

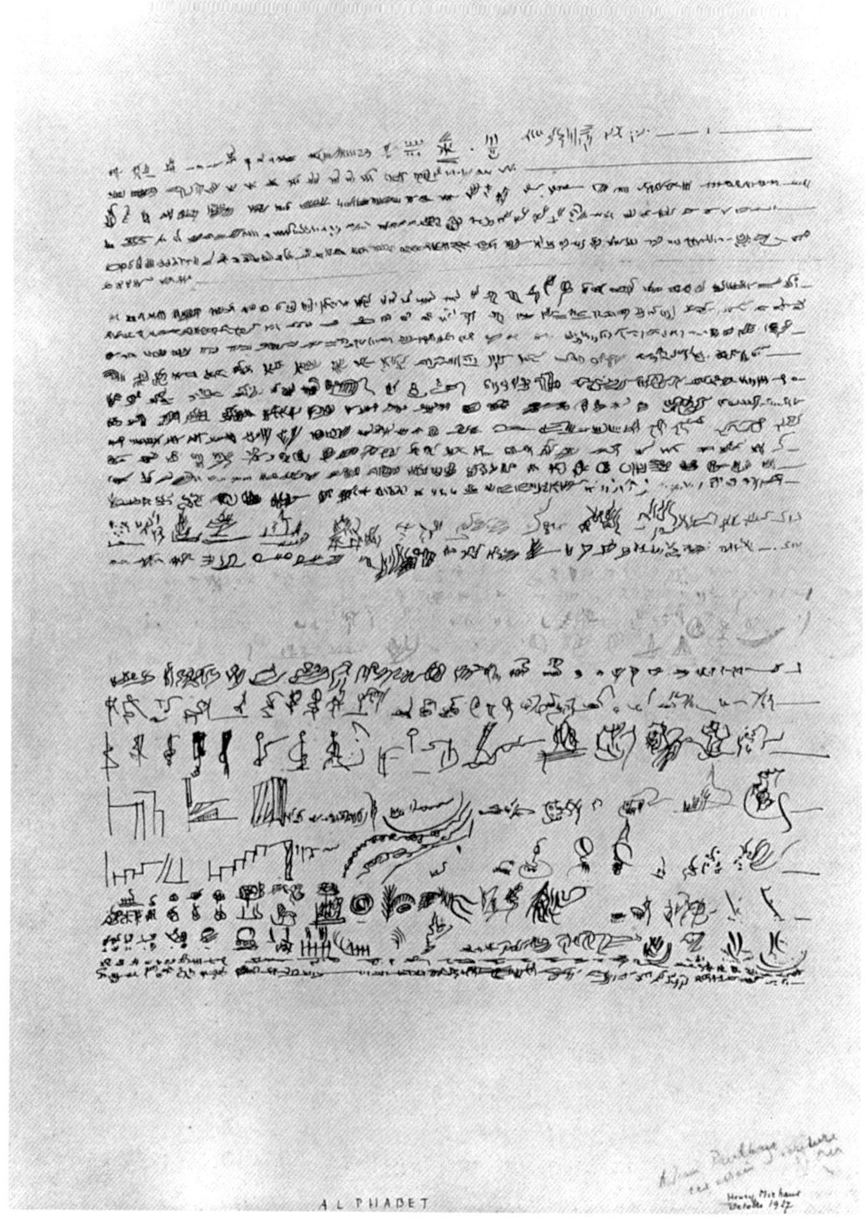

61 Henri Michaux, *Alphabet*, 1927, ink on paper.

words across an imaginary landscape of the mind.

In the debate that unfolded over the very possibility of a Surrealist painting after the publication of Breton's *Manifesto*, Pierre Naville took a hard-line stance, insisting 'No-one can ignore that there is no *surrealist painting*.' By way of alternatives, he proposed photography, cinema, and the street with its 'kiosques, automobiles, rotating doorways, and street lamps radiating skyward'.[62] Like Delaunay and Léger, Surrealist artists and writers, in their turn, gleaned a new poetry in the urban fabric, though it was not in the main the spectacle of modernity that attracted them, but rather the interstitial pockets – flea markets, old-fashioned arcades – that had resisted the pressures of modernization. The city of Paris was, wrote Walter Benjamin, 'the most dreamed-of of their objects'.[63] This phantasmatic conception is articulated by Max Ernst in *Painting-Poem* (illus. 64) of 1923–4 as a layering of linguistic signs upon a Chirico-esque vista. The text begins: 'In a town full of mystery and poetry . . .'. Louis Aragon's *Paris Peasant* (1926) was the apotheosis of this genre. Whilst not immune to the seduction of posters and hoardings – one thinks of the Mazda lightbulb advert in Breton's *Nadja* (illus. 65) – they were inclined to discover a hidden personal significance in the solicitations of these signs. Referring to Baudelaire, Breton wrote in *Mad Love* that: 'Interpretive delirium begins only when man, ill-prepared, is taken

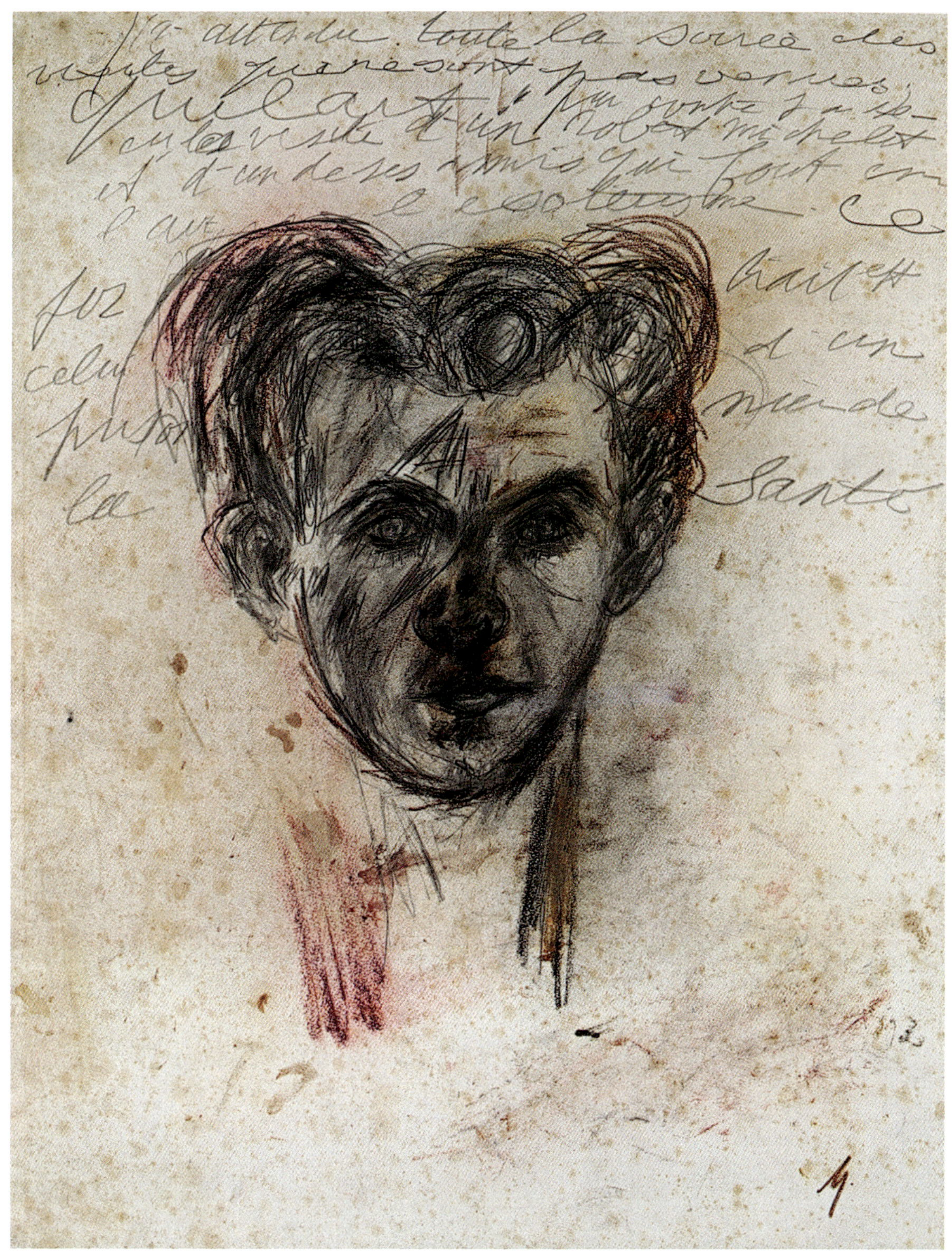

62 Antonin Artaud, *Portrait of a Man*, 20 June 1947, graphite and wax crayon.

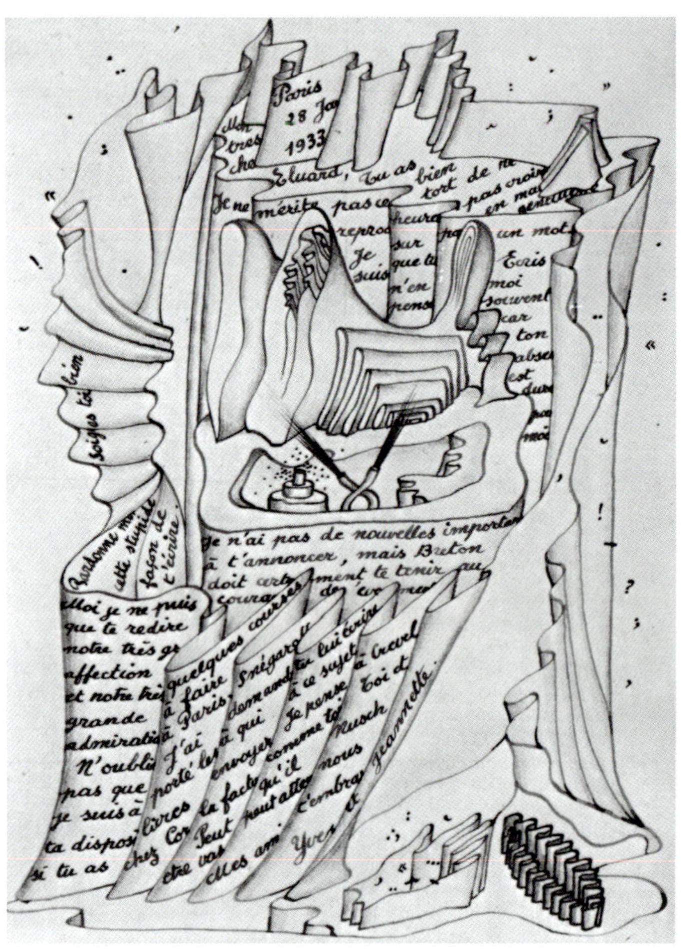

63 Yves Tanguy, *Letter to Paul Eluard*, 1933, ink and pencil on paper.

by a sudden fear in the *forest of symbols*.' Strolling in the city was a popular pastime for the Surrealists, and it provided the theme for Joan Miró's *Music, Seine, Michel, Bataille and I* (illus. 66) of 1927. Explaining the latter, Miró recalled how he would go for strolls with his friends along the banks of the Seine in all weather. He would throw a coin into the water as a custom to ward off bad luck and was mesmerized by the resultant ripple patterns.[64] Indeed, strolling may be regarded as an extension of automatism, and of an idea associated with Klee of drawing as a line going for a walk, into a realm beyond art and poetry.

For the Surrealists, the static nature of the visual image was a serious drawback from the point of view of registering the flux of unconscious thought. For that purpose, language was better adapted. An alternative to painting that promised to overcome this inherent limitation was the moving image, i.e., film. The Surrealists were avid filmgoers and they placed enormous hopes in this still youthful medium. Whether their hopes were actually fulfilled is more of a moot point as the number of indisputably Surrealist films is surprisingly few. Many more film scenarios were written than were produced, often because they were unfilmable. Here again, Apollinaire proves to be entirely prescient, as the author of several unrealized film scenarios.[65] The Surrealist film scenario, as a genre of writing, has a lot in common with automatic writing (indeed, if there is an element of automatism in film, it must be at this point), and with the *récit de rêve*, or dream narrative, a number of which are published in the first issue of *La Révolution surréaliste*. Film also provided Dalí with an effective means for realizing his paranoiac-critical method, a technique for provoking an irrational concatenation of images. In accordance with a Freudian dream logic, Dalí employed intertitles in *Un Chien andalou* so as to actively disrupt the co-ordinates of time and space that regulate waking life: two scenes that apparently follow each other in the film, for instance, are separated by an intertitle

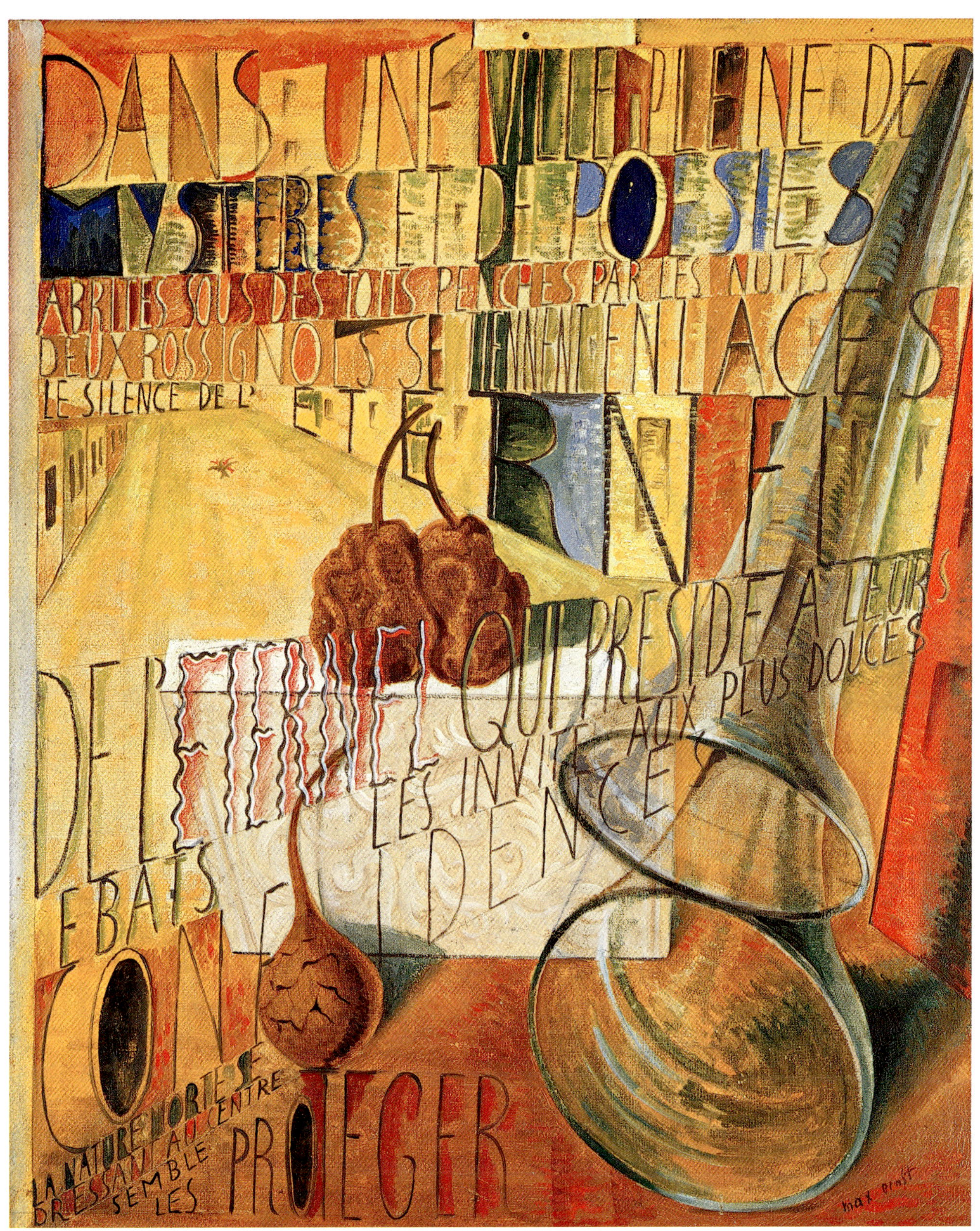

64 Max Ernst, *Painting-Poem ('Dans une ville pleine de mystères…')* 1923–4, oil on canvas.

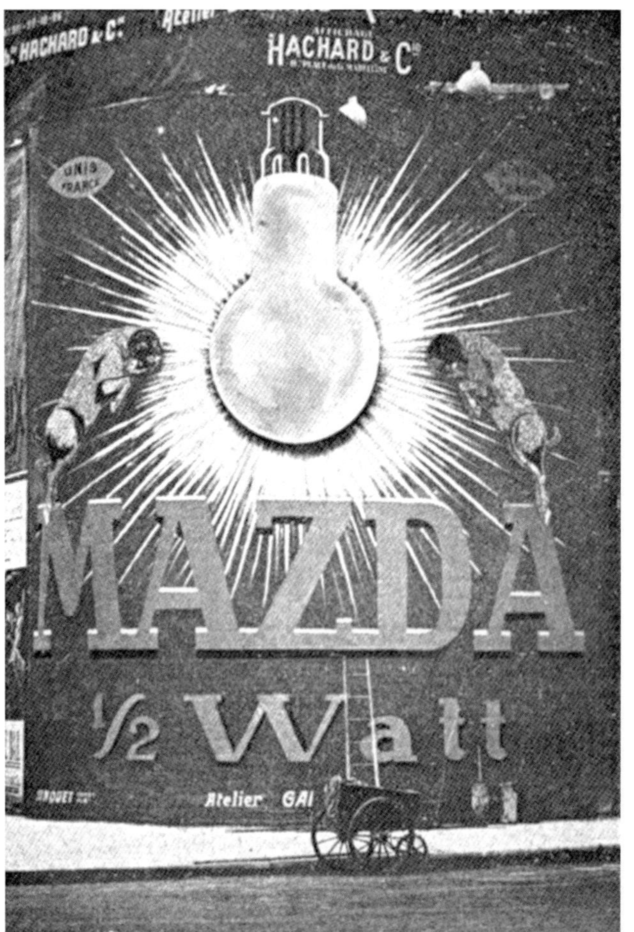

65 Jacques-André Boiffard, 'The luminous "Mazda" sign on the boulevards', illustration for André Breton, *Nadja* (Paris, 1928).

that reads 'Seize ans avant' (sixteen years before).

Returning to Joan Miró, let us conclude this section with a sequence of etchings that were begun in March and concluded in September 1938. *Portrait of Miró* was carried out in the printmaking studio of Louis Marcoussis, erstwhile Cubist painter, and results from an intriguing collaboration.[66] Miró had been introduced to Marcoussis by Tristan Tzara in 1932. Following this date, until 1939, the majority of his printmaking was carried out at Marcoussis' studio. One can well imagine the two artists conversing at length about Apollinaire as they worked side by side: Marcoussis' best-known etching is his Cubist *Portrait of Apollinaire* (1912–20) and, in 1934, he made etchings for a re-edition of Apollinaire's *Alcools*. He was also Miró's favourite poet and a main inspiration for his aesthetic of *peinture-poésie*. The two artists worked together on the plate in a kind of medley; the earliest states by Marcoussis portray Miró in a realistic manner in front of a canvas armed with the tools of his trade. Using the prosaic likeness as a springboard, Miró set to work covering the plate in automatist fashion with a profusion of graffiti-like marks: flames, stars and so forth. Comic-book creatures that appear to leap out of Miró's head inhabit the space that surrounds him. Interwoven with this visual iconography are assorted written inscriptions: the artists' names at the bottom of the plate in fancy lettering rather like the stencilled words on Marcoussis' etching of Apollinaire; the wistfully Romantic lines 'pluie de lyres / CIRQUES DE MÉLANCOLIE' that might almost have been penned by Apollinaire himself; and an automatic poem about colours recalling Rimbaud's 'Voyelles' that appears fleetingly on the artist's palette in the eleventh to thirteenth states, only to disappear again. Thereafter, a spider's web of lines slowly radiates outwards from several nodal points to produce a dense criss-crossed mesh in the final state. There is a final irony too, since it is Miró's contribution that nearly effaces the portrait of him.

WORDS AND THINGS

'The chance encounter of an umbrella and a sewing machine on a dissection table': this oft-repeated phrase, culled from Lautréamont's *Les Chants de maldoror*, an extraordinary book by one of Surrealism's most revered precursors, encapsulates the Surrealist conception of the image as poetic metaphor. André Breton borrowed from the formalist poet Pierre Reverdy a definition of the poetic image as 'a pure creation of the mind' born 'from a juxtaposition of two more or less distinct realities'.[67] Conceived initially as an encounter of linguistic terms, the notion of the encounter is taken up and generalized by Breton: as the chance encounter, it is one of his core metaphysical ideas. The ambiguity that inheres in the very word 'image', which can refer equally to poetry or to painting, holds within itself an encounter of sorts, a convergence and intertwining of words and

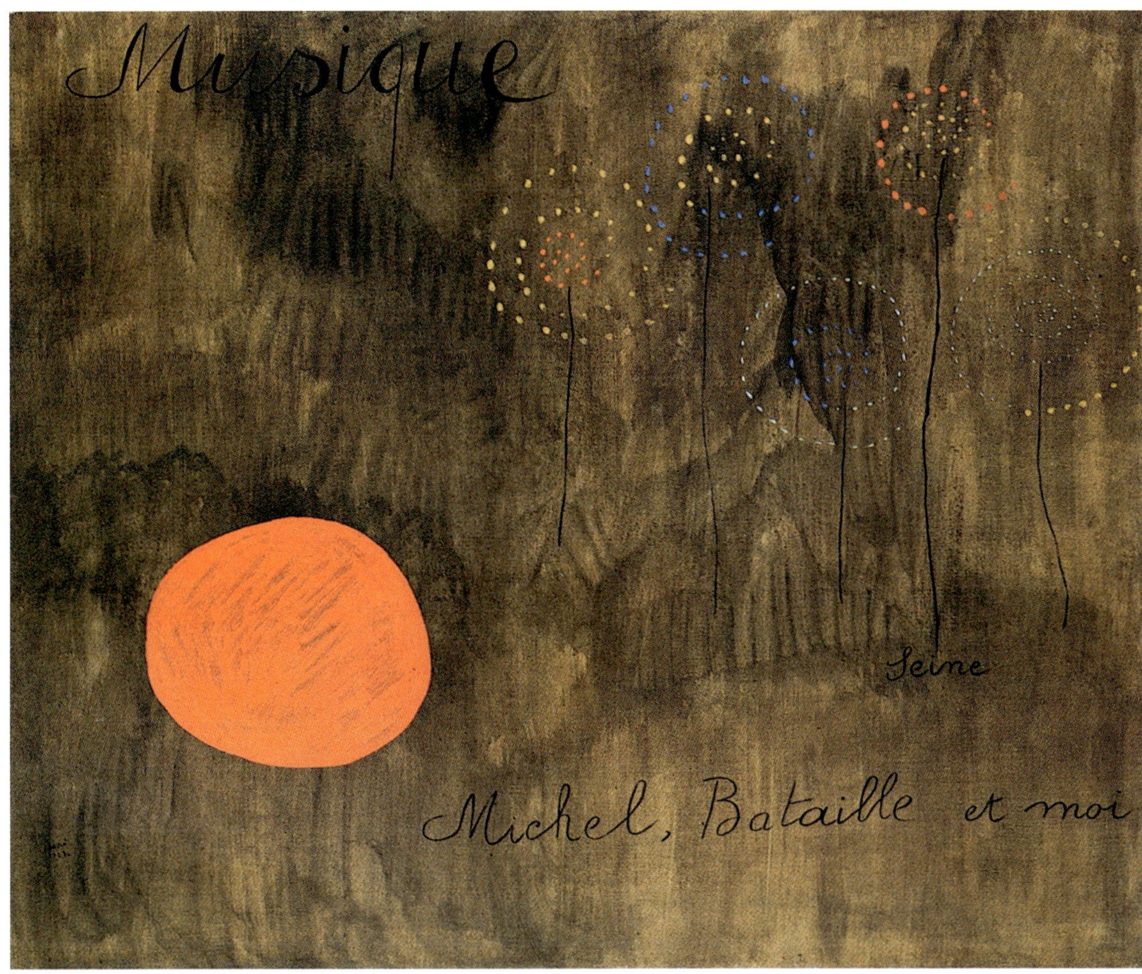

66 Joan Miró, *Music, Seine, Michel, Bataille and I*, 1927, oil on canvas.

images that is definitional of Surrealism. The word–image nexus within Surrealism comprises a system of attractions and interferences, the net effect of which is to subvert the purity and formal autonomy of Reverdy's late Cubist aesthetic.

René Magritte's *The Submissive Reader* (illus. 67) of 1928 dramatically represents the activity of reading and, by extension, the relationship of painting to literature. One imagines the startled woman is reading Edgar Allan Poe or another of the writers from whom Magritte regularly drew his inspiration. More systematically than any other Surrealist artist, Magritte probes the relation of words to images, and to the things they purport to represent. He confronts the viewer with visual brainteasers that provoke a quasi-philosophical reflection upon the nature of language and representation, leading to comparisons of Magritte with the Viennese philosopher of language, Ludwig Wittgenstein. Others consider him as a precursor of conceptual art. A lot of Magritte's uncanny and surreal effects are due to the arbitrary character of linguistic signs. Consistently thwarting our expectation that words and things should affirm each other, the Magrittean word-image is more akin to an unravelled calligram, as Michel Foucault remarked. He also subverts the orderly relation that is meant to obtain between an image and the object it represents: through the use of doubling and other pictorial devices, Magritte introduces doubt in our mind as to which is the model and which is the copy. Not for nothing was one of his most recognizable works titled *The Treachery of Images*.

In the December 1929 issue of *La Révolution surréaliste* (illus. 68) Magritte summarized his diverse experiments in this domain in a series of pithy aphorisms accompanied by simple line drawings.[68] 'An object does not hold onto its name so tightly that one cannot find another which suits it better': *The Key of Dreams* (illus. 69) of 1930, a

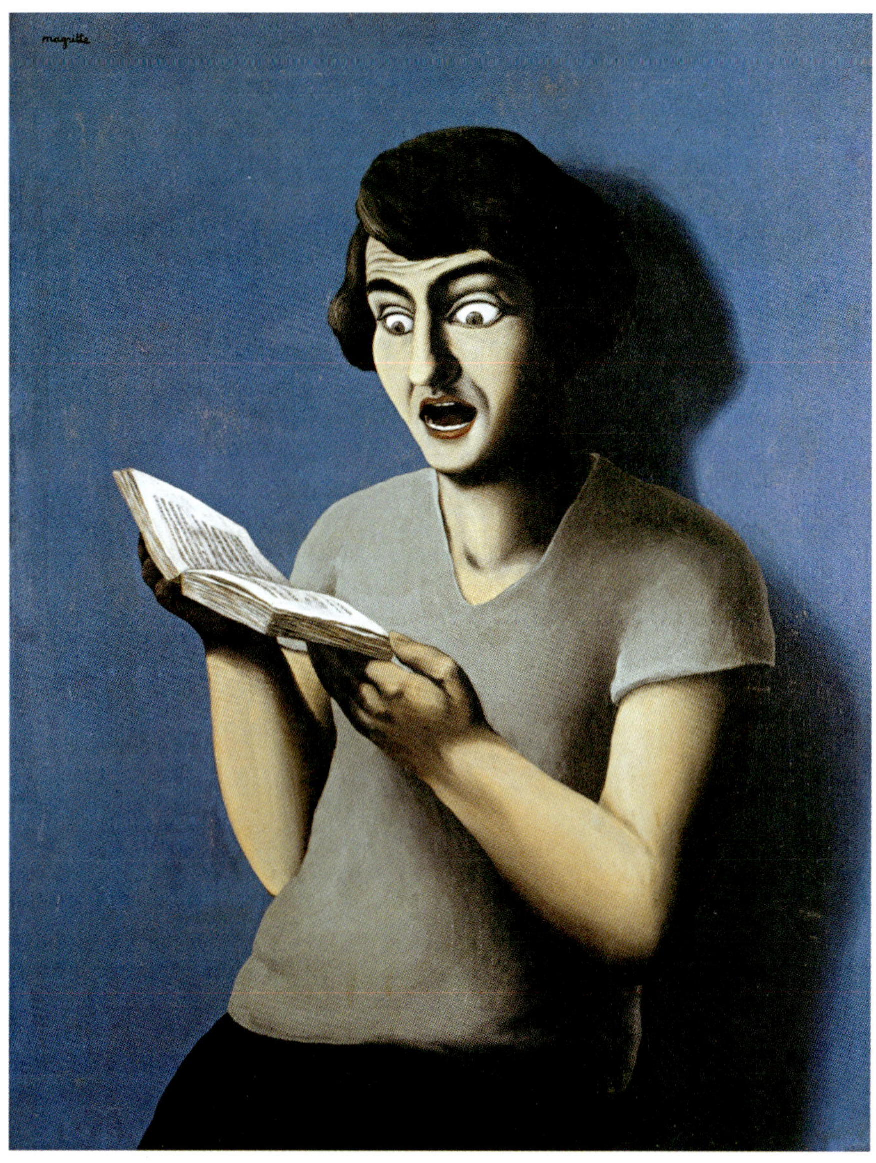

67 René Magritte, *The Submissive Reader*, 1928, oil on canvas.

picture that alludes to the Freudian concept of dream symbolism, illustrates this maxim. 'Everything tends to make one think that there is little relation between an object and that which represents it', declares another: *The Treachery of Images* (illus. 70) tests out this proposition. Michel Foucault elegantly outlines the conundrums, the traps for comprehension, posed by this iconic Surrealist image. It is painted deceptively in the manner of an elementary primer for schoolchildren designed to inculcate knowledge of the proper relations of words to things. Foucault imagines a teacher explaining to his sceptical pupils:

> Scarcely has he stated 'This is a pipe,' before he must correct himself and stutter, 'This is not a pipe, but a drawing of a pipe,' 'This is not a pipe but a sentence saying that this is not a pipe,' 'The sentence 'this is not a pipe' is not a pipe,' 'In the sentence "this is not a pipe", *this* is not a pipe: the painting, written sentence, drawing of a pipe – all this is not a pipe.' The students fall about in laughter at their teacher's bewilderment.[69]

It is perhaps not a coincidence that Foucault turned to Magritte as he was writing *Les Mots et les choses* (1966), in which he analyses the historicity of knowledge in terms of specific configurations of words, ideas and things. Foucault opens with a description of a Chinese system of classification that is utterly alien to a European mindset. Surrealism, likewise, sought to reclassify objects, freeing them from their utilitarian meaning and function. As early as 1924, Breton envisaged the materialization of certain unusual objects that had appeared to him in dreams. Given impetus by Salvador Dalí, the craze for Surrealist objects reached its apogee with an exhibition at the Charles Ratton Gallery in 1936. As with the ready-

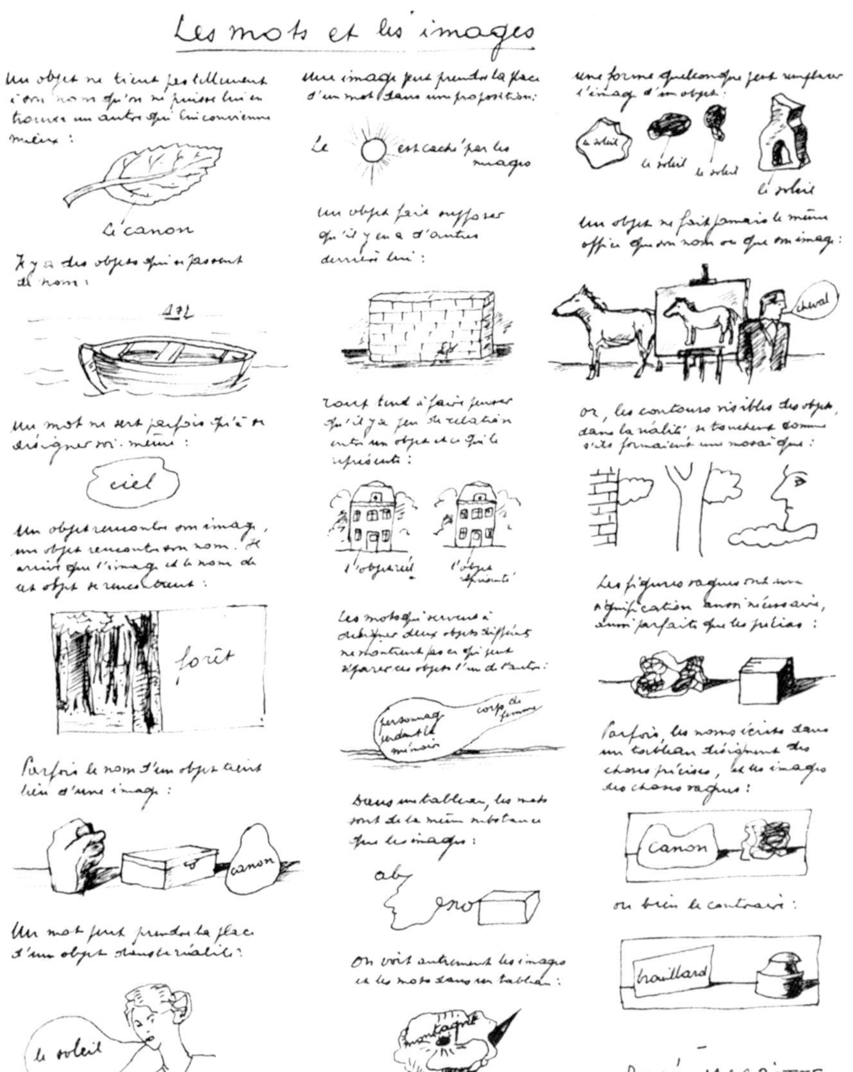

68 René Magritte, 'Les Mots et les images,' *La Révolution surréaliste* (15 December 1929).

made, one of the precursors for the Surrealist object, language as title or inscription not infrequently plays an ancillary role. The box assemblages of Victor Brauner from the early 1940s, such as *Portrait of Novalis* (illus. 71), incorporate magical and fetishistic materials along with cabbalistic inscriptions, some written in Hebrew. A Jewish artist who fled anti-Semitism in Romania, Brauner once more found himself in mortal danger. Produced while he was in hiding in Vichy France, these unique objects have an apotropaic or magical function: they are designed to ward off danger and protect the artist from a hostile and threatening world. One finds the book itself treated as a veritable Surrealist object, indeed one of the dream objects recalled by Breton was 'a rather curious book' with pages of black cloth grafted onto a garden gnome. A number of *livre-objets* by Georges Hugnet, bespoke cover-frames for literary works by his fellow Surrealists, were reproduced in the magazine *Minotaure*.[70] The most startling example of this genre was created by Duchamp as the catalogue cover for a Surrealist exhibition in 1947. Consisting of a cast of a female breast, it is provocatively titled *Please Touch*, a rejoinder possibly to the modernist definition of artistic reception in terms of 'pure opticality' – a detached mode of aesthetic experience enshrined in the universal interdiction against touching works of art in museums. Coinciding as it does with the international spread of Surrealism from the mid-1930s, object assemblage was readily taken up in the far-flung places where Surrealism took root. A 1937 exhibition, *Surrealist Objects and Poems*, at the London Gallery was premised on a belief in the equivalence of these two modes of expression. A wistful, poetic sensibility infuses the work of New York-based Surrealist convert Joseph Cornell, whose trademark glass-fronted boxes

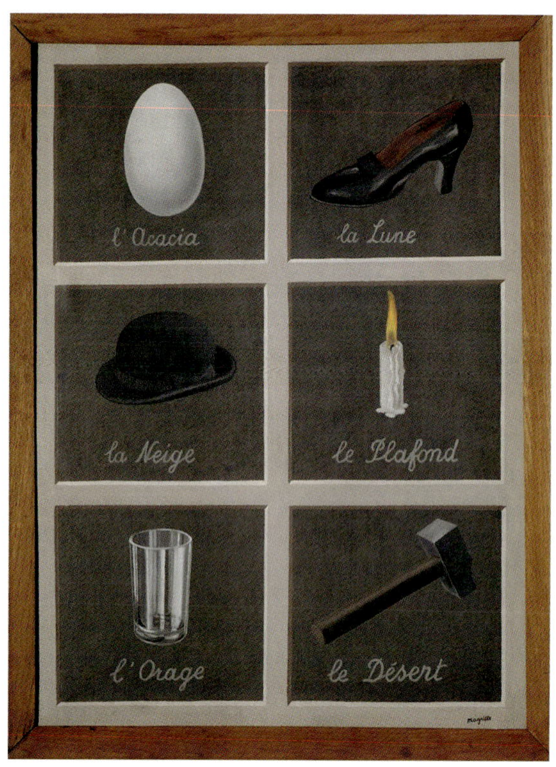

69 René Magritte, *The Interpretation of Dreams*, 1930, oil on canvas.

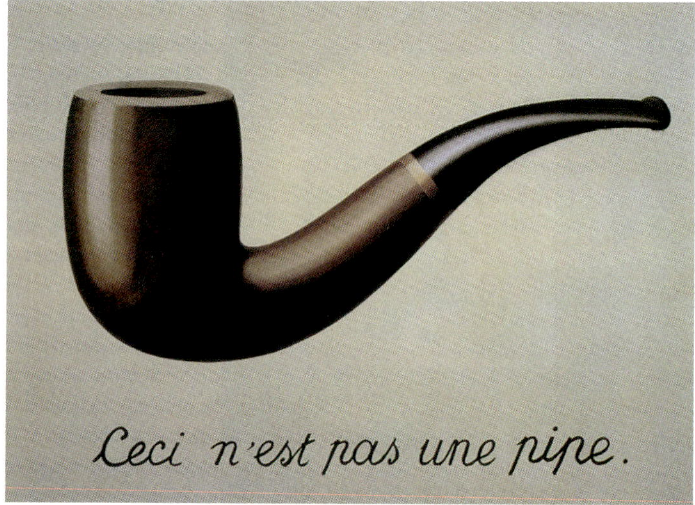

70 René Magritte, *The Treachery of Images*: '*Ceci n'est pas une pipe*', 1929, oil on canvas.

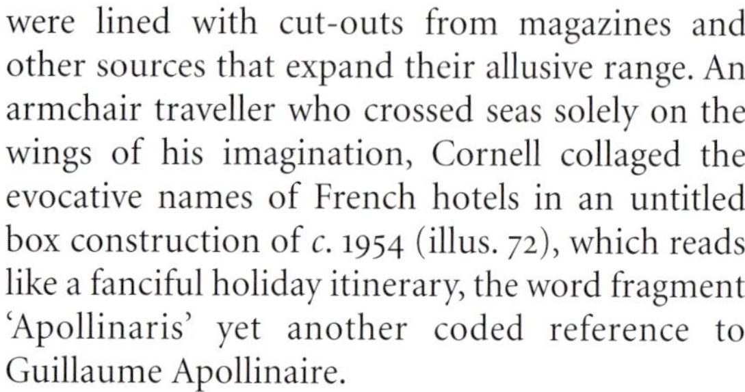

were lined with cut-outs from magazines and other sources that expand their allusive range. An armchair traveller who crossed seas solely on the wings of his imagination, Cornell collaged the evocative names of French hotels in an untitled box construction of *c.* 1954 (illus. 72), which reads like a fanciful holiday itinerary, the word fragment 'Apollinaris' yet another coded reference to Guillaume Apollinaire.

In the mid-1930s, when the vogue for Surrealist objects was at its height, Breton inaugurated a new genre, the *objet-poème*, which seemingly took to heart Magritte's contention that words have the same *substance* as images. 'The object-poem is a composition which combines the resources of poetry and plastic art, and thus speculates on the capacity of these two elements to excite each other mutually', Breton wrote.[71] Formally resembling objects created by the mentally ill, as well as the use of captions in museological displays, the object-poem represents his most significant contribution to Surrealist visual art. The earliest examples date from 1935. In a passage from a lecture delivered at Prague in that year concerned with the issue of how the unconscious can become conscious, which is the core problematic of Surrealist art, Breton makes reference to a highly technical discussion in Freud about the relationship between words and things that it is tempting to see as affording a theoretical underpinning of the poem-object. From the point of view of psychoanalysis, it is the job of interpretation to re-establish the broken connections between words and things. In a manuscript dated 27 February 1942, Breton undertook a detailed elucidation of an object-poem that would otherwise have been entirely refractory to interpretation owing to the personal and recondite nature of the associations underlying it. The piece (dated 1941), which is no longer extant, was shown the following month in the exhibition *Artists in Exile* at Pierre Matisse's New York gallery and was reproduced in 1942 in a catalogue of Peggy Guggenheim's personal collection (illus. 73). The text inscribed on this object reads:

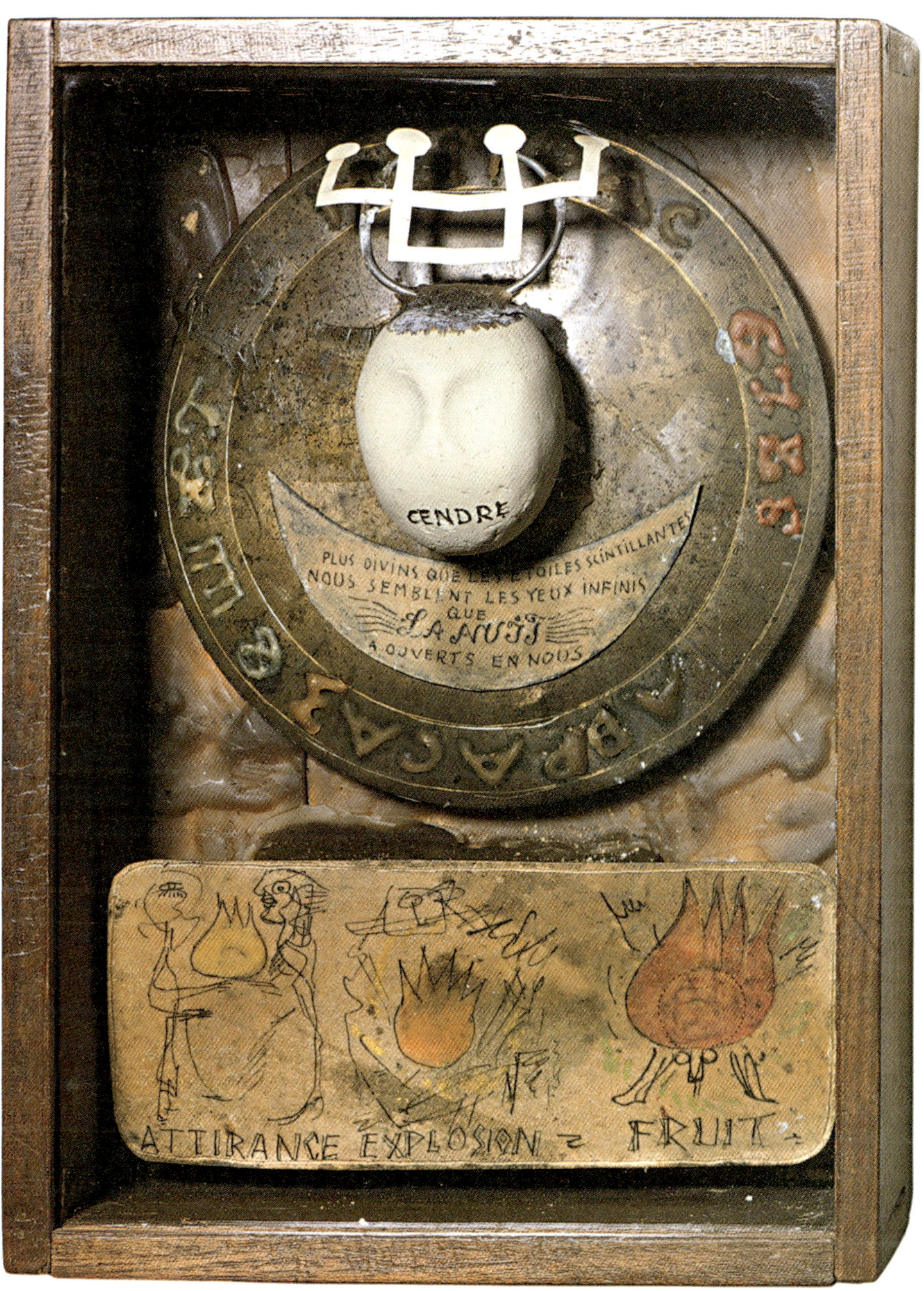

71 Victor Brauner, *Portrait of Novalis*, 1943, copper, plaster, wire, metal thread, wax, india ink and bodycolour on paper.

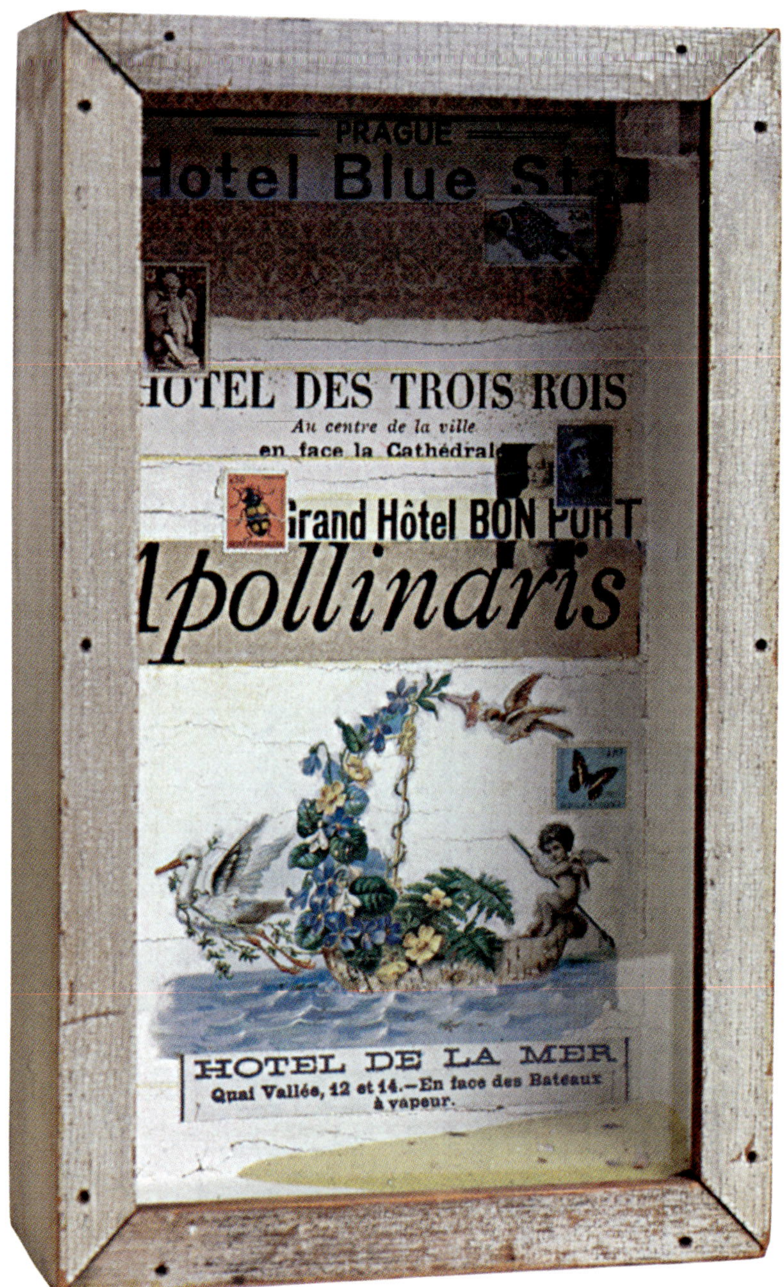

72 Joseph Cornell, *Untitled* (*Apollinaris*), *c.* 1954, box construction with collage.

Portrait de l'acteur a b
dans son rôle mémorable
l'an de grâce 1713
D'un judas de Port-Royal détruite mais
invulnérable
Je te vois pape Clément XI *vieux chien…*

Unpacking this work, which interweaves personal references to Breton's unhappy plight (a tiny suitcase hangs poignantly from the assemblage) with the historical events that culminated in the episode of the Jansenist convulsionaries at Saint-Médard cemetery, we see Breton decompose his initials A B into the numerals 1713. Looking into this association, he discovered that 1713 was the year of a Papal order that declared the Jansenist faith heretical. Although destroyed on the order of the King, the abbey of Port-Royal – a Jansenist stronghold – endured as an anti-authoritarian symbol. Alluding to the Jansenists, Breton in exile identifies with their persecution and their defiance.

Inspired in part by Offenbach's opera, *Tales of Hoffmann*, based on 'The Sandman', in which the hero Nathaniel falls in love with a lifeless doll, the German artist Hans Bellmer began assembling dolls in 1933. Bellmer, who saw his perverse fascination with dolls as expressing opposition to the father and Fascist authority, was welcomed into the Surrealist

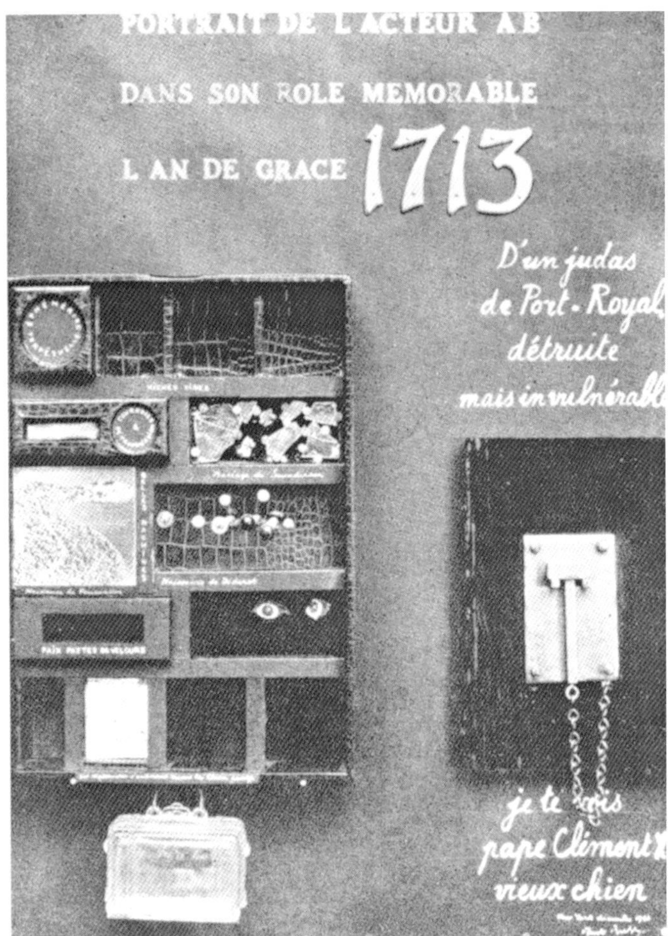

73 André Breton, *Poem-Object (Portrait of the Actor A.B.)*, 1941, destroyed.

fold. A selection of Bellmer's photographs, sub-titled 'Variations on the Montage of an Articulated Minor', was published as a double-page spread in the Surrealist journal *Minotaure* in 1935. A doll, in the form of a pubertal girl, is obsessively dismembered and reassembled with sadistic, or possibly masochistic, delight (illus. 74). Bellmer cites as a crucial discovery a wooden ball-joint that enabled him to reconceive the body as a mechanistic assemblage in which arms/legs, breasts/buttocks, armpit/eye/sex are all potentially exchangeable. In 1946 Bellmer made illustrations for Georges Bataille's pornographic novella, *Story of the Eye* (1928), which similarly revolves around textual equivalences of eggs, eyes and testicles. Bellmer posits a series of parallels between his vision of the body as an infinitely malleable plaything, reversible and interchangeable, and language in the essay *Little Anatomy of the Physical Unconscious: Or, The Anatomy of the Image* (1957). He claimed the existence of a fundamental psychophysical tendency to reversal within the human nervous system, citing mirror writing and the pleasure children derive from pronouncing words and phrases backwards. He also lists various examples of palindromes. Dilating on this vision, the body, he contends, 'is comparable to a sentence that invites you to disarticulate it, for the purpose of recombining its actual contents through a series of endless anagrams'.[72] Bellmer goes on to enumerate a sequence of permutations on the phrase 'Rose au coeur violet', taken from a poem by Gérard de Nerval. The anagrams, a tour de force in French and German, won praise from Man Ray, who telegrammed Bellmer with the succinct response: 'IMAGE = MAGIE.' In a similar vein of erotic transgression, Dalí – who came to Surrealism already imbued, he says, with the spirit of Sade – created an alphabet out of male and female couples engaged in sex acts of all descriptions, a subversive take on Breton's lofty notion of 'les mots font l'amour'.

The Marquis de Sade, one of Surrealism's deities, was paid homage by Man Ray in a sequence of imaginary portraits. The first version took the form of a line drawing in a collaborative volume with Paul Eluard, *Les Mains libres*, of 1937, accompanied by a statement by the poet about the absence of any known likenesses of Sade (only more recently has a portrait engraving of Sade as a young man come to light). Man Ray also produced a very striking painted version, of which at least two copies exist (illus. 75). Sade appears as a monument built out of the stones of his one-time prison – those of the Bastille were indeed reused by the Revolutionaries as building materials – implying that Man Ray's symbolic effigy is a provisional construction that might at some future point be dismantled and reconstructed. In the background, the Bastille burns as the Revolutionary crowd surges around it. At the bottom of the portrait Man Ray inscribed some lines from Sade's will: 'In order that … the traces of my grave should disappear from the surface of the earth, just as I take pride in the notion that my memory will be wiped from the minds of men … D.A.F. de Sade.'

In 1936 Breton gathered a series of texts for an anthology on the subject of black humour (*humour noir*), which he had come to see as a necessary ingredient in any artistic expression of a modern sensibility.[73] Jacques Vaché, a nihilistic character imbued with a deeply felt sense of the pointlessness of everything, coined the term 'umor' – one source of inspiration for Breton's

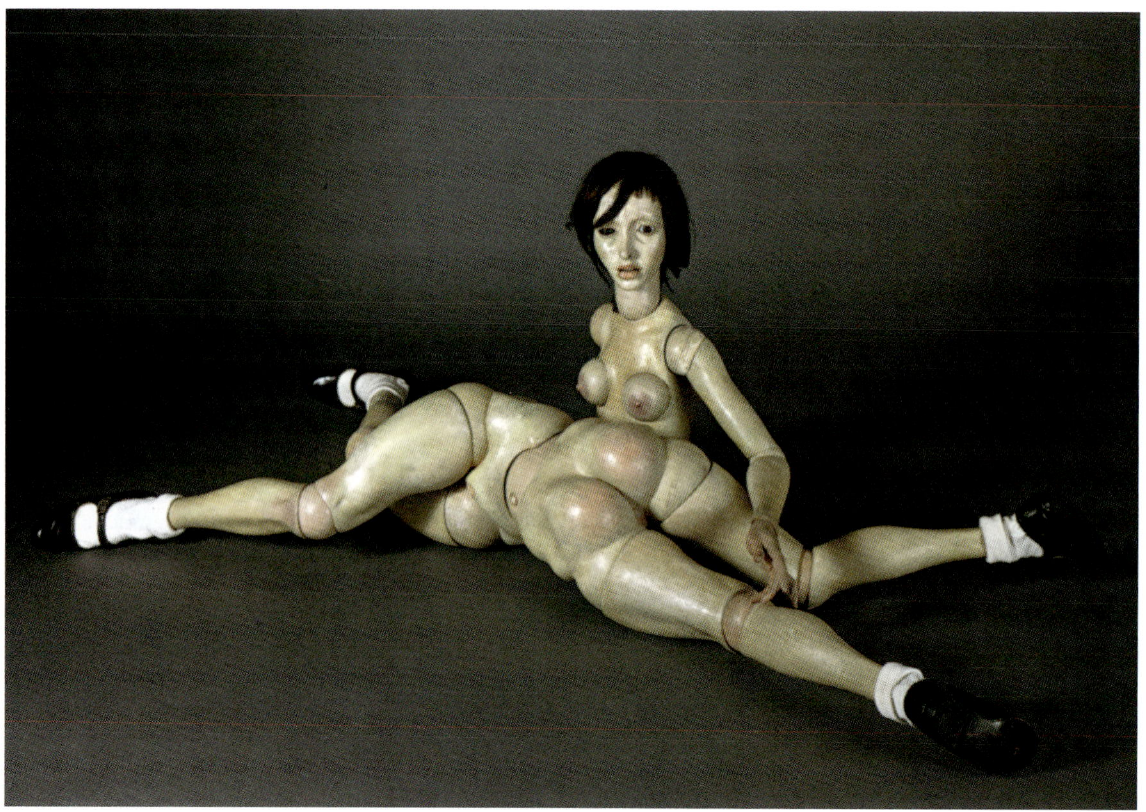

74 Hans Bellmer, *The Doll*, *c.* 1935–6, painted wood, paper maché, hair, shoes, socks.

idea. Black humour expresses a spirit of insubordination, a superior revolt of the mind; citing Freud, it represents, Breton states, the triumph of pleasure over reality. Black humour manifested first in literature and only subsequently in art. In the modern era, cinema is an important domain for the expression of this spirit (Breton mentions, amongst others, the comedies of Mack Sennett, the Marx Brothers' *Animal Crackers* and Dalí's and Buñuel's *Un Chien andalou*). Beginning with Jonathan Swift, Breton includes more writers than visual artists in his genealogy. Among the former are all the expected Surrealist precursors, including of course, the incomparable Lautréamont. Among the artists is Picasso, represented by two automatic, stream of consciousness poems. Picasso had begun writing poetry in 1934 during a year of personal turmoil and uncertainty in which he virtually ceased painting. Breton had brought Picasso's new creative outlet to public attention for the first time in an article, 'Picasso poète', in *Cahiers d'art* in 1936. Picasso went on to write several plays, notably *Desire Caught by the Tail*, remembered for having been performed by a famous cast in Paris under the Occupation. Breton's anthology encompassed the Dadaists Picabia, Duchamp and Arp, but only two Surrealist artists, Salvador Dalí and Leonora Carrington, though Ernst's three collage novels are singled out in the theoretical introduction as examples of sardonic black humour. Irrationality and unpredictable outbursts of savage violence reign supreme in these books. Carrington was represented by an excerpt from her mythological tale *La Dame ovale* of 1939.

Dalí was a major new recruit to Surrealism at the end of the 1920s, offsetting the expulsions and defections at that time. Dalí's brilliance as a writer equals that of the inventor of soft watches and lobster telephones. He was also very funny, as Breton discovered, since he was more than once at the receiving end of Dalí's humour. A love of word-

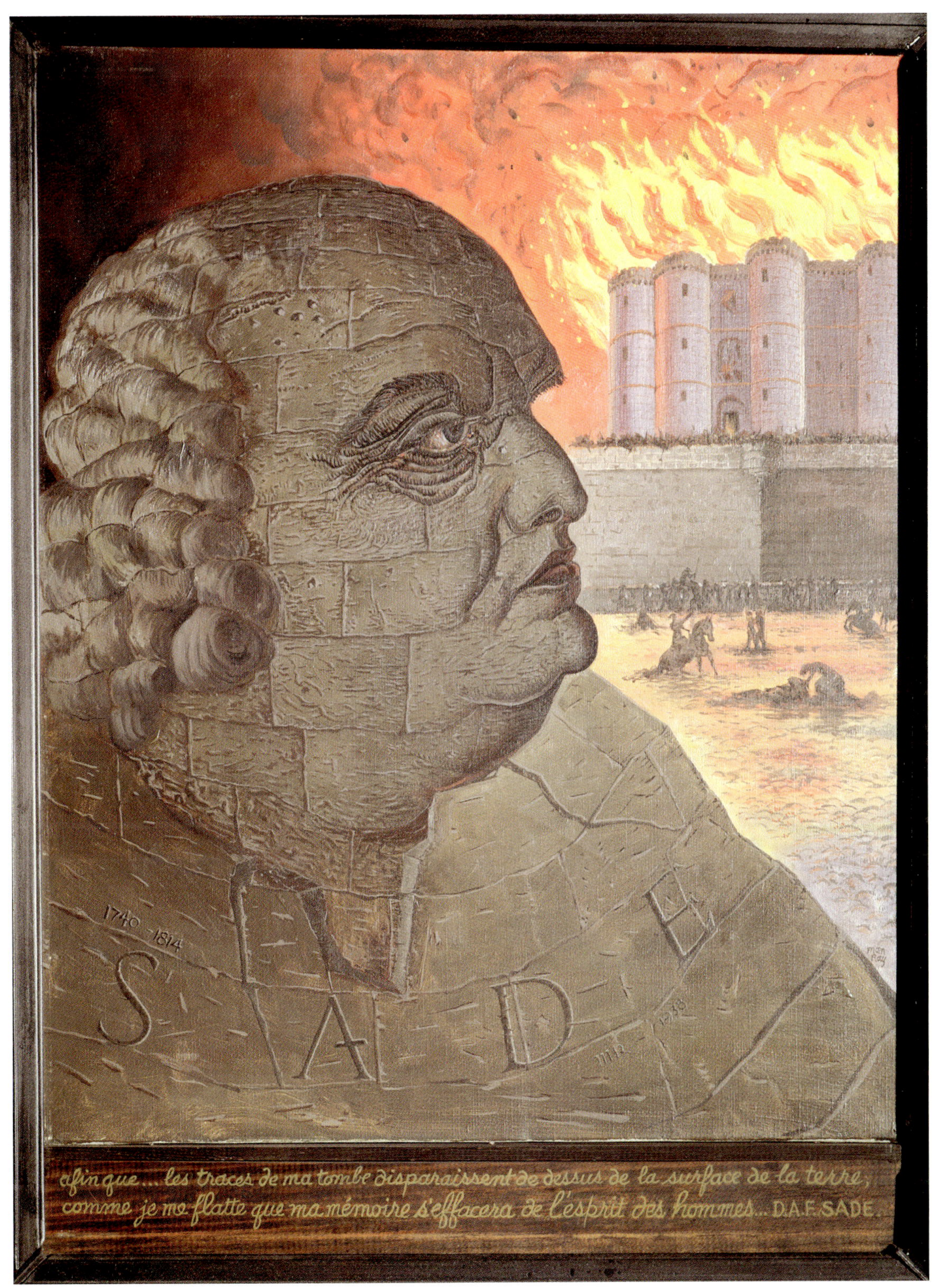

75 Man Ray, *Imaginary Portrait of D.A.F. de Sade*, 1938, oil on canvas, with painted wood panel.

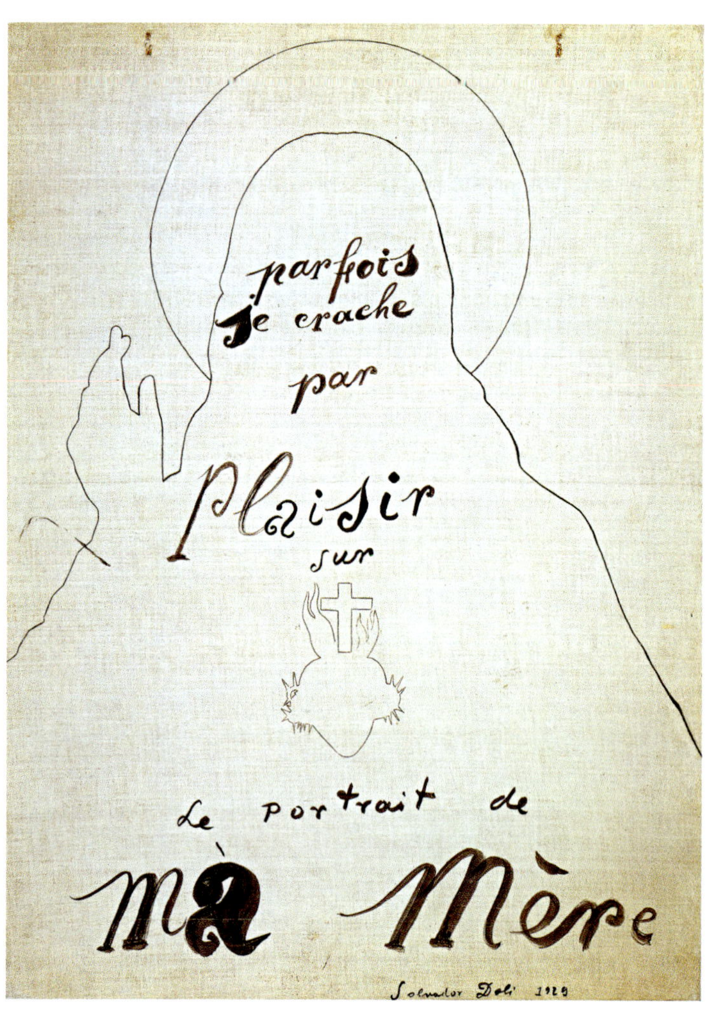

76 Salvador Dalí, *Sometimes I Spit with Pleasure on the Portrait of my Mother,* 1929, india ink on canvas.

plays, mixing English, Catalan, Spanish and French, obscured by the corrected versions of his texts and revealed only lately by the study of the original manuscripts, point to Dalí's affinity with Duchamp, one of the very few modern artists for whom he maintained an unqualified regard. Duchamp's L.H.O.O.Q. and Picabia's *La Sainte vierge* were inspirations for Dalí's *Sometimes I Spit with Pleasure on the Portrait of My Mother* (illus. 76). One has to imagine that Christ, whose hand is raised in benediction, is the source of this blasphemous utterance. Catering to a Surrealist taste for profanation, this incendiary image precipitated Dalí's forcible ejection from his father's household. A later, no less scurrilous exercise in the ready-made genre took as a source image a commercial photograph by Gutman & Gutman, New York. Dalí's handiwork transforms the saccharine photograph of a placid infant into a malcontent who vents its seething cannibalistic impulses on a rat dangling helplessly from its teeth. The title 'Contentment' is amended to 'Le Pervers Polimorf [sic] de Freud'. The visceral disgust provoked by this untoward action is a measure of the degree to which Freud's theory of infantile sexuality countermanded bourgeois stereotypical notions of childhood, to which the source image panders.

Dalí was already thoroughly cognizant of Freud's study of Leonardo when he made an ink sketch for his 1942 autobiography, *The Secret Life of Salvador Dalí,* to accompany the account of his visit to Freud in London in July 1938 (illus. 77).[74] A number of features of this heavily citational drawing are reminiscent of Leonardo: the combination of multiple variant images on a single sheet, for example, is highly typical, a manifestation of Leonardo's restless intellect, which was never satisfied with just one solution. Dalí said of his meeting with Freud that he had wanted to appear a 'kind of dandy of "universal intellectualism"' (like Leonardo) but learned later that the impression he produced was exactly the opposite! The grimacing profile repeated three times at the left of the sheet exacts his revenge, recalling the pitiless caricatures in which Leonardo poked fun at the ravages of old age; Freud was already ill with cancer at the time of Dalí's visit. Another signature trait is the inclusion of notation upon the sheet, in this case explaining that the drawing represents the morphology of Freud's cranium according to the principle of the

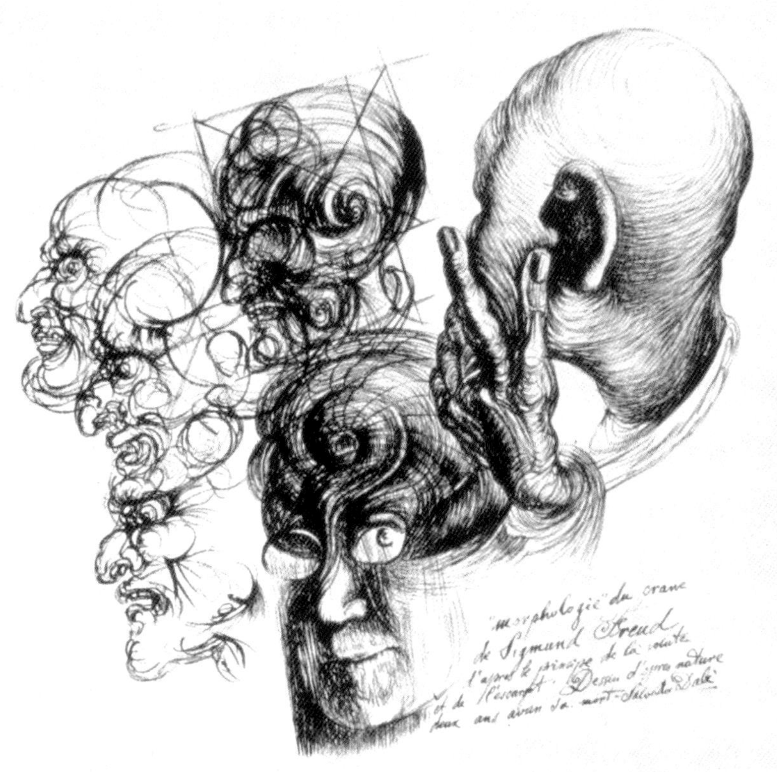

77 Original drawing for *The Secret Life of Salvador Dalí* (New York, 1942), india ink on paper.

spiral of a snail shell. The adjoining text in *The Secret Life* compares Freud's brain with that of Leonardo, which Dalí says is like a walnut. The spiral or vortex is, moreover, a nearly ubiquitous leitmotif in Leonardo's art. By deliberately and self-consciously depicting Freud in the manner of Leonardo, Dalí alluded in 1942 to a complex set of psychic investments in Leonardo and a play of identifications in which he too participated.

The *Metamorphosis of Narcissus* (1937), which Dalí took with him to his meeting with Freud, is the outstanding example in his work of a parallel between poetry and painting. It was, he claimed, 'THE FIRST POEM AND THE FIRST PAINTING OBTAINED ENTIRELY THROUGH THE INTEGRAL APPLICATION OF THE PARANOIAC-CRITICAL METHOD.' The English Surrealist collector and would-be poet, Edward James, who was staying with Dalí at Zürs in the Austrian Alps when he embarked on the picture, recalls that narcissi were everywhere in flower. James's presence might have been a factor in Dalí's choice of the narcissus subject and his decision to write the poem, which in part serves to explain the complex iconography. Given the homoerotic connotations of the narcissus myth, the story of a beautiful youth who falls in love with his own reflection after spurning the nymph Echo, it is of interest that Dalí also refers explicitly in the poem to Federico García Lorca, who had been murdered in August of the previous year, in the early months of the Spanish Civil War. Whilst students in Madrid, Dalí and Lorca enjoyed an intense friendship and their creative exchanges, revolving around St Sebastian, were tinged with homoerotic overtones.[75] The poem begins by narrating the thawing of the snow at springtime, and goes on to describe the melting of Narcissus, in thrall to the 'dionysiac call' of his own reflection, which gradually absorbs him 'with the digestive slowness of carnivorous plants' until he becomes invisible. The final stanza describes the metamorphosis of Narcissus into the flower that bears his name, and retrospectively confers on the whole poem an autobiographical meaning. Referring to the famous double image of the hand holding an egg, Dalí writes that when that head bursts open, 'it will be the flower, the new Narcissus, Gala – my narcissus.'[76]

It behoves us to recall the tradition of ekphrasis, the creation of a mimetic equivalent in words for a painting or sculpture, as a model for the word-image relation here. The narcissus subject, which throughout history has been treated in literature and the visual arts, seems to have been especially conducive to this form.[77] It was the subject of an ekphrastic poem by the Greek sophist Philostratus the Elder in his *Imagines*. Closer in time to the Surrealists, the narcissus subject was popular in Symbolism, with texts by Gide and Valéry, and paintings by Gustave Moreau and many others. Narcissism, and related tropes of mirroring and doubling, are prominent in the photography of the Surrealist Claude Cahun, who

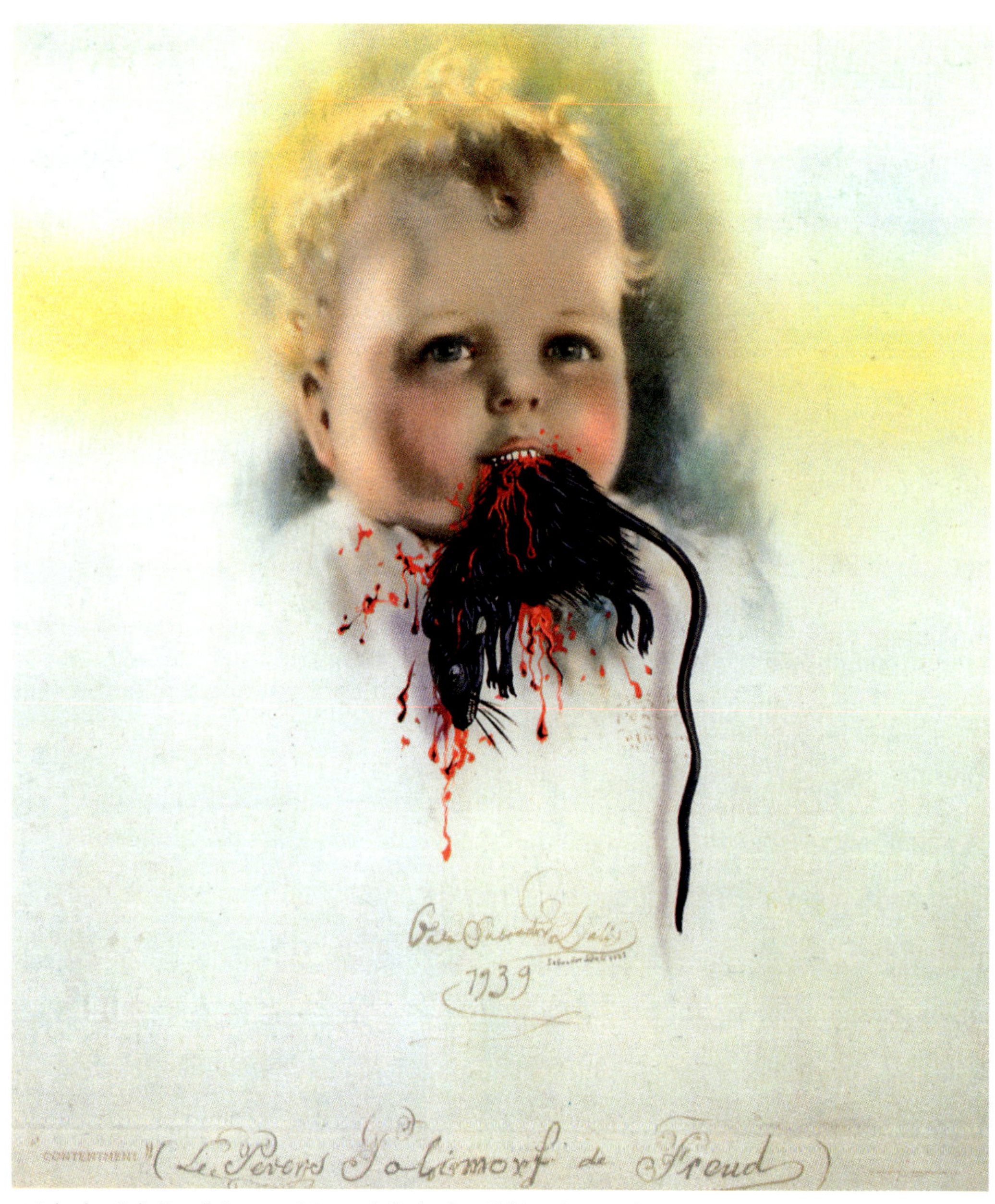

78 Salvador Dalí, *Freud's Perverse Polymorph (Bulgarian Child Eating a Rat)*, 1939, gouache on a photograph.

came from a literary family and was steeped in a symbolist literary heritage. Cahun's *Aveux non avenus* [*Avowals Disavowed*] contains an excursus on narcissism that may be regarded as an ekphrastic commentary on this aspect of her imagery. Cahun was one of a considerable number of gay and lesbian artists and writers who were drawn to Surrealism, for whom the movement provided a clearing, a space wherein they could explore relations of desire, identity and the image. This was despite Breton's notorious intolerance of homosexuality. Cahun elaborated a performative notion of identity, confounding normative signifiers of gender, in an extensive body of self-portrait photography that was produced collaboratively with her lifelong partner, Suzanne Malherbe. An inscription on one of the collages in *Aveux non avenus* (illus. 79) states: 'Behind this mask another, and another, and so on.'[78] The San Francisco-based, Surrealist artist Jess (Collins) also produced a major work on the narcissus theme that occupied him over a very lengthy period. There are many crossovers with literature in the work of Jess, whose partner, Robert Duncan, was a major twentieth-century American poet. Jess, who experienced an epiphany after Duncan gave him a copy of Ernst's collage novel *Une Semaine de bonté* (1934), mostly worked in the medium of collage.[79] We have seen many instances of how collage permitted a stratum of private meanings and innuendo to be layered into the image. The resultant interplay of disclosure and concealment – of avowals disavowed – had enormous practical utility for artists who could not openly declare their homosexuality.[80] It is significant that Jess drew inspiration from Ernst, whose *oeuvre* has the pictorial structure of a rebus or puzzle. Ernst also spoke about himself indirectly, in the third person, as individuals whose sexuality did not conform to prevailing norms were forced to do.

Secretly inscribed on the back of *Men Shall Know Nothing of This* (illus. 80) of 1923 is a poem, together with a dedication to the picture's owner, André Breton, that purports to explicate the inscrutable iconography of the work:

The crescent (yellow and parachutic) stops the
little whistle falling to the ground. The whistle,
because people are taking notice of it, thinks it
is climbing to the sun.
The sun is divided into two so that it can spin
better.
The model is stretched out in a dreaming pose. The
right leg is bent (a pleasant exact movement.)
The hand hides the earth. Through this action the
earth takes on the importance of a sexual
organ.
The moon runs through its phases and eclipses
with the utmost speed.
The picture is curious because of its symmetry.
The two sexes balance each other.[81]

Commentators have discerned an allusion to the alchemical *conjunctio oppositorum* in the motif of a copulating couple suspended in mid-air. There may also be references to Freud's study of Judge Daniel Schreber, whose autobiography recounts a severe psychotic illness in the course of which Schreber believed he was transformed from a man into a woman and was fertilized by the sun's rays, a God-father symbol. Ernst plays subversively with genders (male–female) and genres (poetry–painting), destabilizing their separate characters and presenting an image of their creative union. It is tempting to see this fusion of opposites as revealing something fundamental about the Surrealist project as a whole.

Surrealism, with its unapologetic literariness, was, not surprisingly, Clement Greenberg's *bête noire*. Writing in 1940, in 'Towards a Newer Laöcoon', the formalist critic chided 'the young orthodox Surrealists' for a 'confusion of literature with painting as extreme as any of the past'.[82] Aligning his own critical stance with that of Lessing, who had deduced what belonged properly to poetry and visual art from the different character of verbal and visual signs, Greenberg argued that the task of modernist art has been to purge itself of everything that is foreign to it, a process of purification that resulted from the 'willing acceptance of the limitations of the medium of the specific art.'[83] For painting, this meant a rejection of mimesis and storytelling: of literature, in short. Greenberg claimed Cubism as a crucial staging post on a path leading from Manet to abstraction.

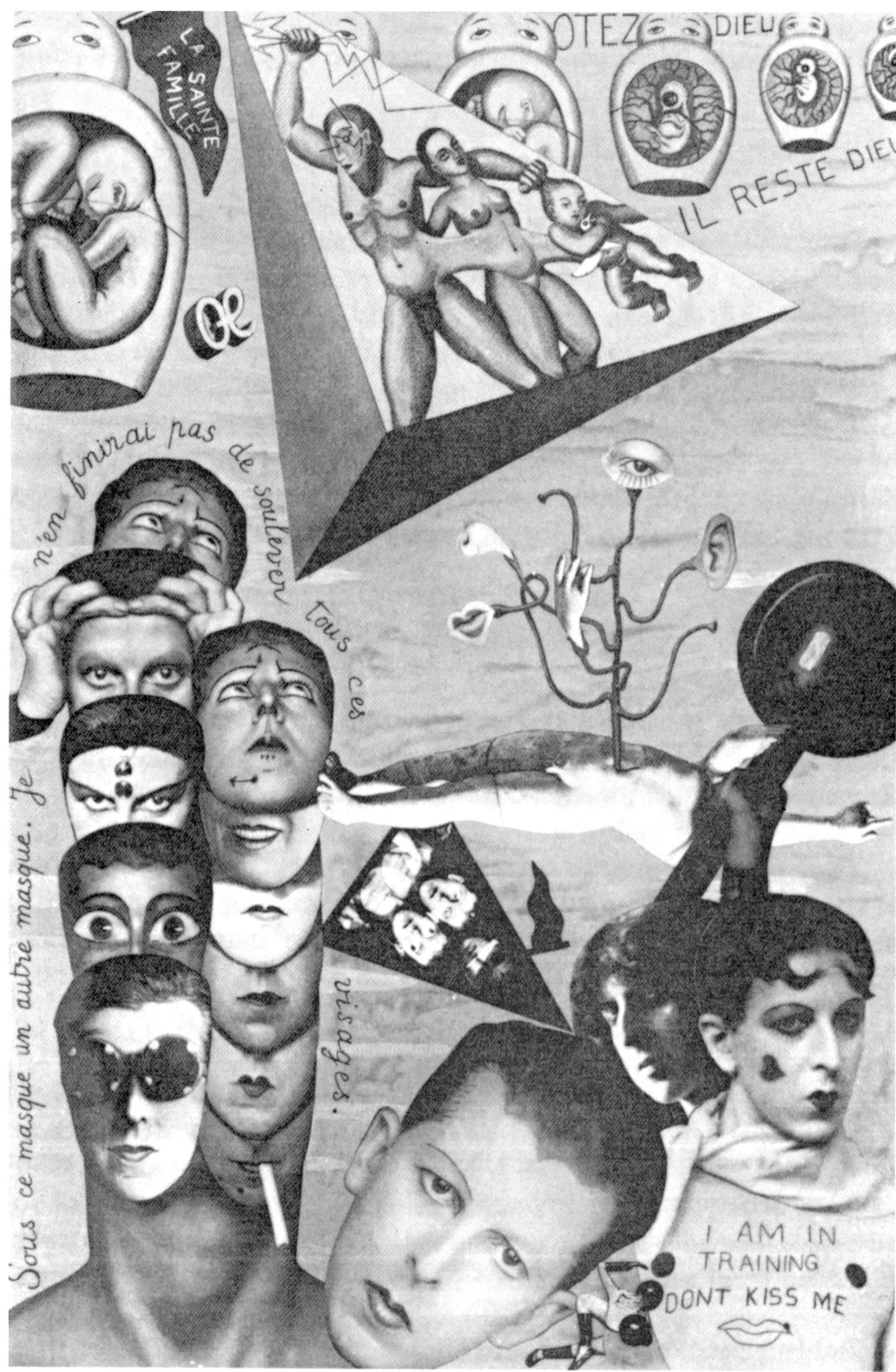

79 Claude Cahun, Collage from *Aveux non avenus* (Paris, 1930).

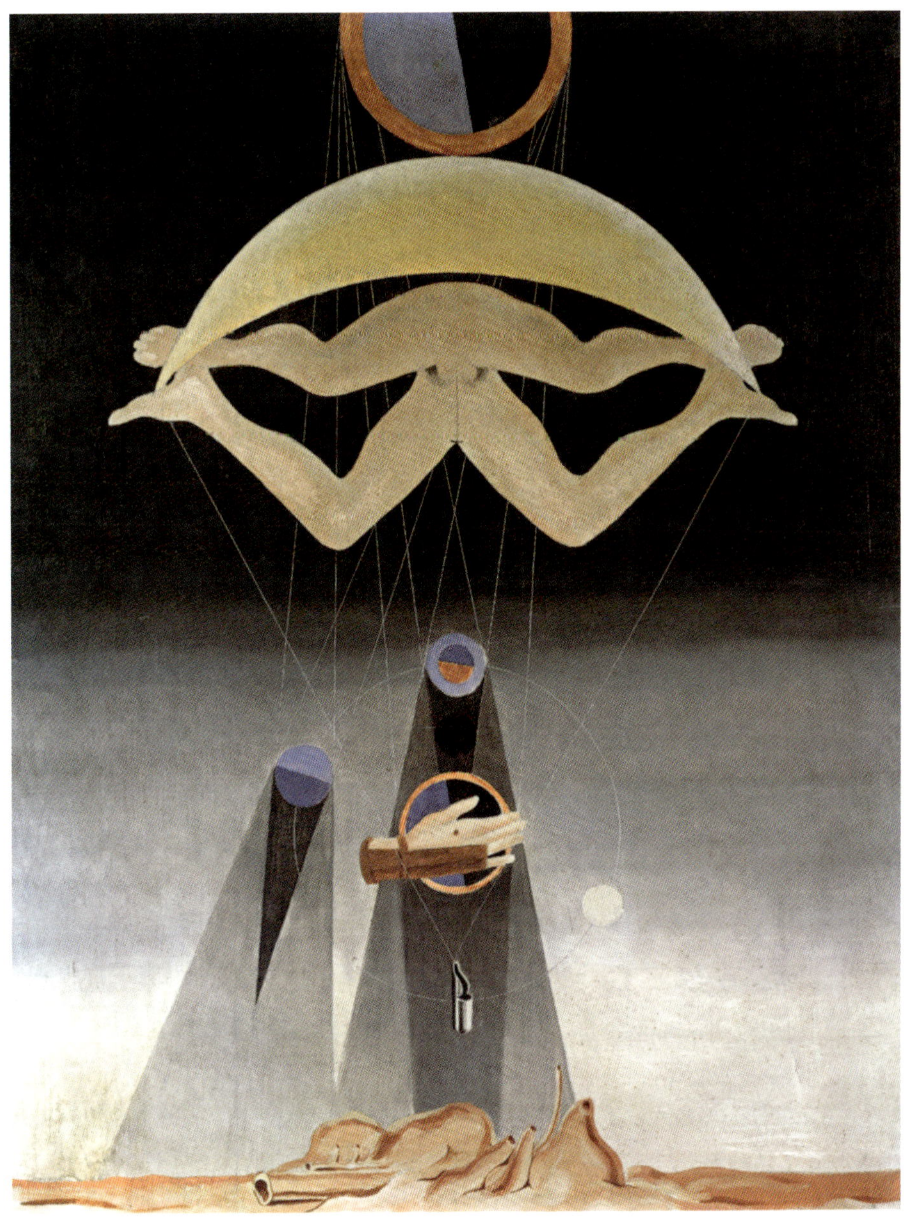

80 Max Ernst, *Men Shall Know Nothing of This*, 1923, oil on canvas.

What we have observed repeatedly, in a survey covering a similar period, is evidence that, on the contrary, artists refused to be so constrained. The stencilled letters of Cubist painting were a Trojan horse, an augury of what was to follow as the floodgates opened and words poured into the field of painting. Foucault discerned the radical subversiveness of this inauspicious operation, writing that: 'the linguistic signs which seemed to be excluded, which prowled at a distance around the image … have surreptitiously reappeared: they have introduced into the plenitude of the image, into its meticulous resemblance, a disorder'.[84] With the eclipse of modernism, it is possible now to look back and see that the true character of experimental avant-gardes in the first half of the twentieth century was to have provided an inter-medial space where verbal and visual modes of expression collided, overlapped, intersected and conjugated in a rich profusion of hybrid forms. Modern art really was postmodern all along.

2

Paul Klee as 'Poet-Painter'

JEREMY ADLER

The early twentieth century witnessed a major change in the relations between word and image, evident in the invention of collage, in which printed words form a part of the meaning, and also in Apollinaire's calligrammes – poems shaped like objects – as well as in the Futurists' words-in-freedom, in which the shape of words, the visual dimension, forms part of the overall sense. These new works reflected a far wider paradigm shift, as can be seen in Freud's attention to symbols or in Wittgenstein's notion of language as a picture. Paul Klee occupies a seminal place in this intellectual revolution, though his innovations were less obviously radical than those of his contemporaries. To understand precisely where his contribution lay, it is worth recalling the position at the start of the twentieth century.

Whereas Oriental art habitually merged word and image, whether in Islamic inscriptions or Japanese paintings, the Western tradition since the Renaissance distinguished more sharply between the two spheres. In spite of innumerable artefacts that crossed the divide, one tended to perceive alphabetic script, and especially the Roman variety, as opposed to pictoriality. Any attempt to cross the barrier and encroach on the territory of the letter ran up against an unspoken taboo: visual poetry, rebuses, grotesque calligraphy and other means of harmonizing word and image met with acceptance only under certain circumstances, such as illuminated manuscripts or childrens' books, but, by and large, to pictorialize the alphabet in the West was – until the twentieth century – treated as an assault on Reason by forces of the irrational. This can be inferred from an optical trick to which Michel Butor draws attention: the same image can be interpreted as a picture or pictogram (illus. 1), or as a letter (illus. 2), yet the two different perceptions of the same image are separated by a binary opposition. There seems to be no common ground, no fuzzy area to unite them. It is precisely this inchoate realm, the meeting-place of script and image, that, as Marc le Bot argued, forms a central strand in Paul Klee's mature painting.[1] In focusing on this ambiguity, Klee in fact recuperates what in the West would once have been called a more primitive attitude, invoking older concepts of the notion 'writing', which in the Greek *graphein* could also mean 'to engrave, scratch or scrape'. Klee

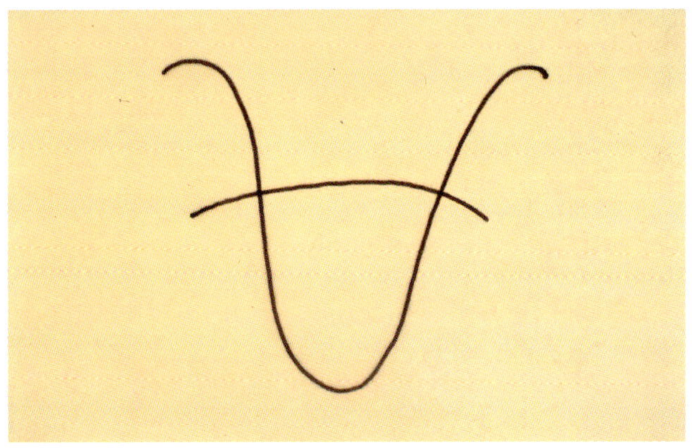

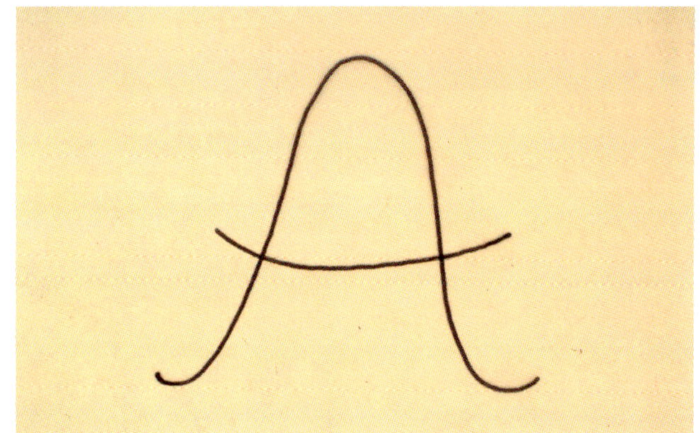

1 After Michel Butor, Conference on Word and Image, Berlin, 1989, pencil on paper.

2 After Michel Butor, Conference on Word and Image, Berlin, 1989, pencil on paper.

preserves this archetypal quality both in theory and in practice by working towards an ultimate harmony, even an identity, of image and script.

In a diary entry of 1908 Klee characteristically speaks of '*writing* a drawing' ('Ich *schrieb* ... eine Zeichnung').[2] In his drawings and paintings, not just the shaping of lines but the actual ductus, the handling of the pen, frequently recalls writing as much as it creates visual art, effecting what Klee once called 'psychic improvization' (Entry 842). The contiguity of script and alphabet in the line can be observed in alphabetic drawings like *Beginning of a Poem* (*Anfang eines Gedichtes*) of 1938 (illus. 3), which returns to the pre-verbal level,[3] or in *Album Piece* (*Albumblatt*) of 1935, which explores beyond script and writing (illus. 4).[4] Certain words stand out here, like Klee's name and the time of year, or the words 'und einmal ein Gemüsegarten' ('and once a vegetable garden'); these create a horizon of semantic sense, yet the squiggles probe beyond the words, into an inarticulable area of meaning.

Twentieth-century art is rich in word–image relations, but it is at least arguable that Klee explored more aspects of it than his contemporaries. In contrast to Braque's use of script, for example, Klee explored language throughout his career; in comparison with Miró, he pursued more aspects; and unlike Picasso, he made the problem fundamental to his project. This can be seen from some reflections on art, written in 1902. Summarizing his early interests Klee notes that his first artistic efforts were poetic rather than painterly ('nicht bildnerisch, vielleicht wohl dichterisch'); and that his chief aim was to harmonize the architectural or constructive elements in painting with the poetic ('architektonische und dichterische Malerei in Einklang ... zu bringen'; Entry 429). His concern with poetic painting was programmatic.

In truth, Klee's painting is embedded in language to a unique degree: beginning with the use of the line, and advancing through letters, words, sentences and allegories, he explores the entire gamut of linguistic possibilities, from simple signs to fully developed stories. His titles give almost every painting a semantic location, and imbue the images with verbal meaning; and the pictorial dimension itself is saturated with signs that recall scripts, runes, symbols, pictograms and ideograms. German literature and aesthetics form a background to this verbo-visual theme: Klee enters into a dialogue with Classical figures such as Lessing and Goethe as well as with Romantics like Novalis and Hoffmann, whose ideas shine through his work like signs on a palimpsest – one of his own chosen media.[5] As Porter Aichele has shown, Klee also embedded his work in contemporary practice, echoing the French modernists, such as Apollinaire, other poet-painters, notably Schwitters, and the German Expressionist poets, including Trakl and Stadler. Furthermore, of course, Klee wrote his own poetry and other texts, such as his diary and pedagogical notebooks, which further contribute to the verbal context of his art.

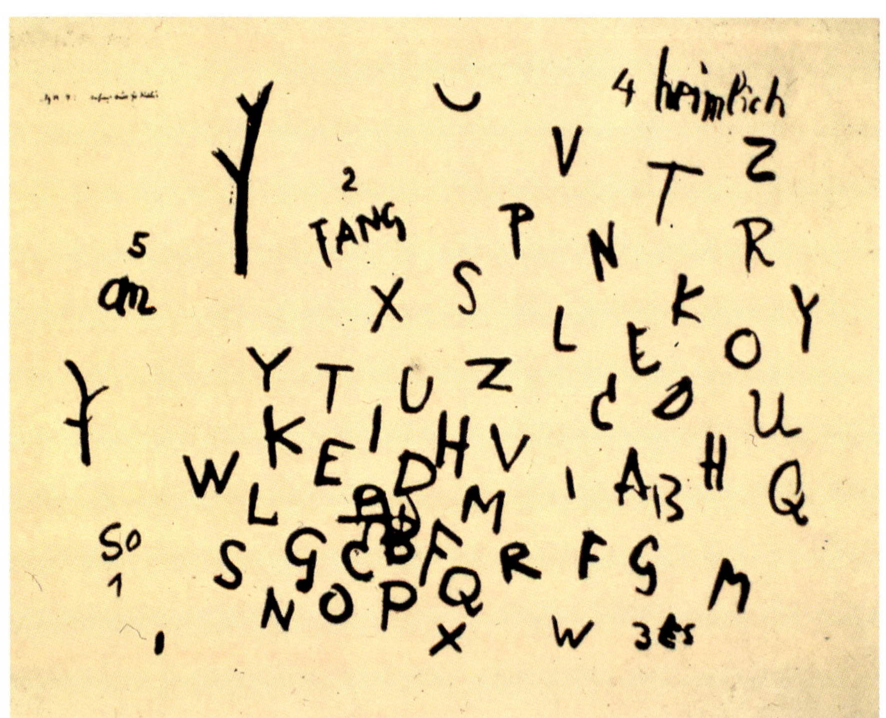

3 Paul Klee, *Beginning of a Poem*, 1938, no. 189, paper on cardboard.

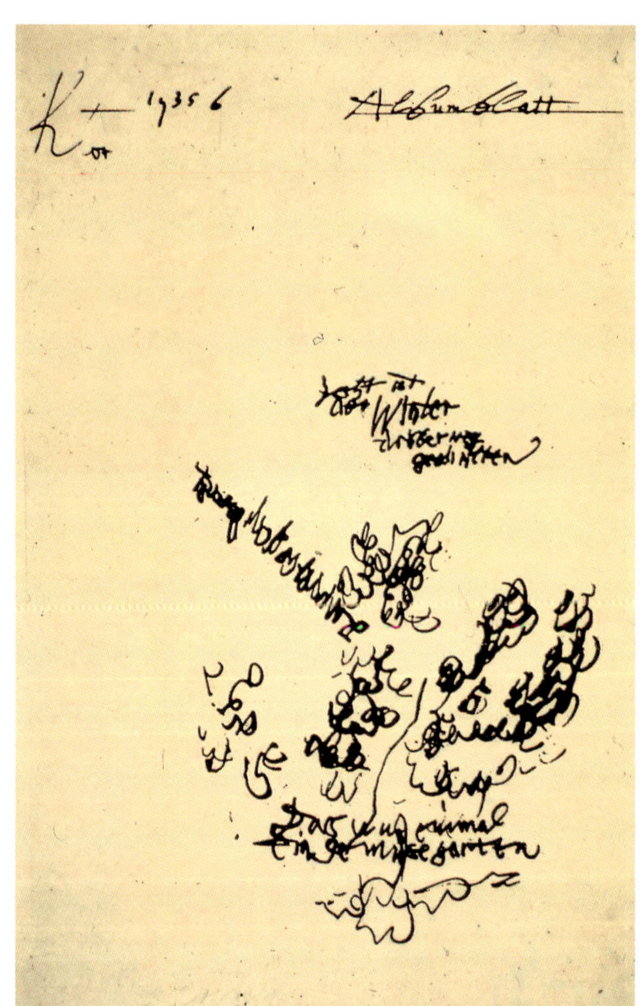

4 Paul Klee, *Album Leaf*, 1935, no. 6 pen on paper on card board.

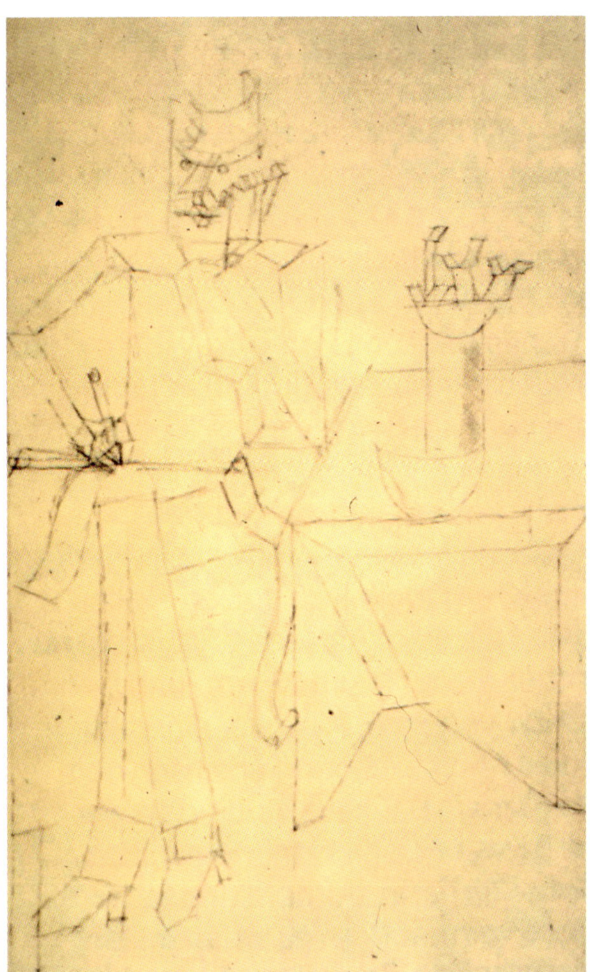

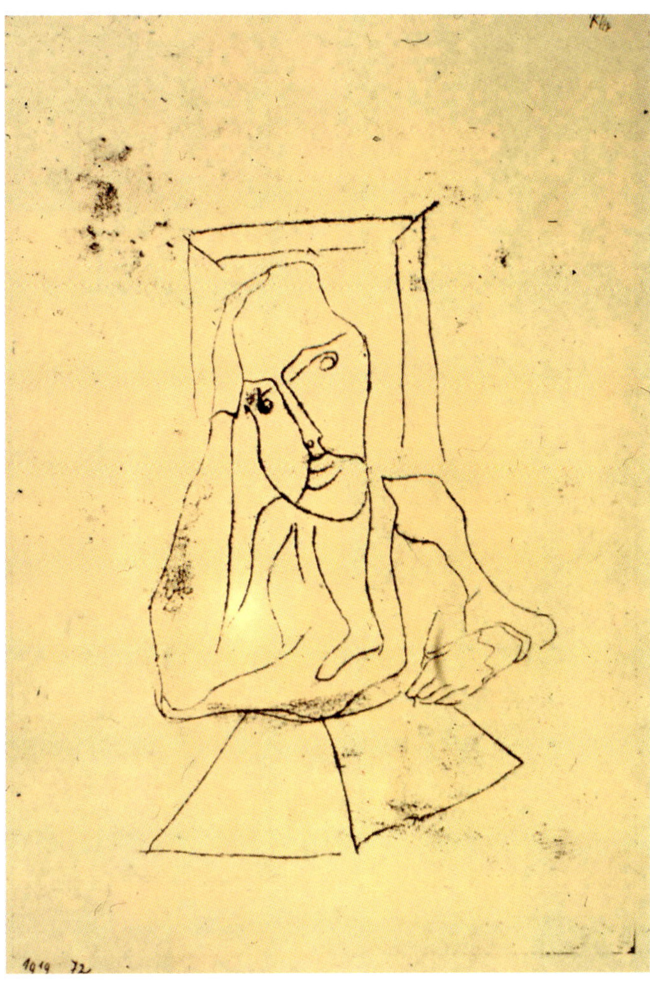

5 Paul Klee, *Poet-Draughtsman*, 1915, no. 195, pencil on paper on cardboard.

6 Paul Klee, *Feeling Artist*, 1919, no. 72, oil transfer drawing on paper on cardboard.

Klee himself pinpointed the conjoint duality of word and image in his own aesthetic in a lost painting of 1908 entitled *Poet-Painter* (*Dichter-Maler*); he took up the subject again during World War I in a remarkable drawing of 1915 (illus. 5) called *Poet-Draughtsman* (*Dichter-Zeichner*).[6] The Cubistically conceived figure representing Klee himself wears a military uniform, a sartorial image that reflects Klee's situation as a soldier but more generally also suggests the embattled avant-garde; the head propped on the left hand implies the thinker or poet; and the eyes, looking ahead, indicate inspiration as much as observation, which flows uninterruptedly through the artist's body into his energetic, active right hand. The scroll of paper he works on is an Oriental symbol for unified poem-painting. It evokes both the continuity of his activity and the merging of poetry and graphic art. Later drawings from 1919 return to this same motif, for example, *Feeling Artist* (*Empfindender Künstler*) (illus. 6). Here, the changed positioning of the hand suggests a dreamer. The lines are fluid; the right hand rests on the head, and it is the passive left hand which holds – or rather, barely touches – the pen, having become the vehicle of passive inspiration.

There is a series of subtexts to these images. These run back to Goethe's novel about the failed painter who writes such brilliant letters, *Die Leiden des jungen Werthers* (*The Sufferings of Young Werther*), to the thinking painter, Conti, in Lessing's tragedy *Emilia Galotti*, and beyond Lessing to the Renaissance. Raphael (Conti's reference in *Emilia Galotti*) provides a notable example of eye-hand imagery in his portrait of Michelangelo in the *School of Athens*. It is widely believed that the curiously isolated figure to our left of the

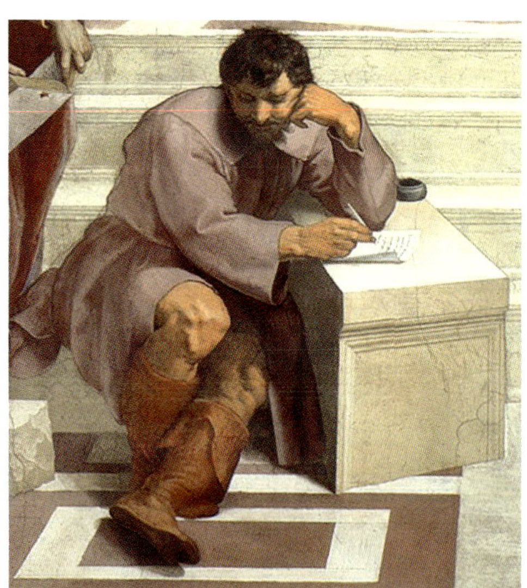

7 Raphael, *School of Athens* (detail), begun 1508–9, fresco.

centre in this painting is Michelangelo (illus. 7). The striking pose, which varies that of the classical 'thinker', provides a likely antecedent for Klee's portrait. Raphael chose to show Michelangelo as a sculptor-poet: wearing craftsman's clothes, he combines the muscular body of an artisan with the gentle, dreamy look of a poet who, turned away from his piece of paper, seems to be writing with his eyes closed, following his inspiration; his right hand holds the pen like an artist's brush; his open left hand relaxes on the side of the head, completing the figure of a circle in the composition, which thus symbolizes the harmony of hand and head.

Klee's *Poet-Draughtsman* (*Dichter-Zeichner*) also sits with a table to his left, but exhibits a more nervous, tense mood. He grips a pen, clutches his fingers: he is an anguished modernist. Michelangelo's harmonious compositional circle is replaced by Cubistic angularity, but the steps connecting the right shoulder and the left elbow still suggest a linking of eyes, hands and head. The image, I would venture, may be read as a response to both Raphael and Lessing: a recurring problem within a traditional aesthetics is, of course, the hand's inability to reproduce the vision of the eye; for within the aesthetic of mimesis, the hand cannot exactly reproduce the vision, and hence Lessing laments 'that which gets lost on the long way from the eye to the hand'. Goethe's poet-painter, Werther, remains tragically divided, unable to harmonize poetic imagination with painterly expression, and ultimately turns his own hand against his head in suicide. Klee's poet-painter breaks with the whole tradition. While looking straight ahead as an observer of nature, he also possesses a second source of knowledge, which can *replace* that which 'gets lost': note how the poet-painter's head is shaped like a tumbler, open on the side and on the top, thus creating the image of the poet as what Hölderlin calls a 'divine vessel'. Klee's embattled modernist replaces mimesis with conceptualization and poetic inspiration. In Klee's vision, non-representational art overcomes a traditional problem of visual aesthetics by fusing poetry with painting.

The ideas embedded in Klee's notion of painter-poet, as conceived around 1908–16, mark the crucial transition in his career, propelling him towards the abstraction attained around 1914 and the subsequent conceptualization of his art. They settle a long-standing quest for artistic identity and usher in Klee's major phase by enabling him to harness his literary ability wholly to his art. The need for such harmonization had long been implicit. In a diary entry of 1898/9, Klee reflected on his three artistic talents – for music,[7] painting and writing – and despaired of them all. Echoing a similar diary entry of E.T.A. Hoffmann's, he observed (Entry 67):

Die Musik ist für mich wie eine verhexte Geliebte.
Ruhm als Maler?
Schriftsteller, moderner Lyriker? Schlechter witz,
so bin ich beruflos und bummle.

Music is for me like an enchanted lover.
Fame as a painter?
Writer, modern poet? Bad joke,
so I'm jobless and footloose.

When Klee resolved this dilemma by incorporating language into his art, it is noticeable that his poetic production largely dried up. Although it spans most of his working life – he wrote around 100 poems – he produced the majority *before* his breakthrough as a painter in 1914, with only occasional examples from the 1920s and '30s.

The tendency of Paul Klee's poetry was towards an expression of silence; towards an intellectual and spiritual content that he only fully accomplished by submerging his poetry in his painting.

The first elements on which Klee's poetry feeds are the common stock of German verse since the 1770s: ballads and, above all, Goethe. An amusing sign of Goethe's hold over later culture is a photograph of Kandinsky and Klee playing at Goethe and Schiller. In 1901 the young Klee unequivocally if ironically defined his own position in a poem which alludes to Goethe's *Prometheus*. Klee's variation is entitled *Eine Art Prometheus*. It is written as a free verse hymn, divided into longer and shorter stanzas after the manner of Goethe's *Ganymed*, but in a more soberly restrained style; lacking the scorn of Goethe's Prometheus, Klee's Titan sets out to complete the divine task:

Gross bist Du,	Great art thou,
gross is Dein Werk.	Great are thy works.
Aber nur gross im Anfang,	But only in the beginning,
nicht vollendet,	not completed,
Ein Fragment.	A fragment.[8]

If in form Klee's early poetry echoes the young Goethe's, he already exhibits a greater sobriety, typified by his characteristic *Zeilenstil* (end-stopped lines), his abruptly truncated sentences and his abstract vocabulary. By 1908 this style had matured into an attitude of recognizable modernism. A poem like *Magic* (*Zauber*) of 1908 begins by recalling the Goethean hymnic manner. It evokes a natural scene that it uses as if to anticipate a philosophical dilema in the manner of Goethe's *Harzreise im Winter*. The poem begins lyrically:

Fernab von dir	Far beneath thee
Dicht davor ein Weg steigt	Close before a path ascends

The word-play, repetition and assonance, however, quickly introduce a strangely jarring note:

Verzweigt,	Divided,
Kein weg neigt	No path tends
ein weg neigt jach erloschen	A path tends suddenly extinguished
sachte wach:	gently awake:
Durch Nacht und Sonne.	Through night and sun.

The poem now completely undermines the Goethean lyric mode by introducing inappropriate imagery, creating an impression of absurdity:

Was Licht jetzunder,	What lights now,
Was Wunder!	What wonders!
Was für Fêten,	What fêtes
Was Nuditäten,	What nudities.
Freund mit Bechern,	Friend with goblets,
Damen mit Fächern …	Ladies with fans …

With its sense of speed and excitement, the poem epitomizes a modernistic fracturing of reality, juxtaposing the sublime with banality; even the linguistic detail evidences the process, when the characteristically *Sturm und Drang* compounds do new service in words like 'flammenbehaart' ('hairy with flames'). A single phrase epitomizes the modernist situation in two key words: 'schocks-chwere Not' – 'shock-heavy anxiety'. Klee takes up the classical Western tradition as represented by Goethe, but finds it to be unworkable in an age governed by the anguished aesthetics of shock.

The main resolution to this dilemma lies in Klee's adoption of a *non*-Western aesthetic in his poetry. This Orientalism enables him to couch mystical statements in his work in an idiom that is acceptable to a modern Western sensibility. The turn appears in a poem of 1901 that rejects religion and the classical Western experience in favour of a mute spirituality. In two contrasting stanzas, Klee juxtaposes an ironic rejection of the twinned palliatives – religious faith and Weimar Classicism – in order to install his own, child-like and individualistic mysticism:[9]

In solchem Zustand gibt	In this condition
Es schöne Mittel.	There are attractive methods.
Gebete um Glauben	Prayers for faith
und Kraft.	and strength.
Auch Goethes' Italienische	Goethe's Italian Journey
Reise gehört hierher.	Also belongs here.
Aber vor allem ein glücklicher	But above all a lucky
Stern. Ich sah ihn oft.	Star. I often saw it.
Ich werd ihn wieder entdecken.	I will discover it again.

The calculated casualness of the opening words implicates something unnamable anterior to the poem, around which the whole text revolves; whilst the naive conclusion, in turn, evokes an intimate faith in unmediated experience. Thus the crystalline distance in the words achieve that quality which Bachelard calls 'intimate immensity'.

Klee's strength as a poet resides in the clarity with which he masters the art of abrupt silence, a mode that implicates the unsayable by means of highly polished, pointed style. The best of these poems graft the lessons on Oriental poetry to a language honed in the German classical tradition. The method frequently depends on a balancing of linguistic parts with an almost geometrical exactititude, bringing to the fore a constructive tendency in the architecture of sound, syntax and sense. The effect can be almost magical, as with the charm of incantation. Take the following little poem, that, with its sixteen syllables, almost exactly recalls a Japanese haiku:[10]

nur eines allein	only one alone
ist nah	is near
im Ich ein Gewicht	in the I a weight
ein kleiner Stein.	a little stone.

The symmetrically placed rhyming words 'eines allein' and 'kleiner Stein' pivot around the central 'Ich' and 'Gewicht'; while the apodictic 'nur eines allein ist *nah*' empowers a further, absent rhyme – 'nur eines allein is *wahr*'; similarly, the image of the 'Stein' within the 'Ich' begins to resonate, dialectically invoking an unstated opposite, the human soul. Characteristically, the poem establishes an imaginary space, comprising a concrete symbol within a conceptual framework.

Even in as fine a poem as this, though, there remains a problem that Klee only resolved in his painting. His language depends on the hard edge of precision. Though spiritually evocative, it lacks the fuzziness of sensuous connotation. In such writing, the intellectual control precludes the invocation, not to say the eruption, of the irrational: dependence on the spirit and the intellect exclude both feelings and the unconscious. Klee uses language not so much for human ends as for seeking out a metaphysical reality. The silence that he writes towards can be better accommodated in painting. This emerges in what I find a moving but ultimately misguided piece of writing, a kind of meta-poem that defines Klee's own poetic dilemma:[11]

Öffne Dich, Du Pforte in der Tiefe,
Verlies im Grunde, gib mich frei,
den Belichtung Witternden.
Und helle Hände kommen, die mich greifen,
und Freundes Worte sagen froh:
Her ihr Bilder schöner wilder Tiere,
entsteiget Eurem Zwinger,
dass lieblich gleiten Finger
durch Flammend Fell.
Und eins ist man wie ehedem
in Gottes Garten
Tag und Nacht
und Sonn' und Pracht der Sterne.

– Im Paradies der Dichtung – Zitternden –

Open up! Oh you gate in the depths,
Dungeon in the lowest ground, set me free,
I who sense the illumination.
And bright hands arrive that clasp me,

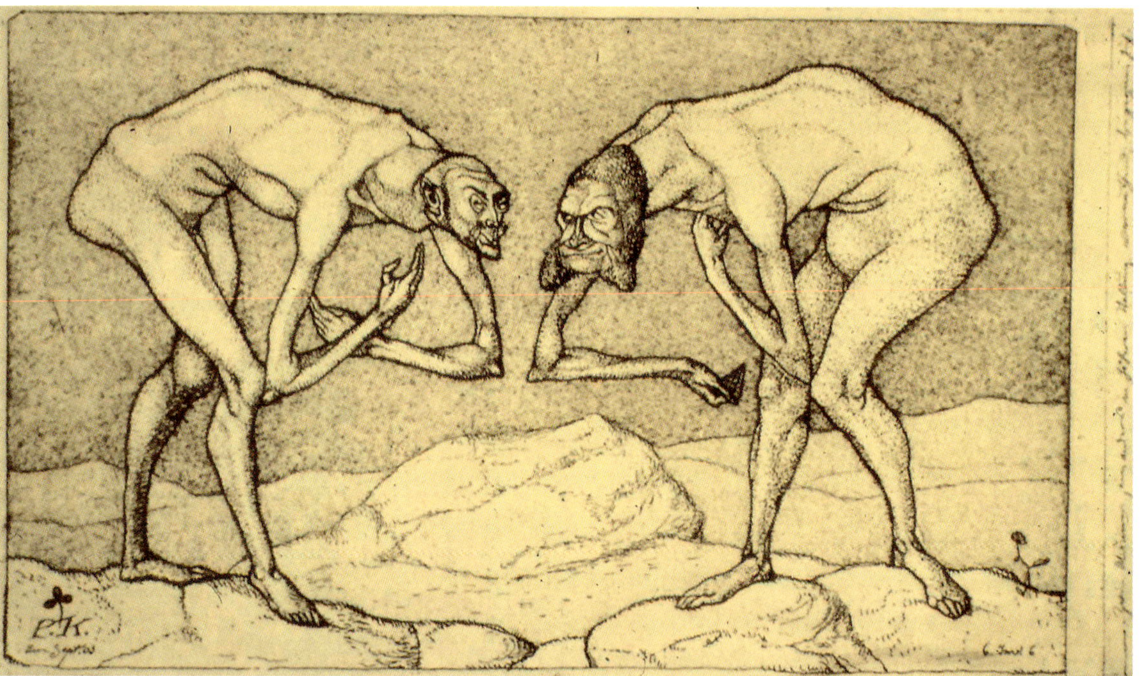

8 Paul Klee, *Two men, each believing the other to be in a superior position, encounter one another*, 1903, no. 5, etching.

And a friend's word happily says:
Come here you images of beautiful wild animals,
Climb out of your prison,
So that fingers may glide lovingly
Through flaming fur.
And I am one again as long ago
In God's garden
Day and night
And sun and splendour of the stars.

– In the paradise of poetry – trembling –

The problem here enunciated remains unresolved in Klee's poetry: Klee, as a *writer*, cannot break into the realm of pure images. He can conceive of a vision, the 'Paradies der Dichtung', but it remains beyond verbal representation.

The first and most abiding resolution that Klee found was, of course, in his use of picture titles. As commentators from Roman Jakobson to E. H. Gombrich have pointed out, these titles do not just name the pictures but provide interpretations – often witty or whimsical – or describe some event. They thus enter into a complex semantic relationship with the visual image. The technique is fully apparent in Klee's first aquatint of 1903 (illus. 8), *Two men, believing each other to be in a superior position, encounter one another (Zwei Männer, einander in höherer Stellung vermutend, begegnen sich.)*

This striking etching contains sundry layers of meaning and constitutes an early high-water mark in Klee's *oeuvre*. As has been pointed out, at one level, the etching had a personal meaning for Klee: its satire on the upper classes, in Klee's words, provided *Trost* ('comfort') for his own lowly social position. At another level, it offers a political satire: the etching caricatures Kaiser Wilhelm (left) and Kaiser Franz Josef (right). At a third level, however, the title sets the image into a universal social context, and turns it into a more general satire on social pretension: the vanities of rank and class appear grotesque before the nakedness of the human condition. The title perfectly explicates the engraving: the syntax, which balances the main clause on either side of a subordinate clause, reflecting the image's own absurd symmetry, by which it unmasks the similarity of the two men. This results in a symbiosis, what Jakobsen calls a 'dialectic', between text and image. The technique remains one of the key ways in which Klee embeds visual meaning into a semantic context.

Here and elsewhere, word and image do not just interact as two contrasting realities: for the image exhibits a distinctly calligraphic quality, which invites further exploration. The posture of the two men and their facial expressions create no serious difficulties for the interpreter, denoting subservience and hypocrisy. Yet the curious positioning of their arms and legs cannot be fully explained by such a reading. The initials 'P. K.' in the lower left-hand corner provide a clue. On closer inspection, it will be seen that the men's grotesque gestures, the position of arms and legs, stems not simply from the satirical intent: the posture recalls a human alphabet. Most obviously, perhaps, the legs of the two figures imitate a 'K'; a corresponding 'P' may be found in the left hand figure; an inverted 'A' in the crook of his right arm, a 'U' in his left arm, and an 'L' in the right-hand figure's right arm: the two men spell out Klee's own name. This completes the satire. The naked emperors are men, worth no more than the artist, and indeed they depend on his artifice: the final 'point' of the etching is then that the obsequious gentlemen are humanly equal, but otherwise inferior, to the creative artist. Just as the artist bridges word and image in a single artefact, his persona comprises opposites, and the whole human and spiritual world finds expression in his art. The underlying conceit of this image, that the Book of Nature is written in alphabetic script, is a dominant motif in Klee's later paintings.

The most substantial documents of Klee's which embed his work into a literary context are, of course, his diaries and other writings on art. The *Tagebücher* also contain some of Klee's poems. Far from being a spontaneous and intimate diary, they are a stylized exercise in self-creation.[12] Klee the diarist modelled himself partly on Grillparzer and Hebbel. Commenting on Grillparzer's *Selbstbiographie* (Autobiography) and *Tagebuch* (Diary), Klee announced them as his major discoveries in the spring of 1904: 'Dieses Buch ist ein ungeschriebenes Drama: wäre es geschrieben, so ware es jedenfells sein bestes' ('This book is an unwritten drama: if it had been written, it would certainly have been his best'). Then, in 1905, he observes: 'Hebbel ist ganz mein Dichter, den ich nur achte wie einen Goethe und Shakespeare.' ('Hebbel is my writer entirely. I admire him like a Goethe or a Shakespeare'.) It was perhaps the numbering of Hebbel's diary entries in the critical edition Klee owned and annotated that stimulated his own obsessive numbering of his *Tagebücher.*

Revealingly, Klee announced: 'Ein Edler arbeitet an der Knappheit des Wortes, nicht an seiner Vielheit' ('A noble man works on the brevity of his words, not their number') (Entry 13).[13] His successive re-working of his diary not only improved the pith of his style, but also his self-image. This can be surmised from the way he handles his emergence as a modernist painter-poet when he offers a narrative of the avant-garde. It is worth dwelling on the diary to see how carefully Klee crafted his self-image as a painter by using literary techniques. In so doing, he tacitly connects his project to the great modern isms – Cubism and Futurism – that are typified by a strong interest in word-image relations.

Klee opens the entries for that *annus mirabilis*, 1912, by quoting from one of his own letters in entry 905. This letter in effect offers a manifesto of primitivistic modernism summed up in the key words 'Uranfänge der Kunst' ('primordial origins of art'). Other slogans he uses include the references to children, mental illness and Kandinsky's *Über das geistige in der Kunst* ('On the Spiritual in Art'). This sets the stage. Then, Klee laconically alludes to the protagonist in Entry 907: 'Der blaue Reiter, so heisst das Ding' ('The Blue Rider. That's what the thing's called'). Only at this point – having argued the precedence of German art – does Klee introduce the French innovators, such as Picasso and Braque. Tongue-in-cheek, then, Entry 908 proposes a visit to Paris, described in Entries 909 and 910. Thus the diaries continuously adjust Klee's image to imply his own priority or that of German art over French.

A comparison with the description of Klee's first visit to Paris of 1905 reveals how both his taste and his style have changed. Puvis de Chavannes is out. Manet is decidedly in. As to his writing, Klee's habitual brevity has now absorbed the techniques of French Cubism and Italian Futurism. His style veers between that of a genuine diary and the artistic *parole-in-libertà* pioneered by Marinetti:

> *909. In Pontarlier stieg ich in einen Personenzug ... Dort waren viele Soldaten eingestiegen. Sie hatten immer noch ihre roten Hosen an, drehten ihre Zigaretten und waren vergnügt, ohne besonders zu stören. Die Bahnbeamten waren etwas wenig soigniert. Auf ihren Mützen stand* PLM.
>
> *An allen Stationen hielt dieser edle Zug ... Die Landschaft bei Dijon ist reizvoll. Steinberge und mitten in diesem Gestein die schönsten blühenden Bäume ... Allmählich verlor die Landschaft den fremdartigen Reiz und wurde grün, sanft, abendlich. Man sah ruhige Ströme, hie und da ein fernes, weidendes Pferd. Irgendwo mußten wir zwei Expreßzüge voraus lassen. 'Ah, les directes!' gruselte eine Frauennstimme und 'Wumm!', brach ein solches Biest an uns Durch. Nach zehn Minuten: 'Schuff!', der zweite. Wahre Explosionen!*

> 909. In Pontarlier I got into a slow train ... Many soldiers had climbed in. They were still wearing their red trousers, rolled their cigarettes, and were cheerful, without disturbing. The railway officials were not very well groomed. On their caps were the letters PLM.
>
> This noble train stopped at every station ... The landscape near Dijon is charming. Stony mountains and in the midst of this stone the loveliest flowers blossom ... Slowly the landscape lost its foreign charm and grew green, gentle, evening-like. There were peaceful streams, here and there a grazing horse. Somewhere we had to let two express trains overtake. 'Ah, les directes!' a woman's voice moaned and 'Wumm!', one of these beasts burst past us. After two minutes: 'Schuff!', the second one. True explosions!

The seemingly naive private diary, on closer inspection, reveals some very contemporary techniques. The casual reference to the three letters on the railwayman's cap imitates the Cubist use of letters and words as visual icons. The sound painting in the expressions 'Wumm!' and 'Schuff!' recalls Marinetti's use of onomatopoeia. Indeed, the whole emphasis on the train itself in the description of the journey is typical of the Futurist cult of the machine, while the final exclamation, 'wahre Explosionen!' ('true explosions!'), makes the link almost explicit in rehearsing the Futurist love of violence. Thus Klee absorbs contemporary influence whilst hiding his sources, and jockeys for position among the avant-garde.

The apparent factuality of many statements can be seen to manipulate the actual events to achieve the appropriate picture. Take for example the Entry for 3 April 1912:

3.4 Boulevards, Seine, Notre Dame, große Boulevards, Opéra, Louvre. Nachmittags im Musée Luxembourg: Degas, Manet, Balcon usw., Luxemberger Park.

The entry treats the Parisian experience like a poem. Much is surely omitted – there is no reference to a café, for example – by which device Klee stylizes the trip, and makes it appear like an artistic pilgrimage. The words in his diary heighten his image as a painter. Taken in one way, the little entry suggests the modernist concept of 'simultaneity' pioneered by the Futurists. Taken in another, the entry can be read as an ascent, leading from the city (boulevards), through religion (Notre Dame), and classical art (Louvre), to the temple of modernism (Musée Luxembourg) with its iconic masterpiece (Manet's balcony painting). This is followed, finally, by relaxation in Nature: the day is designed to represent a spiritual pilgrimage. The whole sequence of events in the Paris diary has something of this quality, pointedly following the visit to Delaunay with the ascent of Notre Dame, and culminating in the visit to Uhde, to view the objects which were – after all – intended as the occasion for the whole visit: the paintings of the French Cubists.

The Paris diary is as remarkable for what it omits – for example, Klee's developing thoughts on technique, or the import of the momentous meeting with Delaunay – as for what it includes. The use of reference works connotatively and symbolically as much as literally and descriptively. Delaunay's name, for example, evokes his concept of 'simultaneity': his handling of the canvas as a series of planes, which will provide Klee's path to abstraction; but the name may also suggest that most remarkable poem-painting of early Cubism, Sonia Delaunay's illustrated version of Blaise Cendrars' *Trans-Siberian Railway*, published in 1913.

The diary thus manipulates biographical and historical data as if they were volumes and masses in a painting, foregrounding certain features, moving others into the background, in order to place the young Klee (who has yet to distinguish himself as an artist) among the modern masters. There is a distinct hierarchy in this presentation, which reverses historical developments, whereby Klee leaves his reference to the key innnovators – the Futurists – until the last, in Entries 914 and 916, where he introduces Carrà and an extract from a Futurist manifesto. Although the Futurist idea informs his treatment of the train journey to Paris, Klee downgrades the movement's role, though this section forms the climax to his narrative, suggesting a hierarchy that runs from German art (the Blue Rider) via French Painting (Cubism) to Italian theory (Futurism).

The crux of Klee's Parisian experience is elliptically placed in a bracketed

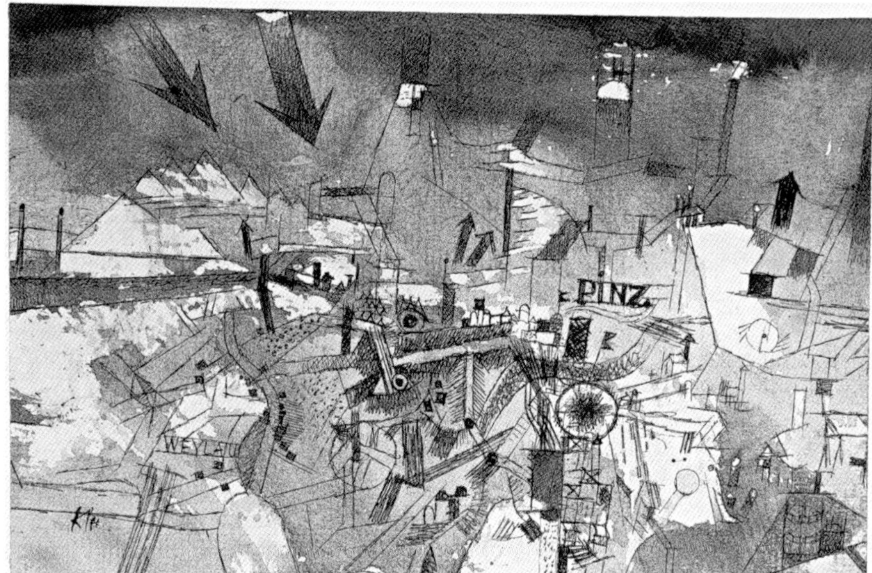

9 Paul Klee, *View of the Severely Threatened City of Pinz*, 1915, no. 187, pen and watercolour on paper on cardboard.

exclamation at the end of Entry 914: 'Heiliger Laokoön!' ('Holy Laocoön!'). The reference is to Lessing's seminal book on aesthetics that overturned the classical doctrine formulated by Horace, *ut pictura poesis* – 'a poem is like a picture'. It is clear from the exclamation that, in Klee's opinion, Futurism spells the end of Lessing's view. The division between poetry and painting upon which Lessing's aesthetics depends, and which was promulgated at art schools throughout the nineteenth century, is now seen to collapse. For Futurism, as Klee recognizes, reinvigorates the time-honoured ideal of *ut pictura poesis*, and thereby paves the way for the innumerable explorations of word–image relations that typify twentieth-century art and design.

By 1914 at the latest, in *Carpet of Memory* (*Teppich der Erinnerung*), Klee had come to incorporate linguistic elements in his painting, and subsequently absorbed contemporary methods of doing so, from Picasso to Schwitters. He mainly built on the two early modern movements: Cubism and Futurism. Picasso and Braque inserted letters into their paintings to introduce a level of genuine reality, as in drawings like *Girl with Violin* of 1915, a technique Klee developed in his drawings of that year. Both Braque and Klee also confronted the problem of decorativeness, with Braque often choosing to use the verbal element for a catchword, as in *Violin and Handbill* of 1912, where the language mediates between real world and picture; by a related but contrary device, as in *17, IRR* of 1923, Klee uses the alphabet hieroglyphically to face the reader with a conundrum: the picture confronts the viewer with some extreme emotional situation, possibly jealousy, or the end of an affair, equivocally detonated by the cipher '17, IRR' ('17, MAD'). The eye restlessly circulates through the picture, from the numeral to the faces, across to the arrowheads and back to the single word. The arrows implant a narrative temporal dimension, hinting at an unexplained story that might account for the man's grim look and the woman's tearful yet smiling face. If the red arrow signifies passion, the black may possibly imply anger or jealousy. The numerals which may or may not denote age and the letters which spell madness multiply the problems, destabilizing meaning in the very act of implying it: they enable the picture to enact the precise ambiguity of an emotional dilemma. The success of the imagery depends on its curious semiotics in that it conflates three different communicational categories: pictorial representation, abstract signs and alphabetic script.

This technique of heightening tension by mixing different categories to produce a unique kind of poem-painting looks back to Futurism rather than

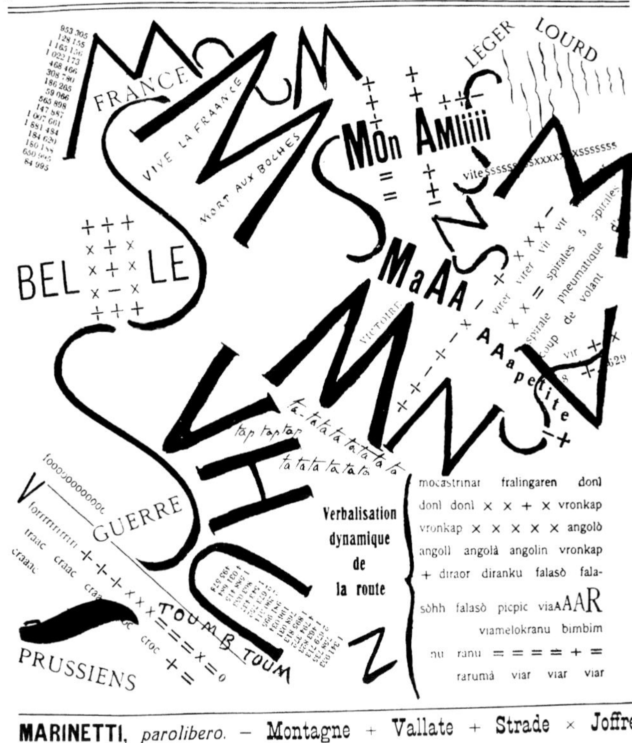

10 F. T. Marinetti, *Words in Freedom*, 1915. (After the Battle of the Marne in 1914, Joffre, the French Commander-in-Chief, visited the Front by car.)

Cubism. For whereas Braque and Picasso reinstated the aesthetic viability of the alphabet, Marinetti and his followers developed its analytic potential in their 'free-word paintings', like *Words in Freedom* by Marinetti of 1915 (illus. 10) in which language constitutes the entire image, evoking a battle both in sound and sight, simultaneously in plan and elevation.[14] Carrà exploited this visual 'vocabulary' in a more painterly manner in his *Atmospheric Envelopment-Exploding Shell* of 1914. This in turn provides a context for Klee's attempt to portray total war in *View of the Severely Threatened City of Pinz* (*Ansicht der schwer bedrohten Stadt Pinz*) of 1915 (illus. 9): as in a Futurist image, the use of words, plan and elevation recall military maps, while arrows used as signs of violence extend the visual vocabulary. The approach undergoes various transmutations in Klee, culminating in *Formula for a War* (*Formel für einen Krieg*, 1936) (illus. 12).

The use of alphabetic script quickly became a standard device in Klee's painting. A single letter may act as an isolated, enigmatic signifier of human meaning, as with the letter E of 1918, or stand alongside other elements. Three years later, for example, the E recurs as the abbreviated name of a village in *Landscape near* E *(in Bavaria)* (*Landschaft bei* E *(in Bayern)*) (illus. 13). This later 'E' attracts the eye as the dominant signifier among child-like pictograms for conifers and runic deciduous trees in a cubistically conceived pictorial space that conflates plan and elevation into a strangely unsettling, dynamic image. All these works operate on two levels simultaneously, the pictorial and the linguistic, thereby introducing a suggestive ambiguity into Klee's art. Whole words or names may also occur to similar effect, as in the whimsical *Bavarian Don Giovanni* (*Bayrischer Don Giovanni*) of 1919 (illus. 14). The painting's structure

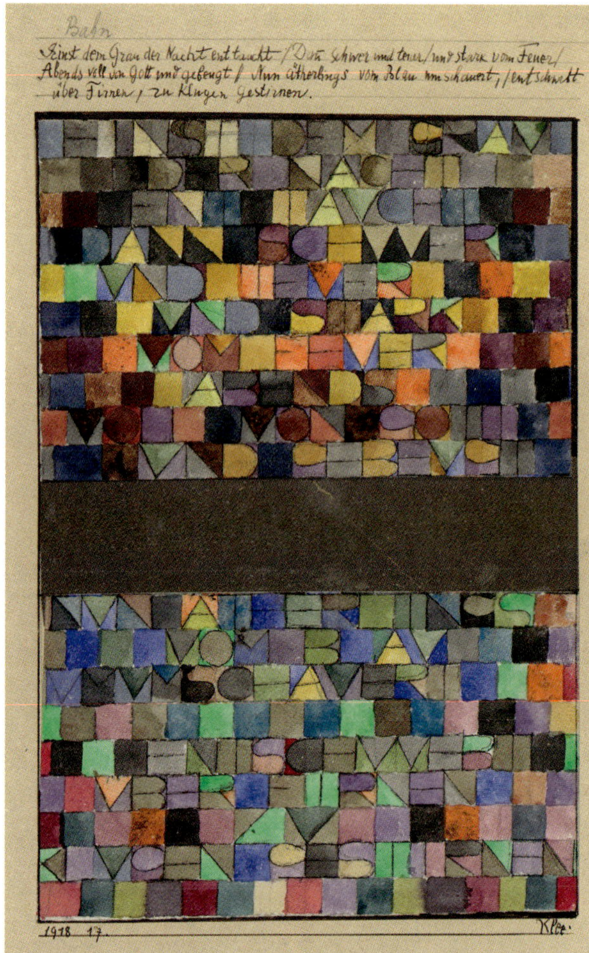

11 Paul Klee, *Once emerged from the grey of night . . .*, 1918, watercolour and pencil strengthened by pen and ink on paper cut into two parts with a strip of silver paper, all mounted on cardboard.

ironically varies Delauney's window-pictures, using language to highlight the absurdity of a *local* Don Giovanni and to deflate the impersonal nature of Don Giovanni's desire. Elsewhere, language can have an opposite function, drawing attention away from physicality to the spiritual, as in *Agnus Dei qui tollis peccata mundi* of 1918 (illus. 15), where the words act as a mystical bridge to the Divinity. Although Klee enters into a dialogue with the other modernists who married word and image, whether they worked from poetry towards imagery – as in the case of Apollinaire's calligrammes – or vice versa – as with Schwitters's collages – his own word-image combinations have a unique stamp, not least thanks to his Orientalism.

Central to this development were a series of picture-poems begun in 1916 under the influence of Hans Heilmann's belief that Chinese script was wholly pictorial. Klee began a series of poem-paintings based on Chinese poems which culminate in his best-known poem-painting, done in 1918 (illus. 11). The centrality of this picture in Klee's *oeuvre* is suggested by its choice for the cover of Will Grohmann's Klee monograph (1954). It is a milestone on Klee's path to abstraction. Nothing concrete is 'represented', for the painting's entire pictorial space is filled by squares and words; more than any previous work of his, the poem-painting overturns Lessing's aesthetics in *Laocoön* by reverting triumphantly to the doctrine of *ut pictura poesis*. The text itself is probably Klee's own – very suggestive – poem, written in the Chinese manner.

> Once emerged from the grey of night
> Then heavy and dear
> And strong from the fire
> In the evening bowed down
> And full of God
> Now heavenly surrounded by blue
> Soars away over snowfields
> To intelligent stars.

The words' evocative power derives partly from the imagery, partly from the complete absence of a grammatical subject. As a whole, the poem-painting depends on the interaction of word and image, on the intricate resonances they trigger: the method of box-like display recalls Klee's early study of checkerboard

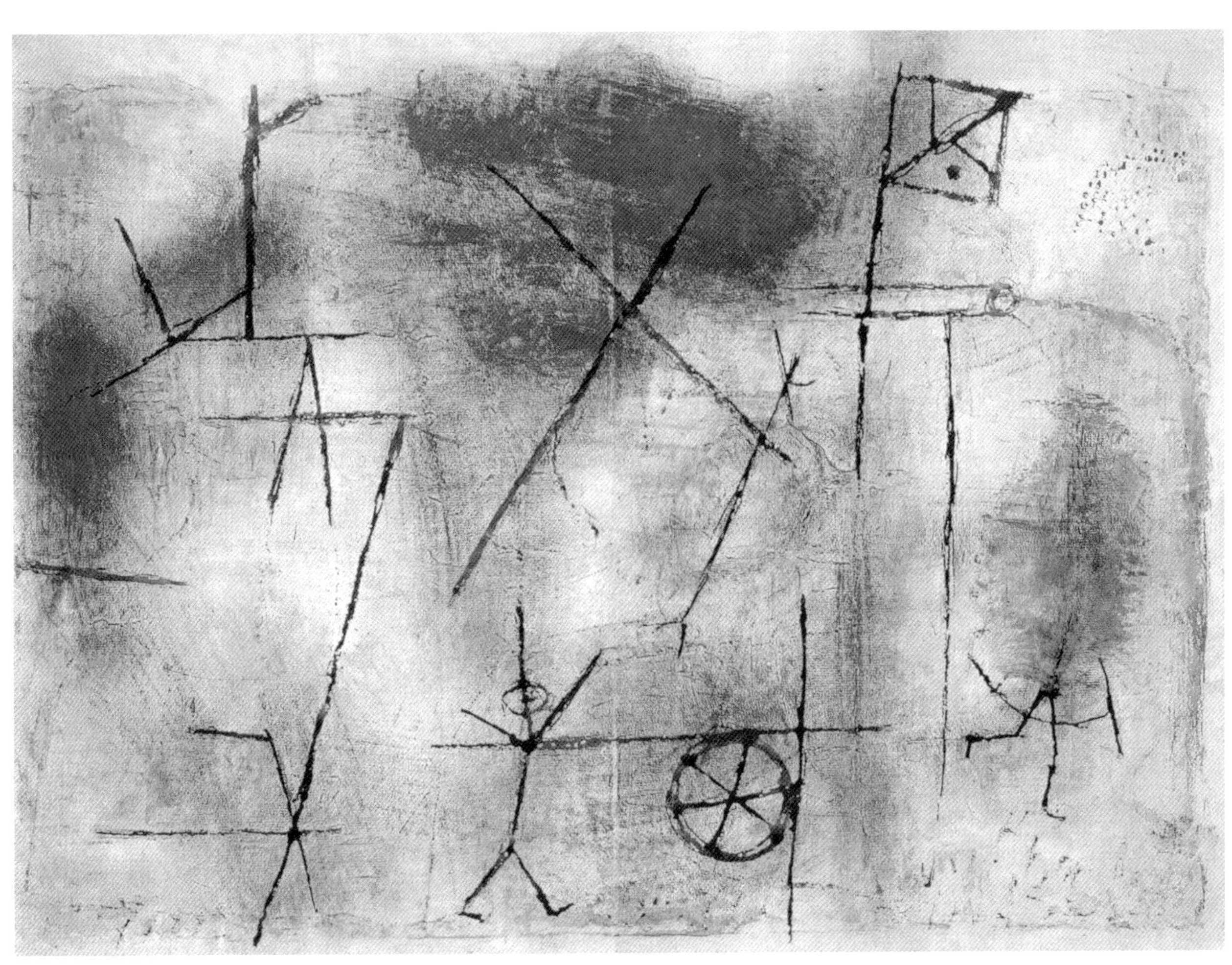

12 Paul Klee, *Formula for a War*, 1936, no. 2, oil and watercolour on paper on cardboard.

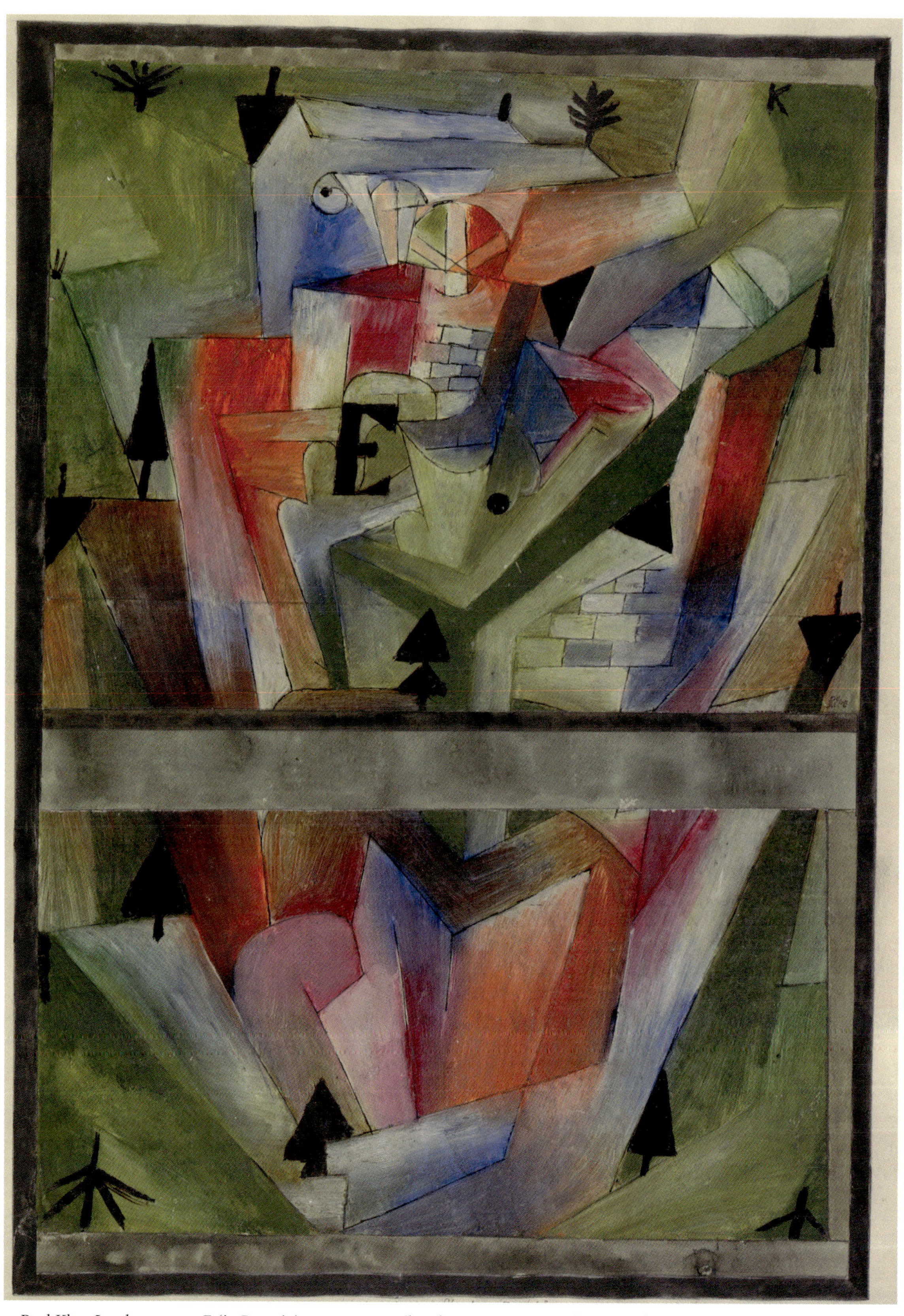

13 Paul Klee, *Landscape near E (in Bavaria)*, 1921, no. 116, oil and pen on paper, cut in two and mounted on card, with additional watercolour.

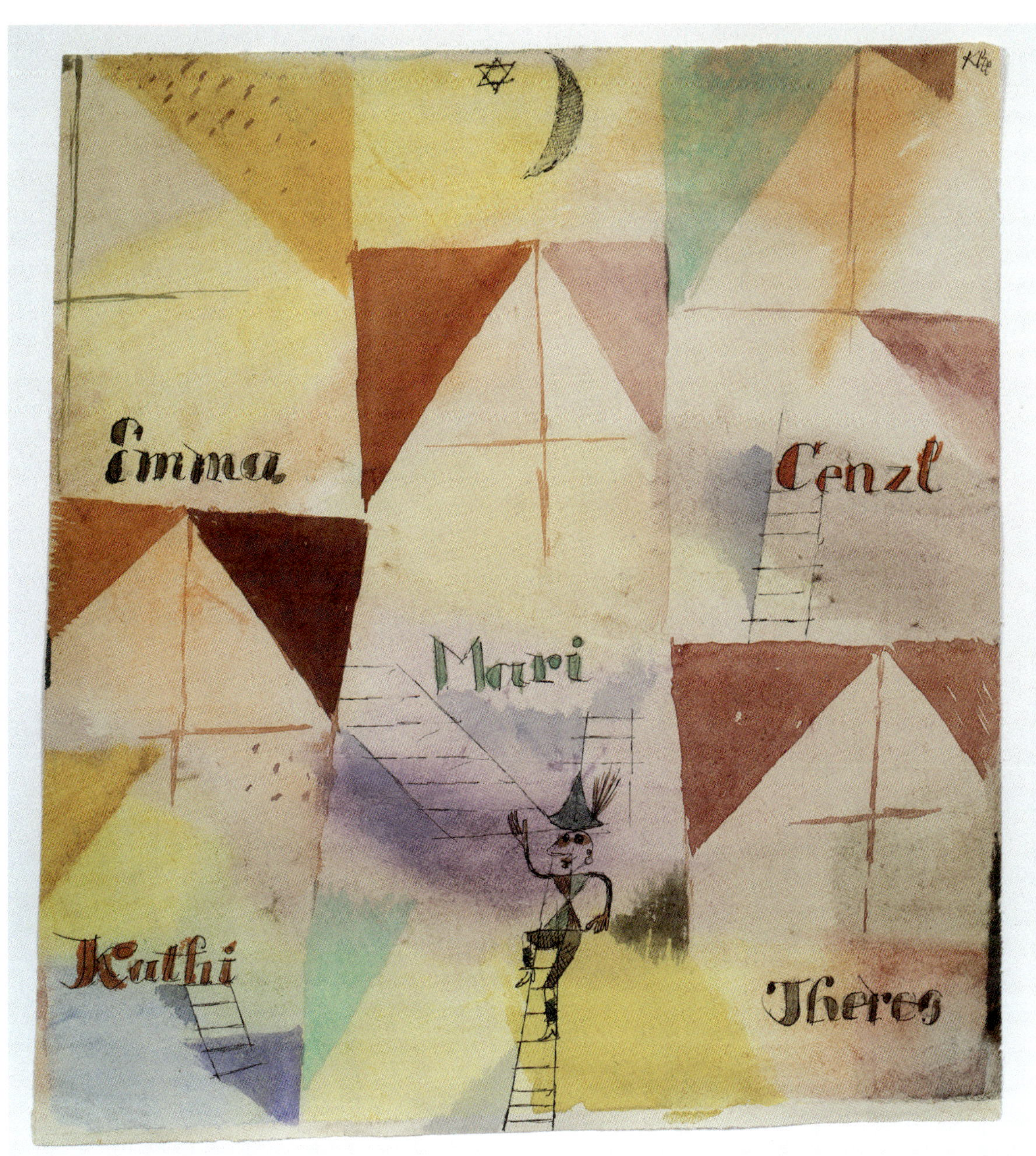

14 Paul Klee, *The Bavarian Don Giovanni*, 1919, no. 116, watercolour and pen on paper.

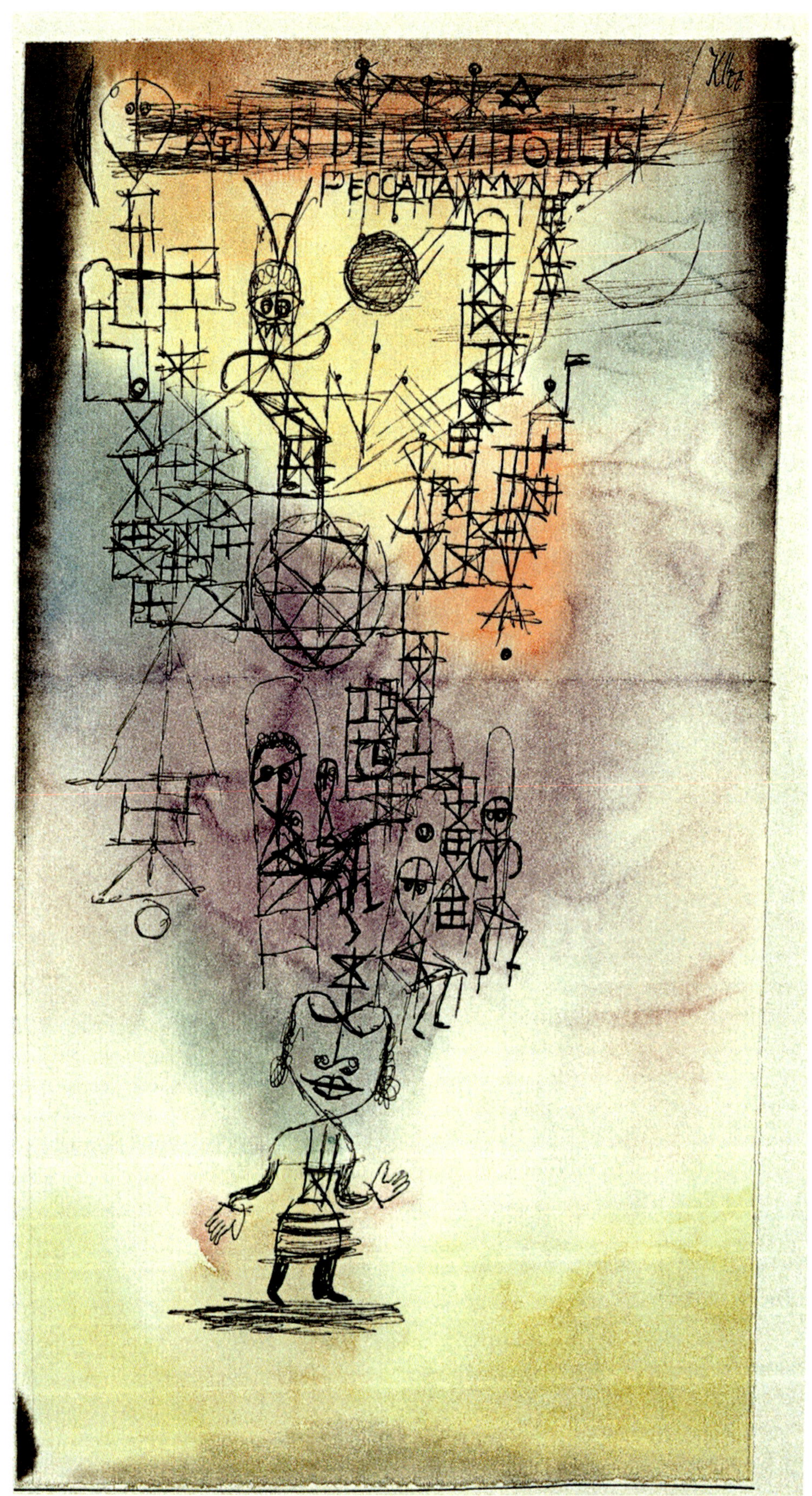

15 Paul Klee, *Agnus Dei qui tollis peccata mundi*, 1918, NO. 20, pen and watercolour on paper on cardboard.

effects and anticipates his later 'magic squares'. It also evokes a child's writing-book, while the layout suggests a Roman inscription: this duality produces an effect of simplistic sophistication. The lettering itself is a modernistic sans serif in the style of the later *Bauhaus* script. It is illuminated by a colouristic patchwork that partly echoes the meaning, as in the use of grey (named in the opening line), red (for fire) and blue, but also puts forward new meanings (as with the colour green). The words present a cycle of emergence, becoming, and departure, from 'Einst dem Grau der Nacht enttaucht ...' (Once emerged from the grey of the night) at the outset, to the conclusion: 'zu klugen Gestirnen' (to intelligent stars) (illus. 11). Throughout there is a reciprocal relationship between word and image: the latter moves from greyness at the top into fuller, warmer colour where fire is mentioned, and descends into cooler colours with evening and stars. If the poem intimates a life history, the prismatic emergence of colour monumentalizes the narrative into a creation myth. As regards style, by alphabetizing almost the entire pictorial space, the poem-painting does justice both to the starkness of Roman script and to the evocativeness of Chinese poetry. Standing at the centre of Klee's *oeuvre* as poet and painter, the poem-painting balances two conflicting traditions. Never again did Klee accomplish quite such a perfect balance of a poem with its pictorial space, although by developing other techniques he went on to create quite different, equally harmonious syntheses of word and image.

As is evident from other works, however, Klee was not just concerned with uniting word and image, but with integrating a far wider range of hermeneutic possibilities. Among the traditional devices, Klee also resurrects allegory as a vital dimension in his painting, although there are relatively few 'pure' examples, such as that in his *Hoffmannesque Tale* (*Hoffmanneske Erzählung*) of 1921 (illus. 16). Commentators have rightly connected the painting to Offenbach's opera, *The Tales of Hoffmann*, which is based on *The Sandman* (*Der Sandman*), *Counsellor Krespel* (*Rat Krespel*) and *The Adventures of New Year's Eve* (*Die Abenteuer der Sylvesternacht*). There are also strong links with *The Golden Pot* (*Der goldne Topf*). The tripartite division in the painting clearly recalls the three tales in the operetta, but the allegory follows the story of Anselmus in *The Golden Pot*. The grid structure in the painting indicates movement along horizontal and vertical axes, suggesting movement in time and space. This is Anselmus's symbolical spiritual journey. The poles of the grid externalize Anselmus's inner conflict.

At the lower left of the painting stands Hoffmann-Anselmus, the hero. Before him rises a tree, representing the natural world; it is perhaps the elder-tree from which Anselmus hears the sound of the three little snakes. But the trio also suggests the three women in the opera. Amusingly, Klee represents them by three hairpins in the heart rising from the lily. The diagonal pin evokes Anselmus's beloved Serpentina. The lily is an icon drawn from the creation myth in *The Golden Pot*. The squiggly line running up from Anselmus's head presumably evokes the hieroglyphic script he is enjoined to copy before he can enter into the higher world. Whereas the boat at the lower left comes from *The Adventures*, the central alembic or bottle is a prop from *The Golden Pot*. Thus Klee mixes his references and playfully celebrates the spiritual ascent of a brother artist – Hoffmann himself – who shared his own triple talent for poetry, painting and music.

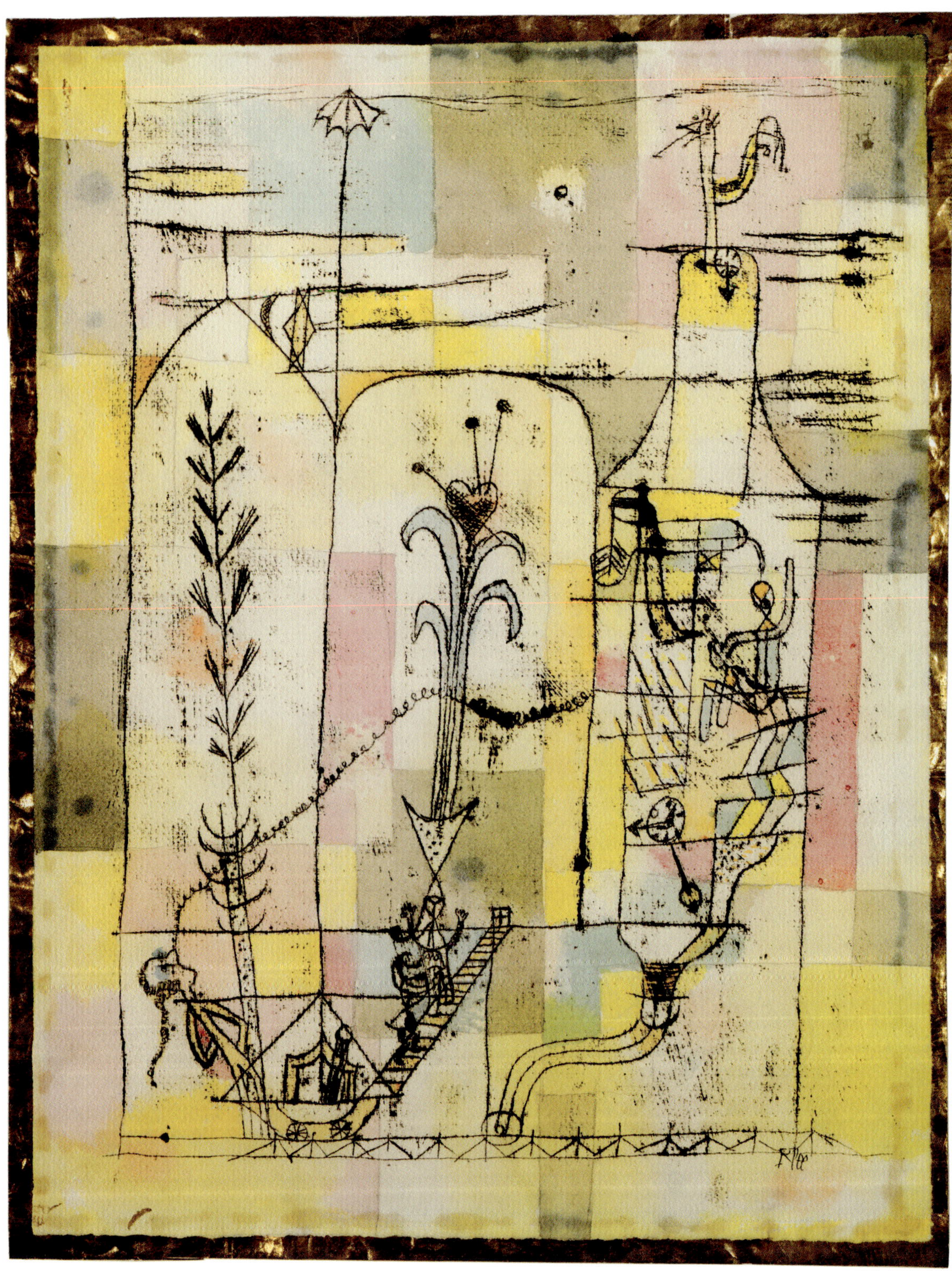

16 Paul Klee, *Hoffmannesque Tale*, 1921, no. 18, oil transfer drawing and watercolour on paper on cardboard.

In works like this, and throughout Klee's *oeuvre*, it is not the alphabetic script but the pictogram or hieroglyph which provides the primary constituent of meaning – signs which occupy the borderline of meaning between the visual and the verbal. As his work matures, it approaches ever more completely a synthesis of word and image, in which pictograms may determine the entire visual space. A late drawing like *Pond with Swans* of 1937 permits of no ready distinction between verbal and visual (illus. 17). Klee began to collect pictograms in his diary as early as 1903 (see illus. 18),18ut it was only in maturity that he learned to master them in his pictures, by which time he had quite literally returned to writing as 'scratching' and 'inscribing'.

The problem of script, then, remains a constant in Klee's work. By the 1930s at the latest he had set himself the insoluble task of squaring the circle in his attempt to merge the alphabet with picture writing in his own form of hieroglyphic pictograms. Runes also feature in this process. In his palimpsest *Dokument* of 1933 Klee successfully integrates runic and alphabetic elements (illus. 19): his own signature at the bottom right is barely distinguishable from the collection of runes and signs.

Klee's final works attain an affecting synthesis of letter and image in a kind of pictogram, notably in the very late *Death and Fire* (*Tod und Feuer*) of 1940 (illus. 20), and in a series of connected drawings. In all these works the image is made up from the letters of the German word for death, *Tod.* This can clearly be seen in *Death and Fire*: on the left stands the letter T with an O sitting on it, perhaps evoking a raised arm with a flat hand and a ball, while a capital D gives the outline of a skull, within which the letters 't o d' once again spell out mouth, nose and eyes. On the right stands a figure with a stick, whose head and trunk also derive from the same three letters. This may, as has been suggested, be the Ferryman; or it may be the figure of Death himself. The angular lettering used for the figure's trunk (note the linear 'D') evokes rigidity, and contrasts with the organically shaped letter of the central human head. Death is both beating the figure in the centre, and 'breaking the stick of life', a play on the German idiom for death by execution, 'den Stab brechen': the violently contrasting straight lines create a sense of fracture. The face of the dying man is white; that of Death, black; while the ball, in yellow, evokes the sun, the fiery realm to which the dying man will return. The threefold use of the word 'TOD' as a structural element is echoed in the three lines at the top of the picture, which recall the letter E, possibly suggesting a single letter from the other title-word, FEUER: the three bars evoke, once again, a region beyond language: a fiery realm which presupposes and yet lies beyond life. The fusing of the pictogram with the alphabet thus also produces an allegory, apparent even in such details as the arrangement of the letters in the central head: Death first attacks the physical self (the mouth) and ascends to the spiritual (the eyes): the first, right eye looks down; the second, the left, upwards, to the higher world. Together, they express a combination of pain and sublime humour. The material on which the work is painted, a rough kind of jute, adds a flickering sensation by its texture, evoking a vital living fire. Yet throughout, the original exudes an unusual gentleness. Thus the work implies the inevitable fulfilment of a quest that Klee – possibly echoing Novalis – had outlined long before, in 1916:

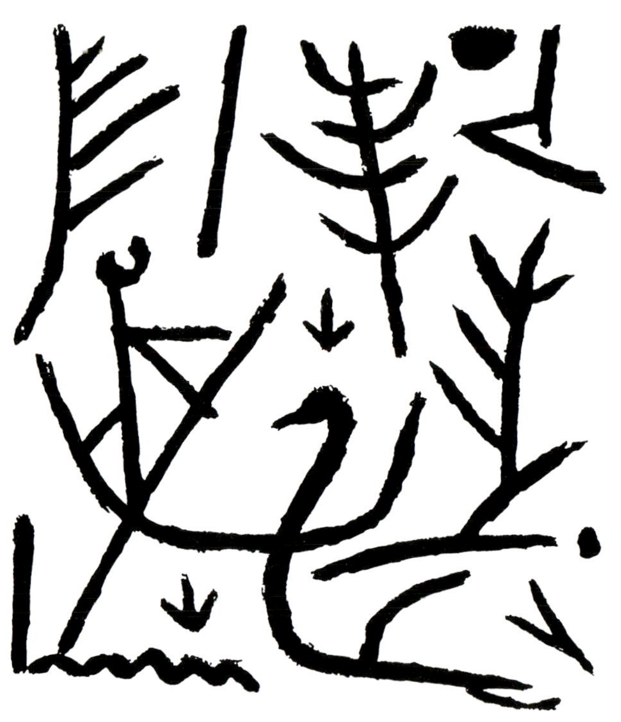

17 Paul Klee, *Pond with Swans*, 1937, no. 221, coloured paste on primed paper on cardboard.

18 Paul Klee, *Pictograms, Diary*, 1903, pen and ink.

19 Paul Klee, *Document*, 1933.

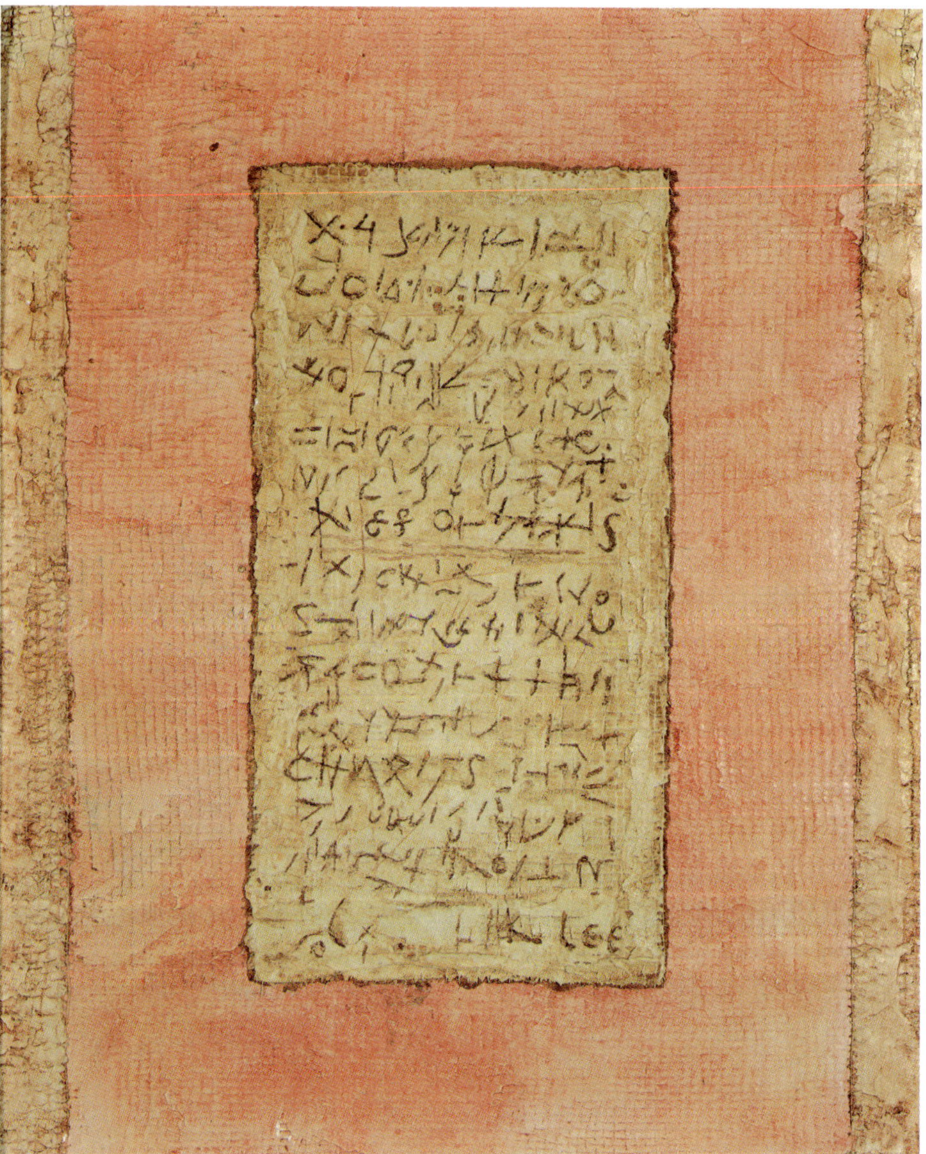

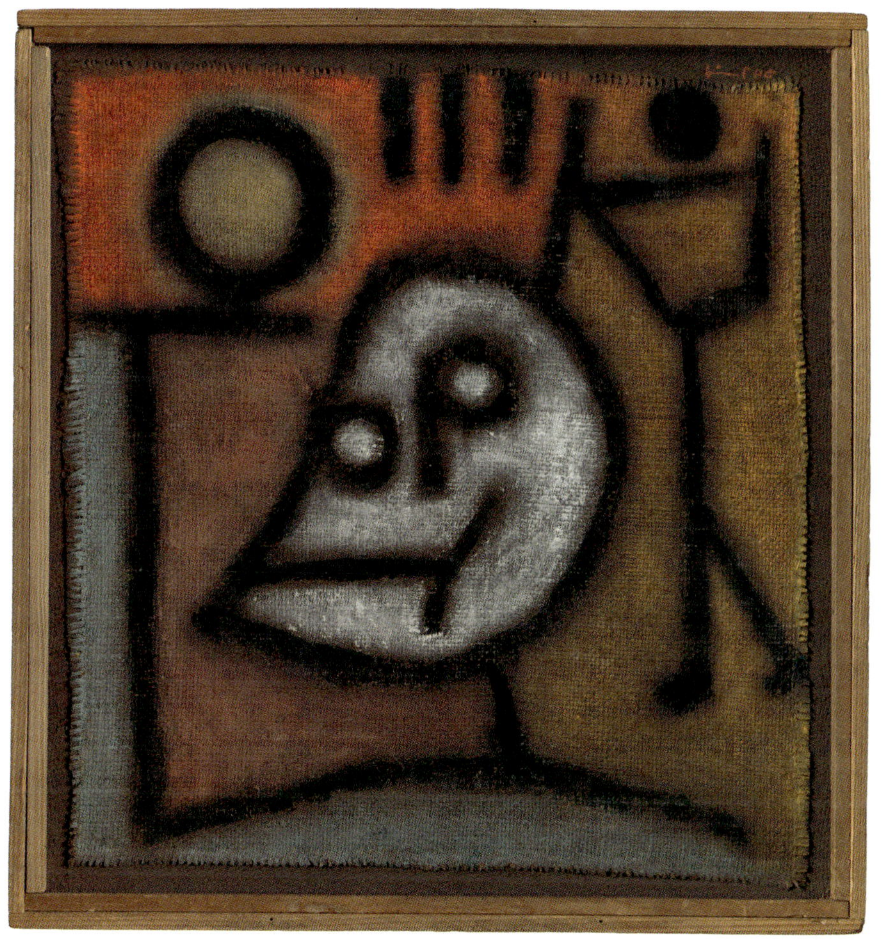

20 Paul Klee, *Death and Fire*, 1940, no. 332, oil and coloured paste on burlap; original frame.

ich nehme einen entlegenen, unsprüngliche Schöpfungsakt an, wo ich Formeln voraussetze für Mensch, Tier, Pflanze, Gestein und für die Elemente, für alle kreisenden Kräfte zugleich …

Geht Wärme von mir aus? Kühle?? Davon ist dort, jenseits der Weissglut, nicht die Rede … Der Mensch meines Werkes ist nicht Spezies, sondern kosmischer punkt.

I assume a distant, original act of creation, in which I presuppose simultaneous formulae for man, the animals, plants, stone and for the elements and the circulating forces …

Is warmth emitted from me? Coolness?? There is not a word of this beyond the white heat … The man of my works is not a species, but a cosmic point.

The painting *Fire and Death* represents just such a formula for a human being. As a matrix of life and death, it is a pure cosmic point.

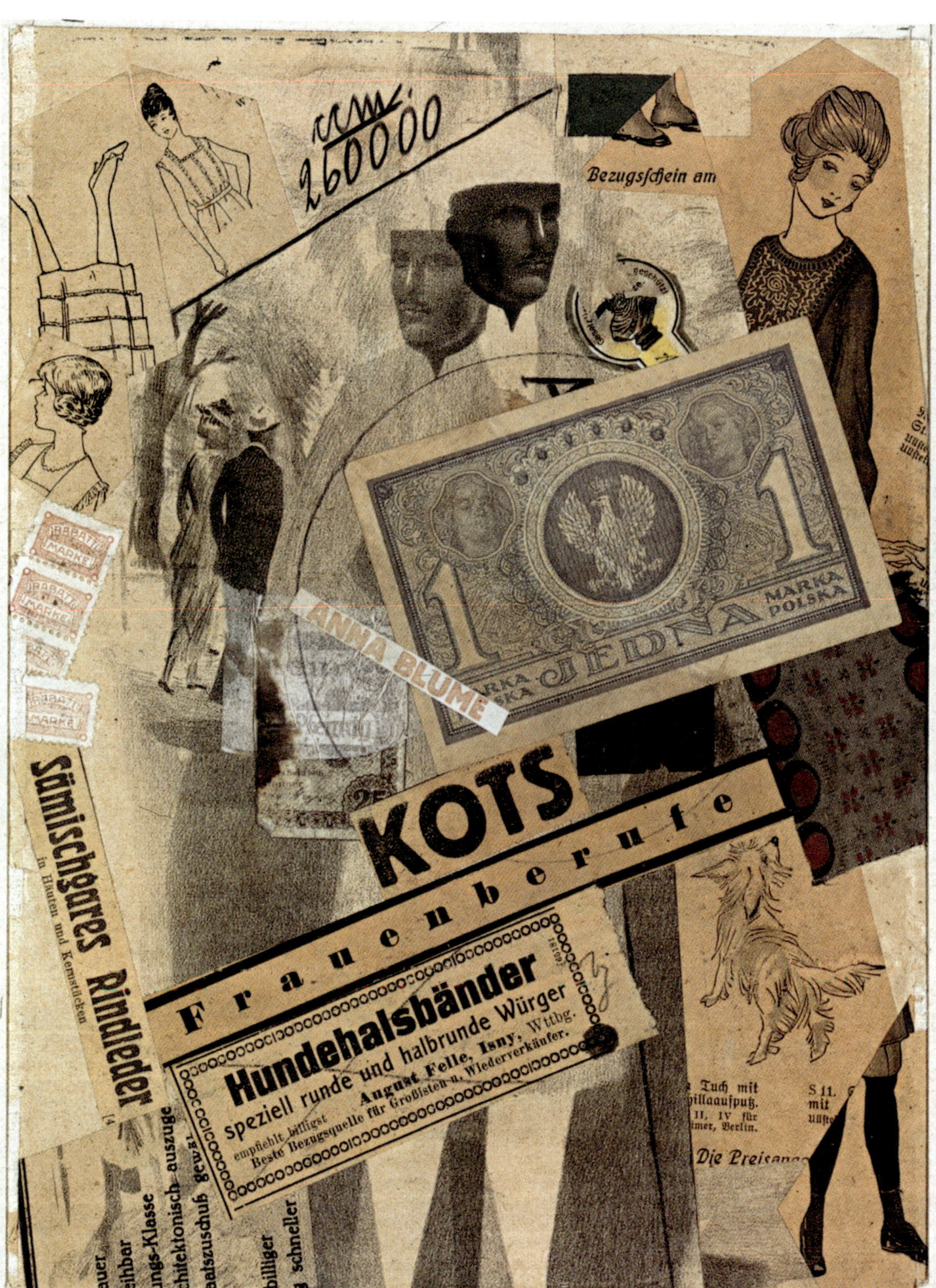
260000
Bezugschein am
1
JEDNA
MARKA POLSKA
ANNA BLUME
RABATT MARKE
KOTS
Frauenberufe
Hundehalsbänder
speziell runde und halbrunde Würger
empfiehlt billigst August Felle, Isny, Wttbg.
Beste Bezugsquelle für Großisten u. Wiederverkäufer.
Sämischgares Rindleder
in Häuten und Kernstücken
billiger
schneller

3

Sense and Nonsense in Kurt Schwitters

MICHAEL WHITE

As is the case with his fellow Dadaists and close friends Raoul Hausmann and Hans Arp, Kurt Schwitters's reputation as a writer and poet is almost as high as it is as an artist. Moreover, just as they did, Schwitters persistently interwove textual and visual elements in both his poems and his collages. This essay will concentrate on the formative moment of his one-man art movement *Merz* at the end of the First World War and investigate how the interchange between word and image in Schwitters's output was connected to the very possibility of an object or a text being meaningful. Where Dada has often been seen as profoundly negative in outlook and an assault on the investment of art objects with superior values such as beauty, truth and humanity, Schwitters's version of it retained a role for the artist as an individual empowered to salvage meaning from the apparently meaningless, to find significance in a disenchanted world. The interaction between words, letters, images and materials we find continually in his works is linked both to a holistic world view that sought connections between apparently unrelated things and to the widening of the definition of art to incorporate all forms of creative activity beyond customary disciplinary boundaries.

To interpret Schwitters's works is to engage in similar processes of sense making. The problem we face is distinguishing the meanings we make out of them from something that the artist may have concealed for us to find. The viewer/reader is often vexed by the question of whether to take a particular absurdity seriously or not, to invest it with great significance or disregard it as accident. This was precisely what prompted the wide-scale popular reaction to Schwitters's 1919 poem, 'An Anna Blume' ('To Anna Blume') (illus. 2), replete as it is with nonsensical phrases, grammatical errors and paradoxical statements, typified by the 'prize question' halfway through the poem: '1. Anna Blume has a bird. 2. Anna Blume is red. 3. What colour is the bird!'[1] The opening line, 'O thou beloved of my twenty-seven senses, I love thine!', should have alerted the reader to the problem. As in English, the German word *Sinn* (sense) connotes both 'meaning' and 'feeling'; the 'twenty-seven senses' mentioned by the poet indicate an abundance of both and the poem prompts manifold interpretations and

1 Kurt Schwitters, *Mz 158, Das Kotsbild*, 1920, collage.

AN ANNA BLUME

Merzgedicht 1

O du, Geliebte meiner siebenundzwanzig Sinne, ich liebe dir! — Du deiner dich dir, ich dir, du mir. — Wir?
Das gehört (beiläufig) nicht hierher.
Wer bist du, ungezähltes Frauenzimmer? Du bist — — bist du? — Die Leute sagen, du wärest, — laß sie sagen, sie wissen nicht, wie der Kirchturm steht.
Du trägst den Hut auf deinen Füßen und wanderst auf die Hände, auf den Händen wanderst du.
Hallo, deine roten Kleider, in weiße Falten zersägt.
Rot liebe ich Anna Blume, rot liebe ich dir! — Du deiner dich dir, ich dir, du mir. — Wir?
Das gehört (beiläufig) in die kalte Glut.
Rote Blume, rote Anna Blume, wie sagen die Leute?
Preisfrage: 1. Anna Blume hat ein Vogel.
2. Anna Blume ist rot.
3. Welche Farbe hat der Vogel?
Blau ist die Farbe deines gelben Haares.
Rot ist das Girren deines grünen Vogels.
Du schlichtes Mädchen im Alltagskleid, du liebes grünes Tier, ich liebe dir! — Du deiner dich dir, ich dir, du mir, — Wir?
Das gehört (beiläufig) in die Glutenkiste.
Anna Blume! Anna, a-n-n-a, ich träufle deinen Namen. Dein Name tropft wie weiches Rindertalg.

5

Weißt du es, Anna, weißt du es schon?
Man kann dich auch von hinten lesen, und du, du Herrlichste von allen, du bist von hinten wie von vorne: „a-n-n-a".
Rindertalg träufelt streicheln über meinen Rücken.
Anna Blume, du tropfes Tier, ich liebe dir!

MOLKENSCHWERE SILBERBLÄTTERBLÜTE

Gedicht 27

Glant zersieden Zeterzacken
Rieselbäume schiffen grinsen Blumen
Lenzen duftet Fackeln loh
Sprühen Blasen Rindertalg (infolge Papiermangels)
Flinken Beine Schwefel Arme Marc Chagall
Mir
Mir Fontänen
Fließen in sich und ersticken stak
Paare du mir
Blättre klettre sprießen fließen
Paare du mir
Deine Ströme glänzen gieren
Elend schwängert Seegelboote (Puppenküchenein-richtungskasten)
Ich umnachte mir

6

2 Kurt Schwitters, 'An Anna Blume' in Schwitters's *Anna Blume: Dichtungen* (Hanover: Paul Steegemann Verlag, 1919).

sensations. It has a strong degree of pattern, produced by the repetition of certain lines, breaking it into distinct sections, the declension of pronouns, which provide its strongest rhymes, and the rhythm of the spelling out of Anna Blume's forename. Whatever assistance such regularity offers conventional interpretation is confused by reference to powerful and irrational feelings, such as frequent mention of intense colour ('red I love you Anna Blume'), physical texture ('your name trickles like soft tallow') and to sound ('the people say . . . what do the people say?'). Hints at standard poetic structure are also thrown by the possibility of reading in different directions: 'One can also read you from the back and you, most glorious of all, are from the back as from the front: "a-n-n-a"'. Schwitters may be ridiculing the emotive rhetoric of the traditional love poem and mocking the representational power of language; 'having a bird' in German signifies madness and we could dismiss the whole thing as deranged. Yet the appeal to sense and the senses is too strong and we cannot reject it as mere foolery.

Such sensate richness is also a feature of the collages Schwitters began to make around the same time as he wrote 'An Anna Blume', and it is therefore surprising to discover how few attempts there have been to produce detailed individual interpretations of them. Scholars have tended to cling to the artist's early written account of his practice, where he stated that 'The medium is as unimportant as I myself. Essential is only the forming.'[2] Arguing here for the abstraction of both his collages and his poems, Schwitters explained that he had abandoned naturalistic representation in favour of the arrangement of pictorial elements which could be of any substance. He christened the process of production *Merz*, a word that 'had no meaning when I formed it. Now it has the meaning which I gave it', and his definition focused on the 'evaluation' of material against material.[3] By extension Schwitters considered that 'Meaning is important only if it is employed as one such factor. I evaluate sense against nonsense. I prefer nonsense but that is a purely personal matter. I feel sorry for nonsense, because up to now it has so seldom been artistically moulded, that is why I love nonsense.'[4] Connecting sense to representation, Schwitters further commented on the frequent appearance of representational fragments in the collages, which he 'evaluated' against other, non-representational elements, suggesting that no import should be derived simply from the appearance of a figurative image or a recognizable word in the midst of abstract coloured shapes and individual letters. As Werner Schmalenbach put it, 'Meaningless elements stand alongside the "clues", and no importance is attached to decoding.'[5] Others have been even more cautious, warning that interpretation might be 'intrusive and in the end destructive of its [a *Merz* picture's] fine-tuned equilibrium'.[6]

Still, some 'clues' have been irresistible for detectives such as Annegreth Nill, who has engaged in some remarkable interpretative work, starting with her extensive account of what is generally regarded as Schwitters's first known collage, *Drawing A2: Hansi* (illus. 3), based on the wrapper of a Hansi chocolate bar.[7] Although the collage is dominated by trapezoidal, coloured shapes, the brand name, *Hansi-Schokolade*, remains clearly legible in the bottom right-hand corner and slightly obscured upside-down at the top. Along the left-hand edge Schwitters left the word Dresden exposed, as he did with the last three letters of the word *Schokolade* (chocolate) on the right, forming the new word *ade* (farewell). Nill initially suggested that this was a reference to the shortage of luxury goods at the end of the war: 'farewell chocolate!' It is well known that Schwitters was extremely interested in the marketing of commodities and later worked for many years as an advertising designer.[8] Furthermore, he revealed in 1927 that the term *Merz* was a fragment of the word *Kommerz* (commerce).[9] But, according to Nill, this historical context is not all the collage alludes to and she goes on to argue that the references to Dresden and 'farewell' were a comment by Schwitters on his abandonment of the academic training he had before the First World War in Dresden in favour of radical experimentation. A significant influence on Schwitters's decision to forge a different artistic path was his encounter with the Dadaist Hans Arp in 1918, and Nill suggests that *Hansi* is also something of dedication to his fellow artist. Finally, she suggests that these textual references support us seeing the red paper forms as a cross shape, indicating Schwitters's demise as an academic artist and rebirth as a member of the avant-garde.

Such a comprehensive iconographic interpretation of the collage is very persuasive, but places its emphasis on the straightforward content of the text with only a modicum of attention to its arrangement and appearance. Words offer meanings to 'solve' the collage but a problematic excess is left unconsidered. For example, what of the numbers *200.11.20* that appear at a slight angle in the top right? The eye-catching black and yellow forms and the curious piece of tracing paper in the middle are also rather irrelevant, it seems.[10] Are they the nonsense to the sense Nill makes of the object? If so, in what way are they being 'evaluated'? And what significance might be derived from the repetition of *Hansi-Schokolade*? Interesting though attempts at decoding are, we obviously need to think very hard about the interaction between what we see and what we think we see in such collages and what we are doing when we 'read' them in these ways. For example, there is something very

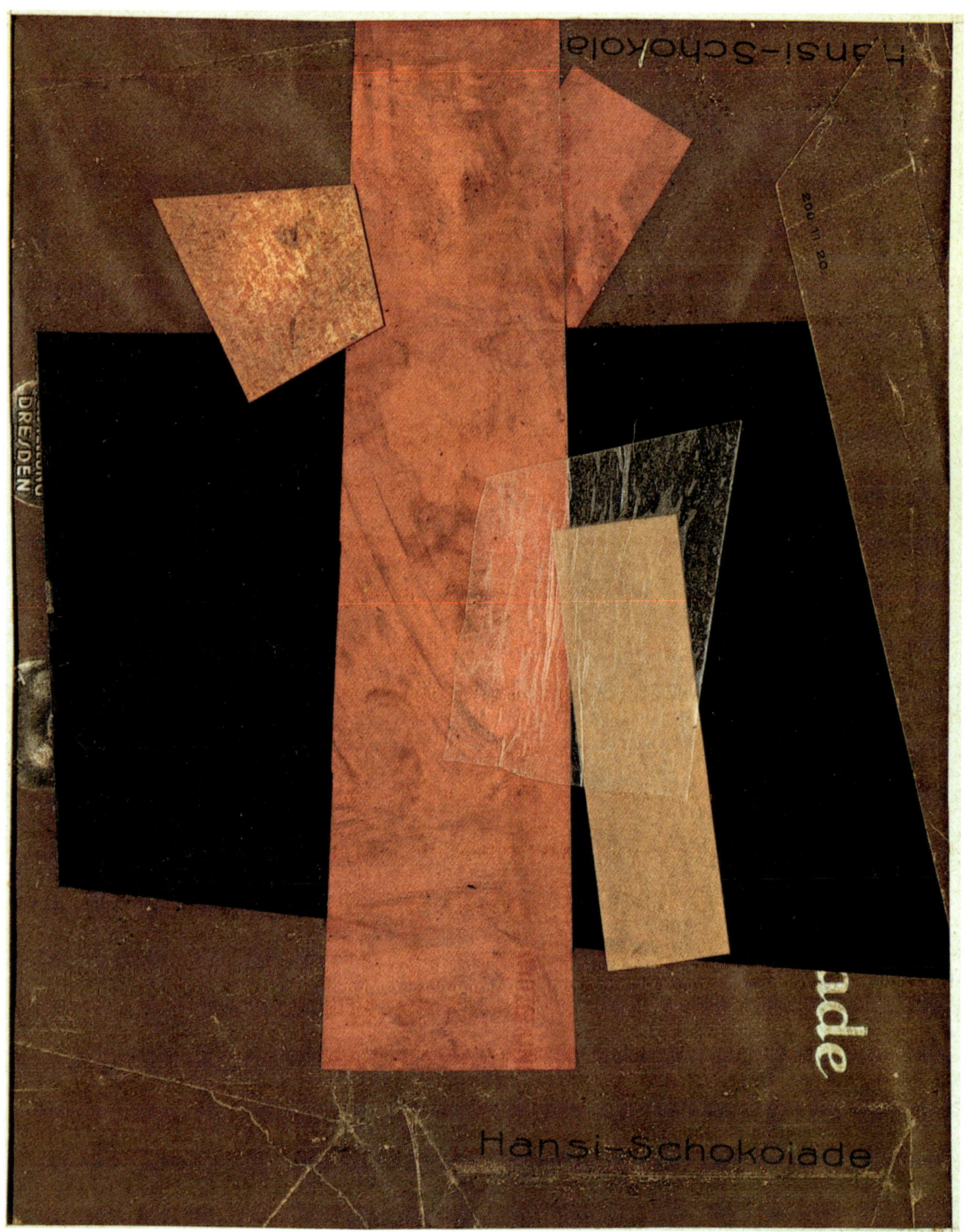

3 Kurt Schwitters, *Drawing A2: Hansi*, 1918, collage, paper and transparent paper on paper.

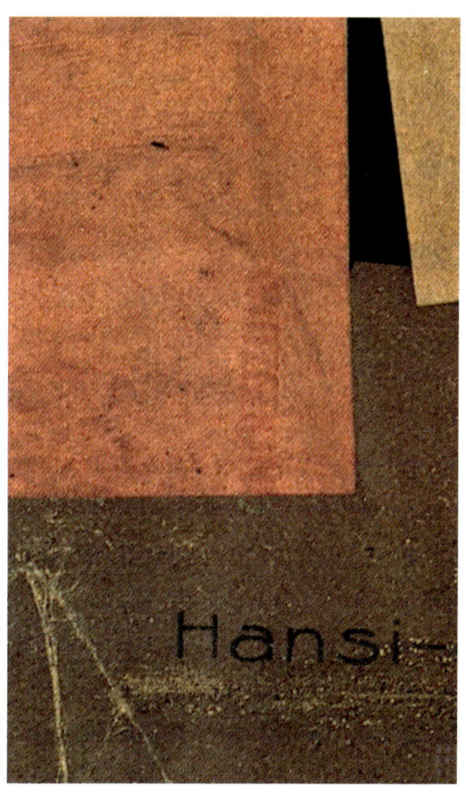

4 Kurt Schwitters, *Drawing A2: Hansi* (detail), 1918, collage, paper and transparent paper on paper.

interesting occurring here in our tendency to complete the partially obscured words in our minds, perhaps the most intriguing example being the very faint presence of the letters *WITZGRUN* on the lower part of the vertical red rectangle (illus. 4), which Nill has identified as the textual remnant of the place just outside Dresden, Lockwitzgrund, where Hansi chocolate was produced. She has therefore interpreted it as the neologism *Witzgrund*, comprised of the German words *Witz* (joke) and *Grund* (ground or foundation), and concluded that it is another reference to Schwitters's rejection of his past artistic training.[11] This does not take into account the fact that the *D* is disconnected from the end of *WITZGRUN*, leaving us actually with a 'joke' *GRUN*, which might be read as *Grün* (green). Whether *GRUND* or *GRÜN*, the 'sense' that we make here is derived from such oscillating effects as seeing 'ground' lying on top rather than underneath and 'green' in red letters.

This gets us much closer to the activity of making the meaningless meaningful that was observed earlier in 'An Anna Blume'. It also helps keep in view the qualities of the materials used. For example, the unfolded wrapper which prompted the collage in the first place no doubt attracted Schwitters's attention because of its combination of symmetry and asymmetry (the rotational repetition of the brand name at top and bottom but the dissimilarity of left and right). Schwitters placed the dominant, red rectangle almost exactly on the central vertical axis, emphasized by the left-hand edge of the transparent paper, which works to disguise the horizontal symmetry that he exaggerated by placing the large black quadrilateral so that it left exposed an almost identical band above and below it. Each shape does its job by the partial cancellation of the word *schokolade*; by blocking out most of the large white letters, the black quadrilateral helps the eye focus on the words above and below, but these are then made dissimilar by the placement of the red rectangle. What is occurring visually and abstractly combines with Schwitters's play with language; the transformation of *schokolade* into *ade*, a word derived from the French *adieu*, involves a change in sound to the final 'e'. Missing its final 'de', the *Hansi-Schokola* at the top of the collage would be pronounced like the French *chocolat*. Playing on German and French sounds, we might also note that the title 'A2' in French would be *A deux*, another near rhyme, which might also be read as *à deux* (in unison).[12] The structural qualities of the collage are based on the desire to see symmetry and hear rhyme but each is slightly confused and frustrated, mimicked in the otherwise irrelevant number series *200.11.20*, which seems to set up a pattern that is then interrupted.[13]

Words that appear in Schwitters's collages, even when used as titles for the works themselves, are never purely transparent but structurally integrated and draw attention to the 'material' qualities of language and the 'legible' qualities of materials. We can see this at work again in *Merzpicture 32A, The Cherry Picture* of 1921, which takes its title from a card placed centrally on it labelled with the words for cherries in both German and French. Scrawled above is the handwritten text 'Ich liebe Dir!' (I love thine), instantly recognizable as the

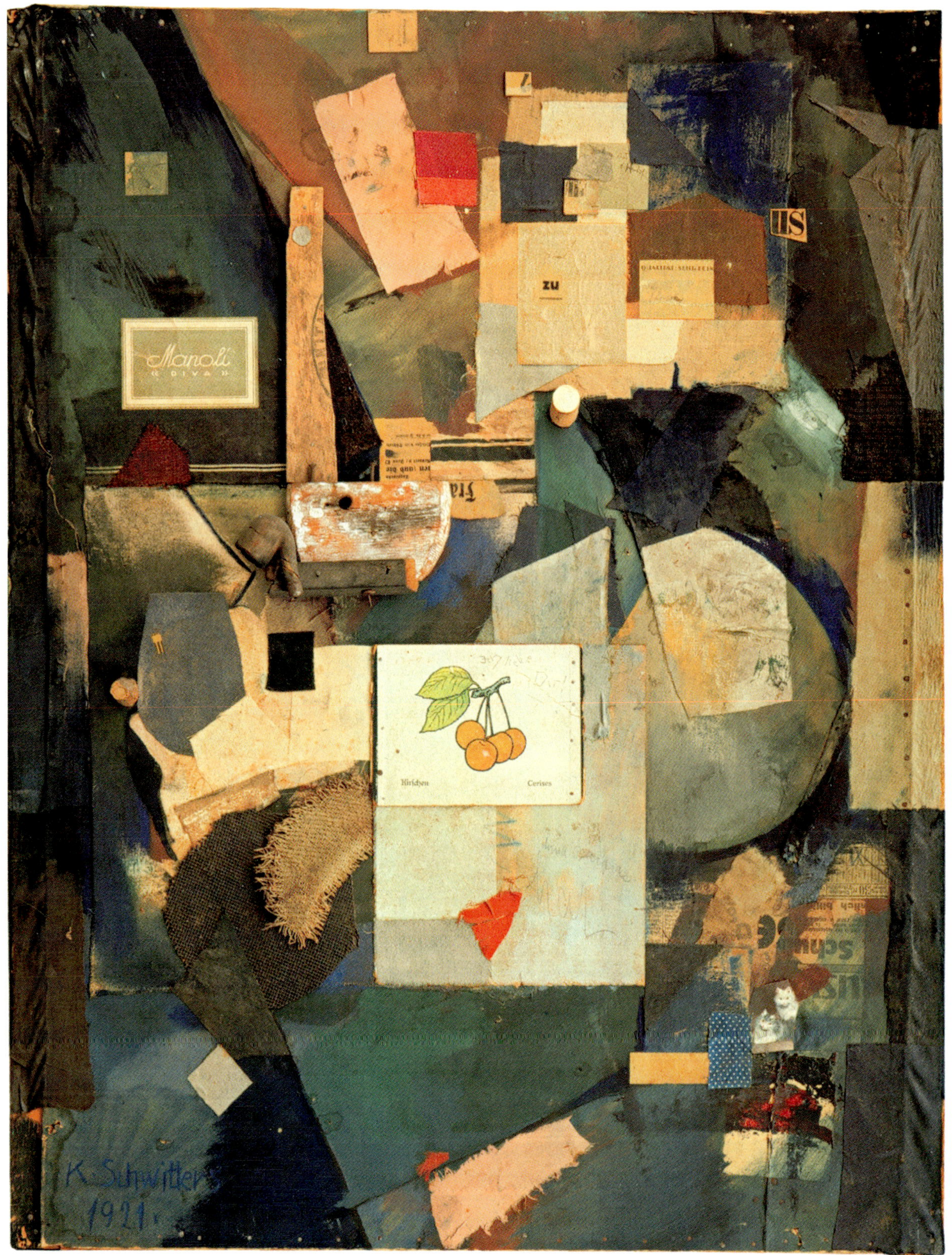

5 Kurt Schwitters, *Merzpicture 32A, The Cherry Picture*, 1921, assemblage, oil, paint, tempera, fabric, wood, cork, paper, card, cardboard on canvas nailed on board.

incorrect grammar of the first line of 'An Anna Blume'. Just below the card to the right is more handwritten text, another abbreviated line from the poem, 'Anna Blume hat' (Anna Blume has [a bird]). Nancy Perloff has taken this as a cue to link the collage to the fictional woman Anna Blume and to Schwitters's 'sense of humor, his delight in veiled sexual references through pictures of cherries, rosy lips, and cards saying "very fine quality". All are puns of the association of good fruit with enticing female sexuality.'[14] Quite where Perloff sees rosy lips I am uncertain, but we could add to her list the 'Diva' brand cigarettes that might link a glamorous woman associatively to lips.[15] However, balancing the reference to quality is one to cheapness (*billig* in the lower right). The cigarette advert is juxtaposed with a pipe (a crude reference to the male anatomy?). Rosy-red touches contrast with the dominant green of the ground.

The picture card in the centre combines the overall colour scheme of the collage with text. Red cherries on a stalk with green leaves are given two names, 'Kirschen' and 'Cerises'. The latter is particularly interesting in that it could hardly have escaped the attention of an artist and the son of a ladies' fashion merchant that 'cerise' is more than the French name of a fruit; it identifies a colour, used internationally often in the context of textiles. The red patches on the collage are predominantly pieces of fabric in shades of red. If we think of Anna Blume, we might recall that she was red. Not only that, 'red is the colour of [her] green bird', while 'blue is the colour of [her] golden hair'; she is only to be apprehended through sensuous contrast. Meanwhile, as John Elderfield has suggested, 'Kirschen' (cherries) may be a pun on 'Kurtchen', the diminutive of Kurt by which Schwitters was commonly known.[16] We might even see the two words together, 'Kirschen Cerises', as something of an alternative signature in the middle of the collage. Schwitters often signed his works K. S., which would match the sounds of the initial letters. What was so straightforward, a picture of cherries simply labelled that might have started life as a teaching aid, becomes potentially an abstract portrait of either or both Anna Blume and Kurt Schwitters in the context of the collage as a whole. Text and image are brought together not to identify the word cherries definitively with a particular object, and not as a witty form of iconography in the way Perloff suggests, but to spark off multiple meanings through association.

Hammering home this lesson is another early collage, *The And Picture* (illus. 6). In his major statement on *Merz* quoted from earlier, Schwitters wrote, 'The expression of a picture cannot be put into words, any more than the expression of a word, such as the word "and" for example, can be painted.'[17] So what are we to make of this? As in *The Cherry Picture* and *Hansi*, *The And Picture* derives its title from text that appears in it, in this case the dominant letters *und* (and) in the top centre of the collage. As a conjunction, the word 'and' on its own is meaningless, although it can be used singularly as a quizzical interjection 'and?' implying 'so what?' or 'what next?' As if to highlight the redundancy of 'and' alone, Schwitters has collaged in other 'ands', an ampersand joining *Sökeland & Söhne* and an abbreviated 'u.' joining *Eckstein u. S[öhne]*. Combination is figured directly in the collage by its very visible marks of assembly, much of it coarsely nailed together as if forcing the materials into coexistence with each other. And then, almost in self-parody, we are given one of the most obvious links imaginable, the fragment of the word *Pferde* (horses) and a horseshoe

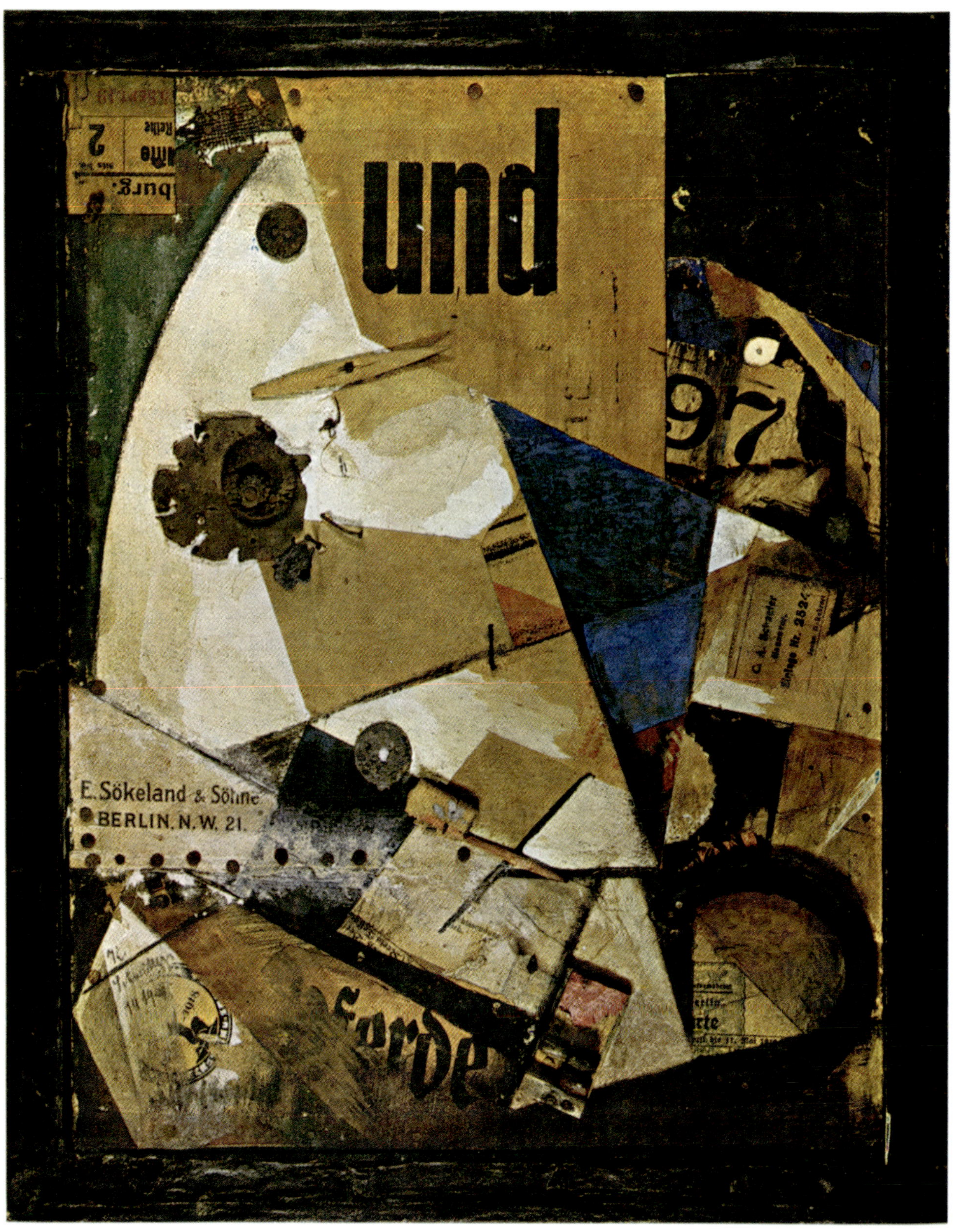

6 Kurt Schwitters, *The And Picture*, 1919, assemblage, gouache, paper, cardboard, wood, metal, leather, cork and wire nailed on board.

shape in the lower right of the collage. Such highly visible linkage is then 'evaluated' against invisible conjunctions, most notably in the many numbers that appear on the collage. Some, such as *97*, imply an 'and' (*siebenundneunzig* in German), while others, such as *19* (*neunzehn*), do not.[18]

One of Anna Blume's most attractive features to Schwitters was that she could read backwards. Composite numbers in German are written out and enunciated in reverse order to the appearance of the digits; 97 is spoken as 'seven and ninety'. On close inspection of *The And Picture* we can note that most of the fragments and objects are arranged in a rough circle with the centre fairly empty. The bold *und* is perhaps what initially catches our eye, but do we then read clockwise or anticlockwise? The *97* is ambiguous in this regard, as just explained. The horseshoe shape is a dead end and once we have realized this, the eye is liberated to travel in every direction, finally reading upside-down. *Und* becomes *pun* and takes us to a commentary on subtraction rather than addition this time in the top left-hand corner. Here we find half a ticket to a theatrical performance, the date of which appears in the diametrically opposite corner to where it might normally be expected on a traditional painting. On the top line of the ticket, what is missing from the word *burg* is *Schau* and, to try to translate this little game, what has been removed from sight is the 'show' or 'demonstration'. I would say that contrariwise the collage is decidedly demonstrative. It draws attention to the patterns of sense-making we engage in as our eye scans over surfaces but does so by literally and figuratively cancelling out a view through or beyond the picture.

The abstract approach to reading staged in *The And Picture* through the cancellation of representation is repeated even more dramatically in Schwitters's poem of 1923, the 'Pornographic i Poem'

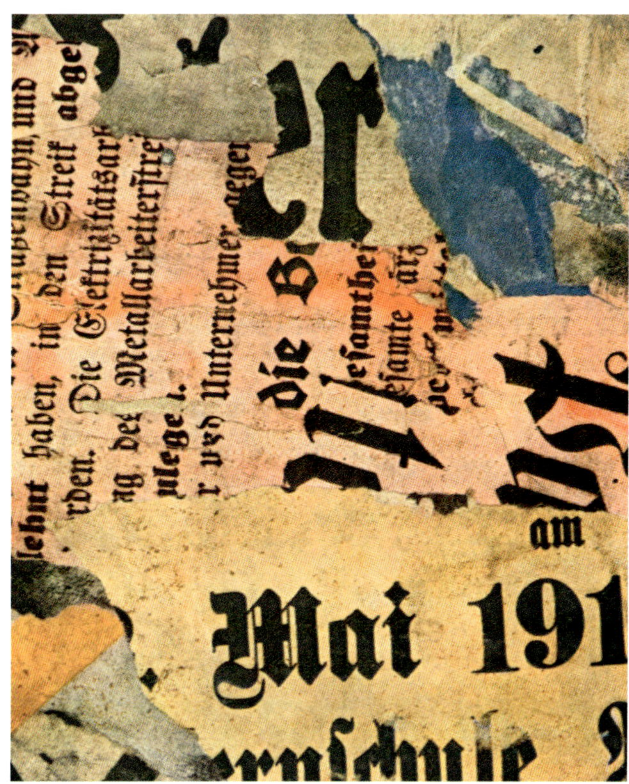

7 Kurt Schwitters, *Untitled (Mai 191)*, 1919, collage.

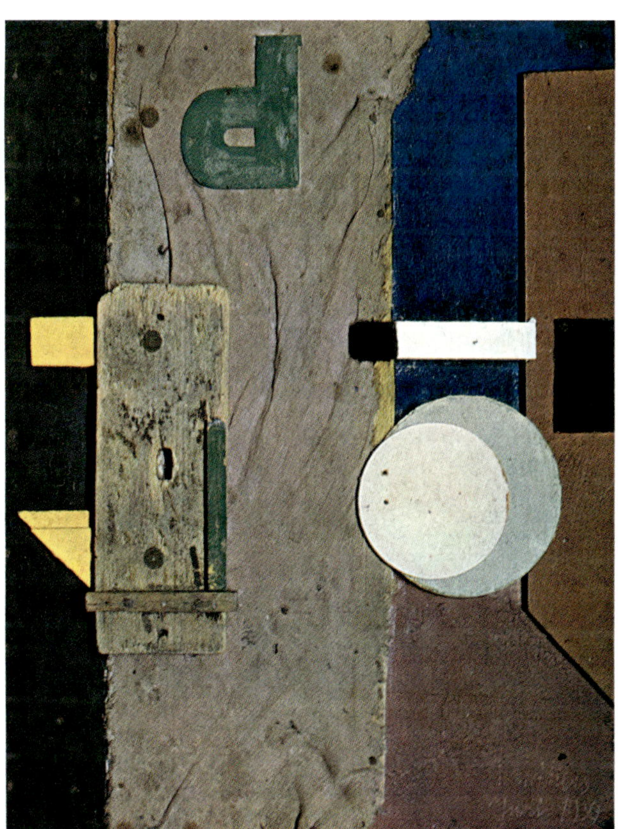

8 Kurt Schwitters, *Merz P. rose*, 1930, assemblage, oil paint, board, fabric and wood nailed on wood.

ppppppppp

pornographisches i-Gedicht

Die Zie |
Diese Meck ist |
Lieb und friedlich |
Und sie wird sich |
Mit den Hörnern |

Der Strich zeigt, wo ich das harmlose Gedichtchen aus einem Kinderbilderbuch durchgeschnitten habe, der Länge nach. Aus der Ziege ist so die Zie geworden.

Und sie wird sich | nicht erboßen,
Mit den Hörnern | Euch zu stoßen.

9 Kurt Schwitters, *Pornographic i Poem*, *Merz* 2, April 1923.

(illus. 9). As the text itself explains, it was written (made?) by cutting a child's poem in half: 'The line shows where I cut the innocent little poem out of a children's book lengthways.' The original, of which Schwitters gives the final two lines in full by way of demonstration, concerns a goat (*Ziege*), transformed into the meaningless 'Zie' in the truncated version, 'whose bleat is kind and friendly'. The potentially pornographic element concerns what she (according to the pronoun) will do 'with the horns' in the final two lines and we are invited to imaginatively fill in the blank space on the right with suitable possibilities. The line that stands in for Schwitters's cut is very interesting in this regard, as it prevents the poem being read conventionally while opening it to new implications. It makes the poem more suggestive but can also be seen as censoring 'Mit den Hörnen Euch zu stoßen' (to butt you with its horns), which is in itself quite suggestive in German. The black line is neither textual nor pictorial, but stands in for the framing activity central to Schwitters's collaging activity.

Schwitters began producing his 'i' works in 1920. Similar to Duchamp's 'ready-mades', the 'i' works re-present objects and texts with minimal transformation on the part of the artist; 'i' stands for intuition and Schwitters relied on his ability to perceive value in something that was essentially valueless. One of the first 'i- drawings' was *Drawing I6. Fashion I*, whose title is typically confusing regarding the status of I as a letter or number. The 'drawing' began life as a proof sheet or the product of a printing error that had misplaced a text advertising a manufacturer of building materials over an image of smartly dressed people wandering in a park, perhaps itself an advertisement for clothing. The text, running vertically, describes building costs and the processes and transport of materials, and is obviously disjunctive with the well-attired strollers behind it. The functional, bare typeface clashes with the refinement of the fashionable promenaders. The last line, 'AMBI-Massiv ist' (AMBI-Solid is), has been cut off, leaving an adjective hanging. We do not find out what qualities the product has but instead read reflexively that 'AMBI is solid', a quality echoed in the bold, plain font used, contrasting again with the lightness and superficiality of the modishness represented in the background. Yet for all these disparities, the spacing of the lines does chime with some parts of the pictorial composition, such as the single column of text just to the left of the centre that runs through the point where the elbow of the male figure in the foreground meets that of the dark-suited man in the background. There is a curious relationship between the downward fall of the text and the upright nature of the figures and the trees, which is focused by the base line, once again, a line that hovers between textual and pictorial. It acts as a border and a cut, but also the ground, and makes the 'i-drawing' into a collage even though there has been no pasting, only framing.

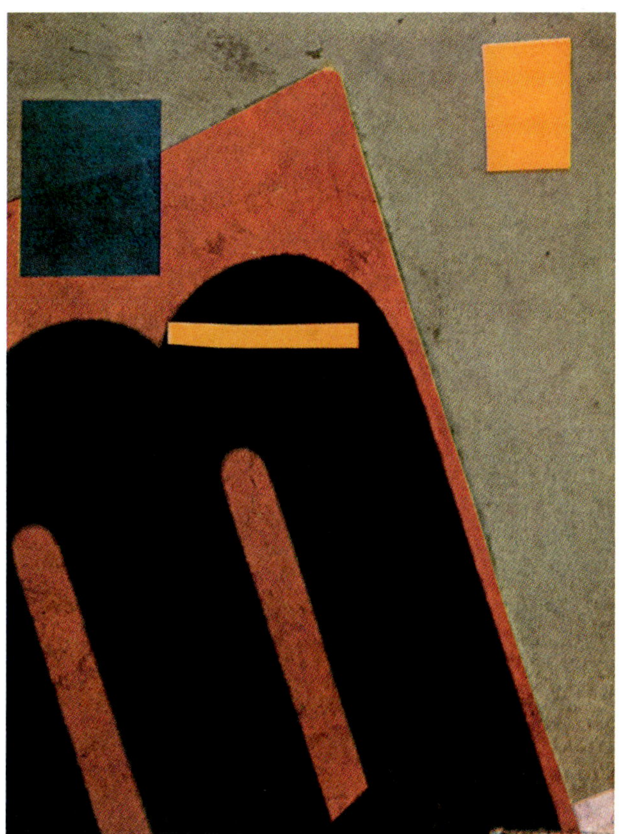

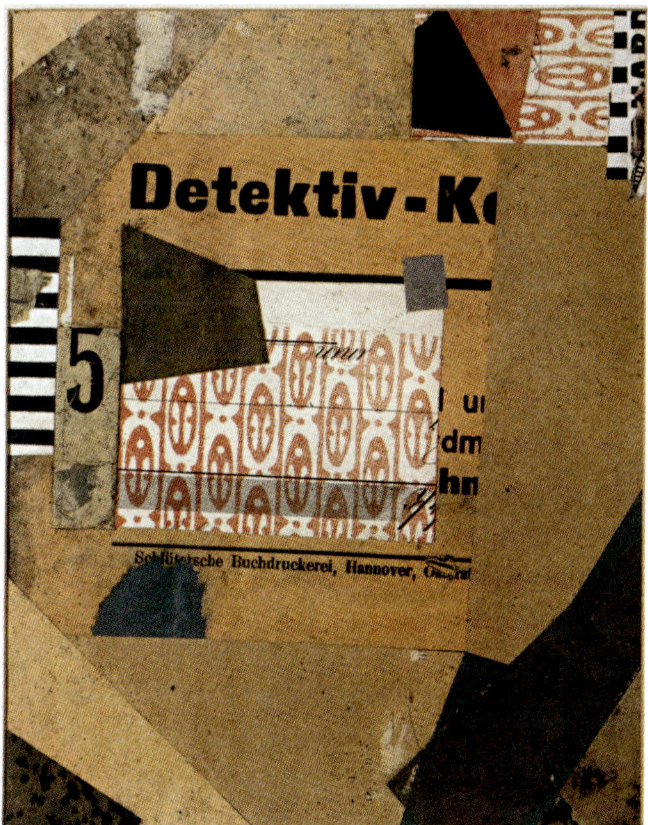

10 Kurt Schwitters, *Mz 1926, 12 liegendes emm*, 1926, collage.

11 Kurt Schwitters, *Mz 212, fuer Moholy-Nagy*, 1921, collage.

Returning to Schwitters's comment quoted above, 'The medium is as unimportant as I myself. Essential is only the forming', we can now start to see what he was getting at. The first part of the statement warns us against 'decoding' the collages in search of some expressive content Schwitters might have hidden there. The 'i-drawings' were his most obvious renunciation of that kind of authorship. On the other hand, when he goes on to speak about 'forming', we should be careful about confusing this with 'formal' and viewing the collages merely as attractive arrangements of colour and shape. 'Forming', for Schwitters, was always accompanied by *Entformung*, a neologism which has been translated as 'dissociation' but also has connotations of 'metamorphosis' or even 'deforming'.[19] If the 'forming' makes the medium unimportant, it is because it dissociates textual elements from their habitual contexts and permits us to see them pictorially, and similarly we find ourselves 'reading' pictorial elements. As the 'i-drawings' and 'i-poems' demonstrate, the interchange between text and image lies at the very heart of the principle of collage, where fragments are recombined into new wholes. As interpreters of them we are encouraged to be similarly creative in our abilities to associate and dissociate, seeking the sensible in the nonsensical, the representational in the abstract and vice versa. Schwitters's ultimate vision for *Merz* was that it would encompass all creative activity, spilling over into the realms of architecture, theatre and music. However, the interaction between word and image remained paradigmatic to his theory of bursting the boundaries of conventional artistic practice and the collages were the place where it was demonstrated to its fullest effect.

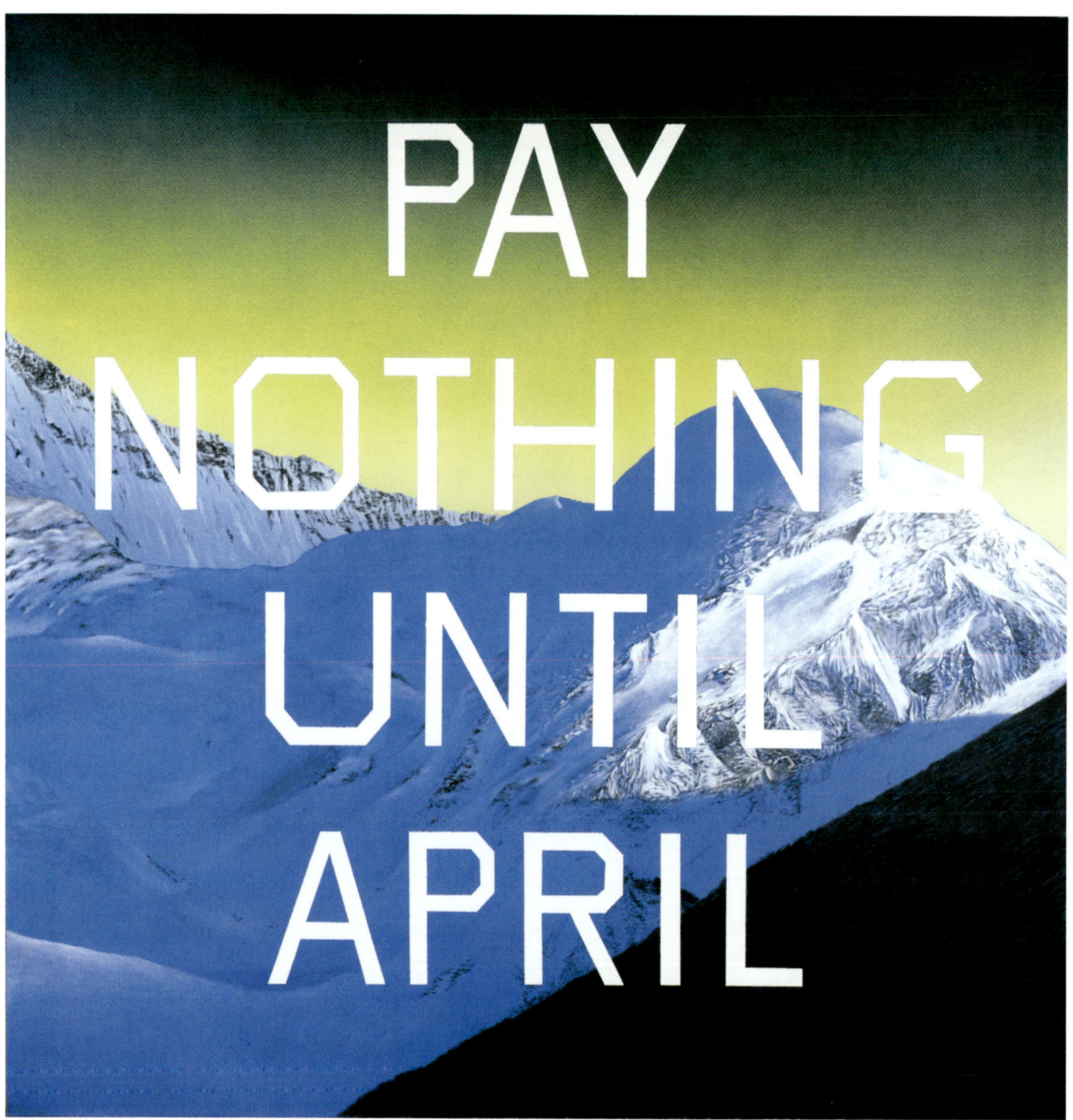

1 Ed Ruscha, *Pay Nothing Until April*, 2003, oil on canvas.

III

Word and Image in Art since 1945

MICHAEL CORRIS

THE PLAY OF RESOLUTION

What did the conjunction 'word' and 'image' mean to art produced in the aftermath of the Second World War? What possibilities did these two pillars of expression conjure up for artists still struggling to come to grips with the enormous cost, in human and material terms, of that historic conflict?

The prospect of a cornucopia of civilizing virtues lurking deep within the categories 'art' and 'literature' seemed doubtful after the experience of total war. Art and literature proved to be fluid, rather than foundational, markers for the future. While creative expression has always been in dialogue with currents of ideological conflict, the status of art and literature was challenged by the extreme polarization of left and right characteristic of the interwar period and extending into the post-war era in the shape of the Cold War. The ideological mobilization of societies for the sake of war or Communism or capitalism from the 1930s through the '50s left its mark on art while bringing home the lesson that the promise of culture's autonomy – a condition linked to the autonomy of the subject – rested largely upon a certain understanding between power and society at large.

The events of the Second World War taught the world that the individual was expendable. In particular, it was the Shoah that demonstrated precisely how autonomy could be obliterated using the available tools of Enlightenment rationality and capitalist efficiency. Art of the immediate post-war period could not remain indifferent to this history, to these truths. Yet, it was caught in an irresolvable situation: while it was art's ethical duty to bear witness to the disasters of genocide and war, art could not be certain that it possessed adequate means to do so. A benchmark of horror had been installed in the history of civilization; not just art, but life itself was in question.

This chapter begins at a point of crisis: in art and society. If 1945 marks the end of the autonomous subject, then it also signals the beginning of a reaction against the post-war aporia of representation so brilliantly addressed in the writings of Theodor W. Adorno. Without trivializing Adorno's conclusions or remaining indifferent to the historical events that gave rise to them, it can be said that the aporetic relation between word and image in art presented artists of the post-war period with a means to stave off cultural paralysis. In this context, the dialogue between word and image in a single artwork becomes a symbol of compensation; a symptom of the acknowledgement of the impossibility of art and literature to represent the collapse of the autonomous subject. The condition of the possibility of art is exemplified by the closing utterance of the protagonist in Samuel Beckett's 1953 novel, *L'Innomable* (*The Unnamable*): 'I can't go on, I'll go on.'

If the dialogue between word and image within a work of art is best left unresolved because it preserves the uncomfortable reality of irresolution

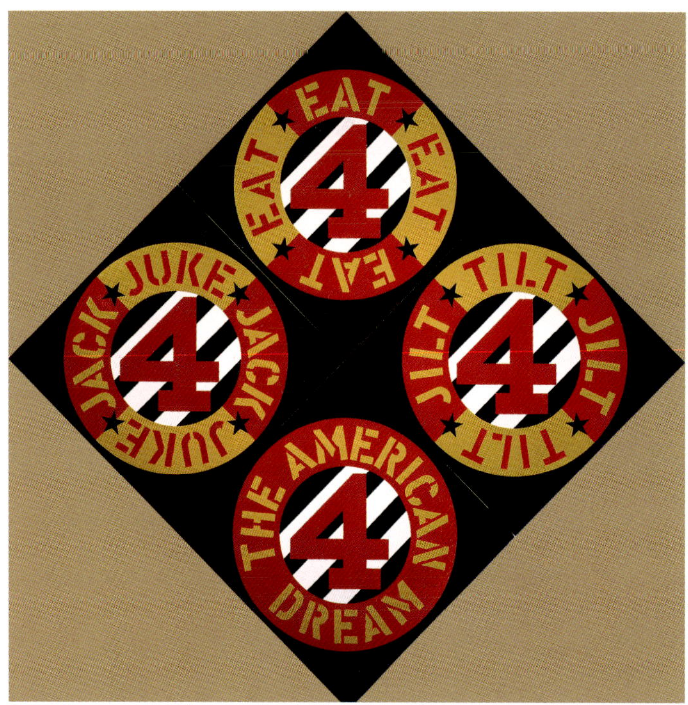

2 Robert Indiana, *The Beware-Danger American Dream, No. 4*, 1963, oil on canvas.

in life itself – that is, if the dialectical tension of this conversation between art and culture is allowed to live and flourish in unexpected ways and to occupy unexpected sites – then a possible criterion presents itself for deciding which works of art employing word and image deserve our attention.

If advertising may be said to exemplify the false resolution of word and image, then perhaps the most readily accessible example of a negative response to this charade of word and image thrown up by advertising is to be found in American Pop art. It is important to note that Pop art is simply one of several artistic engagements since 1945 to address the reified dialectic of mass consumer society. While Pop art was by no means the most virulent in its condemnation of this false dialectic nor the most successful in reintroducing a necessary tension into the word and image constellation, recent revisionist accounts have enabled us to reconsider its significance. This new interpretation of Pop art's ambiguous relation to consumer culture has lent much needed depth to an analysis of works by iconic figures such as Andy Warhol. Yet it also invites us to reconsider the practices of other, lesser known or marginalized figures, such as Robert Indiana, Joe Brainard and Elaine Sturtevant. Indiana's early emblematic paintings express vividly under cover of satire the underside of the American post-war promise of affluence (illus. 2). Brainard's misappropriations of the newspaper comicstrip character *Nancy* created by Ernie Bushmiller shows how it is possible to derail the comfortable resolution of word and image through the expedient of taboo content (illus. 3). Sturtevant – a model for many post-feminists – undercut the authority of the visual in art by remaking through a process of recollection the works of Warhol, Marcel Duchamp, Jasper Johns, Joseph Beuys and others.

Even more trenchant is the historically prior example of the programme of resistance to the reification of everyday life offered by the concept of the *dérive* as articulated by Guy Debord, Ralph Rumney and others associated with the Situationist International. Here, voluptuousness is reintroduced to an everyday life drained of meaning and given aesthetic form through the documentation of aimless wanderings across the city (illus. 4).

During the period under discussion, one might

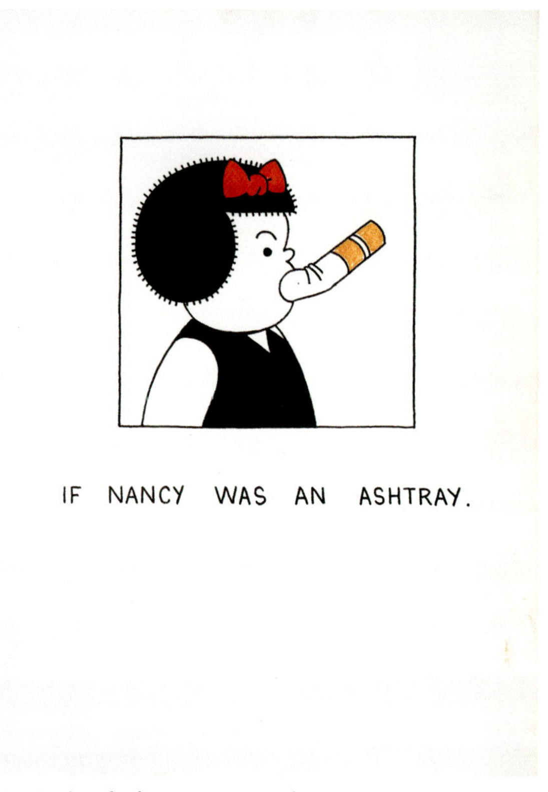

3 Joe Brainard, *If Nancy was an Ashtray*, 1972.

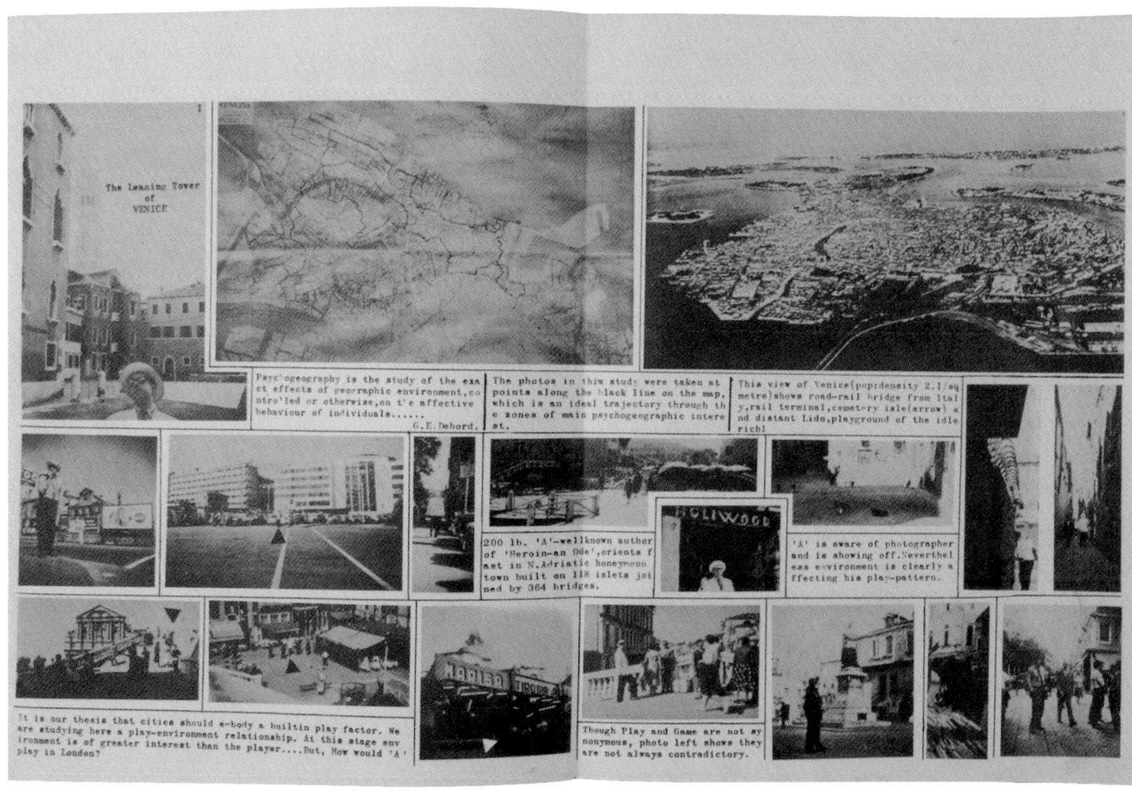

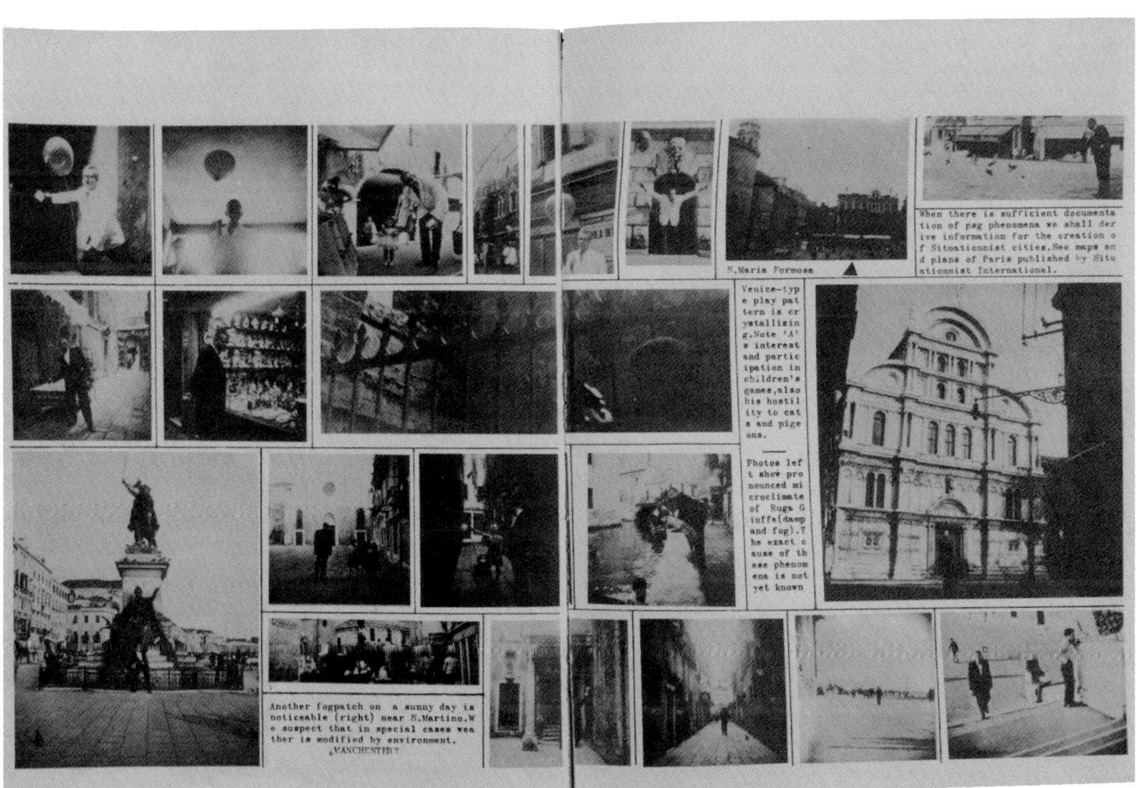

4 Ralph Rumney, *The Leaning Tower of Venice*, 1958.

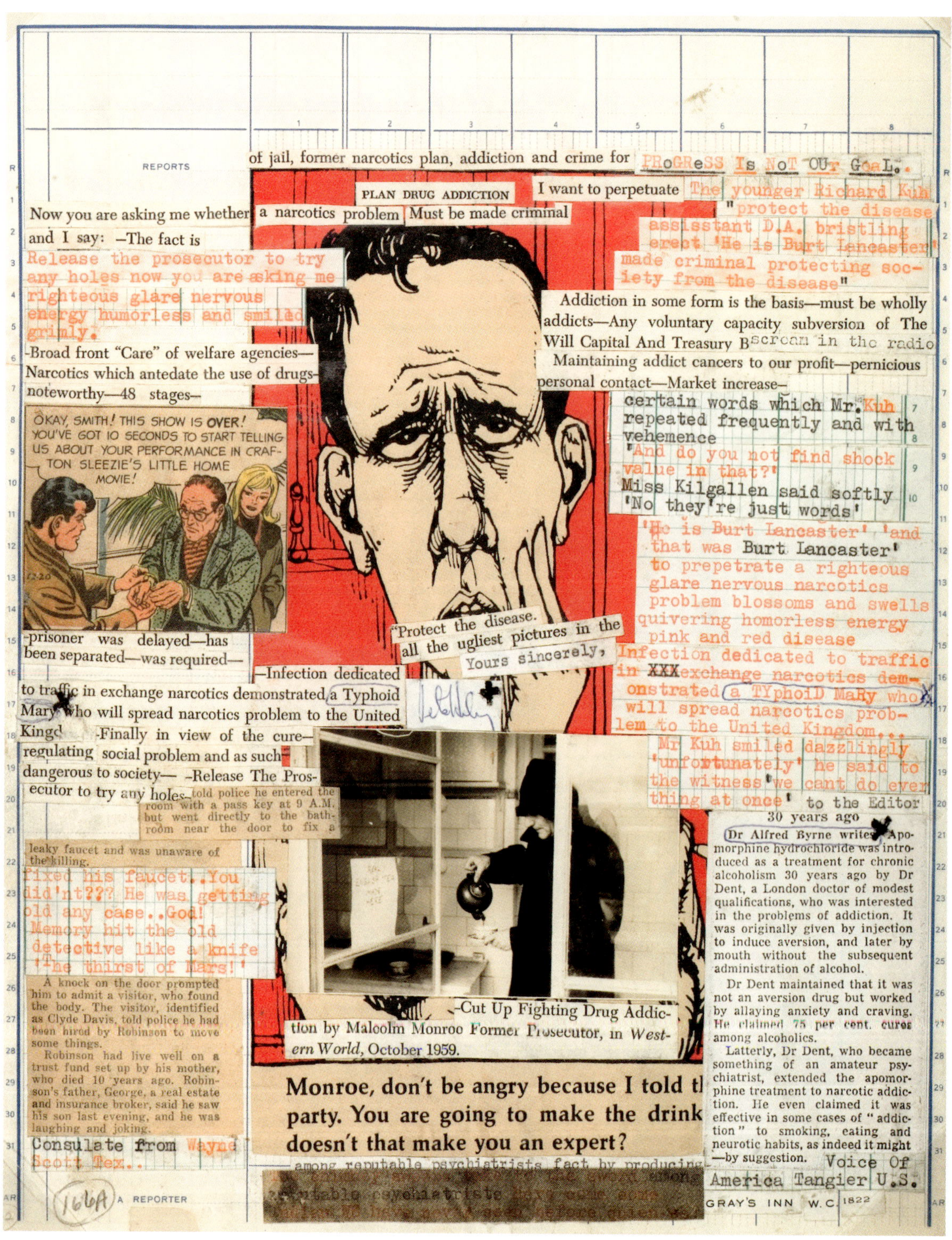

5 Brion Gysin (1916–1986) and William S. Burroughs (1914–1997), *Plan Drug Addiction*, *c.* 1965, from *The Third Mind ('Of Nuclear War Danger')*, 1959–70, gelatin silver print, typescript, offset lithography, newsprint, crayon and ink on paper.

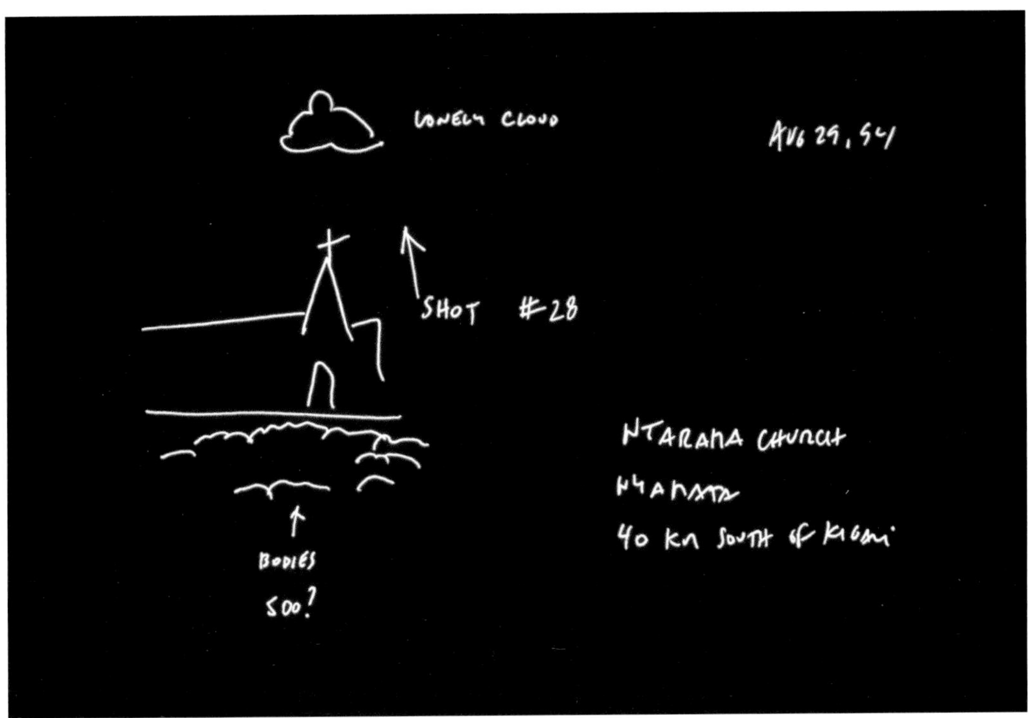

6 Alfredo Jaar, *Field Road, Cloud*, 1997, ink on paper.

say that for every artistic assertion of the agency of the subject – for every call for the creation of an immersive, visceral art employing the means of word and image – one can identify a countervailing plea for the symbolic intensification of indifference or even the obliteration of the word. This strategy, realized through the application of chance or the 'cut-up' to the composition of the work, gave rise to some stunningly layered images of erasure (see illus. 5).

Even as the trauma and loss of the Second World War and the conformism of everyday life threatened to transform 'word' and 'image' into ciphers, art continued to affirm its obligation to bear witness rather than remain silent. In a sense, much post-war art pursued the reconstitution of a dialectic that would offer the hope for the further continuation of art. Among other perspectives, this chapter highlights the work of artists who have employed word and image in various ways within the field of visual art for just such constructive, dialectical purpose.

It is well known that the relation of word and image in art has been conceptualized as an agonistic one in which each term represents the fullness of a rich, competing cultural tradition. This is a hierarchical conception that invites one to start from the premise that pictures are subordinate to literature or vice versa. Yet, this is not necessarily the only way to understand the relation in art between word and image. Contemporary visual artists are not likely to respond to the suggestion that they are either iconophiles or iconoclasts, although they may take on the mantle of one or the other opportunistically, as the situation demands. For many artists since the 1960s, the markers of place, lived experience, and the encounter with the common culture or the culture industry are more pertinent to the shape of their practice than an identification with the historic cultures of literature or image-making.

A substantial proportion of artists working with word and image during the 1970s and '80s did so in order to engage in a meaningful way with new developments in media technology; this trend continues, as seen in the work of younger artists such as Joe Scanlan. In contrast, an artist like Frances Stark takes a far more 'low tech' approach, reinvent-

HOVELS AND PALACES: 1

Dave Rushton and Paul Wood

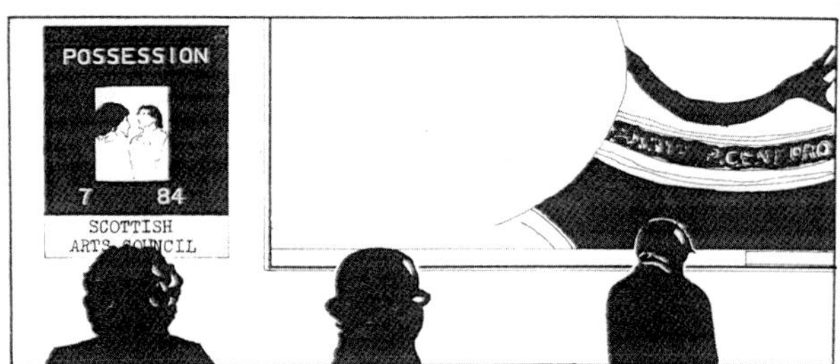

ANTICIPATION

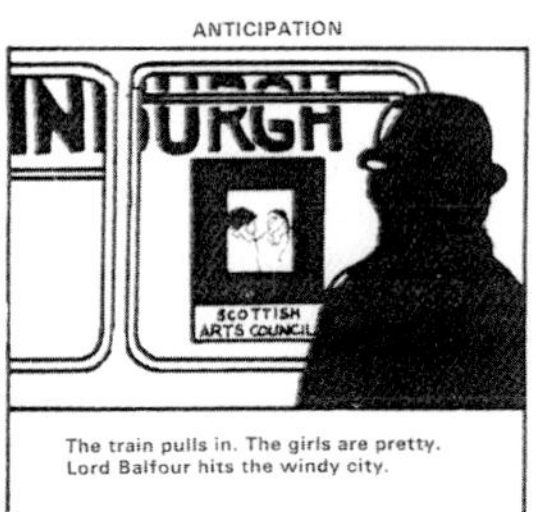

SHOCK

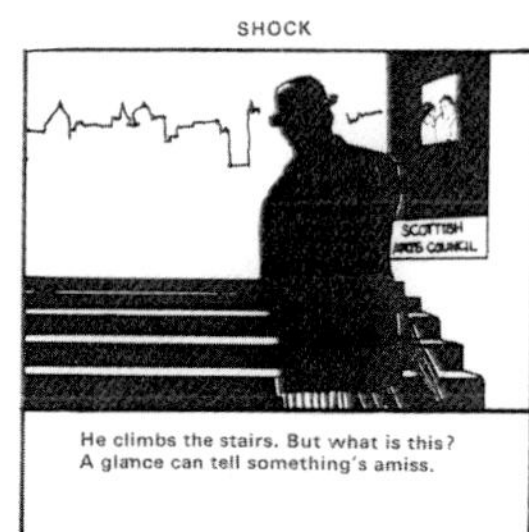

ANGER

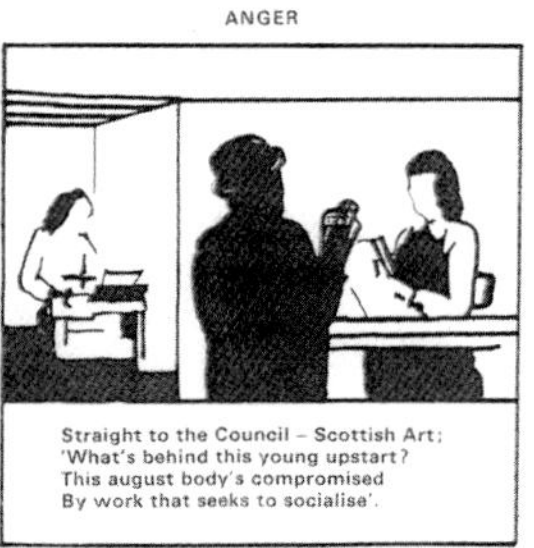

PERSUASION

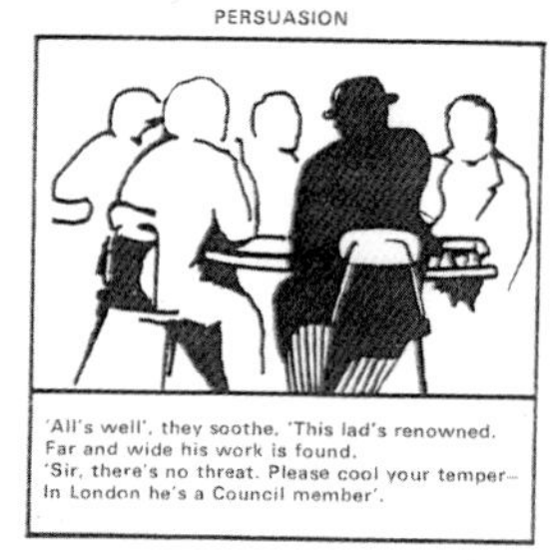

REASSURANCE

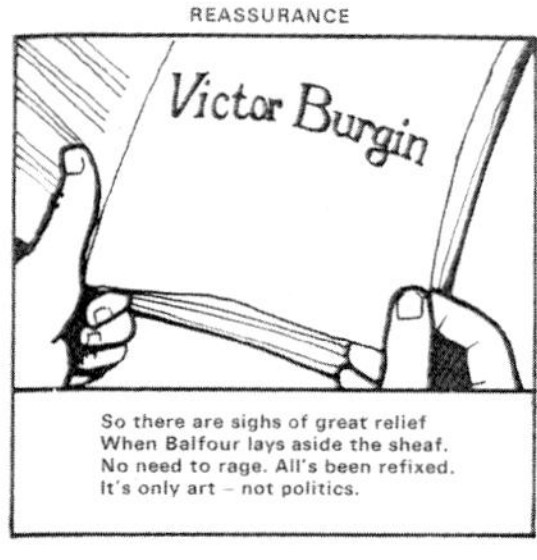

MOLLIFICATION

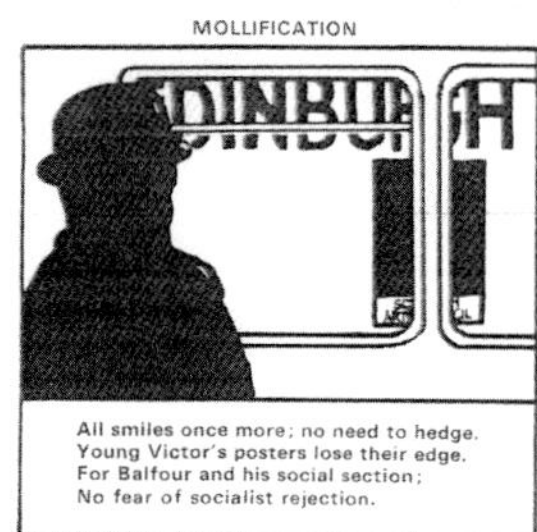

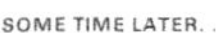

DESPERATION

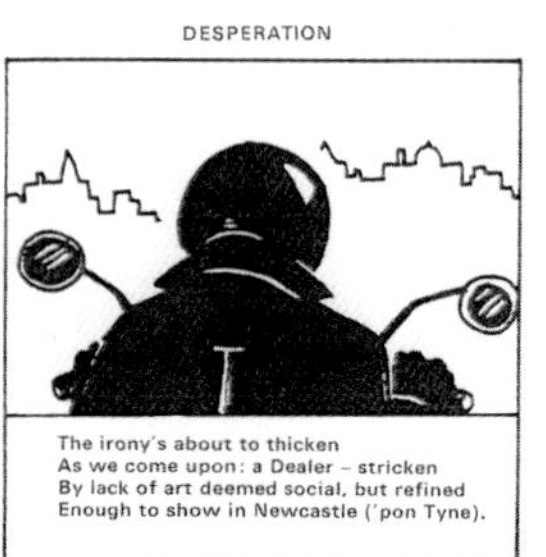

SOLICITATION

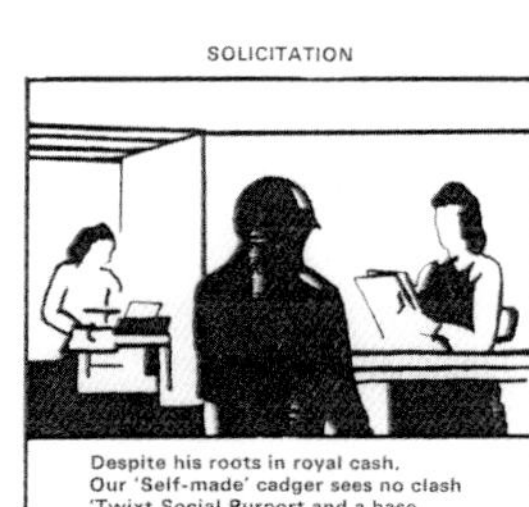

APPROPRIATION

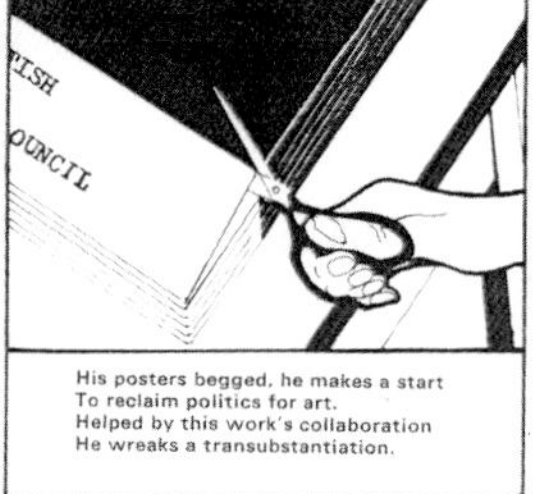

REGURGITATION

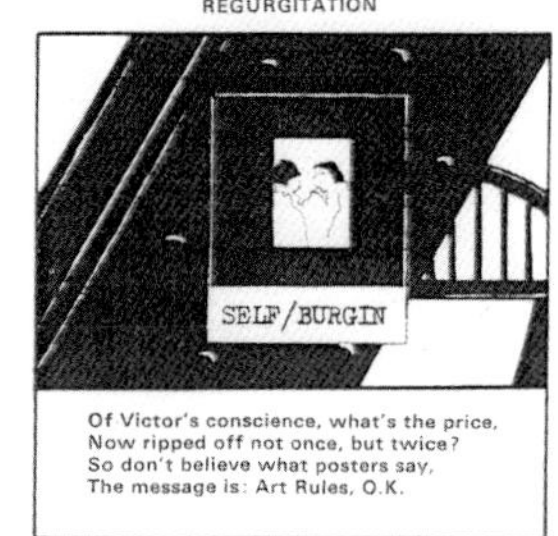

7, 8 Dave Rushton and Paul Wood, *Hovels and Palaces 1* and *2*, 1976.

ing collage and exploiting off-the-shelf presentation software to exemplify the anxieties and dilemmas faced by the artist working in a post-media culture of art. The tremendous impact on artistic practice caused by a collision of visual cultures – the cultures of documentary and journalistic photography or the language of cinema – is felt strongly in the work of artists as varied as Martha Rosler, Carole Condé and Karl Beveridge, and Alfredo Jaar (illus. 6). These artists have benefited from the example of earlier practitioners concerned with the semiotics of word and image and the cultural import of subverting the act of reading. Using various strategies of disruption, artists of the 1960s and '70s, such as Victor Burgin and Carolee Schneeman, provided models of cultural resistance that often blended imperceptibly into the realm of political resistance. In the case of Burgin's work, the claims made on behalf of semiotics were brutally satirized by artists who sought to expose the idealism of this particular conjunction of theory and politics (illus. 7, 8).

THE HABITS OF SPECTATORSHIP

What happens when a work of art makes extraordinary demands on the spectator? This is precisely the question posed by the Australian artist Ian Burn (1939–1993) in a curated project of the early 1990s, *Looking at Seeing and Reading*. The exhibition asks us to reconsider the act of spectatorship

HOVELS AND PALACES: 2

Dave Rushton and Paul Wood

I

1 The various disciplines which get taught in educational institutions and which are presented in terms of their own integral problems, methods, etc, reinforce capitalism. This is axiomatic, there can be no argument, just the injunction 'go and look'. Art and its connected 'practices' is one of these and the same applies; bullshitting trivia about 'beauty', 'timelessness' and 'pleasure' notwithstanding. Furthermore, in some cases 'reinforces' can be substituted by 'serves'. This much is so, and there's an end on't.

2 Recently manifested para-practices, such as appear in these pages under rubrics like Art – Photography, Art – Video, Avant-garde Film, Art – Performance are, face-values and much expenditure of jargonised special pleading to the contrary, in exactly the same position.

3 The reification of media-practices as practices ipso facto, or as sufficiently end-like in themselves to support social transformation epiphenomenally, is mistaken insofar as it relies on precisely the history of the activities of a thoroughly bourgeois social section which it ostensibly wishes to negate.

4 Liberal boom-induced social consciences are not trustworthy in terms of the historical class struggle, and moreover are not to be mistaken for class consciousness. It might be argued that left-liberal practices have emerged with crisis, not boom. On the contrary their preconditions were formed at the end of an era of expansion. Crisis provides the 'subject-matter' in terms of which these preconditions are realised. It is the boom-crisis conjunction which has provided the conditions for a criticism of orthodoxy and its sub-structures. This is the same for all of us. What differentiate a putatively socialist from a left-liberal position are the ends developed from considering this determination. The socialist practice works to develop a trans-specialist class consciousness, aware of the sectional nature of its own history, and it attempts to construct a practice whose identity is sought not in terms of the merely sectional history, but whose links are with the historical tendency of the class-against-capital: to resolve class contradictions into the class-for-itself. This is set against the left-liberal interest in a utilisation *of* the historical contingent features of that sectional history, induced (although it is unaware of this) by the condition of capital as a whole, in order essentially to preserve culture *in* capital.

5 In such contexts the repugnant but entirely predictable para-media reification of Social Purpose can only be looked on as actively negative against the possibility of reflexive critical practice. Social Purpose as a style?? All that is demonstrated is the desire for, and assumption of, the continuing (?) viability of the notion of a practice sufficiently (and mistakenly) pure as to enter into alliances, *ie* mistaking constitutional forms for contingent adjuncts. The fact that this is the expected reading to be derived from modernist history absolves nothing in the face of the erstwhile complicity of such organs and authors in the adumbration of that history.

6 Remonstrations about a 'feeble grasp' of implications are hardly adequate. In the context as just spelled out the left-liberal rush to proselytise can't be sustained as an ironic pinch on the corporate arse. Notwithstanding all the gauchiste semiological fervour, making points about class by scabbing off media presentations of class-stereotypes reads as a straightforward continuation of the thrust of previous policy: to ensure the modernist succession.

7 The sanguine spectacle of one media-practice choreographing social commentary out of Rimbaud and semiological niceties is offensively deployed as camouflage for the political thrust when put in the circumstance of confrontation (billboards, hoardings). The theorification of the relations of class confrontation provides the step-down into orthodox art practice at the merest hint of class penetration.

8 Whether the authors, promoters and culture-crats involved are aware of such a contradiction between the appearance and the reality of their practice is another matter. Clearly, the categories in which Social Purpose is understood are offensive to anyone really dealing with that range of implications for practice — practice which, moreover, has been inherited in a state that militates strongly against prospective success in such an enterprise. To underline the point: the world view which lies behind 'Art & Social Purpose' (etc) is *the same one* that brought about in the first place the execrable state of practice in which 'social purpose' was susceptible to excision.

9 The founding principle of *Studio*, as well as of similarly motivated general publications, is the defensibility of a notion of 'modern art'. The only thing that seems to be up for debate is 'modern'. What is demonstrated is merely the false consciousness of a collectivity of collectivity-denying aspirants whose Purpose (*sic*) is located and defined essentially in terms of social graduation.

10 'Art & Social Purpose', rather than transparently addressing itself to a problem after the manner of a philosophical problem, is making a mess of a problem which has a history: the relation of sectional interest to sectional interest located in the network of a social structure of a developing and specific kind. This cannot be entertained in ignorance of the problems as sectional, firstly, and sectional rooted in class, secondly.

II

1 A defensible practice is firstly an organised practice; it will not be composed of the litter of earnest young conceptual artists with half a conscience and half an eye for opportunity.

2 The artist as petit bourgeois social sectionalist: forget about an artist class. Look at the artists' economic base in the schools and in the galleries and question why Social Purpose neatly draws a boundary round the places of work and leaves them treacherously hollow.

3 Look at the way in which a crisis of national capital was invoked as a quasi-rationalisation for an examination of Italian Art and taken no further (*Studio*, Jan/Feb '76): neither into an examination of private patronage in that context nor an examination of state patronage in this one (silly buggers at the Arts Council) — but used as an excuse for celebration-by-default. Much the same can be said for the failure to entertain scepticism in the face of the obvious collaboration involved in entering industrial corporations, in a context supposedly devoted to Social Purpose (APG, *Studio*, March/April '76). If cross-criticism from article to article is effectively debarred by the editorial policy (or lack of it), how can it be expected to be engendered in the audience? The reading which is indicated is more significant by virtue of what is left out than what is included; but that which *is* included is determined by its omissions . . . so where does that leave the possibilities of learning? The only thing you can learn from this is how to be as big an arsehole as the limp-wristed, 'some-of-my-best-friends-are-proletarians' fops who conjure such treatments.

4 The obvious stumbling-block for the organisation of a student collectivity is the persistence of the conception that the interests, problems and so forth of that body lie in a different social section (*ie* teachers, artists, etc), with respect to which they conceive themselves as unproblematically transitional. Not until interests are conceived as integrally sectional – conceived as emerging out of interest-conflict with those other sections – is there a possibility of a transformational process.

5 It's comparatively easy to retain a sense of a transformed 'teaching'. But art is a notion so thoroughly capitalistic in its day-to-day practice that the expression 'socialist art' is self-contradictory. Whereas with practices that can sustain a notion of subject-matter and a consideration of ends 'transformation into' at least follows as a possibility, with art per se ('High Art') it's a case of 'transformation out of' . . . but we don't have to go about constructing bulldozers-for-lemmings.

6 Another tack. Organising for the production of local magazines in art schools is not a misplaced re-emergent yearning for consumables. They are a platform for the articulation of local and sectional issues which are the (at present mystified) foundations of media-practices. The trivialities and superficialities of practices constructed around the dictates of an international or essentially metropolitan style cease to be the horizon-to-horizon possibilities for filling out time. With organised production centred on the characteristic institutional infrastructure encountered by a more or less ephemeral section, student action in those stages can be substantial and non-trivial. Development is no longer mystical individual proprietorship but a function of changes in sectional commitments of which one is conscious. Sectional consciousness is not to be mistaken for class consciousness. But the question *is* one of organisation towards such sectional consciousness as a viable basis for transformation, such as is not offered by an individualist (and therefore implicitly not sectionally conscious) perception of working. Local magazines can facilitate jointly discursive purchase on jointly – since institutionally – determining problems. Such magazines shouldn't be seen as a style – 'Art & Magazines' – but as avenues for the questioning and sorting out of the axioms of that kind of (prevalently sponsored) conjunction. These conjunctions are not dialectical but a subordination of media in/under/to the ends of 'art'. As for Art & Social Purpose . . . the same. That's just a mistake; but these are commonplace enough.

7 Look at the scope of the injunctions (*cf Studio*, March/April, p. 154): 'Investigate semiology', 'investigate political economy', etc; then look at some other ways of putting ethereal coaches before phantom horses. There can't *be* much examination or such forms of art practice wouldn't be surviving. The hovel of Social Purpose is still the gatehouse to the palace of Art.

8 Which is the social section which constitutes the reference class for considerations of Social Purpose? *Studio*'s assumption is one of an undifferentiated receptivity. On the contrary, a necessary prerequisite is the location of diverging sectional interests. But then a Black Hole to be borne in mind is the vested interest of *Studio* in apparently remaining without sectional interests. What is the social purpose of *Studio International*?

9 Social purpose is co-emergent with an articulation of section and locale. The international art magazine, by virtue of its structural generality, deflects and distorts the foundation of that which it ostensibly promotes. How efficacious can the work be said to be in terms of the blunt directives advocated for it, when around all you see is stepping-down at intimations of conflict? (See Part I).

10 Students should start to examine the working relationships of these new theorists-as-artists who cry social practice from the roof-tops. The students can sort out how the 'practice' advanced emerges in the 'artists' working context. Under the bravado and veneer of the recent contributions to *Studio International* the economic routines of those participants remain hidden.

11 Back to the axiom of the defensibility of modern art. You can't start to articulate its indefensibility from within its postulates – *eg* of individualism. Organised collectivity around a point of production which addresses the common problems of being in a particular history, and faced by the specific contradictions generated by that history and its collision-points with other histories: only this offers points of access. But just as a listing of problems remains trapped by bases which escape review, so does organisation qua organisation: there's nothing to be salvaged from(*eg*) APG. Organisation is necessary insofar as it mediates the resolution of substantive problems which are extant in the class society. Reformist organisations also exist. They are part of the problematic for the putatively socialist organisation. Its work resolves itself as the dialectic between its organisation of (access to) problems and the (reflexive) problem of organisation.

III

1 We seem to be faced by a simple framework. On the one hand there is available a more or less refined notion of objective problems. That in fact has been hinted at by people like Burgin. The reason for the inadequacy of that is a neglect of the essentially determining factor — namely that the approach to handling the problems has to be mediated organisationally within each section. The normative audience of *Studio International* is composed of several economically conflicting social sections, and a blanket appeal in terms of purposiveness avoids the fundamental economic issues on which the appeal rests for coherence.

2 The artist's courtship of the working class can only delay and confuse the furtherance of the working-class movement. Artists are at best condemned to sectional problems directly. From the base of an organised sectional consciousness artists can demystify the determining structure of the section they occupy, the ambivalence of teaching as a 'support' to art, and perhaps deconstruct the pseudo-interest of students who are presently affirmed in their ignorance of the mediations of the economic sphere through the cultural.

3 For their part, students can cease the fetishised consumership of de-historicised, de-contextualised norms, and organise collectivities of production around the focus of (*eg*) local magazines, conceived as integral to the resolution of the concrete tasks which face them in the practice of emerging from the debris of hopeless and trivial wanderings which are all that attend disreputable perpetuation of the disorganised and angst-ridden section they have inherited.

134 135

by presenting an array of word and image works foregrounding the relationship between visual art and language. Some works, like Jasper Johns's *Target* (1970), employ language to label image. In others, language frames the work, guiding the interpretation of an otherwise puzzling visual experience (illus. 9). Inscribed language may be absent altogether, encouraging one to think about the spectatorial act as a kind of framing in its own right, analogous to the way a camera viewfinder picks out an image, or a caption labels a picture. In visual art, then, language polices as much as completes. For Burn, language in art is construed more radically: word and image or text and object are important mainly as mediators of perception, which 'in its *critical* capacity realises the visual density of art-making'.[1]

Burn's understanding of the relation between word and image in visual art was shaped by his participation in the discourse on art and language that took place within the early analytic tradition of Conceptual art. At the same time, it is clear that Burn – returning to this theme nearly three decades later – wished to propose that *something other* could be made of the lessons learned from the intensely self-reflexive art of the mid- to late 1960s. During the late 1980s, Burn's own artwork took as its subject a constellation of politically charged issues, from the status of the amateur to the problematic representation of the Australian

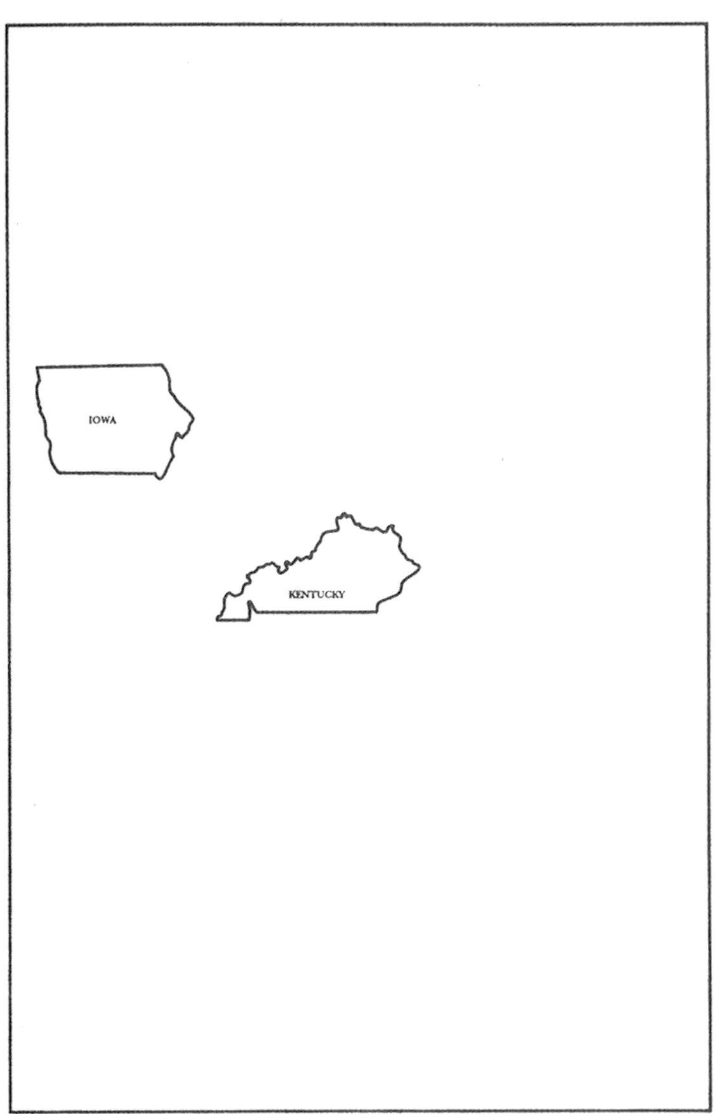

9 Art & Language, *Map to not indicate: Canada, James Bay … Straits of Florida*, 1967, letterpress print.

outback. The complex material configuration of this body of work of the late 1980s to the time of his death in 1993 juxtaposed word and image in an effort to ensnare the spectator and frustrate her direct perceptual encounter with the image (illus. 10, 11). Burn had no doubt that the act of *consuming* a landscape as an aesthetic object was inextricably linked to other constructs, such as theories of land ownership and nationalism. Thus it was important to draw attention to these salient connections by interrupting through the intercession of text the pleasure of looking. The text in Burn's work introduces an alien, antagonistic element to the encounter. It was Burn's intention that the experience of looking under such circumstances would inexorably cascade into self-reflection and doubt. The structure Burn designed forced the spectator to perceive the image of the landscape through a veil of text; it was impossible to *see* without *reading*. In this way, the work was transformed into a miniature theatre of vision that illustrated the conclusions of philosopher of science N. R. Hanson's important 1967 book on the theory-ladenness of observation languages, *Patterns of Discovery*. The strategy of forcing the spectator to simultaneously read and look had already been well established in Burn's practice during the mid-1960s.[2] What Burn was searching for through the *Value-Added Landscapes* of the early 1990s was the means to make a work of art that functioned as the nexus for a philosophical inquiry into the cultural practice of looking at pictures and the political discourse around conflicting concepts of land ownership as articulated by the Australian state and the Aboriginal peoples. For Burn, an artwork comprised of word and image was the most efficient means to bring into proximity these two vital conversations.

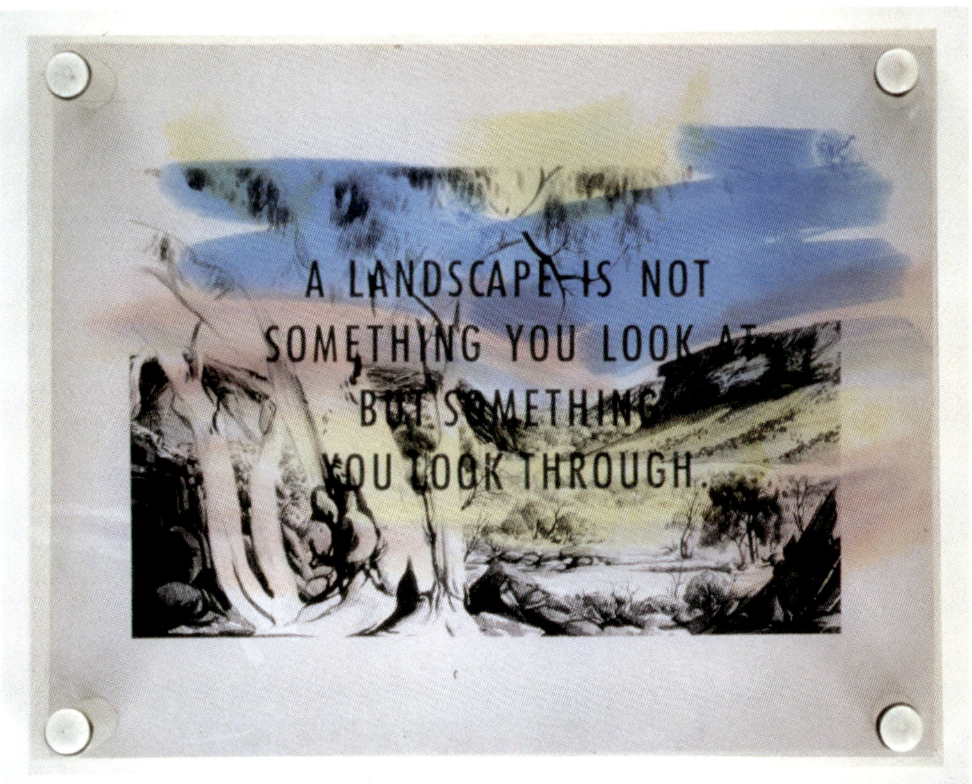

10 Ian Burn, *Homage to Albert (South through the Ranges, Heavitree Gap 1952)*, 1989, acrylic on canvas, serigraphy on acetate, plexiglas, metal fasteners, wood.

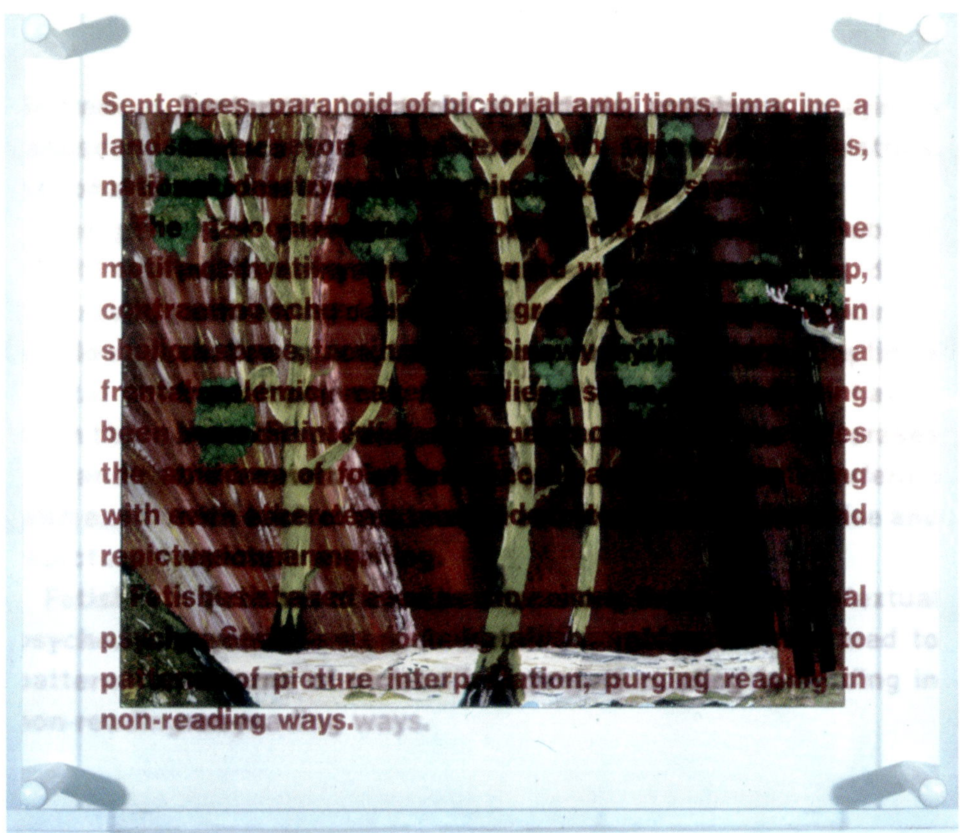

11 Ian Burn and unknown artist, *Value Added Landscape No. 4*, 1992, found canvas, serigraphy on acetate, plexiglas, metal fastners, wood.

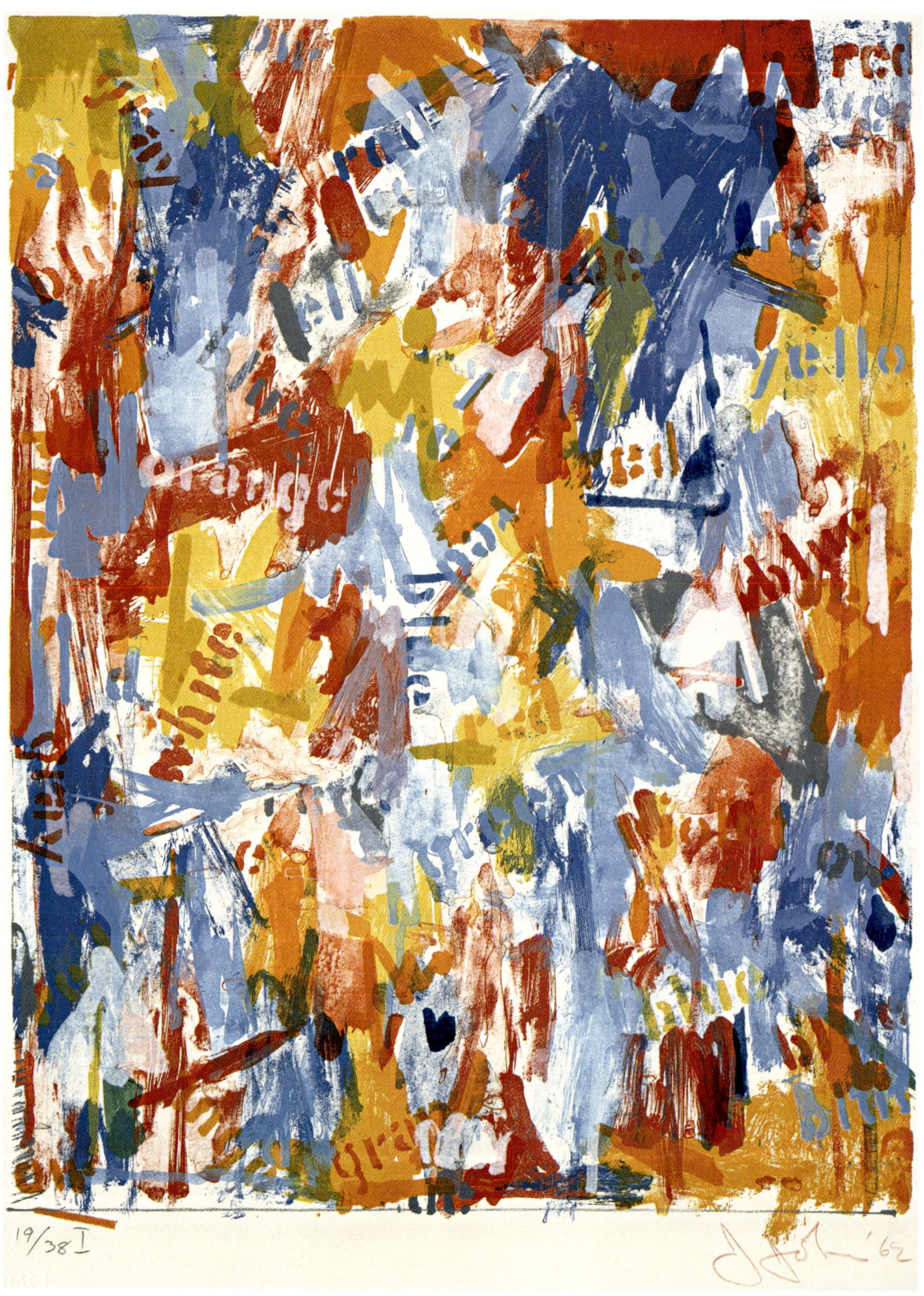

12 Jasper Johns, *False Start 1*, 1962, 11-colour lithograph on paper.

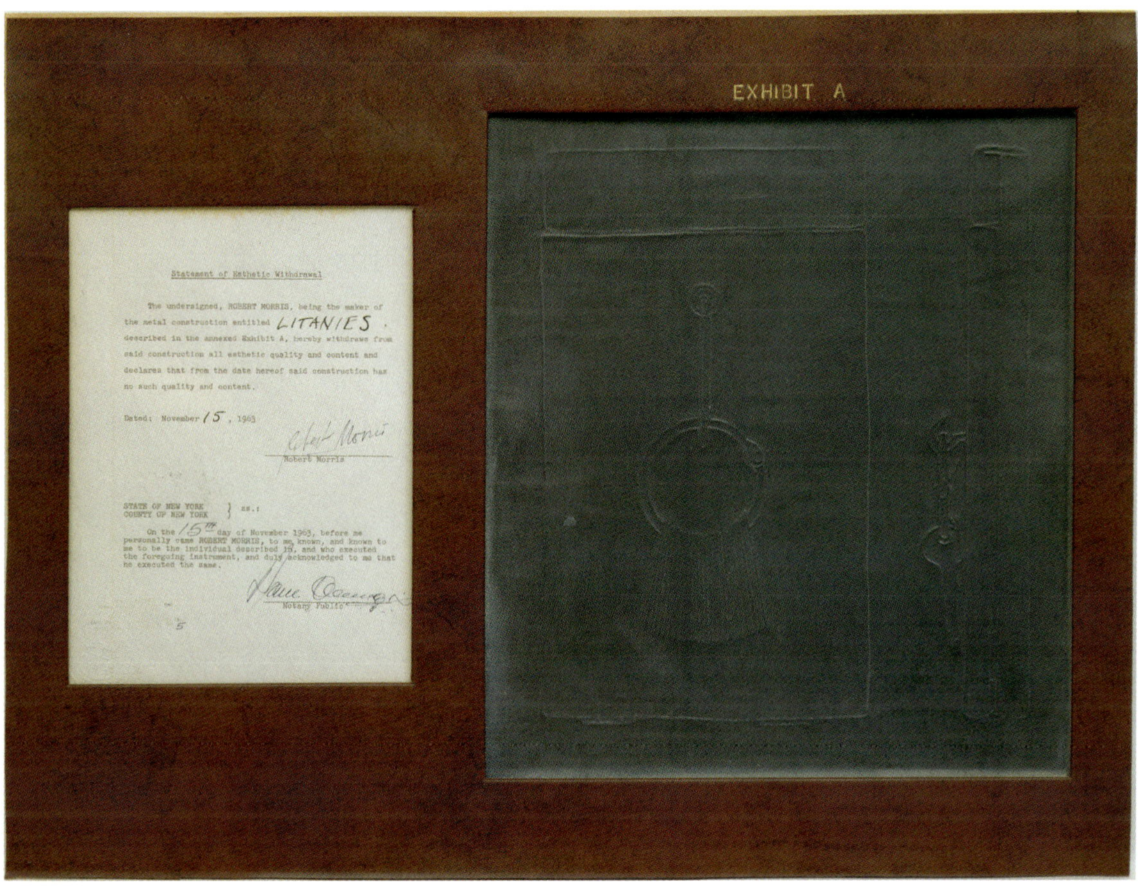

13 Robert Morris, *Document*, 1963, typed and notarized statement on paper and sheet of lead mounted in imitation leather mat.

THE ARTIST SPEAKS

It is possible to select a number of artistic practices of the late 1950s through the '60s that take as paradigmatic the rendering of vision as a self-conscious act. So many of the works of that period – for example, the paintings of Jasper Johns and early works by Robert Morris – press the spectator to consider the act of looking as an experience profoundly determined by language (illus. 12, 13). A degree of subtlety is required here to distinguish how artists themselves interpreted this shift in the culture of art. For many artists, works comprised of word and image address the fundamental conventions that surround the 'consumption' of visual art. In many of these works, the relation between word and image is found to be neither illustrative nor analogical. Rather, it is critical and negative insofar as the conjunction of word and image functions more as an occasion for re-education than as an opportunity for the enjoyment of sheer visual pleasure. Entire practices of art since 1945 have been based on the proposition that there is nothing about the encounter with visual art that may be considered to be *self-evident*; that is, no aspect of visual art remains opaque to language.

Described as a kind of research project for visual artists, word and image in art might be understood as a systematic exploration of the problematic nature of seeing.[3] But the history of word and image in visual art since 1945 is more than a chronicle of artists' engagement with the problem of reading or interpretation. While some art since the beginning of the post-war period points to the paradigmatic status of language in visual art and the need to take seriously the link between art and language, other less visible inquiries introduced into artistic practice the themes of gender, sexuality, race and class, and asserted a role in art for photography, the vernacular image, and other forms of mechanical reproduction. The interest by artists in word and image since 1945 cannot be adequately understood without reference to the mass media. It is within the particular articulation of word and image in advertising that a social power presumed to have escaped the grasp of art was to be recovered. Artists in Europe during the post-war period tended to approach this discovery with ambivalence; artists in the US were less sceptical of the conformist values and worldliness reflected in the growing consumer society. The story of word and image in art, then, is not necessarily a tale of the victory of iconoclasts over iconophiles, or vice versa.

The visual culture theorist W.J.T. Mitchell identifies the 'other' of the so-called linguistic turn as the *pictorial turn*. Mitchell defines this as a shift in orientation within the visual arts founded on 'the realization that *spectatorship* (the look, the gaze, the glance, the practices of observation, surveillance, and visual pleasure) may be as deep a problem as various forms of *reading* (decipherment, decoding, interpretation, etc.) and that visual experience or 'visual literacy' might not be fully explicable on the model of textuality.'[4] The postmedia tendencies of artistic practices of the mid-1980s – rather misleadingly dubbed 'Neo-Conceptual Art'– are instanced as marking the beginning of this shift. Within the early practices of artists such as Jenny Holzer (b. 1950) and Barbara Kruger (b. 1945), reading intervenes in the experience of engaging with visual art in a manner that recalls earlier strategies of Conceptual art (illus. 14, 15). But in these latter works one discerns an unmistakable desire to break free of earlier analytic constraints; to leave behind, as it were, what a younger generation of artists took to be Conceptual art's impossibly clotted, allegedly elitist philosophical agenda.

Holzer and Kruger are representative of a generation of artists who have rejected the idea that art might refuse to be a mode of public address. The point of artistic practice, in their view, is to centre *in a timely and efficient manner* on the

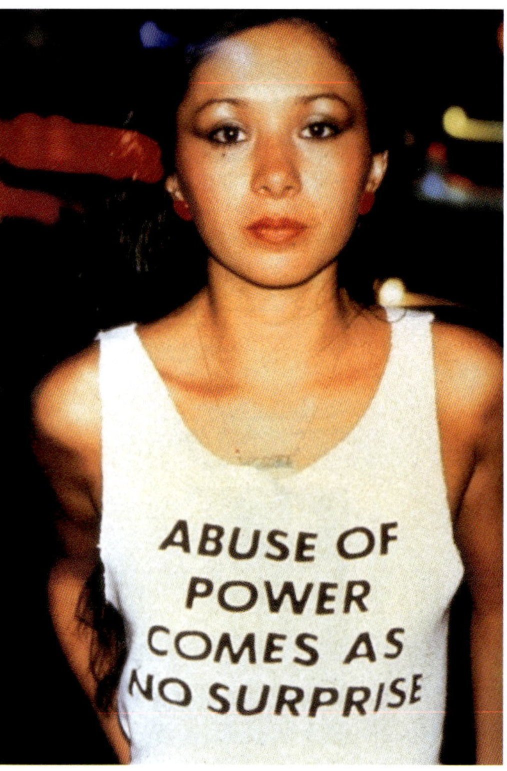

14 Jenny Holzer, from *Truisms*, 1983, Lady Pink.

development and projection of a public voice. Such art fashioned itself after aspects of the mass media, mimicking in appearance and public placement the assumed power and reach of advertising, television and popular magazines. And timeliness is no hyperbole here, as both Holzer and Kruger launched their careers mindful of the erosion of political liberalism in the United States – especially during the Reagan presidency (1980–88) – setting themselves in opposition to the resurgence of conservative values of representation as expressed through the work of Neo-Expressionist painters and sculptors. This was not a time for understatement or deference in the visual arts. What is fascinating is how Holzer and Kruger have transformed language into a spectacular material presence in its own right through an increasingly grandiose and congenial conversation with technology and architecture. By comparison, the earlier work of Holzer of the late 1970s and of Kruger of the early '80s seems more austere and politically pointed.

Alongside a handful of earlier Conceptual

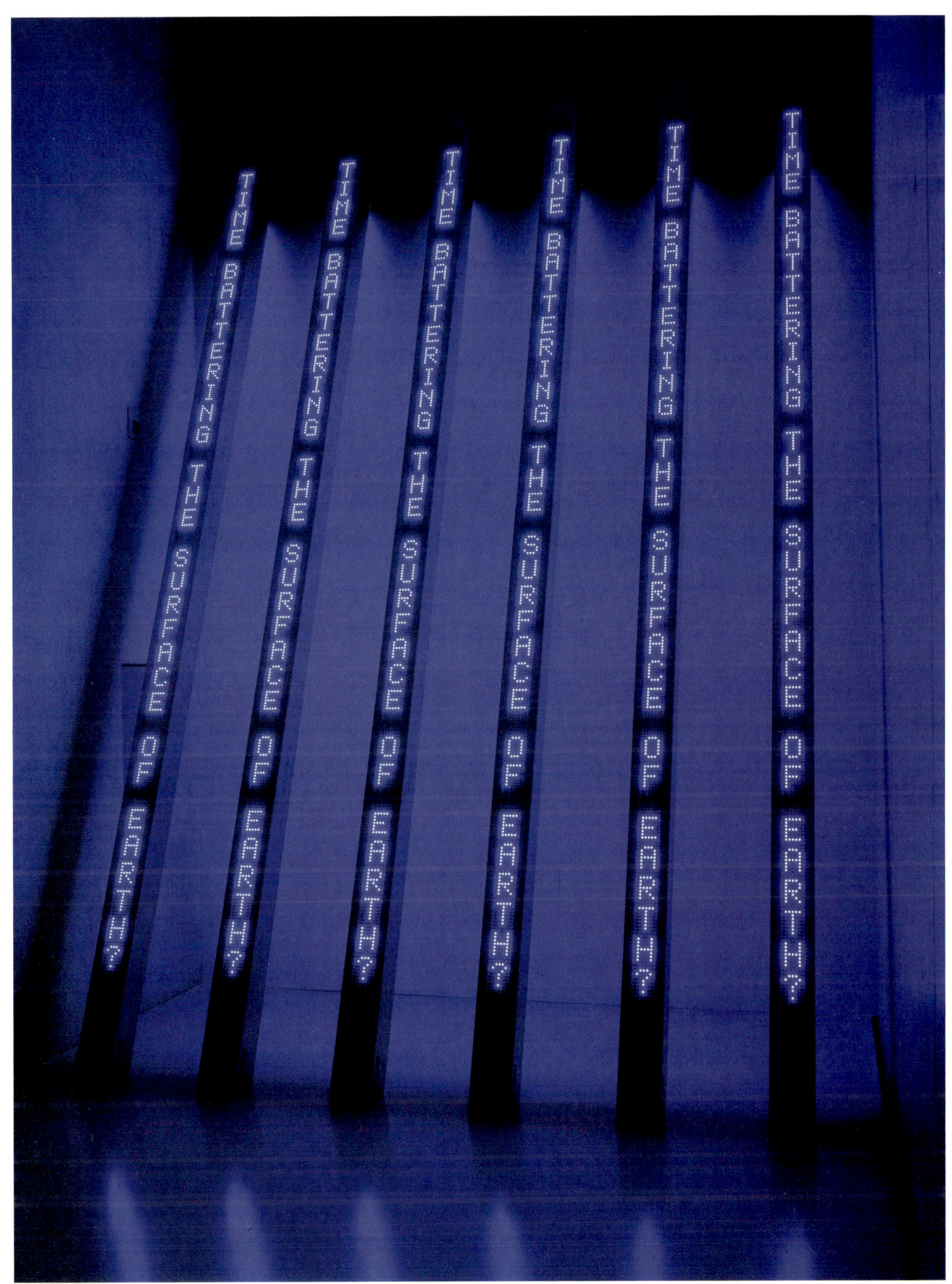

15 Jenny Holzer, *Blue Tilt*, 6 doubled-sided electronic LED signs with blue diodes.

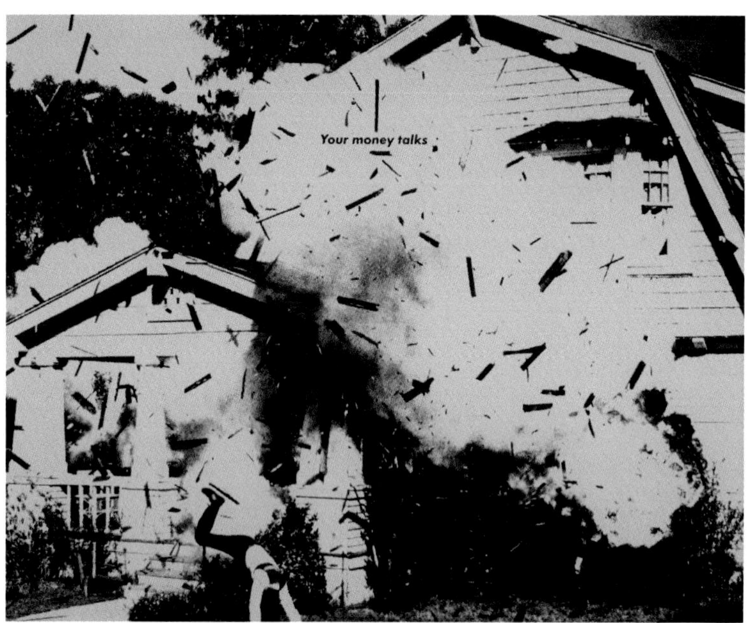

16 Barbara Kruger, *Untitled (Your money talks)*, 1984, photograph.

artists, Holzer was among the first to exploit the urban public space as the principal site of artistic practice. Holzer's *Truisms* (1977–present) and *Inflammatory Essays* (1978–9) existed outside the conventional gallery setting of art and remind us that works of art incorporating word and image need not be tied to the sumptuous *livre d'artiste* or the art gallery, or even the printed page of the relatively inexpensive and portable artists' book.

The implications for artists of this fact are manifold. It can no longer be taken for granted that the spectator will encounter such works in a state of attentive repose principally in the cloistered space of the library or gallery. For those artists emerging since the 1960s, dissemination of their work in any particular form, then, is no longer a given. Rather, the mode of distribution of art is one of several factors to be considered during the course of practice.

The contemporary artist is mindful of the context in which artworks compete for the beholder's attention. The image flux that fills our urban spaces is but one aspect of our overall exposure to urban visual culture. Beside public displays of image and text, from advertising to graffiti, one must surely take note of the more personal, though no less significant, exposure to image and text displayed on the LCD screens of laptops and smart phones. Scanning, rather than close reading, is the pre-eminent mode of consumption of word and image. Some contemporary art employing word and image seeks to exploit this ability of the urban dweller to selectively scan her environment while in motion and engaged in other activities.

But the act of scanning needs to be anchored to a more considered reception if the artist is to allude to more than the *flâneur*'s experience of the city and the world. To this end, the Chilean artist Alfredo Jaar has conjoined word and image to create a public work of art that introduces an entire unseen world to unsuspecting commuters. Works produced to mimic the form of advertising posters were installed by Jaar in 1986 in a New York subway station well known for its proximity to galleries of contemporary art (illus. 18). Displacing advertisements using public art immediately transformed the public's perception of the nature and role of the social space of the station platform. The dramatic amalgam of photographic images of Brazilian open-pit gold miners and textual quotations of the price of gold as traded in centres like London, Frankfurt and Zurich served to link the relative affluence of the New York commuter to an unseen reality of misery and exploitation half a world away. It is not likely that images or words alone could have forged this bond with such passion and immediacy.

Within the field of visual art, the conjunction of word and image clearly serves many agendas. In this essay, many of the examples will focus on the critical potential of word and image in art to mark a genuine break in flow of cultural values. Such work may even adopt the mantle of interventionist or radical political forms to establish its cultural space. Yet as one approaches contemporary practices, a nagging question remains: what is

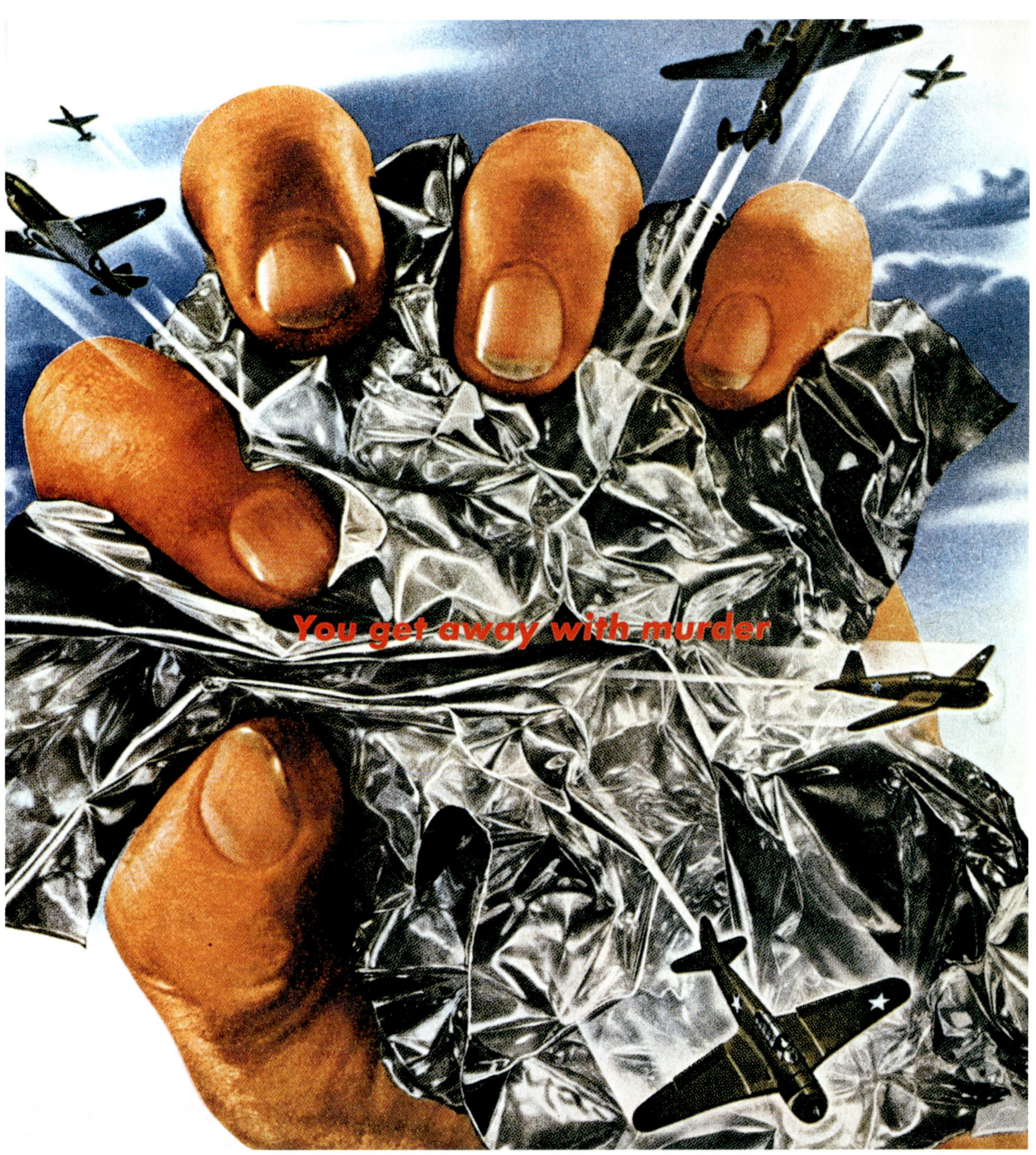

17 Barbara Kruger, *Untitled (You get away with murder)*, 1987, dye-coupler print with silkscreen lettering.

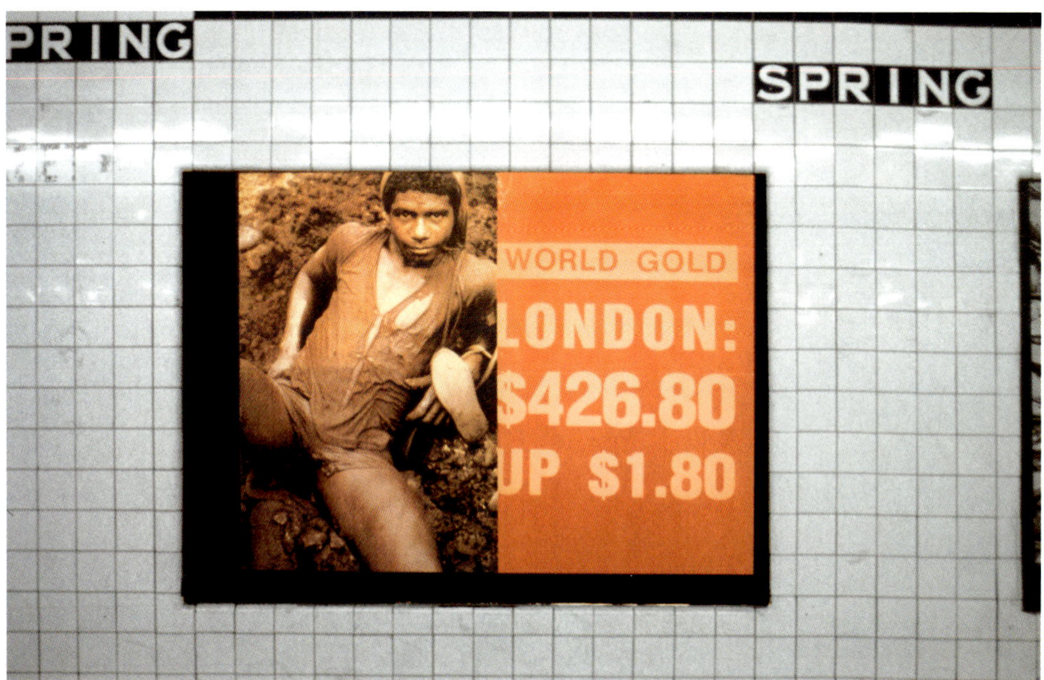

18 Alfredo Jaar, *Rushes*, 1986, oversized photographs installation.

to be gained through a self-conscious alignment of one's artistic practice to those of the historical avant-garde? Certainly, there continued to be a strong urge among artists to do so; this, despite the possibility that such overt identification with a historical past threatens to stifle imagination and risk transforming word and image art into a *generic* form (illus. 19).

From our vantage point at the beginning of the twenty-first century, it may appear as though most of the contemporary variations of word and image in art are redundant or late. Such historicism must be resisted; otherwise we risk becoming blind to the impact that, say, digital technologies have had on fostering in word and image art a new emphasis on narrative and performative function. The meaning of word and image in art today – even when it is static – bears witness to formal and technological innovations as well as various traditions of storytelling and narrative themes. Artists working since the new millennium have eagerly appropriated visual forms ordinarily encountered in the graphic design field (illus. 20). Such forms – which were developed for the effective visual display of information or the production of complex network diagrams and sociograms – are regularly plagiarized and customized by artists eager to map a corner of the rhizomatic world as conceptualized by futurologists and philosophers from Marshall McLuhan to Deleuze and Guattari. The introduction or suggestion of the temporal – literally through the use of animation and video, or implicitly through the cinematically driven graphic novel or the simple device of the timeline – has also refreshed the conjunction of word and image in art. The graphic novel is a particularly interesting development, as one strand of its prehistory in the context of artist-activism of the 1970s is beginning to be more fully appreciated (illus. 21). Contemporary versions of the graphic novel are routinely adapted as film; an acknowledgement of the form's intimate connection to the visual language of cinema. One may also begin with a stock of still images, sutured together using intervening text panels and a cinematic language of jump cuts, fades and flashbacks, to construct a silent video that balances the experience of reading and looking (illus. 22).

Postmodernism has given us the ironically

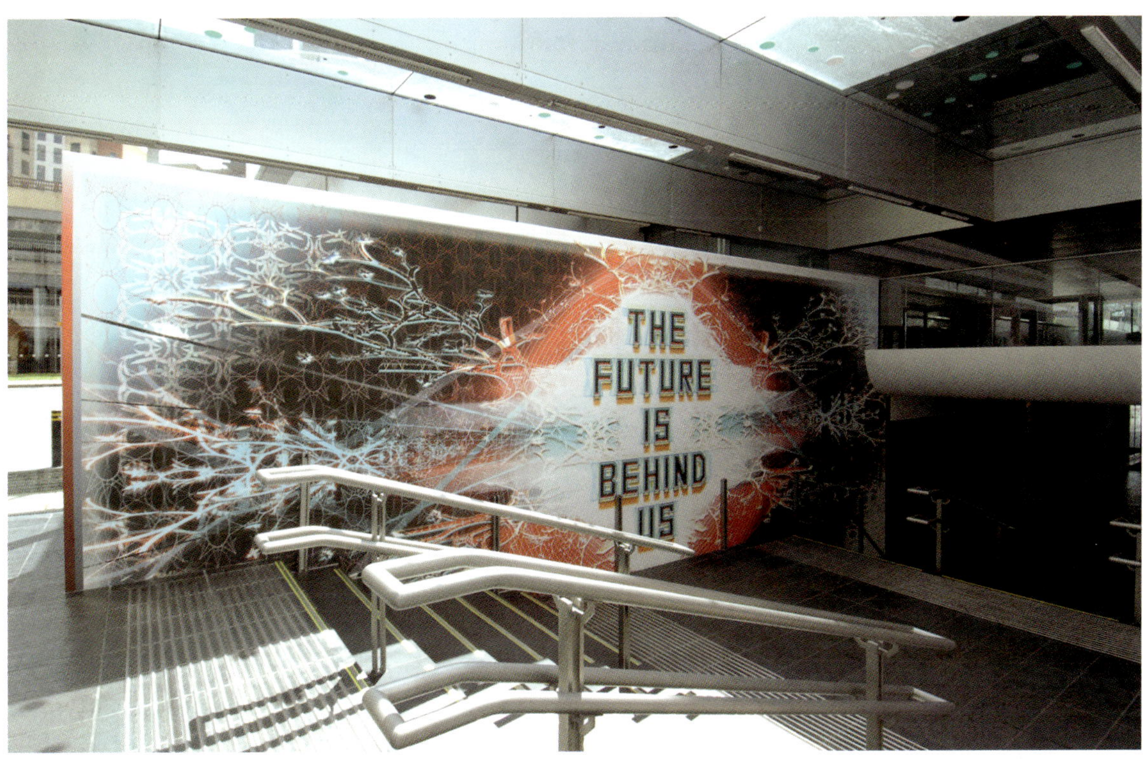

19 Mark Titchner, *The Future is Behind Us*, 2007, inkjet print.

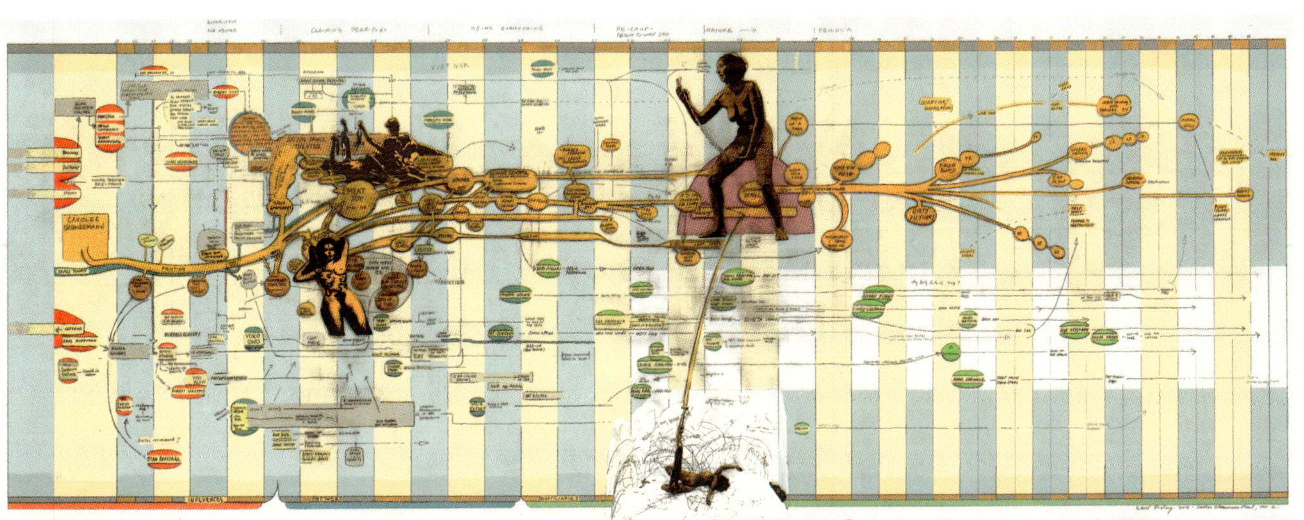

20 Ward Shelley, *Carolee Schneeman Chart, version 2*, 2005, oil and toner on mylar.

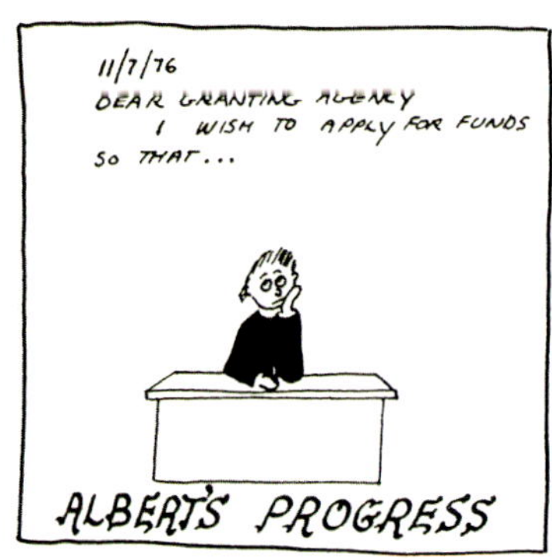

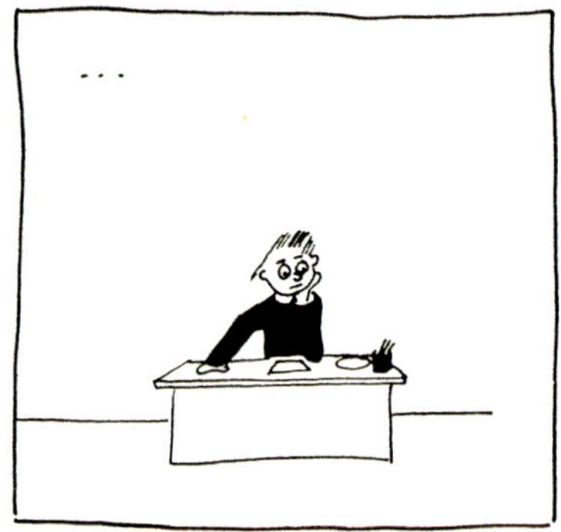

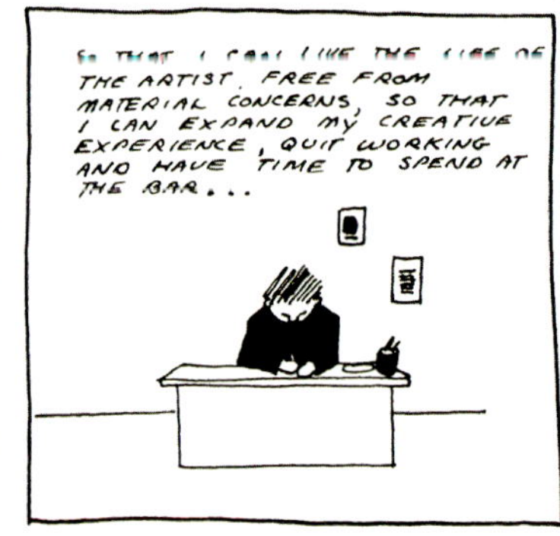

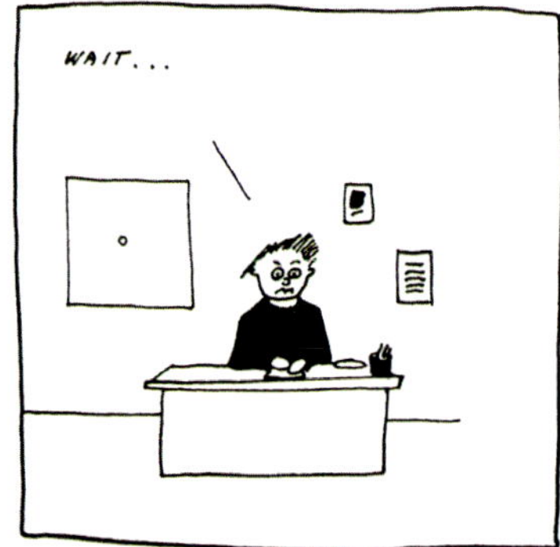

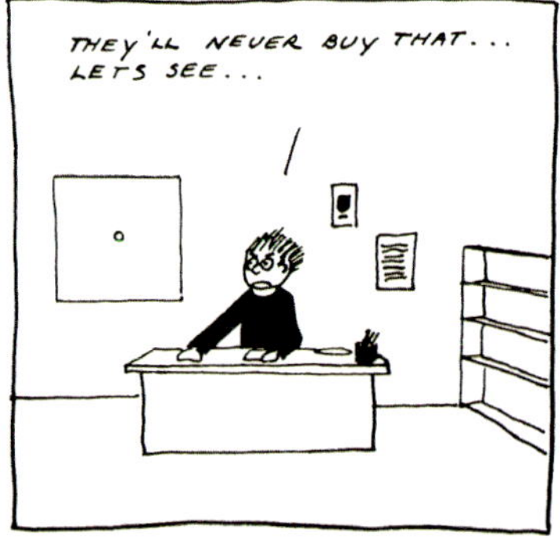

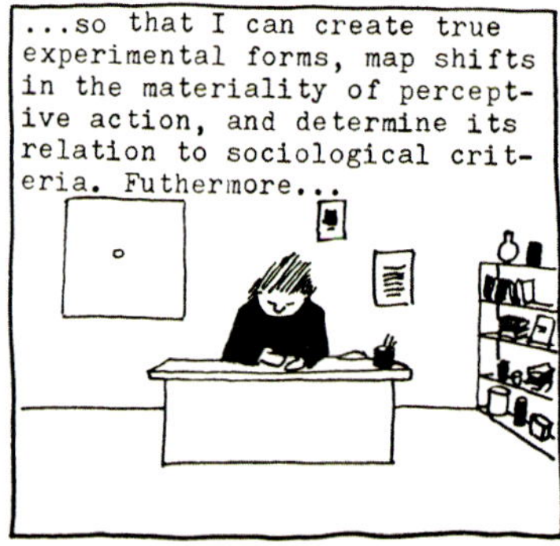

21 Carole Condé and Karl Beveridge, *Albert's Progress*, 1976, collage and ink on paper.

enduring notion of accelerated change, alongside a social demand for radical human adaptability. What the critic Robert Hughes colourfully described some time ago as the 'shock of the new' now seems a hopelessly quaint idea. The point is that the 'new' is no longer shocking; if it is, no one is so unsophisticated as to let on to that fact. The ideology of the 'new' new implies that culture does not grow in any organic sense; rather, the culture of the present seems to behave according to the well-rehearsed tropes of the rhizomatic, the network, the mob and the viral attack. In this cultural climate, the simple conjunction of word and image seems almost antique; an emblem of a bygone cultural era. Its quaintness bespeaks, perhaps, an attachment to sustained attentive seeing that engages our capacity to map disparate elements and discordant semantic fields onto each other – in other words, to continue to be able to puzzle with satisfaction and with no thought of art's utility the difference between a meaningless pattern and a meaningful detail.

'BUT TODAY, WE COLLECT ADS'[5]

During the early years of this century, an advertisement for the international banking giant HSBC appeared throughout the passageways connecting terminals at, among other international airports, London's sprawling Heathrow. The important point about this advertising campaign is that it was conceived as a global campaign; advertisements had been placed simultaneously in major airports around the world to be viewed by travellers in transit or en route to their departure terminal. Typically, one reads the advertisements while on the move. The elements of the advertisement are not grasped as individual static images as much as successive frames of what might be termed a rather short and minimal animation sequence. The advertisement succeeds because a constant mapping and remapping of word and image is actively required on the part of the viewer in order to 'see' and understand the advertisement's message.

The first version of this campaign was launched in 2002 under the slogan 'never underestimate the importance of local knowledge'. The advertisements illustrated cultural variations on a single theme, such as 'lucky numbers'. By 2004, the campaign was deploying two images and two captions in combination as a quadriptych. An image of an elderly Asian man, for instance, may be variously captioned 'wise' in one frame and 'old' in another. In between these two poles of meaning resides the opposing term subtending an opposing image; in this case, an elderly person clearly identifiable as Western. This game of 'positive'/'negative' connotation is used to systematically generate a host of captioned images. A close-up photograph of a medicinal capsule alternates with an equally saturated and seductive colour photograph of a vegetable. In the first pair of images, the pill is labelled 'poison' while the veg-

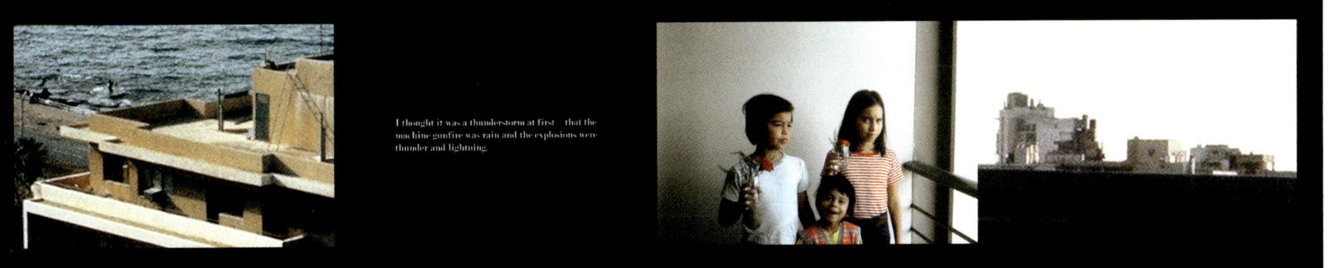

22 Madeline Djerejian, *The Last of Beirut*, 2006, stills from a single channel video.

etable is labelled 'medicine'. The second set of captioned images reverses the labelling. And so it goes, until one is left wondering if there is anything of substance left to Roland Barthes's classic and trenchant distinction of the image/text relationship as either 'anchor' or 'relay'. That is, does the caption explain the image in a relatively straightforward manner, or does the caption function dialogically, as a lever, hurtling the beholder's imagination into new realms of meanings?

Advertising is routinely criticized for its simple-minded flattening of experience; the hallmark of mass-marketing being the reductive, memorable formula. This, of course, is a generalization and hardly true of the most sophisticated advertising. At least since the 1960s, advertising has introduced campaigns in print and television that rely far more on semantic indeterminacy, double entendre and self-deprecation. In this context, the HSBC campaign exploits our ability to puzzle the relation between word and image, however crude the juxtaposition employed might be. In other words, advertising assumes a set of competences on the part of the target audience. Moreover, these are competences routinely thought to be appropriate principally to the appreciation of high art.

The repetitive placement of the campaign along the seemingly interminable transitways of London's Heathrow airport takes its toll on our nerves; this is saturation advertising at its most irritating. Throughout, HSBC is offered as a memorable brand, despite the fact that the corporation's logo is generally not centre stage. The disembodied image of 'local' culture delivered by this campaign is in fact a kind of generic culture that is intended to reconfigure a new, global subject.

'AN EXAMPLE OF WHAT CAN BE DONE WITH A STUB PEN'[6]

A recent version of the campaign presents a triptych of captioned images (illus. 25). In this case, a single image is subject to the semantic pull of three different captions; alternatively, three differing images may be identically captioned. The HSBC campaign employs a system of coding that bridges the separate worlds of mass media and art. As the dialogue between art and advertising has existed throughout the twentieth century, it is not surprising that the HSBC campaign would become a rich vein for parody; especially by groups of political activists intent on targeting global corporations and utilizing strategies that are part of the legacy of visual art of the 1950s and '60s. The Yes Men – a collective of political activists working in a way that may be described as an enlightened form of media hacking – recently published a facsimile edition of *The New York Times* (illus. 26). Dated 4 July 2009, the newspaper announces boldly on the front page: 'Iraq war over.' Not only are all the news stories and editorial opinion fabricated, all the advertisements are as well. And they are all designed impeccably, masquerading as the real column, the real news item, and the real advertisement. Turning to an inside page spread, one finds a parody of the latest HSBC advertising campaign; it is the same campaign that adorns the passageways of Heathrow or the streets of Manhattan, yet subject to the kind of culture jamming that pervades our urban environment and the Internet. In the version of the HSBC advertisement found in the facsimile newspaper, President-elect Barack Obama's image is reproduced in triplicate and subtended with a variety of captions designed to put his administration on notice (illus. 25). The Yes Men

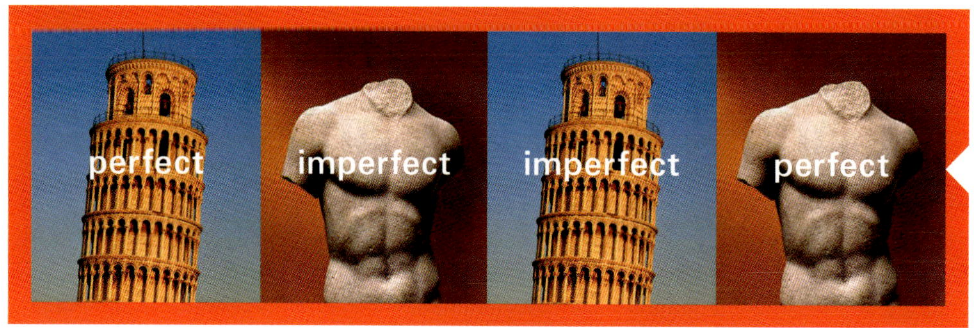

23 HSBC advertisement, *c.* 2004.

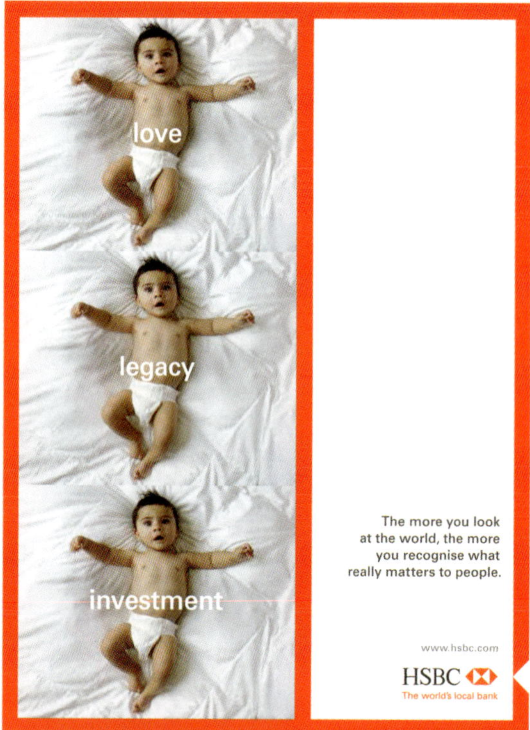

24 HSBC advertisement, *c.* 2008.

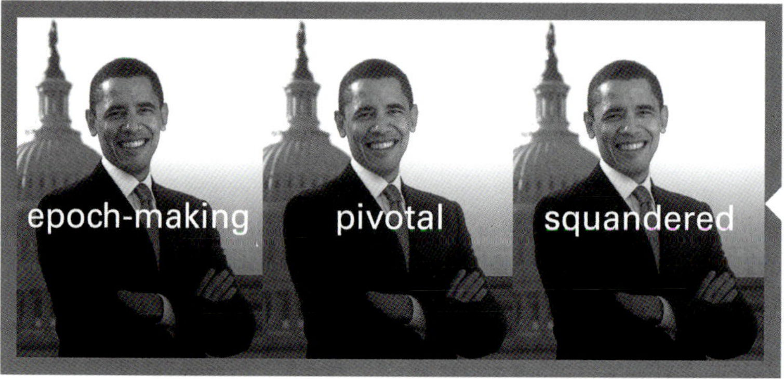

25 The Yes Men, *The New York Times, 4 July 2009*, 2008, detail of parodied HSBC advertisement.

"All the News We Hope to Print"

The New York Times

Special Edition
Today, clouds part, more sunshine, recent gloom passes. **Tonight,** strong leftward winds. **Tomorrow,** a new day. Weather map throughout.

VOL. CLVIV . . No. 54,631 | NEW YORK, SATURDAY, JULY 4, 2009 | FREE

IRAQ WAR ENDS

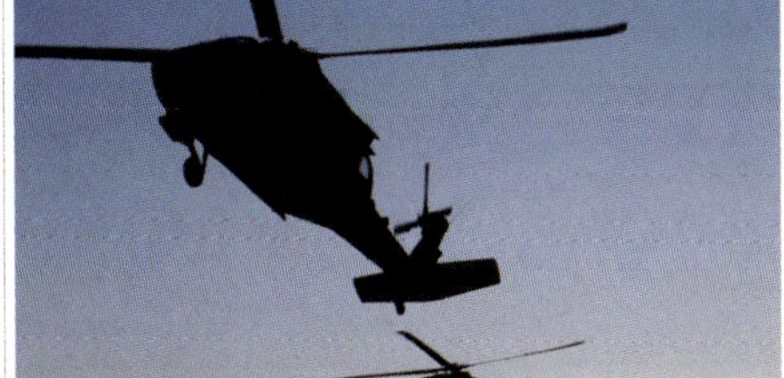

COURTESY ARMY.MIL

U.S. Army helicopters begin moving troops and equipment from Saddam Hussein's former Baghdad palace.

Nation Sets Its Sights on Building Sane Economy

True Cost Tax, Salary Caps, Trust-Busting Top List

By T. VEBLEN

The President has called for swift passage of the Safeguards for a New Economy (S.A.N.E.) bill. The omnibus economic package includes a federal maximum wage, mandatory "True Cost Accounting," a phased withdrawal from complex financial instruments, and other measures intended to improve life for ordinary Americans. (See highlights box on Page A10.) He also repeated earlier calls for passage of the "Ban on Lobbying" bill currently making its way through Congress.

Treasury Secretary Paul Krugman stressed the importance of the bill. "Markets make great servants, terrible leaders, and absurd religions," said Krugman, quoting Paul Hawken, an advocate of corporate responsibility and author of "Blessed Unrest, How the Largest Movement in the World Came into Being and Why No One Saw It Coming."

"At this point, the market is our leader and our religion. No wonder the median standard of living has been declining so much for so long."

Krugman said that the new Treasury bill seeks to ensure the prosperity of all citizens, rather than simply supporting large corporations and the wealthy. "The market is supposed to serve us. Unfortunately, we have ended up serving the market. That's very bad."

Much as Roosevelt, after the Great Depression, put the brakes on C.E.O. wages and irresponsible banking practices, administration officials claim that today we need to rein in the industry that has caused such chaos and misery.

"The building blocks of post-World War II American middle-class prosperity have all been swept away," said House Speaker Nancy Pelosi, who initially op-

Continued on Page A10

Troops to Return Immediately

By JUDE SHINBIN

WASHINGTON — Operation Iraqi Freedom and Operation Enduring Freedom were brought to an unceremonious close today with a quiet announcement by the Department of Defense that troops would be home within weeks.

"This is the best face we can put on the most unfortunate adventure in modern American history," Defense spokesman Kevin Sites said at a special joint session of Congress. "Today, we can finally enjoy peace — not the peace of the brave, perhaps, but at least peace."

As U.S. and coalition troops withdraw from Iraq and Afghanistan, the United Nations will move in to perform peacekeeping duties and aid in rebuilding. The U.N. will be responsible for keeping the two countries stable; coordinating the rebuilding of hospitals, schools, highways, and other infrastructure; and overseeing upcoming elections.

The Department of the Treasury confirmed that all U.N. dues owed by the U.S. were paid as of this morning, and that moneys previously earmarked for the war would be sent directly to the U.N.'s Iraq Oversight Body.

The president noted that the Iraq War had resulted in the burning of many bridges. "Yet our history with our allies runs deep," he said, "and we all know that friends forgive friends for anything. Or nearly." A spokesperson for the French Ministry of Defense confirmed that France would assist the U.S. withdrawal. "The U.S. helped the Soviet Union defeat Hitler. We do recognize that."

In conflict zones worldwide, leaders and rebels pledged peace. (See "In Conflict Zones Worldwide, Peace Moves," on Page A4.)

On Wall Street, reactions were mixed, with the Dow Jones Industrial Average up 84 points, to close at 4,212. While KBR stock was quickly downgraded to a "junk" rating of BBB-, defense contractors such as Lockheed Martin and Northrop Grummon started up.

Continued on Page A5

Maximum Wage Law Succeeds

Salary Caps Will Help Stabilize Economy

By J.K. MALONE

WASHINGTON — After long and often bitter debate, Congress has passed legislation, fiercely fought for by labor and progressive groups, that will limit top salaries to fifteen times the minimum wage. Tying the bill to a plan of overall reform of the U.S. economy, the bill echoes a similar effort enacted by President Franklin Roosevelt in 1942, which was followed by the longest period of growth for the middle class in U.S. history.

"When C.E.O. salaries remain stable thanks to high taxation of high salaries, there's little incentive to take big risks with shareholders' money, and the economy remains in a steady growth mode," said Senator Barney Frank, one of the bill's co-sponsors. "But when C.E.O. salaries can fly through the roof, there's a very strong incentive for C.E.O.s

Continued on Page A10

TREASURY ANNOUNCES "TRUE COST" TAX PLAN

By MARCUS S. DRIGGS

The long-awaited "True Cost" plan, which requires product prices to reflect their cost to society, has been signed into law.

Beginning next month, throwaway items like plastic water bottles and other items which are wasteful or damaging to the environment will be heavily taxed, as in many developed countries. Steep taxes will also apply to large cars and gasoline.

The new plan calls for a 200 percent tax on gasoline, comparable to the one long in effect in most European countries. Companies and consumers are already switching in droves from inefficient gas vehicles to new electric cars. "We suddenly have a waiting list 200 names long for the EV1," said Jake Cluber, the owner of Cluber Chevrolet in

Continued on Page A10

Recruiters Train for New Life
As a ban is imposed on recruiting minors, ex-recruiters nationwide look for new work. The Times follows one on his job-hunt odyssey through Manhattan and surrounding areas.
BY BARRY GLOAD, PAGE A12

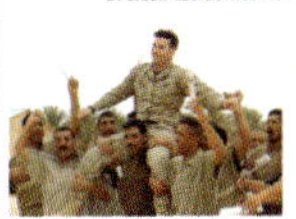

Last to Die
Two proportional monuments — one to the Iraqi dead, 300 feet high, and one to the American dead, 15 feet high — are unveiled in Baghdad, and a five-year-old boy whose lifespan coincided with that of the Iraq War is remembered.
BY J. FINISTERRA, PAGE A5

USA Patriot Act Repealed
Eight years later, a shamefaced Congress quietly repeals the much-maligned USA Patriot Act, unanimously… or almost.
BY SYBIL LUDINGTON, PAGE A8

Evangelicals Open Homes to Refugees
Up to a million Iraqi exiles — nearly half of the total — will find sanctuary in Christian homes across the U.S., vows the National Association of Evangelicals. Other denominations are expected to follow.
BY W. WILBERFORCE, PAGE A7

Public Relations Industry Starts to Shut Down
The public relations industry has been criticized for misleading the American people, corrupting politicians, and even helping to start wars. Now, it's beginning the process of shutting down for good.
BY LOUIS BECK, PAGE A10

Ex-Secretary Apologizes for W.M.D. Scare

300,000 Troops Never Faced Risk of Instant Obliteration

By FRANK LARIMORE

Ex-Secretary of State Condoleeza Rice reassured soldiers that the Bush Administration had known well before the invasion that Saddam Hussein lacked weapons of mass destruction.

"Now that all of you brave servicemen and women are returning, it's important to us to reassure you, and the American people, that we were certain Hussein had no W.M.D.s and that he would never launch a first strike against the U.S.," Ms. Rice told a group of wounded soldiers at a Veterans' Administration hospital yesterday.

"I want you to know that if we had had the slightest suspicion that Saddam could use W.M.D.s against you, we never would have sent hundreds of thousands of you to be sitting ducks on the Iraqi border for several months."

Mr. Rice was referring to the fact that by August 2002, eight months before the ground invasion, the US had over 100,000 troops stationed in countries throughout the Gulf, a number that grew to over 300,000 shortly before the 2003 attack on Baghdad. Most of these were within range of the Scud missiles used by Mr. Hussein in the 1991 Gulf War, that could easily have been fitted with chemical or biological weapons if they had existed.

Rice noted that in the 1991 Gulf War, Hussein had used missiles to launch attacks on Israel, which made him popular with Arab citizens throughout the Middle East.

"Do you really think we would have given Saddam a major public relations coup by allowing him to annihilate tens of thousands of you right there on holy territory?" asked Ms. Rice.

Former Secretary of State Henry A. Kissinger responded to Ms. Rice's revelation without surprise. "Of course this was the case. When Israel believed Iraq had nuclear weapons in 1981, they didn't attack on the ground — they bombed from the air. That's a preemptive attack. If you believe deterrence will not prevent an attack and that your enemy has W.M.D.s, then the last thing you do is station your troops right next door."

ABC's George Stephanopoulos

Continued on Page A5

Nationalized Oil To Fund Climate Change Efforts

By MARION K. HUBBERT

Congress has voted to place ExxonMobil, ChevronTexaco, and other major oil companies under public stewardship, with the bulk of the companies' profits put in a public trust administered by the United Nations, and used for alternative energy research and development in order to solve the global climate crisis.

While unusual, this is not the first time the government has chosen to take control of large corporations. From 1942 to 1944, U.S. car factories were retooled in order to produce tanks for the war effort. And Fannie Mae and Freddie Mac were both created as "government sponsored enterprises" with a significant amount of government oversight.

"We can do what needs to be done," said Senator Charles Schumer, Democrat of New York. "Our planet's survival is at stake. Plus, public pressure hasn't given us much of a choice."

Not everyone felt the move was a good idea. "The climate crisis may or may not be real," declared Senator Kay Bailey Hutchison, Republican of Texas. "I'm an agnostic and I'm staying that way. But sea

Continued on Page A5

Popular Pressure Ushers Recent Progressive Tilt

Study Cites Movements for Massive Shift in DC

By SAMUEL FIELDEN

The spate of reform initiatives undertaken by the Administration and both houses of Congress can be attributed directly to grassroots advocacy, according to a comprehensive study due out this month.

"In education and health care, most notably, but also in housing, banking, and the environment, we have documented unprecedented responsiveness on the part of political leaders," said Dr. Joyce Wellmon, director of the Plains Institute for Policy Analysis, a New York-based think tank. "Our data show a direct correlation between the level of activity of particular coalitions, on the one hand, and specific legislative action, on the other. It's popular pressure that is responsible for the swiftness and scope of legislation emerging from the White House and Congress."

The institute's report shows a three-fold increase in the incidence of letters, phone calls, faxes, and email received by congressional offices, 88 percent of which were from people who identified themselves as new members of particular activist organizations.

See nytimes-se.com for more

The report includes extensive interviews with House and Senate staff, who speak of "unimaginable change," a "dramatic policy shift," and "a new era of accountability" since the elections.

"Not since the Great Depression has the interaction between popular movements and public leaders been so robust," said Jorge Lazaro, head of the U.S. Government Accountability Office. Lazaro cited, in particular, the Wagner Act, also known as the National Labor Relations Act of 1935, which recognized the right of workers to organize and bargain collectively with their employers.

"Roosevelt showed no interest in the Wagner Act until it became clear the unions were going to force it through regardless," Mr. Lazaro noted. "At that point he jumped on it and helped push it into law."

Mr. Lazaro also pointed to the Depression-era organizing of the Farmers' Holiday Association, when farmers refused to sell or bid on crops, blockaded roads, and even once used a torpedo to halt a train carrying livestock into Iowa. Such direct actions helped push courts and legislatures to adopt measures that granted relief from debt caused by low crop prices.

"The similarities between the two periods are remarkable, and the lesson that emerges is simple: if you want change, keep our feet to the fire."

Dr. Wellmon agrees. "The only reason the current President and Congress have been able to implement all these changes, was because of pressure from popular movements that made them have to."

The Plains report, due out next month, cites the work of groups associated with United for Peace and Justice, an umbrella for anti-war groups, for galvanizing public support for ending the war, and for pushing the Administration to resist the oil lobby and other interest groups. It also cites the work

Continued on Page A6

KC IVEY/THE NEW YORK TIMES

Protests organized by Witness Against Torture helped pave the way for the close of the Guantánamo facility.

INTERNATIONAL A4-5

Gitmo, Other Centers Closed
The notorious Guantánamo Bay, Cuba detention camp will be closed, along with a network of secret C.I.A.-run facilities in Eastern Europe, Afghanistan and elsewhere. PAGE A24

Iraqi Refugees Worldwide Celebrate Withdrawal
Two million Iraqi exiles, and three million internal refugees, celebrated the end of hostilities and began making plans to return to their homes. PAGE A4

NATIONAL A6-9

Conflict of Interest Law Will Stop Revolving Door
The "Revolving Door" bill will prohibit high-ranking corporate officers from holding public office for ten years upon leaving their companies, and public officials from accepting management positions at large corporations for the same period. Coupled with the Ban on Lobbying bill, the bill will reduce the influence of large corporations on public policy. PAGE B1

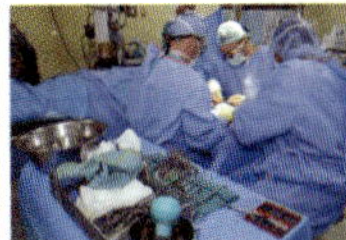

Health Insurance Act Clears House
While almost all are celebrating the passage of the National Health Insurance Act, which finally brings the U.S. up to par with other developed nations, representatives of Kaiser, Cigna and other health insurance companies are vowing to "fight tooth and nail" to protect their interests. PAGE A7

Bush to Face Charges
Most observers weren't surprised by the high treason indictment itself, but rather by the party that brought it. The case could also provide an unexpected boost to the International Criminal Court, paving the way for more indictments. PAGE A5

BUSINESS A10-11

Corporate Personhood Gets Real
An initiative to abolish limited liability will make shareholders pay for the crimes their corporations commit — even if they only own one or two shares in a mutual fund. PAGE A11

NEW YORK A12

Bicycle Lanes Inaugurated
With the completion of the 9th Avenue bike lane and groundbreaking on other avenues, New York is on the (bike) path to becoming as livable as other world cities. PAGE A12

EDITORIAL A13

A Lobbyist Defends Lobbying
The Ban on Lobbying bill is not with out victims. PAGE A13

Thomas L. Friedman
The columnist resigns, and will put down his pen to take up a screwdriver. PAGE A13

A Baboon Troop's Experience
A particularly peaceful baboon troop may have lessons to teach us. PAGE A13

More Inside The Times.
PAGE A2 ►

26 The Yes Men, *The New York Times, 4 July 2009*, 2008, offset lithography on paper.

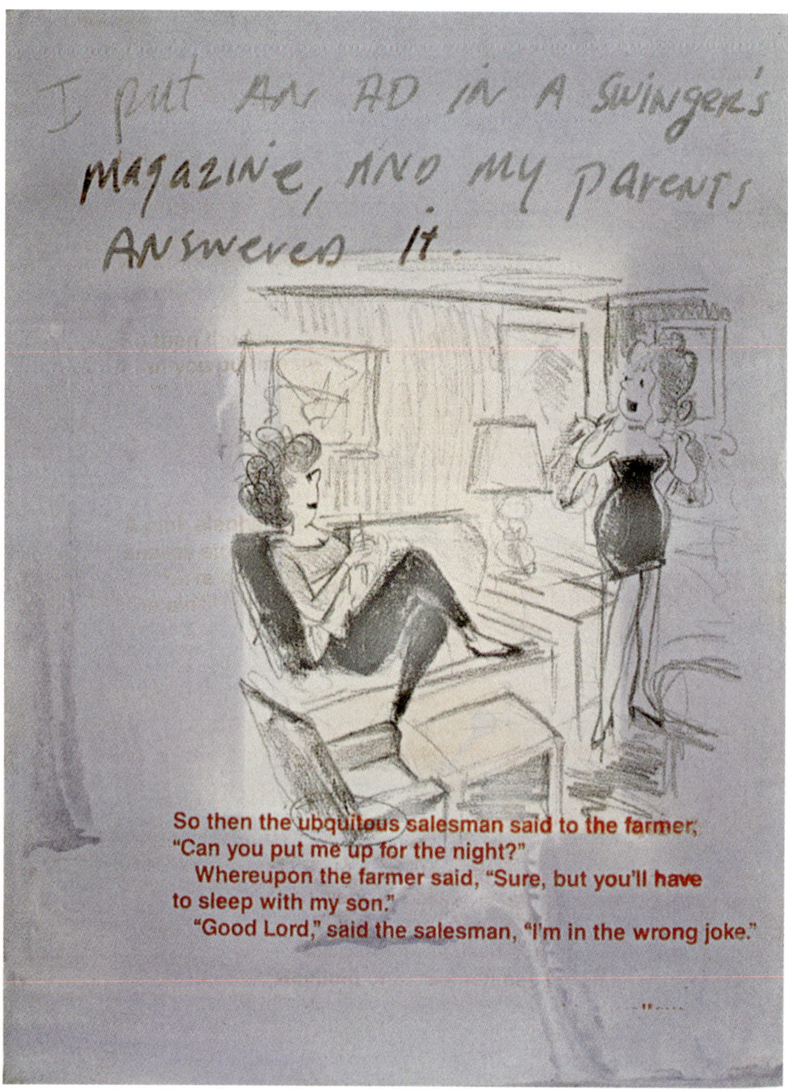

27 Richard Prince, *The Salesman and the Farmer*, 1989, acrylic, silkscreen, charcoal and marker on canvas.

aim to temper the celebratory moment of this most historic of US Presidential elections and transform the proactive mood of the original HSBC advertisement. The optimism and hope generated by Obama's election as the first African American president is qualified abruptly as one reads from left to right across the triptych. By the final frame, we have received a rather stark and cautionary tale. It will undoubtedly be perceived by some to be little more than a message of despair from a disenfranchised, rancorous left. It simply says – quite unremarkably if one is willing to read between the lines – that the American body politic must remain vigilant and continue to hold their politicians to account. The entire project – as The Yes Men have said trenchantly of previous efforts – is both a total success and a complete disaster. Its importance for the present account of word and image in art is twofold: it demonstrates how the boundary dividing art and media may be breached and introduces us to contemporary versions of agitprop art. In the discussion below we shall reconsider how artists involved with the Situationist International and figures such as Joseph Kosuth, Jenny Holzer and Alfredo Jaar have used this strategy to develop new models for public art. At the same time, it is important to acknowledge the work of artists like Richard Prince, for whom advertising imagery and popular culture have a different resonance as resources for the reimagining of painting (illus. 27, 28).

The semantic relation between a picture and a name introduces a new perspective for our understanding of the relation between image and text in art. But this inventory of connections – so brilliantly philosophically drawn by Nelson Goodman in *Languages of Art* – may reduce unnecessarily the internal complexities and cultural associations to be discovered in works of word and image art. The

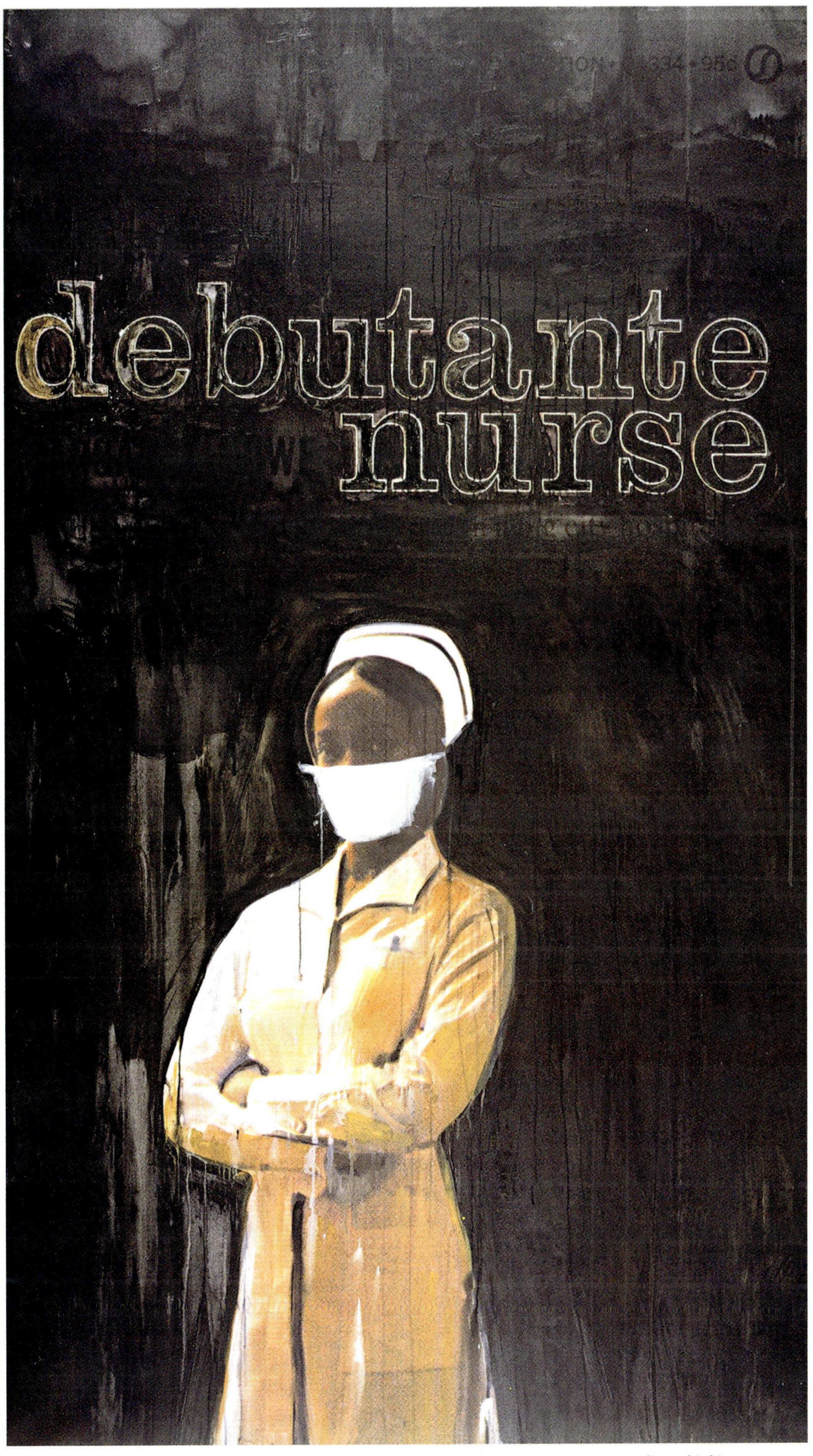

28 Richard Prince, *Debutante Nurse*, 2004, acrylic and inkjet on canvas.

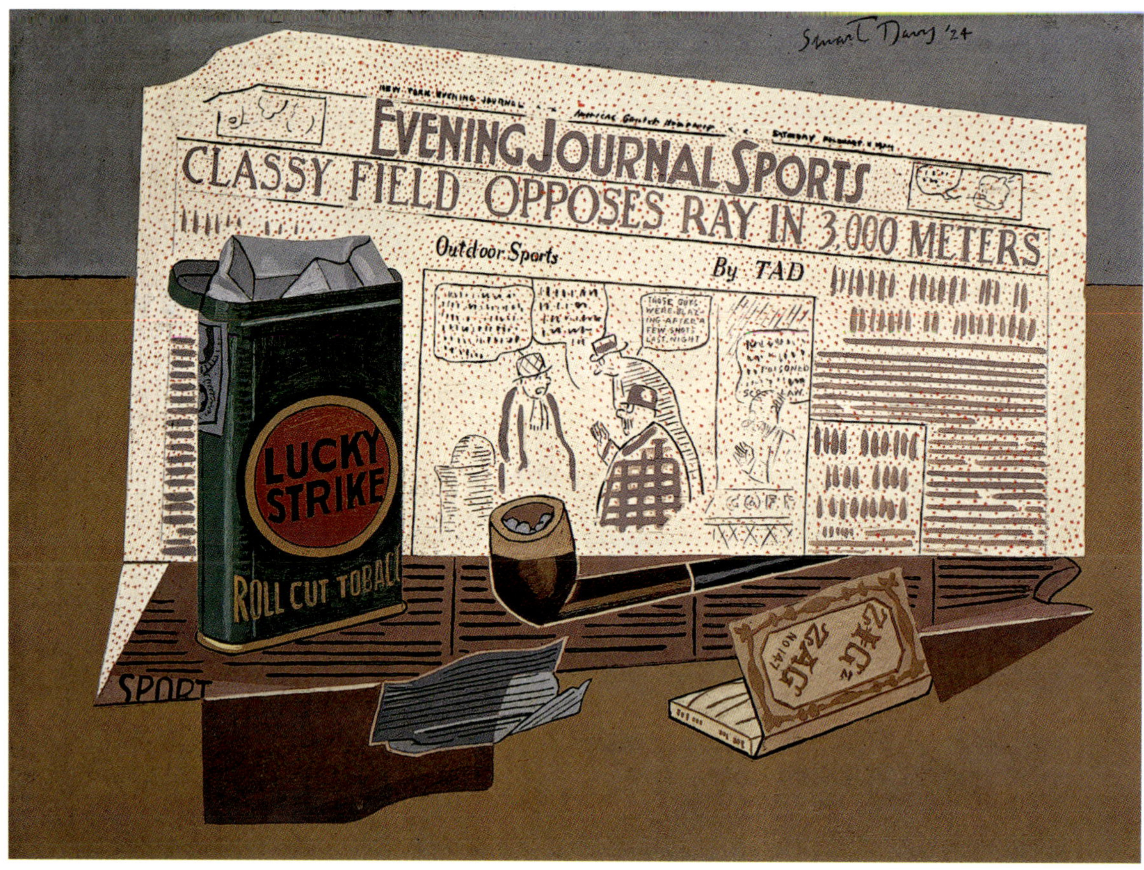

29 Stuart Davis, *Lucky Strike*, 1924, oil on paperboard.

presence of inscribed language as a component of an image is a powerful trigger for seduction and confusion. However, we are so inured to the collocation of image and text in all visual media, principally through advertising, that the corresponding disposition of apparently incongruous signs in a work of visual art provokes our curiosity but not necessarily our ire. It could be argued that such a condition increases the level of pleasure of spectatorship.

It is also important to consider how 'text' and 'image' are themselves signs for complex entities, and not simply self-contained components that might be fitted together as an assembly. If, as W.J.T. Mitchell has pointed out, the term 'image' connotes a 'far-flung family which has migrated in time and space and undergone profound mutations in the process', then the 'text-and-image' constellation in art can be no less complex and various.[7]

THE GREAT AMERICAN VOICE

The American painter and political activist Stuart Davis (1892–1964) was noted for his productive engagement with commercial packaging and branding; his work *Lucky Strike* is perhaps the first example of a painting to integrate product branding and newspaper comics (illus. 29). During the 1920s, Davis identified strongly with the expansive democratic vision of American poets such as Walt Whitman and considered the representation of commercial logos an expression of his American identity and a token of his modernity. As Davis wrote in 1921, reflecting on his first paintings that figured tobacco packages as subject matter, 'In poetry we have Lindsay, Masters, Sandburg and Williams, all in some way direct descendants of Whitman our one big artist. I too feel the thing Whitman felt and I too will express it in pictures – America – the wonderful place we live in.'[8]

Knowing what we do of Davis's long-standing political views, it is difficult to take his unqualified approval of American life at face value. By the 1930s, as the Great Depression took hold, Davis became increasingly involved in radical politics and artists' organizations with strong connections to the American Communist Party and other left-wing political groups. Davis's paintings were by no means explicitly political, but they did demonstrate the artist's desire to forge abstraction as a new type of realist art. The curator Lowery Stokes Sims admires Davis for trying to assert social content through subject matter while maintaining an allegiance to abstraction. According to Sims, Davis attempted to achieve this synthesis by employing 'themes culled from the consumer, media-inflected urban culture of America', by correlating his aesthetic theories with 'dialectical reasoning', and by 'reintroducing the figure into his work in order to express more overtly political commentary'.

By 1940, Davis had ceased his engagement with the American Artists Congress, but remained attached to a highly schematic abstraction that never completely renounced its origins in realism. Davis had already mastered synthetic Cubism and set about to depict the urban environment as an overall pattern of interlocking forms and high-keyed hues and text. The actual vectoring of urban space by skyscrapers and the grid layout of Manhattan supplied the initial inspiration that linked the city to modernist art. To appreciate the specific visual impact on Davis of the city, one need only consider how the dispersal of geometricized urban space is effected through neon lighting and animated advertising exemplified in districts such as New York's Times Square, the Ginza of Tokyo, or London's Piccadilly Circus.

Impressed by how this new conjunction of elements could be mobilized to express modernity, Davis sought to remake abstract art into the image of the new reality of the modern city. Davis, equally enamoured of jazz, utilized the slang of the jazz musician and the jazz devotee as a marker for his aesthetic achievement. Jazz bespoke dynamism and modernity, but also ethnic difference and the exotic margins of a multicultural cityscape. Some of Davis's titles, like *Owh! In San Pao* (1951), are not simply labels but sharp onomatopoeic puns that mimic the cries of delight voiced during a particularly hot jazz performance (illus. 32).

Davis learned from the School of Paris and reinvented synthetic Cubism as an American pictorial idiom, which he memorializes in his painting, *Colonial Cubism* (1954), a self-conscious assessment of achievement expressed in an ironically self-deprecating manner. In the same way a jazz musician can take a theme of a popular song and 'jazz' it up, so too could Davis 'jazz' up and distil to great effect the compositional prerogatives of word and image. With these 'cover versions' of Picasso, Braque and Gris, Davis transforms the familiar Cubist collage, with its inclusion of text in the image, into something far more specific. Davis integrated text into the overall formal structure of the painting, submerging it in the fabric of the composition rather than simply placing it within the composition as wayward counterpoint. One might say that there could be no such thing as a sombre painting by Davis. Language, when represented in the artist's painting, is pictorial; its form is configured ecstatically within the mosaic of the painterly surface. The text becomes, in effect, a scintillating grace note urging us forward. At the beginning of the 1950s, Davis was the only American painter to treat text as an image in this way and to continue to treat it as a central aspect of his art.

POST-WAR CHALLENGES TO 'DISORDER AND DISINTEGRATION'[9]

For the North American artist, the immediate post-war period was a time of promise and anxiety. New York artists were painfully aware of the growing confrontation between the United States and the then USSR and the danger posed by the existence of atomic weapons. Artists on the left viewed the close of the Second World War as a political opportunity, and continued to agitate for a return to government-funded arts and cultural projects and for a new dispensation of wealth redistribution and an array of social services such as health care. For some, there was a sense that the end of the war heralded a new beginning for American society; the tumultuous political activity of the immediate pre-war era of the 1930s, suspended for the sake of the war effort, would now be resumed. All the issues that seethed in American social life – racism, anti-Semitism, exploitation of workers and the inequality of women – would be addressed with renewed vigour and purpose. This is seen vividly in '. . . *Is It True What They Say About Cohen?*', a pamphlet co-authored by Bill Levner and Ad Reinhardt in 1948. It is a richly communicative 'mirror image' of prejudice, thanks to Levner's accessible and engaging text and Reinhardt's simple yet effective illustrations. The pamphlet demonstrates one means of combating unacceptable stereotypes: stressing the stereotype to the limit of credibility by mapping it

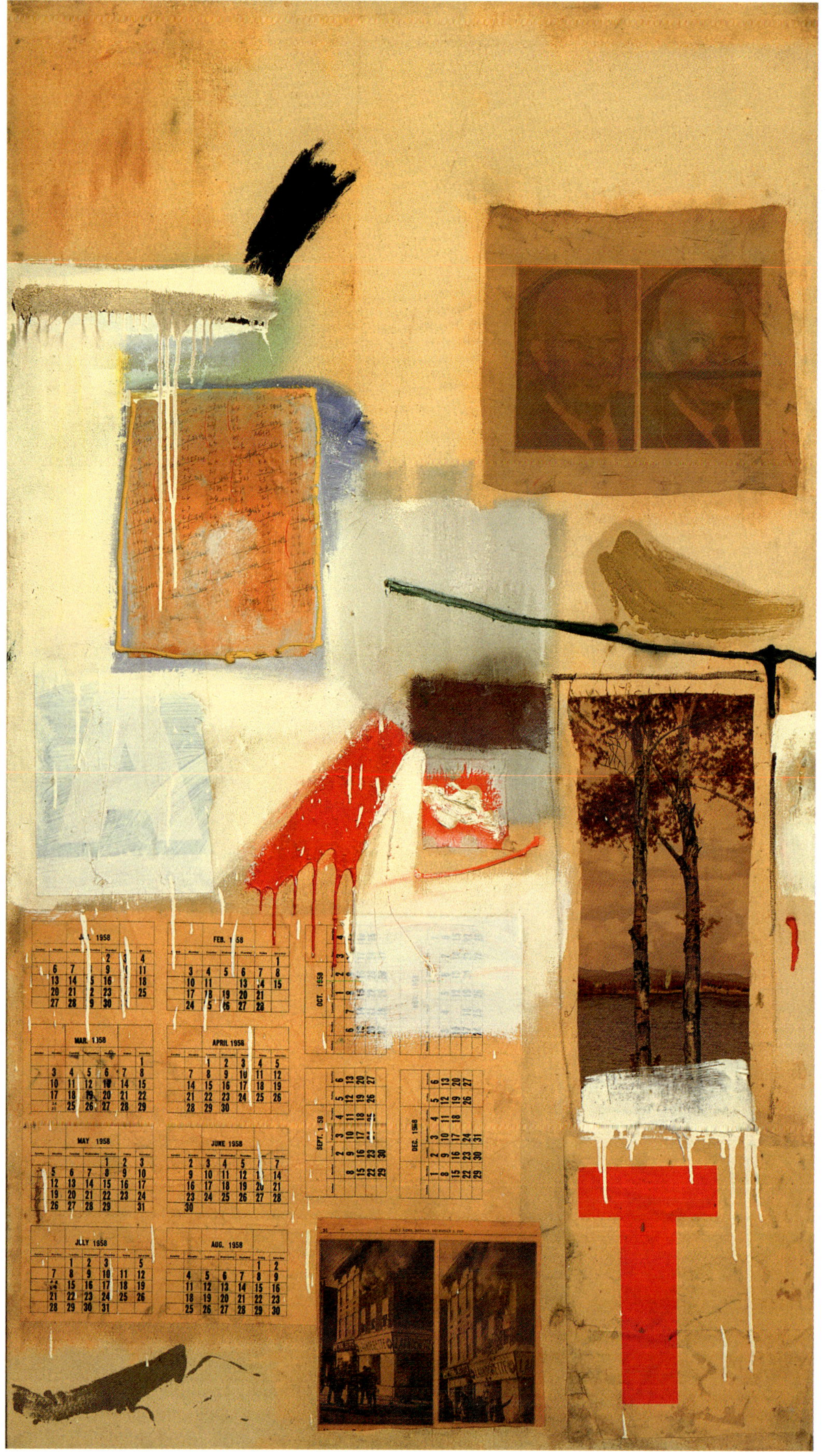
FEB. 1958
APRIL 1958
MAY 1958
JUNE 1958
AUG. 1958
OCT. 1958
DEC. 1958

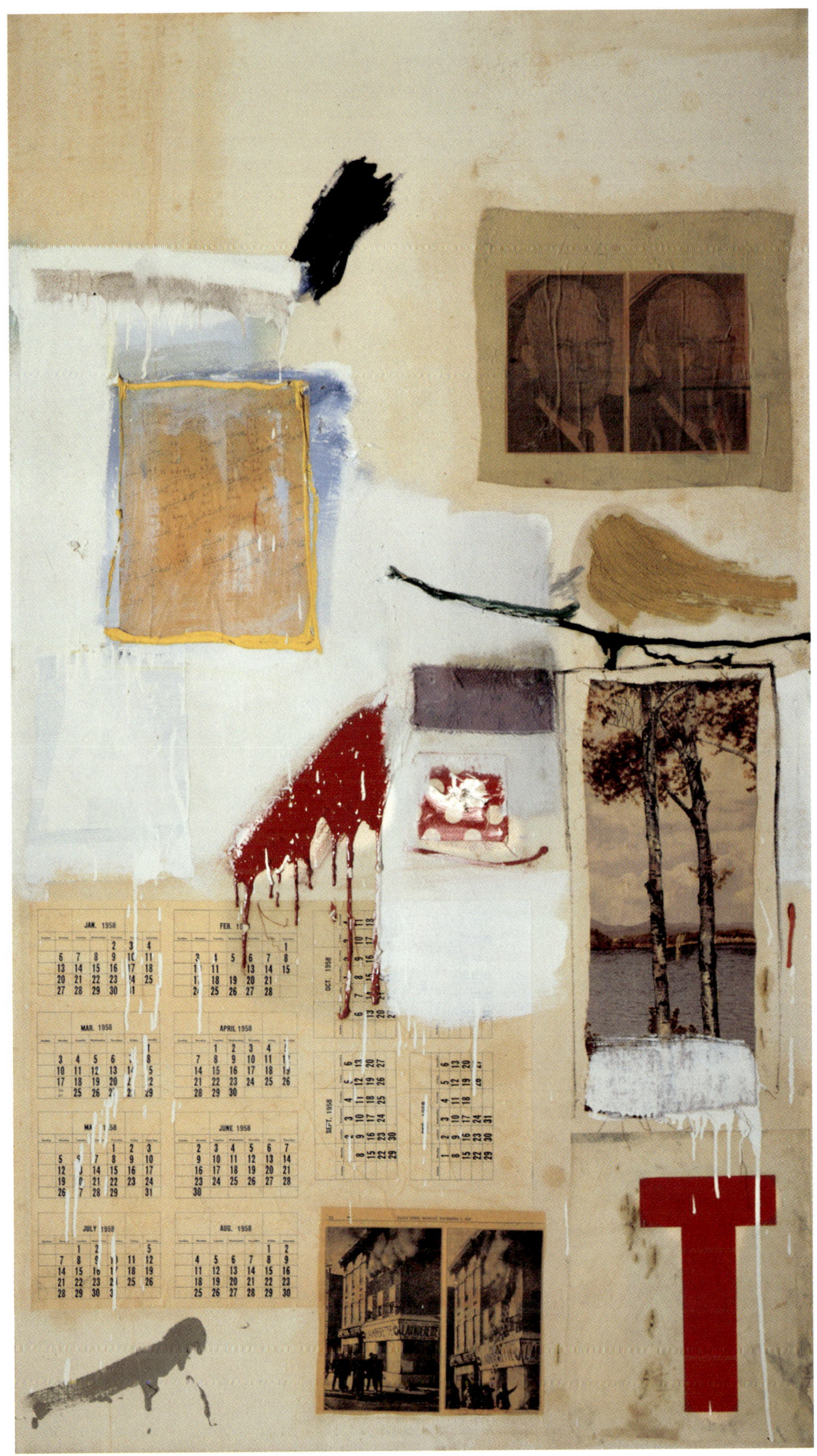

30, 31 Robert Rauschenberg, *Factum I* and *Factum II*, 1957, oil and enamel on canvas, printed papers, serigraphy.

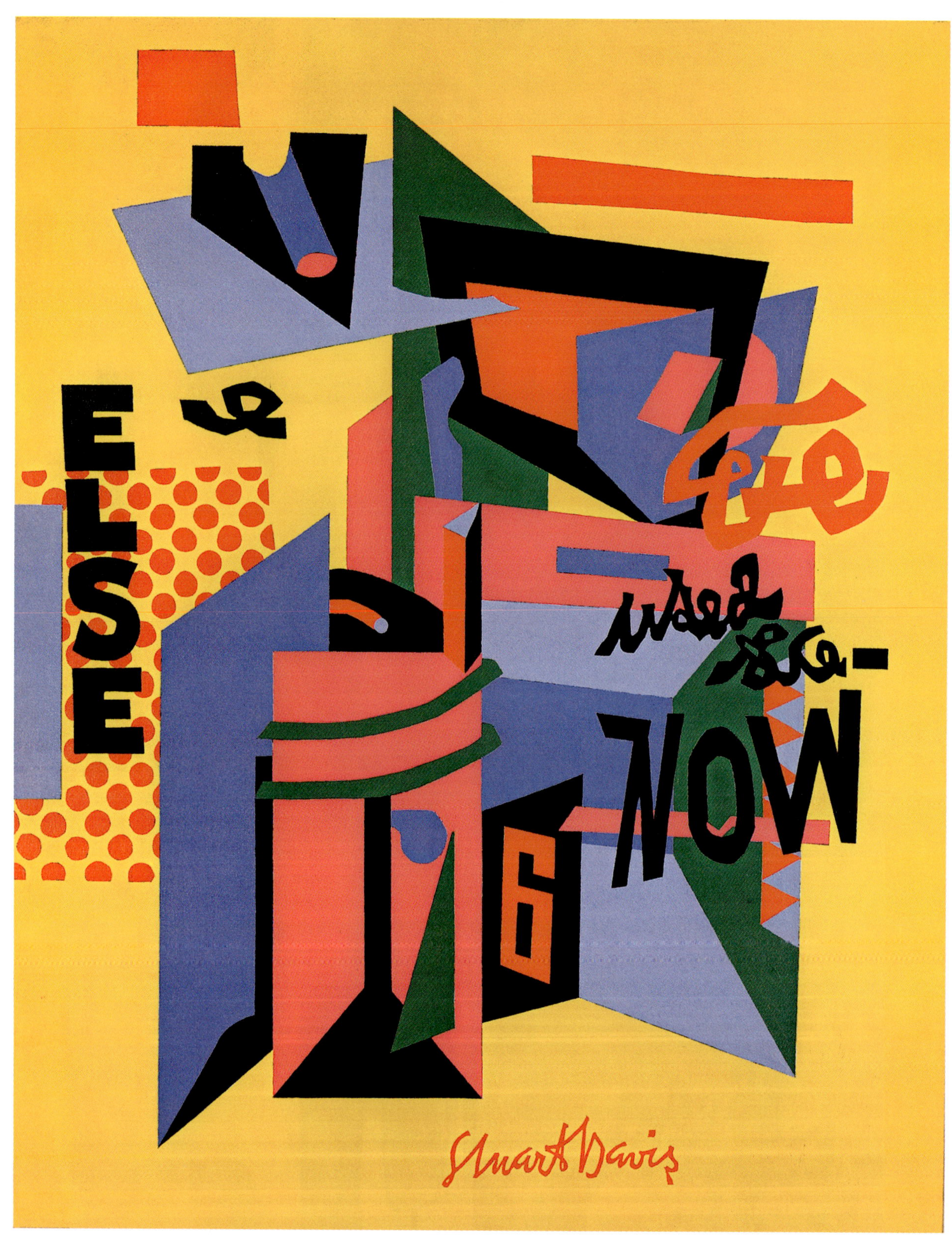

32 Stuart Davis, *Owh! In San Pao*, 1951, oil on canvas.

onto another version of reality; one which personalizes the other and appeals to an individual's real experience with others.

The post-Second World War world ushered in a new balance of power; a shift away from the great imperialist empires of Britain and France of the early twentieth century to the burgeoning military-industrial complex represented by the United States. But the argument in support of this new global political order was not only economic and military in nature; the cultural superiority of the liberal democracy that the United States represented would be foregrounded in the struggle for global supremacy and influence.

In a well-known study of the emergence of the New York School, the art historian Serge Guilbaut addresses the de-Marxification of American art during the 1940s and the ascendancy of New York as the new capital of modern art. While Guilbaut's book was highly controversial at the time of its publication, the main point of *How New York Stole the Idea of Modern Art: Abstract Expressionism, Freedom and the Cold War* is now generally accepted. By 1950, American artists considered themselves to be the leading proponents of modern painting and sculpture, having usurped Paris as the undisputed centre of modern art. As art historian Meyer Schapiro remarked: 'It wasn't automatism that the Americans learned from the Surrealists, but how to be heroic.'[10]

As US artists began to explore the possibilities offered up by liberation from the values and aesthetics of European art, other cultural obligations began to emerge and come into sharper relief. The significance of a specifically 'American' identity in art took hold and the entire experience of post-war life in the US asserted itself as a legitimate subject for art. What is relevant to our concerns is that some of this new art, drawing once more on the widest possible cultural landscape, found creative potential in the use of word and image. The combine paintings of Robert Rauschenberg of the mid- to late 1950s, to give one example, employed word and image to sustain a convincing allusion to the complexity of American identity (illus. 30, 31). In most cases, the judicious placement of a fragment of text would be enough of a foil to the equally fragmented images and objects that Rauschenberg would work into his playful assemblages of 'poor' materials. With these works, Rauschenberg announced his allegiance to a revivified avant-garde art; a tendency that invited comparison with the great formal achievements of the historical avant-garde of the early twentieth century while simultaneously undermining the profound metaphysics surrounding the reception of Abstract Expressionist painting and sculpture. Notwithstanding Rauschenberg's celebration of collage as unbridled conjunction, there is something darkly moody and conflicted about the way in which these combine paintings picture the culture of the US during the 1950s.

THE TIME OF LEAN COWS

For French artists and intellectuals, the immediate aftermath of the Second World War meant having to come to terms with a far different palette of social and moral issues: reconstruction, the impact of Marshall Plan aid (1948–51) and a rapidly flourishing anti-American sentiment. Jean-Paul Sartre's terse dismissal of Surrealism as a relevant form of art for post-war Europe reflected the harsh realities of life during the late 1940s and declared the new political battle lines that were to be drawn between the various factions on the left. Not long after André Breton's 1946 return to Paris from exile in New York, Sartre wrote: 'in the time of the fat cows, they were prophets of disaster; in the time of lean cows they have nothing to say to us.'[11] The emigration to North America by the group's leading members during the early 1940s contributed to Surrealism's waning influence in Paris. Artists and intellectuals who had remained in Paris were deeply resentful of those who had fled, first to Vichy France, then to New York. Breton – the chief architect of Surrealism – was aware of the political turmoil immediately following the end of the war and delayed his return to Paris until May 1946 to gain the best possible advantage. Soon after his arrival, Breton began to initiate a number of new alliances with artists not directly engaged with the pre-war Surrealist project.

When the young Romanian artist Jean-Isidore Goldstein (1925–2007), known as Isou, arrived in Paris at the end of the war, it was evident that the battle lines had already been drawn. Isou aimed to challenge Surrealism directly with his new pro-

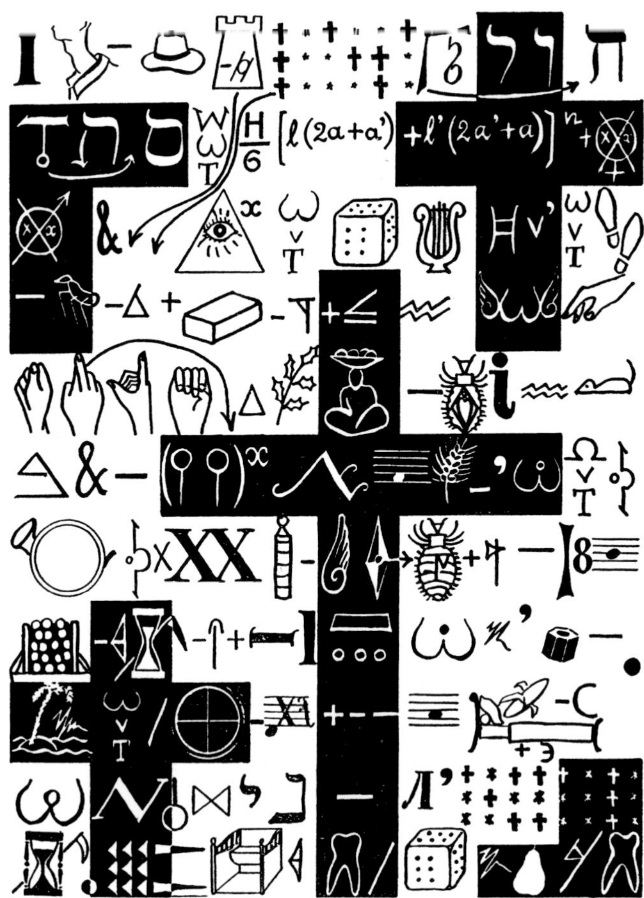

33 Gabriel Pomerand, *Saint Ghetto des Prêts*, 1950, collage on paper.

gramme of artistic practice that depended on the manipulation of language and was named, appropriately enough, Lettrism. Isou – forever an outsider to the Parisian art world – did manage to reconstitute the art of word and image by making the intentional manipulation of literary texts through typographic and other means the central formal tenet of his movement. The unconscious, erotic desire and the body as a field of endless play were displaced by language, but in the greatly reduced form of the individual letter. Isou was first a sound poet, producing poetry that was reminiscent of the Dadaists Tristan Tzara and Raoul Hausmann. Later, Lettrism embraced the possibilities of inscribed language – a form he called *hypergraphy* – and a mixture of letterforms and symbols. The significance of Isou's attack on Surrealism may be said to turn on whether or not *Lettrism* was able to convincingly frame a new kind of subjectivity, rather than simply propose a meaningless babble as a corrective to Surrealism.

The high point of Lettrism was likely during the early part of the 1950s, when the group included artists such as Maurice Lemaître, Gabriel Pomerand (illus. 33), François Dufrêne and Guy Debord. In some respects, the most successful work of Lettrism was its films, which offered up a radical, content-less, deracinated cinema. Works such as *Hurlements en faveur de Sade* (1952) by Debord demonstrate the power of an artistic strategy that conjoins different modes of expression or worlds of experience for the sake of a great effect. The concept of *détournement* – characteristic of later Situationist International works – is precisely the aesthetic that Debord is groping towards in this film.

Détournement – especially when realized through the use of found or stock photographic or cartoon images to which is applied suggestive or subverting text – has proven to be a durable conceptual strategy of contemporary art and may be found in the early work of Dennis Adams, the found photographic work of Lutz Bacher and Tacita Dean's storyboards for imaginary films also constructed from found photographic prints (illus. 34, 35, 36).

In one sense, the notion of an artwork as that which is constituted by internal difference, rather than internal unity, is already implicit in earlier Lettriste works that pit the formal qualities of letterforms against their potential as meaningful

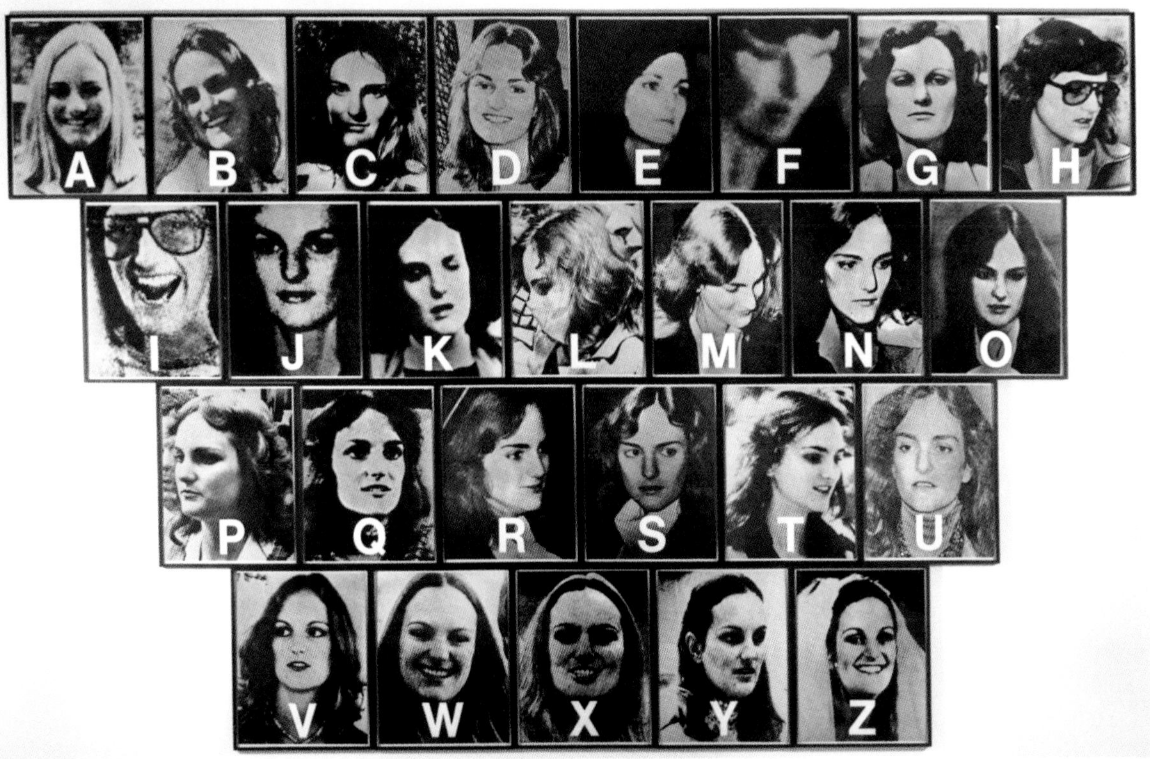

34 Dennis Adams, *Patricia Hearst, A–Z*, 1979–90, portfolio of 26 two-colour serigraphs and 4 text sheets.

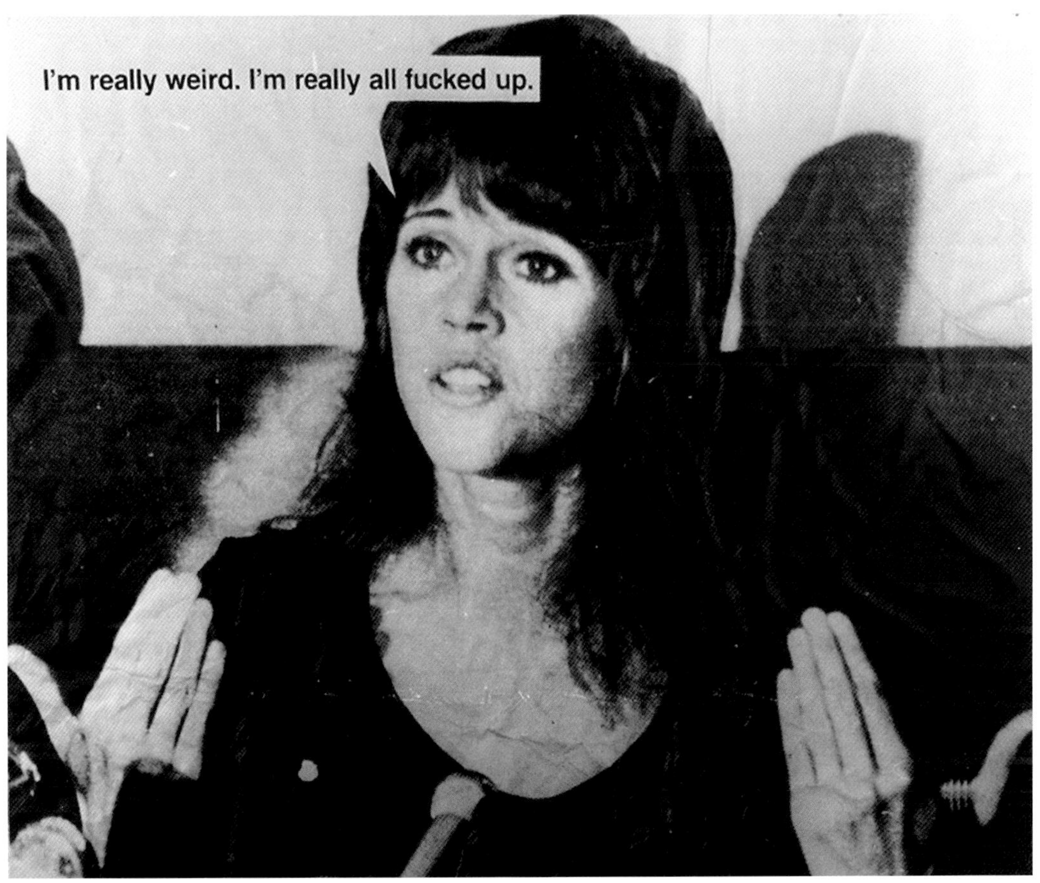

35 Lutz Bacher, *Jokes (Jane Fonda)*, 1985–8, found images.

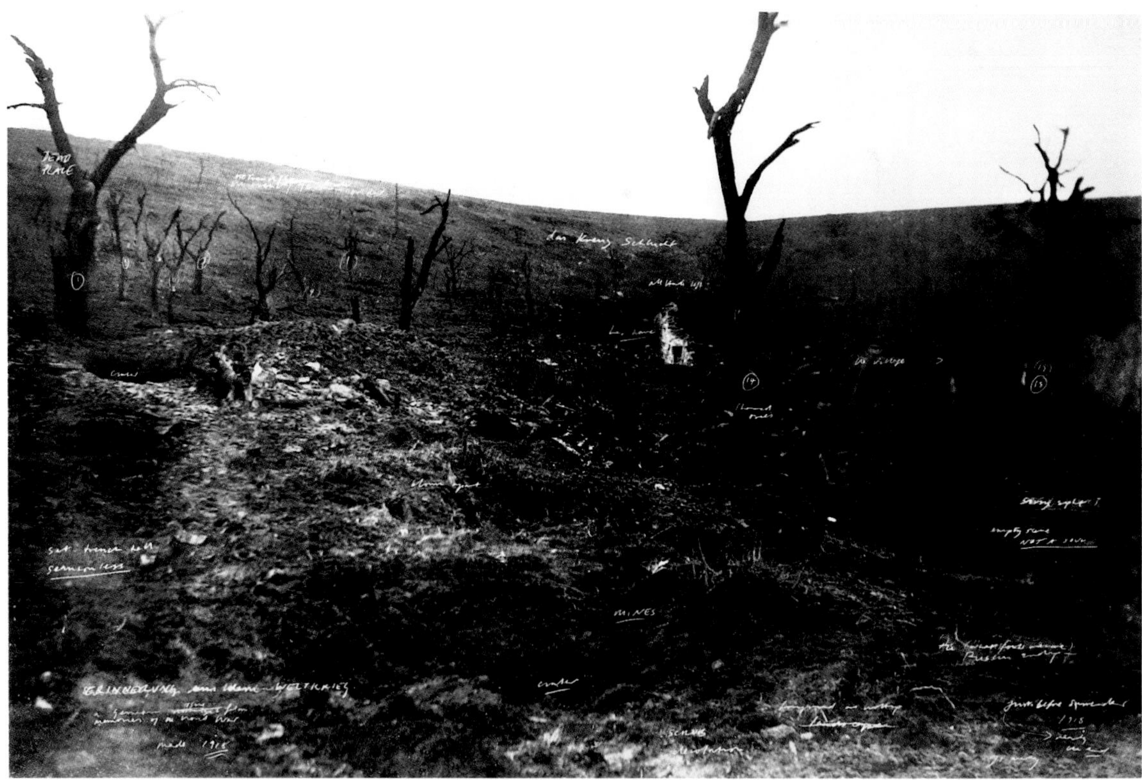

36 Tacita Dean, *Memory from the World War*, from *The Russian Ending*, 2001, photogravure.

components of language. Lettrism, with its chaotic arrays of letterforms, pictographs and symbols – the hypergraphic or metagraphic approach pioneered by Isou and Maurice Lemaître in the early 1950s – could be said to have provided more than simply an appropriate model for artists interested in redescribing the public language of consumer advertising as private nonsense.

Another response to the opportunities and challenges posed by the post-war period is found in the work of Jean Dubuffet. Having coined the term *l'art brut* – literally, raw art – Dubuffet enjoyed a long and successful career that included a brief flirtation with the Surrealists, a collaboration with Asger Jorn on a musical composition, and numerous high-profile municipal and corporate commissions for publicly sited sculptures. An early work by Dubuffet, *Wall with Inscriptions* (illus. 37), pictures a defaced wall upon which a cartoon image of a figure is rendered opportunistically from the stains and distresses of the surface. The primitive figure is not yet an autonomous image, but merges with the ground itself; an image, perhaps, of what the rough, post-war city had to offer art as a subject of spontaneous, anarchic self-renewal. The inscribed wall, then, reveals a complex truth about the city as it inclines towards reconstruction and reconciliation: the sheer materiality of the surface of the wall stands in for the very matter of the city, while its presence is confirmed as a space for inscribing dreams, marking territories or to declare with 'genital urgency', as Robert Hughes put it, one's undying love. The unsanctioned incursion into social space by an anonymous citizenry marks the very fabric of the city as an actor in the construction of urban life. Yet, for Dubuffet, the impetus that allowed inscription and figuration to coexist in this manner did not blossom into an enduring interest in word and image in art. Rather, the reverse turned out to be the case; the *act*, rather than the substance, of graffiti insinuates the superiority of untutored creativity. Graffiti as *performance* strengthens its association with a particular kind of urban lawlessness and retains its lustre as a mode of expression residing tantalizingly outside the bounds of respectable art culture. It remains highly visible today as a vernacular to memorialize traumatic events (illus. 38).

By 1948, Dubuffet had located an even more powerful model for this fantasy of unrecoverable, incorruptible creativity. At this point, in conjunction with André Breton, he dissociated his art from the city and its characteristically public forms of life in exchange for the private and inscrutable work of solitary psychiatric patients. The compulsively patterned work of asylum inmates such as Adolf Wölfli was deemed by Dubuffet to be far more suitable as a model for a form of expression that would remain resistant to the recuperative pull of culture.

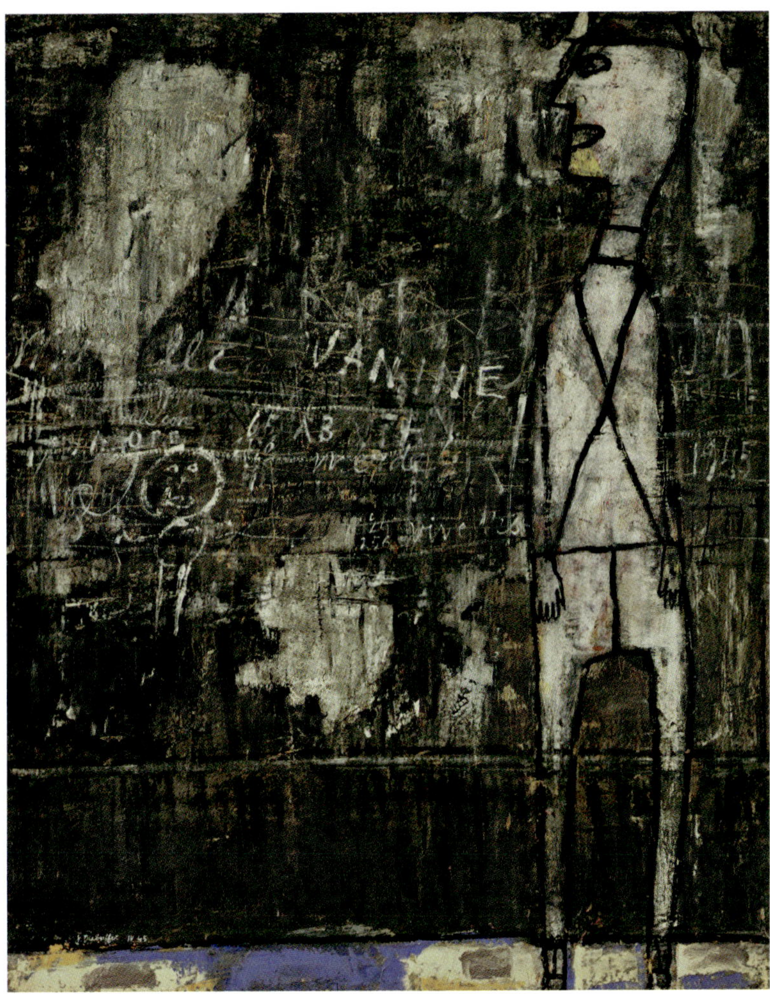

37 Jean Dubuffet, 'Wall with Inscriptions', from the *Walls* series, 1945, oil on canvas.

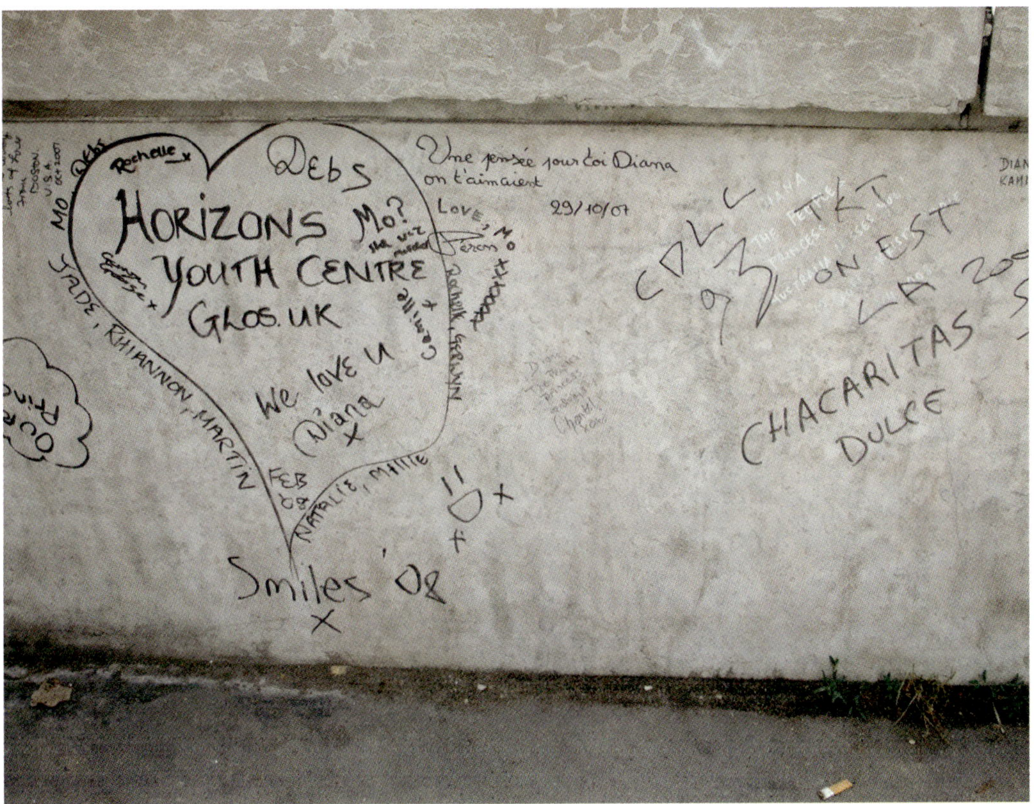

38 Graffiti on wall of an overpass near the tunnel Pont de l'Alma, Paris, site of Princess Diana and Dodi Fayed's 1997 fatal car crash, 2008.

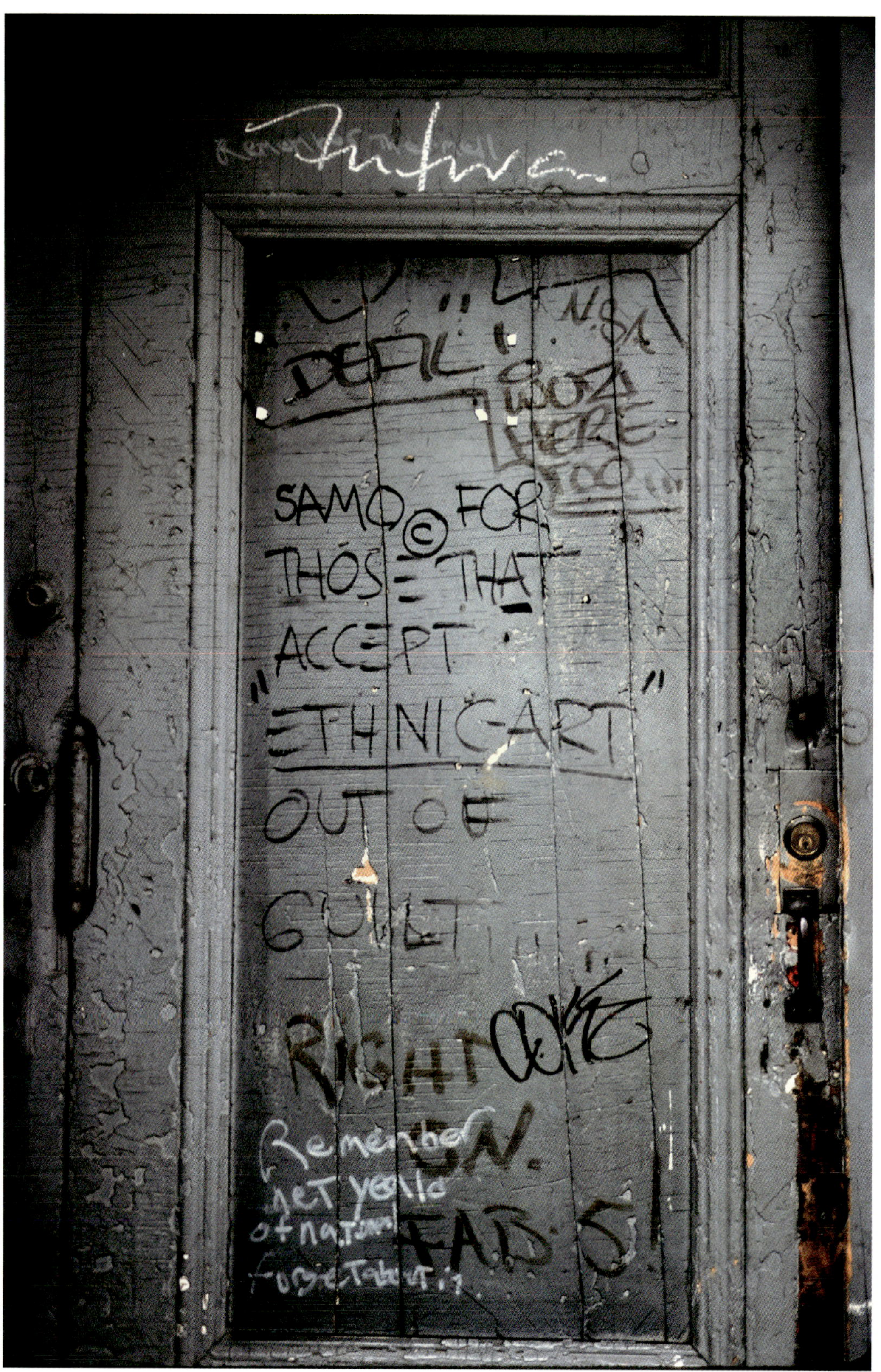

39 Jean-Michel Basquiat, *Shannon Dawson* and *Al Diaz*, example of graffiti inscription in situ: *Samo © for those that accept 'ethnic art' out of guilt*, photographed in 1997–8.

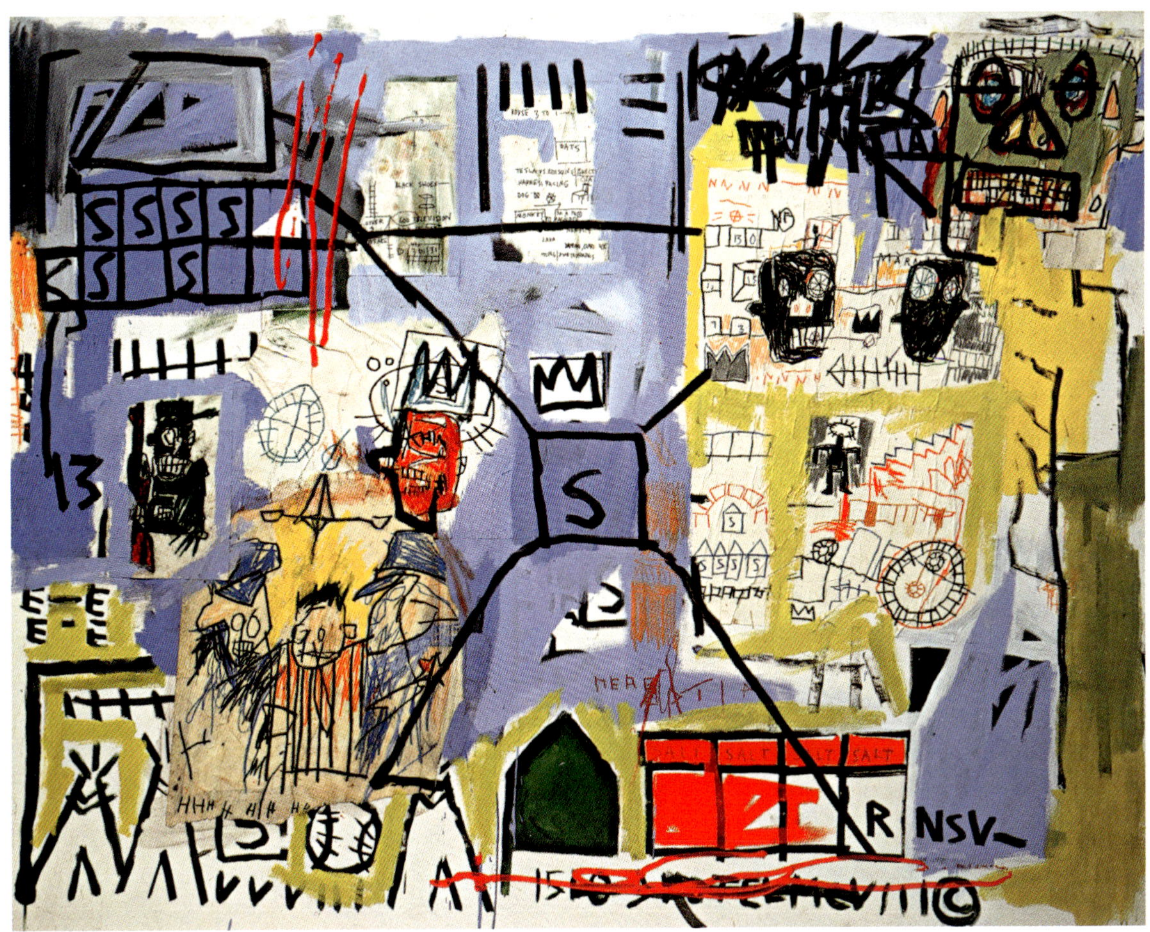

40 Jean-Michel Basquiat, *Untitled*, 1981, acrylic, marker, paper collage, oil stick and crayon on canvas.

Urban graffiti and the work of *outsider artists* – the term favoured by the Anglophone world – would continue to fascinate contemporary artists eager to find energetic alternatives to overly sophisticated, media-saturated forms of art comprised of image and text (illus. 39, 40, 42). The self-conscious embrace by the avant garde of the primitive in all its guises – African tribal sculpture, the art of children, the insane or urban youth gangs – has been a persistent feature of modern art since the nineteenth century. During the past two decades, the naivety and intimacy of scale characteristic of outsider art has likewise imprinted itself on much contemporary drawing and painting. The appropriation of the appearance of outsider art, in particular, has been repeated far too often and struggles to exist as anything other than a cliché. Through a self-conscious association with the untutored inventiveness of outsider art – which already exists as a kind of visual brand and a highly desirable art commodity – the work of knowing naïfs is rendered contradictory. It is already decided that there is no hope for a vivid cultural expression of unalloyed conformism. Rather, the point of this new exploration of naiveté is to proclaim another programme; one marked by a real fascination with the melancholy – sometimes coldly sullen, at other times faintly hysterical – induced by the overbearing presence of mainstream culture and its power to strip meaning to the bone (illus. 41).

WHEN WRITERS DRAW

An untitled drawing executed in 1948 by Saul Steinberg (1914–1999) shows how the mutability of the line may serve as an emblem for art's potential for self-reflexivity. Steinberg could sometimes be profound, but he was always amusing; and he had no problem developing his gifts in the parallel worlds of fine and applied art. Because of this, the artist's position within the New York School remains eclipsed by his fame as a cartoonist and illustrator. But Steinberg was a well-known figure in the milieu of the New York School whose gifts for intelligent satire and the ability to produce stunning pictures-within-pictures earned him the approbation of his peers, who considered him to be something of an 'artist's artist'.

An obvious student of Paul Klee and an equal to Ad Reinhardt's graphic achievement, Steinberg pre-

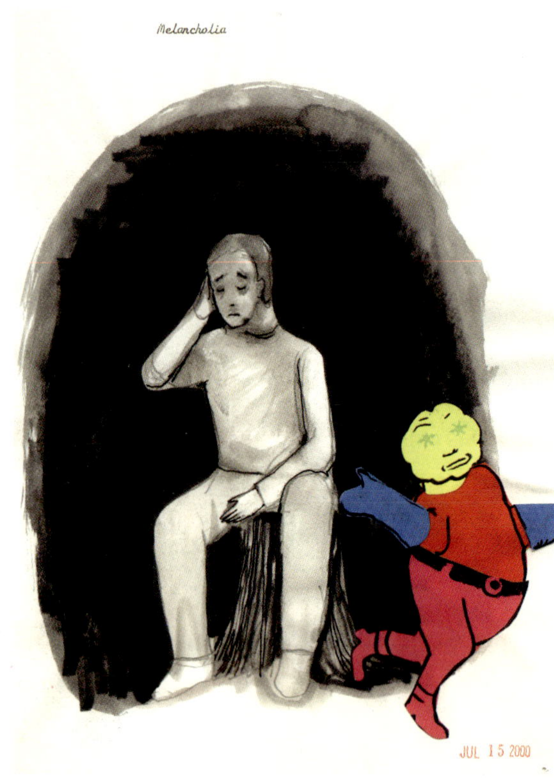

41 The Royal Art Lodge, *Melancholia*, 2000, gouache on paper.

ferred to describe his calling as a writer who draws. Certainly, the prevailing currents in Steinberg's drawings are literary and the narrative impulse of his work relies upon a deep structure rooted in an appreciation and mastery of literary tropes. But Steinberg's work is essentially an elaborated form of the comic strip genre. The artist's decision to blur the boundary between high art and mass illustration really distinguished Steinberg from his peers. By remaining steadfastly devoted to a comic figuration – the likes of which would not appear in the precincts of high art in any concentration until the advent of Pop Art or Philip Guston's return to figuration – Steinberg created a working space clear of the hairy-chested polemics of the American avant-garde art of the 1950s. At the same time, his art refracts the many vehicles of word and image that were in circulation throughout the visual culture of the time – cartoons, comic books,

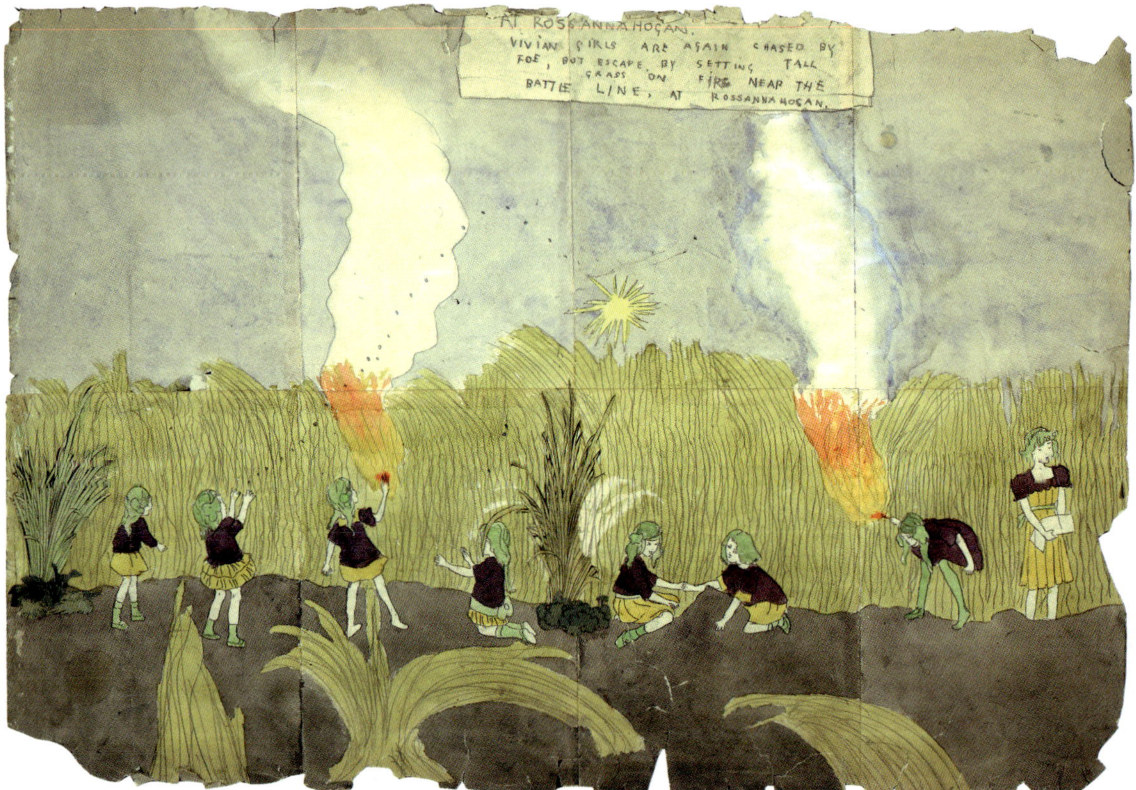

42 Henry Darger, *Untitled (At Rossanna Hogan. Vivian Girls are again chased by foe, but escape by setting tall grass on fire near the battle line)*, n.d., watercolour, pencil and carbon tracing on pieced paper.

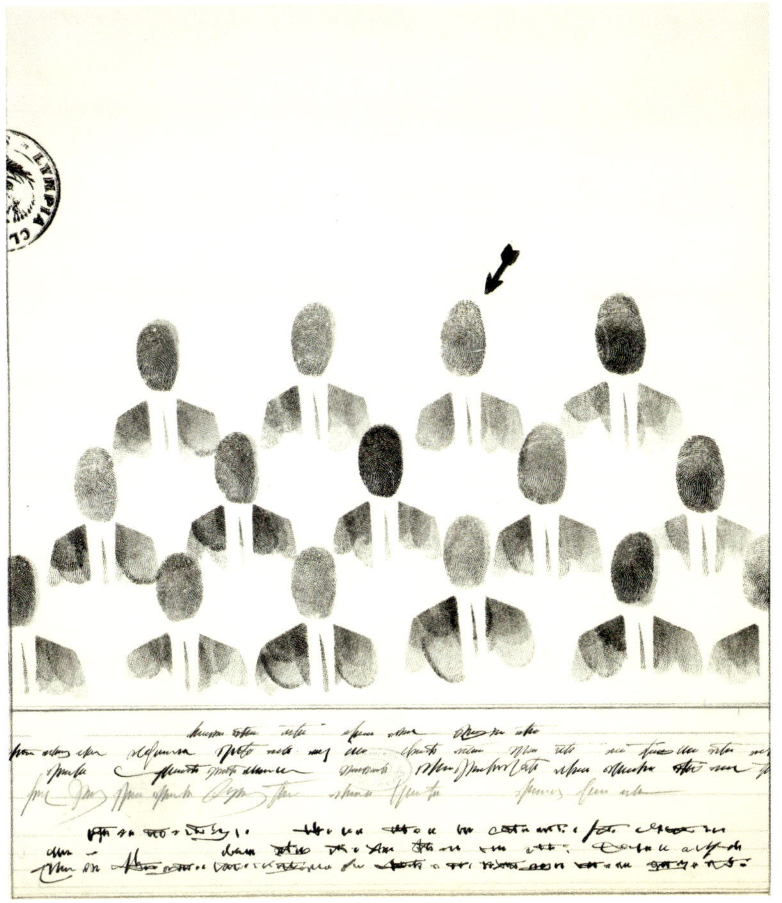

43 Saul Steinberg, *Group Photo*, 1953, ink, thumbprints and rubber stamp on paper.

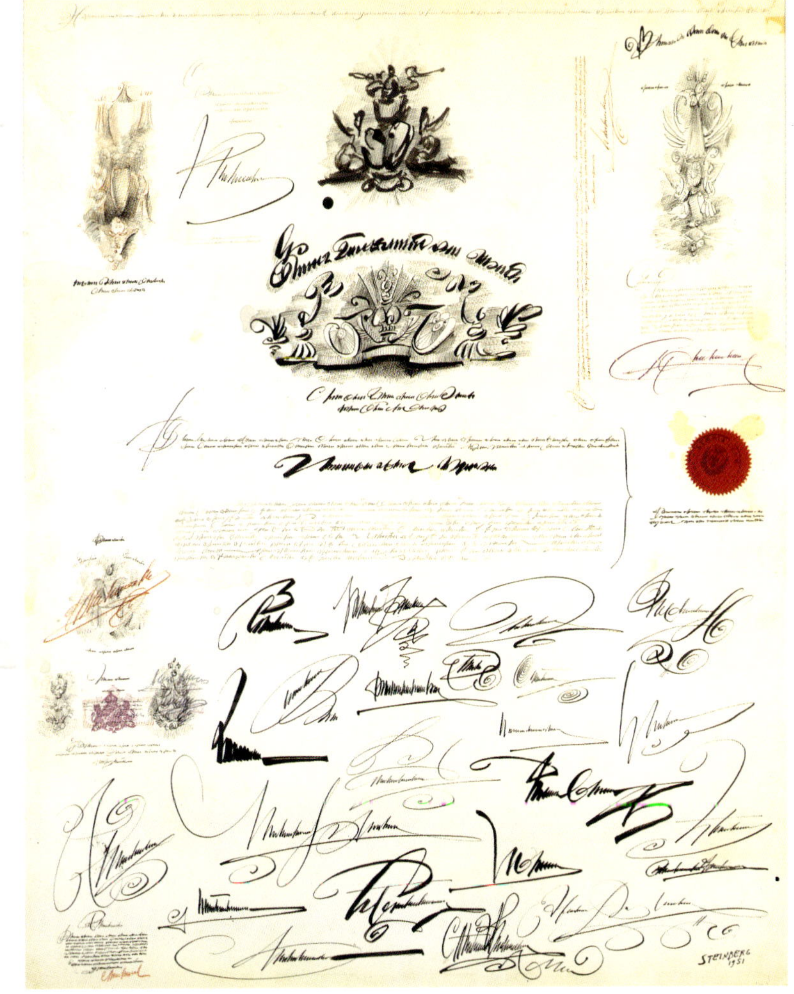

44 Saul Steinberg, *Large Document*, 1951, ink, rubber stamp and collage on paper.

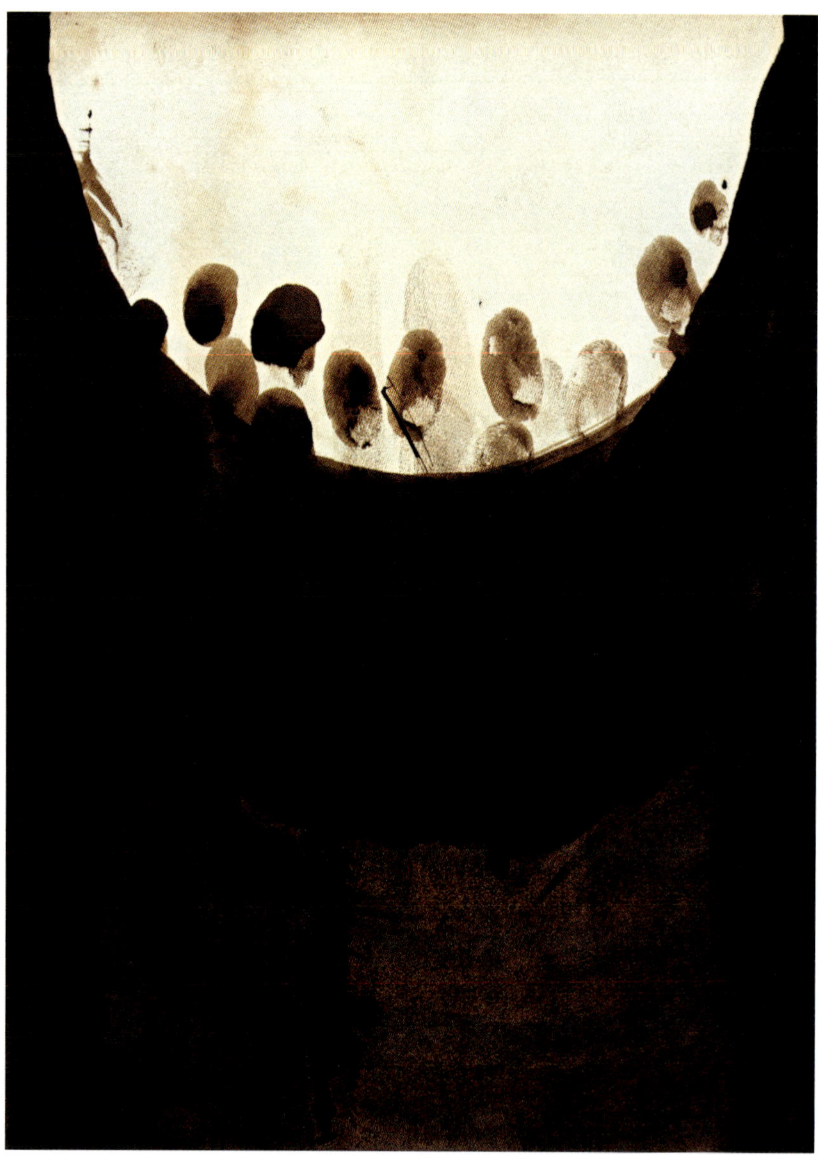

45 Victor Hugo, *Drawing with Fingerprints*, 1864–65.

advertising and images of architecture – with little regard for their status as building blocks of serious culture or commerce.

The essential quality of Steinberg's art is its use of hyperbole and caricature in the service of the joke. The graphic signs of authority are misapplied, deconstructed and reassembled with a child-like playfulness. The artist's gags are never inaccessible: a fingerprint stands in for a face (illus. 43); masses of meaningless arabesques are arranged as authoritative signatures on passports or other legal or historical documents (illus. 44). In *Fingerprint Landscape*, the link from fingerprint to identity to police surveillance suggests we are all suspects. The image is not such a paranoid vision in the context of Cold War America and not unlike the kinds of images produced by another 'writer who draws', Victor Hugo. Hugo's *Drawing with Fingerprints* (illus. 45) realizes a suggestive image through the play of hand and materials, as significant form emerges from the accidental encounter with the formless. What looks to be a bit of clowning by Steinberg at the expense of the authority of state institutions in *Large Document* is dark enough and equally resonant with the times of its making. Once you get past the wit, the effect is chilling.

'IT IS THE DESTINY OF THE POPULAR ART TO BECOME OBSOLESCENT'[12]

Since the 1950s, mass-produced commodities, their packaging and advertising have been popular subjects for artists on both sides of the Atlantic. The British artists, architects and critics who formed the Independent Group in London – Eduardo Paolozzi, Alison and Peter Smithson, Nigel Henderson and Lawrence Alloway – were the first to use the term 'Pop' art. The term features prominently in Richard Hamilton's well-known collage produced for the seminal 1956 exhibition *This Is*

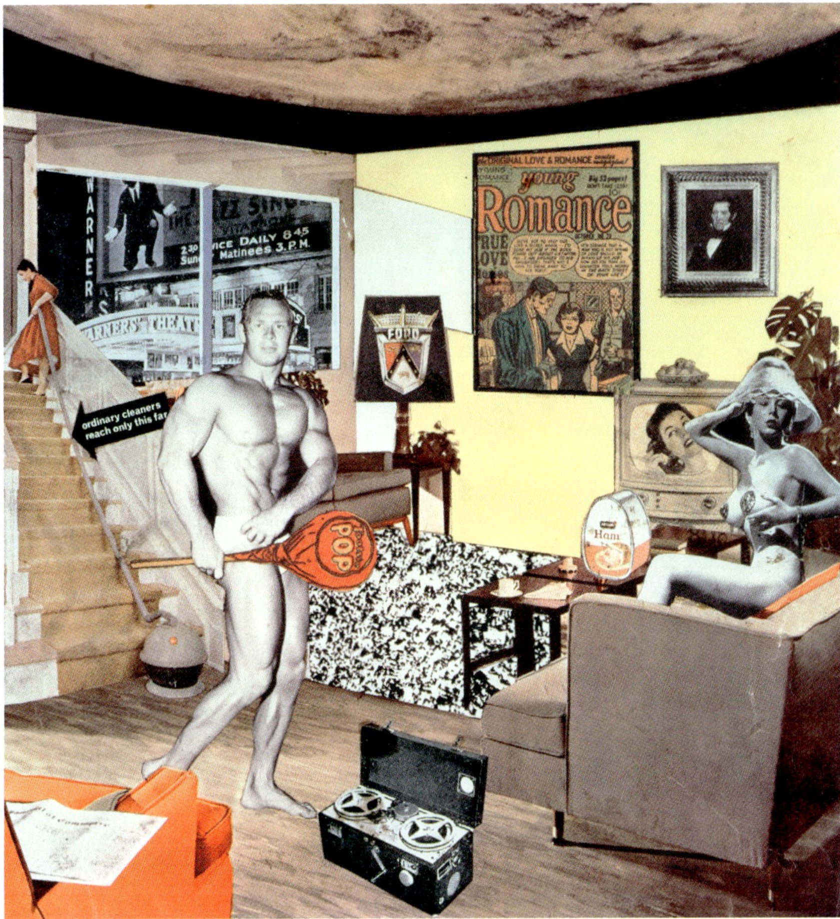

46 Richard Hamilton, *Just what is it that makes today's homes so different, so appealing?*, 1956, collage.

Tomorrow at the Whitechapel Gallery, London (illus. 46); it may be read off the enormous 'Tootsie Roll Pop' that shields the genitals of the Italian-American body-builder Charles Atlas. Hamilton's collage is likely a condemnation, rather than an affirmation, of British post-war enthusiasm for consumer goods, proposals for rationalized urban housing, and the notion of the leisure society. If Hamilton's work, as art historian Thomas Crow argues, proposes a topography of the dark side of the Independent Group's 'aesthetics of plenty', then it would occupy an opposing position with respect to American Pop art of the early 1960s.[13] Despite its reputation as an inventory of visual and textual elements that anticipates the iconography of American Pop art of the 1960s, the appropriated images of consumer goods, contemporary advertising, comic books, Hollywood and hyper-eroticized male and female bodies found in Hamilton's collage offer a very different sense of the future of Western affluence. When we think of Pop Art, we perhaps tend to have other images in mind; works of art that are more vividly Americanized and less ambiguous in their embrace of popular visual culture as a resource of artistic expression.

Regardless of the ideological weakness of the Independent Group and its failure to raise a stronger critique of the state-supported consumer society of the later 1950s, Paolozzi and Hamilton redescribed art as a means to depict the continuum of visual culture, embracing high art, science fiction, mass-produced forms of entertainment and kitsch. The desire in art to shift the register from the appearance of the aesthetic to that of the social also took root most strongly in France, Italy and Northern Europe. In these contexts, one finds some of the most extreme reactions in art to post-war consumer culture.

Working in France, Jacques Villeglé (b. 1926) and Raymond Hains (1926–2005) sought to redescribe collage through the use of the found material of street posters. The practice of pasting new posters over old, as a means to renew the advertising or to aggressively compete for precious wall space, provided Villeglé and Hains (and later, the Italian artist Mimo Rotella) with a rich vein of materials with which to fashion their spectacular denunciations of commodity culture and the unwelcome Americanization of French popular culture (illus. 48). As early as 1949, Villeglé and

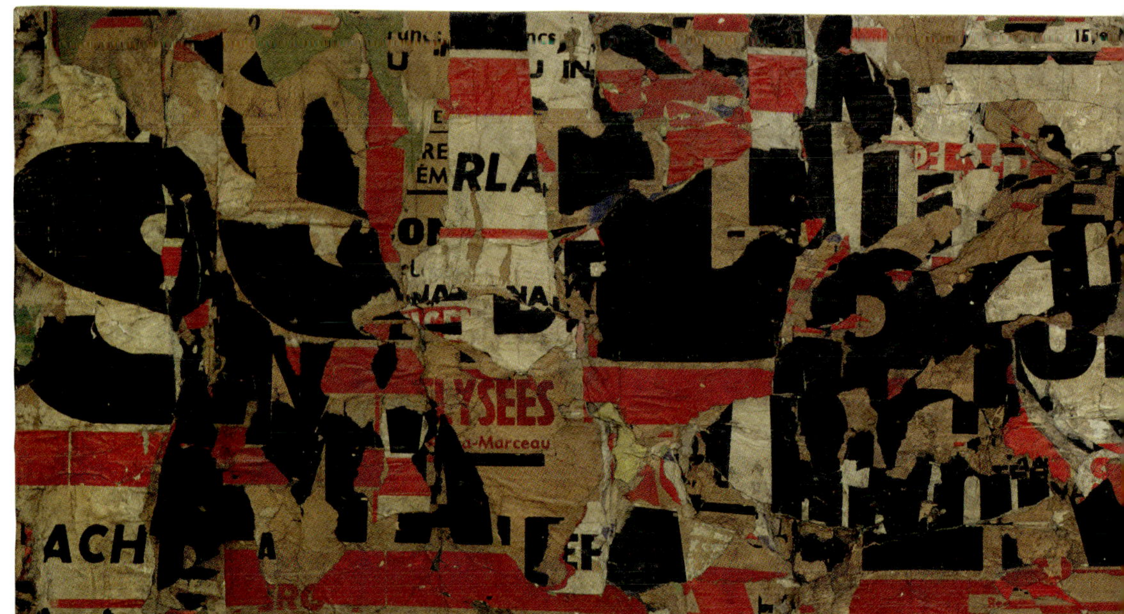

47 Jacques Villeglé and Raymond Hains, *Ach Alma Manétro*, 1949, collage.

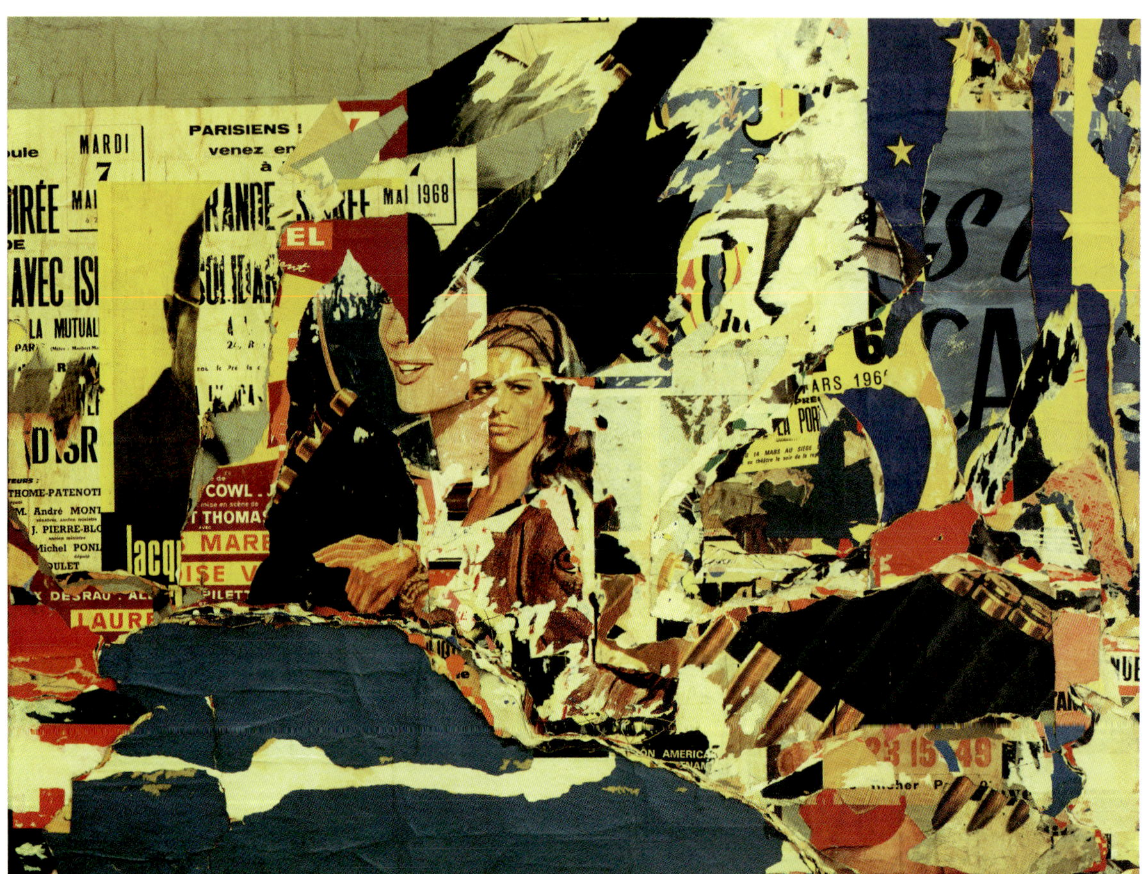

48 Jacques Villeglé, *122 rue du temple*, 1968, collage.

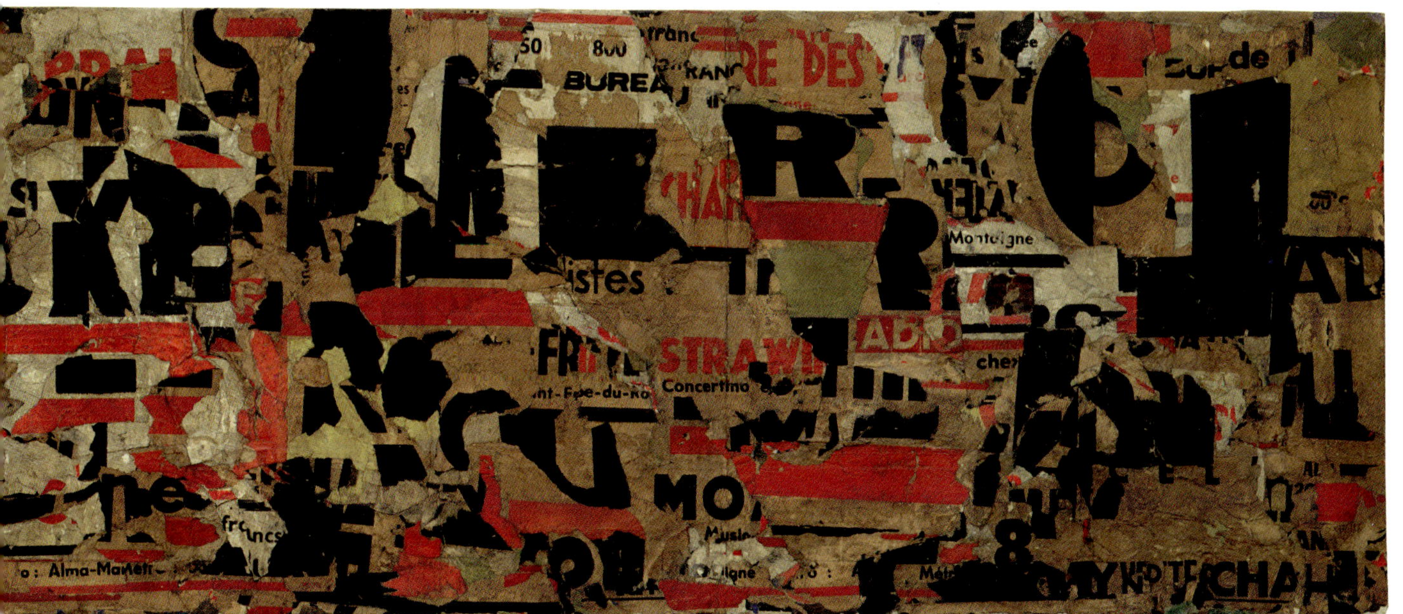

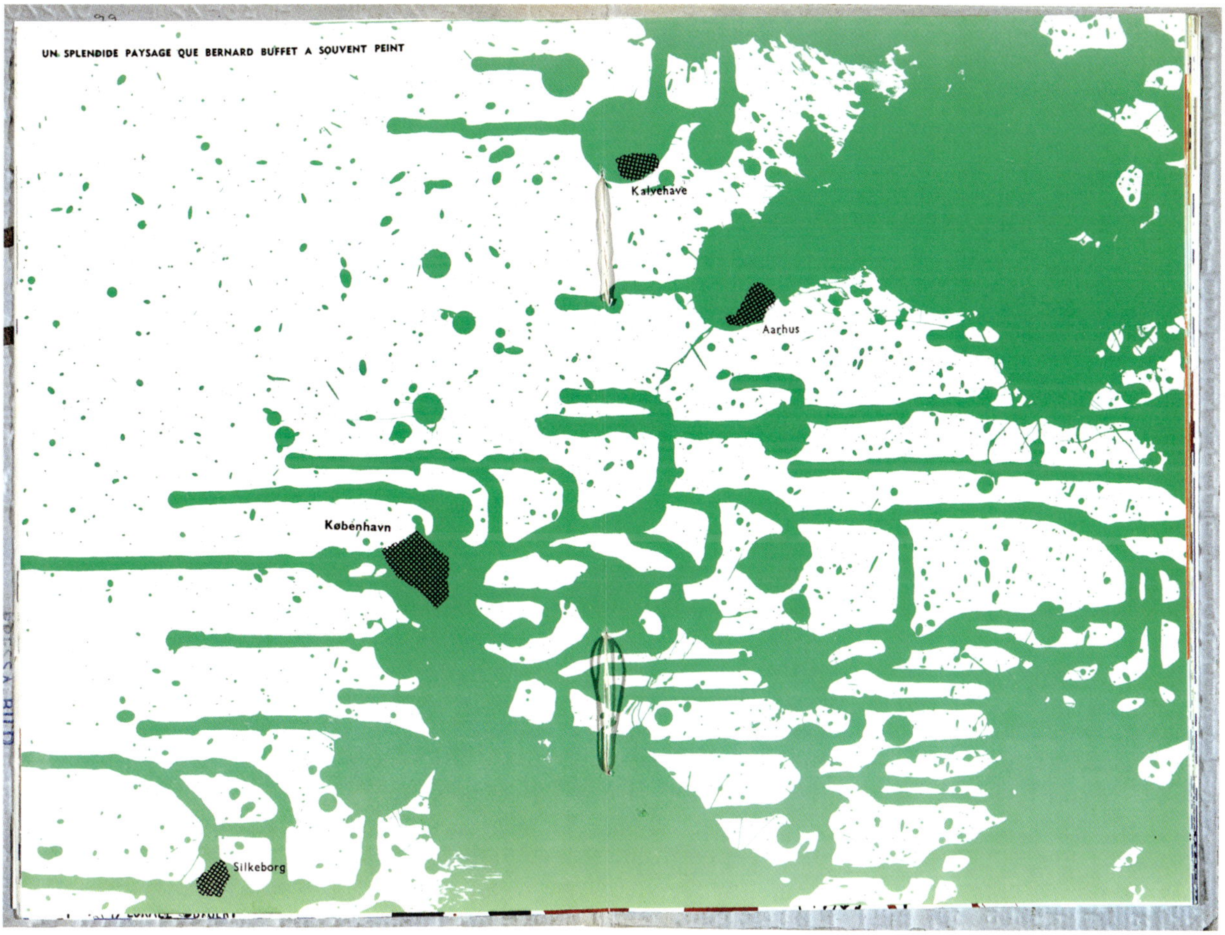

49 Asger Jorn and Guy Debord, *Fin de Copenhague*, 1957, a collage of text and images, poured over with lithographic ink.

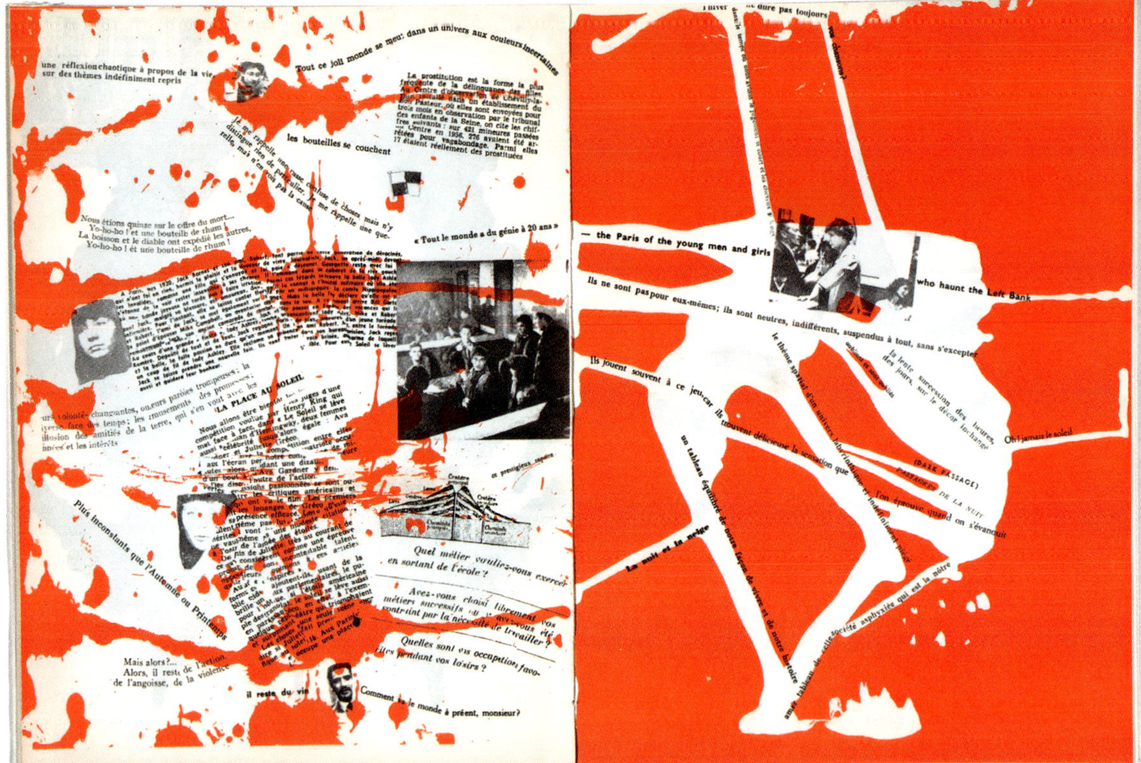

50 Guy Debord and Asger Jorn, *Mémoires*, 1959.

Hains collaborated on an enormous *décollage*, *Ach Alma Manétro* (illus. 47). In 1959 the *décollage* artists Villeglé, Hains and François Dufrêne were invited to exhibit their work in the inaugural Paris Biennial. The following year, this trio – alongside Yves Klein, Arman, Martial Raysse, Daniel Spoerri and Jean Tinguely – were included in the initial constitution by critic Pierre Restany of a neo-avant-garde movement, dubbed 'Nouveau Réalisme' (New Realism).

The works of the *décollage* artists were filled with a cacophony of unexpected imagery; a composite resulting from the random juxtapositions of word and image that emerged as each section of poster hoarding was selectively lacerated. The chaotic overall image is disorienting and was intended to disrupt the sensible interlocking of image and text. Text emerging in this way becomes a thing within the picture; one thing among many and just as forgettable.

'BASEBALL OR AUTOMATIC WRITING, WHAT DOES IT MATTER?'[14]

In the context of a symbolic disruption of the wheels of commerce, Guy Debord in 1952 split from Lettrism and went on to form a breakaway group, the Lettriste International, with Michèle Bernstein and Gil J. Wolman. The new group published *Potlatch*, a bulletin to disseminate ideas about new relations between art and everyday life, such as the *dérive* – the aimless excursion – and *détournement* – a kind of subversive plagiarism.[15] The publication's title refers to the ceremony of property redistribution and destruction practised by indigenous peoples of the Pacific Northwest coast and serves as a powerful metaphor for the more radical anti-consumerist analyses that would inform the ideology of the Situationist International.

As Debord wrote retrospectively in 1955 of their differences with Lettrism, 'our business is not a literary school, a new form of expression, or a modernism. We are concerned with a way of living that will take place through explorations and provisional formulations, which are themselves only exercised in a provisional way.'[16] During the late 1950s, the Danish artist Asger Jorn (1914–1974) and Debord collaborated on the production of two books: *Fin de Copenhague* (1957) and *Mémoires* (1959). Both were characterized by vibrant drips and splashes of colour that either obscure or support the texts or images.

The publication of *Fin de Copenhague* (illus. 49) marks the beginning of a period of Jorn's collaboration with Debord and the latter's role in the founding of the Situationist International. Jorn and Debord are reputed to have put together the book's 32 collaged pages in a haze of intoxication, mixing items sourced from a random collection of consumer magazines and newspapers. After print-

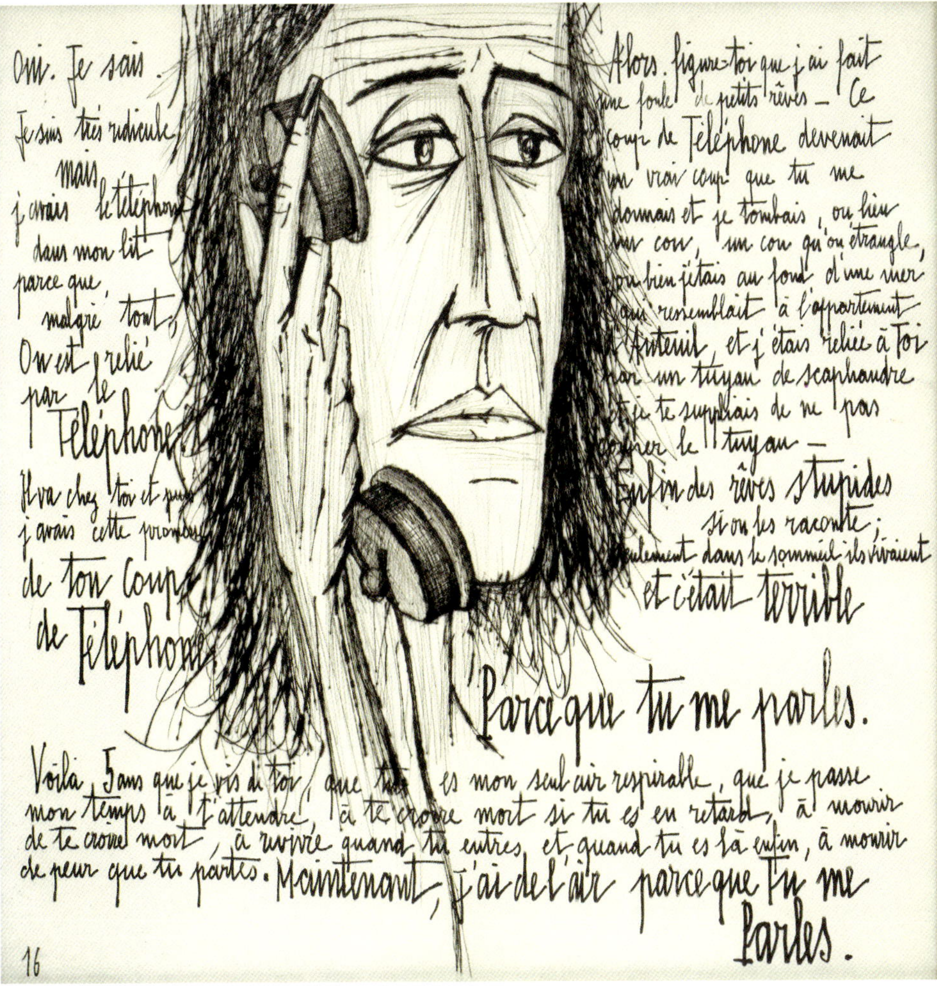

51 Bernard Buffet, *La Voix humaine*, 1957, ink on paper.

ed plates were produced from photographic negatives made of the collages, the plates themselves were subjected to a barrage of India ink. One double-page spread, showing skeins of green ink running horizontally across the page, is captioned with a text that reads: 'A splendid landscape that Bernard Buffet often painted.' The place names Copenhagen, Göteborg and Aachen are visible between the drips, suggesting an inverted map of Northern Europe.

Often described as a 'psychogeography' of Debord's thought informing the Lettrist International, *Mémoires* (illus. 50) is renowned for its cover made of heavy sandpaper; presumably a device with which to abrade and damage any book placed in its proximity. Principally the work of Debord, *Mémoires* is as close to a *bildungsroman* as Lettrist principles allow. The 64 pages are divided into three sections, each signifying one month of the period June 1952 through September 1953, during which time Debord's work, especially his imageless film *Hurlements en faveur de Sade*, was increasingly criticized by conservative factions within Lettrism and the artist distanced himself from Isou's programme. Later, Debord would retrieve some of the intellectual resources developed during the formation of the Lettrist International through a demonstration of the *dérive* and *détournement*. *Fin de Copenhague* and *Mémoires* stand as the antithesis to the *livre d'artiste* and represent a challenge to the form and content of other word and image works of the period, such as Bernard Buffet's 1957 reinterpretation of Jean Cocteau's 1932 one-act play *La Voix humaine* (illus. 51).

Buffet's stylized treatment of figurative subjects using a succession of slashing strokes to define contours and to express an evacuated presence must have been regarded by Debord as an embarrassing holdover from the late 1940s. Against the sharply polemical inventions of Debord and Jorn, calling for the creation of new emotions, Buffet's work seemed to be a mannered rendering of privation and angst; a fantasy of existential dread, neurosis and individualism that was no longer appropriate to the moment and certainly could no

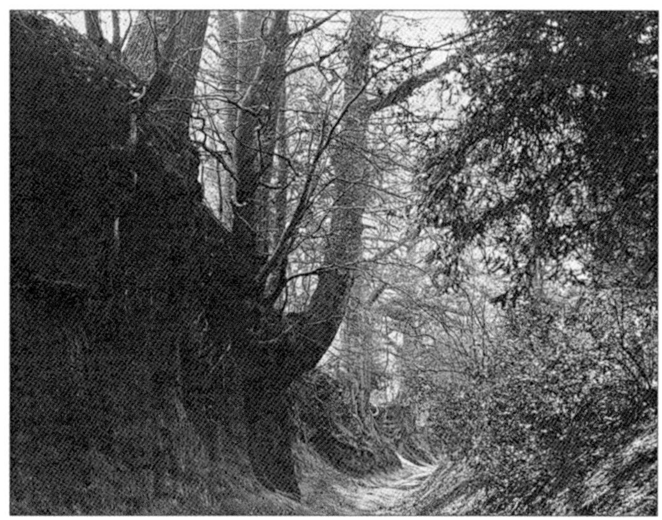

52 Hamish Fulton, *The Pilgrims Way*, 1971, photoprint and letterpress.

longer be represented except as bathos. Cocteau's melodrama describes an intimate human relation as a doomed enterprise. The plot is the final telephonic meeting – interrupted due to repeated technical failures of the Parisian telephone system – between a woman and her lover, who is about to leave her. Such a theme would be unthinkable for Debord and his collaborators, whose focus on everyday life depended on the elevation of free play and the unimpeded search for what the group termed 'new emotions'.

Beyond the unacceptable theme, however, one must consider how the self-managed artist's book and its counterpart in the artist-published bulletin responded to an important political and cultural need recognized by Debord, Jorn and others at the time. The desire to collapse avant-garde art and revolutionary politics stood at the base of the Situationist International programme. From the important early experiments in 'psychogeography' by British artist Ralph Rumney (see illus. 4) to Jorn's 'modification' paintings of the late 1950s and early '60s, the notion that pervaded artistic practices aligned to the Situationist International grasped art as a socially critical practice fashioned from the existing visual and intellectual resources of urban culture, rather than an inspired calling, expressive of human verities and essentially the work of isolated, alienated human beings.

The works of these artists also helped to establish a new lexicon of avant-garde stratagems, many of which were elaborated by artists of the 1970s and '80s. One finds echoes of Rumney's 'Psychogeography of Venice' (1958) – a photographic record of the artist's overt surveillance of the American Beat author Allan Ansen, referred to as 'A' in the captions – in the work of Sophie Calle. From the peripatetic works of Stanley Brouwn, the documented walks of Richard Long and Hamish Fulton (illus. 52), to the 'narco-tourism' of Francis Alÿs, the strong precedents of the Situationist International have undergone numerous revisions and thereby suffered their own recoding as art. At the same time, the work of later artists like Brouwn, Long, Fulton and Alÿs is not entirely circumscribed by the museum. If we grasp this class of works – commonly presented in the form of photograph and text – as models of activity rather than aesthetic objects, it becomes an invitation to the spectator to withdraw from the gallery environment and to experience the exhilaration of the outside world. In keeping with the legacy of the

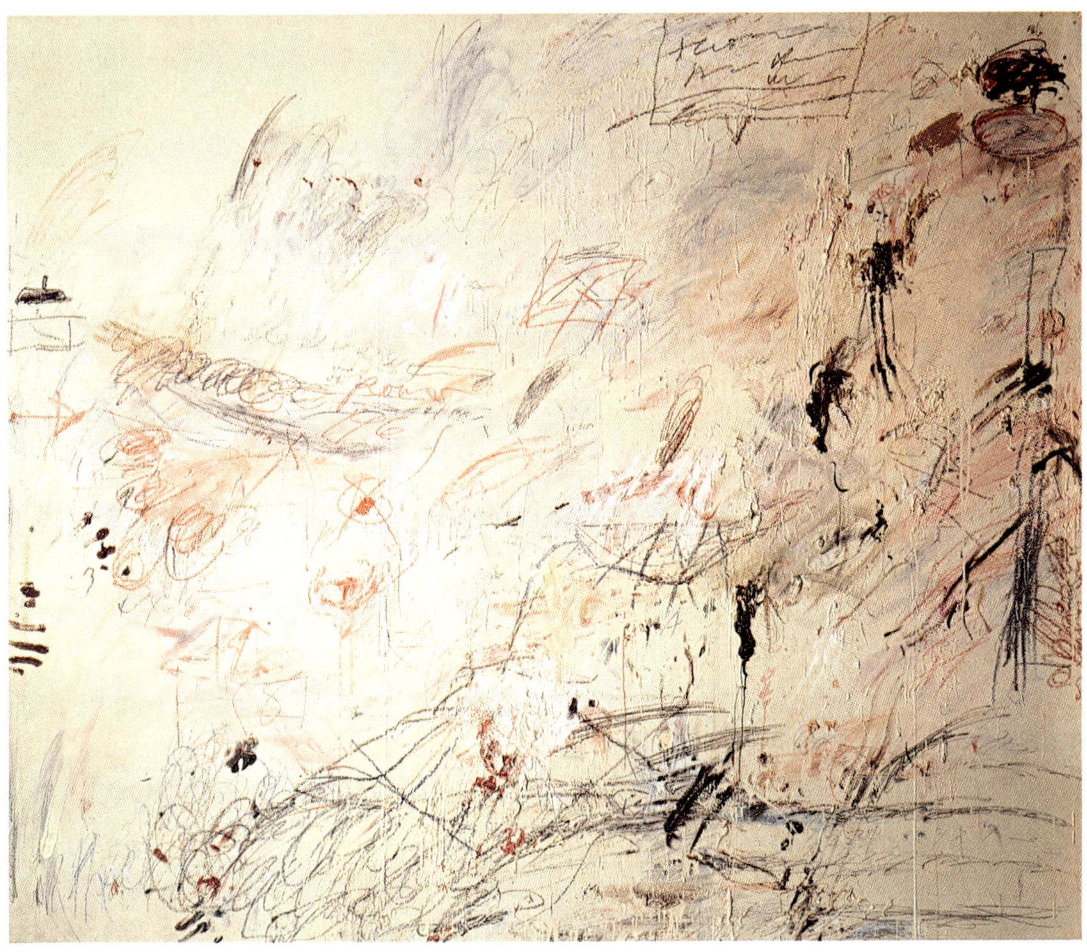

53 Cy Twombly, *Untitled*, 1961, oil, pencil and crayon on canvas.

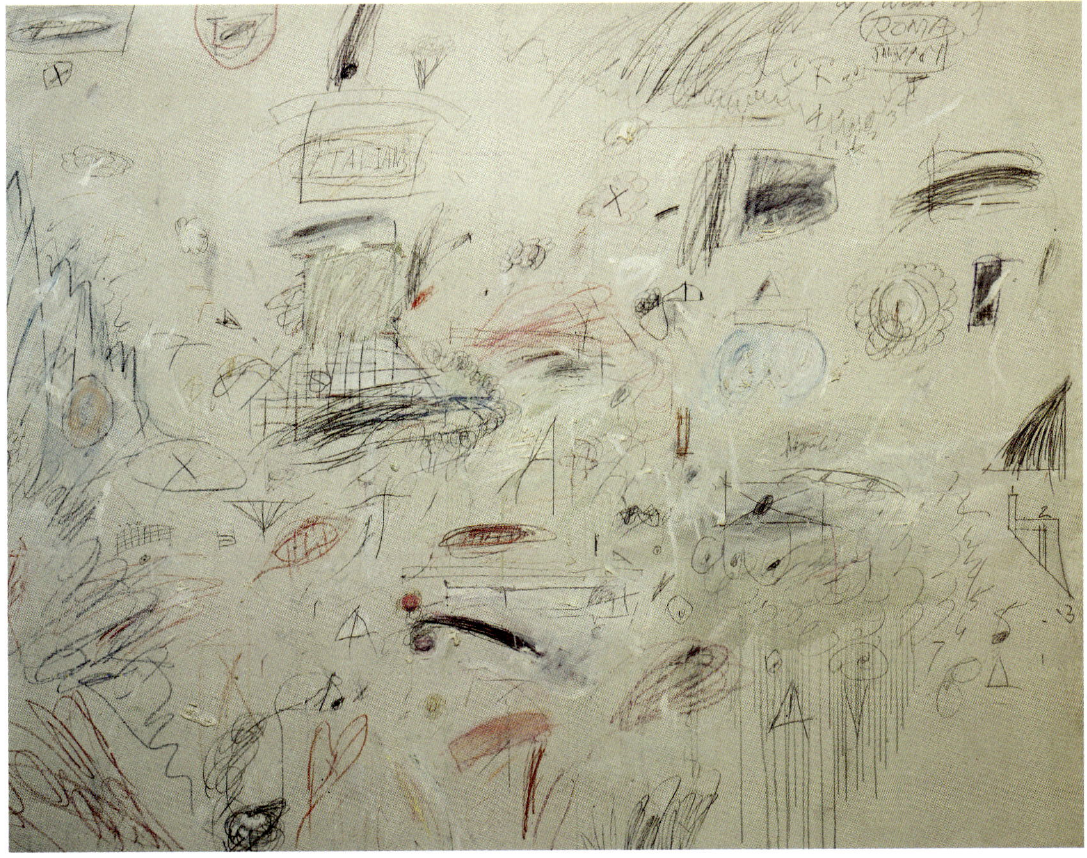

54 Cy Twombly, *The Italians*, 1961, oil, pencil and crayon on canvas.

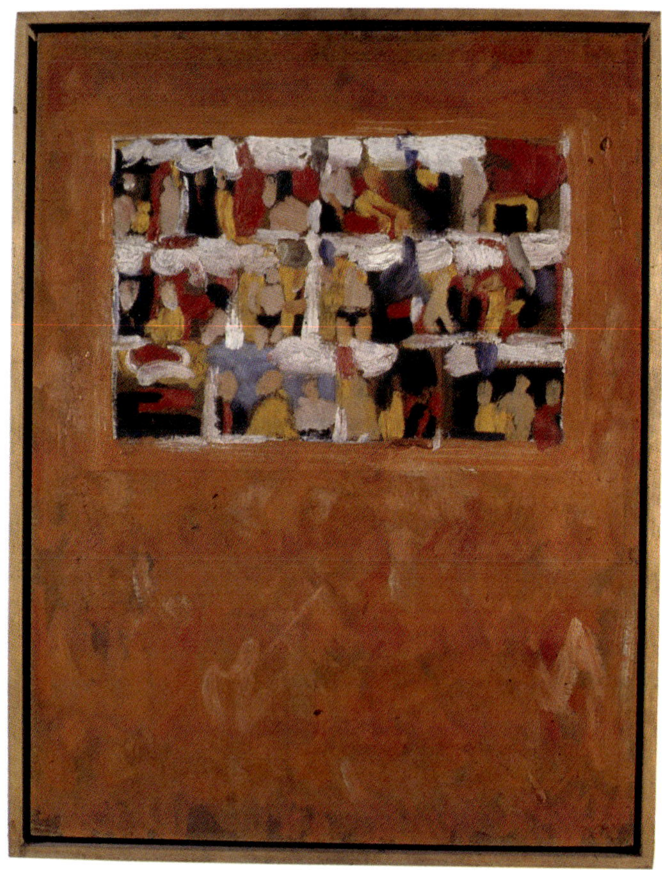

55 Jasper Johns, *Alley Oop*, 1958, oil and encaustic on paper mounted on canvas.

Situationist *dérive*, the 'outside' may be constituted through one's contact with the creative disorder of the city. Alternatively, an earlier Romantic tradition of landscape may be evoked through an account of a walk in the countryside.

SCRATCHING, SMUDGING AND SMEARING; CHILDISH, IRREGULAR AND CLUMSY[17]

Shorn of its political intentions and valued for other qualities, imagery drawn from a variety of mass-produced or vernacular sources can be viewed as either mild satire or a celebration of the very values and mode of social life reviled by the Situationists and other artists of the European avant garde. For artists working in the US during the 1950s, the influence of Abstract Expressionism and the domestic repression of the left amounted to another kind of tension. For Cy Twombly (b. 1928), the attraction of the Antique was a pretext through which to frame an anti-expressive visual language; a practice that shuns representation and embraces performance, thereby short-circuiting the tiresome quest for meaning in the (perhaps meaningful) detail. In the words of Rosalind Krauss:

> [G]raffiti makes clear that the idea of the painting as the mirror of the painter – an idea suggested by Harold Rosenberg's theory of Action Painting – is an impossible utopia, the dream of an art of presence. Even as graffiti's graphic lash strikes in the present, it registers itself as past, a mark whose violence dismembers the very idea of the image in the mirror, the whole body, Narcissus. Graffiti's character is to strike against form, ensuring a field in which the only way the image of the body can survive is as part-object, a concatenation of obscene emblemata, the genital splatter that Twombly went on to enact in his Roman paintings from the early '60s.[18]

Twombly's decision in 1957 to establish himself as an expatriate American artist in Italy was an atypical response to the rise of New York as the dominant force in modern art. Twombly's move encapsulates a rejection of the artistic self-image cultivated by Abstract Expressionism. Twombly's fixation with the graffiti of Rome led him to an indexical form of mark-making that was just detached enough from the self to produce a strangely cold vision of painterly virtuosity (illus. 53). Handwriting in Twombly's work may be seen as indexical of the artist who inscribed it; the

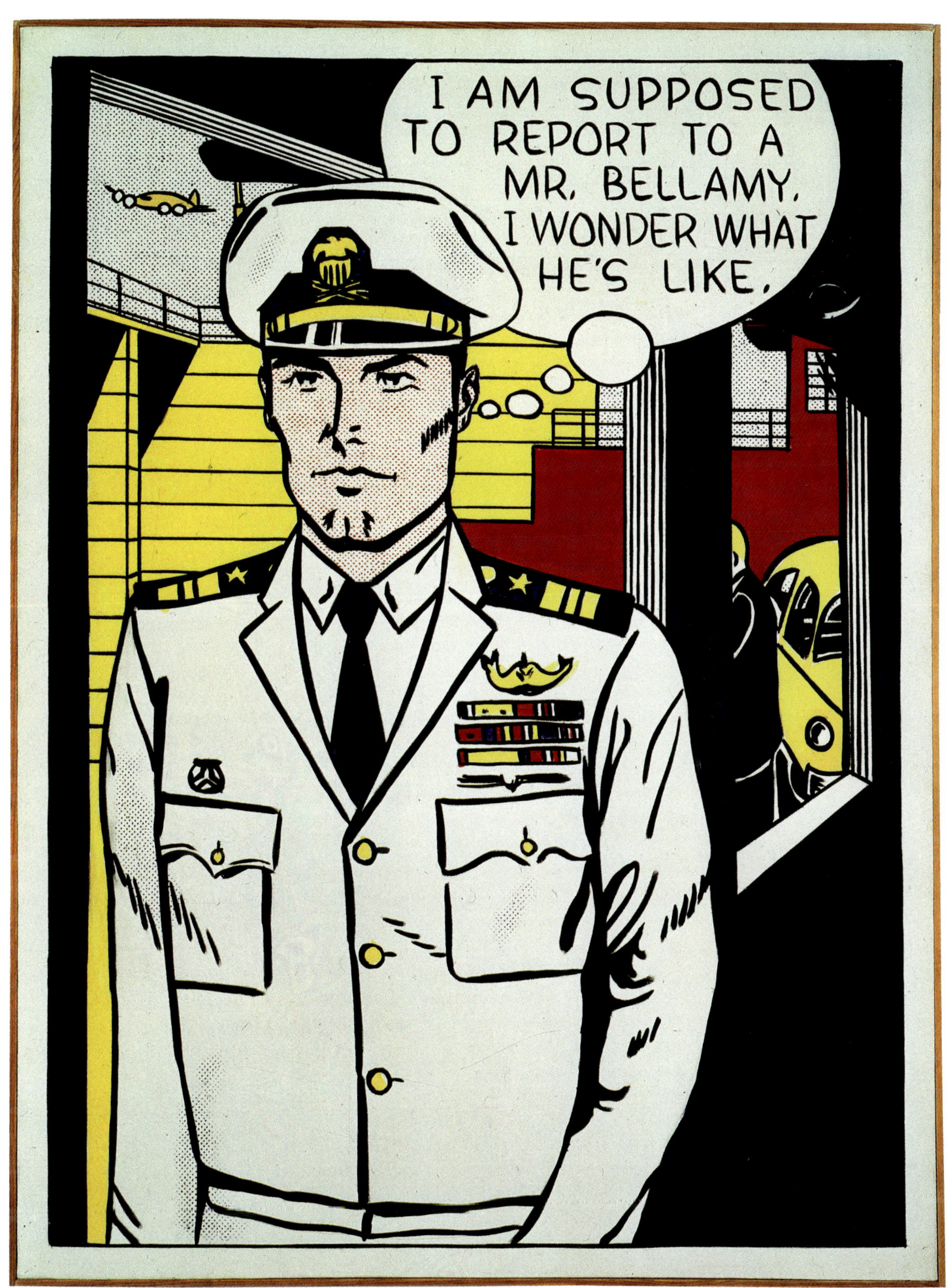

56 Roy Lichtenstein, *Mr Bellamy*, 1961, oil on canvas.

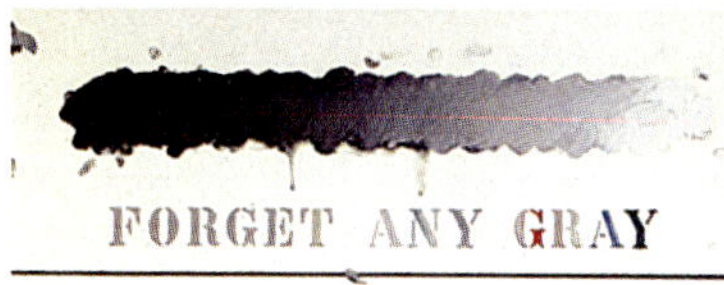

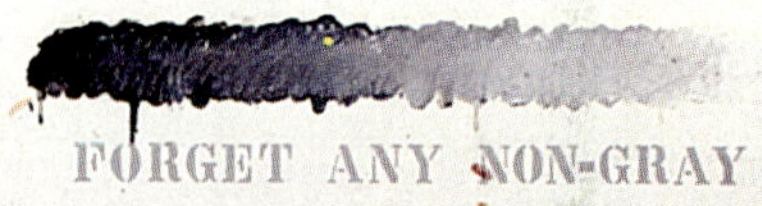

57 Arakawa and Madeline Gins, panel from *The Mechanism of Meaning*, 1963–73.

inscription represents 'nothing' but signifies a great deal. The informality of the chalkboard like scrawl promulgated by Twombly is impish in comparison; playful, rather than 'primitive' and heroic (illus. 54). Some would even say 'gauche'.[19]

'FIRST, I WOULD PICK A CARTOON...; THEN, THE "VERTIGINOUS SADNESS" OF A REPLICATED CLICHÉ'[20]

The fascination of comics for art critics and historians may have to do with their intermediate position between the categories of word and image. Comics are capable of presenting other worlds in which the philosophical conundrums of our existence, like the problem of other minds, are dissolved. Comics also supply fertile ground for the analysis and exposition of the puzzles of representation and meaning.[21] But the most common value attached to the comic in the context of the 1950s and 1960s is its association with 'low' – which is to say, mass – culture. The newspaper comic strip and the comic book had been naturalized as signs of cultural difference long before North American artists like Jasper Johns, Roy Lichtenstein and Andy Warhol had appropriated them. Johns's early painting of an Alley Oop comic-strip which eliminates text from the dialogue balloons provided him with a model for the construction of a painting whose meaning remains elliptical despite the presence of recognizable objects and inscribed language (illus. 55). As Johns remarked in a 1973 interview, 'my work is in part concerned with the possibility of things being taken for one thing or another – with questionable areas of identification and usage and procedure – with thought rather than with secure things.'[22]

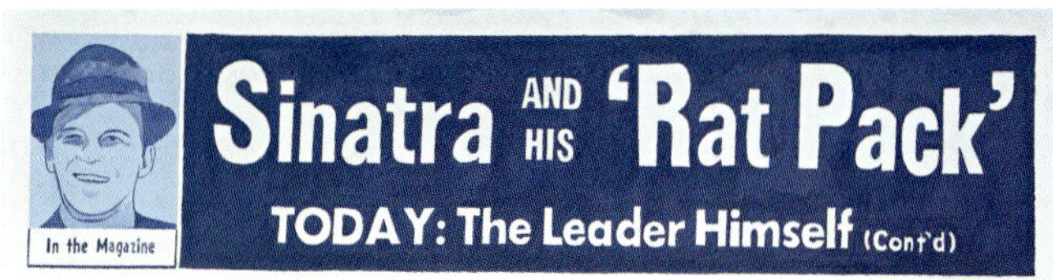

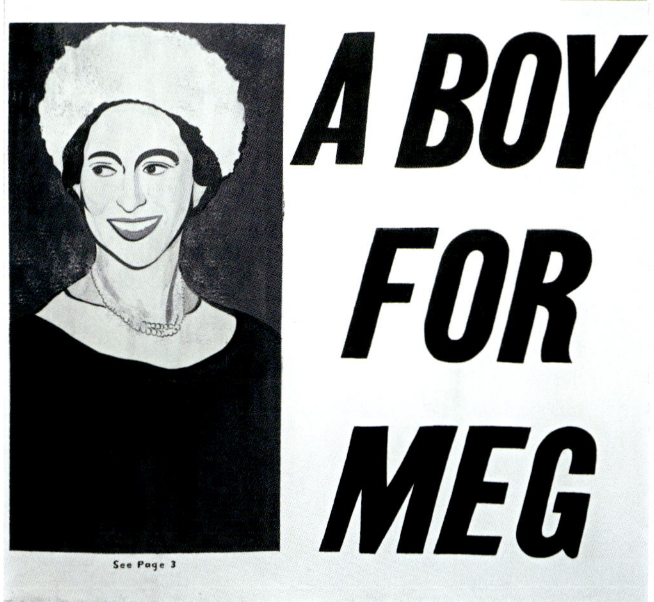

58 Andy Warhol, *A Boy for Meg*, 1961, oil on canvas.

Lichtenstein and Warhol, however, appropriated the individual cell of the comicbook for different reasons. Faced with the competition of Lichtenstein, Warhol's use of comicbook and newspaper comicstrip images was short-lived, but it did seem to provide him with an entry into the realm of representing other aspects of a naturalized conception of everyday life, such as the front page of tabloid newspapers, Campbell's soup cans and popular celebrities (illus. 56, 58).

Warhol's adoption of serigraphy – an inexpensive commercial art printing process used for signage and posters – foregrounded a primitive type of mechanical reproduction that enabled the artist to forego the need for drawing. Warhol's customization of identical silkscreen images – the characteristic swathes of non-local colour that appeared to be so casually and indiscriminately applied to portraits of Marilyn Monroe and Mao Zedong – yields an *image* of art that reads simultaneously as hot and cool. Lichtenstein's chosen technique, far more handcrafted than serigraphy, appeared to produce a more deathly icon of self-conscious American materialism.

The success of Lichtenstein's paintings is owed to more than the artist's judicious selection of individual comic book cells. These were scrupulously traced, cropped and simplified in order to heighten a sense of anonymity of the finished work. Lichtenstein, defending himself against the charge of plagiarism voiced loudly by professional cartoonists, repeatedly referred to his studio practices as the locus of his art. Using simple tools, Lichtenstein devised a means whereby he could convincingly reproduce the Ben Day dot patterns characteristic of the commercial printing process of half-tone reproduction; a stencil fashioned from a sheet of perforated aluminum was sufficient to lay down on canvas a field of precisely uniform dots. But the process of image revision was crucial to Lichtenstein's ownership of the work.

One may argue that commercial artists undertake their practice with the same dedication to craftsmanship and the same desire to make their work their own. But this is not the point of the significance of comic strip imagery to Lichtenstein's art. Lichtenstein's early attempts to render popular imagery hint at what was at stake; these are pictures of popular comic strip figures *in the style of* Willem de Kooning. The artist's decision to make his art out of isolated comic-strip cells may evoke portentous claims of cultural levelling but the

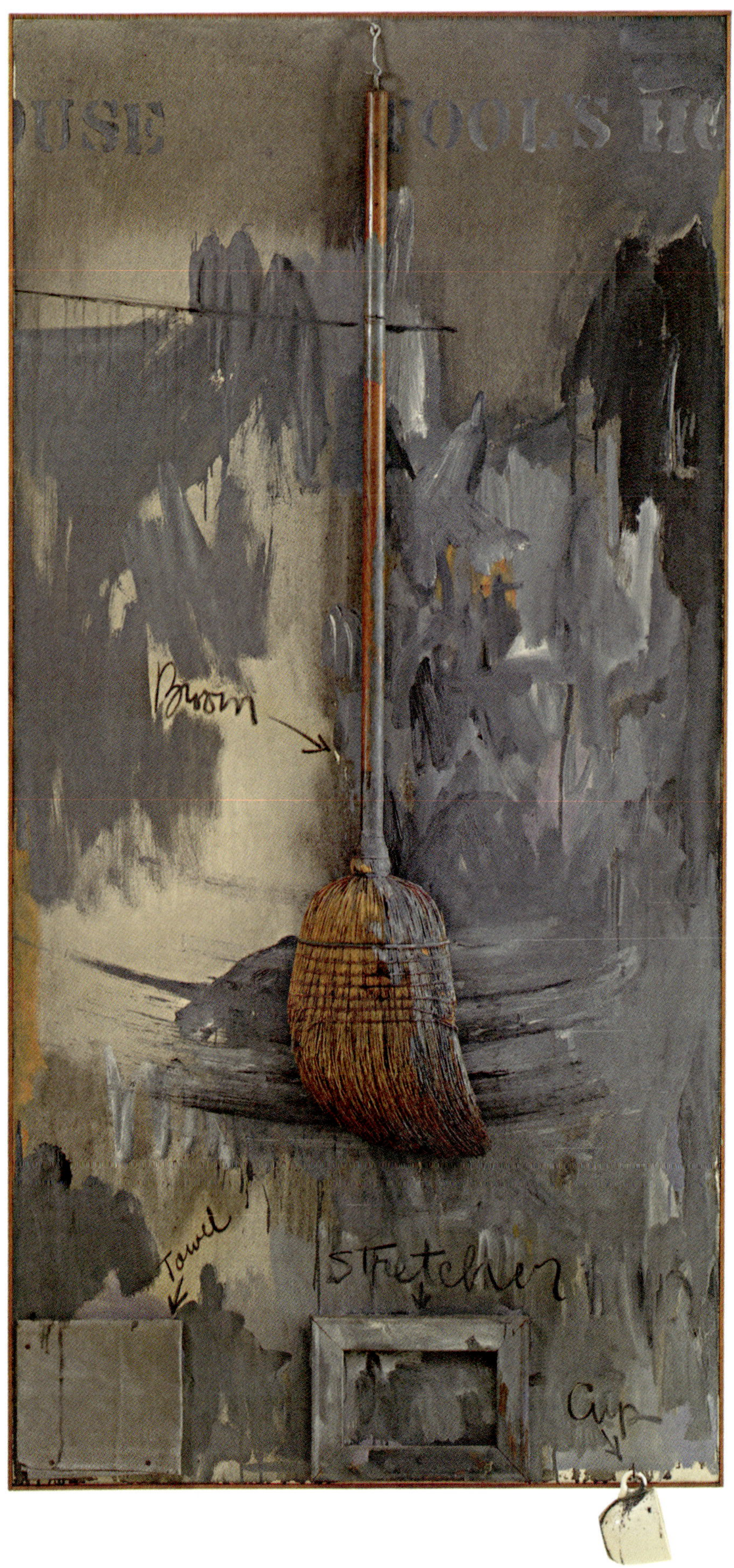

59 Jasper Johns, *Fool's House*, 1962, oil on canvas with objects.

principal effect is the destruction of the narrative complexity of the original material. The single cell is less than a detail; it is a fragment, and it is not yet meaningful as a narrative, but certainly adequate as a picture. Lichtenstein's violation of the very sequence from which the individual comic-strip cell derives its meaning turns out to be a paradoxical act of recovery and effacement. While much has been made of the dialogue in Pop art between high and low, it would be difficult for me to consider Lichtenstein's art to be an unqualified endorsement of popular visual culture. The artist's work of the early 1960s represents a powerful visual summary of one class of popular imagery; yet it does so in the name of art and offers us *fragments as icons* or, as the artist noted, portraits of clichés. What Lichtenstein and other Pop artists achieved was a means to trump the visual rhetoric of Abstract Expressionism. By the time this had been accomplished, many more instances of word and image drawn from the common culture would figure in the pursuit of artistic ambition.

IMAGE, TEXT AND SOMETIMES, BODY

'The Mechanism of Meaning' is the title of a complex, ambitious and on-going project initiated by Arakawa and Madeline Gins in 1963 (illus. 57). The subject of this project is the nature and habit of mind, where mind and matter are conceived as equal determinants in the sphere of human life. Throughout a series of panels combining word and image, meaning is presented in all its multiplicity as the outcome of interactions between the individual and the world. These interactions are presented as an outline that serves to conceptually organize the many elements of the work. The outline presents a number of non-standard interpretations of meaning, expressed using neologisms that are reminiscent of the strange mixture of poetry and technocratic language found in the classic Modernist manifestos of the avant garde of the early twentieth century.

The contents of this first series (1963–73) are numbered one through nineteen, the subsequent series being reorganized around a more condensed system of sixteen headings. The panels are diagrammatic in style; the text is stencil-like (although there are also handwritten entries). The panels combine text, image and objects, as well. The imagery may be painted or photographic. What we see are elaboratedly designed instructions, presenting the spectator with simple tasks or problems to solve.

Arakawa and Gins began their project at the moment when Fluxus first made its presence felt in New York; the strategy they employ has some resonance with the artworks collected by George Macuinas in *Fluxus 1* (1964, the first *Fluxyearbox*) and *Fluxkit* (1965–6). The difference, of course, is that 'The Mechanism of Meaning' is presented in the form of a series of conventional paintings, rather than on a series of, say, index cards, as George Brecht did in his 'event scores'. The relation of this project to the aims of Fluxus or Conceptual art seems strained; blocked, perhaps, due to the very means by which Arakawa and Gins seek to communicate with the spectator and effect her transformation. The panels simply do not extend a convincing invitation to the spectator to become anything more than a compliant actor.

How might we explain this contradiction? It might be more informative to consider 'The Mechanism of Meaning' as a response to the image-object-text constructions produced by Jasper Johns; one that tries to literalize the aesthetic achievements of Johns without regard to the semantic properties of the works themselves, but which may, nevertheless, harbour some of the semantic models of the original. In other words, the *look* of Johns's heterogeneous canvases is redescribed as a Fluxus funhouse, with some *errors of transcription*.

Despite the presence of text, painting-constructions by Johns such as *Diver* (1962) and *Fool's House* (illus. 59) are not meant to read as analogies or representations. Even in *Fool's House*, in which words function as labels for the objects to which they are obviously attached, no sensible narrative is to be recovered through a decoding of the elements. One item of text – notably, the title of the painting itself – is stencilled at the top of the canvas and characteristically broken up to suggest a continuation of the space of the painting beyond the margins of the canvas part of the work. As the title of the painting, it is also a kind of label, but in *Fool's House* it is also a part of the painted field. The critic Philip Fisher argues persuasively that

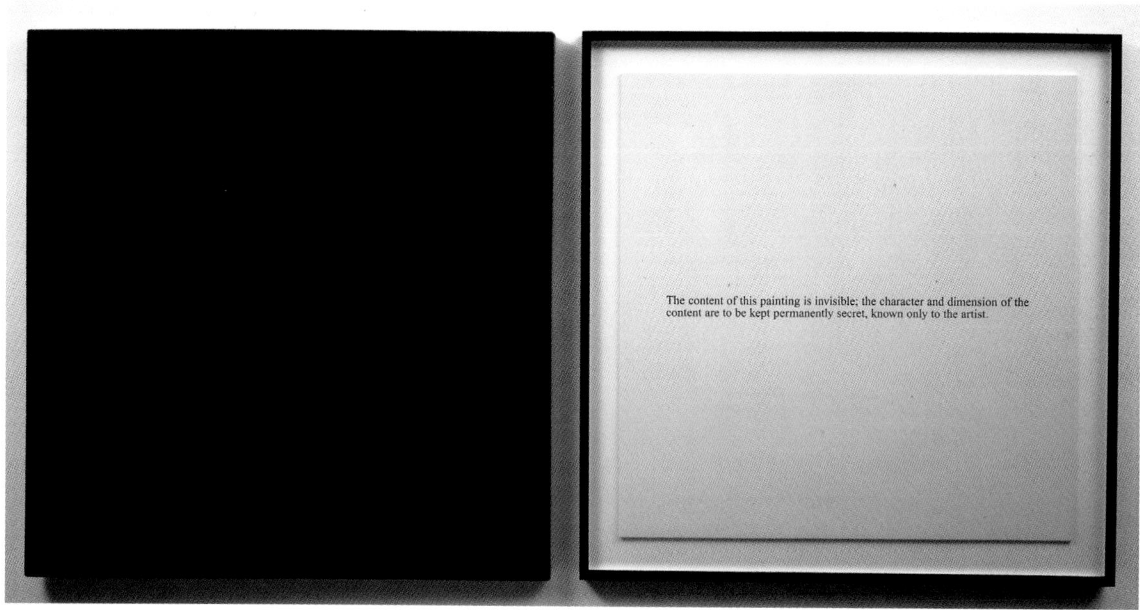

60 Mel Ramsden, *Secret Painting*, 1967–8, Liquitex on canvas and printed texts.

these works take on the character of an autonomous space, like a room, in which one finds a number of heterogeneous objects in proximity. The condition that this arrangement mimics, and therefore sets out to embrace, is that of the museum of fine art. That is, the space in which different orders of objects and different modes of meaning mingle and impinge on each other. The key element in leading our thinking in this direction is the presence of text and object in the painting. The text presents us with a dilemma: Do we 'read' it? Or 'look' at it? Or 'follow' it, as one would follow road markings or directional arrows or other symbols? Fisher writes:

> The strategies of effacement and aggregation that occur as content within Johns's works – along with the creation of a script for looking at the works that draws on, while rivalling, the set of formulas for looking that are culturally untroubled within the modern period – make up, in combination, an appeal within the work addressed to the future… . These futures all concern the work's own aftermath. They make up a set of instructions for how it might be used. There is a final museum strategy within Johns's paintings, one that might be called a cultural strategy, because it involves an inventory of resources, a display of possibilities for representation.[23]

'The Mechanism of Meaning' aspires to be encyclopaedic, but its content is full of comic elements and the action, so to speak, takes place outside the frame. The work does not pretend to offer the full measure of profound self-reflexivity to be experienced in the work of Johns. It tends to mention concepts like 'irony', 'ambiguity' and 'paradox' rather than deploy them in the making of the work. These modes of meaning are among the first that Arakawa and Gins identify in their project outline, under the heading of 'presentation of bases for selection'; an informal bit of advice to the viewer that suggests an entry into the project. Taken as a whole, the projects display a degree of redundancy; the participant-viewer is meant to explore the terrain of meaning in a variety of ways. There is even a section titled 'review and self-criticism', introducing a pause to remind us how important the literalization of self-consciousness was to artists of the 1960s even if only as a ground for satire.

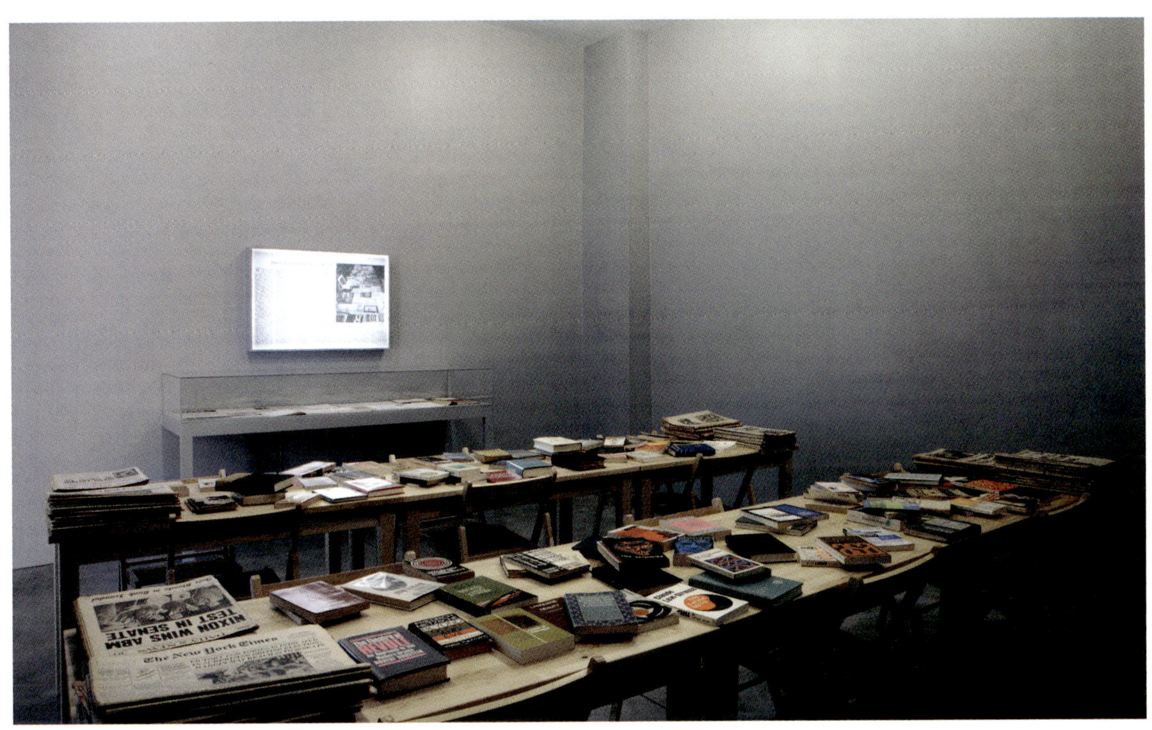

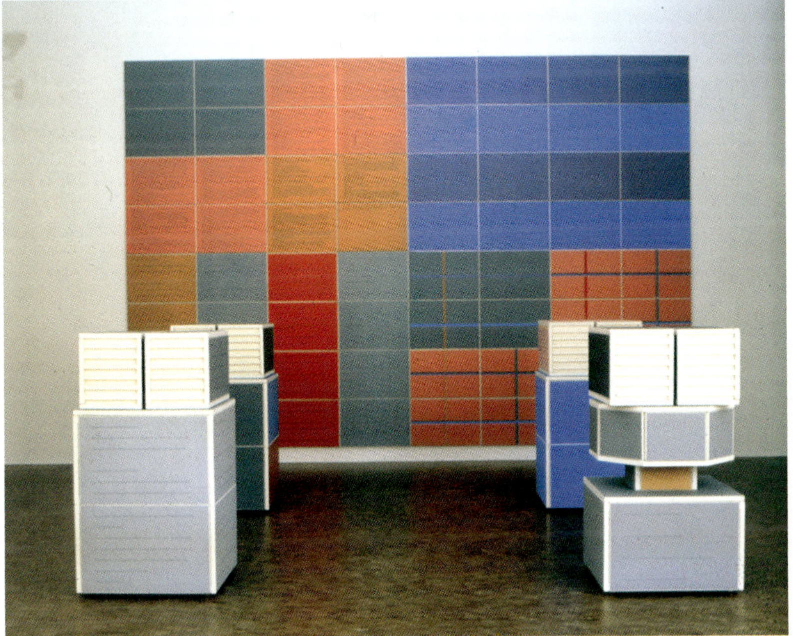

61 Joseph Kosuth, *Information Room (Special Investigation)*, 1970. chairs, tables, various reading matter.

62 Art & Language, *Index: Wrongs Healed in Official Hope*, 1998–9, alogram on canvas over plywood and mixed media.

63 Roman Opalka, *Detail*, 1965, acrylic on canvas.

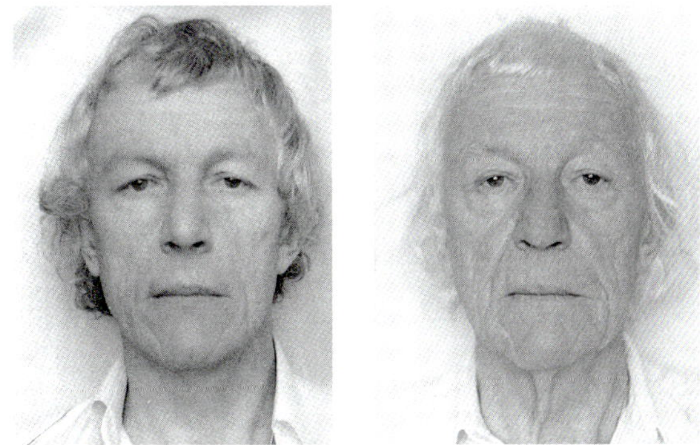

64 Roman Opalka, Self-portraits.

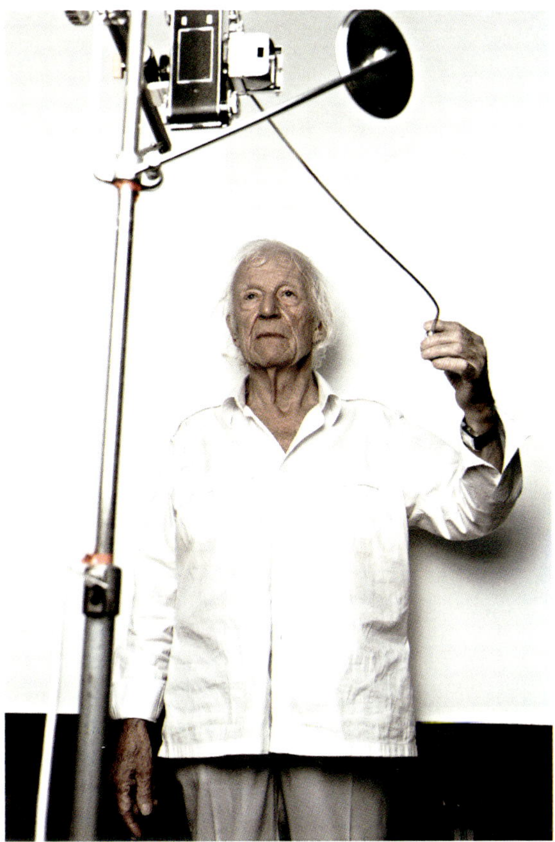

65 Roman Opalka.

'The Mechanism of Meaning' was the founding collaborative project for Arakawa and Gins. Commentators have interpreted this project as epistolary, suggesting that they may be read as letters addressed from the artists to the viewer-participant. But the historical precedent of Johns's practice inclines us to appreciate more fully the dual nature of 'The Mechanism of Meaning' as paintings that employ word and the image of text. It is perhaps this more significant class of paintings that critics had in mind when they likened the work of Arakawa and Gins to a display of signs, or 'a maelstrom of signification that goes nowhere but into itself'.[24]

INFORMATION/DISINFORMATION

There are iconoclastic works produced during the late 1960s that we can point to that reflect actively on the conventional relationship between a picture and what it stands for. The numerous works by Mel Ramsden titled *Secret Painting* are one such example (illus. 60). In this series, produced around 1967–8 in New York in the company of the Australian artist Ian Burn, Ramsden presents us with a black monochrome and an accompanying text; often a 'certificate of authenticity' that guarantees the content of the adjoining monochrome to be known only to the artist and / or his co-conspirator. The black monochrome is not a picture of anything, but it is a performative image insofar as the actual structure of the painting is a smaller black rectangle within a larger one. At least this is what we are led to believe. If this is the 'secret' of the *Secret Painting*, then we must conclude that the nothingness of the monochrome is not exactly 'nothing'. Looking, as Ad Reinhardt remarked, is not as simple as it looks. The accompanying text invites us to consider such a prospect; its purpose is to make the easy identification of image and text problematic in the extreme. In so doing, it opens up an entire world of possible relations between image and text in art. Roman Opalka physically separates image and text, rendering each in two simulatenous bodies of work. Opalka's well-known painterly performance of counting sits alongside an open-ended series of daily photographic self-portraits (illus. 63, 64, 65). Considered as a pair, these works remain an ascetic, unforgiving record of the passing of time; literally, in the case of the painted integers, a measure of one person's mortality.

The display of information, in the context of its unregulated retrieval and use, became a hallmark of some Conceptual art. This tendency diverged into two distinct paths: one seemed to be more about a fetishized librarianship, while the other presented the viewer with an invitation to collaborate. The *Information Room (Special Investigation)* of Joseph Kosuth (b. 1945) redescribes the artist as a worldly intellectual. One is immediately confronted with two trestle tables upon which are piled books, newspapers and articles drawn from academic journals (illus. 61). *Information Room* can be considered a depiction of the artist's studio, which has now been transformed into a reading room or academic study. The point is that the new expertise required of artists engaged in Conceptual art practices must be radically different than the skills required of the painter, sculptor or printmaker.

In one sense, Kosuth's work is indebted to Duchampian stratagems: the 'information' presents itself as an aggregate of readymades, as much to hand as the artist's earlier dictionary definitions. Yet the intellectual pathways mapped by artists of the late 1960s represented a new kind of education; Kosuth, like other autodidacts at the time, went about retrieving these new resources in a manner that was highly opportunistic. The seemingly chaotic array of materials suggests that there is no curriculum to be found here and no guide to indicate the 'correct' study of the materials on offer. *Information Room* is a territory waiting to be explored, rather than a prop in a pantomime of conventional academic knowledge acquisition and transfer.

The *Index* projects of Art & Language[25] (illus. 62) attempted to transform items of discourse into shifters or indexical terms, like the pronoun 'I'. The project invited users to create pathways through fragments of reading material; yet the matter on view was of a different order than that presented by Kosuth. Rather than use complete books and academic articles, Art & Language presented fragments and the means to create strings of bits of information. The administrative features of both approaches did not escape those art critics intent on anathematizing certain strains of Conceptual art thought to be beyond the pale of the institutional critique. In fact, Art & Language's history of engagement with text and word and image might also be described as a long endorsement of the positive value of linguistic terrorism, rather than an attempt to develop an alternative pedagogy of art.

'TOTAL ENLIGHTENMENT'

It's 1968. In Paris, students are occupying the Sorbonne, calling for a united front with the working class and the overthrow of de Gaulle, capitalism, and everything associated with the decadent bourgeois spectacle of consumption. In New York, the Students for a Democratic Society are battling with police and the Weather Underground – a short-lived revolutionary splinter group – is running amok in Chicago. In Venice, artists and activists are rioting in San Marco, temporarily calling a halt to the biennale. In Moscow, Illich Ramírez Sánchez (alias 'Carlos the Jackal') hits the books, trying hard not to get expelled from Patrice Lumumba Peoples' Friendship University. In East Germany, Roland Matthes – king of the backstroke and future gold-medallist – is gearing up for his appearance at the Olympics in Mexico City.

In 1968 throughout the West everything is explained by 'class struggle', a concept that no one outside the ultra-Left understands; throughout the East everything is explained by 'ideology', a concept that no one outside the Politburo understands, either.

According to one story, Conceptual art emerged in the liberal democracies of the West in defiance of the commodification of art and culture. In the USSR and the Eastern bloc – states where the commodification of art and culture was said to be non-existent, unthinkable – there lived another type of enemy, called totalitarianism. During the 1960s, artist-poets such as Jiří Kolář produced a variety of highly lyrical, collage-based word and image works in the former Czechoslovakia (illus. 66). Kolář utilized a wide repertoire of collage techniques to displace and transform the conventional meaning and authority of the targeted object. Bank notes became the ground for vignettes of erotic art; it's been said that contraband Western pornography briefly became a

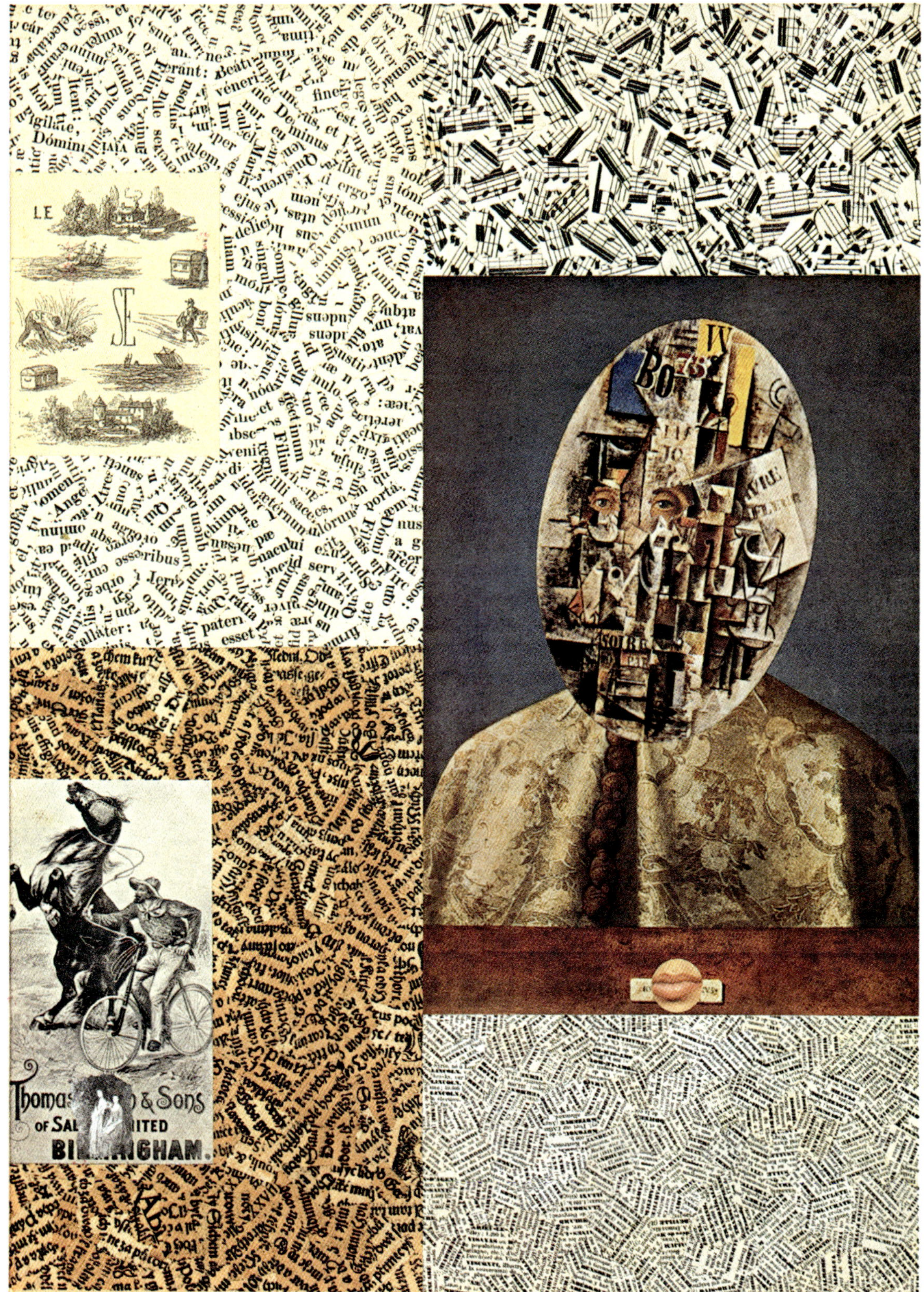

66 Jiří Kolář, *Puzzle*, 1967, collage on paper.

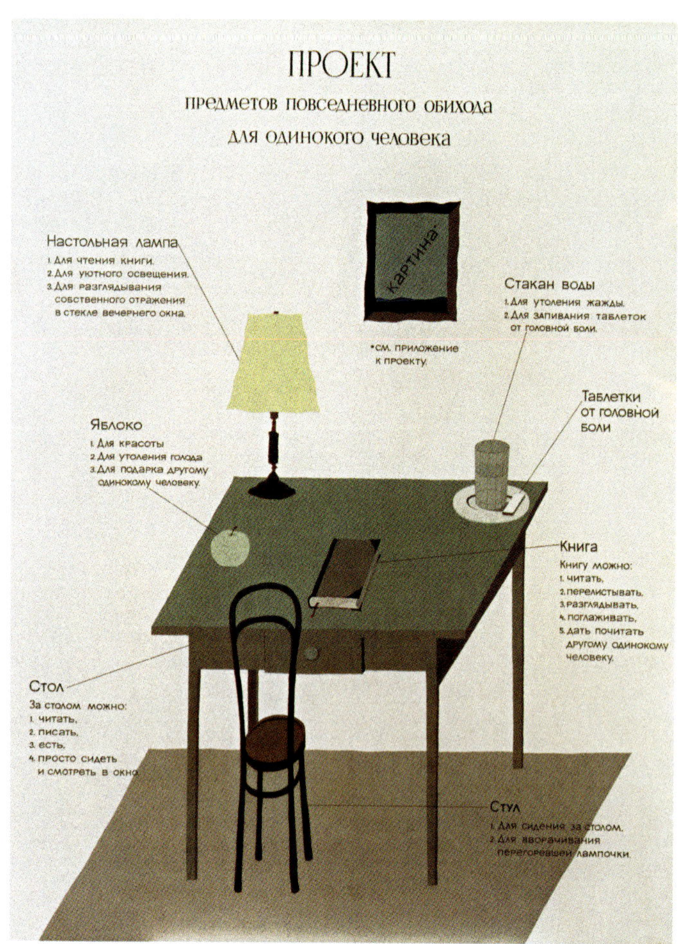

67 Viktor Pivovarov, *Plan for the Everyday Objects of a Lonely Man*, 1975, enamel on fibreboard, one of 6 panels from the series *Projects for a Lonely Man*, 1975.

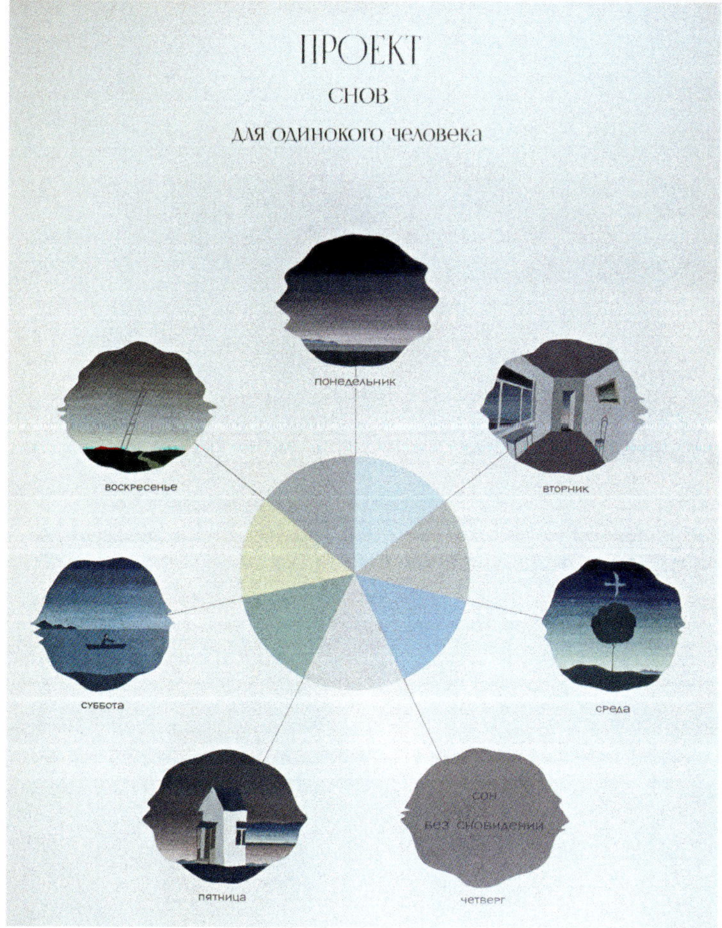

68 Viktor Pivovarov, *Plan for the Dreams of a Lonely Man*, 1975, enamel on fibreboard, one of 6 panels from the series *Projects for a Lonely Man*, 1975.

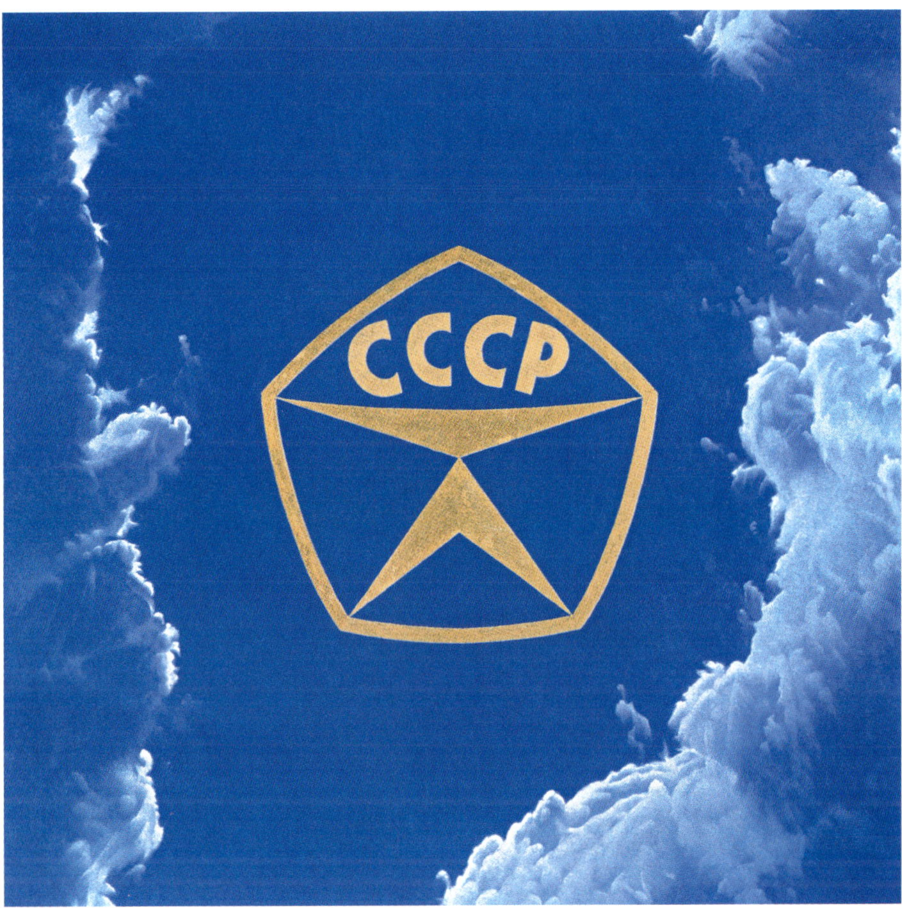

69 Erik Bulatov, *Trademark*, 1986, oil on canvas.

symbol of intellectual freedom during the Prague Spring of 1968. Even more prosaic is Kolář's metonymic portrayal of innocence: a child's rubber boot festooned with lyrics and musical notation.

For artists residing in Eastern Bloc countries, these seemingly innocent displacements delineated a world of subversive intent. But what's a young *Russian* artist to do? Those who did not become *samizdat* artists and political dissidents invented their own kind of Conceptual art, a sort of 'through the looking glass' Conceptual art that merrily proliferated versions of dissent appropriate to the command economy of the USSR. Where Western conceptualists sought to 'make meaning', these artists proceeded to destroy meaning. Against the Cold War image of life in the Soviet Union as intricately ordered and rigid, these artists supply us with a picture of life as essentially anarchic and corrupt. If anything, it was their mission to project upon that chaos their own brand of madcap bureaucratic order. This explains the obsession with systems and archives that one sees in the work of artists like Ilya Kabakov, Viktor Pivovarov and Grisha Bruskin. Their target was not the market or the commodification of art; rather, the 'rules of the symbolic economy that governed life in the Soviet Union in general'.[26] Pivovarov's 1975 series, *Projects for a Lonely Man*, may be reminiscent of the event scores produced by Fluxus artist George Brecht, but is conceived through the mind of a subject who is socially isolated yet still susceptible to disciplinary guidelines (illus. 67, 68). Pivovarov's helpful illustrated guides depict domestic interiors wherein everyday items such as a book, chair or tumbler of water are labelled with an acceptable set of uses. For exam-

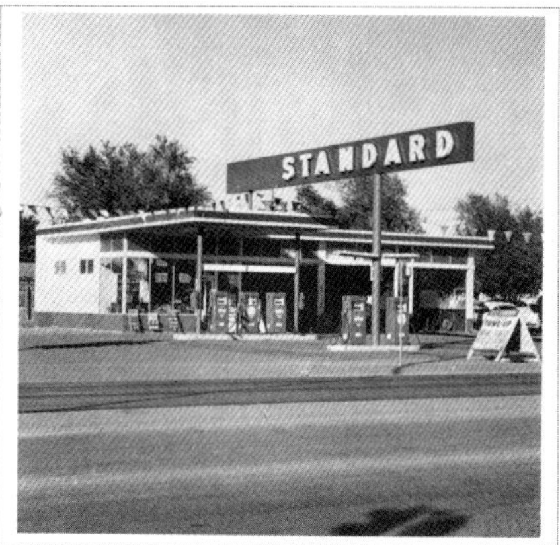

STANDARD, AMARILLO, TEXAS

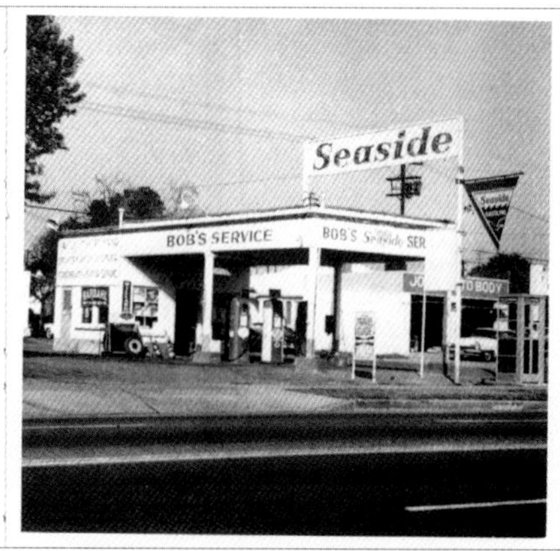

BOB'S SERVICE, LOS ANGELES, CALIFORNIA

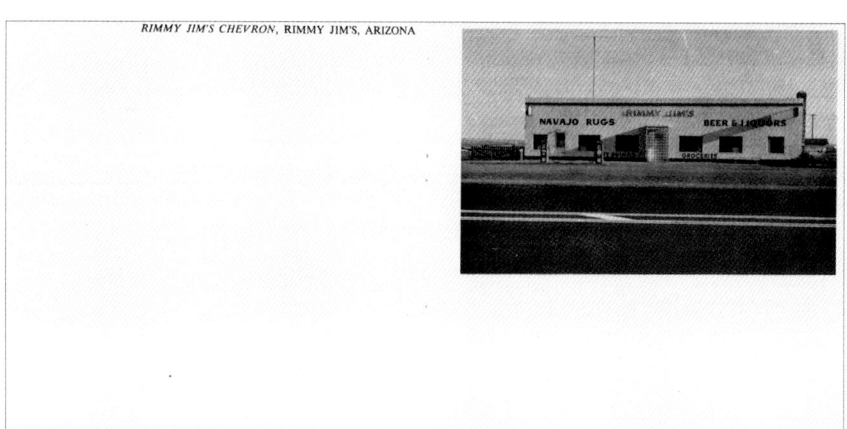

RIMMY JIM'S CHEVRON, RIMMY JIM'S, ARIZONA
NAVAJO RUGS
BEER & LIQUORS

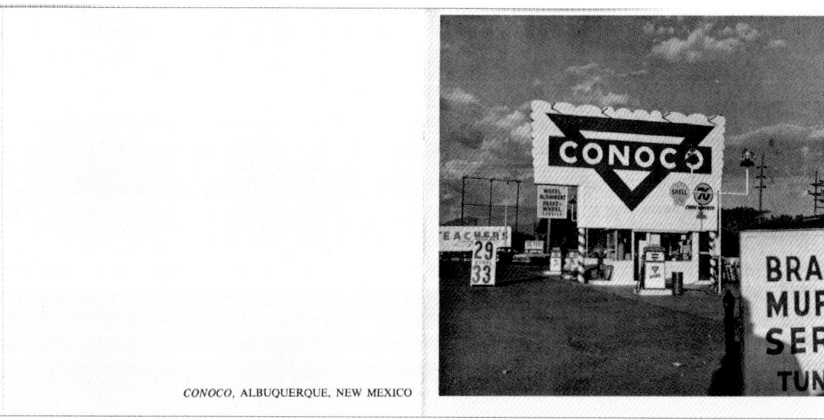

70 Ed Ruscha, *Twentysix Gasoline Stations*, 1962, interior spreads.

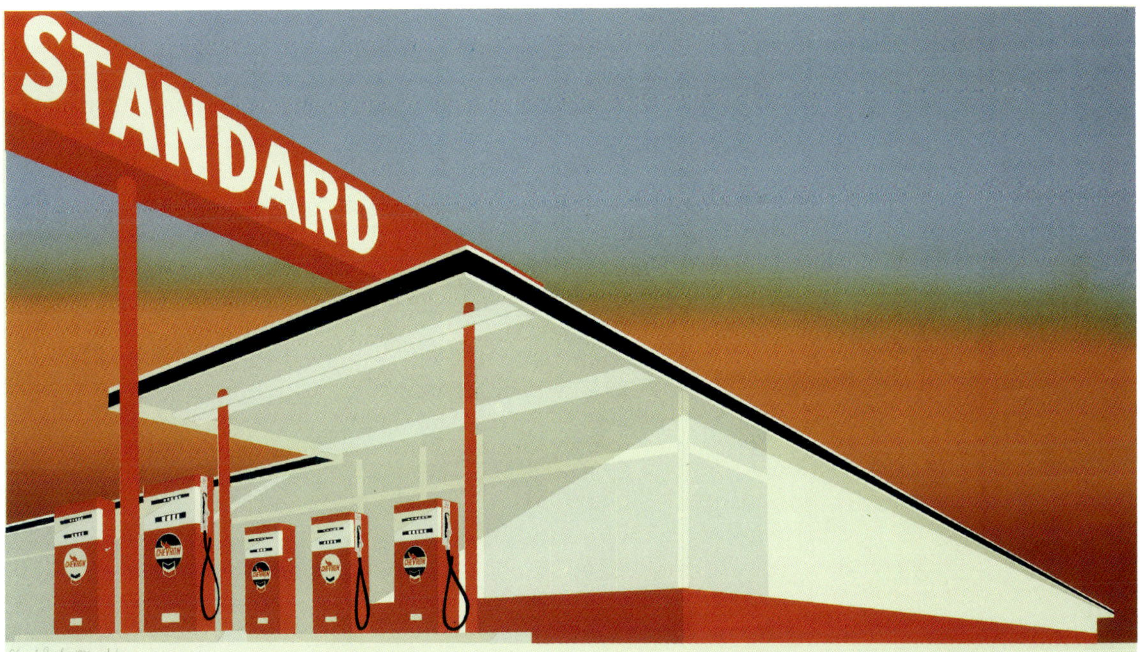

71 Ed Ruscha, from *Four Standard Stations*, 1966–9, screenprint.

ple, the book possessed by the 'lonely man' may be 'read, leafed through, looked through, stroked, or given to another lonely person to read'. Not even the subject's subconscious can escape this regimentation, as one of the artist's panels illustrated suggested themes to occupy one's dreamtime each night of the week.

Conceptual art in Moscow proved to be a durable, cohesive, multi-generational avant-garde art movement; perhaps the most important wave of art to have emerged from Moscow since the early twentieth century. The names of artists who have been associated with this group are now, mostly, well known: Erik Bulatov, Vitaly Komar and Alexander Melamid, Ilya Kabakov and Ivan Chuikov. Yet, until the late 1980s, the art of this second Russian avant garde was relatively unknown outside Moscow. With the exception of artists who had emigrated to the West – Komar and Melamid, for instance, who became US residents in 1978 and have been represented since 1976 by a New York art gallery that pioneered the exhibition of dissident Russian art – no public for this work existed outside that formed by the collectivity of Moscow artists themselves and a few clandestine collectors. There was no open domestic market for this work and no support from the state; officials bulldozed an unofficial exhibition of avant-garde art in 1974. Until the late 1980s, when Mikhail Gorbachev's policy of *glasnost* began to bite the apparatchiks hard, the majority of these artists remained obscure to the Russian public. By 1988, however, the British auction house Sotheby's was given permission to hold a sale of contemporary and modern Russian art in Moscow; it made millions. One year later, *Flash Art International* published its premier Russian-language edition, displaying on its cover a painting by Erik Bulatov (b. 1933) satirizing the Soviet Communist ideal (illus. 69).

Enforced obscurity in a hostile environment encouraged the production of a fabulously absurdist art; the oppressive weight of the Moscow political atmosphere was the crucible that gave birth to an art of profound humour deeply engaged with the everyday. The amelioration and eventual disappearance of the Communist monolith, along with the growth of an international market in Russian art of the period from the 1960s to the '80s, effectively disarticulated the movement and signalled its historical conclusion.

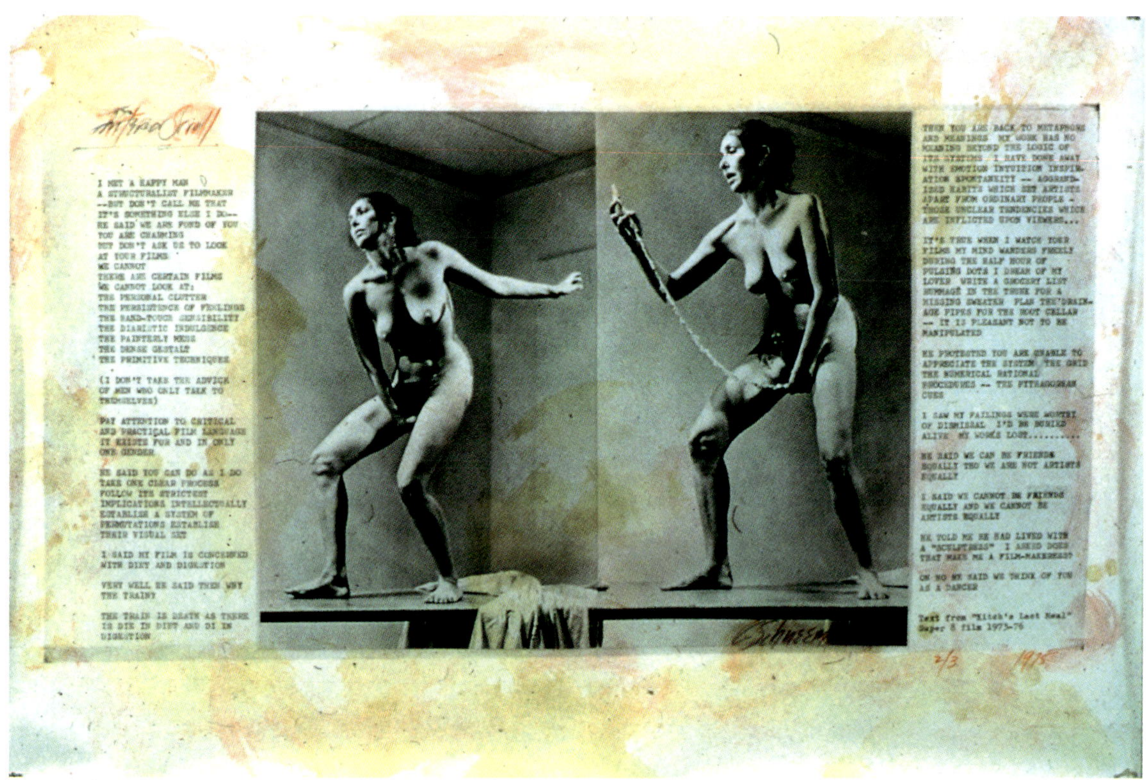

72 Carolee Schneeman, *Interior Scroll*, 1975, photo collage with text, beet juice, urine and coffee on photographic print.

When it was a vibrant underground movement, however, the practices of Moscow Conceptual art were inventive and expressive in ways that would have scandalized Conceptual art purists of the West. Moscow Conceptual art stands alongside other practices of the 1960s and '70s that fall under the rubric Conceptual art; they represent a counterweight to Anglo-American Conceptual practice by contextualizing the latter as one among many outpourings of post-media art on a global scale. The intensity of Moscow Conceptual art is exemplified by the practices of Collective Actions, a group of artists who organized a two-minute performance in 1976, *The Appearance*, and then spent two years documenting, discussing and elaborating that original act.

IMPOSSIBLE DOCUMENTS: PHOTOGRAPHY AND PERFORMANCE

In 1963 Ed Ruscha published his first book of images, titled *Twentysix Gasoline Stations* (illus. 70). Ruscha intended to catch his audience unawares, playing with the conventions of documentary photography, the photographic book and – most importantly – the concept of the readymade inherited from Marcel Duchamp. Ruscha's book defied documentary photography's claim to realism while at the same time presenting the reader with a perplexing array of visual content.

On the face of it, there is no structural logic to Ruscha's inclusion of gasoline stations, their sequence in the book, or even the number of images that eventually comprise the work. It has been noted that Ruscha's collection of gasoline stations – which lined the route travelled along the legendary Route 66 highway by the artist on his frequent visits to his parent's home in Oklahoma – has much in common with Warhol's series *Campbell's Soup Cans*, exhibited at the Ferus Gallery in Los Angeles in 1962. In both works, the artists seek to establish a mass-culture typology, to present objects as signs, and to retrieve the ordinary from the flux of everyday life. This may be seen in Ruscha's early paintings of signs and commercial buildings. A suite of four prints, *Four*

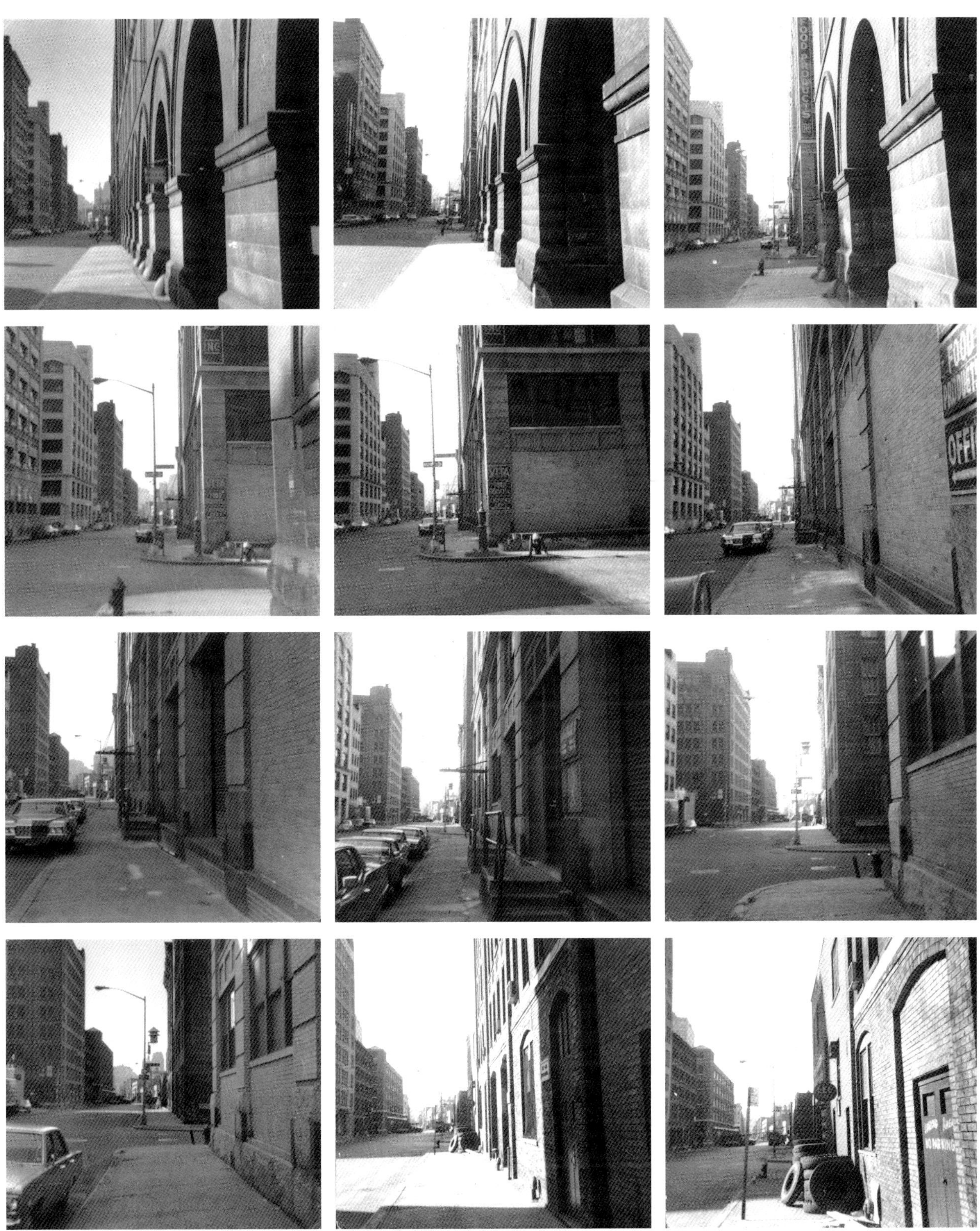

73 Vito Acconci, *Blinks, November 23, 1969, Afternoon*, 1969, photographic prints.

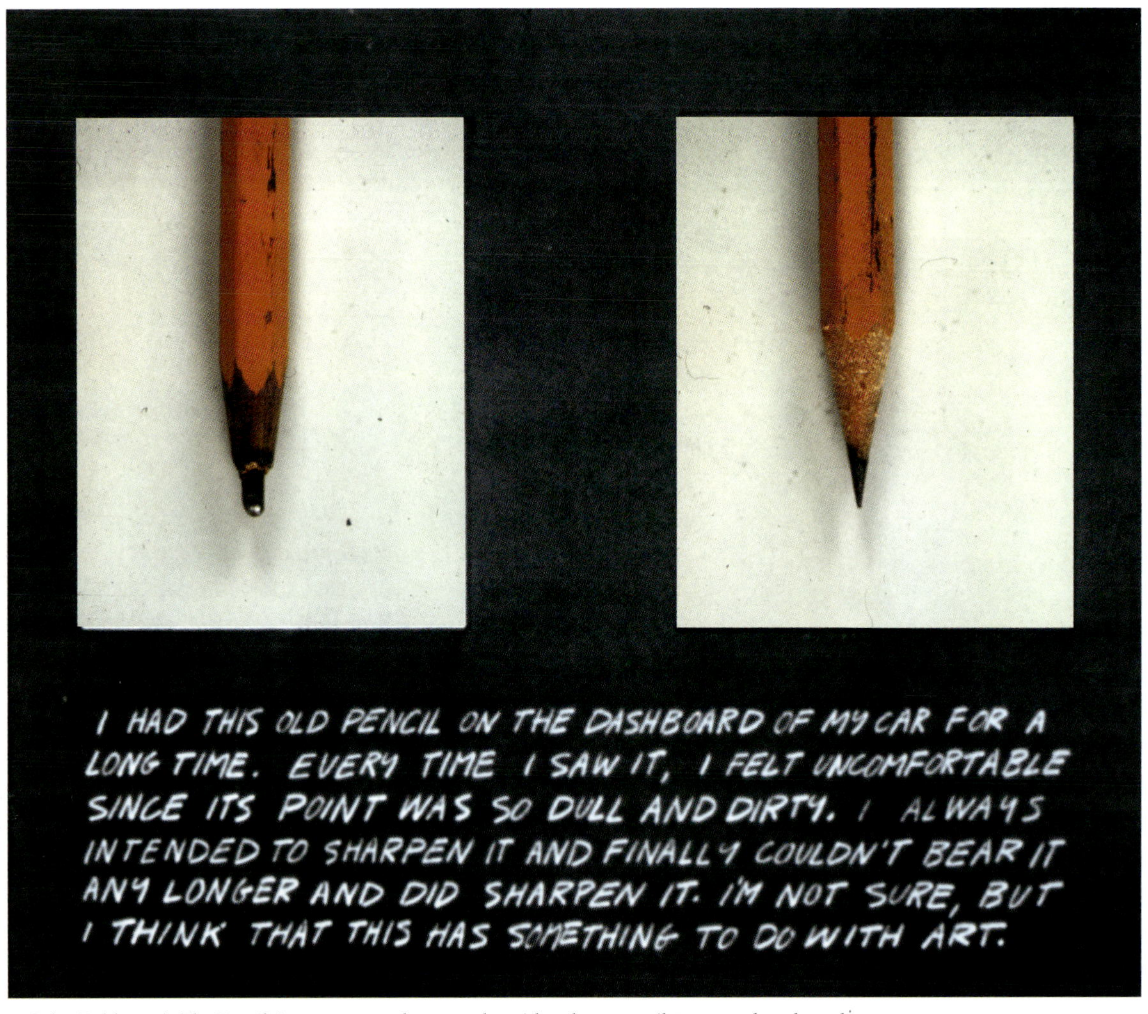

74 John Baldessari, *The Pencil Story*, 1972–3, photographs with colour pencil, mounted on board.

Standard Stations (illus. 71), depicts the same view of a Standard gasoline station using a different palette (save one in which the logo 'Standard' is doubled and set across the image). The title describes the object depicted – a Standard Oil gasoline station – while providing a punning reference to Duchamp's 1913–14 readymade, *Trois Stoppages Etalon* (*Three Standard Stoppages*). Ruscha knew of Duchamp's work from the artist's first retrospective organized by Walter Hopps in 1963 for the Pasadena Art Museum. *Four Standard Stations* underscores Ruscha's extension of the application of the concept of the readymade to vernacular, large-scale commercial structures.[27]

The subject matter of Ruscha's paintings and books of the 1960s are invariably indexed to Los Angeles. Subsequent artists found this conjunction of documentary-style photography and place compelling. From the mid-1960s onwards, the captioned photographic image styled after documentary photography or, better, the most ordinary technical photography was a dominating form in Conceptual art and its cognates. The typological approach, with or without accompanying text, persisted well into the 1970s and was adapted repeatedly to serve a number of critical agendas, such as class, gender and race. Carolee Schneeman, a pioneer since the early 1960s in the use of photography in body art, staged a performance in 1975 entitled *Interior Scroll*. During this performance the artist read from a text inscribed on a scroll that was slowly extracted from her vagina (illus. 72). The text is a cautionary tale about the fate of women artists in a patriarchal world. Around 1969, Vito Acconci began to document his so-called task-oriented performance works using a photo-text format. In *Blinks, November 23, 1969* (illus. 73), Acconci presents a grid of twelve photographs that were shot, according to the descriptive caption appended by the artist, 'while walking a continuous line down a city street'. The description of the task, then, functions as an extended caption that makes sense of the sequence of images.[28] Similarly, the Californian artist John Baldessari employed this strategy to contrive a series of humorous photo-text scenarios that gently satirize the progressive deskilling of art under the rubric of conceptualism (illus. 74).

A more acidic use of the photo-text format is to be found in the early work of the British duo Gilbert and George. Diaristic and scathingly critical of homophobia, the 'living sculpture' works of Gilbert and George index an ongoing performance of the couple in the guise of free-spirited Edwardian dandies (illus. 75, 76). In a statement by the artists published in 1970, the bittersweet legacy of Oscar Wilde's exuberant aestheticism is plainly visible: 'Oh Art, what are you? You are so strong and powerful, so beautiful and moving… . We really do love you and we really do hate you.'

Keith Arnatt, an artist responsible for the introduction of documentary photography into the curriculum of the Newport School of Art and Design during the 1970s, used photo and text to document himself as a form of sculpture. *Trouser-Word Piece* (1972) depicts the artist supporting a sign that reads: 'I'm a real artist.' The accompanying text panel – rarely shown in reproduction – is an excerpt from the work of the noted philosopher of language, John L. Austin. Here, Austin discusses the idea that the true meaning of the word 'real' is not to ascribe a quality of being 'real' to an object, but to exclude the number of ways in which the object may possibly be 'not real'. Austin – famous for propounding the theory of the speech act – was widely read by Conceptual artists at the time. By citing Austin's text, Arnatt was aligning himself, if only peripherally, to a tendency that valued an analysis of the linguistic framework supporting art over the actual production of objects. Decades later, Arnatt's strategy of using text as an ambiguous label in a performative setting would reappear in the work of younger British artists, such as Gillian Wearing, who also shared a belief in the body as the fundamental ground of art (illus. 77).

'WRITING IS USED TO IRRITATE VIEWERS'

The 'overcoming of active forgetting' of Germany's Nazi past that defined Anselm Kiefer's project from the 1970s through the '80s introduces a number of interesting problems for interpretation,[29] specifically, according to critic Andrew Benjamin, the status of representation: that which is represented and the image that comes to be *the* representation. Kiefer's paintings of the 1970s and '80s do not, in this view, portray an event; they do, however, show us an example of how historical and ideological concepts may be staged imaginatively as though actors in a history painting. Part of the problem with Kiefer's use of word and image is the odd way in which history is *inscribed* in the paintings; the text that appears in some of Kiefer's paintings is never sufficient to open up history to scrutiny. They are allusive voices. The artist claims to use text to irritate the spectator, in order to generate awareness of another layer of memory. There is an urgency to put *something down*; to stake a claim for remembering the past.

At times, Kiefer's inscription reaches back to the pre-modern origins of Germania. The entire sweep of German history – from the mythic to the modern era – becomes a resource. Everything about Germany is placed under the injunction of having to be changed *immediately* and *completely*. The encrustation of Kiefer's paintings makes these anything but pictures; they are hulking assemblages, enormous collages of heterogeneous elements. Works of the early 1980s such as *Paths: March Sand* (1980) and *Your Golden Hair Margarete* (illus. 78) – the latter inspired by Paul Celan's poem 'Death Fugue' – incorporate straw and sand along with oil paint. Yet they are not the work of an artist in love with painting; rather they

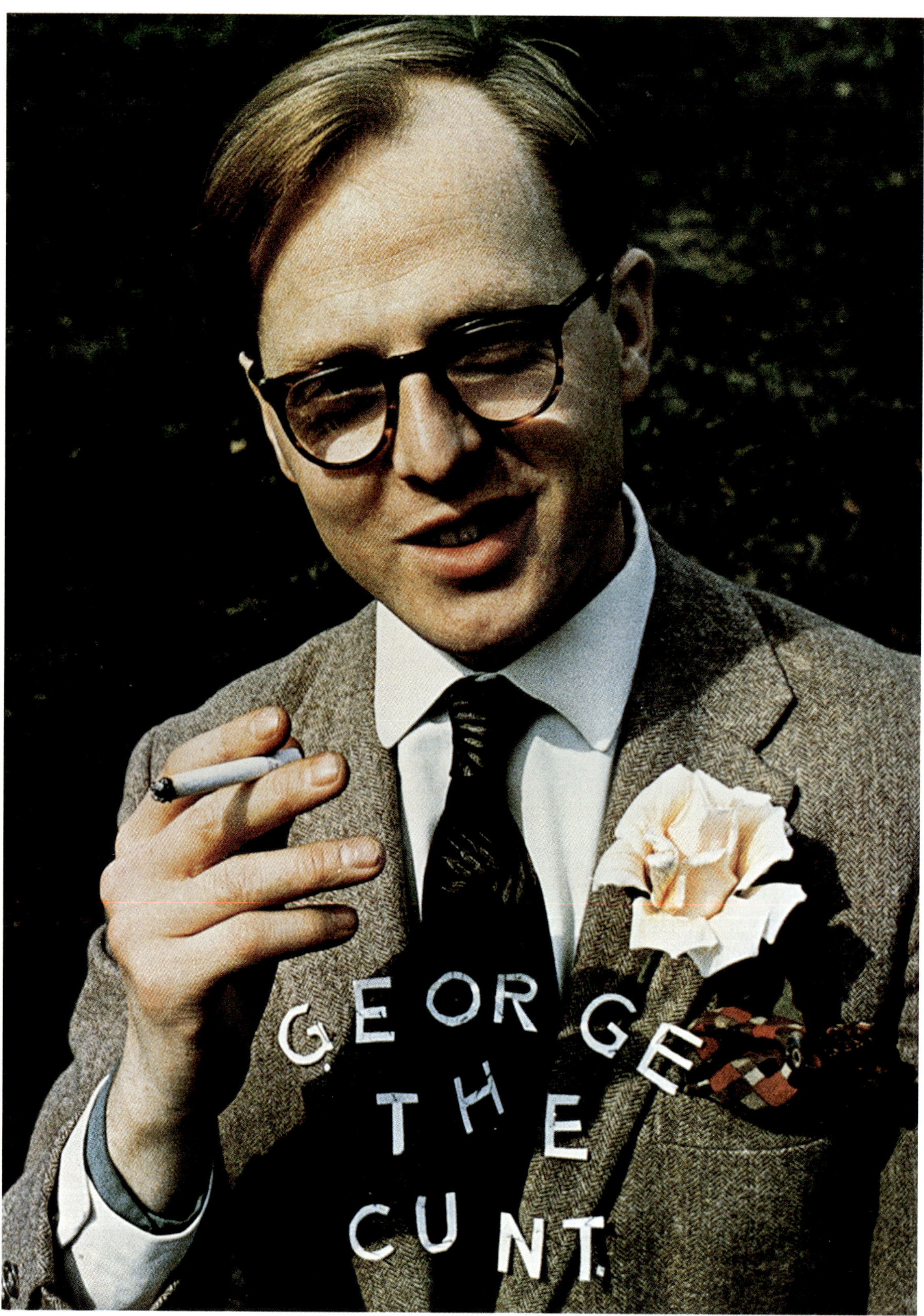

75, 76 Gilbert & George, *Magazine Sculpture*, 1969, photographic prints.

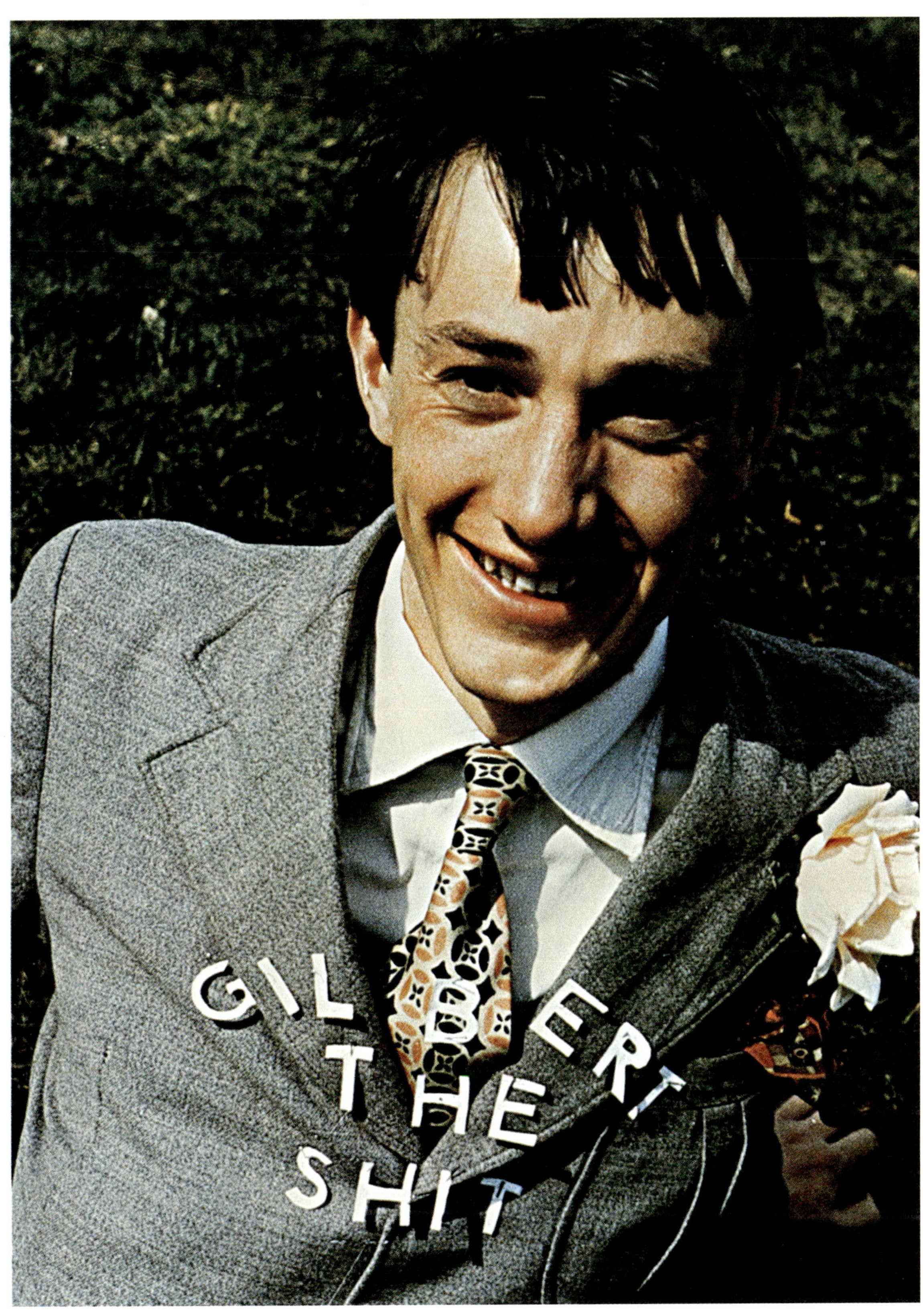
GILBERT
THE
SHIT

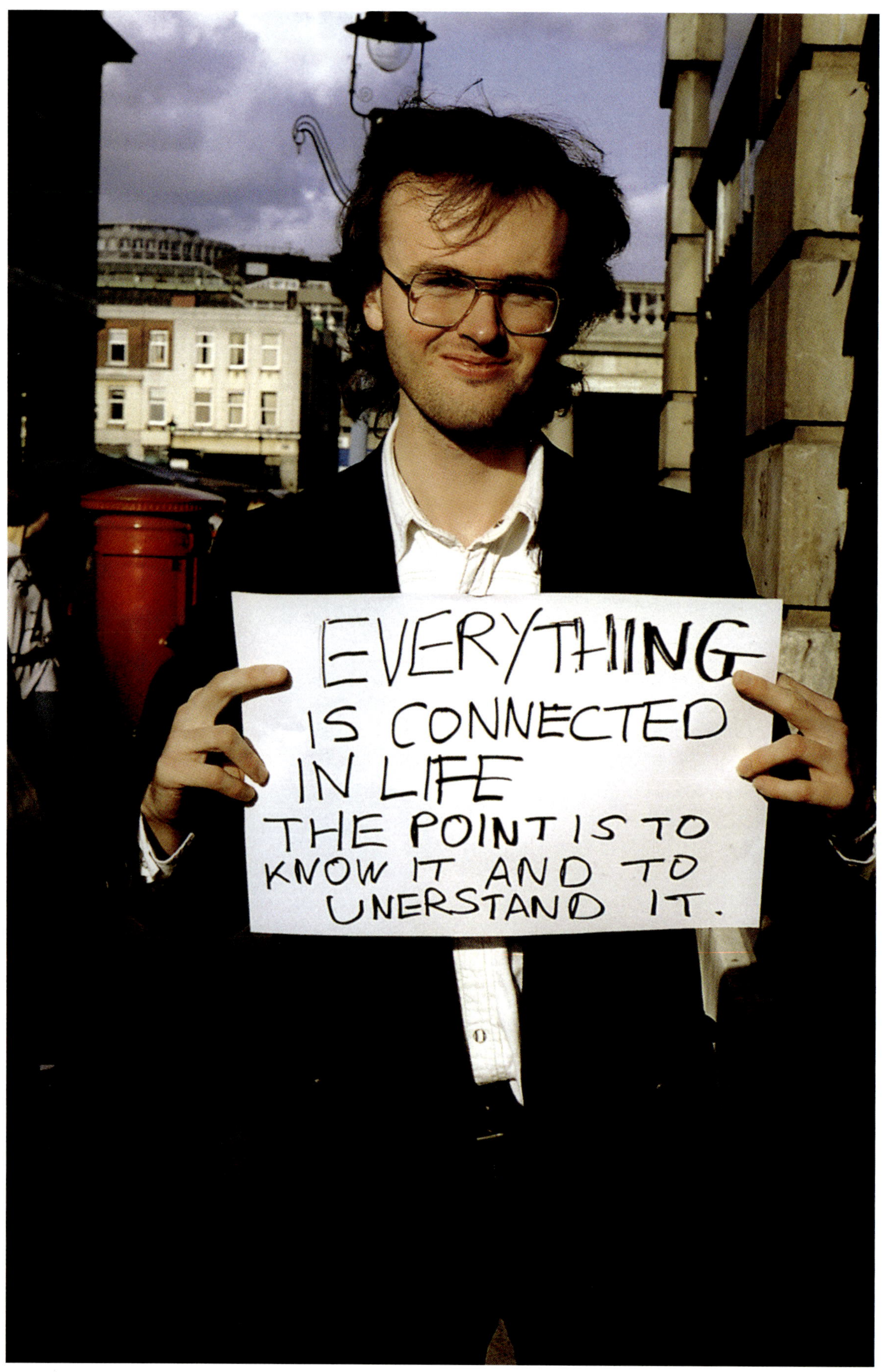

77 Gillian Wearing, *Signs that say what you want them to say and not signs that say what someone else wants you to say*, 1992–3, photographic print.

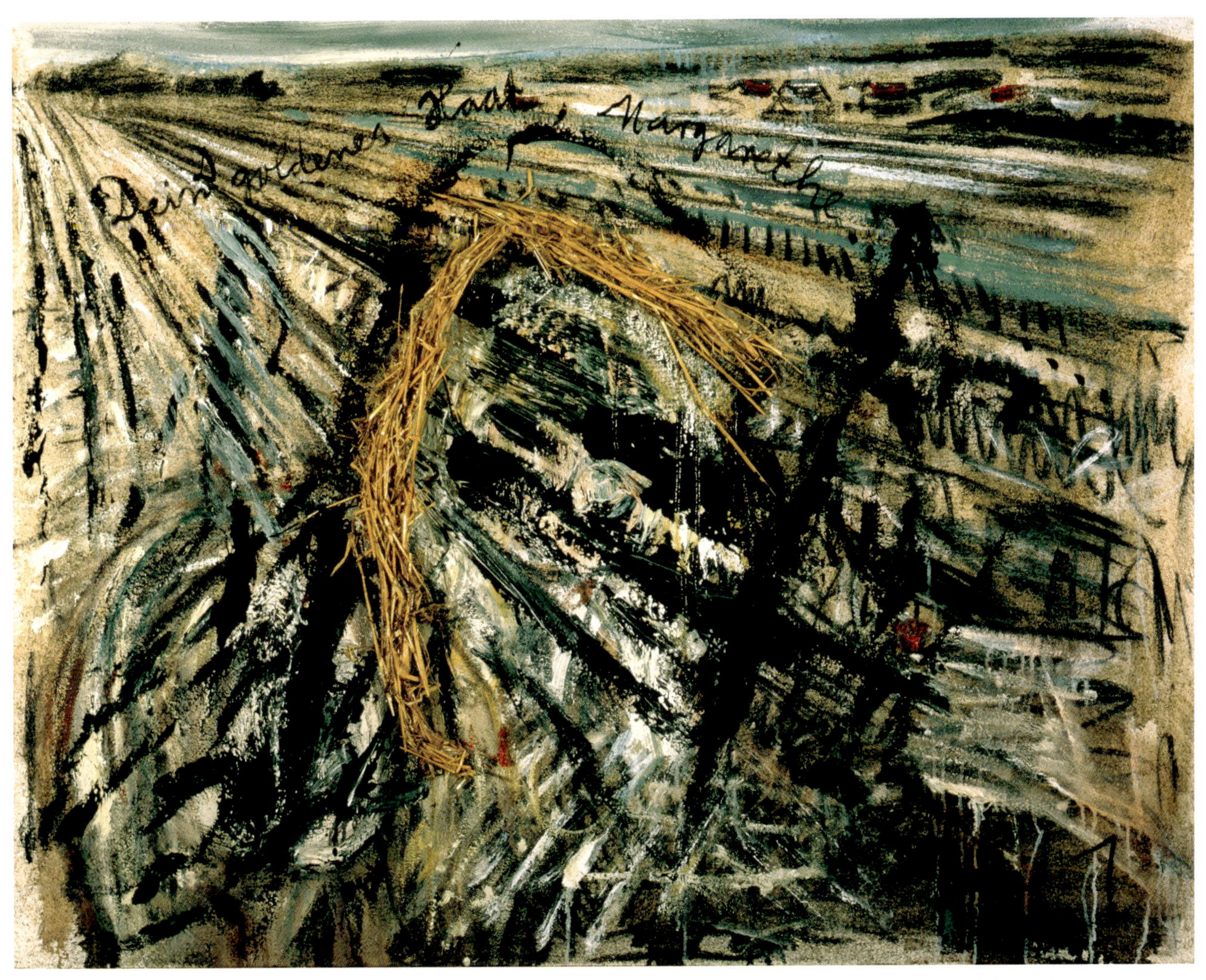

78 Anselm Kiefer, *Your Golden Hair, Margarete*, 1981, oil, emulsion and straw on canvas.

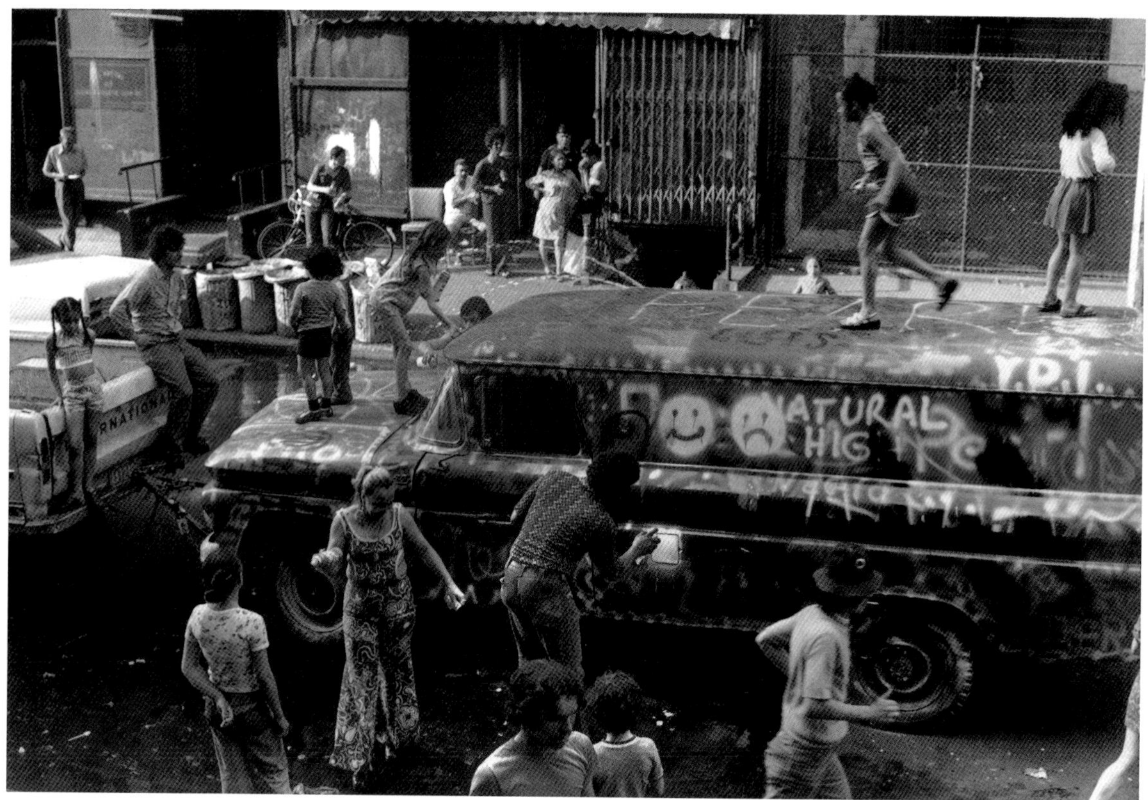

79 Gordon Matta-Clark, *Graffiti Truck*, 1973.

seek to destroy painting. They are monumental icons that revel in their heterogeneous nature. The texts in these agglomerations are painted titles; their presence gives the spectator something to latch on to, conferring conceptual shape on what would otherwise read as an inflated version of the unformed.

Kiefer's art aims to overcome the repression of German history. Kiefer's rough inscriptions of proper names and titles are aesthetic elements of the work. This doubling, which is also present in the paintings of Jasper Johns, speaks to the way in which modes of representation and representational conundrums have become internalized as artistic conventions across a relatively brief span of time. In Kiefer's practices of the early 1980s, the point seems to be to reconstruct a new order of symbols for German culture in its entirety. The painting becomes a crucible in which all elements of German history are mixed and fashioned as such.

Kiefer's position on the representational function of art and his rejection of the analytic frame of Minimalism and Conceptualism is much beloved by art students. For them, Kiefer reasserts what they see as the artist's right to invest objects with emotional power, to transgress the aesthetic dicta of art movements, and to play with material processes. The results of this newly found freedom are often startling; very quickly, the overdetermined reading of surface as a repository for iconographic fragments begins to pile up, literally and figuratively. At some point, the process of symbol formation becomes lost, overwhelmed by a complete disregard for difference. In Kiefer's works, that difference is often supplied by inscribed language, which inhabits the artist's works like a plume of smoke or a passing breeze.

TAGS

In 1973, in the South Bronx, Gordon Matta-Clark invited local residents to graffiti his delivery truck. The truck was then driven downtown to Mercer

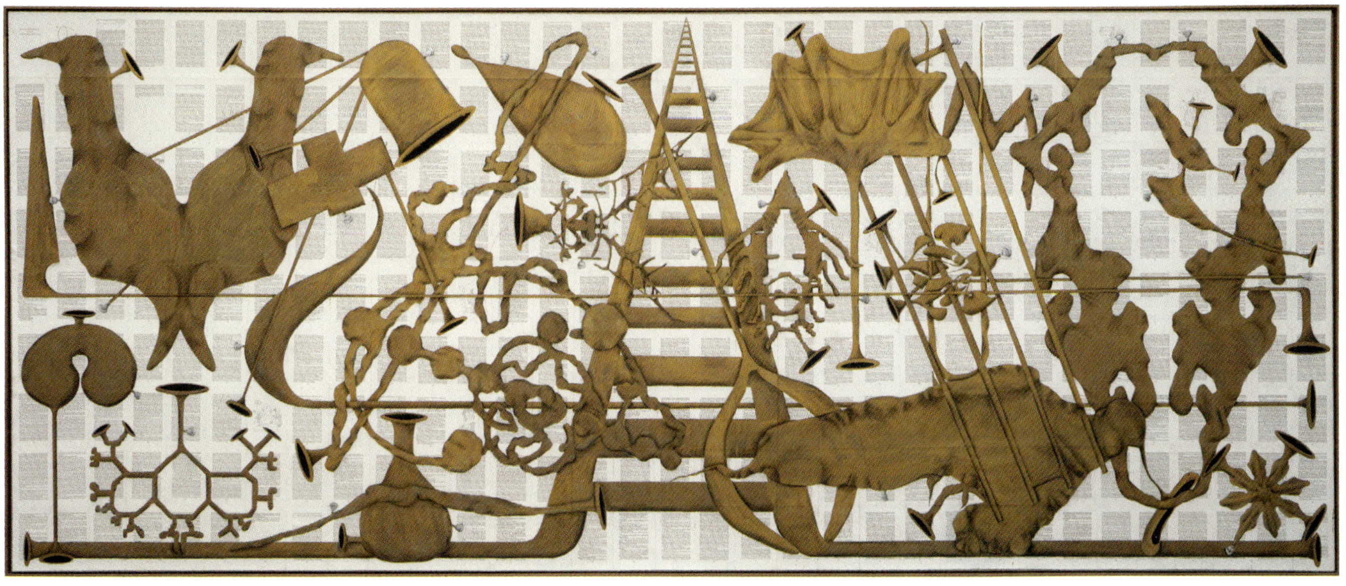

80 Angel Abreu, Jose Burges, Robert Delgado, George Garces, K.O.S. (Kids of Survival), Richard Lulo, Nelson Montes, José Parissi, Carlos Rivera, Tim Rollins, Annette Rosado and Nelson Ricardo Savinon, *Amerika VIII*, 1986–7, watercolour, charcoal, synthetic polymer paint and pencil on book pages on linen.

Street where it became part of the 'Alternatives to the Washington Square Art Show'. Matta-Clark's *Graffiti Truck* (illus. 79) anticipated the art market's interest in unsanctioned forms of territorial marking and informal urban expression. Along with the truck, Matta-Clark presented large format photos of subway graffiti, and 'offered sections of his work cut out on the spot with an acetylene torch'.[30]

Graffiti, particularly in New York during the 1970s, became the emblem of urban vandalism and a visible reminder of the decline of services at a time when the city faced bankruptcy. The tag 'Taki 183' – the work of a Greek-American teenager – received wide press coverage and resulted in an explosion of graffiti activity across New York. Graffiti writers concentrated their efforts on the subway system, 'bombing' entire subway cars at night in terminal yards. Graffiti was also seen as the heroic vernacular art of African-American urban youth subcultures, specifically groups involved with hip-hop and rap music. During the late 1970s Jean-Michel Basquiat, Al Diaz and Shannon Dawson entered into this fray, using the tag 'SAMO©', ironically accompanied by a copyright symbol, to 'bomb' locations in Manhattan's SoHo artist district. The well-known Fluxus artist, Henry Flynt, created a comprehensive photographic archive of these tags. The name 'SAMO' was a jest meant to signify a magical cure-all. In the event, it sounds like a condensation of the refrain 'same old, same old' (itself a polite version of the scatological expression of resignation, 'same old shit').

Graffiti was awash with the cachet of outlaw cool and soon became the subject of a number of documentary films of the early 1980s, including *Wildstyle* (Charlie Ahearn, 1982) – the term refers to the so-called 'bubble' lettering that dominated graffiti at the time – and *Style Wars* (Tony Silver and Henry Chalfant, 1983). Inevitably, graffiti found its way into art galleries, beginning in 1979 with an exhibition of work by Lee Quinones and Fred Braithwaite in Rome. By the early 1980s, when Basquiat was producing some of his most interesting work, graffiti-based art was on display in galleries throughout the Lower East Side and becoming increasingly common in the works of artists eager to establish a link to this celebrated urban subculture. Basquiat no doubt traded on this association, but also attempted to recover the spontaneity of graffiti as brash political and social commentary.

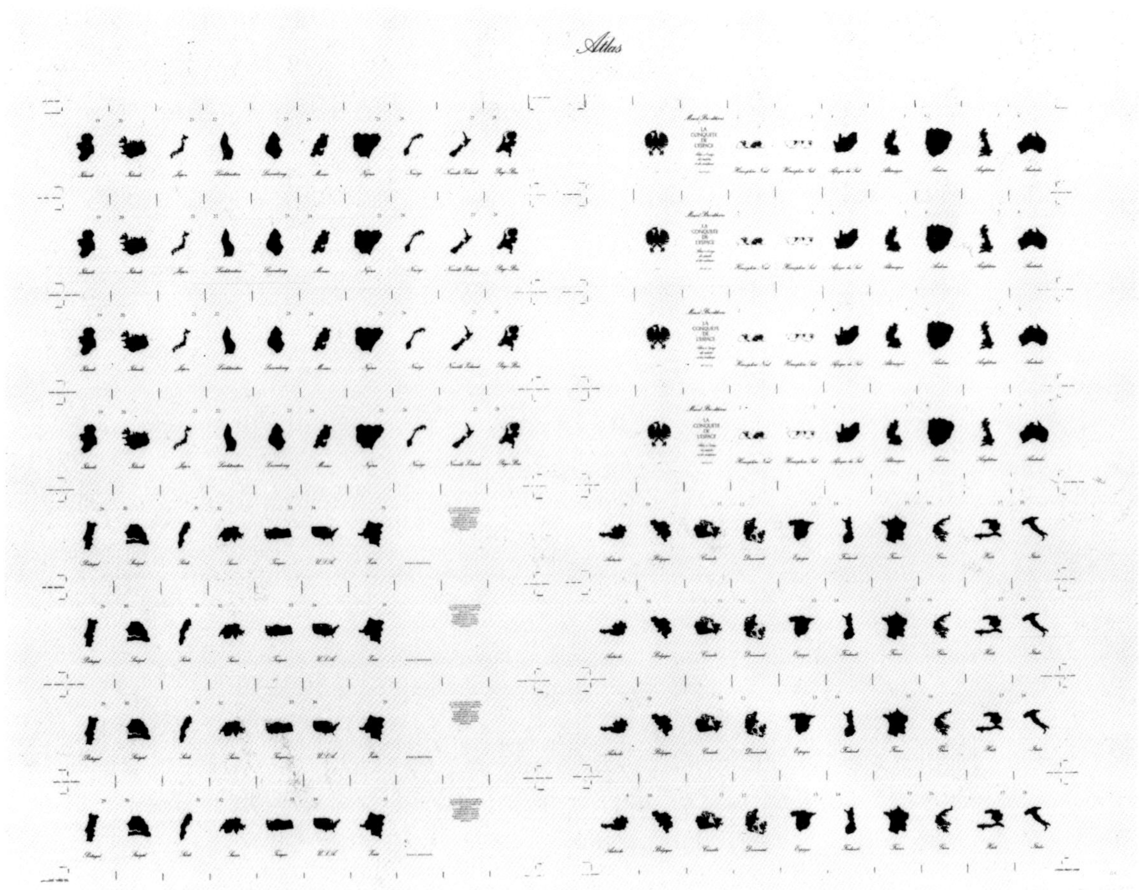

81 Marcel Broodthaers, *Atlas*, 1975, relief print on paper image.

More significant than the commercialization and recuperation of graffiti by the media intent on developing persuasive new youth branding was Fashion Moda, a Bronx-based exhibition and community space initiated by Stefan Eins in 1979. Artists like Tim Rollins, Justin Ladda, John Ahearn, Jenny Holzer and Christy Rupp began working at the gallery with neighbourhood residents; in many cases the experience had long-lasting effects on their practice (illus. 80). In 1980 a nineteen-year-old graffiti writer, CRASH, curated Fashion Moda's first exhibition of graffiti; a few years later, the project space was invited to exhibit work at *Documenta 7* (Kassel, Germany), where a Fashion Moda 'store' was installed featuring the work of artists associated with the Bronx project. Lucy Lippard, a strong supporter of Fashion Moda's activities, called the artistic activities that took place there a 'genuine mesh of [the artists'] own interests and those of its audience'.[31] Lippard's sentiment echoed that of many artists, for whom art's use as a tool for social cohesion was particularly important at a time when gentrification was threatening to destroy the working-class neighbourhoods of the Lower East Side and divert attention from the needs of impoverished areas like the South Bronx.

ART AS DIRECT SPEECH

Artists emerging during the 1980s and '90s were aware to some extent of the politicized art of the 1960s and '70s. As they began to devise their own version of engaged art, it became clear that one of their goals was to avoid what they saw to be the fatal flaw of an earlier generation's probing of the common culture: the demonization of mass communication. The use of word and image that

Sensation

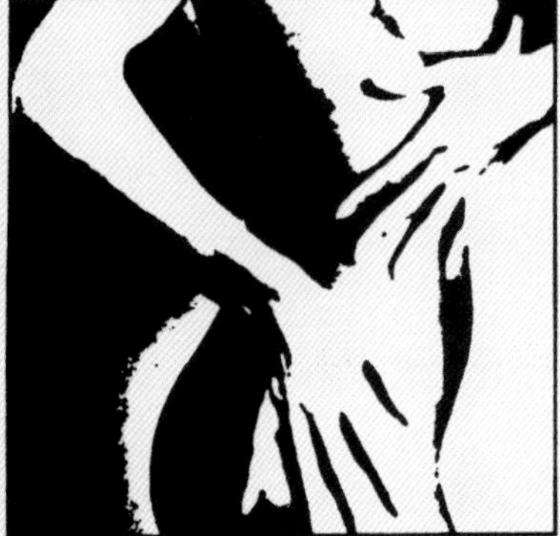

ContraDiction

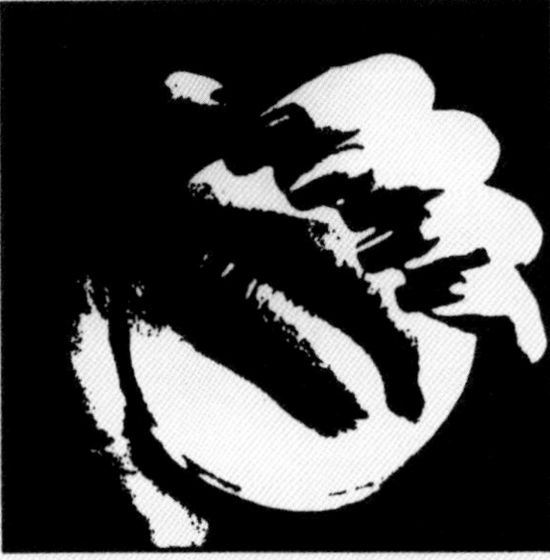

Logic

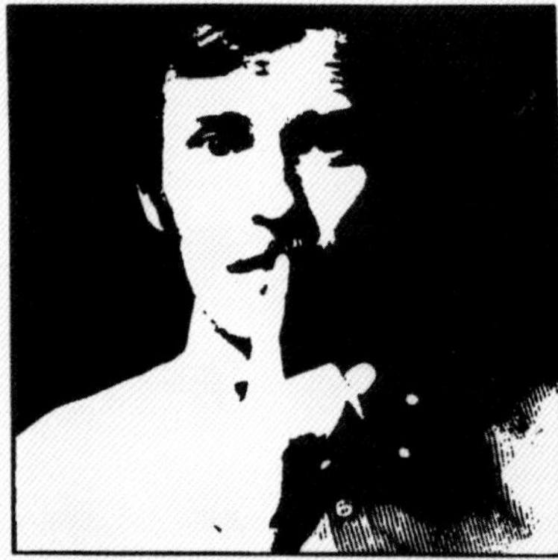

82 Victor Burgin, *Sensation*, 1975, photographic prints.

would be reproduced in a variety of media and displayed in a variety of settings, from the gallery to the billboard, was strongly associated with historical Conceptual art. Yet Conceptual art was often opaque and rarely addressed a general public. The artists of the 1980s who sought to realize the full potential of word and image as public media were far more interested in learning from the forms of media rather than to demolish it uncritically. Where some historical Conceptual art was intent on deconstructing the cultural prestige and coded authority of the advertising image, artists of the 1980s who incorporated word and image in their work looked to the media as a salient model of cultural power. Of course, these artists could also point to the work of Marcel Broodthaers, Victor Burgin, Hans Haacke, Lawrence Weiner and Martha Rosler for models of artistic practice of critical import (illus. 81, 82, 83). Yet the figure of Andy Warhol seemed to have enduring influence on the generation of artists who had emerged during the 1980s. Quite simply, Warhol was the avatar of the savvy media artist. From this eclectic mix of Conceptual art, semiotic theory and institutional critique, artists ranging from Alfredo Jaar to Lorna Simpson would find suitable resources of expression appropriate to their very different projects. The history of attempts to create out of art a socially efficient tool in the service of progressive causes is undoubtedly an interrupted narrative. Nevertheless, the broad ideological lineaments – the elision of art and artefact, the desire to level cultural hierarchies and the need to position artistic practice in a social setting – constitute something of a cultural tradition that harkens back to the time of the *soixante-huitards*.

Beginning in 1980, Group Material – a New York collective – organized a series of thematic exhibitions that mixed art, artefact, documentary images, consumer goods and information.[32] While inspired by the example of the innovative exhibitions mounted by the Independent Group, the founders of Group Material were responding explicitly to the most accessible models of artistic practice: the highly politicized artist collectives of the 1960s and '70s, such as the Guerrilla Art Action Group, the Los Angeles Womanhouse and Artists Meeting for Culture Change. Group Material focused principally on political issues and embraced the semi-public space of the art gallery as a retort to the growing climate of political and social reaction that defined the years of the Reagan administration and the so-called Culture Wars (illus. 84).

Other artists who have reconsidered the example of Conceptual art to construct an ideologically pointed archive include Peter Fend and Renée Green (b. 1959). Green's installations construct a dense web of relations around an artefact, a work of art or architecture, or a cultural phenomenon. *Import-Export Funk Office* (1992) maps the cultural context of hip-hop music across three disparate geographic locations: New York, Los Angeles and Cologne. *Partially Buried in Three Parts* (1996), deconstructs the locality of Kent, Ohio, circa 1970, through the filter of three points of reference: the making of Robert Smithson's *Partially Buried Woodshed*, sited at Kent State University in Ohio; the shooting of four students by Ohio State National Guard militia during an anti-Vietnam War demonstration on 4 May 1970; and the author James Michener (illus. 85). Using video clips, photographs, recordings and textual material, Green shows how history eludes us, becomes myth and fades into another sort of depiction. This is achieved through the design of the installation, which presents the beholder with an overlapping display of image, text and sound. Here, we are shown how the details of historical events become obscured as different commentators report on the same event, or different events are conjoined by chance. We learn that shortly after the shooting of the students, Smithson's installation was daubed with the date 'May 4, 1970' in commemoration of the deaths. On a small, circular table, Green has place a sample of asphalt gathered from the purported site of Smithson's installation, an aerial photograph of the site on campus of the confrontation between militia and students, and a suggestively defensive array of paperbacks authored by Michener.

SPECTATOR GAMES

The collection and production of documentary materials and their presentation in the form of an archive has not been limited to artists intent upon exploring the personal dimension of public events or the separation and texture of private recollection and socially available myths. Sophie Calle (b. 1953) – dubbed an unacknowledged heir to the legacy of the Situationist *dérive* – employs text and a means to stage work that calls into question the veracity of language itself. Calle's earliest works may be considered exemplars of the art of drifting; her aesthetic has been summed up by an unwitting subject of one of her inquiries as modelled after police surveillance and espionage. Language may fix the target or establish motive, but the visual and verbal evidence never seem to add up.

If this is the case, then the relationship between word and image in Calle's practice is conceivably, if not enticingly, forensic: one has the report, duly noting with precision and succinctness the time, place and subject of one's observations. The written report is supplemented by the visual evidence; the often poor-quality image of the subject photographed clandestinely, caught in the act, compromised and now prey to the authorities, her minder, spouse, boss or whomever launched this sordid investigation. In fact, for Calle, the distance from the event is usually guaranteed by the nature of the contact: at first, she simply went along with the tide of events while keeping track of everything of interest. She subverts the notion of surveillance by implicating herself at every turn. Speaking of her first major project, published as *Suite Venitienne* in 1983, she explains: 'At the end of January 1981, on the streets of Paris, I followed a man whom I lost sight of a few minutes later in the crowd. That very evening, quite by chance, he was introduced to me at an opening. During the course of our conversation, he told me he was planning an imminent trip to Venice, I decided to follow him.' Calle shadows her mark all the way to Venice, where she records sightings of her subject, comments on her own state of mind, and attempts to photograph him covertly. Calle's practice tells us more about the stalker than the target.

Calle's practice has been criticized as solipsistic; an unwanted public exposure of the self with no discernible purpose other than the celebration of one's self-absorption. For some, this position seems to have defined much of the art of the 1990s. Yet Calle's work can respond to such criticism only if it provides evidence of a bridge that links the act of clandestine surveillance and the pleasure of voyeurism to a larger public. Are Calle's works subtle and complex enough to slough off the charge that they are merely instances of exhibitionism and therefore not worthy of serious consideration?

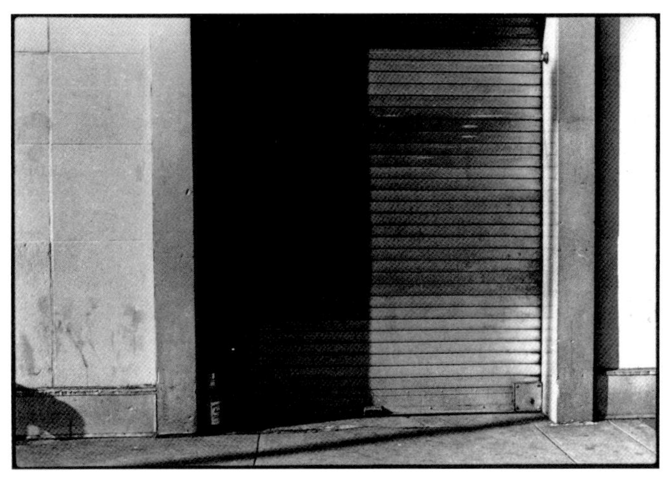

loopy groggy boozy

tight steamed up bent

folded flooey

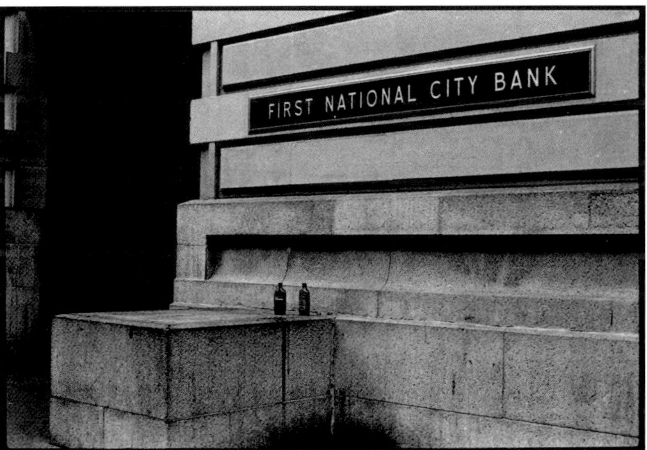

plastered stuccoed

rosined shellacked

vulcanized

inebriated

polluted

83 Martha Rosler, *The Bowery in Two Inadequate Descriptive Systems*, 1974–5, photographic prints, typewritten text on paper.

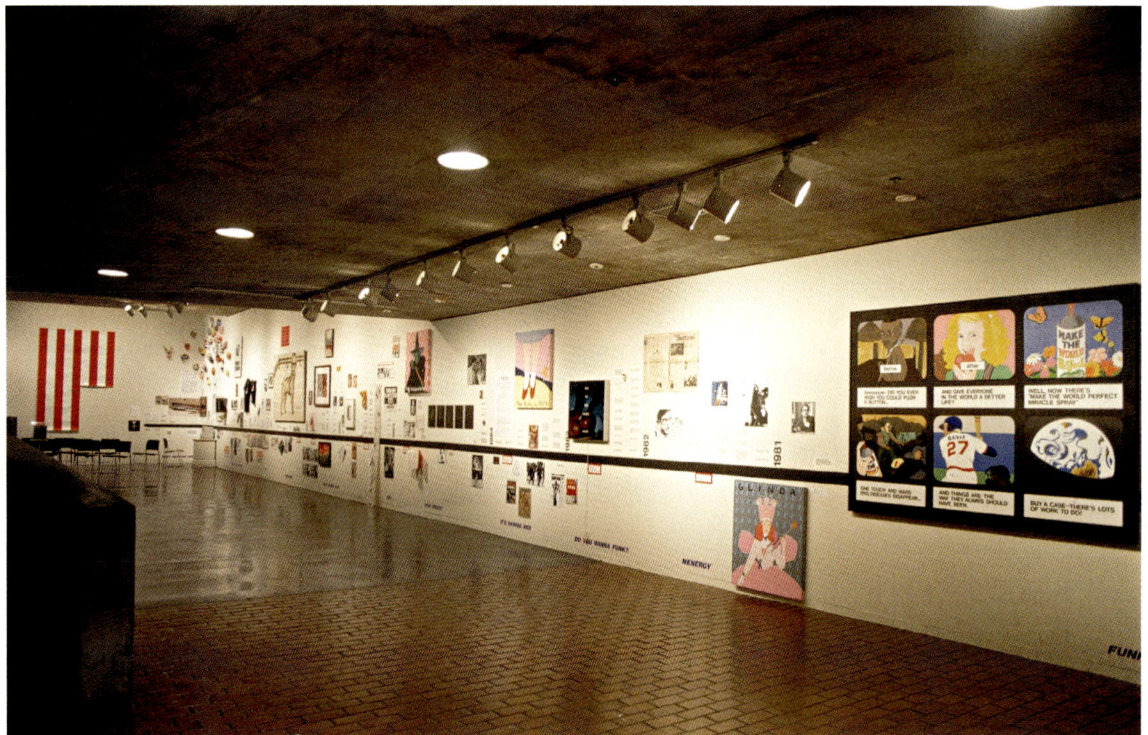

84 Group Material, *AIDS Timeline*, 1989, mixed media.

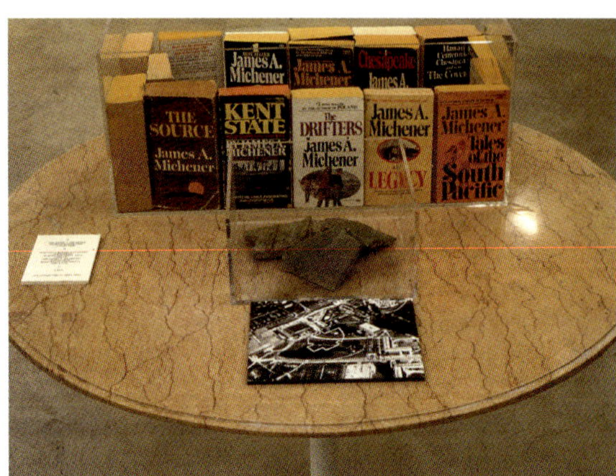

85 Renée Green, *Paperbacks by James Michener and Fragments from Partially Buried Shed*, 1996, mixed media.

Voyeurism, role-playing and a talent for displacing reality with fantasy have enabled Calle to interrogate the certainties of public and private life to the fullest. Jacques Rancièrre speaks to this despised modality, suggesting that spectatorship is an activity that should not be so readily devalued. To make the personal public was the battle-cry of 1960s feminism. Calle's response is to do just that, but in a manner that tests the limits of the public expression of our private lives and thoughts. That one has something like a 'private life' or 'private thoughts' is both indisputable and open to contention, as the private in this context can be something like a pose: an invagination of a socially acceptable subject position. The secrets revealed by Calle in her relentless investigations of strangers or her spectacularization of the inner life-worlds of others turn out to be somewhat unsurprising. The problem of 'other' minds is, for Calle, not really a philosophical or epistemological one, but a practical challenge: where does one find such an entity?

In Calle's highly celebrated work of 2007 for the French Pavilion at the Venice Biennale, she once

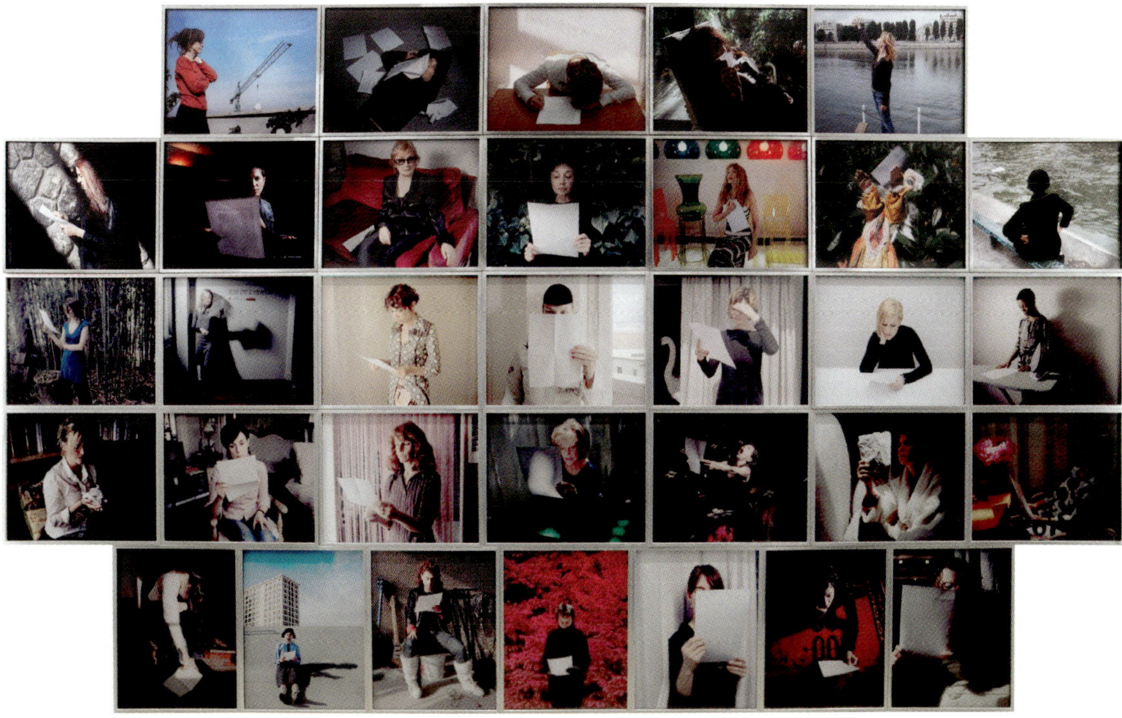

86 Sophie Calle, *'Prenez soin de vois' ('Take care of yourself')*, 2007, photographic prints.

again places herself in a position of trust and opens herself up to strangers (illus. 86). Overwrought in its proliferation of views and approaches, Calle's project is a powerful and ultimately successful topology of personal loss that quickly expands into a profound meditation on the role of women as guardians of emotional life. In fact, there is no emotional core here; rather, this outward-looking proliferation of redescriptions and interpretations is implosive and filled with uncertainty. The work's title – 'Prenez soin de vois' ('Take care of yourself') – is said to be the phrase employed by Calle's boyfriend to close an email message that abruptly, unceremoniously severed their romantic relationship. Calle presents this email to 107 women professionals and enlists their help in building a profile of this man, her former lover. Artists, philosophers, copy-editors, dancers and psychoanalysts all rise to the occasion to provide Calle with raw material for an elaborate documentary project. In one sense, Calle's work is a collective act of rage and healing – *female* rage and *female* healing – that quickly undermines the crude stereotype of women as beings of extraordinary emotional literacy but rather limited rational capabilities. Calle composes an extraordinary social landscape of dialogue obliquely, as it were, by holding the entire experience at bay. The spectacle of scores of other women using their professional expertise to create, reflect upon, analyse and criticize the instigator of the artist's distress is breathtaking; after a while, it is no longer relevant to the viewer whether the offending email presented by Calle is truth or fiction. We are more engaged and immersed with what confronts us; nothing less than a cross-section of contemporary social life, attitudes, aspirations and varieties of emotional and intellectual expression. All this has the effect of showing that if one is prepared to step outside one's habitual responses, something surprising and wonderful may result. Beyond this, one has the sense of an elaborate social ritual unfolding before us; a logical ordering of incredible energies for the sake of one person's passage through a broken relationship. It is, perhaps, one of the most comprehensive pictures of the moral climate of our time that any artist has had the ambition to create.

That the work is composed of such relatively unexceptional parts – unexceptional in the sense of normal forms of visual media, such as the video, the text-on-the-wall, captioned photography, etc. – adds to its sense of veracity. The work as a whole is eminently accessible. Everyone but Calle registers the responses to her being dumped by her boyfriend. Estranged from the very situation that provokes the work, Calle presents us with an inventory of possible emotional responses without ever having to betray herself. Paradoxically, were she to do so, the entire edifice would collapse, because we would no longer feel the need to keep the figure of 'Sophie Calle' in circulation. The forms Calle uses – particularly word and image – add to the sense of estrangement from the original trauma that is the presumptive basis of this work. The multiplicity of media engages the spectator in a sensory and intellectual experience of intoxicating richness; a strategy, needless to say, that was pioneered by feminist artists of the past several decades. The effect, it seems, mirrors the flux of consciousness and emotional affect that constitutes our experience of the everyday. Ultimately, one still must take responsibility for sifting through reams of vagrant opinion, expert advice and a cornucopia of networked texts, performances, theatre and visual imagery.

LABELS

The visual stereotype aims to denote its subject as a particular kind of being. With its nefarious, dehumanizing purpose in mind, the stereotype works through the exaggeration of physical characteristics and social custom, muddling what the philosopher Nelson Goodman describes as the subtle distinctions between 'representation' and 'representation-as'. The woman, the African American, the Jew, the Pakistani become 'objects classified by or under various pictorial labels'.[33] The labels, in turn, are subject to further classification and in the realm of picturing pose two questions: 'what is represented?' and 'what sort of representation is it?' The class of images of racial stereotypes might seem an extreme type of representation, but in its active classification and characterization it exemplifies the constructive nature of representation. That stereotypical images may come to be seen as truthful imitations is a matter of social reinforcement; the social group imposing the stereotype finds it to be useful for the pursuit of other aims. The stereotype, like the religious icon, is a powerful tool of social cohesion; a rallying point and a warning. It identifies the Other and justifies his alienation from our social world and the means of domination used to enforce such a separation. The representation of the Other as less than human, less than civilized, weakens the bond of human solidarity and diminishes our own humanity in the bargain. By narrowing our own frame of social reference, we deny the possibility of unexpected social encounters and new opportunities for learning and adaptation; in short, we deduct something from our own sense of identity.

What is at stake when an artist consciously adopts caricature as a critical tool with which to reflect on the role of representations in the formation of identity? The artist enters quite directly into the discussion about race and ethnicity in order to affirm the value of visual representations in the construction of identity. In the visual culture of the West, the celebration of racial superiority and ethnic identity is widespread and persistent. According to Karla Holloway, there is an important distinction to be drawn between the concepts of 'race' and 'ethnicity'. It is, as Holloway points out, 'an issue of agency'; 'ethnicity is a self-determined and defined construction' while 'race is a politically conferred and simplistic abstraction that is easily co-opted into systems of abuse and domination'. The desire on the part of artists to understand this distinction has led to the creation of some of the most harrowing and powerful works of modern and contemporary art. Some works that take racial stereotyping and ethnic identity as their subject do so in a softer register, in order to analyse the subtler points of 'representation-as'. Clearly, the conjunction of word and image in these works, such as the photographically based art of Lorna Simpson of the late 1980s, aims at directing our attention towards the ambiguities in the act of visual and verbal labelling (illus. 87). The work already ensures that certain images will be read directly and therefore the placement of a dissembling caption frustrates the efficiency of the image while pointing out its

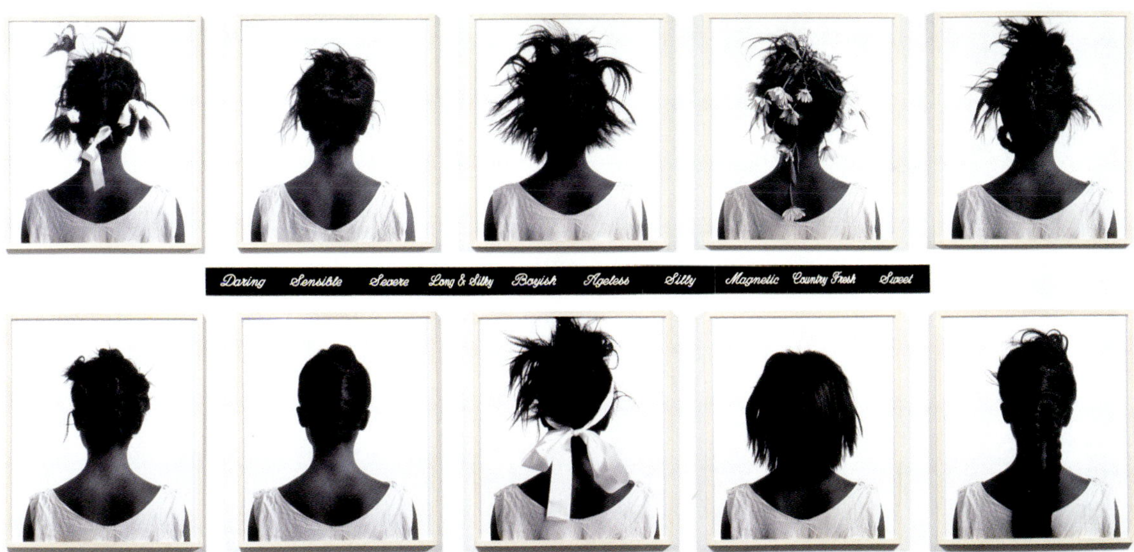

87 Lorna Simpson, *Stereo Styles*, 1988, 10 Polaroid prints, 10 engraved plastic plaques.

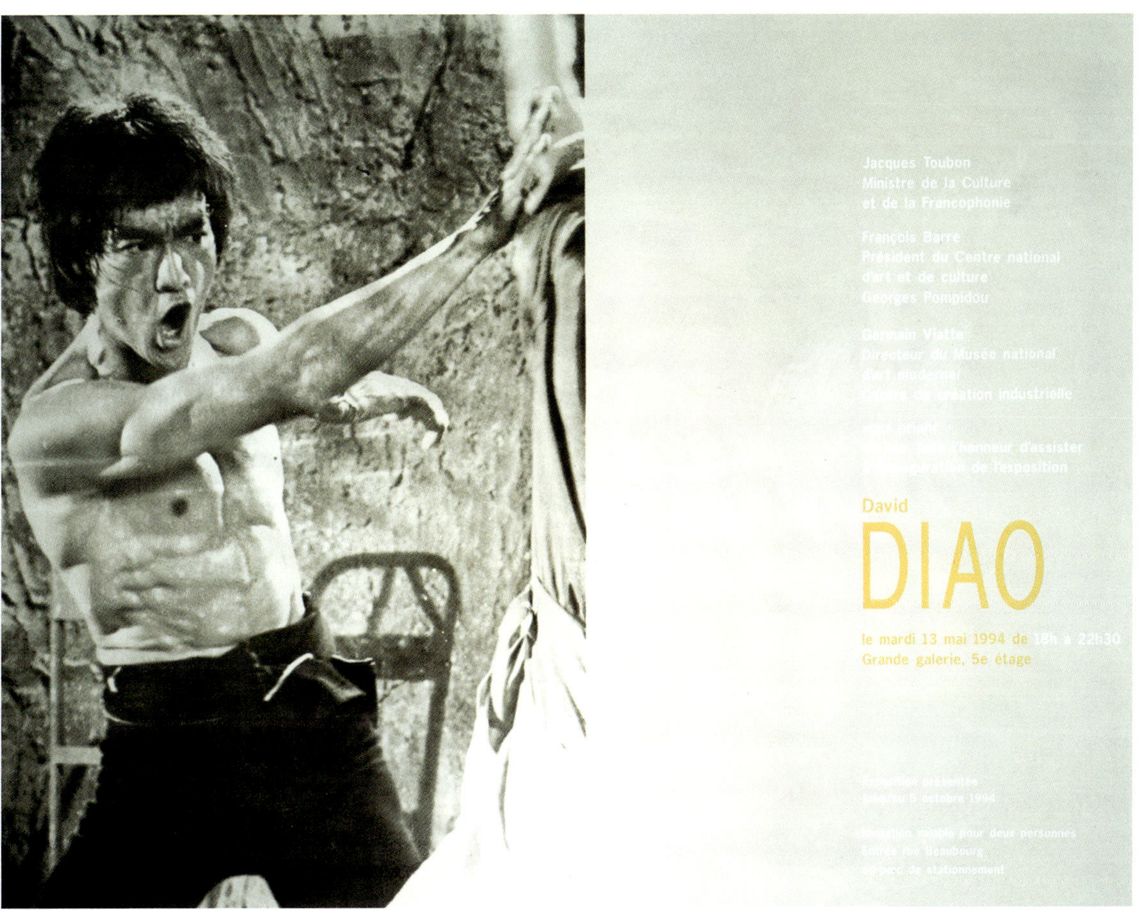

88 David Diao, *Carton d'Invitation*, 1994.

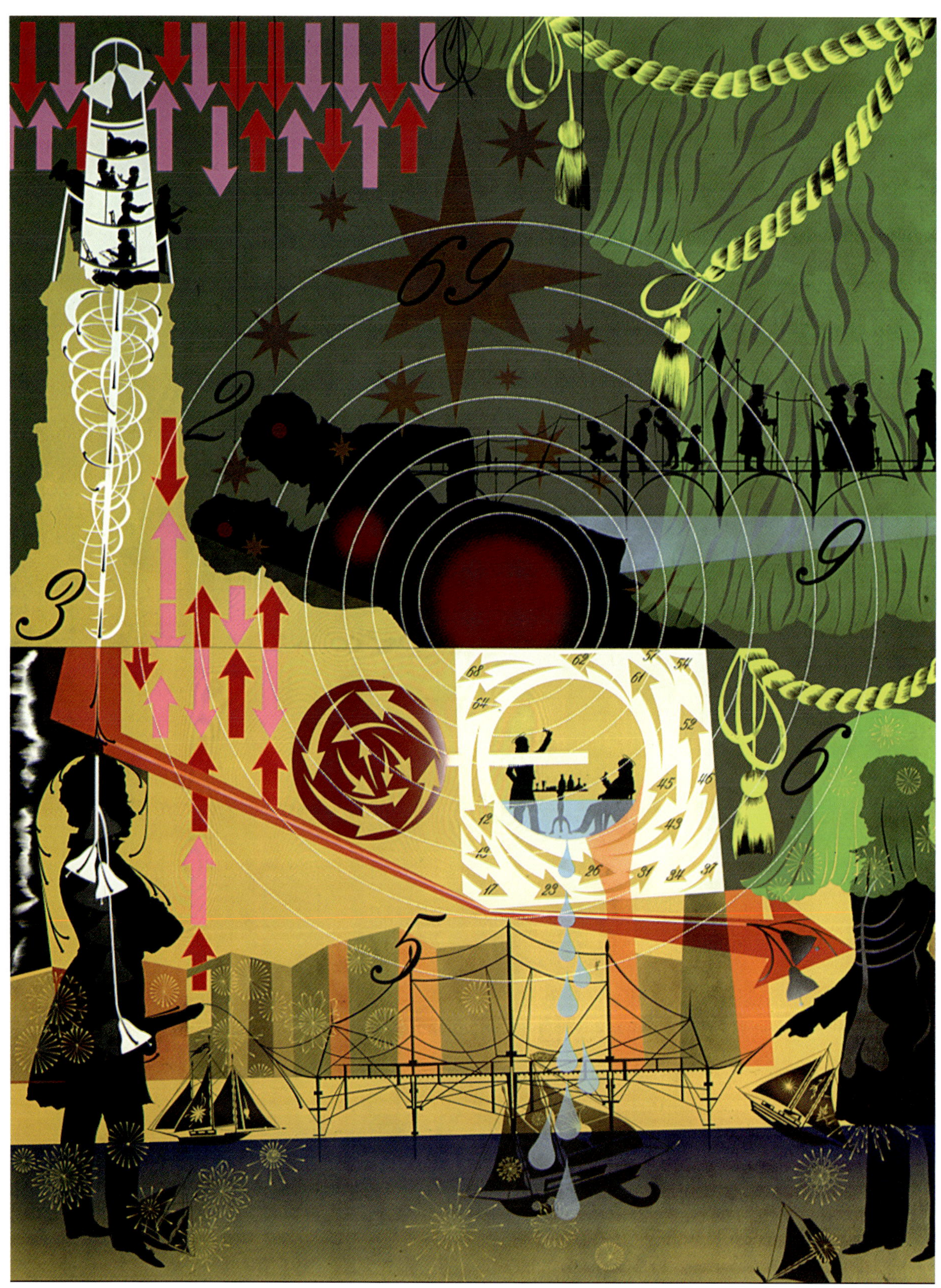

89 Lari Pittman, *This Wholesomeness, Beloved and Despised, Continues Regardless*, 1989–90, acrylic and enamel on two mahogany panels.

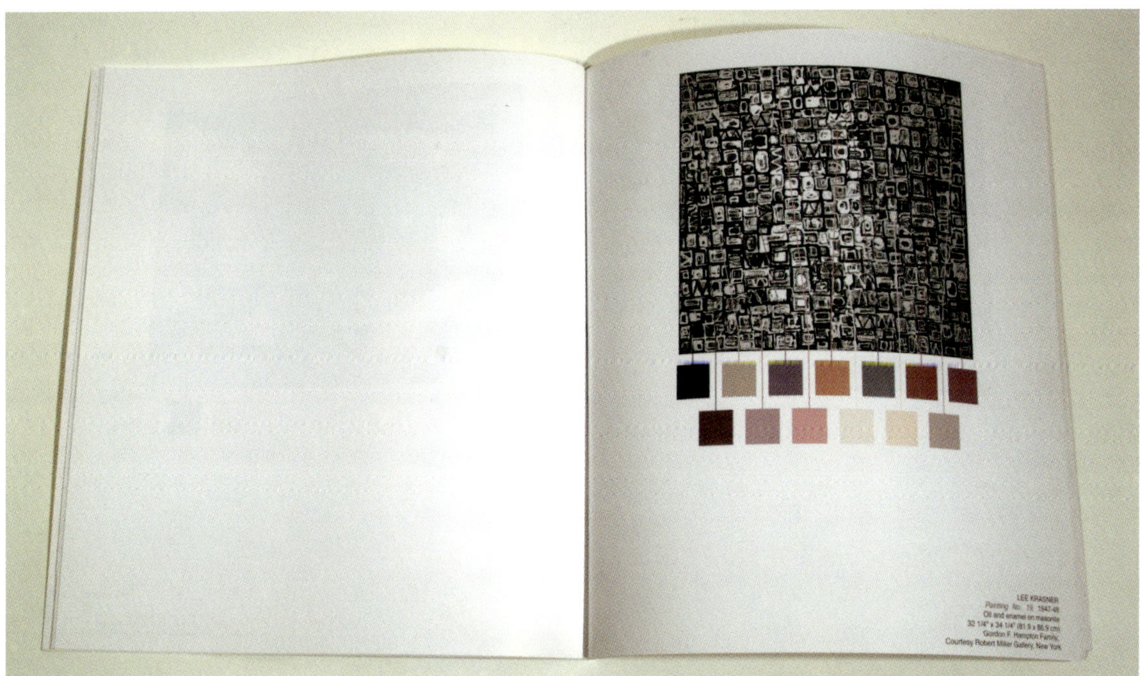

90 Brian Kennon, *Lee Krasner, Painting No. 12*, 1948–9, from *Black and White Reproductions of the Abstract Expressionists* (2003).

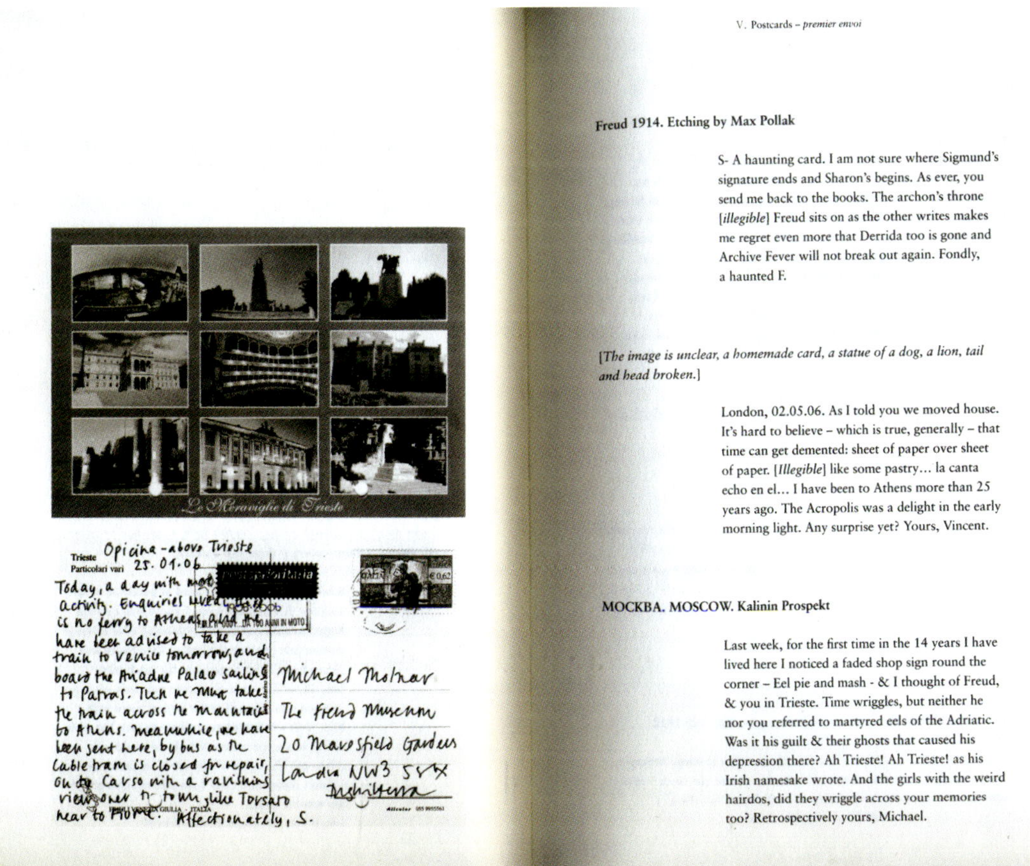

V. Postcards – *premier envoi*

Freud 1914. Etching by Max Pollak

S- A haunting card. I am not sure where Sigmund's signature ends and Sharon's begins. As ever, you send me back to the books. The archon's throne [*illegible*] Freud sits on as the other writes makes me regret even more that Derrida too is gone and Archive Fever will not break out again. Fondly, a haunted F.

[*The image is unclear, a homemade card, a statue of a dog, a lion, tail and head broken.*]

London, 02.05.06. As I told you we moved house. It's hard to believe – which is true, generally – that time can get demented: sheet of paper over sheet of paper. [*Illegible*] like some pastry… la canta echo en el… I have been to Athens more than 25 years ago. The Acropolis was a delight in the early morning light. Any surprise yet? Yours, Vincent.

MOCKBA. MOSCOW. Kalinin Prospekt

Last week, for the first time in the 14 years I have lived here I noticed a faded shop sign round the corner – Eel pie and mash - & I thought of Freud, & you in Trieste. Time wriggles, but neither he nor you referred to martyred eels of the Adriatic. Was it his guilt & their ghosts that caused his depression there? Ah Trieste! Ah Trieste! as his Irish namesake wrote. And the girls with the weird hairdos, did they wriggle across your memories too? Retrospectively yours, Michael.

91 Sharon Kivland, *Freud on Holiday*, 2008.

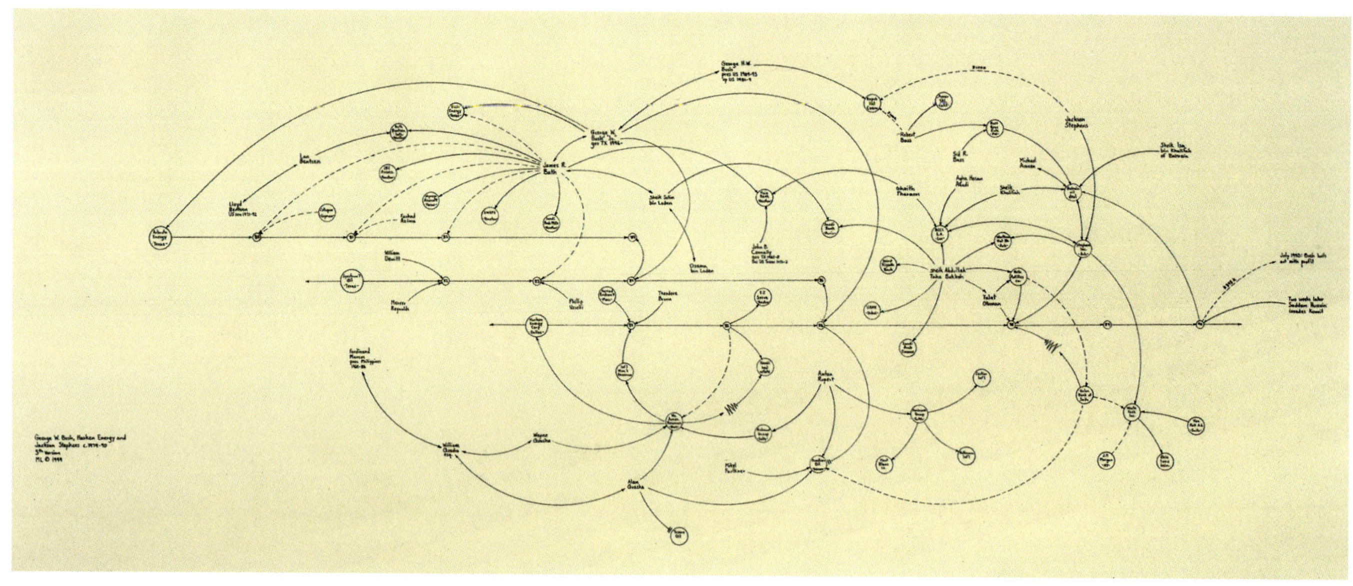

92 Mark Lombardi, *George W. Bush, Harken Energy and Jackson Stephens*, *c.* 1979–90, 5th version, 1999, graphite on paper.

invidious message. As such, the disclosure through visual art of the mechanisms of reproduction of race prejudice and ethnic identity has taken a variety of forms and moods, from the brutality of Kara Walker's representations of both African-Americans and whites in the setting of the antebellum South to the fey contrivance of David Diao's depiction of the artist's erstwhile alter ego, Bruce Lee (illus. 86).

KNOWLEDGE WORK

With the means of digital form building and dissemination firmly entrenched in the armoury of contemporary artistic techniques, the boundary between word and image is routinely breached. Lush arabesques flow seamlessly into distorted but recognizable alphabetic characters that, in turn, morph into figurative compositions of astonishing complexity, sometimes in real time in the form of an animated image (illus. 89). Confronted with imagery that appears to be supplemented with notations drawn from the visual culture of scientific displays of quantitative and qualitative information, contemporary interpretation is forced into new and often unfamiliar territory. But hybrid forms can be easily 'decoded'; what is required is an awareness of the ways in which a variety of historical practices may be collected in one form, like the artist's book, and are then transfigured and mapped onto one another. For Brian Kennon, the bookworks of Ed Ruscha and the subversive practices of Guy Debord comprise important resources of expression that are brought to bear on unlikely subjects, such as a reflection on the status of reproductions of works of art (illus. 90). For Sharon Kivland, the corpus of Sigmund Freud's writings and episodes from his life serve to organize a complex series of bookworks masquerading as travel guides yet marked by the structure of the dream as wish-fulfilment (illus. 91).

Where once the print-based media provided a stable ground for the presumptive subversion by dynamic semiotic theories of the word and image complex, the contemporary critic and historian of art must delve into the theory of the cinema, of digital media and other theories of visual culture to elaborate their analyses. What is almost a given amongst a new generation of artists and theorists is how so many of these fields of inquiry have already internalized the figure of globalization within their semantic matrix.

Mark Lombardi (1951–2000) produced enchanting pictures of corruption. The artist's large-scale network drawings chronicle the interlocking

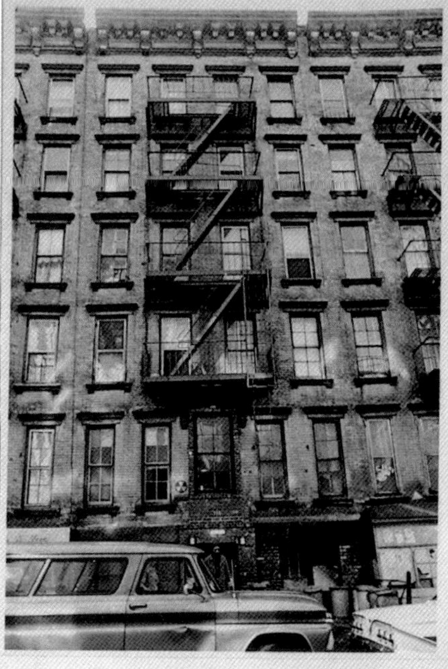

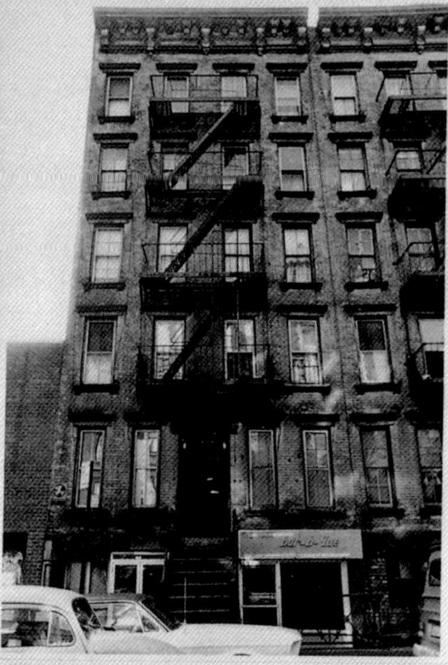

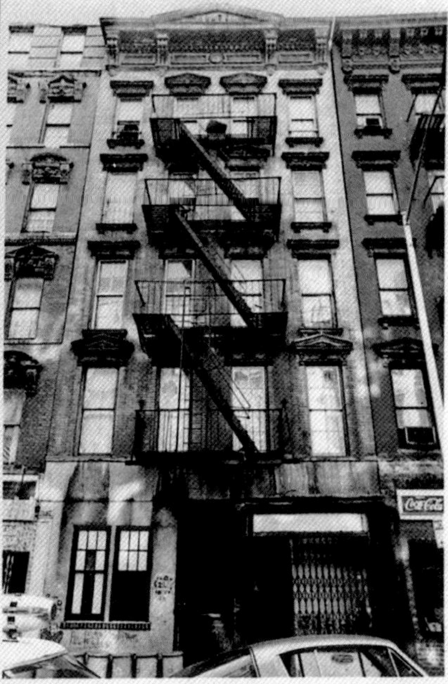

93 Hans Haacke, Shapolsky et al., *Manhattan Real Estate Holdings, a Real Time Social System as of May 1, 1971*, 1971, photographic print.

corporate relations, dubious financial transactions and criminal spheres of influence that defined scandals such as the Whitewater controversy (involving former President Bill Clinton and Secretary of State Hillary Rodham Clinton), the Iran-Contra affair (made public in 1986), the implication of the Vatican bank (named the Institute for Works of Religion) in the 1982 collapse of the Banco Ambrosiano, and the savings and loan debacle of the 1980s and 1990s (illus. 92).

Lombardi's sociograms are often large, spanning over ten feet in length. Lombardi gathered the material by researching published sources of information, such as newspapers, magazines and websites. This information was then transcribed onto index cards, resulting in, at the time of his death, an archive of more than 12,000 items. Lombardi's first major exhibition was mounted at The Drawing Center (New York) in 1997; two solo exhibitions followed in 1998 and 1999. In 2000, at the age of 48, Lombardi committed suicide.

Lombardi's link to historical Conceptual art is often mentioned because of the artist's interest in depicting documentary information in an aesthetically engaging visual form. The German-American artist Hans Haacke utilized this approach in the creation of an early work that sought to reveal the sordid real-estate holdings of Harry Shapolsky, a trustee of the Guggenheim Museum, New York. Haacke's project – 'Shapolsky et al. *Manhattan Real Estate Holdings, a Real Time Social System as of May 1, 1971*' (illus. 93) – prompted the cancellation of the artist's solo exhibition at the Guggenheim. This incident became a *cause célèbre* for proponents of freedom of speech and the work itself a touchstone for artists and writers on art interested in the accountability to a wider public of cultural institutions.

The conjunction of political revelation and the delicate, sensuality of drawing is the hallmark of Lombardi's brief practice. In this regard, the artist's practice is related to a number of others within the generic field of 'Neo-Conceptual Art' that play on the seduction of the beholder by various dramatic visual means in order to deliver a sobering political message. The aesthetic impact of Lombardi's serpentine pictures of corruption is due to the distance between the nature of the activities being depicted and the style in which such depiction occurs. While not strictly speaking readymades, Lombardi's sociograms encapsulate a wide range of unspecified social and political relations as a graphically coherent entity. They are reified representations of dynamic social relations; maps that permit a kind of analysis but which do little to illuminate the dialogical relations that lie beneath the contingent relations of association. One critical commentary of Haacke's practice that is applicable to Lombardi's likened the former's politically charged work to a form of homeopathy: the social 'body' would be 'cured' through exposure to a measured dose of the same 'poison' to which its sickness could be traced.

Both Haacke's and Lombardi's practices assume the existence of a democratic *public sphere* in which the revealed truths of corruption and exploitation would be subject to free and uncensored rational debate by informed citizens. They are highly burnished tools; but will they be admired for their utility or their elegance? Perhaps the image of social relations and interactions as an objective *thing* offers the beholder a rhetorically powerful reminder of the realities accompanying the exercise of economic and political power in the United States. Equally, such an image can function as a powerful closure on debate, with no guarantee that the art will be an 'efficient' cause of either political reflection or action.

In many ways, the delicately traced sociograms of Lombardi evoke the less confrontational metaphor of the *rhizome*, a concept coined by the French philosopher Gilles Deleuze and French psychoanalyst Félix Guattari in their collaborative text *A Thousand Plateaus* (1980; English translation, 1987). The rhizome as shorthand for unfettered, non-hierarchical connectivity has been eagerly embraced by artists, theorists and cultural managers alike and used to describe and legitimize a strategy of artmaking or curating that aims to create links across heterogeneous fields of knowledge, experience and practice. The rhizome has also served as a powerful metaphor for the alleged social effects of the Internet, standing in for a liberated spirit of 'connectivity' in general.

THE RETURN OF THE NARRATIVE

Frances Stark (b. 1967) has been producing word and image works since the late 1990s. *Structures That Fit My Opening and Other Parts Considered in Relation to Their Whole* (2006) incorporates a wide array of textual and graphic materials, including Stark's own writings, into the structure of a PowerPoint presentation. Coincidentally, in 2003 Edward R. Tufte – the doyen of the graphic representation of quantitative and qualitative data – produced an incisive and humorous diatribe against the unthinking use of PowerPoint presentations. In 'The Cognitive Style of PowerPoint', Tufte assesses the eponymous slideware and finds it wanting, asserting that it 'reduces the analytical quality of presentations', weakens 'verbal and spatial reasoning' and 'almost always corrupt(s) statistical analysis'. The problem with PowerPoint presentations is that they suppress dialogue: 'PowerPoint is entirely *presenter-oriented*, and *not content-oriented, not audience-oriented*.' Serious analysis is replaced with 'chartjunk, over-produced layouts, cheerleader logotypes and branding, and corny clip art'; in short, Tufte writes, 'PowerPointPhluff'.[34]

Stark is no corporate presenter. What interest does her use of PowerPoint hold for us? The indelible association of PowerPoint with corporate culture clearly articulated by Tufte seems irrelevant to Stark's practice, which is virtually a point-by-point negation of these values: 'the metaphor behind the PowerPoint cognitive style is *the software corporation itself*. That is, a big bureaucracy engaged in *computer programming* (deeply hierarchical, nested, highly structured, relentlessly sequential, one-short-line-at-a-time) and in *marketing* (fast pace, misdirection, advocacy not analysis, slogan thinking, branding, exaggerated claims, marketplace ethics).'[35]

Tufte asks why 'the structure, activities, and values of a large commercial bureaucracy (should) be a useful metaphor for our presentations'. It is pretty clear that no metaphor could be worse than the 'hierarchical market-pitch approach'.[36] But Stark's use of PowerPoint and her framing of word and image, too, is to communicate a very different cognitive style; one antithetical to the world of business but also, and perhaps more pointedly, a rebuke to the fantasy world of 'art world' expectations. Stark's Derridean premise demands that the process of deferring or repudiating 'X' results in something akin to the actual production of 'X'. Stark's repudiation of alienated art-making unavoidably results in the making of art. In her collaged works especially, the arduously achieved 'wholeness' is never quite convincing, as it is never allowed to look as if it is 'finished', or, better, 'settled'.

The restless Stark has been called 'an artist who writes or a writer who makes primarily text-based artworks'. Saul Steinberg, you may recall, also described himself as a writer who draws. There is an intriguing ambivalence to such pronouncements, as though committing one's self to this or that role is an act of self-betrayal. Indeed, it may very well be felt as such. However, here as elsewhere in the contemporary field of word and image, there is ample scope for the creation of metapictures, that is, pictures about the process of making pictures.[37] Stark's self-reflexive monologues 'write' her work while declaring her refusal to do so. Stark's images are not illustrations to her texts; some of the artist's images are made of text contorted into a more or less recognizable representation of something else. And Stark's texts are not necessarily captions underpinning the meaning of her images. Stark's *Structure That F(its My Opening)* (illus. 95), for example, consists of the text-image of a snail shell, while the snail's body is represented by a fragment of a silk shirt.

The question of whom or what coaxes this organism out of its shell has been mooted, as if this picture were symbolic of Stark's famous deferrals of writing. Clearly, it is a body-like depiction that invites many associations, some of which are intentionally romantic with respect to the situation of the artist in the world. Still, Stark's work is far from flabby or sentimental. Her playful combination of word and image rehearses nothing less than the ingenuity of the highly pragmatic *bricoleur*. The double entendre ('opening' as sexual or bodily orifice or premier of an exhibition) is hastily cast in the title through the use of a parenthesis, which functions as a cut that ruptures the syntactical flow. Everything is left hanging and the impression is of a work that was thrown together at speed. Many of Stark's works show the literal suturing of elements

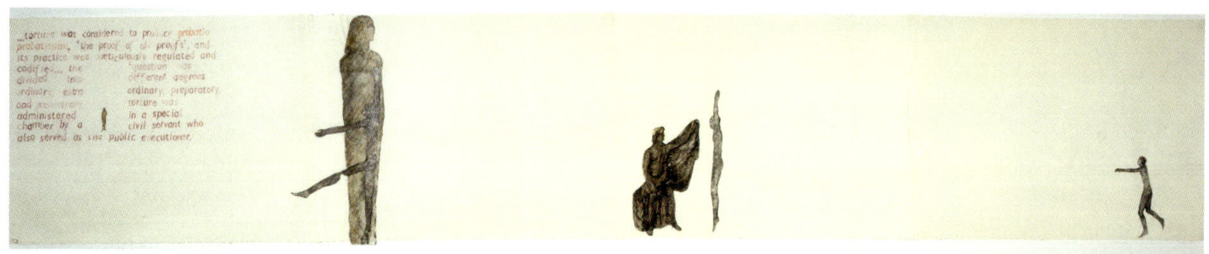

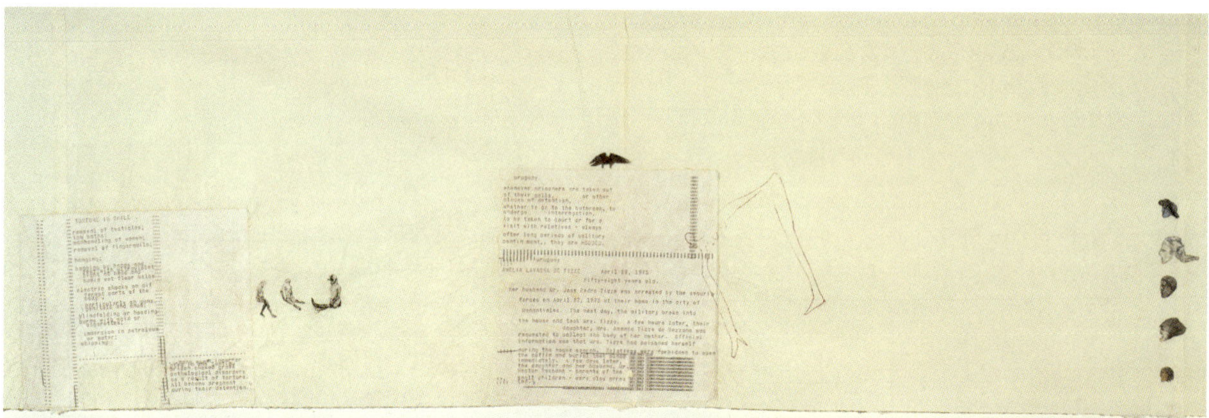

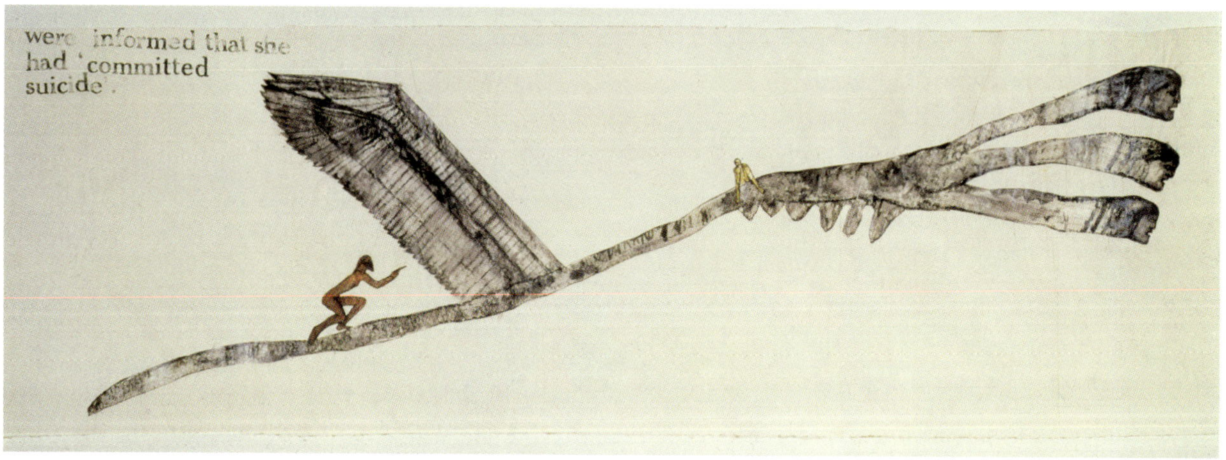

94 Nancy Spero, *The Torture of Women* (detail), 1976, gouache, typewritten notes, collage and handwriting on laid paper.

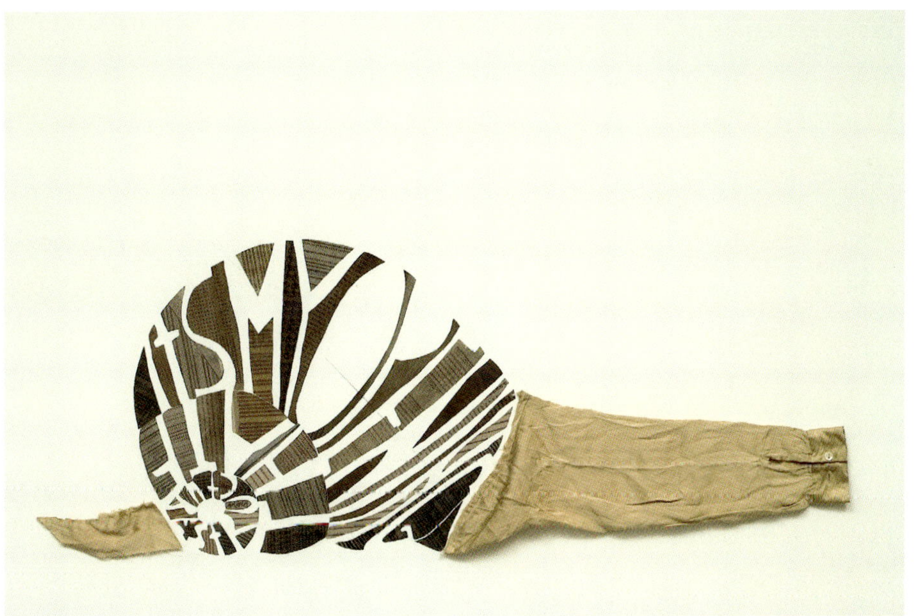

95 Frances Stark, *Structure That F(its My Opening)*, 2006, gouache on paper with silk on panel.

and elicit a disregard for sophisticated finish; they are more graphic collision than composition. The collage and the drawing are all direct means of making, giving force to the artist's claim to wish to 'reflect on why . . . urgency in terms of production increasingly seems to overshadow urgency in terms of expression.'[38] The problems of the visual and the verbal are nothing compared to those faced by the artist who orchestrates their union.

AFFECTIVE MAPPING

In the wake of 9/11, the use of drawing gained ground as a tool specifically charged with communicating the subjective experiences of the artist. An urgent need for a vehicle to help one overcome trauma was sincerely felt; drawing, as the most indexical of tools for the creation of visual art, was the preferred mode of expression. In effect, the conventional view of representation as analogy or mirroring became the dominant mode of meaning.

Through her use of blotting as a self-consciously inept technique of drawing, Tracey Emin simultaneously draws attention to the rich tradition of expressionist drawing in twentieth-century European modernism while also recalling Andy Warhol's blotted illustrations, which were produced with the assistance of the artist's mother. The splayed naked figure, presumably a self-portrait, is accompanied by a sprawling caption, spelling errors intact. These combined markers serve to relocate drawing as a specifically gendered resource of self-expression (illus. 97). It is also not surprising that needlepoint – a conventionally feminized craft practice – exists alongside drawing in Emin's practice as one of her most convincing artistic suits.

During the early part of the twenty-first century, artists continued to choose drawing and other obviously autographic and labour-intensive processes as the preferred media for works that intend to signify the least distance between personal observation and reaction and the public domain in which such works were to find a home. In the work of Annabel Daou (b. 1967) the intensity of artistic effort and the specificity of subject matter combine to create a series of highly detailed redescriptions of the idea of the USA as seen through the texts of its founding documents. Daou's *America* (2006) is a large drawing pieced together of hand-transcribed excerpts from important political addresses and social documents. As a compound 'textimage' it presents an abstract example of visual poetry, where the principal formal effect is one of graded tonalities that reduce text to undifferentiated matter. Done entirely using graphite pencils, the density of Daou's transcription yields an array of grey tones across the surface of the drawing. The resulting pattern resembles nothing so much as a cross-section of a crystalline or geologic strata. Once more, the artist's choice of the scale of the work – in this instance, 88 x 150 inches – pushes to the limits the resolve of the artist to maintain focus and quality of mark-making and the resolve of the beholder to remain attentive.

In *Ruined Cities* (illus. 100), Daou creates a poignant map of towns and villages across the world and throughout time that have been destroyed; some identify those destroyed during the course of Lebanon's civil war. Here, place names are rendered with delicacy and informality

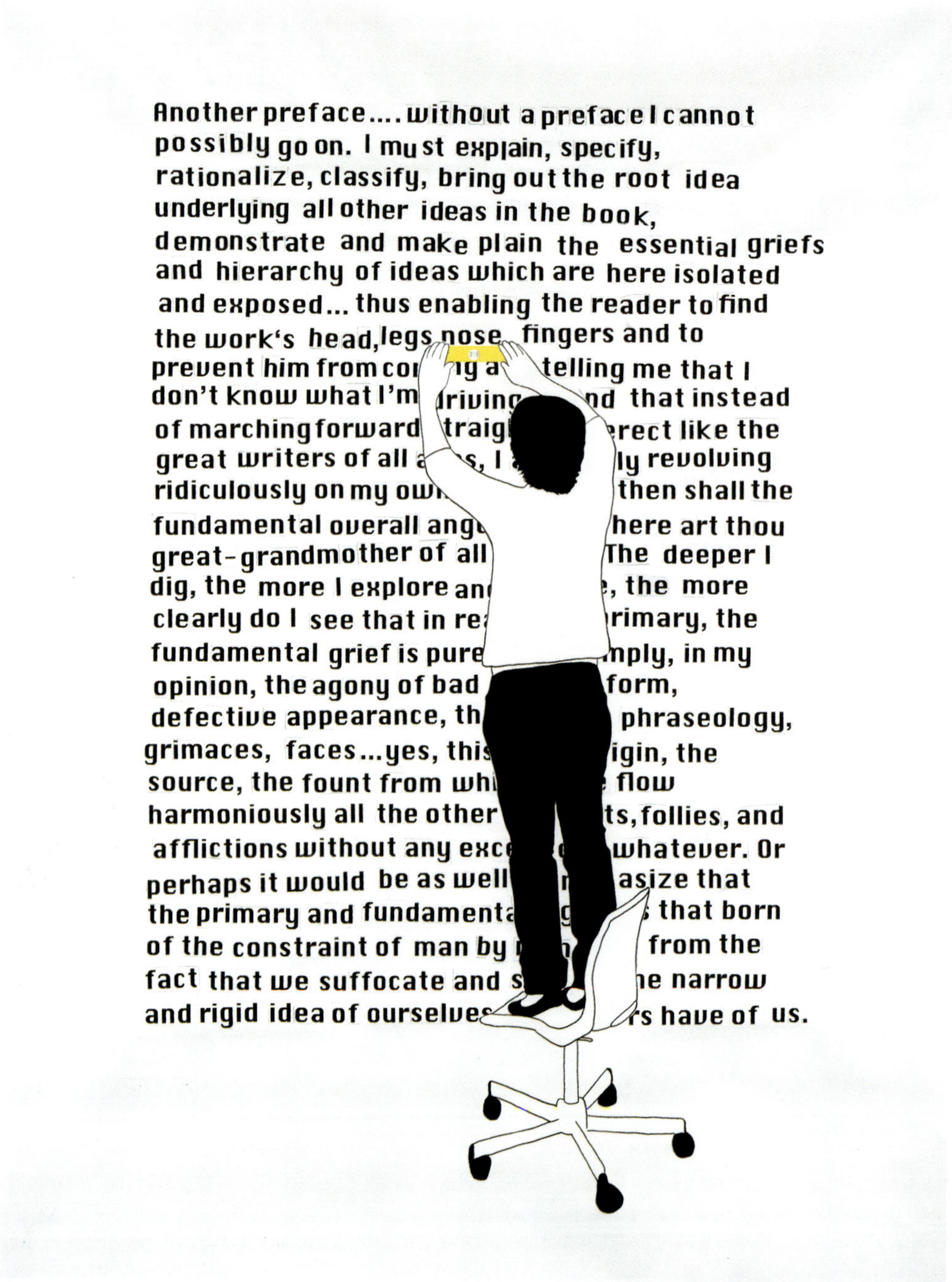

Another preface.... without a preface I cannot
possibly go on. I must explain, specify,
rationalize, classify, bring out the root idea
underlying all other ideas in the book,
demonstrate and make plain the essential griefs
and hierarchy of ideas which are here isolated
and exposed... thus enabling the reader to find
the work's head, legs nose fingers and to
prevent him from co ng a telling me that I
don't know what I'm driving nd that instead
of marching forward traig rect like the
great writers of all s, I ly revolving
ridiculously on my ow then shall the
fundamental overall ang here art thou
great-grandmother of all The deeper I
dig, the more I explore an , the more
clearly do I see that in re rimary, the
fundamental grief is pure mply, in my
opinion, the agony of bad form,
defective appearance, th phraseology,
grimaces, faces...yes, thi igin, the
source, the fount from wh flow
harmoniously all the other ts, follies, and
afflictions without any exc whatever. Or
perhaps it would be as well asize that
the primary and fundament that born
of the constraint of man by from the
fact that we suffocate and s e narrow
and rigid idea of ourselve s have of us.

96 Frances Stark, *I must explain, specify, rationalize, classify, etc.*, 2007, vinyl paint and inlaid laser print on paper; text is taken from Witold Gombrowicz's novel of 1937, *Ferdydurke*.

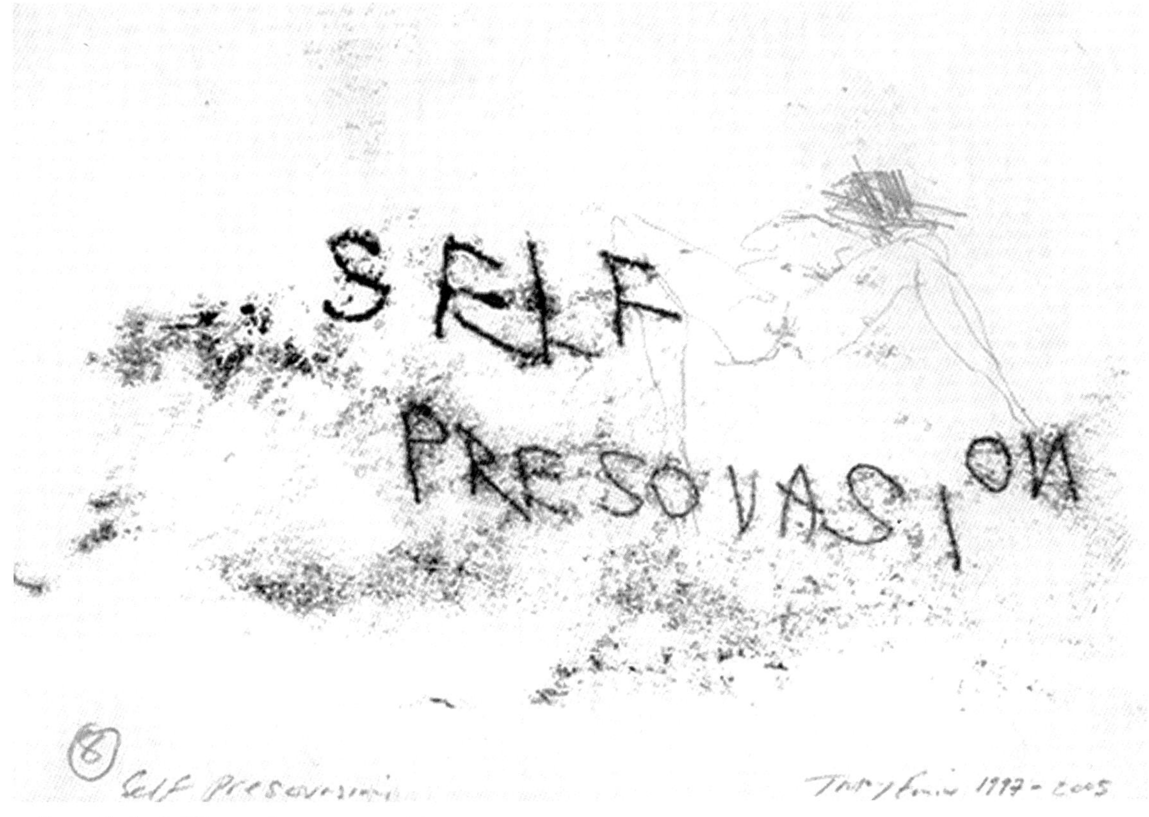

97 Tracey Emin, *Self Presovasion*, 1997–2005, ink on paper.

using pen and ink. Their clustering, more or less from memory, suggests a map of one area of the country of her birth. The drawing is a collection of irregularly torn pieces of paper that have been fastened together with tape. The work invites us to compare the shattered integrity of the Lebanese nation during this period, and also leads us to mediate on the selective construction of memory. In both readings, the compromised substrate of the map-like drawing encourages an analogical interpretation. It may be pointed out that the evocative fragmentation of the drawing's ground is overstated. Yet the acting out of destruction and renovation is an essential part of Daou's artistic process. In general, the performative element of drawing is always present in our interpretation and prevents the work from being seen as simply an *image*. The relative informality and directness associated with drawing and collage imbues Daou's work with an enormous optimism. The artist's deft orchestration of techniques has produced a token of great empathy.

The success of drawing over the past decade, then, does not necessarily turn on an appeal to tradition or a reinstatement of academic artistic skills and competences. Rather, drawing *works* – especially in the context of word and image art – because it announces a difference between art and media. The calligraphic hand is a trace of human writing and, however devalued by overuse, persists as a powerful symbol of authenticity (illus. 98, 99).

During periods of great trauma, uncertainty and insecurity, the reassertion of human mastery over technology or nature seems reassuring and necessary. Just as ekphrasis employs the pretext of description to overwrite the visual for the sake of the literary, systems of notation that translate or codify physical processes or actions over time, like choreographic or musical scores, may be viewed as aesthetic forms in their own right. The judicious choice of notational conventions will yield something other than a perspicuous map of an unfamiliar territory or a reliable guide for the performance of a ballet or a symphony. Like Daou, the New York-based artist Brian Lund (b. 1974) is also interested in personal systems of notation and drawing where the appearance is far removed from any kind of usable representation or diagram (illus. 101). Lund's work, however, begins from the rather different position of the cinema spectator. The artist's task is to translate the structure of moving pictures into a serpentine diagram of abstract symbols. The symbols do not conform to any professional shorthand used by cinematographers or directors to indicate the various kinds of edits that move the action from scene to scene, but they do correspond to the fundamental structural elements of the film. Lund develops these

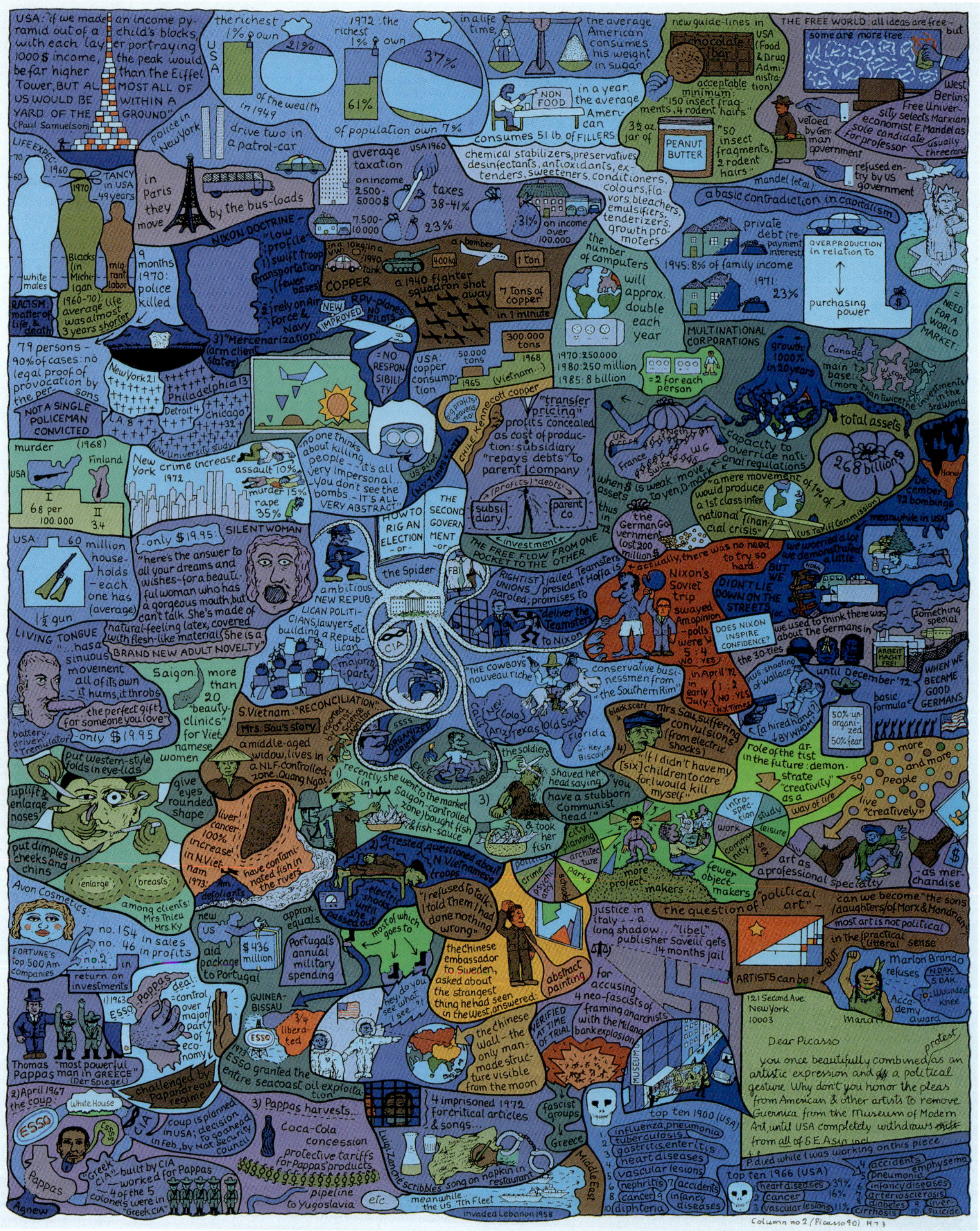

98 Öyvind Fahlström, *Column no. 2 (Picasso 90)*, 1973, screenprint on paper.

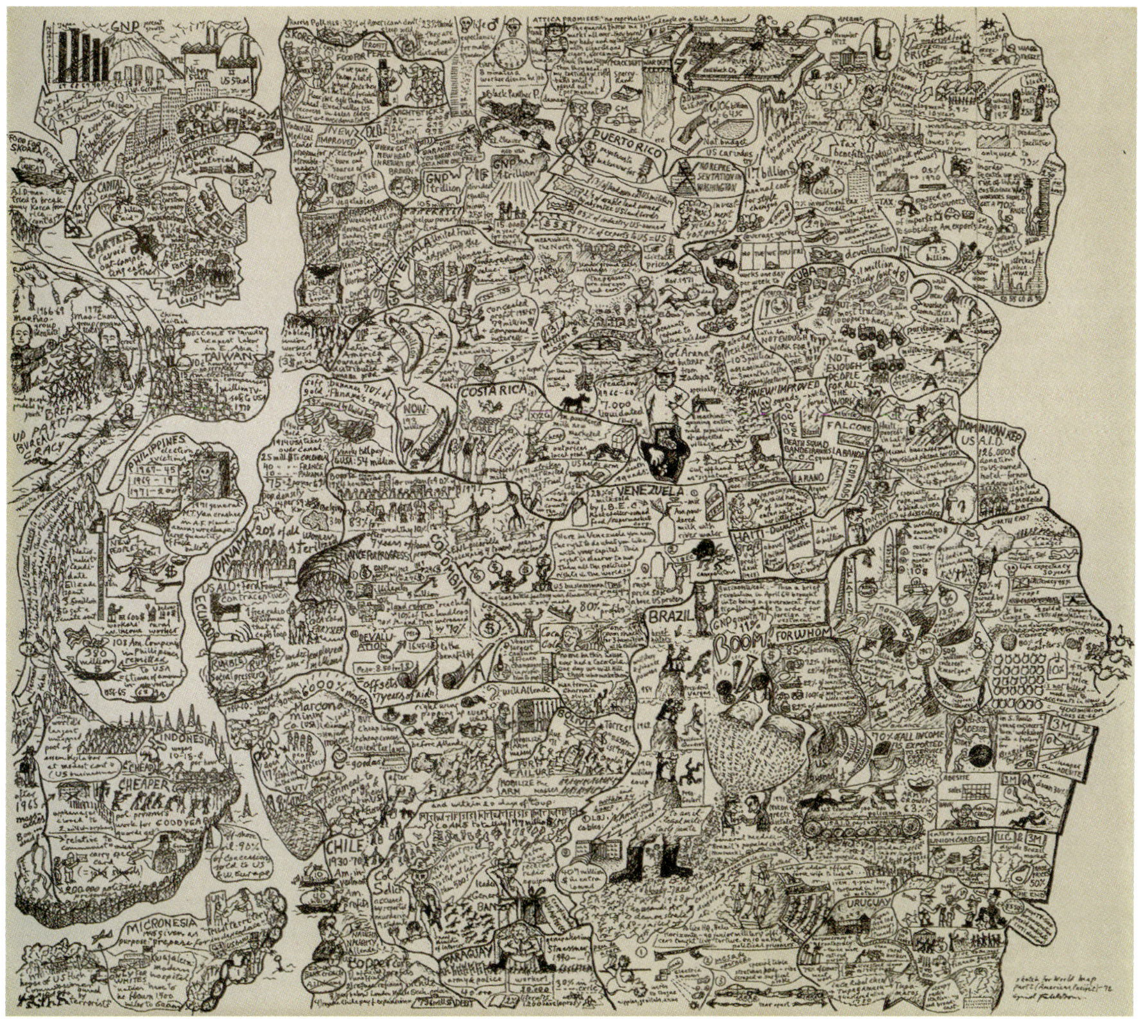

99 Öyvind Fahlström, *Sketch for World Map Part 1 (Americas & Pacific)*, 1972, lithograph on paper.

maps by drawing from the resource of the film script, storyboards and other production information, as well as repeated viewings of the film itself. The temporal element is not simulated; the illusion of movement is reduced appropriately to a set of repeating symbols and colours. The motion picture itself is redescribed as a repetitive structure, nearly distilled to the indivisible unit of the single frame.

THE NETWORKED INTIMACY OF THE INTERNET

It is being argued that the ubiquity in contemporary art of handwritten text, drawing and the use of the traditional draughting materials is symptomatic of a desire on the part of artists to differentiate the personal and intimately accessible work of art from the larger environment of mechanically produced and mass-distributed works of media. Intimacy expressed as a function of scale and through the reintroduction of traditional tools of artmaking has established itself as a powerful index of the interpersonal link that binds audience to artist. To draw is a powerful cultural code signalling the redescription of experience in symbolic form. Even when the scale of the work is relatively heroic, as in Lombardi's case, the tension between size, the relative fragility and impermanence of paper, and the labour-intensiveness required to realize the work becomes a paramount factor in its reception. Paradoxically, such work remains unintimidating despite its scale and our engagement is characteristically that of the curious

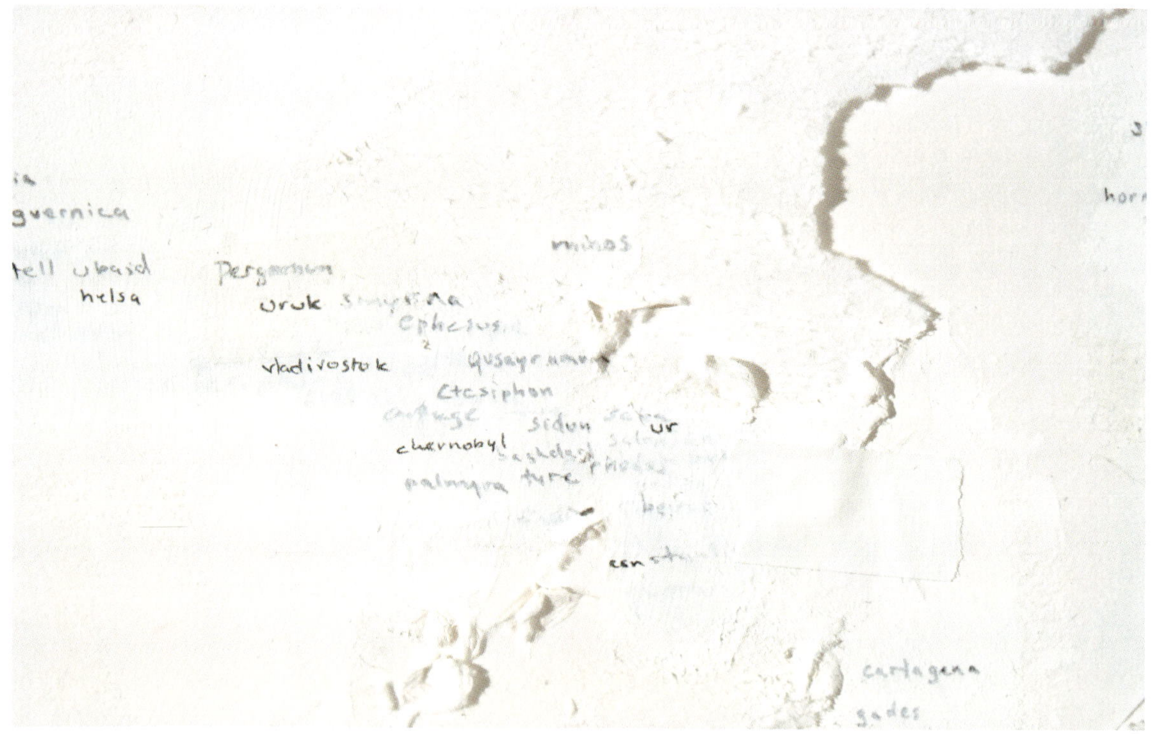

100 Annabel Daou, *Ruined Cities*, 2005, pencil, gesso and tape on paper (detail).

reader. However it is mediated, the effect aimed for is one of intimacy and communion. But it is also suggested that the contemporary vogue for drawing is not achieved without a cost: that of narrowing the range of modes of meaning in art and naturalizing one convention of representation above all others.

It is salutary, therefore, to consider word and image work that uses the platform of the Internet to garner resources of self-empowerment. The proliferation of Internet-based artists, along with the appearance of myriad websites of varying eccentricity and innovation, holds the promise of a new sort of technologically induced space for social interactions. The digital environment of the Internet is seen by some artists as an opportunity to create a highly specific social web. Much has been said about the false promise of community promoted by social networking sites. Rather than dwell on that aspect of digital technology, I shall turn to the way in which the existence of screen-based information that is portable and small-scale – from the laptop screen to the mobile phone or PDA display – provides us with the opportunity to articulate a link between our experiences of urban (macro) and screen-based (micro) environments. It seems important to understand how marketing attempts to colonize both environments while reconsidering the role of reading as a factor in a *negative* response to both worlds. Specifically, the way in which reading is compromised or celebrated as an intimate activity *regardless of where it takes place.*

The 'private' consumption and enjoyment of literature is a relatively recent phenomenon; during the Victorian era, books were routinely read aloud as a family entertainment. Today, reading, like the experience of listening to music on a personal MP3 player, is principally a solitary affair and only exceptionally a public spectacle. But our privacy is always being invaded; the daily amount of publicly accessible yet *unsolicited* and generally irrelevant, unwanted reading matter (read: information) is vast. From outdoors advertising to junk mail to unsolicited web pop-ups, one is constantly placed in the position of having to both *read* and to *defer reading*. The various intrusions – whether on the intimately scaled laptop screen or the huge animated billboards of Times Square – compel us to seek new ways to avoid being subjected to visual noise. The din of the global village actually encourages self-authoring. The twenty-first century *flâneur* is an entirely different animal from that described by Baudelaire in nineteenth-century Paris and theorized, in turn, by Georges Simmel and Walter Benjamin. During *our* walks through the city, our thoughts turn to *sabotage*.

The desire to resist the conventional demands of cultural authority is definitive of and persistent in artistic practice from the modern period to the present. The city and the structures and institutions of the knowledge economy itself are providing the

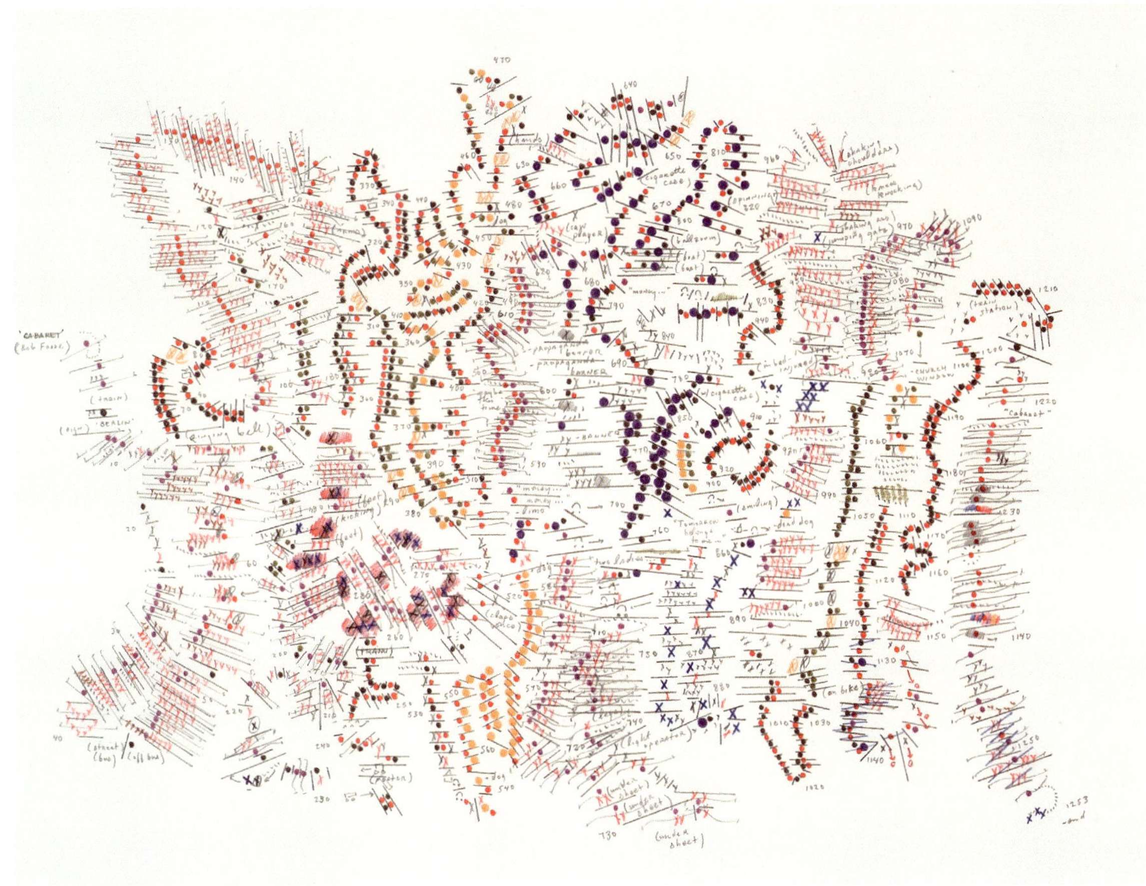

101 Brian Lund, *A Very Real and a Very Dark Time (Bob Fosse's Cabaret, 1200+ Edit Cuts)*, 2008, coloured pencil and graphite on paper.

impetus of this resistance. Earlier in this essay we discussed how a collective enterprise like The Yes Men aims to utilize the form of the modern newspaper to create a contraflow of political ideology. In the context of the Internet, Joe Scanlan demonstrates how to develop urbane, complex forms of resistance appropriate to a contemporary digital environment that most artists would consider to be unproblematic: namely, the convention of the artist's website. According to Alan Liu, 'cool' is the word used to describe 'oblique tactics of resistance'.[39] This is precisely the kind of subversive attitude cultivated by Scanlan and which is hilariously materialized through the various components of his website, 'Things That Fall'. One section – *Bent Light* – consists of texts by Edward Said, Milton Friedman and Joseph Schumpeter, which have been altered by Scanlan to produce an array of meanings antithetical to the originals. Scanlan helpfully indicates the class of revisions made through a system of colour-coding that graphically signals text that has been added, rewritten, moved or left intact (www.thingsthatfall.com/bentlight.php).

Another recent project, Concrete Poetry, conjoins word and image to lampoon the subjects inferred by the title's ambiguity. These include: the debt owed by modern architecture of the early twentieth century to a rather humble yet versatile construction material; the graphical literalization through letterforms of poetic imagery; the metaphorical reference to typography as the architecture of the page; and postmodernism itself. This last subject, exemplified by the works of key contemporary architects such as Frank Gehry, Jean Nouvel and Zaha Hadid, is the deep structure motivating the entire project. With its thoroughgoing embrace of montage easily pushed to excess, postmodernism itself becomes an object of ridicule (see illus. 102–105).

Scanlan's entire website is constructed to confound our expectations about what an artist does and how artwork operates in the world. His point seems to be that marketing artistic production is a form of artistic production that artists need to grasp and control. This is not to suggest that artists merely renovate their self-image and revise their practice by aligning it to the principles of the knowledge industry. In truth, the artist is not necessarily willing or able to join in without asserting her nonconformism. So Scanlan's website offers an

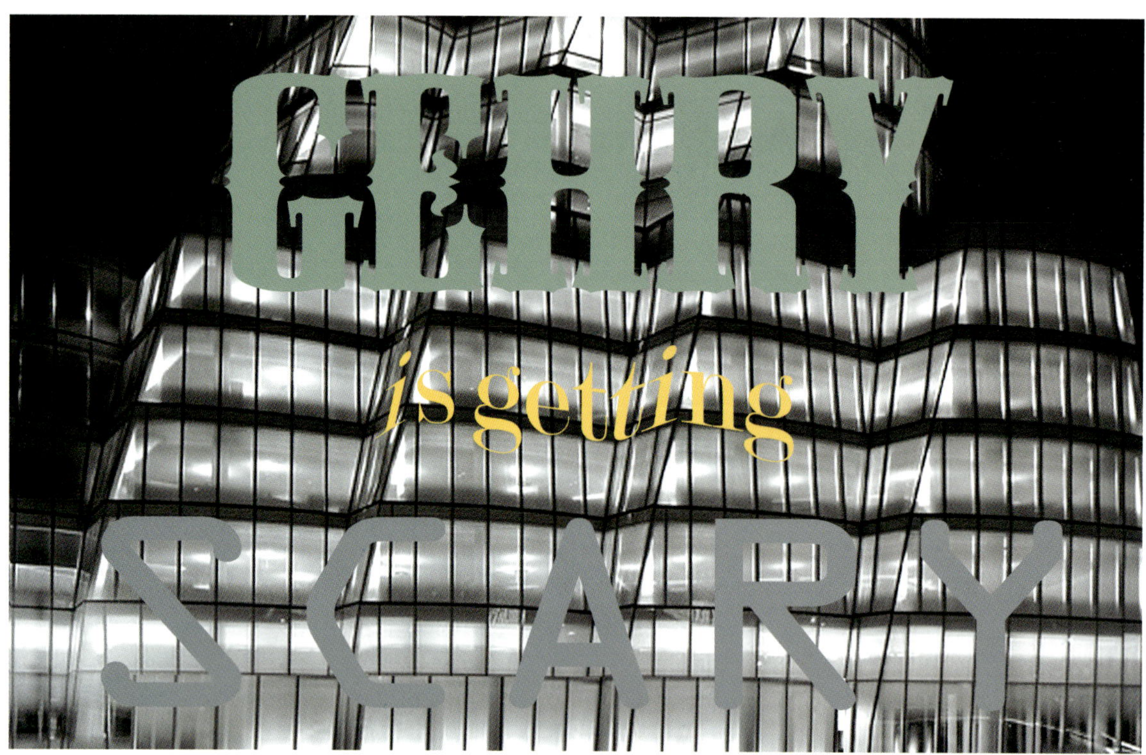

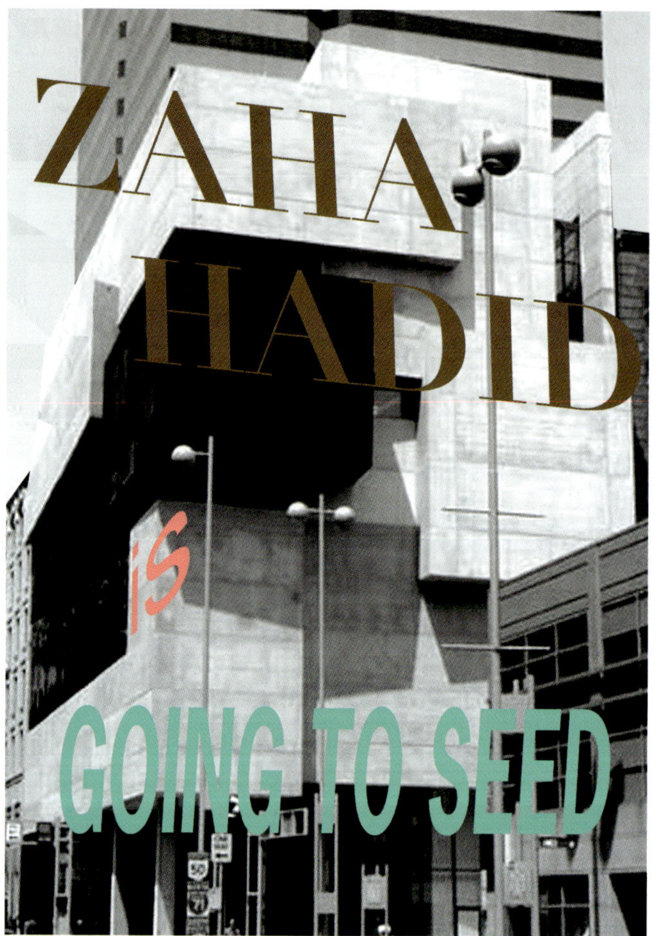

102–105 Joe Scanlan, *Selections from a Concrete Poetry,* 2009, Archival inkjet on Gatorboard. (Thirteen images of famous buildings by famous architects, all defaced with clever rhymes embedded in the images themselves.)

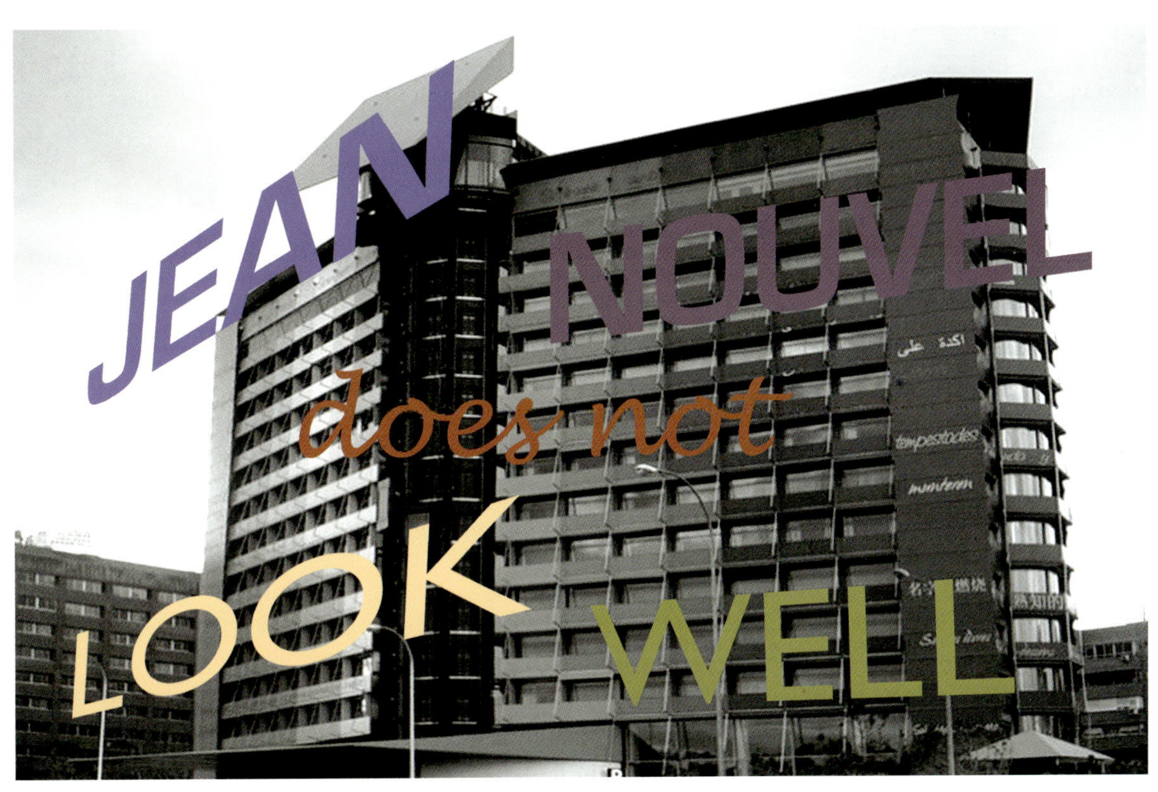
JEAN NOUVEL
does not
LOOK WELL

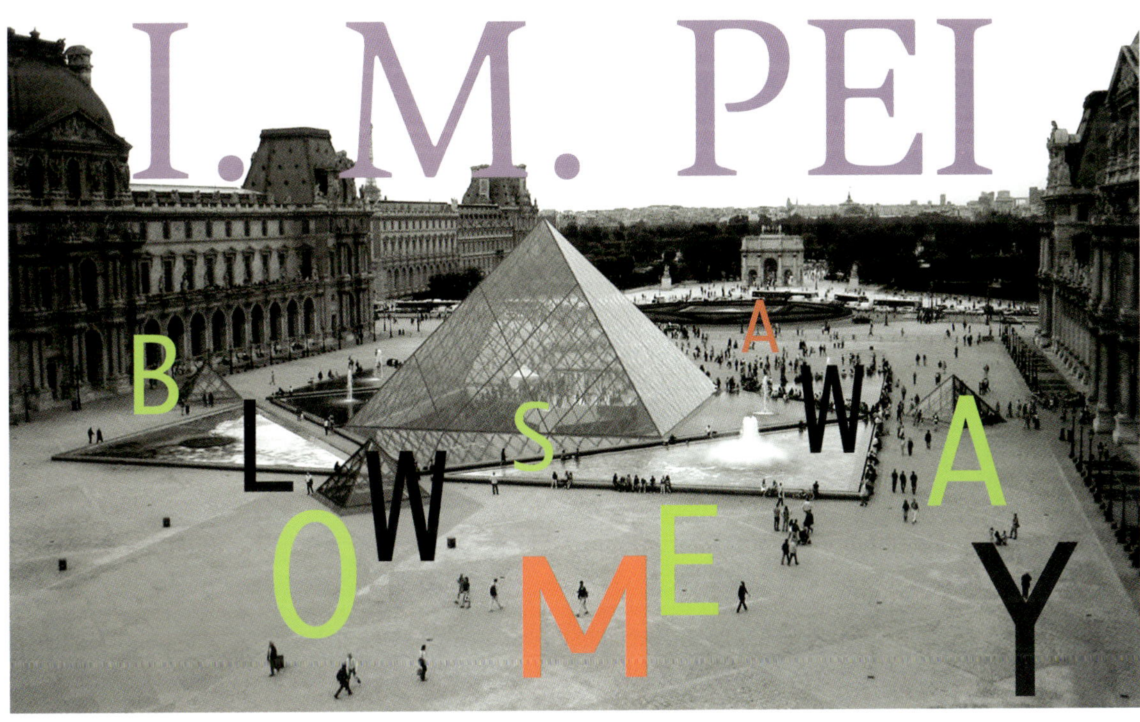
I. M. PEI
BLOWS ME AWAY

incredibly useful model for the techniques of subversive self-authoring. The site itself has a dual function as a portfolio of images of work and related commentary and as a legitimate site of production. Part of Scanlan's appeal is his use of conventional craft-intensive processes to produce critically incisive work. In other sections of his website, Scanlan's work and commentary are intentionally indistinguishable. That's part of the game, where the website becomes a model for artistic practice rather than simply supplying the artist and the art world with an efficient and inexpensive marketing tool.

Scanlan's practice is a model of versatility and self-management; the artist writes, produces art, curates and provides critical commentary on the work of his alter ego. The website's vaguely corporate-style template contributes to its sense of authority, coherence and seamlessness. Scanlan is particularly adept at packaging a convincing version of the edgy hipster art image; a conceit that is supported by scenarios that proclaim the marketing of art by artists to be a viable (Internet) niche activity. The credibility of this message is reinforced through the artist's relentless redescription of contemporary art practice as a species of knowledge work. But the relationship between all this 'text' and his practice is a negative one; a relationship that is hidden by virtue of Scanlan's rhetorical gifts.

Pressing the (general) point of the artist's alienation from her/his output, Scanlan has created an African American female alter ego, *Donelle Woolford*. This fiction had been timed to coincide, more or less, with the centenary of Cubism; one intention, we might surmise, is to parody the recuperation by Picasso of African tribal art and the dogged examination, in the company of Georges Braque, of the late paintings of Cézanne. Exposing this fictional artist, one begins to doubt the 'sincerity' of other aspects of Scanlan's website. This collapse of certainty between reader and text (or beholder and artwork) returns us to a familiar theme of post-1960s art. Yet the irony is inflected with what some might call a political edge, and others would identify as a voice crying in the wilderness. According to Scanlan, the most interesting artists working today are those 'who take matters into their own hands by reframing aesthetics and retelling stories – in general, asserting their power as *aberrant individuals inhabiting a conformist technology*.' (Emphasis mine.) Liu calls this attitude variously 'cool sadness' and 'cool anger'; it remains to be seen if it succeeds as something other than a species of cyberlibertarianism.

AN EMBLEMATIC READING OF THE *FOUR SEASONS*

Artistic practices incorporating word and image undoubtedly define a crowded field. Reflecting on the achievements of the past six decades or more, it would be an insensitive soul indeed who did not enter upon this domain with some trepidation. Clearly, the constellation of word and image presents a real challenge to the artist on many levels. Sensing this, some artists have reached back, excavating older forms of the genre in order to breathe new life into what might seem to be a more or less exhausted field of practice in contemporary art. Moreover, the exhaustion may be conceptual. How many kinds of relations are specifiable by the conjunction of word and image? To what extent, we might ask, is the continued development of contemporary text/image art dependent upon extrinsic determinants such as technological change? To what extent is the periodic efflorescence of text/image art symptomatic of an internal crisis in art? Is text/image art no longer transformatory and innovative, but merely generic and fashionable?

In her collage work *Four Seasons*, the North American artist Kara Walker (b. 1969) casts back to a genre that can be traced to the emblem books of the Renaissance (illus. 106–109). The appropriation of this historical schema is not unusual in recent art, although the intentions of the artist vary dramatically. In 1987 Jasper Johns exhibited an iconographically dense, four-part series of works under the title *The Seasons*. These were celebrated not only as important works of art, but as contributions to the pictorial depiction of autobiography. More recently, Cy Twombly exhibited *Quattro Stagioni (Four Seasons), A Painting in Four Parts* (illus. 110–113). Twombly's variation on this allegorical theme collapses personal and historical narratives. As one journalist wrote, while mindful of

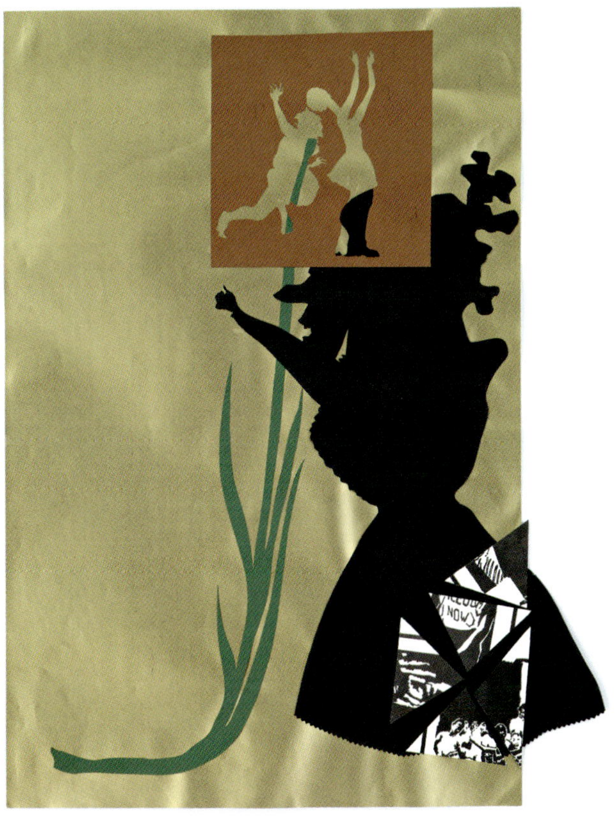

106 Kara Walker, *Four Seasons: Untitled (Spring)*. All four are cut paper on paper, graphite.

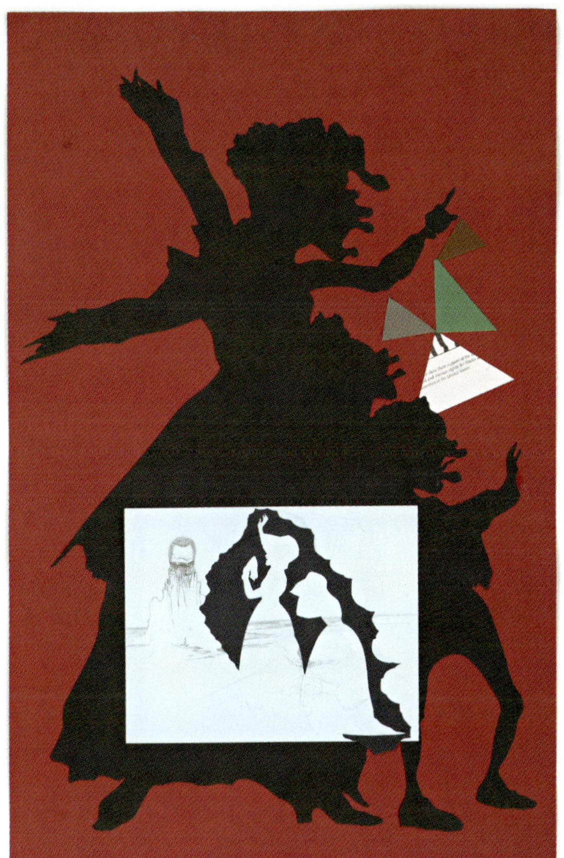

107 *Four Seasons: The Hot Summer.*

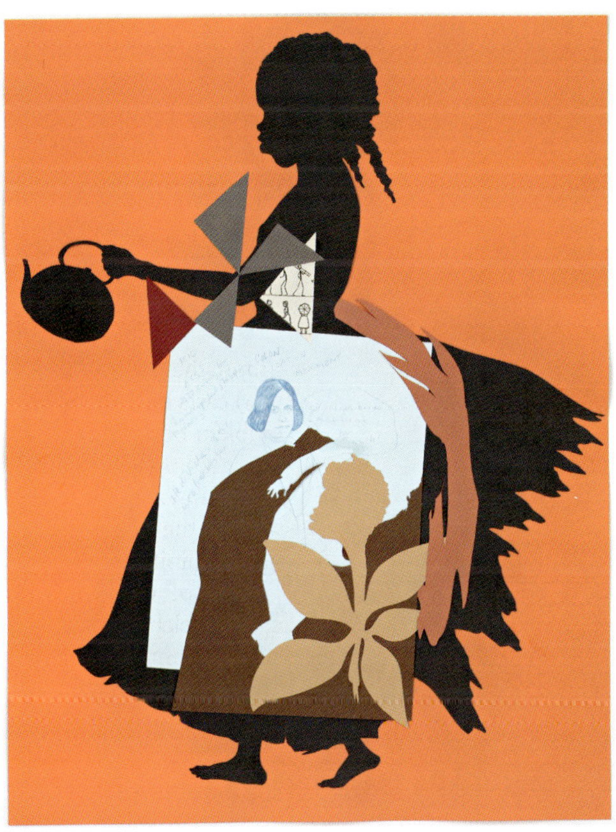

108 *Four Seasons: The Fall.*

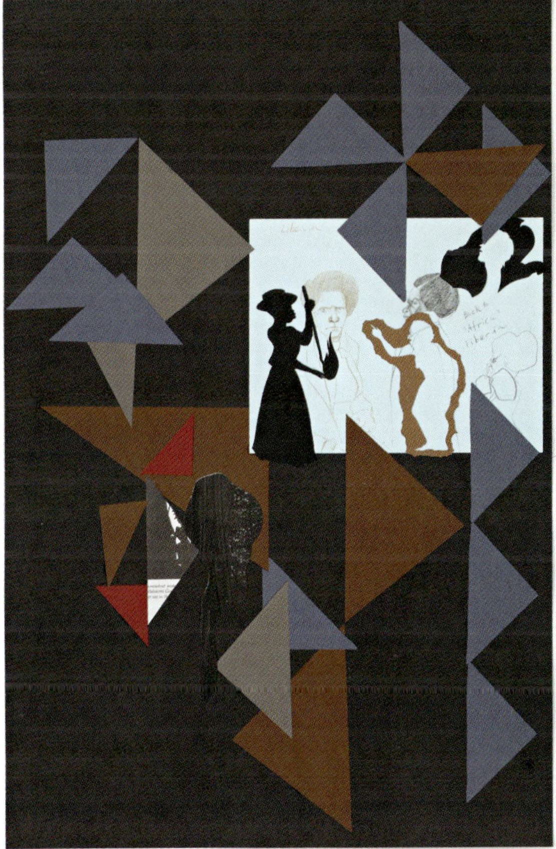

109 *Four Seasons: Winter of Contentment.*

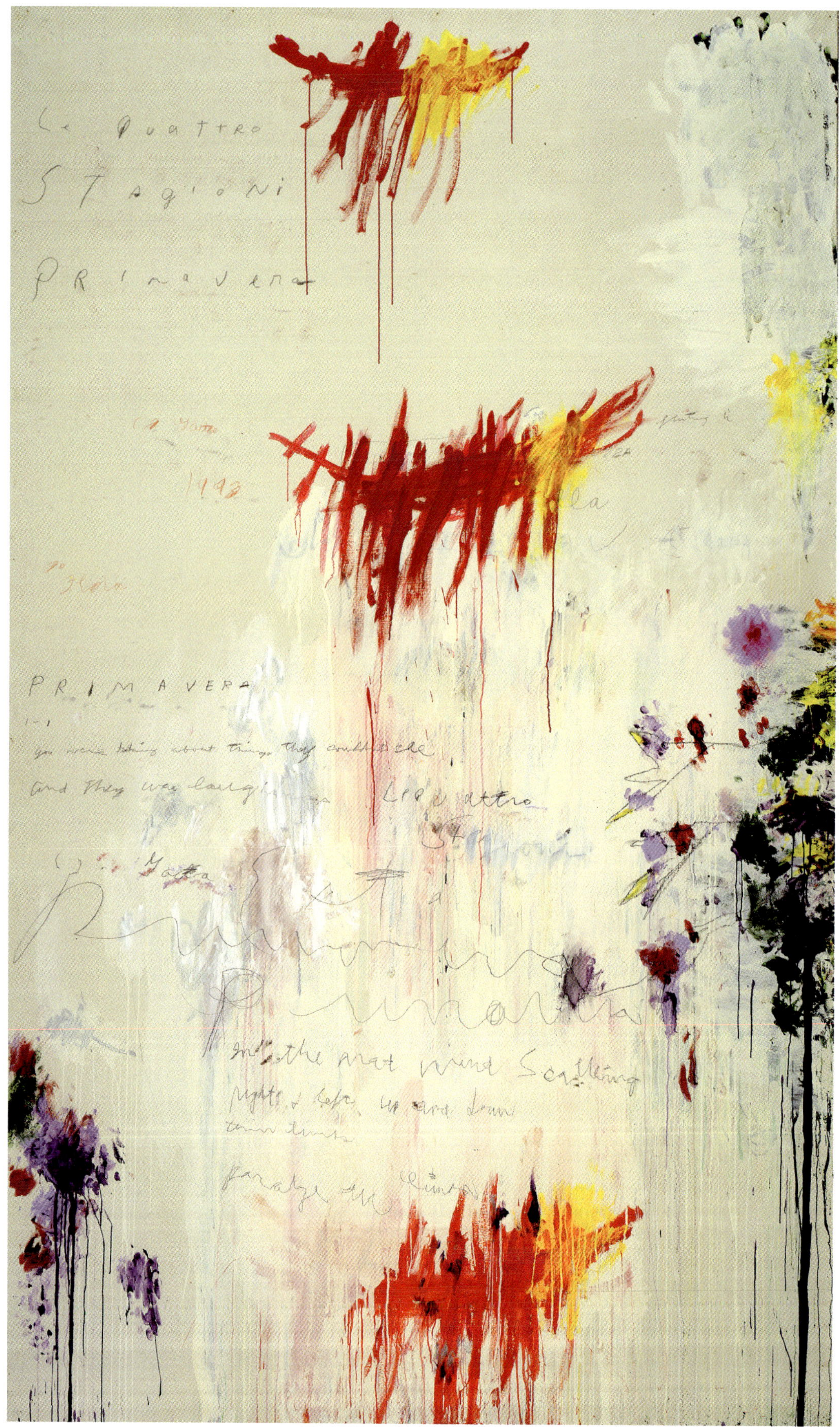

110 Cy Twombly, *Quattro Stagioni (Four Seasons), A Painting in Four Parts*, 1993–5, oil on canvas. *Spring*.

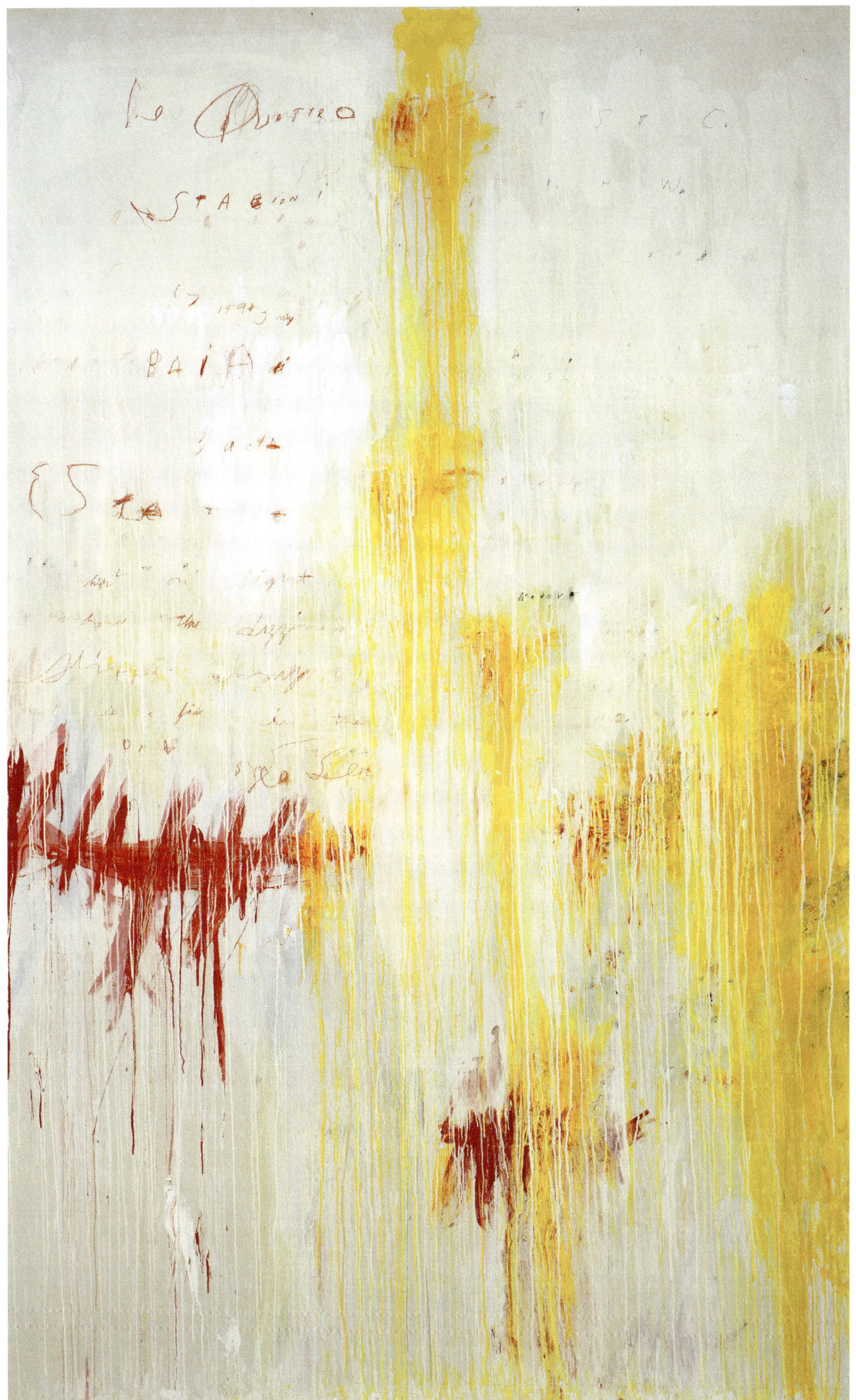

111 *Summer.*

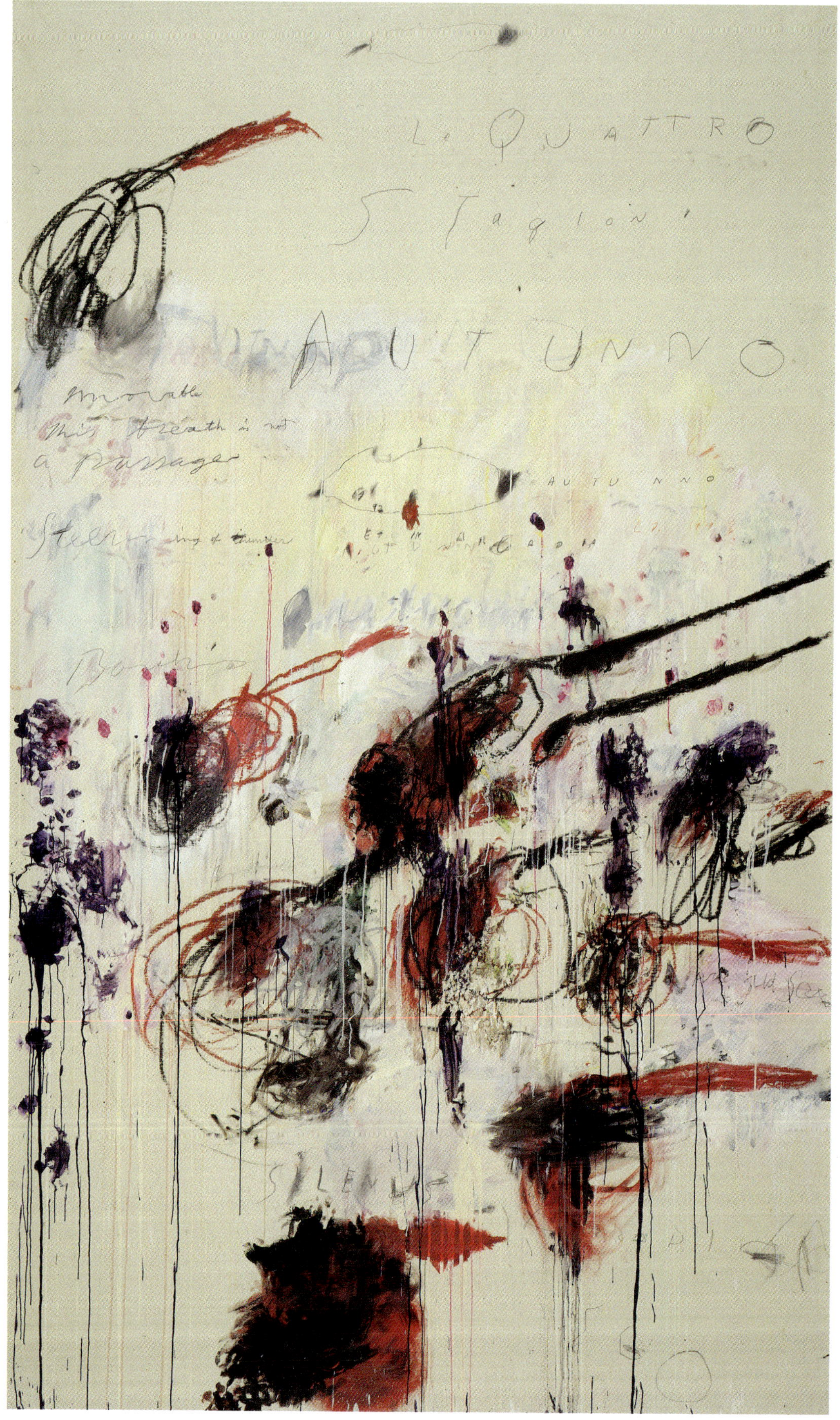

112 *Autumn.*

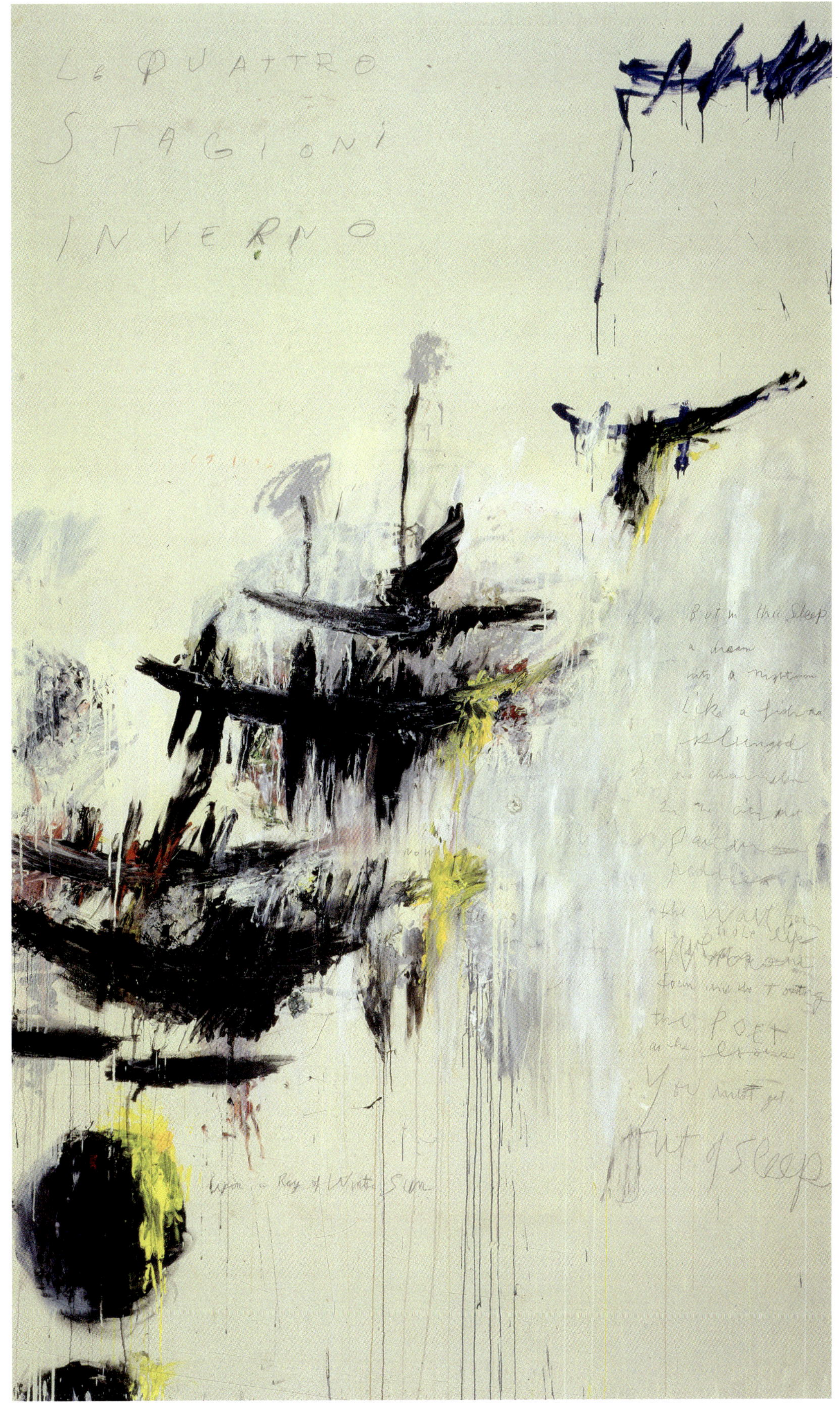

113 *Winter.*

Twombly's expatriate status since 1957, these paintings 'are letters to history from the heart of a corrupt empire'.[40]

Walker's seasons stand in an ambiguous relation to the artist's interest in making work out of an engagement with the antebellum South. *The Four Seasons*, as such, point to the painfully slow movement of liberation through the trope of the eternal return; each cycle bringing one closer to the desired end. Walker's text – a conventional feature of the emblematic form – is fragmentary, abjected and gnomic. This is disconcerting, since the convention of the emblem demands that language remains the point of departure for the interpretation of the moral precept carried by the figure. The confessional text – the quintessential medium of historical narrative through which the liberated bear witness to the trials of their brutal unfreedom – seems to be incomplete in Walker's emblem. It is a dysfunctional emblem, forcing us to reconsider the role of language in making the image intelligible. Our encounter with the work demonstrates the poverty of our own expectations about the relation between language and reality; a reality that no non-African American can know authentically. Walker seems to be saying that despite the fact that the experience of being the object of racial stereotyping cannot be represented through language or images transparently, the ownership of the optimistic message of wholeness inferred by the trope of eternal return must nevertheless be reclaimed and made available for her own expressive ends.

This destabilization proposed by Walker seems to be a world apart from either the paradoxical entanglements of seeing versus reading staged by Johns's visual conundrums or Twombly's tasteful compositions. All the same, there is an important affinity that unites these three heterogeneous bodies of work. In all cases, the conceit of the four seasons becomes a pretext for a specific moment of reflection and summation. As with any proper emblem, there is a moral fixed to the pleasure of seeing and reading. The point of using such an archaic form today, however, must surely lead us to another place. Speaking ethically, it is a realm where the subject is inescapably implicated by whatever is being looked at or read. This is no longer simply a private matter of contemplation, but a full realization of seeing (and 'seeing-as') as a social act. Historically, the Renaissance emblem sought to heal the alienation caused by the disjunction between the worldly and spiritual and thereby lead to the betterment of the individual. In the hands of some artists, the contemporary emblem allows a more considered and critical public rehearsal of the pleasures and obligations of the spectator.

4

August Walla: Devil/God, Image/Text

STEPHEN BARBER

In the Austrian artist August Walla's work, the area of interconnection between word and image forms a zonal landscape of mutation and transformation between two entities which remain equally in irresoluble turmoil and uncertainty. An image alone cannot render the extreme urgency and density that Walla instils into his work, and a word alone has a parallel deficiency; their dual autonomy, in separation, constitutes a defusing of the preoccupations with sexuality, corporeality, divinity, warfare and death that amass to activate Walla's work. By contrast, the intersection of text and image unleashes an unstoppable velocity and volume of conjoined forms that overspill the two-dimensional surface and must exert their presence on whatever environment surrounds Walla's own body: on the walls of his room, on all objects in that room, and on the exterior environment, in the form of road surfaces, trees and derelict buildings. In turn, a three-dimensional object, inscribed with text, held and displayed within Walla's hands, must enter that surrounding environment and, through the medium of a photograph which documents its presence, dislocate the natural or urban world so that it, too, is transformed into image. The presence of the inscribed word, inserted into the natural or urban world, imposes a dislocation on that world, subjugating it to the inscribed word that has entered it, so that it can exist as nothing but image, confronted by text. In that escalating affrontment between word and image, all objects and surfaces become inescapably enmeshed: the natural and urban world is engulfed, metamorphosed into the status of exposed, raw material for the mediation of Walla's preoccupations. The conjunction between word and image leaves nothing untouched, allows no respite: the obsession with magnifying all objects and surfaces into components for a vast terrain of combat between image and text forms the sole tenable medium of survival for Walla.

While Walla's work demands that the world exist solely as an emanation of it, and of its need for infinitely renewed content for the intersection of text and image, that work itself exists in the world by accident, by an aberration in the conjunction between psychiatry and art history that mirrors that between text and image. In the 1950s, at the Lower Austria Psychiatric Hospital in

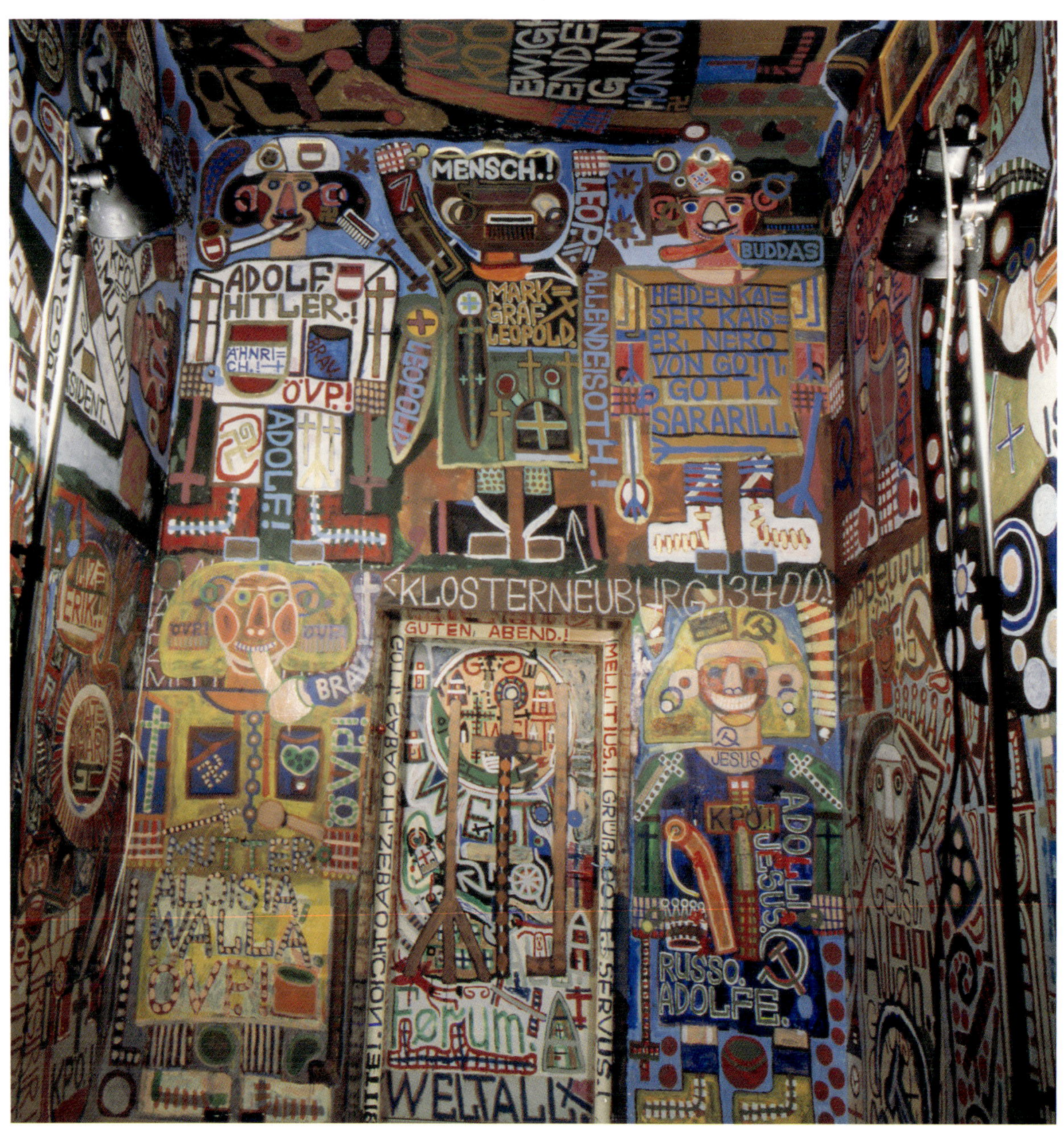

1 Room of August Walla, 1992, laquer paints.

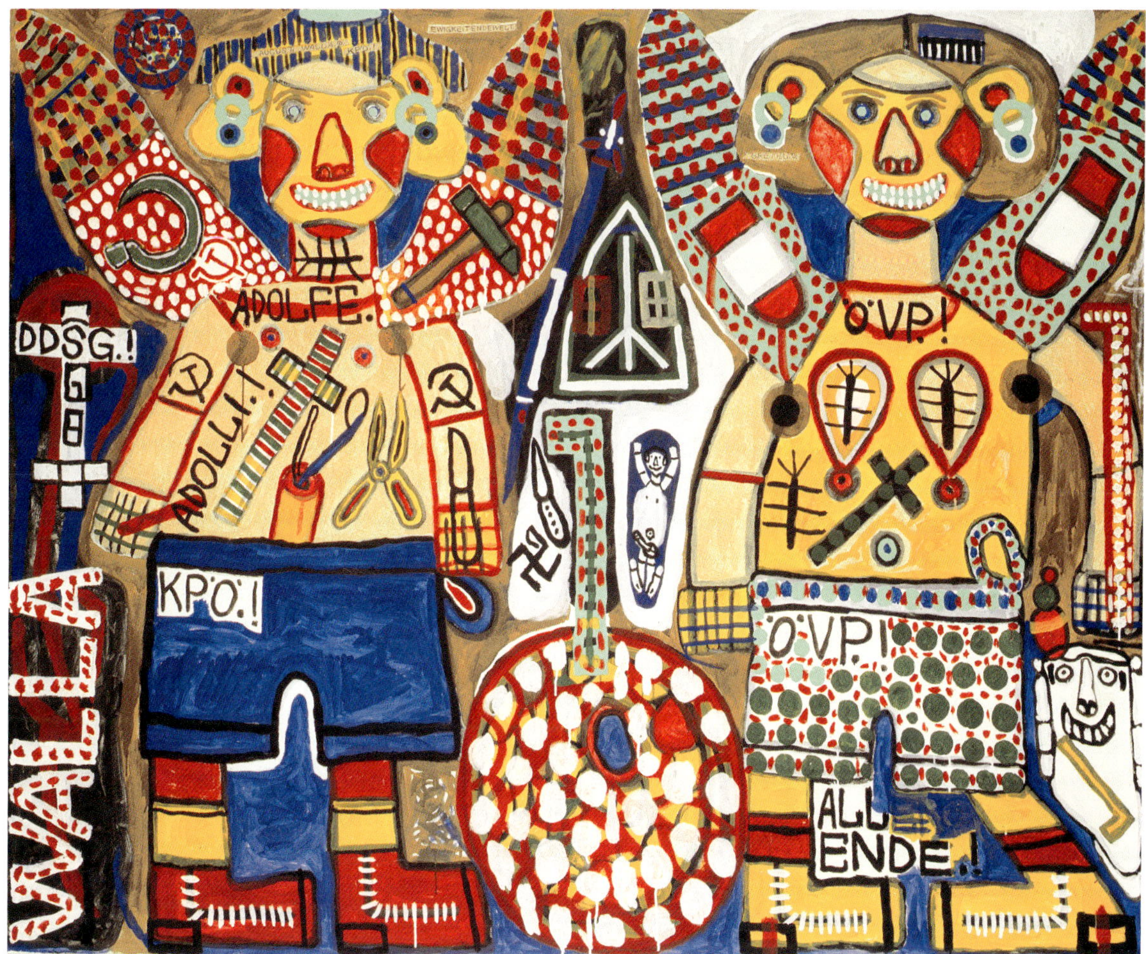

2 August Walla, *Two Angels*, 1986, laquer paint.

Klosterneuburg, a few miles north of Vienna, the Austrian psychiatrist Leo Navratil began to experiment with instructing his patients to draw. Navratil's experiments developed at a distance from the French artist Jean Dubuffet's conception of Art Brut, as encapsulating the work of artists with no artistic training, no social standing and no relationship to the history of art, and from Dubuffet's own collection and promotion of those artists' work; Navratil's experiments also existed at a provocative tangent to the work of psychiatrists who, since the nineteenth century, had been inducing their patients to draw solely in order to gather diagnostic materials. Navratil viewed his patients as existing in a limbo-state between insanity and art, and assessed their drawings as both indicators of psychosis and as art-objects; in the decades until his death in 2006, he wrote a number of monographs on his individual artist-patients, probing the works that held that intractable contradiction.

By the late 1960s Navratil had assembled a small group of institutionalized patients, mostly men in their forties, with diagnoses ranging from schizophrenic catatonia to manic depression. Several of them had fought in World War II and had suffered permanent trauma as a result, such as Oswald Tschirtner (a Stalingrad combatant) and Johann Hauser. In order to move their work beyond the asylum and into the urban art world, Navratil planned an exhibition of his patients' work at a prominent gallery for experimental art and performance art in Vienna, the Galerie Nächst St Stephan, in 1970, with the support of celebrated Austrian artists such as Arnulf Rainer; the drawings to be exhibited often demonstrated acute sexual obsession and focused primarily on excavations of the human figure, depicted as undergoing intensive and hallucinatory upheaval. At this point, Navratil became aware, by chance, of the work of Walla, who was in his early thirties and lived with his mother in extreme

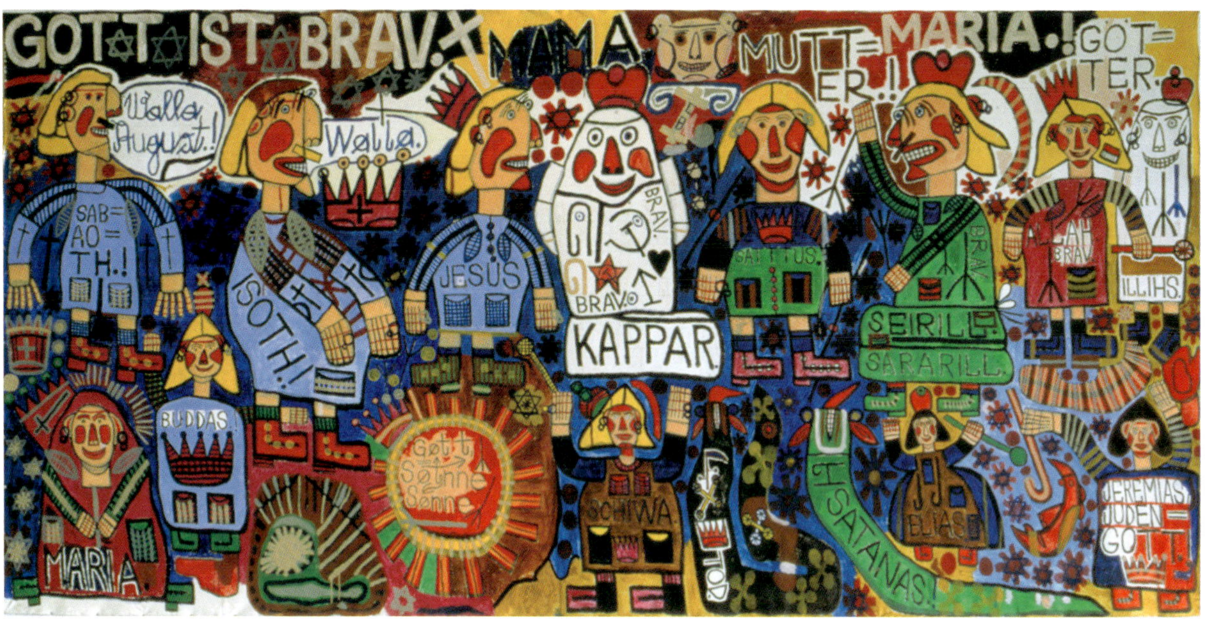

3 August Walla, *Gods*, 1986, laquer paint.

poverty and isolation at an abandoned barracks in the town of Klosterneuburg, rather than in the psychiatric hospital. Although Walla had spent his youth, during the years of World War II, in special schools for maladjusted children in Vienna, and had subsequently been interned in the Lower Austria Psychiatric Hospital between the ages of fifteen and twenty-one, he had since 1957 remained outside the asylum, under the care of his mother. Throughout that period, Walla had worked incessantly, painting and inscribing objects around him, in the dilapidated room he shared with his mother, and also performing actions in the streets of Klosterneuburg and the surrounding countryside that his elderly mother documented in the form of photographs; his work remained unchanged by Navratil's engagement with it. Navratil included Walla's work in the exhibition at the Galerie Nächst St Stephan; although the exhibition created huge international interest, Navratil's project was attacked by young activist art historians, by exponents of the anti-psychiatry movement in Vienna – who accused him of exploiting his patients and called for them to be liberated from their asylum – and also, contrarily, by traditional psychiatrists such as Gaston Ferdière (the psychiatrist of Antonin Artaud), who denounced Navratil for misrepresenting his patients' psychotic scrawls as artworks. Walla himself denied that he was creating artworks, and insisted that his intention in making his image/text works was solely the desire to be obliging ('*aus Gefälligkeit*').[1] Navratil continued to exhibit his elite group of artist-patients' work in art museums, and it gradually became assimilated into the Art Brut movement while also generating art market interest during the early-1980s resurgence in figurative art; in 1981, Navratil created a separate pavilion for twelve artist-patients in the extensive grounds of the psychiatric hospital, and encouraged curators and art historians to visit them. Walla moved to the pavilion in 1983, when his mother became too senile to look after him outside the asylum, and continued his work there until his death in 2001.

Word and image can never remain equivalent in the work of artists, such as

Walla, who intensively explore their point of intersection. A word or phrase may be inserted into the domain of the image to draw out and accentuate the impact of its historical and mythological underpinning (as in the work of Anselm Kiefer), or an image may accompany a text in order to distil a content which an over-accumulation of textual layers has obscured (as in innumerable works of illustration); in either instance, the accompanying word or image is relegated to a role of subjugation, at the service of its counterpart. A number of factors may instigate a combative collision between word and image that negates that illustrative or equivocal rapport; an artist may require the abrasive zone between word and image as the point from which to fire a preoccupation with the disintegration of the status of language and image, or else that area of collision may activate an exploration of corporeality, conflict and sexual obsession which can only take form and be mediated as a direct result of that collision, and would otherwise hold an insufficient visual or linguistic charge. Integral to the intersection between word and image, in work such as Walla's, is the human body. The point of encounter between image and text is one that works to unhinge and dislocate, and without a specific focus for the sensorial velocity generated by the image/text intersection, that velocity dissipates, even when exacerbated by the element of aberrance that attends the mutant conjoining of language and image. In Walla's work, the human body is infinitely vulnerable; text and image must conflictually amass in order to safeguard it, but also to mediate the engulfing, multiple danger that assails the corporeal.

One of the unique attributes of the intersection between image and text is its capacity to mediate historical upheaval, to intimate traumatic memory and to reveal corporeal fissuration and fragmentation, in a way that is closed to any medium that is solely visual, or solely textual. That zone between word and image is one that gathers confrontation, and sensitizes the work to transmit corporeal, political, historical or sexual conflicts. In Walla's work, the history of twentieth-century Europe insurges in an excoriated but awry form, dense with apocalyptic forces and murderous figures, of weaponry and political insignia (interchangeable hammers-and-sickles and swastikas), all of it concentrated around Walla's body, as though it required the acute social withdrawal of Walla's perception to reveal that history, and to expunge that history of all narrative and anecdote. History is urgently exclaimed, by the intersection of text with image, and instilled into the body, rather than recounted or mythologized. In Walla's work, the confrontation between word and image possesses a momentum that has already arrived at apocalypse: the final point has permanently been reached. But at the same time, Walla occasionally conjures angelic presences to accompany that apocalypse, as though, even in its definitive erasure, history still betrays its own negation, and the human body may still escape itself. In many of Walla's works, he exclaims the word '*Halbholle.!*': the 'half-hell' (as intangible and unseizably volatile as the interstice between text and image), beyond death, beyond all devils and gods, inhabited by a body still possessing the remotest chance of miraculous survival if it can project itself, or withdraw itself, away from all danger.

One of the pre-eminent threats to Walla's survival is sex. His work appears simultaneously utterly sexless and naïve – Walla's mother noted to Dr Navratil that her son had never had any sexual experiences: 'nothing at all, thanks be to

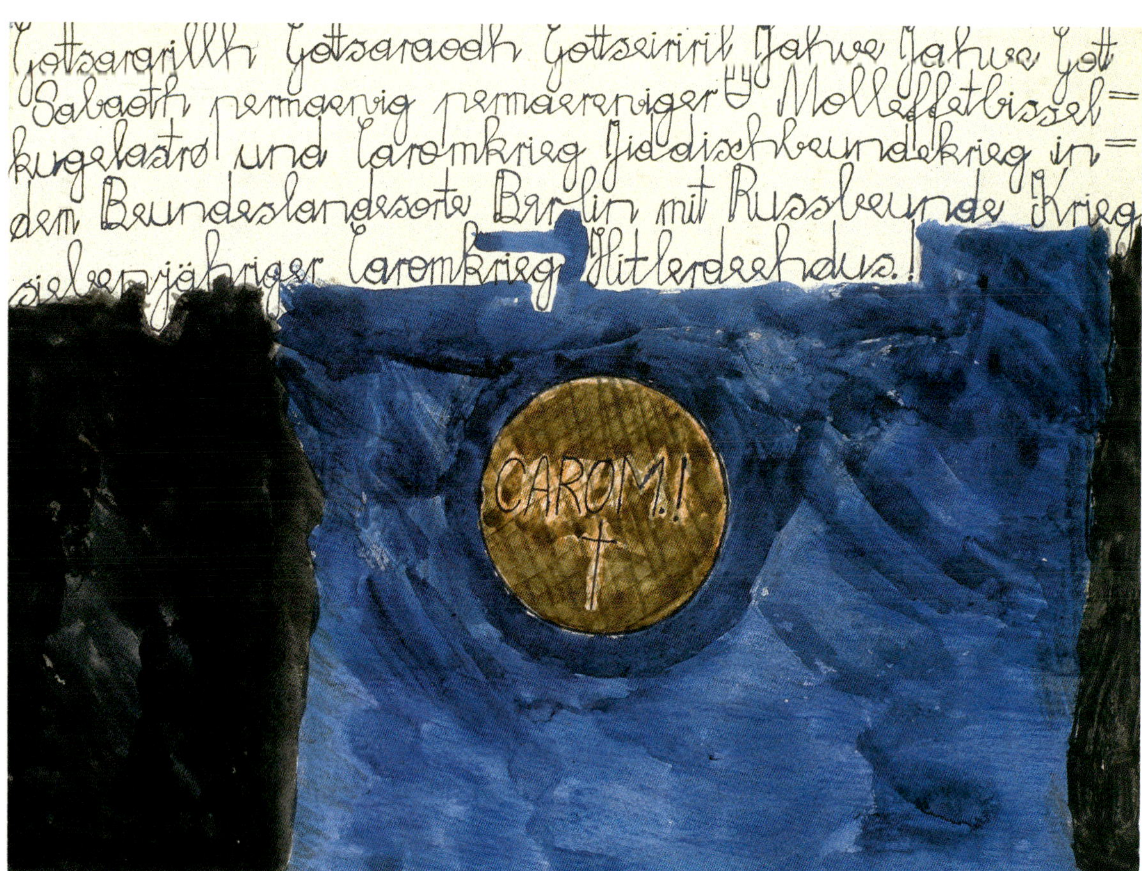

4 August Walla, *CAROM!*, undated, coloured inks.

God!'[2] – and sexually obsessed. Almost all of Walla's male figures possess prominent sexual organs, often doubled (in Walla's work, everything irresistibly duplicates itself, or multiplies itself infinitely) and accentuated by the textual exclamation '*Doppelbube.!*' ('Double-Boy.!'). Sexual fluids and urine, from both male and female organs, are also pervasively visualized in his work, but textually sent off-kilter, in their sexual charge, by their naming as 'condensed-milk' or 'honey'. Walla's sexual self-conception is one of forcible transformation: already dead, he has undergone a kind of transgendering autopsy at the hands of the Russian military occupiers of Austria during his childhood, which has rendered his female sexuality masculine. The visual element of the works depicting this 'Russian Operation' shows an array of surgical instruments and threatened or lacerated sexual organs which resonate – in a parallel encounter between psychosis and the art world – with those surrounding the performance-artworks of the Vienna Aktionists, during the late 1960s, in which Günther Brus and Rudolph Schwarzkögler undertook performances which explored acute sexual vulnerability and rituals of self-laceration. But whereas the Aktionists were denounced and marginalized in Austria as psychotic, antisocial criminals (Brus was given a prison sentence for a performance-action at the University of Vienna in 1968 in which he publicly defecated and then sang the Austrian national anthem while masturbating), Walla's works of sexual obsession took the inverse trajectory, from the context of institutional psychosis and social isolation towards that of artworld acceptance.

The rapport of text with image in Walla's work unleashes spatial disruption that further impels the human body into that volatile interstice. Although much of Walla's work was undertaken in interior spaces, and involved the saturation with his words and images of those spaces' surfaces, he also undertook extensive performance-actions in the peripheral areas of Klosterneuburg (never in the central streets, where he risked provoking the town's conservative inhabitants, who viewed him with hostility – unlike the Aktionist Brus who, conversely,

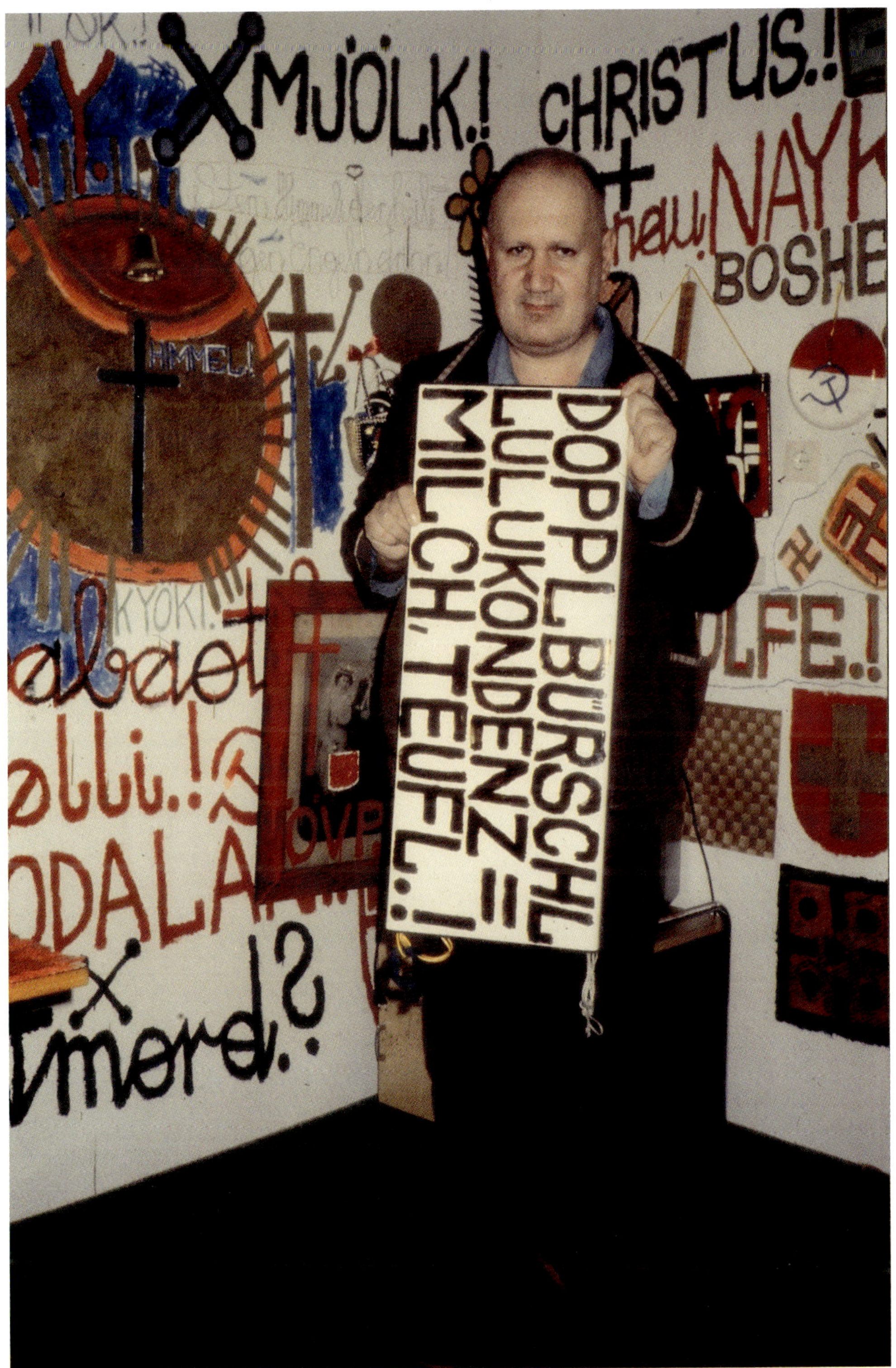

5 August Walla, 1984.

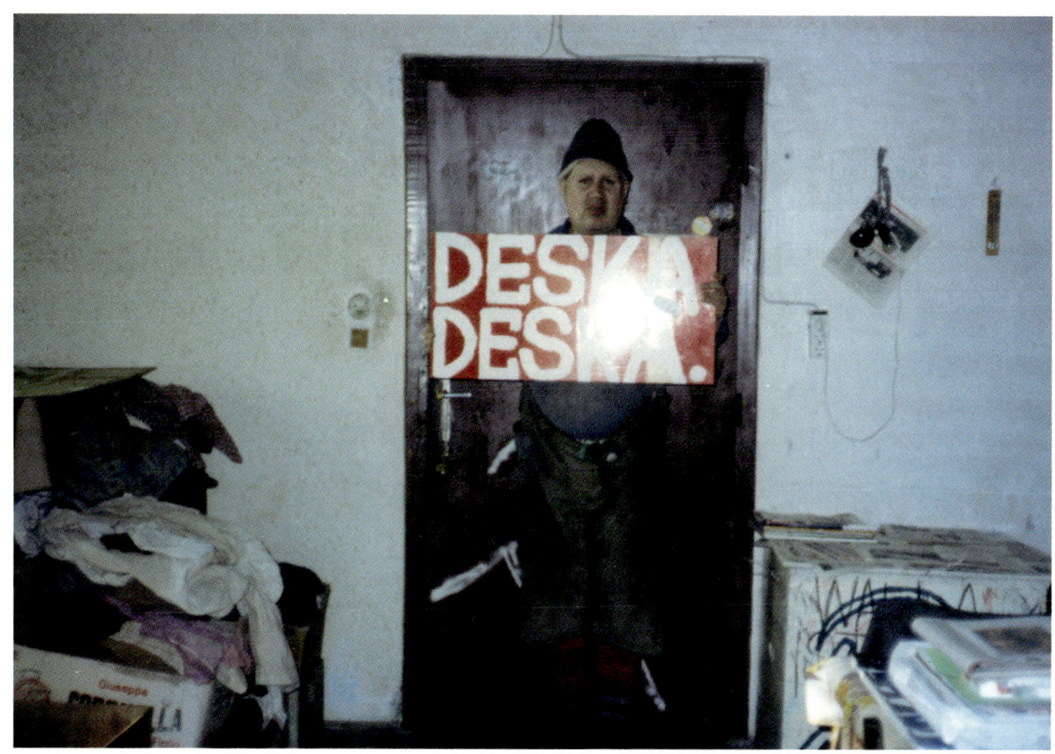

6 August Walla with a board.

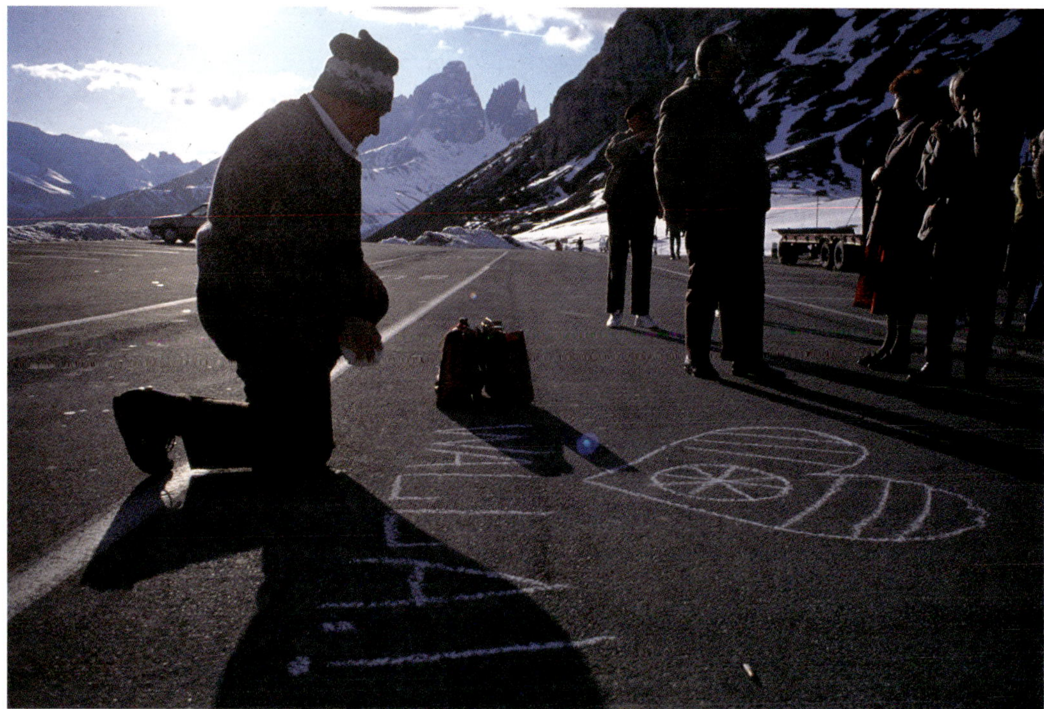

7 August Walla at the St Bernard Pass.

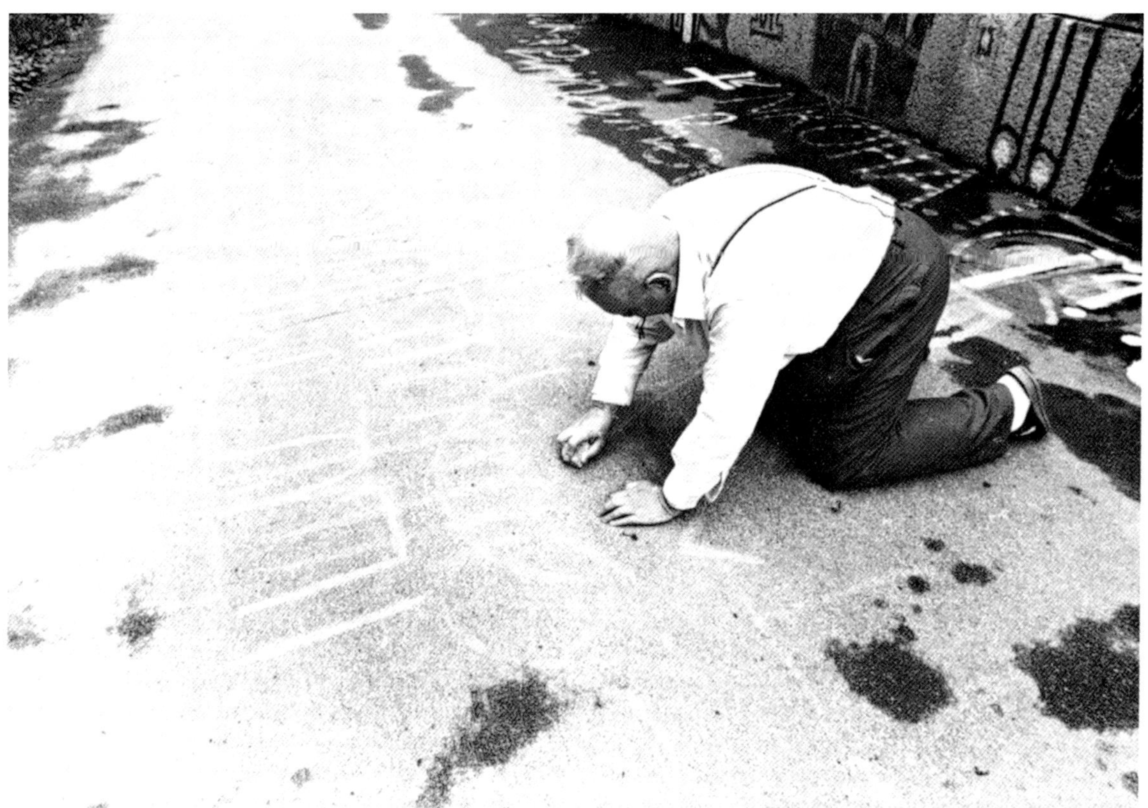

8 August Walla, *Untitled*.

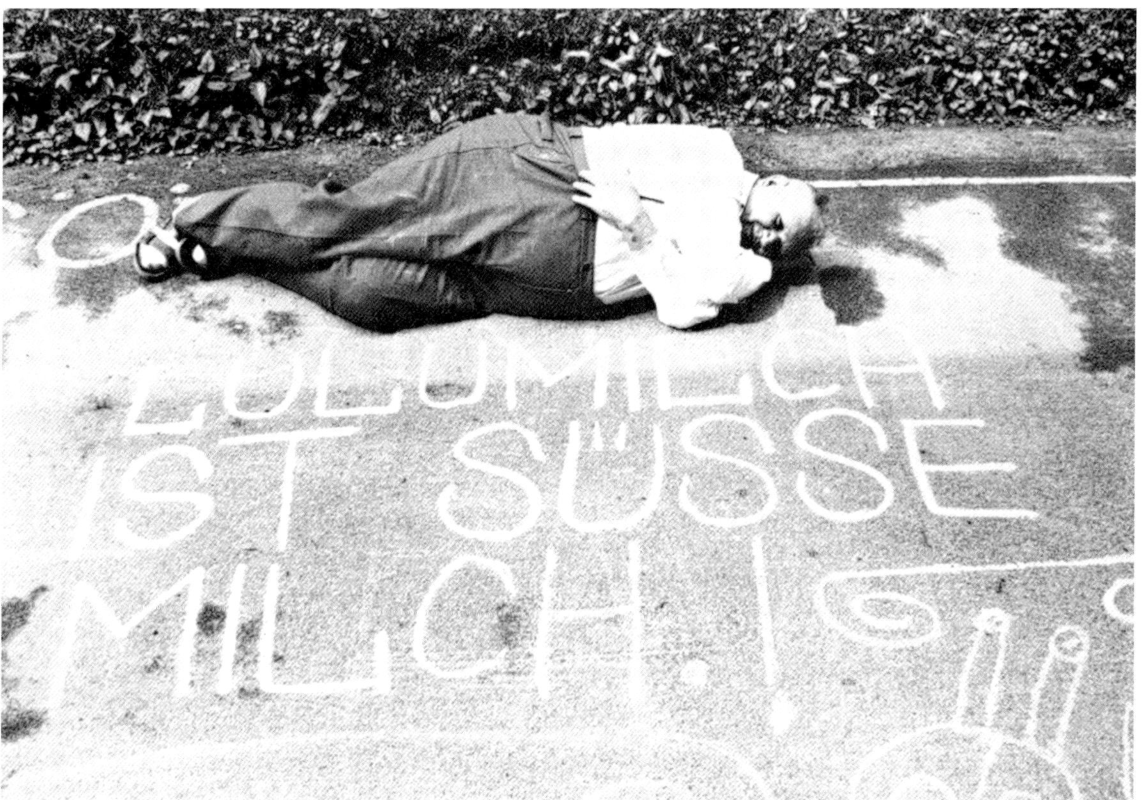

9 August Walla, *Untitled*.

headed directly for the centre of Vienna, and began his *Wiener Spaziergang* (*Vienna Walk*, 1965) performance-action, which would terminate with his arrest, from underneath the palace-balcony where Hitler had announced the annexation of Austria to Nazi Germany). Occasionally, Walla's performance-actions involved his standing directly in front of derelict urban spaces, such as demolition sites, and performing manual gestures, but more usually, the performances integrally cohered his body with textual and linguistic elements. In numerous photographs of his performances (Walla's mother invariably served as the adept documenter of his performance-work, despite her senile dementia), Walla stands and gestures in front of buildings, trees, objects or roads on which he has already inscribed his texts or images in paint; in other performances, he holds placards or other objects on which a text (usually a word from an invented language, or a word drawn from Walla's dictionary-searches) has been inscribed in large letters, so that it mutates into the status of an image in its rapport with its urban or natural context (the placard is often held awry or inverted to destabilize the pre-eminence of text), and thereby enmeshes that urban/natural context into the intricate arena of Walla's preoccupations. Performance-photographs also show Walla in the act of inscribing his texts and images on roadways, in chalk or paint, and then lying on the ground alongside the completed inscription, as though the presence of the body validates that work and momentarily stalls the open confrontation between text and image. During his performances in exterior space, Walla is photographed heavily clothed; in interiors, he is often photographed naked.

In Walla's work, the text/image collision, together with the presence of the body in the painting or performance, exacerbates the need for an ultimate expansiveness that will occupy all space, all bodies, all languages and images, and all histories, so that the dangers they raise for Walla's own body become concurrently lessened and defused. A desire for extreme density is generated by the collision between text and image, and must manifest itself in a maximal spatial pervasiveness. Nothing must escape inscription: the painting's surface shows no space uninscribed by text or image, and the urban/natural world surrounding Walla's body must demonstrate a parallel inhabitation by that body's image/text presence. After Walla had spent a decade or so at the Lower Austria Psychiatric Hospital, in the early 1990s, the entire grounds, roadways, buildings and surrounding woodland held multiple evidence of his work; even six years after his death, the grounds remained constellated by the faded traces of that work.

In order to determine the rapport of text with image in his work, Walla requires the command of all global languages. In his conversations with Dr Navratil and with his visitors, Walla always asserted that he was developing a comprehensive knowledge of every language in the world, and incorporated elements from those languages into his work, combining and deploying them as the demonstration of omniscient textual authority. Any income that reached Walla from sales of his paintings was spent on the acquisition of a collection of foreign-language dictionaries, and any time not devoted to his work was spent in studying those dictionaries. By contrast, the image remains something which is *already* known, by Walla, in its entirety; Walla's supreme indifference to art history and all visual culture ensures that the element of image in his work retains its autonomy. But the cultural autonomy of the image, in Walla's work, will also not be subjugated to his textual authority; that work never shows a body that attains the status, free from engulfing dangers, that Walla desires. Always, the body's image is subject to proliferating exposure and violent fragmentation, to disassembly by scalpels and weapons; text and image form terminally irreconcilable entities.

The axis of text and image in the work of artists probing their intersection is often an intangible zone of slippage in which the status of word and image may fluctuate: as one erases the other, one accentuates the other; the location at which word and image mesh habitually remains in perpetual movement. However, with Walla's work, in which the human body always intrudes or is seized into that intersection, and takes on an essential role as transmitter or exacerbator of the text/image confrontation, that axis possessed a specific and fixed location from which the expansiveness of his work originated and emanated: Walla's room in the pavilion that Dr Navratil had created for his group of artist-patients.

In 1992 I visited Walla in his room, and was shown into it by one of the psychiatric nurses. The entire surface-space of the room, including the ceiling, and all objects within it – the television set, the radiators, the side-table, the chairs – had been saturated with Walla's figures, including those that depicted his own body, together with his textual exclamations of contested identities, of maleficent corporeal threats and of protections. That room possessed an aura both of forming a spatial aperture into engulfing terror, and of constituting an irrevocable refusal: of history, of the human body's vulnerable form, of the relationship between language and image, and of time itself: everything perceived by Walla demanded an immediate repudiation, and simultaneously a transformational overturning, generated by the collision of text, image and the human body. Spatially fixed, the room remained in temporal movement: Walla had constantly reworked his texts and images during the nine years he had lived there, so that the space was becoming ever more saturated, ever more dense. The only element of the room that had been excluded from Walla's reformulation of its time and space was the threadbare, institutional carpet, and the equally uninscribable curtains, pulled back from the window, through which I could see the wooden walls of a storage hut, and the trees adjoining the pavilion, all of them meticulously covered over with Walla's work.

To most questions, Walla responded with exclamations of two or three words that resonated with the texts inscribed on the room's walls. He spoke about an etching he had made in 1970, entitled *Hitler Sein Baum.!* ('Hitler's Tree.!'), in which a huge axe and two swastikas – unintentionally inverted, along with the work's textual element, by the etching process – accompanied a tree inhabited by a lemur. How had Hitler come to own such a tree? All Walla had to say on the matter was that yes, it was Hitler's tree. Then, he spoke of how, as a small boy during World War II, he had heard the voice of Hitler giving speeches on the radio, and had decided that it must be the voice of his father (who was always absent, having abandoned the family before Walla's birth); later, he had discovered that the voice on the radio was not what he had thought it was, and that the world around him was apocalyptic.

In Walla's work, image and text cannot accord with one another, and their mismatched intersection forms a fissuration that transmits a content always focused around the corporeal: one of terror, but also one of transformation, in which corporeal mutation seeks to elude death. Word and image together constitute one variant of an endless proliferation of doubled entities whose imminent threat Walla must exclaim, but whose expansive inscription (in the form of painted surfaces and objects), and performance (in the form of photographed actions), allows him to defuse to the point where, for a moment at least, that threat will not yet reach his body. Text and image, in their rapport, hold an integral presence of monstrousness in Walla's work, like the aberrantly doubled penises of his boy-figures, that resonates – in an intensively amended form – from the exterior world, from the social, institutional and corporeal histories which surround Walla and mediate their apocalyptic potential to him, like radio-static. The combat between text and image, then, is an element in what is literally a life or death struggle, to overturn the world and to survive.

5

'The Sound of Painting': Colin McCahon

REX BUTLER AND LAURENCE SIMMONS

'... try for the sound of the painting'.
– Colin McCahon, 1972

The American art historian Thomas Crow, in his interview with Marja Bloem, curator of the 2002 Colin McCahon show, *A Question of Faith,* at the Stedlijk Museum, made the following apparently hyperbolic assertion: 'A major contemporary of Rothko, Newman, Pollock, Twombly and Johns – an artist fully at their level of achievement – is in the midst of his first major touring retrospective'. However, in the first words of his article, he had already qualified this by suggesting: 'Globalization, our mantra of the moment, only carries so far where art is concerned'.[1] That is, Crow admits, there is only a remote chance that the readers of *Artforum* would have heard of McCahon, and it is unlikely the situation is going to change any time soon. For nothing could more destine an artist to obscurity – even one as admittedly great as McCahon – than being born in faraway New Zealand and making his best work there in the 1950s, '60s and '70s. McCahon's work became well known in his home country for its exploration and synthesis of three major themes: the regional New Zealand landscape, the pictorial use of text and the meaning of Christian faith. But even now the art world seems unready to admit him into the wider canon, or the history of twentieth-century art that would make sense of his work has not yet been written. Indeed, one of the challenges faced by contemporary art history and its promise of a new global or world art is whether the kinds of historical revisionism that would make McCahon visible to the rest of the world are even possible. Can an artist simply be inserted into mainstream art history after an absence of some forty years?

Extraordinarily, however, we would say that it is just this possibility of its future redemption that McCahon's work is *about.* As a number of commentators have pointed out, the 'messianic' is very much one of the subjects of his work – and it is a messianism exactly in Walter Benjamin's sense of a history written from the point of view of its losers.[2] In other words, McCahon's work is not only passively subject to the process of historical revisionism, but also actively involved in it. There thus exists a subtle paradox at the heart of McCahon's work: one of the things it grapples in its present is its future, or to put this the other way around, the work that will eventually gain him his reputation is about the gaining of this reputation. This again is the prophetic or messianic aspect of McCahon's work. It is prophetic in the only proper sense of the word: it seeks to bring itself about, to make itself true. To engage in any way with McCahon's work is already to fulfil its prophecy, to follow the programme it sketched out for itself a long time ago. If it constitutes a certain limit or threshold, something through which we must pass – and 'gates' are another major theme in McCahon's work – it is a threshold in the sense we see in Kafka's 'Before the Law'. It is not something before us which we can decide whether or not to enter. It is rather something that exists only in retrospect, after we have already entered it.

A HISTORY OF WORDS IN McCAHON

It is in terms of its essentially performative nature that we must understand the incorporation of language within McCahon's work. In his interview with Bloem, Crow describes McCahon's work in terms of a 'limitation to the barest kind of sign system and the taking over of so much of the surface of his major canvases with writing – a gradual giving up on painting itself, with language becoming its substitute'.[3] One of the first uses of words in McCahon's oeuvre is the 'Saxa Salt' label in *Still Life with Saxa Salt*, a painting of 1937, completed while he was still at art school. But by 1945 inscribed titles were beginning to occupy a place of prominence, with the oddly large inscriptions in black paint of titles, dates and signatures. His early Georges Rouault-like religious paintings contained words enclosed in speech bubbles, ribands and cartouches, devices that McCahon borrowed from both popular culture (advertising and comics) and the paintings of the Italian Quattrocento. We might think here, for example, of the words 'Jesus King of the Jews' written around the edge of *The King of the Jews* (1947) or the speech balloon that carries the words 'Come from the four winds, O Breath, and breathe upon these Slain, that they may live' in *The Valley of Dry Bones* (illus. 1).

McCahon's first all-word painting appeared in 1954, with the words 'I AM' (illus. 2), followed by the Martin Buber-influenced 'I and Thou' (1954–5), in letters as three-dimensional Cubist objects, echoing the shadow lettering of then-contemporary advertisements. In 1958 McCahon completed his largest word painting, a multi-panel work on unstretched canvas, dominated by the words of a cycle of poems by his friend John Caselberg, commemorating the death of the poet's Great Dane dog. In a significant series made the following year, McCahon dramatized his crisis of belief by drawing on ambiguous words from St Matthew's Gospel, as uttered by the onlookers to Christ's crucifixion: 'Let be, let us see whether Elias will come to save him'. In the early 1960s a body of work known as the *Gate* series employed rich brooding colour and words from the Old Testament that can be read as a searing denunciation of nuclear warfare. In 1961, asking Caselberg for help with this work, McCahon had written: 'I WILL NEED WORDS . . . Words can be terrible but a solution can be given. In spite of a message which can burn I intend a painting in no way expressionistic but with a slowly emerging order'.[4] And in 1969 McCahon began another word series, now popularly known as the *Scrolls*, which were crayon and wash text drawn from the Letter of James on blank wallpaper stock that had been passed on to McCahon in several large rolls by his brother-in-law.

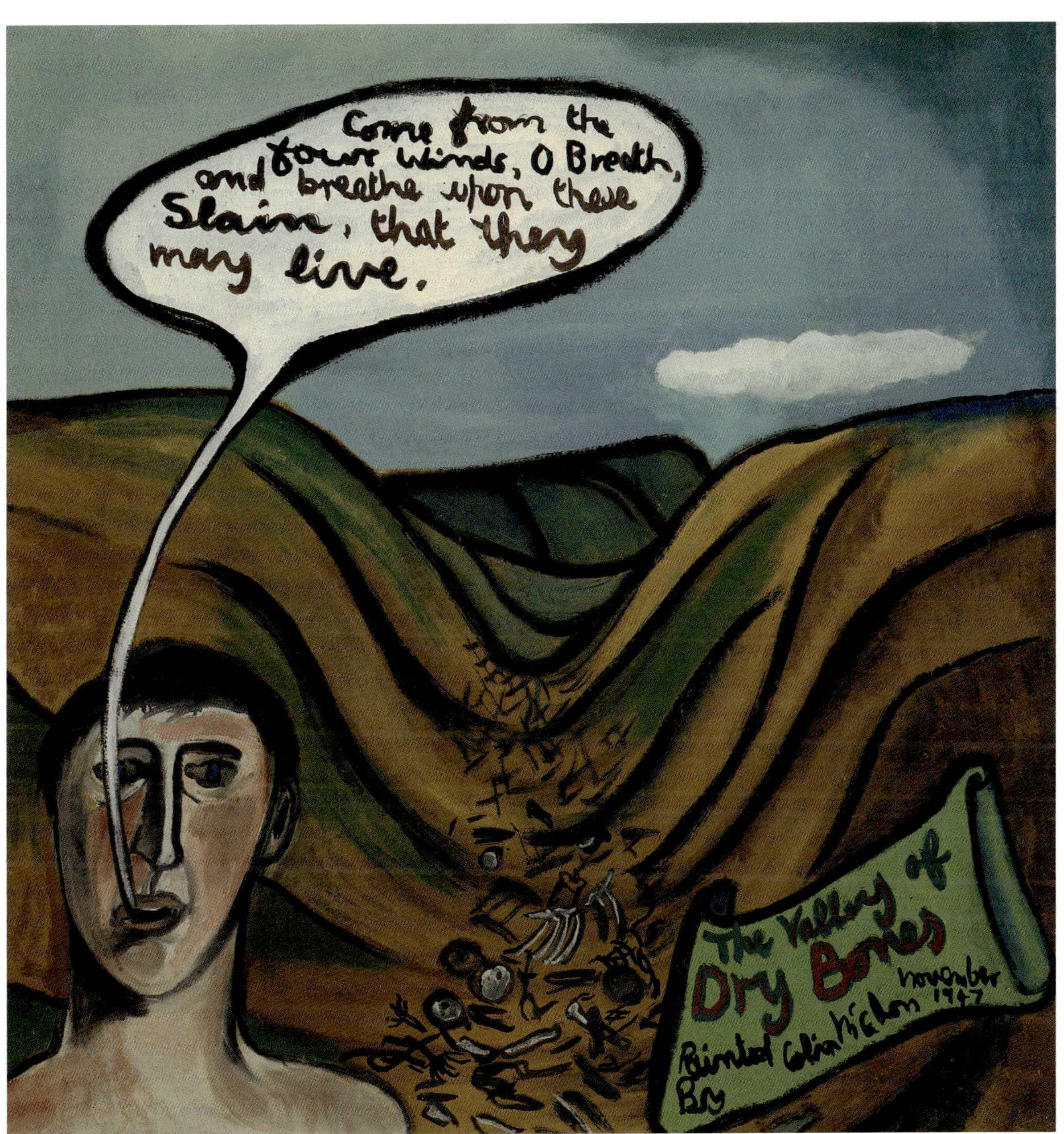

1 Colin McCahon, *The Valley of Dry Bones*, 1947, oil on canvas.

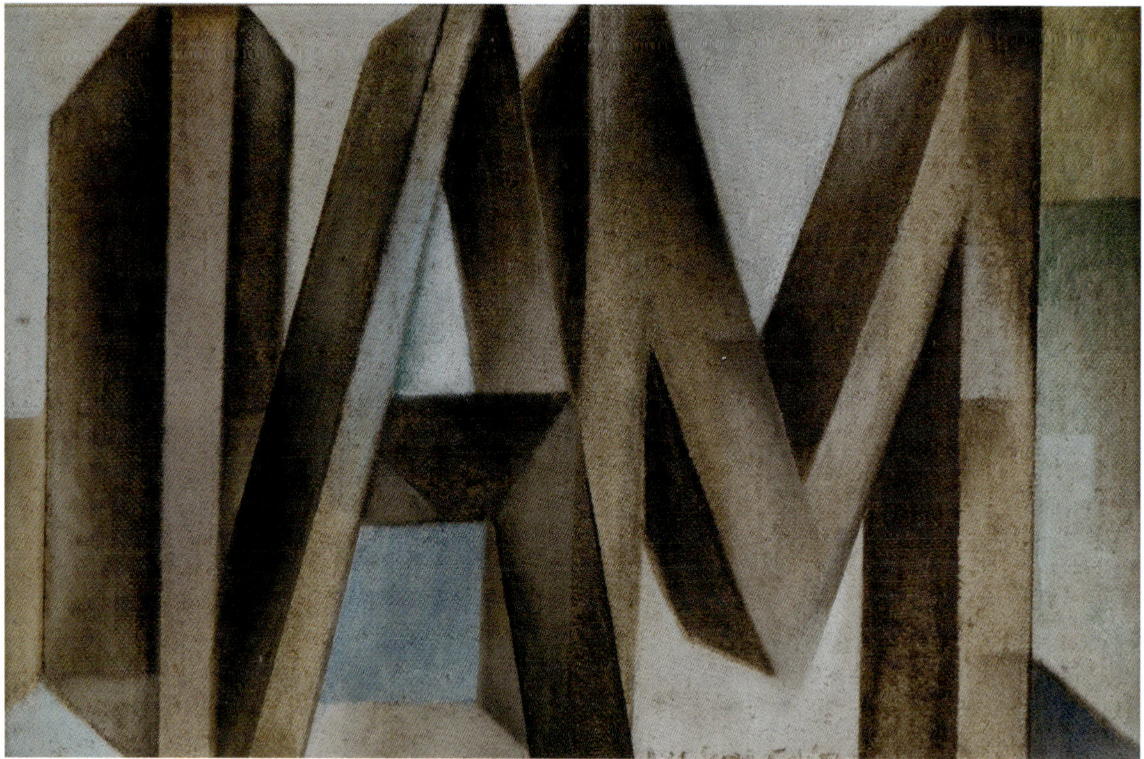

2 Colin McCahon, *I AM*, 1954, oil on hessian.

Most of McCahon's subsequent word paintings from the late 1960s on employ the rough amateur lettering, white on black, found on the roadside fruit and vegetable stalls on the main highway out of his home city of Auckland. Or they recall the biblically inspired graffiti McCahon found scrawled on walls, bridges and even on outcrops of rocks near highways. In the monumental word-covered painting *Victory over Death 2* (illus. 3), which the New Zealand Government presented to Australia before the signing of the Closer Economic Relations pact between the two countries, the lettering, which is based on God's 'I AM' from Exodus, is over seven feet (2.13 metres) tall. In another mural-sized painting, *Practical Religion: The Resurrection of Lazarus showing Mount Martha* (illus. 4), a great hump of landscape is all that remains of the regional, while words from the Gospel of St John run across the black expanse behind, carrying the traces of a repetitively loaded and then emptied brush that produces an incantatory rhythm. These paintings all evidence what McCahon once called, with reference to his *Waterfalls* series (1964), the 'joy' of 'taking a brush of white paint and curving through the darkness with a line of white'.[5] Indeed, towards the end of his career, McCahon's work became virtually nothing more than a series of transcriptions of selected passages from the Bible. The painting found symbolically face down in his studio at the time of his death, *I considered all the acts of oppression* (illus. 5), is a collage of prophetic quotes from Ecclesiastes, recorded in a tight white handwriting on a background that has become nothing but black. This last painting also contains a rectangle of unpainted darkness where no writing appears, a space for words where no words would do, unfinished because unfinishable.

Undoubtedly, this use of language provides something of a way into McCahon's work for those coming from a different cultural context. Critics are able to compare his work to that of other artists from around the world using language at around the same time, as though they shared a similar set of concerns. Rudi Fuchs in his preface to the catalogue for *A Question of Faith* lists Jackson Pollock, Asger Jorn and Joseph Beuys.[6] Crow mentions Johns, Twombly and Pop art, and the way that McCahon might be seen as the precursor to someone like Raymond Pettibon, who 'exploits visionary and prophetic tracts

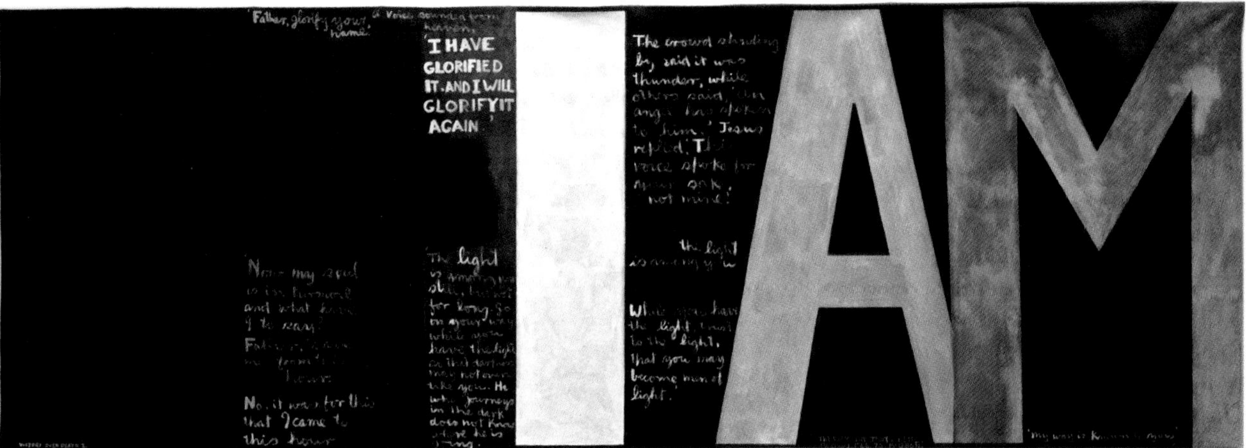

3 Colin McCahon, *Victory Over Death 2*, 1970, acrylic on unstretched canvas.

from American charismatic sects also in a demotic graphic style'.[7] And, for their part, New Zealand critics have also not been slow to make a series of comparisons between McCahon and other artists using language, both contemporary with McCahon and from the past. Comparisons have been made, in terms of individual artists, to Fra Angelico, Francis Picabia, Stuart Davis and Roy Lichtenstein and, in terms of more general art movements, to Cubism, Surrealism, Dadaism and Conceptual art. Indeed, a wide variety of culturally divergent precedents has been put forward to try to explain McCahon's work, from the Italian Primitives to Japanese screens to English Romantic poetry.

There exists in the literature a number of accounts of how McCahon comes to incorporate words in his paintings. There is not only the official artistic inspiration – the well-known story of McCahon acquiring a copy of John Pope-Hennessy's book *Sienese Quattrocento Painting* soon after its publication in 1947[8] – but also, as we have noted, the encounters with language in everyday life: comics, advertising, the signs for roadside fruit and vegetable stands. In what has become a kind of origin myth, McCahon himself claimed that as a young man he once watched a signwriter paint letters on the glass of a tobacconist's shop window:

> The hairdresser had his window painted with HAIRDRESSER AND TOBACCONIST. Painted in gold and black on a stippled red ground, the lettering large and bold, with shadows, and a feeling of being projected right through the glass and across the pavement. I watched the work being done, and fell in love with signwriting. The grace of the lettering as it arched across the window in gleaming gold suspended on its dull red field but leaping free from its own black shadow pointed to a new and magnificent world of painting.[9]

McCahon was a supreme creator of autobiographical fictions, and this is a story that has been repeated many times in the critical literature. But we would argue that McCahon tells the story precisely to make clear that his motivation for using writing in his paintings is not merely artistic, but truly vernacular or

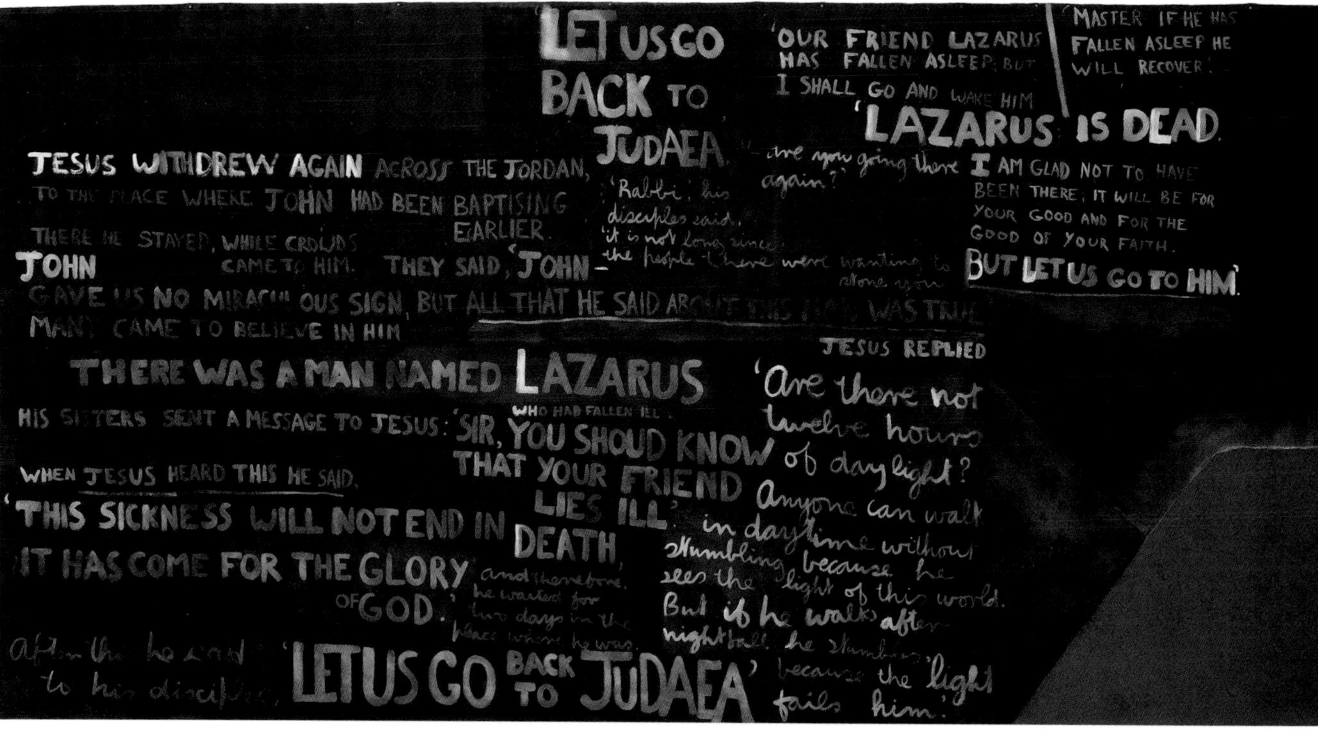

4 Colin McCahon, *Practical Religion: The Resurrection of Lazarus showing Mount Martha*, 1969–70, acrylic on unstretched canvas.

5 Colin McCahon, *I considered all the acts of oppression*, 1980–82, acrylic on unstretched canvas.

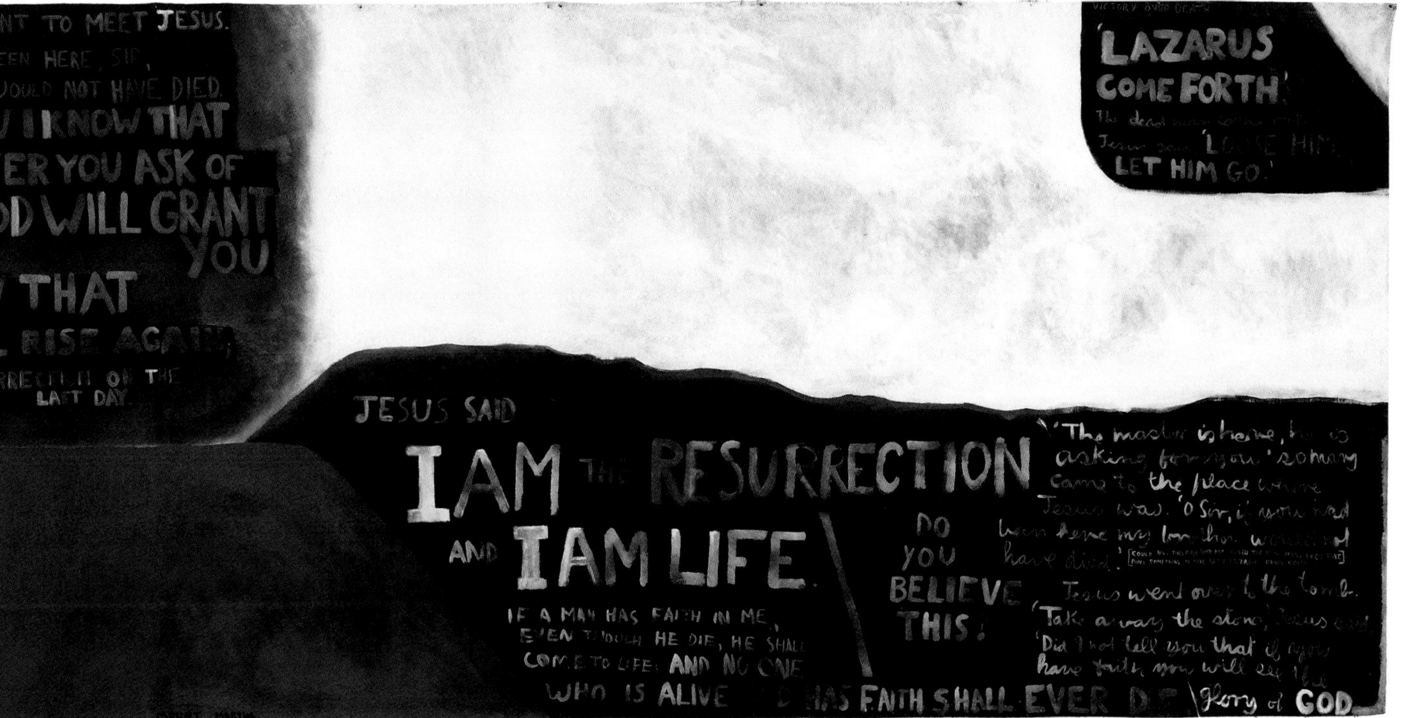

demotic, beyond even the way in which it is employed in Pop art. (In truth, Pop art is an unlikely inspiration for McCahon in New Zealand in the 1960s, for it could only have reached him late and merely to confirm a direction that was already in place.) Indeed, we would want to argue that not only the type of language taken up by McCahon in his work (religious texts) but also his motivations for doing so are profoundly different from many of the artistic comparisons cited. McCahon's reasons for incorporating language in his work are not finally artistic, but religious, instructional, what Crow calls the 'exercise of Catholic catechism'.[10] It is McCahon's employment of language in his work, we would ultimately suggest, that takes it out of the realm of the aesthetic and, 'projecting it right through the glass', out into the world.

THE CRITICAL RESPONSE TO McCAHON'S USE OF LANGUAGE

There are three major accounts of the treatment of language in McCahon's art. The first was written in 1969 by McCahon's friend and biographer Gordon Brown, 'With My Left Hand, I Write: A Consideration of Colin McCahon's Word Paintings'.[11] The second is by the New Zealand English professor and art critic Wystan Curnow for the first McCahon show to go overseas, *I Will Need Words,* which travelled to the Sydney Biennale and then to the Edinburgh Festival in 1984.[12] The third is by art historian and curator Francis Pound, who in the 1990s wrote several essays examining McCahon's relations with living writers, as well as issues concerning quotation and translation in his work.[13]

It is Brown, with his unrivalled access to McCahon, who was the first to set out the broad outline of McCahon's use of text, from his early religious paintings, such as *The Valley of Dry Bones* and *The Promised Land* (1948), which pictorially incorporated the title of the picture or otherwise included speech bubbles for the different Biblical characters depicted, to his transcriptions of various passages of the Bible, which are more or less entirely made up out of words. But it is also Brown, importantly, who was the first to insist on the fact that, even if the paintings incorporated words, they were not simply 'literary' paintings. Indeed, beyond this – and this is part of his long-running elaboration of the relationship of McCahon to modernism in general – Brown was the first to speak of the way that, through his introduction of language, McCahon was implicitly challenging the whole thrust of painterly modernism towards the purely 'visual'. That is, Brown both rejects the idea of taking the 'literary' element of McCahon's work out of the visual setting in which it is found and insists that the introduction of the literary does not indicate any 'failure' of McCahon the modernist to achieve the visual. In a way that remains undeveloped in his text, Brown argues against modernism for the validity of McCahon including language in his work, but with modernism expresses a distaste for merely 'literary' painting, the 'notion that painting should rely for its appreciation on what can loosely be called literary ideas – either as an episode from a story or symbols understandable through reference to some literary source'.[14]

Curnow's text, written some fifteen years later, reveals the influence of semiotics on the study of painting at the time, and is contemporary with the same 'linguistic' turn occurring in literary theory. Employing the Saussurean language of signifier and signified, and the idea that words take on their meaning only in context, Curnow makes two particularly important observations about McCahon's work and the way that language functions in it. The first is that a series of puns or analogies, occurring even between images and words, allows McCahon to construct in effect a number of theologically significant arguments. For example, in *I, One, One* from his *Elias* series (1959), using the visual similarity between the cross on which Christ was crucified and the letter 'I', the 'question of individual identity is linked to the crucified Christ; the self is a cross'. But this letter is also the 'I' of God, that is, 'Jesus and God are the same, they have different names as signifiers but the same signified'[15] (though we would perhaps reverse this and say that what we have here is the same signifier – 'I' – and different signifieds – 'Jesus' and 'God'). The second observation Curnow makes is that the particular meanings produced in one work are carried across to other works, so that each new work brings with it associations built up elsewhere in McCahon's *oeuvre*. The example Curnow points to here is the connection between *I, One, One* and McCahon's later *The Days and Nights in the Wilderness* (1971) (illus. 6), in which not only do we have an iconic resemblance between the 'I' of the self and the 'T' of the tau cross, but both of these are now combined with the bare, misty plains of the New Zealand landscape, in which the darkness of the night makes possible the brightness of the cross (another very common McCahon theme).

Francis Pound, writing slightly later than Curnow, begins by celebrating McCahon as an author, as someone who had a strong literary bent himself and who was generously supported by the New Zealand literati. Indeed, McCahon inscribed the words of many New Zealand writers on his paintings, and illustrated and provided cover designs for their books and set designs for their plays; but Pound notes, ironically, how with his word paintings McCahon left these same literati behind. It was paradoxically his desire to communicate clearly and directly, often in a simple vernacular language, that produced incomprehensibility. Pound writes: 'How much more "direct" could you be . . . than to write your message all over your painted surface?'[16] For Pound,

6 Colin McCahon, *The Days and Nights in the Wilderness: a constant flow of light falls on the land*, 1971, acrylic on unstretched canvas.

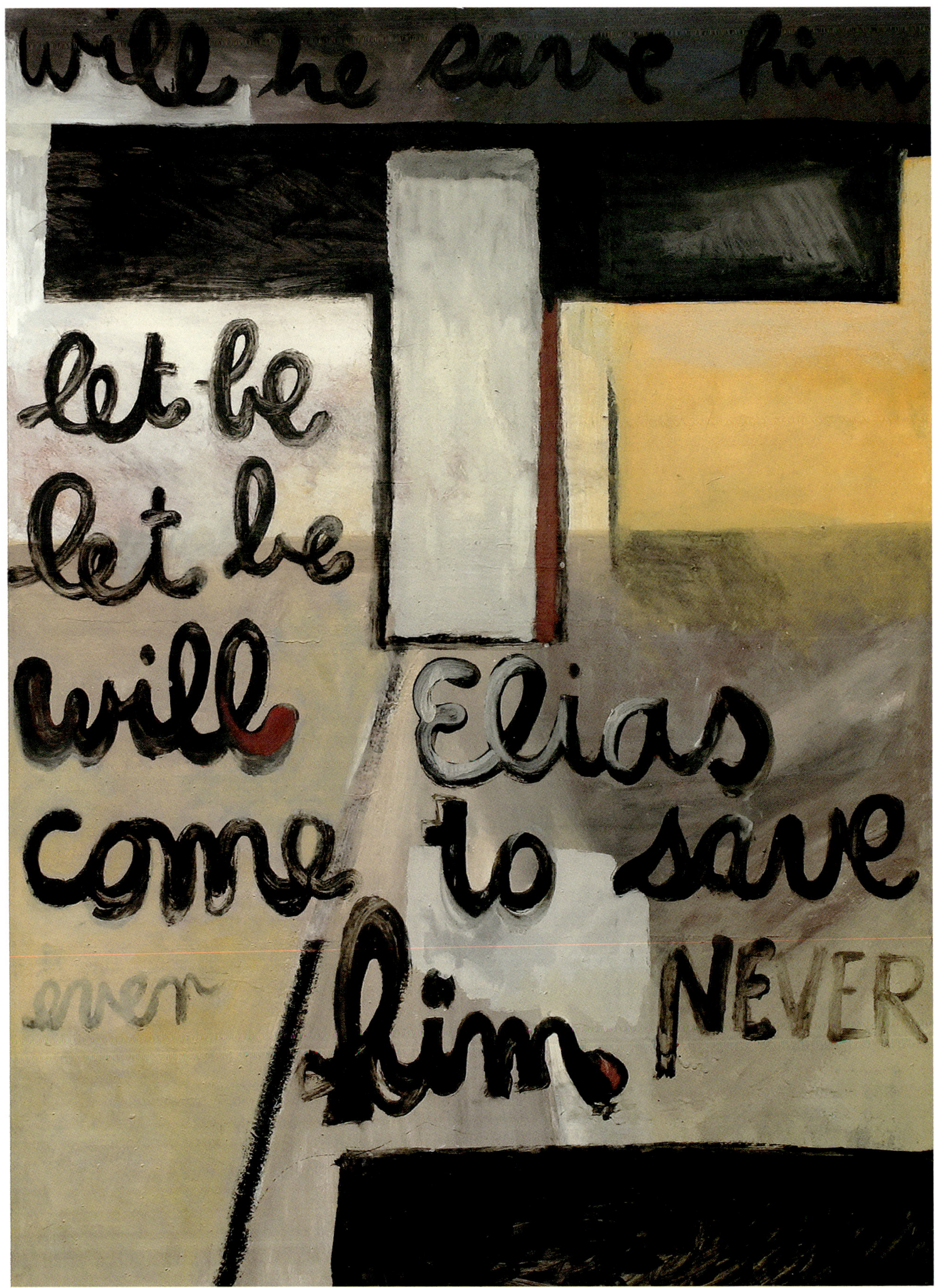

7 Colin McCahon, *Will He Save Him? (Elias series)*, 1959, enamel on hardboard.

McCahon's work is marked by the urgent necessity to communicate, and Pound, like Curnow, focuses on the thematics of translation in his work. Pound is clear that McCahon's adoption of an impassioned, prophetic voice and his choice and incorporation of particular Biblical texts is not merely a 'form of postmodern quotationalism'.[17] These texts are intended to be read for their meaning and for their continued relevance today. For Pound – who for his part is interested in both the biblical and McCahon's 'I' as what linguists call a 'shifter' – McCahon is more a ventriloquist, who selects passages from texts that answer or respond to his own local situation, 'so that they might speak for him, and be, in this sense, his speech'.[18]

All of this is to say that, with regard to the use of language in McCahon, there is no simple distinction we can make between the visual and the verbal. As Brown argues, it is not for McCahon a matter of illustrating 'prior' ideas, which would be 'literary' painting at its worst, in which the visual is merely an adjunct to the verbal. As Curnow stresses, not only is there no way of separating the visual and the verbal in McCahon, insofar as the visual turns into the verbal, but the visual itself already forms a system of signs, and takes on its meaning not so much through its iconic resemblance to any external reality, but through its differential relationship to other elements in McCahon's oeuvre. And, as Pound emphasizes, McCahon identifies his voice with the 'prophetic voice, in the bitter ecstasy of its revelations'.[19] That is, the entirety of McCahon's work is rhetorical or – to use a vocabulary closer to McCahon's religious model – typological. Everything is translated into or substitutable for something else in his work. Indeed, everything in his work even allegorizes or speaks of this. This question of translation is in many ways what the work is about.

But in all of this McCahon's critics seem to have missed two important aspects of his work. The first is that McCahon's work affirms, from the beginning, not translation but *mistranslation* as the productive linguistic mechanism allowing the expression of an abstract truth. Indeed, his interest in the famous mistranslation of Christ's final words on the cross, '*Eloi, Eloi, lama sabachthani?*' ('My God, my God, why hast thou forsaken me?'), as a call for the Old Testament prophet Elias first appears in McCahon's work as early as the painting *Crucifixion According to St Mark* of 1947.[20] And, as we have seen, McCahon goes on to pursue this issue of mistranslation throughout his *Elias* series of 1959 (illus. 7). The question of (mis)translation, and the fact that the onlookers misunderstand Christ's cry, are foregrounded there in the double and opposing meanings of the words 'ever/never'; 'Elias cannot save him/why can't he save himself'; 'will he come?/he will come'; and the confusion between 'He/he' and 'Himself/himself' (McCahon does not employ capitals in the series). Together with the compositional strategies of division and juxtaposition produced by such geometrical structures as the tau cross, the strategy keeps alive the two possible readings of '*Eloi, Eloi . . .*'.

Second, connected with this, we would say that McCahon's interest in the voice is not as a ventriloquist. He is not interested in merely inhabiting another voice from a safe distance; and if he is concerned to create a certain 'voice' in his own work, he is also not wanting the spectator to relate to it in any ironic or second-hand way. Rather, he was, as he said, interested in the 'sound of painting', which we might understand first of all as the voice before any origin, author-

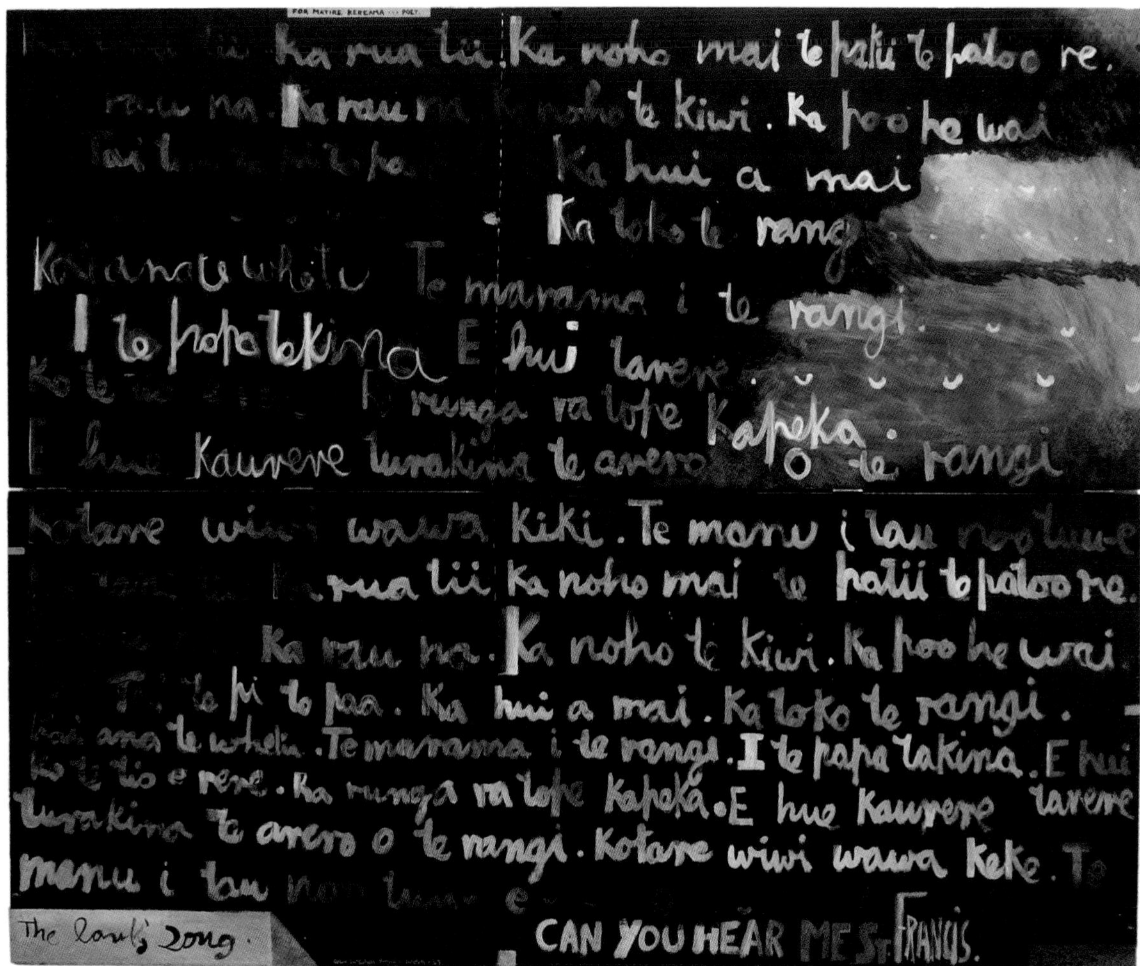

8 Colin McCahon, *The Lark's Song (a poem by Matire Kereama)*, 1969, acrylic on wood.

ship or even meaning is attributed to it. It is a voice that appears before it is translated, or that is able only to be mistranslated. To take just one instance of this, we might think of McCahon's *The Lark's Song (a poem by Matire Kereama)* (illus. 8), which is commonly regarded by critics as one of his definitive word paintings. In *The Lark's Song*, the words are entirely in Maori, a language that McCahon and undoubtedly many of his viewers did not know, except for its final line, 'Can you hear me St Francis?', which comes from a poem by McCahon's friend Peter Hooper. The reference here to hearing is decisive, as McCahon makes clear in his comments on the painting:

> From August to October I struggled with Mrs Kereama's *Lark's Song*. I loved it, I read the poem out loud while I painted and finally the little lark took off up the painting and out of sight. The words must be read for their sound, they are the signs for the lark's song. This whole series of paintings gave me great joy. Please don't give yourself the pain of worrying out a translation of the words but try for the sound of the painting.[21]

'THE WORDS MUST BE READ FOR THEIR SOUND'

What would it mean to represent the voice in painting? Of course, as we have shown, any number of writers have remarked upon the general appearance of language in McCahon's work. And they have, with regard to such works as the *Elias* series or the *Scroll* series, even analysed the complex question of address in McCahon's paintings, the way that McCahon individualizes the speakers of the various Biblical texts he cites (often several in the same painting). But we mean

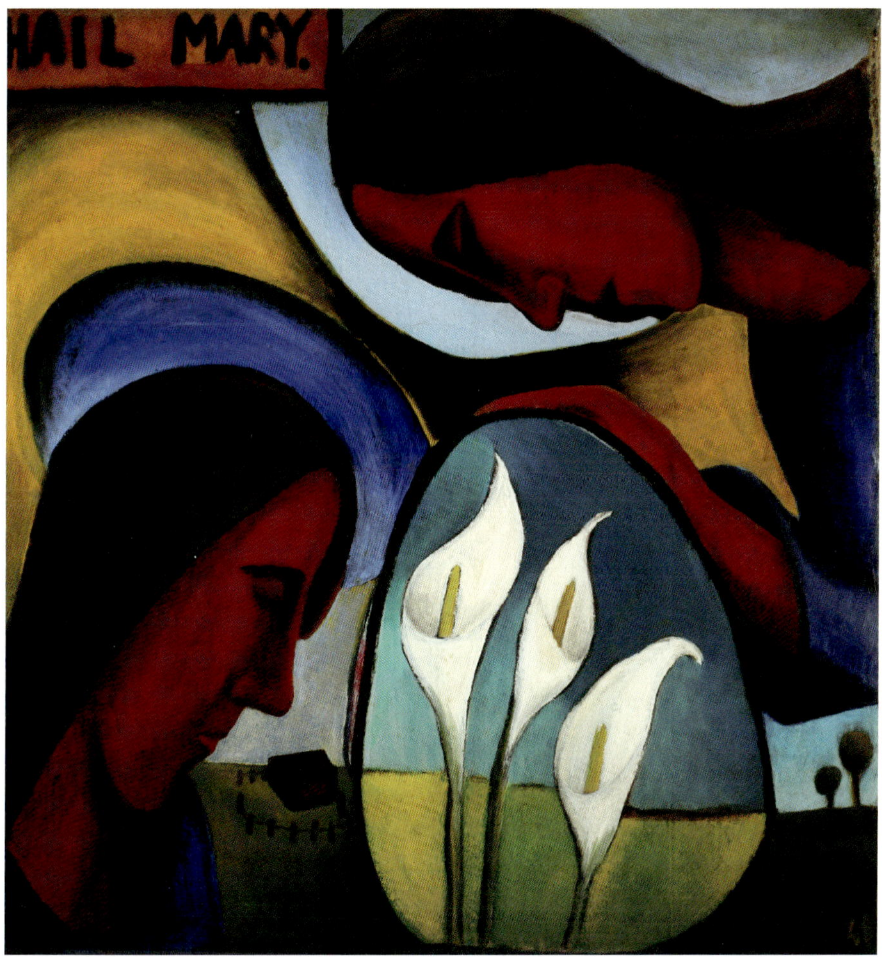

9 Colin McCahon, *Hail Mary*, 1948, oil on canvas.

more than this. The voice appears as a kind of accent or phrasing in McCahon's painting, crossing its writing but not simply to be identified with it. It is something like the breath or rhythm with which its texts and images are inscribed, the 'grain' of McCahon's particular painterly hand. It is this voice that McCahon attempts to make us see in his work, and that would testify to the force of his convictions. And it is this voice that, in the proper religious sense of the word, *interpellates* us into the painting, so that we identify with it, attempt to make it our own. It is this voice, operating not as a description of any currently existing state of affairs but as a prediction of how they will be, that aims to move us from our passive aesthetic contemplation and make us act in the world. When we look at such McCahon paintings as *Hail Mary* (illus. 9) and *You are Witnesses* (1959), which intend a certain performative role for the spectator, it is not a matter of any simple verbal message or even of the transference of this message into any visual form. Rather, its message cannot be represented, or it exists only in the form of the spectator standing in front of the painting.

Of course, as a work like *Hail Mary* reminds us, there is already a long history of the attempt to represent the voice in Western art. As McCahon was well aware, for he did a whole series of works on the topic,[22] in the long-running painterly theme of the Annunciation, in which the angel Gabriel hails Mary and tells her that she is to bear the Son of God, painters had to find a way to represent the Divine Word or Spirit that becomes flesh. Indeed, as painters understood very well, in the visual depiction of this invisible and ineffable Word, they themselves were faced with the problem of transforming the Word into flesh in a kind of Incarnation. And it is this problem that McCahon grapples with throughout the whole of his career. Going beyond the premises of modern humanist scholarship, it might be said that he works within a distinctively Christian economy of the image, in which it is not through any mimetic resemblance or significative equivalence that the image works, but through a certain *non-resemblance* to its subject matter. It is paradoxically through its inability to be expressed – an inability that can take place only through the image – that we might best capture the presence of the Divine within a fallen world. What McCahon's Christian images attempt to open us up to, therefore, is exactly what cannot be seen, what cannot be imaged. To use the language of the Annunciation, we might say that what he attempts to present to us is the *matrix* of the image, that which precedes the visible and meaningful image, that space in which the image can come to be. It is what we might call *light* itself, and we identify with it not because of what it means or what it resembles but in its own right.

However, in order to make this difficult argument a little clearer, let us see how this identification is played out with regard to a work from McCahon's *Practical Religion* series, *As the Body is Dead* (illus. 10). It is a painting that draws upon a section of the Letter of James in order to look at the relationship between faith and reason. But it is particularly the two texts in the lower half of the painting that we want to focus on. McCahon reproduces there the demand ('Prove to me that this faith you speak of is real though not accompanied by deeds') of the unnamed objector, who argues against James that faith and deeds must be inextricably linked. We want to ask, reading this, who is the person speaking? Who is the objector? Is he speaking as a friend or opponent of James? Could the person speaking even be James himself, or a projection of him? The phrase in capitals below this from verse 16 is also freighted with ambiguity. Here 'Good luck to you . . .' seems to be a voice projected on to us by James. But, in another way, it also appears to be us, replying to the image. Although the quotation marks at first function to distance us from the phrase, it can also be seen that they open up the possibility of its successive reiteration, with first James, then McCahon and then us claiming it. In both latter cases, there is a kind of prior meaning or authority that both McCahon and the spectator identify with, and yet at the same time what is shown is that this authority does not exist until they have identified with it. And, crucially, this is the relationship between faith and deeds that the work speaks of. Both James and his objector are ultimately right: deeds can be done only on the basis of some prior faith, but this faith can be seen only after these deeds.

In McCahon's work in general, the theme of prophecy and the way the viewer is drawn to follow the work in line with the Biblical narrative is obviously played out. This is evidently the subject of the work as well as what the work enacts. But there is also something else at stake there. We can look at the way the paint periodically runs out and renews itself, as though it were the reflection of the very waxing and waning of faith. Different voices or figures occupy different positions in the paintings as though it were a play that McCahon were staging. The white paint he uses to inscribe his texts appears like light breaking the original darkness of the world. And, again, it is all this that the work can be seen to be speaking of. But – and this is the truly complex point of the work – even though the work can thematize itself in this way, there is nevertheless a certain *limit* to this. There is a moment when the self-reflection or self-knowledge of the work comes to an end. There is something in the work that cannot be seen or

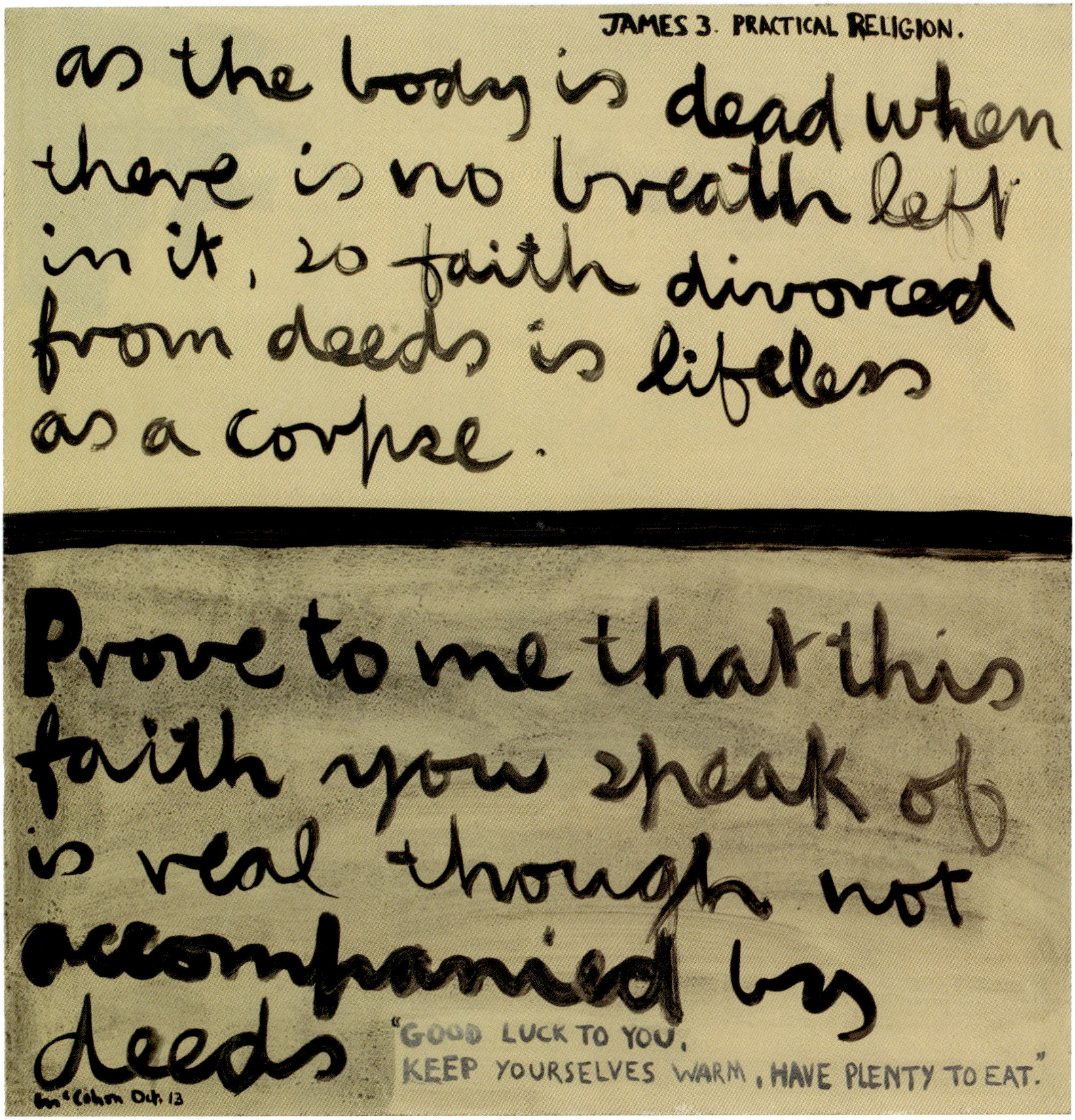

JAMES 3. PRACTICAL RELIGION.

as the body is dead when
there is no breath left
in it, so faith divorced
from deeds is lifeless
as a corpse.

Prove to me that this
faith you speak of
is real though not
accompanied by
deeds

"GOOD LUCK TO YOU.
KEEP YOURSELVES WARM, HAVE PLENTY TO EAT."

McCahon Oct. 13

10 Colin McCahon, *As the body is dead*, 1969, acrylic on hardboard.

spoken of in this fashion. There is something that even following the voice as a coherent iconographical theme in McCahon's work necessarily misses. It is the 'voice' in the sense of what precedes every interpretation of the work, every attempt to understand the work as speaking about itself. And this is the true question of faith raised by McCahon's work: it is what we follow in it before we even know what it means. It is the voice we see in the very curve of the line before we realize that it marks out the figure of Mary. It is the voice we see in the touch of white on the canvas even before it spells out the words that we read.

It is just this sense of the necessary limits to interpretation in McCahon that we argue is missing in the existing interpretations of his work, this abyssal structure in which a kind of pure visibility comes before any attempt to describe the work or to say what it means. (And this applies even to the most sophisticated interpretations of McCahon, which want to speak of how McCahon himself thematizes this voice or light.) It is undoubtedly the case that a series of metaphors or translations occurs between different parts of a McCahon painting or between several different paintings to construct a semiotic or typological system. As in any semiotic system, the meaning of any one term, for example, the landscape of *Days and Nights*, is caught up in the meaning of another term, for example, the cross found in *I, One, One*. And the meaning of the work in that way we have tried to describe arises out of a whole series of such associations, for example, the cross of *I, One, One* that turns into the landscape of *Days and Nights* that turns into the altar of the *Visible Mysteries* series (1968). Indeed, as the very emphasis on translation as a thematic in McCahon's work reveals, it is this transference or metaphoricity itself that becomes the meaning of the work. That is, the intriguing thing is that even though McCahon's critics are able to admit that religious belief is the real subject of his work, this becomes equivalent in their reading of it simply with the immanent movement from one sign or symbol to the next. The actual question of faith is displaced or has no need to be asked. The final term of their analysis is deferred: it is the act of exegesis or interpretation itself that *is* the faith or belief at stake in McCahon's work. It is the following or tracing out of a meaning already there in his paintings – even if ambiguous or equivocal – that is both the proof and activity of belief. In fact, the ultimate meaning of the work is put off just so that this interpretive activity might continue forever.

As we say, we could never go beyond the attribution of meaning to McCahon's work. All we can ever do is add another 'theme' to it, point to the evidence in it for what we say. And yet at every moment, cutting against this and opening it up, there is to be seen an entirely other order of signs or signification (or more precisely of non-signification). For a question haunts the usual analyses of McCahon's work and is literally unaskable within them: what exactly is at stake in this series of equivalences we find throughout his paintings? What exactly motivates them? What requires McCahon always to find another form for what he is speaking of? And it is at this point that we encounter the question of faith or belief in its proper sense. It is a faith not guaranteed by any series of readymade meanings, by the retracing of a symbolic order that is already either in McCahon's paintings or in the world. Rather, it is a faith that there *is* an order before knowing this. It is a kind of faith before faith, without proof or evidence. And, as we say, this is figured in McCahon's work as a moment of seeing before we know what we are looking at, before the essentially linguistic operation that connects word and image. Before the possibility of translation – and perhaps even of mistranslation – there is perhaps simply the fact that there is something to be translated. It is the fact that it is only after we believe that we will be rewarded by evidence. It is this – and here, of course, we would ourselves lose what we are speaking about – that so much of McCahon's work thematizes or better dramatizes, from birds having to jump out of their nests before they know they can fly (the *Necessary Protection* series), to the fact that it is only after we see what is before us as an iconic figure and not an indexical stain that we can pass through it (the *Gates* series), to the whole series of works McCahon did based on biblical episodes of resurrection (the *Lazarus* paintings of 1969).

To return finally to what we began by speaking of here, it is exactly insofar as it takes up the thematics of resurrection that we would say that McCahon's work at its deepest level is about its own future, the possibility of it living on in a revised twenty-first-century art history whose shape McCahon could never have predicted. Although the cliché about great art is that it lives on because of the enduring and unchanging message it passes on to following generations, McCahon knew this not to be true. Rather, the quality that defines great art is almost the opposite of this: its openness to the future, its ability to be re-read by successive generations as a reflection of them and their concerns. And, in a sense, for all of his efforts while alive to ensure his work's continuation – and no one worked harder to place his work in important institutional collections, to have influential critics and collectors backing him – he also knew that it was ultimately not up to him but the other, that his work would survive only in its future spectators. McCahon knew very well the analogous Hegelian idea that Christ endures only in his community of worshippers. Indeed, as we have seen, he made work on something like this very topic. That is to say, there is the following profound paradox at stake in McCahon's work, both in its relationship to its subject matter and in our relationship to it. McCahon finds his own voice, becomes a transferential figure of authority in his own right, only because he thinks he is relaying a series of teachings whose meaning is already clear. And critics, for their part, believe that they are merely retracing a series of connections that already exist, that endlessly evidence each other in a self-referring system of language. But what is revealed in McCahon's work is that the providential guarantee of God, the authority in whose name he makes his work, does not exist until after a kind of pure act of faith by the artist. And in the same way criticism is able to enter the tautological and self-justifying system of McCahon's art only by a moment of unmotivated identification with a 'voice' that summons it without the promise of meaning. This is why that 'voice' we have tried in to describe in McCahon's work is so fugitive or transitory, so difficult to describe or pin down. It is because it exists only between two, in the very moment of its transmission, between a work whose authority comes from its spectators and spectators whose authority comes from the work.

6

Revelation in Image and Word: The Apocalypse according to Horst Haack

BARBARA WEYANDT

'In that single gigantic instant I saw millions of acts both delightful and awful ... What my eyes beheld was simultaneous, but what I shall now write down will be successive, because language is successive. Nonetheless, I'll try to recollect what I can.'[1] What sounds like a commentary on Horst Haack's explosive series of images, *Apocalypse* (illus. 1), is actually taken from Jorge Luis Borges' short story 'The Aleph', in which the first-person narrator reports on that wondrous sphere that contains everything that was, is and will be, and that causes despair in the face of the unfathomable nature of this overwhelming scenario.

Horst Haack's *Apocalypse* (1999), with its kaleidoscopic colourfulness and panoptical density, is as unassailable and overwhelming as that cryptic Aleph. And like the infinite Aleph, Haack's multifaceted array of images, with its quite vertiginous richness and the resulting vortex, confounds linguistic appropriation. The oscillating, indefinable relation between the effable and the visible that we can intimate here leads us directly into the broad terrain of word and image.

On a total of 150 sheets, Haack offers us not only the complete wording of the book of Revelation, that zenith of notions of the apocalypse, but also a dense sequence of somehow visionary images. Each set of 30 sheets forms a portrait-format panel (225 x 54 cm). Together, these five slender panels form a compact block of hermetic coherence.

Images and words combine here to form such a dense texture that we would be justified in speaking of a true *horror vacui*. What we see is no less than the artistic attempt to grasp the infinite whole in a limited frame – *multum in parvo*. Even at first glance, the over-brimming confines created by the simultaneous presentation of countless sheets and images highlight a key side to the book of Revelation: the acute plight of a world *in extremis*.

Haack's *oeuvre* is a prime example of the transgression of the lines dividing the disciplines, or, to be more exact, of the interaction of literacy and visualization. In all his works, word and image meld to form a single visual statement, bearing witness to his marvellous ability to tread the fine lines between things. In the following I shall try to trace the strategies of crossing over and interpenetrating media as innate in the words and images of the *Apocalypse*. I shall consider two aspects in particular. In Haack's *Apocalypse* there is a clear textual reference, so the question will not only be how Haack visualizes the *Revelation of St John the Divine*, but also whether there are structural equivalents between the underlying texts and images that are interartistically motivated. It bears consideration here that in the form of the *Revelation*, Haack resorts to a text that, as the description of a vision, is itself on the fine line between visibility and effability. Alongside the relation of word and image as generated by textual reference, the 'word' is visualized in quite a concrete manner, as script. This also suggests that we should inquire into the visual quality of the word/image linkages, and focuses attention on the visual properties of written language.

While analysing the picture panels I will also of course consider the contents, structure and linguistic particularities of Revelation. Only by direct comparison can we ascertain whether Haack transposes the original text interartistically into an iconic semantic structure.[2] In the process, I suggest there are amazing correspondences between the narrative structure and the pictorial images.

The 150 individual sheets in Haack's *Apocalypse* merge to form a vibrant overall panorama with a dense network of references. However, it is truly impossible to discern a clear structural system underlying it. This is something Haack's work has in common with the literary model. 'There are great differences in opinion on the work's structure', stated Alois M. Haas in a discussion of the Revelation.[3] Many authors have endeavoured to discern a convincing underlying structure, favouring above all a structure in terms of three or seven parts. This is tempting, given the countless numerical series in Revelation, first and foremost the series of the visions of seven. They primarily reflect an enracination in old Judaic mysticism and speculation on the meaning of numbers, but there is no proof for any periodicization by key numeral. Any interpretative stricture based on numerical schemes violates the text of the Revelation and diverts our attention away from the specific qualities of the 'apocalyptic voice'. The latter is characterized by sudden ruptures, unexpected caesurae, insertions, interweavings, pre-emptions and dramatic exaggeration. The text's labyrinthine structure proves to be an aesthetic strategy that reflects in formal terms the prophesied chaos of the end of time and the related collapse of structuring values. It is striking that the artist Horst Haack differs from most exegetes of the Revelation,[4] in which the over-hasty, anarchic narrative structure and the complex self-referential syntax constitute the formal equivalent of the dissolution anticipated at the end of time and the confusion it will bring: this all takes its place in his excessive, seemingly chaotic overall view.

The artist faced the challenge of transforming the successive nature of the narrative text into the simultaneity of an image. Given the wealth of images in John's vision of the Apocalypse, this amounted to squaring a circle. Haack thus from the outset depicts the visionary report as a multipartite panorama, not dissimilar to a large multivision wall on which the action at the end of time unravels. Unlike his major cycles such as the *Chronographie Terrestre* (since 1981) and *The Waste Land* (since 2001), the *Apocalypse* is not a work in progress, but a complete composition that presents the cataclysmic events as an overall

1 2 3

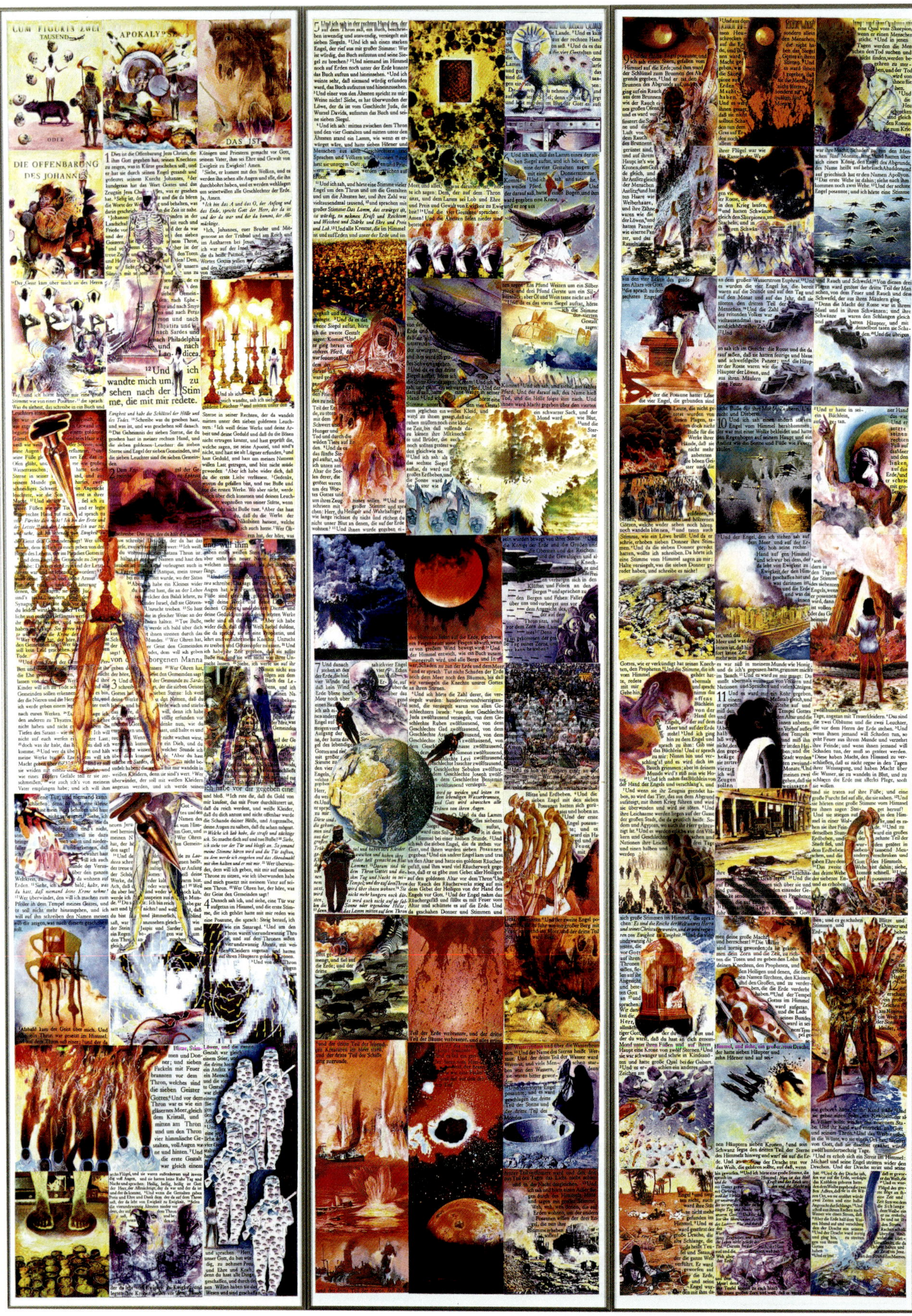

1 Horst Haack, *Apocalypse*, 1999, five panels, transfer drawing, collage, ink and bodycolour on paper.

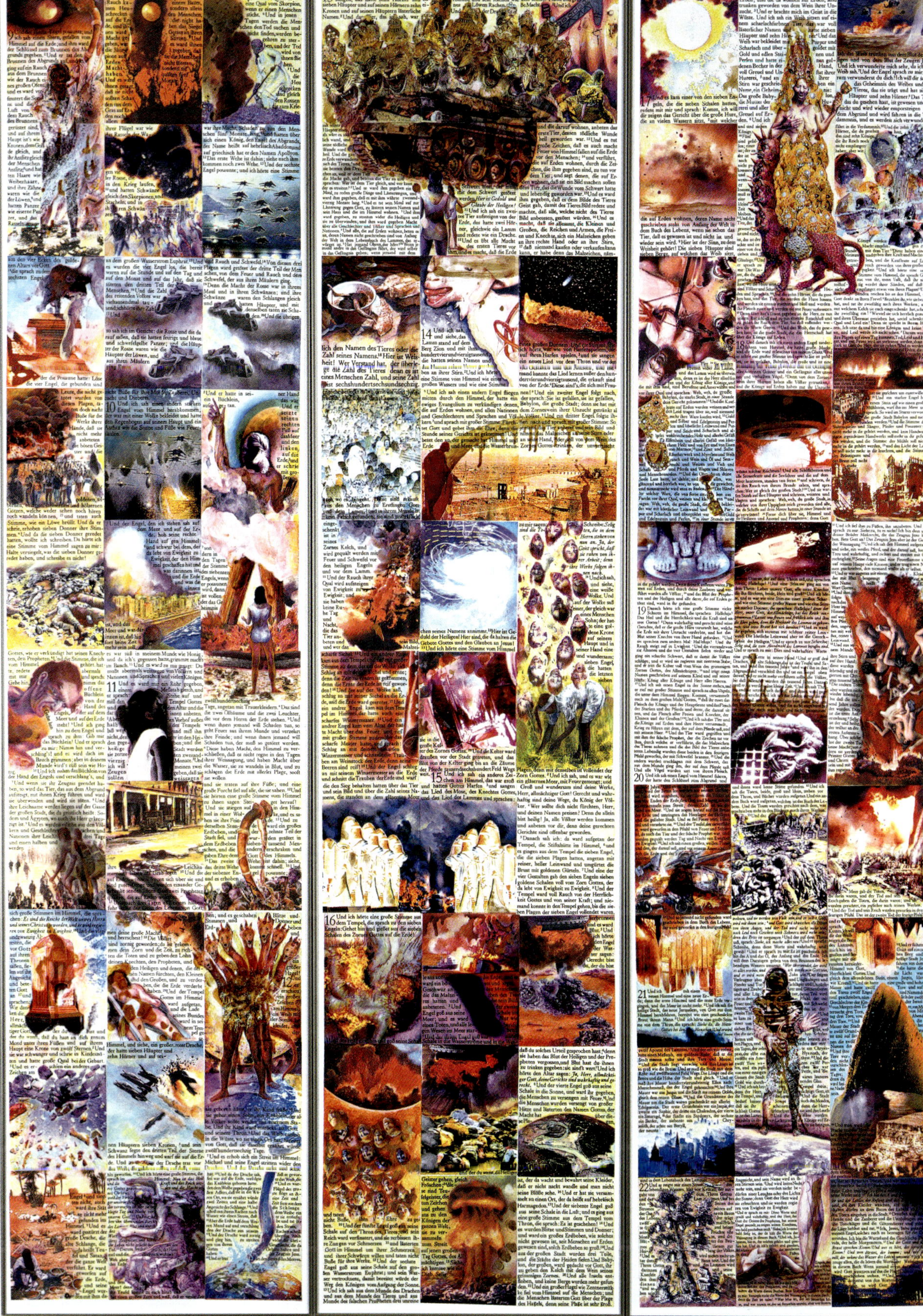

picture. Haack counters the danger that the numerous images might simply add up to some colourful eye-catching spectacle by using a complicated system of formal references that merge to form a complex image sequence that also serves to balance the composition.

Thus, Haack structures his *Apocalypse* by means of a variety of formal approximations, staggered images and repetitions. Sections in which several sheets condense to form a semantic unit, given the concentration of compositional references they contain, alternate with those of a more transitional nature. Here, the sheets are ordered to constitute a compact square, there, they are arranged as two- or three-sheet sequences, some to be read vertically, others horizontally, either overlapping, dovetailing or interweaving.

The first nine sheets of Haack's *Apocalypse*, assuming that we read it from the upper left to the bottom right, summarize the beginning of Revelation, and culminate in the image of the vision John is instructed to write (illus. 2) The vortex of visionary images can already be intimated here, as can the overall apocalyptic topic, death and destruction. Here, Haack introduces the seer, whose female figure is one of the strangest changes he makes to the iconographic stocks of Revelation. She appears in this *Introitus* a total of nine times in changing meditative stances, a process that visualizes our gradual immersion and transition into 'the other reality'.[5] The supernatural dimension to the experience is paralleled by the visionary, light-suffused figure with her psychedelic touch. The striking end point in this composition of nine is the vision of the seven candlesticks, with its clear allusions to Dürer's famous woodcut on the theme. What catches the eye here is the colouring: at the centre of this panel, dazzling, divine light consumes everything. This key scene also forms the foundation for what then ensues, as can be seen from both the colours used and Haack's strategy as regards choice of image. The glowing reds of the vision of the candlesticks run over into the next sheets, as it were, colouring them with the vision.

The candlesticks from the prior scene appear like an echo on the following sheets, leading to the mighty angel of the vision, who is presented from behind and only in fragments. His legs and the repeated depiction of the seer are examples of the repetition of specific themes in Haack's *Apocalypse* (illus. 3) Here, we can discern an allusion to the stylistic principle of parataxis so typical of the tone of Revelation: in a swift, staccato-like sequence, John narrates events and instructions.[6] In this way, his narrative has something hasty and breathless about it, intensifying the forcefulness of the vision he portrays. Comparable to these sequences of words, in Haack *cum grano salis* we find themes repeated, with the images used to visualize the parataxis through adjacency. Among them are the horse rearing up, the seer and the large angelic envoy. As elements that direct our gaze, they function to underline the sequential presentation of the events and set the direction in which things unfold and we read. Such repetitions span the details of the individual panels to form a complex unity and call for cross-reading on the part of the viewer. Serialization also arises from the way he presents the apocalyptic games with numerals. Initially, the young seer juggles with seven skulls in a macabre fashion (see illus. 2), and the four creatures before the throne appear in various guises: at one point the four figures, which the Bible says are 'full of eyes before and behind' (Revelation 4.6),

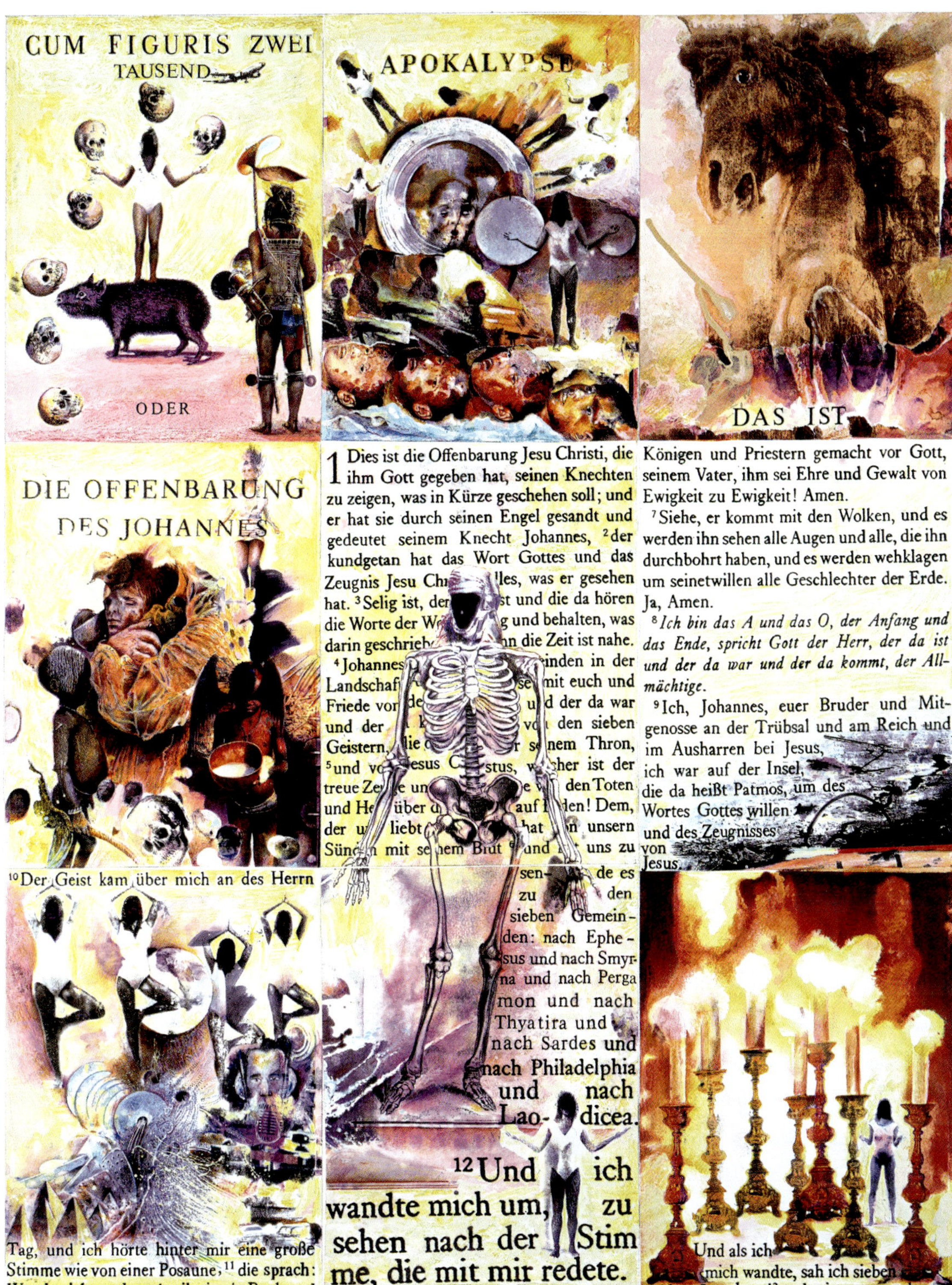

2 Horst Haack, Detail from *Apocalypse*, panel 1.

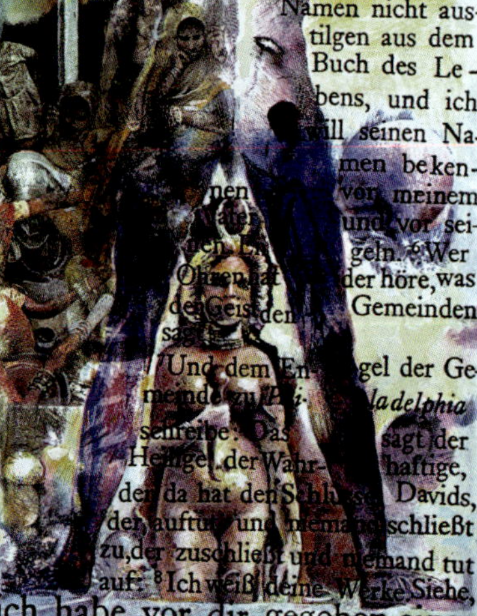

3 Horst Haack, Detail from *Apocalypse*, panel 1.

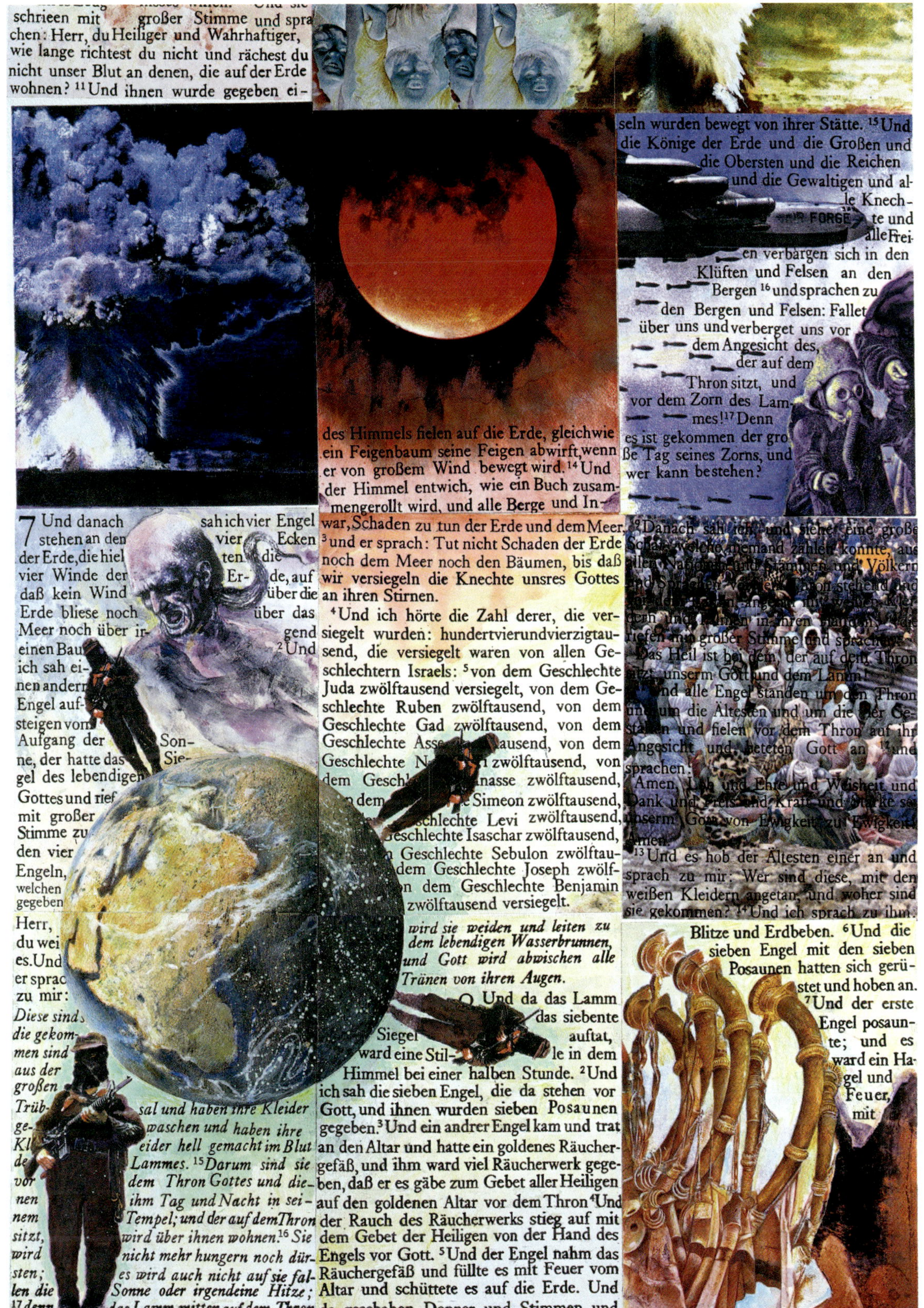

4 Horst Haack, Detail from *Apocalypse,* panel 2.

resemble mysterious heavenly warriors, and then they appear as a line of turbaned heads. At various points, the stencil-like nature of the figures is apparent. Thus the martial-like angels of the wind (illus. 4) 'standing on the four corners of the earth' (Revelation 7.1) resemble the figures with covered eyes in the preceding panel. They are examples of the principle of varying repetition and formal approximation. Such schematic recurrences are reminiscent of Thomas Mann's assertion that the author of the *Apocalypse* 'was delighted by a stencil'.[7]

We should also point here to the hard-edged positioning of most of the sheets. They abut in abrupt disconnection, separated by sharp caesuras, distinguished by differences in brightness and colour contrasts. The rupturing is raised here to the status of a formal principle, reflecting the acuity and mercilessness of the events. The swift alternation of the different images imbues the whole with a pulsating rhythm. The hard contrasts innate in this form of editing and montage are reminiscent of the use of cut-off in a literary context, something used by William S. Burroughs and later members of the Beat generation to connote existential alienation and threats. And there is also a clear similarity to the fast-paced image sequences in video clips or the fast alternation of TV images.

Within this dynamic sequence there are a series of spaces that function like concentrated blocks and form substantive and formal focal points. In Tableau 2, Haack brings together the horrors of the first four visions of the trumpets. Nine sheets present burning ships, fleeing creatures and ruins. The choice of colours specifically reflects the bloody nature of the reality of the vision (illus. 5). The visions from the vials in panel 4 are also worth mentioning here. The world appears as a flaming inferno, tormented by both cosmic and man-made catastrophes. Each positioned at the bottom of their respective panels, these two complexes of images can also be read as the nadir of events, an impression reinforced by the heavy colours (illus. 6). 'One should look at the red tones used in Christian painting, for only few of them do not taste of blood.'[8]

This brings us to Haack's use of colour in his *Apocalypse*. It is decisively influenced by two factors, the first being the hard contrast of dark and light sections. In the tense juxtaposition of bright and dark hues, we can discern at the level of colour symbolism the dualism of good and evil. The juxtaposition of brightness and threatening darkness also brings to mind the external escalation of the conflict before the final battle. Secondly, whether fire red, blood red, blackish violet or deep black, the colours reflect the world's darkening and its mutation into a burning hell. Specifically, the way the red grows darker condenses the disastrous potential threat. The colour is also reminiscent of that awful trumpet red, that colour 'in which the sun radiates during the Last Judgment'.[9] Colour lexicons do not, however, include this tone, as it is solely a literary creation. This horrible, one could say supernatural colour is deployed here as a cipher for the *Mysterium tremendum*: 'Woe unto me for that is no colour of earth and my eyes cannot tolerate it.' These hard-hitting colour tones contrast with the other bright, surreal hues that serve to dematerialize the objective world. Here, it is cool violet, yellow and blue tones that predominate. Detached from all material gravity and weight, they merge to form one continuous colour, a foil against which the visionary occurrences

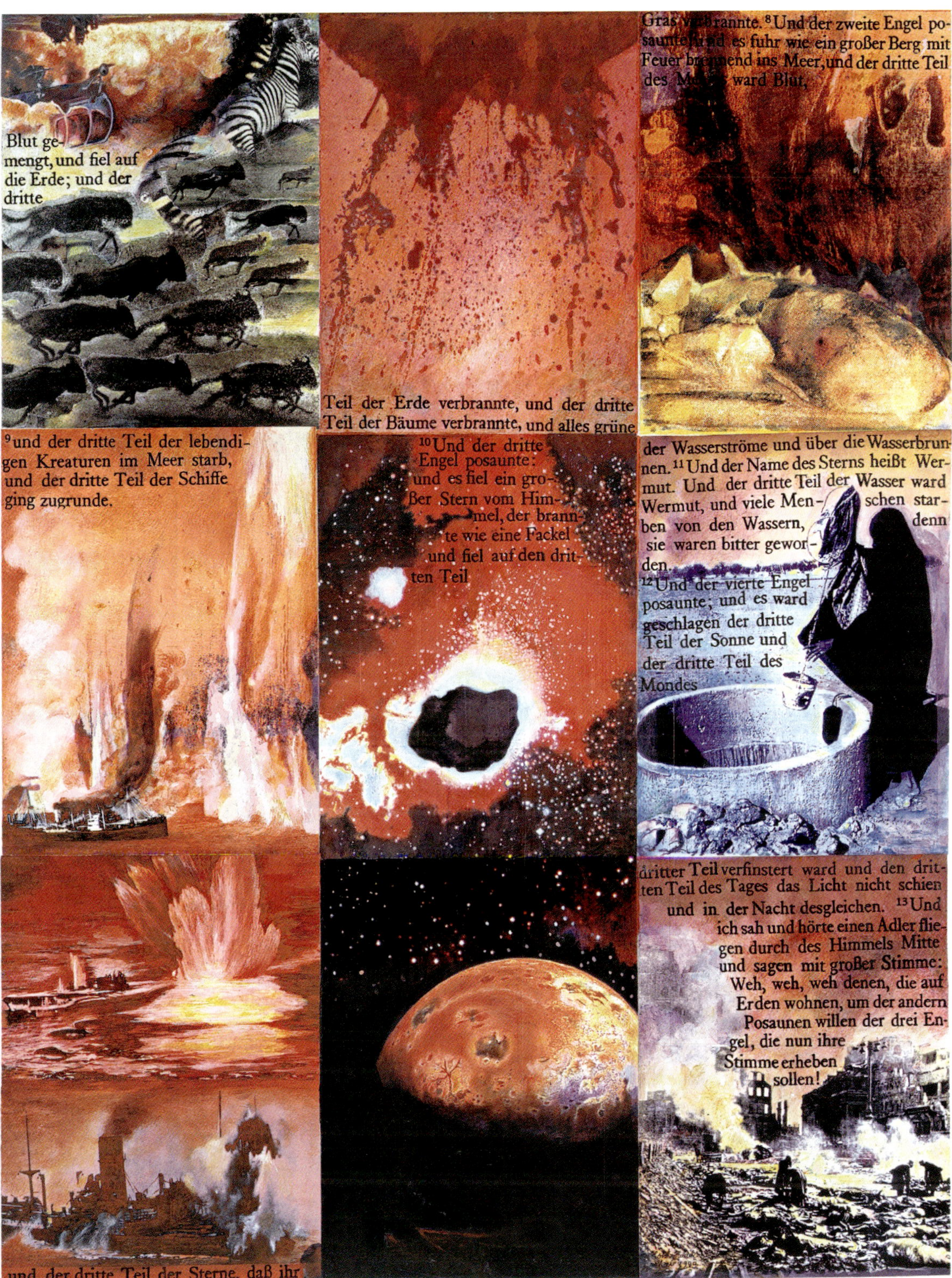

5 Horst Haack, Detail from *Apocalypse,* panel 2.

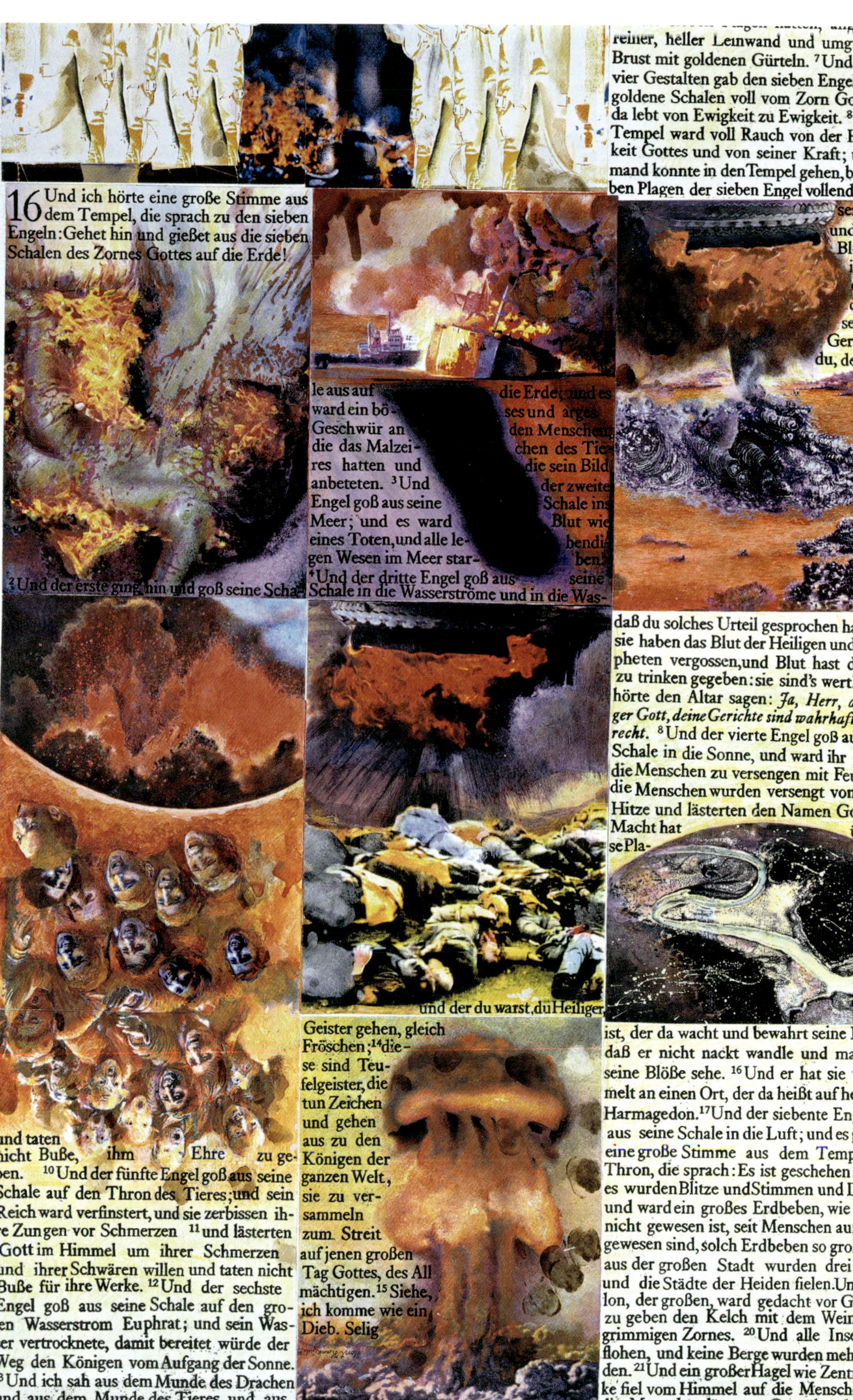

6 Horst Haack, Detail from *Apocalypse*, panel 4.

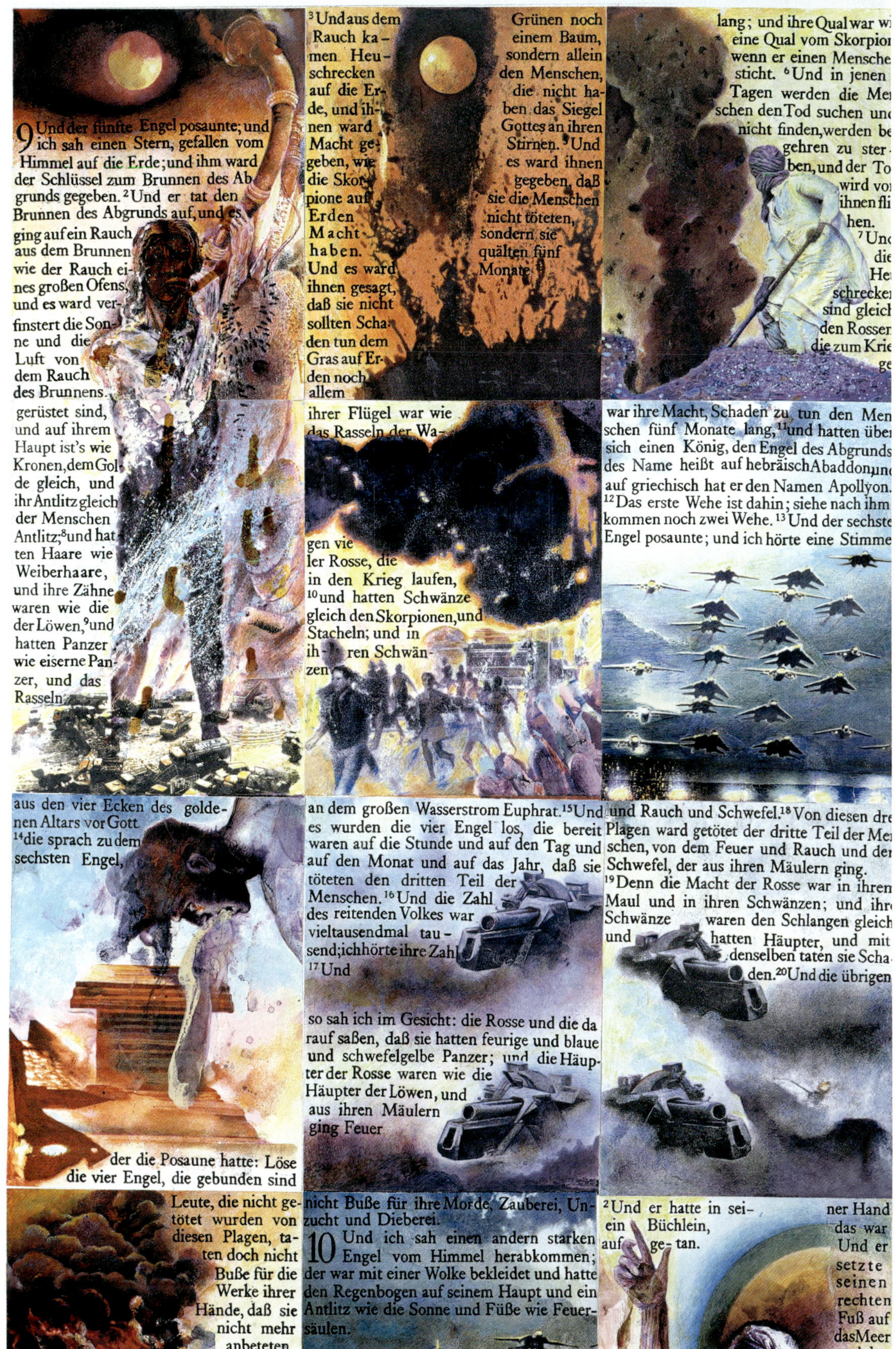

7 Horst Haack, Detail from *Apocalypse*, panel 3.

unfold. Bright clarity and intensified colour can be considered essential features of the visionary experience (illus. 7). The intrusion of the supernatural is visualized in particular by the transitional lucid character of the colour that, as it were, transcends the occurrences. The shape of the light is inseparable from the shape of the colour. Yet the phenomenon is ambivalent. The colouration and the way it melts with the light shows that we have transcended everyday consciousness and entered a state of perspicacity, but can also be read as referencing a nuclear disaster. Haack dresses the angels of the seven plagues in anti-nuclear protective clothing that has the feel of a mysterious aura of light. In some scenes the pale, cool tone given to the colour brings to mind a notion of 'nuclear winter'; others seem to be suffused by the radiation of an atomic explosion. The visions are typified by bright, kaleidoscopic colours.[10] There are plenty of pointers to this in Revelation. John's text is shot through with sometimes quite astonishingly differentiated colour adjectives. Not only are there the colours of the horses of the riders of the Apocalypse, white, red and black (6:2–5), but jacinth and brimstone (9:17), scarlet (17:3) and purple (17:4) are all mentioned. The crystalline clarity and transparency of Haack's palette (visible particularly in the prismatic structures of the final sheets) is preceded in Revelation by the list of the colours of countless precious stones (see illus. 7). Together with the frequent descriptions of various surface properties, John conjures up vivid effects of synaesthetic trenchancy that Haack then visualizes.

The presence and vividness of the images are so strong that they seem to burst forth from the text. Tellingly, this applies both to the script left to us by John of Patmos and to the panels created by Horst Haack. In fact, when reading Revelation, one has the impression that the images are rising up from or breaking out of the text. John marvellously transposes the visual religious imagination that proceeds via rapture into striking linguistic images. His visual images are high points of literary metaphor. Haack takes this up and with great imaginative and creative emphasis transfers the language into 'real' images filled with visionary power. He quite clearly takes his cue here from the rich seam of images that John offers, while at the same time updating them. The apocalyptic riders, the angels of the wind, the seer, the many nameless people who are extras or actors in the processed photos he uses, all wear clothing attesting to their own time: twentieth-century uniforms and garb. The plagues that befall man are transformed into contemporary experience. Instead of locusts, fighter planes and helicopters come out of the earth (illus. 8); the bombed ruined cities stem from our recent past; the ships exposed to destruction are modern. He weaves into the series of images an atomic mushroom as a special cipher of the Fall (see illus. 6). Many motifs stem unmistakably from the tradition of the ancient orient or the Old Testament, including the religious iconography – the throne, the lamb and the beast, all of which play a part in cult. Then, as clear references to the Apocalypse, there are the symbol of the 'great whore' and the scenes of the Last Judgment, all of which Haack renders in contemporary form without losing their mythological framework.

Deliberate additions expand the associations with the present. The lamb is on a slaughter bench reminiscent of a metal dissecting table, the monstrous beast with the seven heads is mounted on a gun carriage and the firepit into which the lost souls crash is nothing other than the fire raging over Dresden

nicht Buße für ihre Morde, Zauberei, Unzucht und Dieberei.
10 Und ich sah einen andern starken
Engel vom Himmel herabkommen;
der war mit einer Wolke bekleidet und hatte
den Regenbogen auf seinem Haupt und ein
Antlitz wie die Sonne und Füße wie Feuer-
säulen.

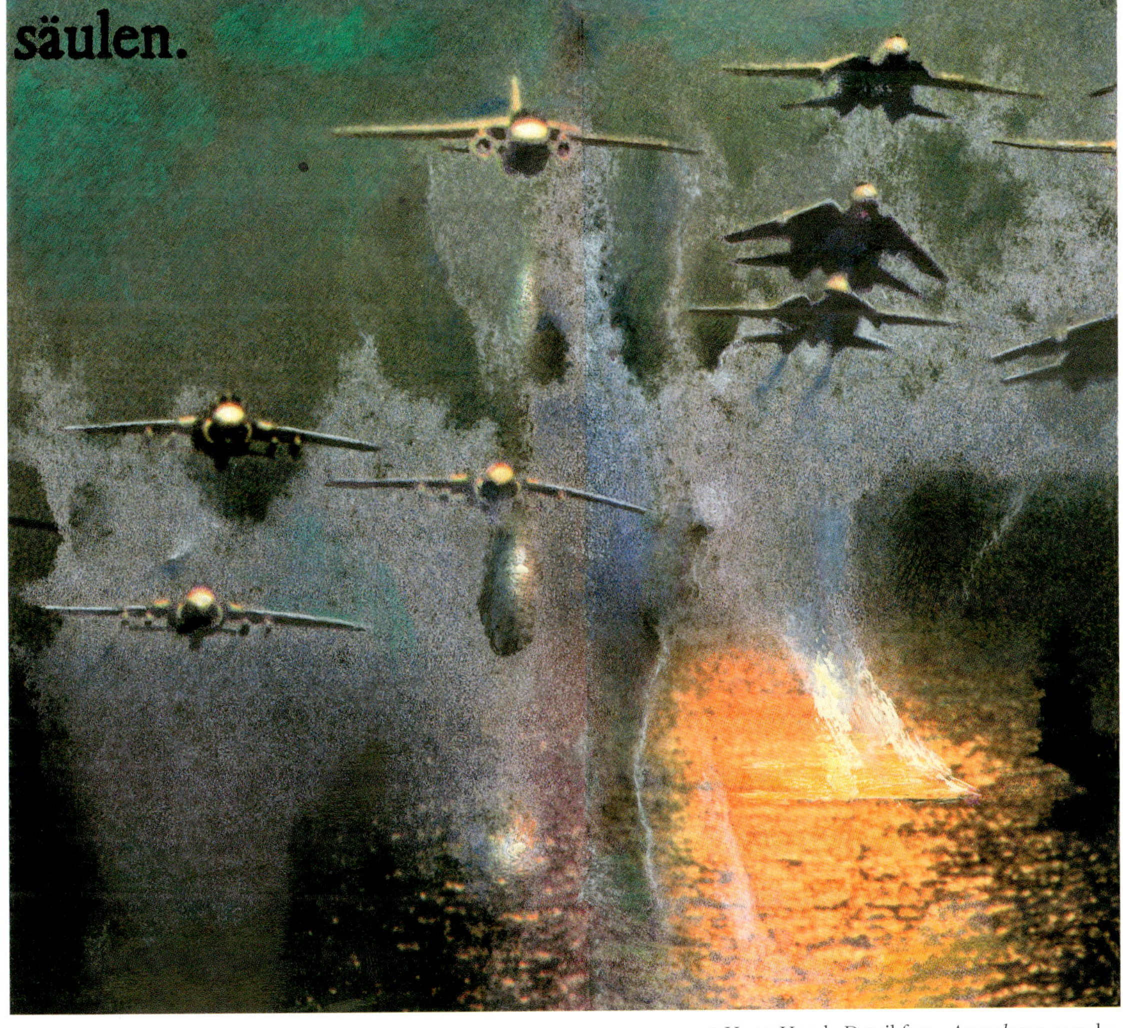

8 Horst Haack, Detail from *Apocalypse*, panel 3.

in February 1945 (illus. 9). This ability to create associative references leads us to the notion of linguistic metaphor, which, owing to its productive ambivalence, is considered as bridging language and image. Boehm even suggests that the metaphor is suited to present the structural pattern of the visualization.[11] Haack makes use precisely of this intrinsic productive oscillation innate in pre-given linguistic metaphors. The exciting interaction between word and image in metaphor, its vacillation between disclosure and shrouding and its specific logic of contrast enable him to 'modernize' the visionary images. 'One central point must never be forgotten: the revelatory text authored by St John is a text of images.'[12]

A text of linguistic images, one might more accurately say, which takes us on to the metaphorical potential of Revelation. The visionary language itself calls for a recourse to visualization, as the experience of the vision cannot be reproduced in language. All visionaries have asserted this through time. Yet visionary experience insists on being communicated.[13] One way out of this dilemma is to resort to metaphorical speech. Metaphor is ideal for describing scenes of transgression and transcendental experience.

Haack thus always remains very close to the text and yet his *Apocalypse* is compellingly topical. This is important to the extent that the apocalypse is not just the product of theological reflection but also of historical interpretations. It is always related to specific historical disasters and is thus an up-to-date text. In the case of Revelation, as written by John in AD 95, the threatening excessive powers of the Roman Empire triggered events, and for Horst Haack it is the twentieth century, with its seemingly never-ending flood of bloody conflicts, violent excesses, genocides and world wars. Be it then or now, we pay attention to them because of their ecstatic tone and their overt representation in the images.

Haack draws on various print media, such as magazines, newspapers, journals or specialist books of all sorts, for his images. In the process, he ignores any line dividing lowbrow material from highbrow, culling images from textbooks, pornographic magazines and the gutter press. By using historical and sometimes well-known photos that have been seared into the collective consciousness as symbols of apocalyptic horror, Haack intensifies the overall impression of authenticity. The panorama of Hiroshima after the atom bomb is part and parcel of this, as is the famous 'angel figure' that looks out over the fire-bombed old town of Dresden. Haack melds the two vistas to form one large image (illus. 10). Elsewhere, the references are less unequivocal, encouraging association. Thus the severed heads above the workers in the paddy field could evoke the infamous Killing Fields. Other sheets seem to pre-empt the events of 9/11.

All the images he uses he has processed, making use, to touch on this briefly, of collage, montage, recombination and overpainting. The image is then photocopied and the settings are deliberately mis-set to create the basis for the special colour tones of the *Apocalypse*. Transfer drawing proves to be the ideal technique here for ensuring the optic permeation of word and image.

I have thus far focused on the interartistic presentation of the text and will now turn to the actual dovetailing of text and image. With Pop art, material images

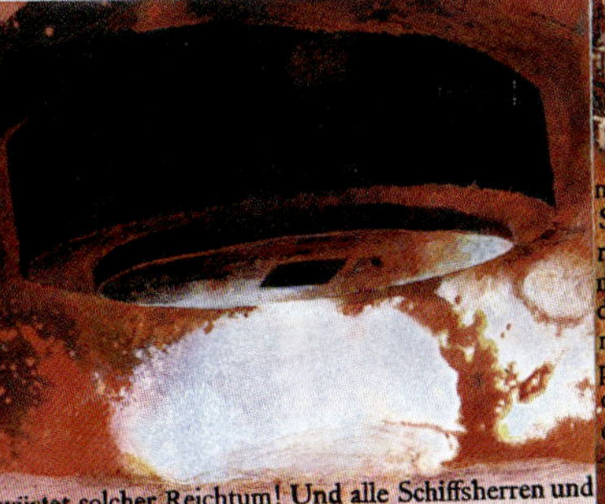

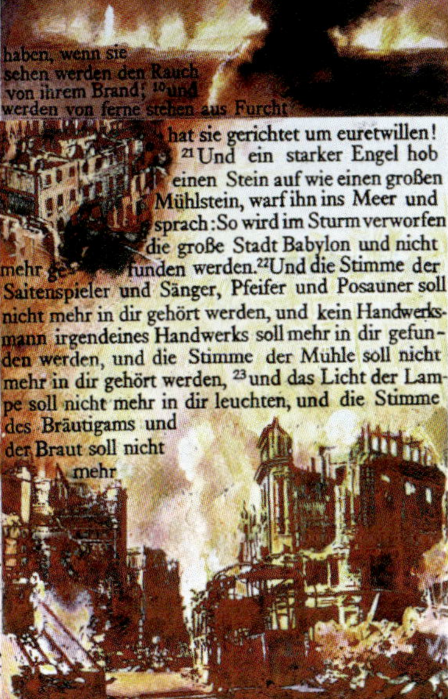

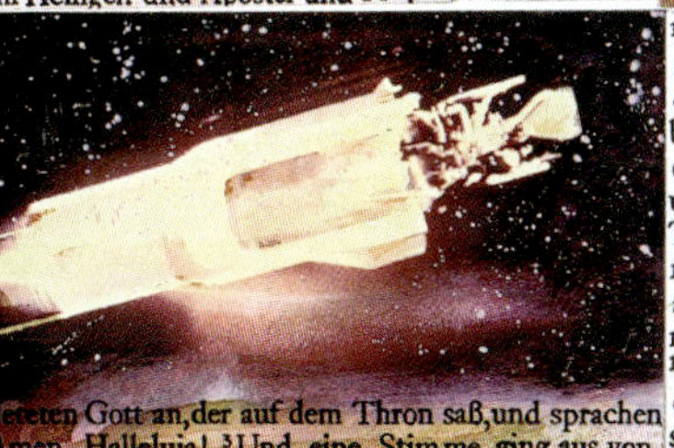

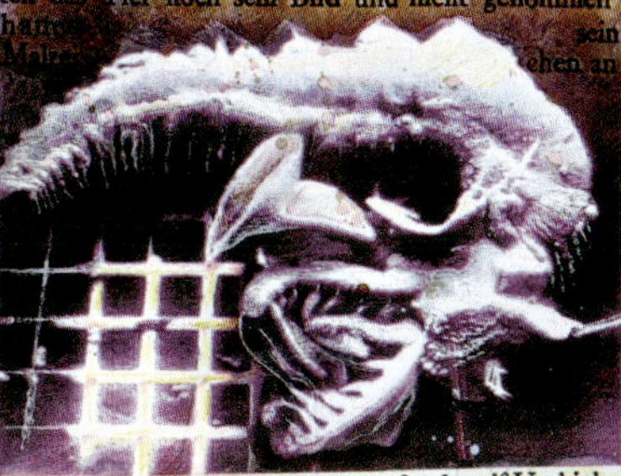

Tier. 14 Sie werden streiten wider das Lamm, und das Lamm wird sie überwinden, denn es ist der Herr aller Herren und der König aller Könige, und die mit ihm sind, sind Berufene und Auserwählte und
len, sie ist gefallen, Babylon, die große und ist eine Behausung der Teufel geworden und ein Gefängnis aller unreinen Geister und ein Gefängnis aller unreinen und verhaßten Vögel. 3 Denn von dem Zorneswein ihrer Hurerei haben alle Völker getrunken, und die Könige auf Erden haben mit ihr Unzucht
getrieben
haben, wenn sie sehen werden den Rauch von ihrem Brand; 10 und werden von ferne stehen aus Furcht
vor ihrer Qual und sprechen: Weh, weh, du große Stadt, Babylon, du starke Stadt, in einer Stunde ist dein Gericht gekommen! 11 Und die Kaufleute auf Erden werden weinen und werden Leid tragen über sie, weil niemand mehr ihre Ware kaufen wird, 12 Gold und Silber und Edelgestein und Perlen und köstliche Leinwand und Purpur und Seide und Scharlach und allerlei wohlriechendes Holz und allerlei Gefäß von Elfenbein und allerlei Gefäß von köstlichem Holz und von Erz und von Eisen und von Marmor, 13 und Zimt und Salbe und Räucherwerk und Myrrhen und Weihrauch und Wein und Öl und Semmel und Weizen und Vieh und Schafe und Pferde und Wagen und Sklaven und Menschenseelen. 14 Und das Obst, daran deine Seele Lust hatte, ist dahin; und alles, was glänzend und herrlich war, ist von dir gewichen, und nimmermehr wird man es finden. 15 Die Händler solcher Ware, die von ferne stehen aus Furcht vor ihrer Qual, weinen und klagen 16 und sagen: Weh, weh, du große Stadt, die bekleidet war mit köstlicher Leinwand und Purpur und Scharlach und übergoldet war mit Gold und Edelgestein und Perlen, 17 in einer Stunde ist verwüstet solcher Reichtum! Und alle Schiffsherren und alle Steuerleute und die Seefahrer und die auf dem Meer hantieren, standen von ferne 18 und schrieen, da sie den Rauch von ihrem Brande sahen, und sprachen: Wer ist gleich der großen Stadt? 19 Und sie warfen Staub auf ihre Häupter und schrieen, weinten und klagten und sprachen: Weh, weh, du große Stadt, in welcher von ihrer Üppigkeit reich geworden sind alle, die da Schiffe auf dem Meere hatten, in einer Stunde ist sie verwüstet! 20 Freue dich über sie, Himmel und ihr Heiligen und Apostel und Propheten: denn Gott
hat sie gerichtet um euretwillen! 21 Und ein starker Engel hob einen Stein auf wie einen großen Mühlstein, warf ihn ins Meer und sprach: So wird im Sturm verworfen die große Stadt Babylon und nicht mehr gefunden werden. 22 Und die Stimme der Saitenspieler und Sänger, Pfeifer und Posauner soll nicht mehr in dir gehört werden, und kein Handwerksmann irgendeines Handwerks soll mehr in dir gefunden werden, und die Stimme der Mühle soll nicht mehr in dir gehört werden, 23 und das Licht der Lampe soll nicht mehr in dir leuchten, und die Stimme des Bräutigams und der Braut soll nicht mehr
in dir gehört werden. Denn deine Kaufleute waren Fürsten auf Erden, und durch deine Zauberei sind verführt worden alle Völker; 24 und das Blut der Propheten und der Heiligen und alle derer, die auf Erden getötet sind, ward in ihr gefunden.
19 Danach hörte ich eine große Stimme vieler Scharen im Himmel, die sprachen: Halleluja! Das Heil und die Herrlichkeit und die Kraft sind unsres Gottes! 2 Denn wahrhaftig und gerecht sind seine Gerichte, daß er die große Hure verurteilt hat, welche die Erde mit ihrer Unzucht verderbte, und hat das Blut seiner Knechte von ihrer Hand gefordert. 3 Und sie sprachen zum andern Mal: Halleluja! Und ihr Rauch steigt auf in Ewigkeit. 4 Und die vierundzwanzig Ältesten und die vier Gestalten fielen nieder und
beteten Gott an, der auf dem Thron saß, und sprachen: Amen, Halleluja! 5 Und eine Stimme ging aus von dem Thron: Lobet unsern Gott, alle seine Knechte, die ihn fürchten, beide, klein und groß! 6 Und ich hörte, und es war wie eine Stimme einer großen Schar und wie eine Stimme großer Wasser und wie eine Stimme starker Donner, die sprachen: Halleluja! denn der Herr, unser Gott, der Allmächtige, hat das Reich eingenommen! 7 Lasset uns freuen und fröhlich sein und ihm die Ehre geben, denn die Hochzeit des Lammes ist gekommen, und seine Braut hat sich bereitet! 8 Und es ward ihr gegeben, sich anzutun mit schöner reiner Leinwand. Die köstliche Leinwand aber ist die Gerechtigkeit der Heiligen. 9 Und er sprach zu mir: Schreibe: Selig sind, die zum Abendmahl des Lammes berufen sind. Und er sprach zu mir: Dies sind wahrhaftige Worte
10 Und ich fiel ihm zu Füßen, ihn anzubeten. Und er sprach zu mir: Siehe zu, tu es nicht! Ich bin dein und deiner Brüder Mitknecht, die das Zeugnis Jesu haben. Bete Gott an! Das Zeugnis Jesu aber ist der Geist der Weissagung. 11 Und ich sah den Himmel aufgetan; und siehe, ein weißes Pferd, und der darauf saß, hieß: Treu und wahrhaftig, und richtet und streitet mit Gerechtigkeit. 12 Seine Augen sind eine Feuerflamme und auf seinem Haupt viele Kronen; und er trug einen Namen geschrieben, den niemand wußte als er selbst. 13 Und er war angetan mit einem Kleide, das mit Blut besprengt war, und sein Name heißt: Das Wort Gottes. 14 Und ihm folgte nach das Heer im Himmel auf weißen Pferden, angetan mit weißer, reiner Leinwand. 15 Und aus seinem Munde
ging ein scharfes Schwert, daß er damit die Völker schlüge; und er wird sie regieren mit eisernem Stabe; und er tritt die Kelter voll vom Wein des grimmigen Zornes Gottes, des Allmächtigen; 16 und trägt einen Namen geschrieben auf seinem Kleid und auf seiner Hüfte: König aller Könige und Herr aller Herren. 17 Und ich sah einen Engel in der Sonne stehen, und er rief mit großer Stimme und sprach zu allen Vögeln, die unter dem Himmel fliegen: Kommt, versammelt euch zu dem großen Mahl Gottes, 18 daß ihr esset das Fleisch der Könige und der Hauptleute und das Fleisch der Starken und der Pferde und derer, die darauf sitzen, und das Fleisch aller Freien und Knechte, der Kleinen und der Großen! 19 Und ich sah das Tier und die Könige auf Erden und ihre Heere versammelt, Krieg zu führen mit dem, der auf dem Pferde saß, und mit seinem Heer. 20 Und das Tier ward gegriffen und mit ihm der falsche Prophet, der die Zeichen tat vor ihm, durch welche er verführte, die das Malzeichen des Tieres nahmen und die das Bild des Tieres anbeteten. Lebendig wurden diese beiden in den feurigen Pfuhl geworfen, der mit Schwefel brannte. 21 Und die andern wurden erschlagen mit dem Schwert, das aus dem Munde ging des, der auf dem Pferde saß. Und alle Vögel wurden satt von ihrem Fleisch.
20 Und ich sah einen Engel vom Himmel fahren, der hatte den Schlüssel zum Abgrund und
eine große Kette in seiner Hand. 2 Und er griff den Drachen, die alte Schlange, das ist der Teufel und Satan, und band ihn tausend Jahre 3 und warf ihn in den Abgrund und verschloß ihn und tat ein Siegel oben darauf, daß er nicht mehr verführen sollte die Völker, bis daß vollendet würden die tausend Jahre. Danach muß er los werden eine kleine Zeit. 4 Und ich sah Throne, und sie setzten sich darauf, und ihnen ward gegeben das Gericht. Und ich sah die Seelen derer, die enthauptet sind um des Zeugnisses von Jesus und um des Wortes Gottes willen, und die nicht angebetet hatten das Tier noch sein Bild und nicht genommen hatten
ihre Stirn und auf ihre Hand; diese wurden lebendig und regierten mit Christus tausend Jahre. 5 Die andern Toten aber wurden nicht wieder lebendig, bis daß die tausend Jahre vollendet wurden. Dies ist die erste Auferstehung. 6 Selig ist der und heilig, der teilhat an der ersten Auferstehung. Über solche hat der zweite Tod keine Macht; sondern sie werden Priester Gottes und Christi sein und mit ihm regieren
tausend Jahre. 7 Und wenn die tausend Jahre vollendet sind, wird der Satan los werden aus seinem Gefängnis 8 und wird ausgehen, zu verführen die Völker an den vier Enden der Erde, den Gog und Magog, um sie zu versammeln zum Streit; deren Zahl ist wie der Sand am Meer. 9 Und sie zogen herauf auf die Breite der Erde und umringten das Heerlager der Heiligen und die geliebte Stadt. Und es fiel Feuer vom Him-
und ihnen ward keine Stätte gefunden. 12 Und ich sah die Toten, beide, groß und klein, stehen vor dem Thron, und Bücher wurden aufgetan. Und ein anderes Buch ward aufgetan, welches ist das Buch des Lebens. Und die Toten wurden gerichtet nach dem, was geschrieben steht in den Büchern, nach ihren Werken. 13 Und das

9 Horst Haack, Detail from *Apocalypse*, panel 5.

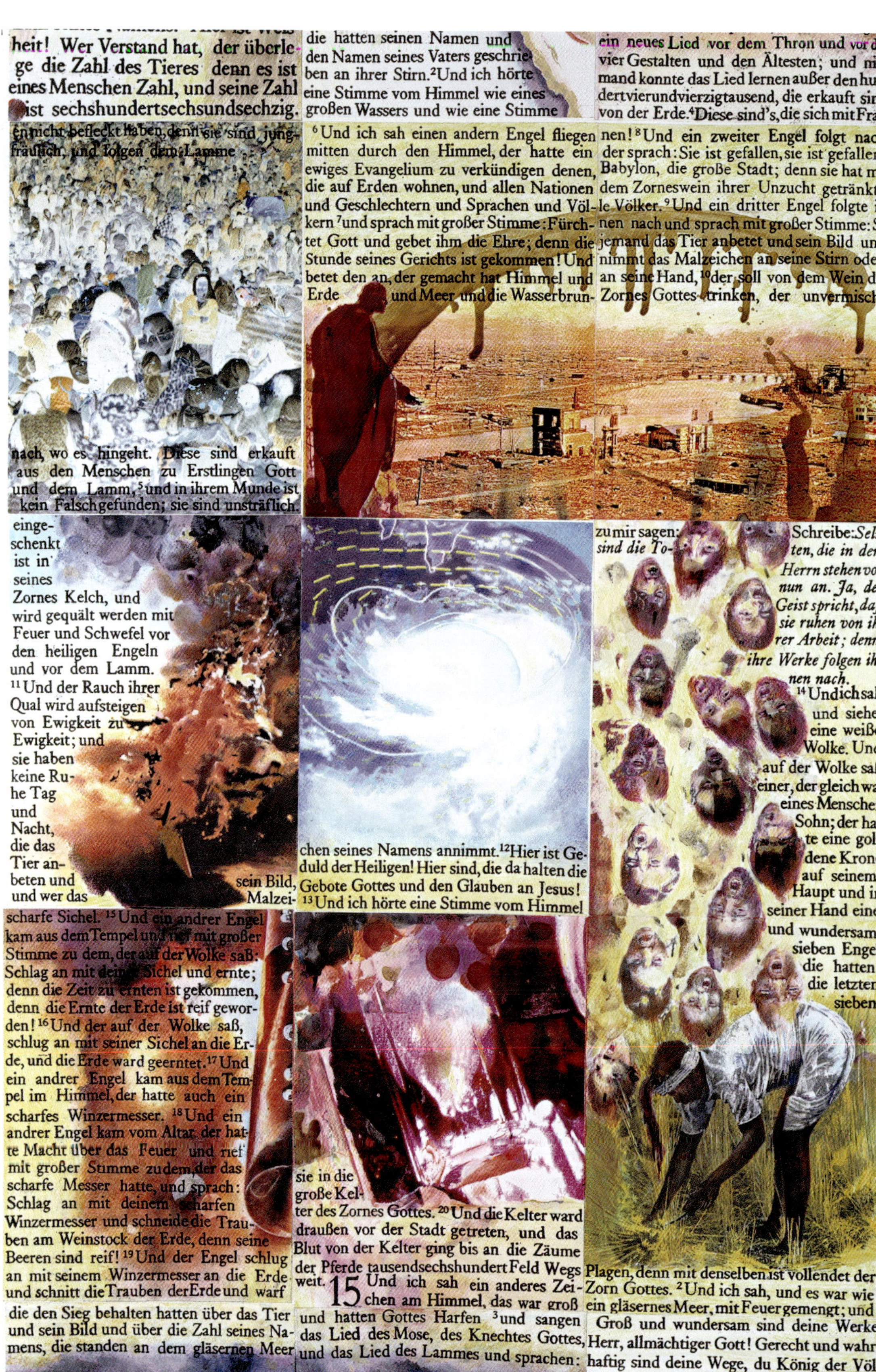

10 Horst Haack, Detail from *Apocalypse*, panel 4.

were incorporated into texts:[14] the work of poet Rolf-Dieter Brinkmann is a prime example.

Hardly any artist exploits the potential afforded by the interface of language and image as consistently as Haack. In the *Apocalypse* he reproduces the entire text. Be it deliberate or not, Haack thus does as the angel bids and bears record of the revelation. The seer is supposed not just to narrate the experiences that pass before his inner eye, but to write them down. Here we can sense the historical paradigm shift from the oral tradition to writing. Today, the pendulum has swung in favour of an image-based media culture. Both aspects are reflected in Haack's version of Revelation.

Initially, one of the most striking features of *Apocalypse* is Haack's insistence on the book-page format. As identical basic modules, individual sheets form the unchanging compositional grid. Given the colourful flood of images, one might at first sight think of a whole host of TV monitors, yet the typical page format Haack uses references the medium of the written word. On these pages, image and script enter into diverse formal relationships that are defined by the content and that focus on the visual character of the text. The result is a single unit in which legibility and visualization coincide, and this happens all the more, the more text and image directly relate to each other. Thus Haack focuses on highly symbolic words that function as signals, facilitating interpretation of the adjacent images. Yet the images and their projective power enforce a specific understanding of the text. Here, word and image do not compete, but are mutually fertilizing 'correlates that constantly seek each other'.[15]

On some pages we see only individual lines of text, not dissimilar to short picture captions or commentaries; then there are also sheets on which the script completely runs over the image beneath it. Often sections of text nestle up to images, with the edges blurred at the transition between text and image. The words run round the images and are set very close to the visual contours so that complementary negative and positive fonts interact. The resulting text formations are reminiscent of visual poetry, contrasting with the stringent, closed blocks of script. Pictorial motifs and script reside on one visual level, attesting to their inner linkage, and whereby technical they are the product of transfer drawing.

The typography of the text passages is by no means normal. While book printers tend, when setting type, to keep it at a certain distance from the edges of the page, creating a certain aura around the script, Haack opts for a different approach. His printed words completely fill the book pages, right through to the margins. One might be tempted here to think of the notion of the *scriptio continua* practised from classical through to medieval times. Haack uses this device to foster a vivid sense of confinement that may possibly correspond to an impression of psychological oppression. This fits with the emotional state of emergency that forms the backdrop to what the seer narrates. The lack of an edge to the pictures robs the reader of distance from the text and visually emphasizes its trenchancy. The density created by using justified print intensifies this oppressive feeling, and the space between the lines is likewise narrow, and uninterrupted by paragraph endings. Occasionally, italics are used, and now and then a large font. The text seems to move along without interruption, reminiscent of the flow of someone speaking without a break.

There is an astonishing overlap here with the remarks by Teresa of Avila, who stated, and here she is representative of many visionaries, that 'these words are thus short, and terse, holding in the most succinct form the richest of content, such that one word contain not only much but even that which can otherwise not be uttered with words.'[16] All these observations show that the script here does more than functioning simply as the 'sober' impression of the text; instead, the specific linguistic gesture of apocalyptic speech is also visualized in the choice of type and print. Textuality and visualization are linked here. Haack thus succeeds in visualizing substantive aspects[17] and moves beyond understanding script solely as the 'graphic fixation of the spoken word'. Here, the text appears as a 'mode of rendering language iconic'.[18]

Haack cuts across the boundaries between the media and is an example of the blurring of the lines between the genres of which Theodor W. Adorno speaks. With his *Apocalypse* he succeeds in representing the visionary experiences that are encoded in Revelation. Haack's realization of the Apocalypse stands out for its great feel for the text on which it draws and the interartistic brilliance with which he manufactures it.

In Revelation the visionary images blend to form a kind of film of consciousness in a striking form. The special achievement of the current *Apocalypse* is to revisualize this 'film in script'.[19] 'Today nothing is as problematic as the attempt to translate St John's visual language into telling images', [20] comments M. P. Maass, who concludes: 'Only the genius of a Dürer can gladly engage in such a daring undertaking and survive.' This judgement is certainly no longer applicable, given Horst Haack's brilliant visual transposition.

Translated by Jeremy Gaines

7

Raymond Pettibon: Words and Images

HAMZA WALKER

Raymond Pettibon's artistic practice consists as much of reading as it does drawing. Constructing a literary spectrum that displays as much respect for the Golden Age of the comic book as it does an historical, modernist literary tradition is perhaps the only way to capture with any accuracy the breadth of his work. Pettibon's practice is deceptively simple and his drawings could be objectively described as singular panels from a comic strip. Pettibon combines hand-drawn images and text taken from a variety of indiscriminate sources and his reverence for the word and image is directly proportional to his irreverence for their context. The style of his drawings ranges from the highly illustrative work of cartoonist Milton Caniff to the fluid brushwork associated with kanji. His eclectic iconography includes Gumby, surfers, trains and dollar signs, to name a few, and he draws as much from pulp fiction as he does from the Bible. The simplicity of means, however, does little to explain the complexity of the results. (He is an aggressive reader, annotating books with a shorthand designating a suitable motif –'baseball', 'trains', 'Gumby', 'surfers' – for a particular text.) Likewise, the familiarity of the form makes it difficult to articulate exactly what separates Pettibon from a clever cartoonist or illustrator. It certainly is not Pettibon's drafting skill, which in many instances he purposefully disregards, opting for an aesthetic of rapid execution that forsakes elegance for urgency. In addition, many of Pettibon's drawings operate in a relatively straightforward manner, delivering their punchline, be it poignant or perverse, by exploiting the irony between what is written and what is rendered. Although their eclecticism and their irony are a source of pleasure, neither qualifies as a characteristic that makes Pettibon's drawings a distinct body of work. Insofar as there is a singular quality that allows the thousands of drawings he has produced to be called a body of work, it is the manner in which they literally draw attention to the act of reading, an act to which he refers incessantly, and an act he skilfully disrupts.

Born in 1957, Pettibon began his career in college as a political cartoonist for the UCLA student newspaper *The Daily Bruin*. It is telling that Pettibon did not begin his career with a sequential narrative format. That would come

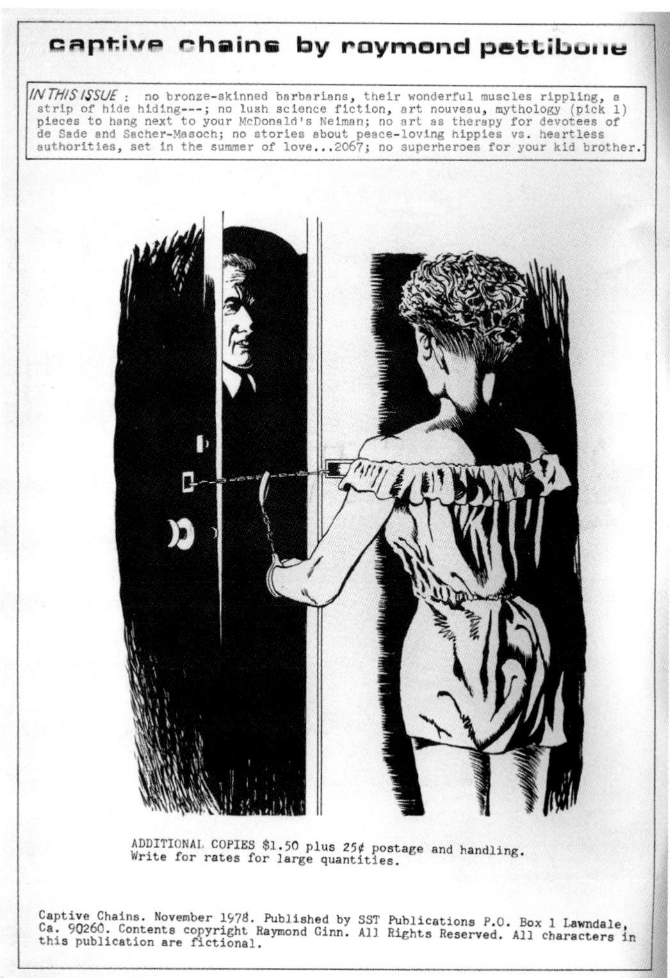

1 Raymond Pettibon, *Captive Chains*, 1978, pen and ink on paper.

immediately after college in 1978 with a self-produced underground comic book entitled *Captive Chains* (illus. 1, 2). Before that Pettibon penned a series of political cartoons over a stylized signature of his real name, Raymond Ginn. These would reveal Pettibon to be squarely a child of the 1970s whose political consciousness as defined by presidencies is post-Nixon and pre-Reagan. Although the political cartoons would announce his commitment to the combination of word and image, it is *Captive Chains* that sets the orientation of Pettibon's career.

A generous 68-page black and white comic with a glossy cover and newsprint pages, its main narrative is a series of vignettes subsumed under the title *City Kids* (illus. 3). As stories of dread and despair set in a bleak, unnamed city, they indulge a rote pessimism regarding the hopelessly irredeemable character of urban centres overrun with crime, gangs and vice. Love offers its characters no salvation.

Similar in mood, the second half features full-page pen-and-ink drawings rendered in a stilted but awkward manner perfectly compatible with their dominant theme, which is that of surreal deviancy straight from the psyche of a late 1970s 21-year-old. Stylistically it is nascent Pettibon with the most telling feature being an absurdly puerile dark streak that revels in, yet deeply regrets, the inevitable loss of adolescent innocence. Strange, kinky, rude, harsh, funny. Despite its resolute cynicism, *Captive Chains*, in looking as though it was produced by a teen for a teen, actually comes across as touching. While it is the legitimate heir to an underground comics movement that blossomed in the late 1960s, *Captive Chains* sets itself apart as a product by youth, for youth and most importantly parodying youth.

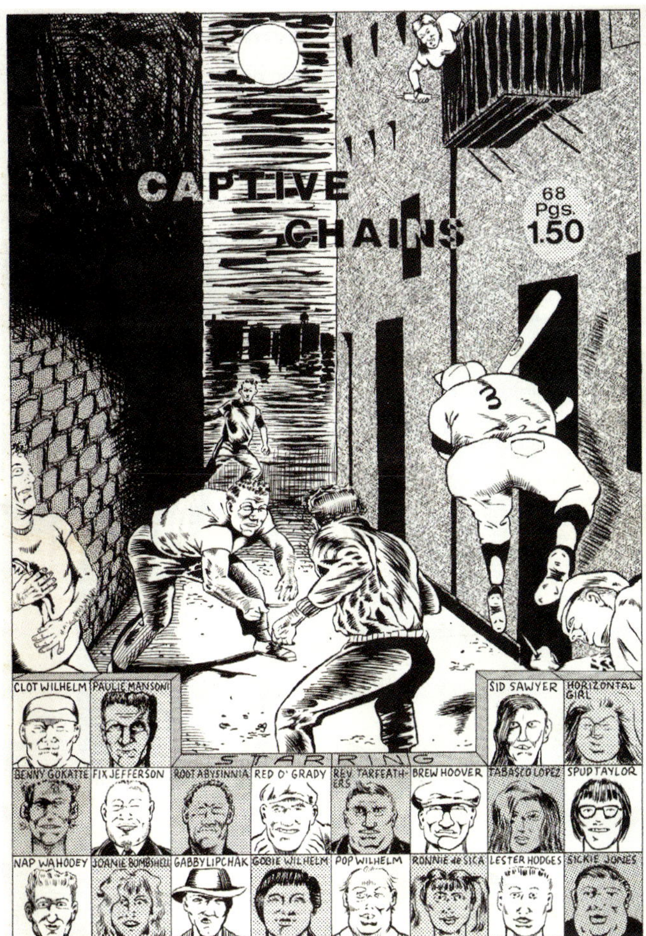

2 Raymond Pettibon, *Captive Chains* cover, 1978, pen and ink on paper.

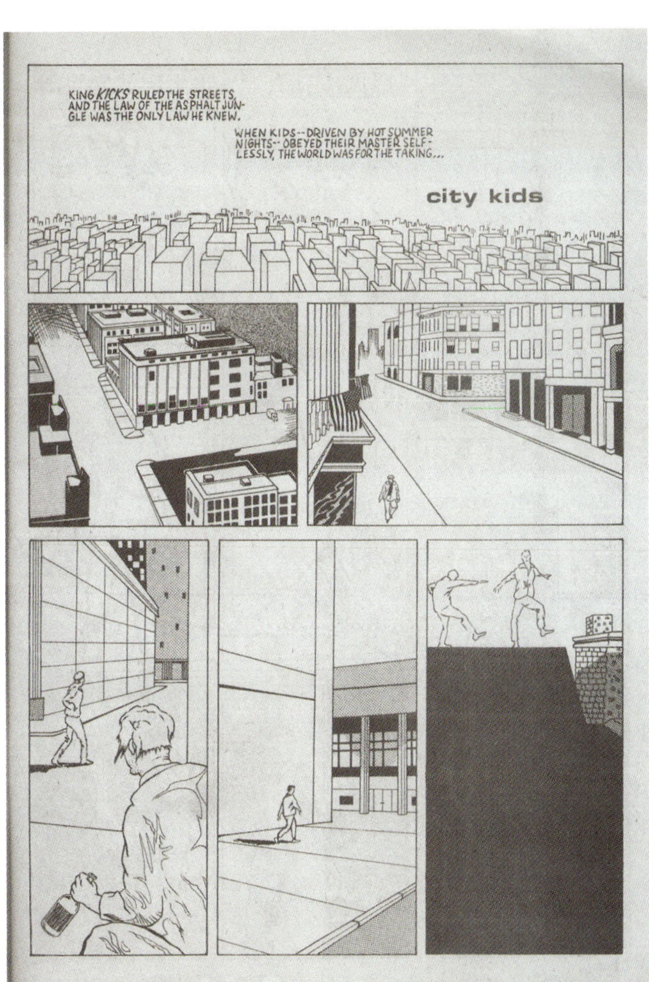

3 Raymond Pettibon, *City Kids/Captive Chains*, 1978, pen and ink on paper.

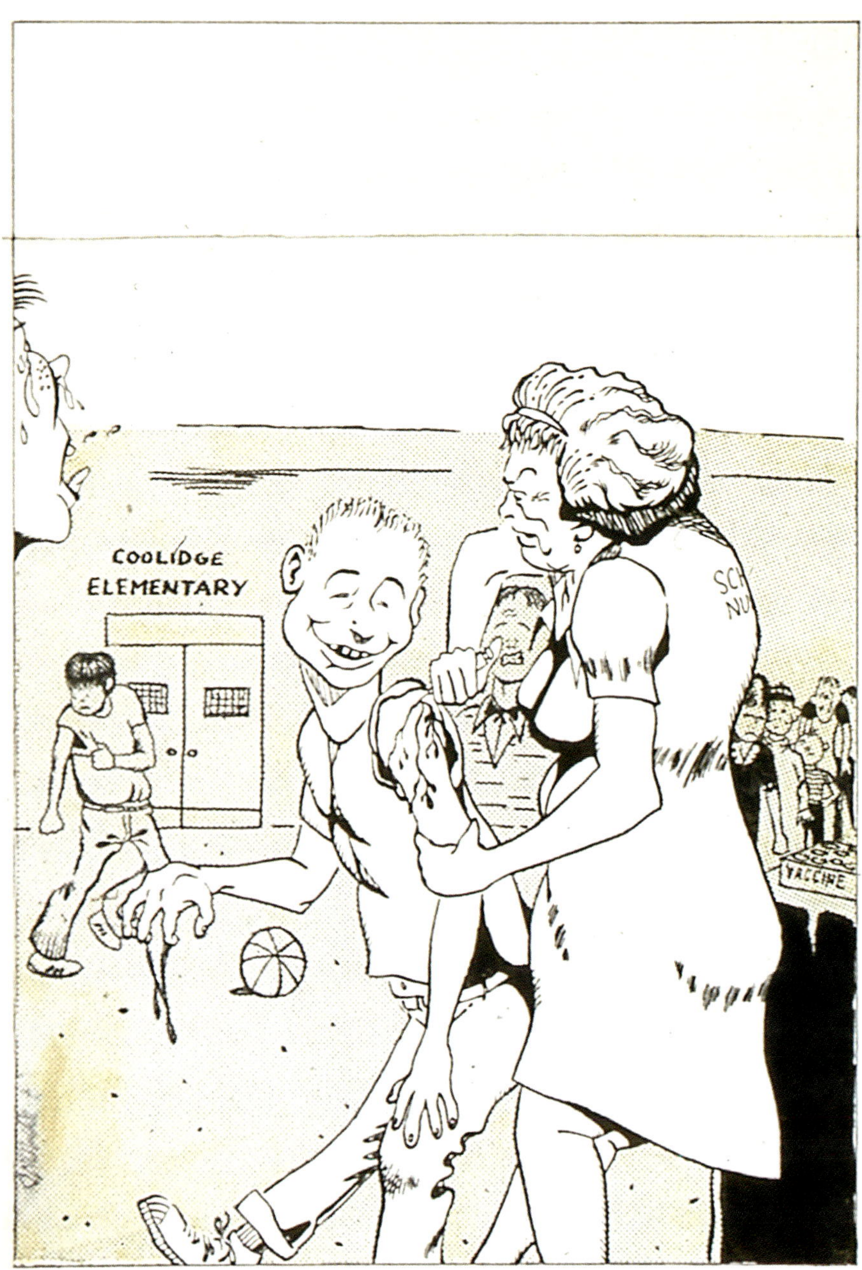

4 Raymond Pettibon, *School Nurse/Captive Chains*, 1978, pen and ink on paper.

Each story takes up roughly a page, broken down into the standard comic book format of around nine panels over which the narrative unfolds. The narratives are dark surreal tales whose irony revolves around the ubiquitous poles of sex, death and occasionally baseball. *Captive Chains* offers itself up point for point as a parody of Wertham's claims regarding the social degeneracy captured in comic books.[1] Fredric Wertham's *Seduction of the Innocent* (1954) was the key document in a vigorous crusade against the comic book publishing industry, a crusade which began as a series of local decency campaigns in the 1930s and '40s and escalated to a national concern in the '50s as efforts such as Wertham's linked comic book reading to juvenile delinquency.

By the time *Captive Chains* was published, however, *Seduction of the Innocent* had become archaic. Comic books had long ceased being considered a menace and the newspapers and television of the mid- to late 1970s far outpaced the graphic depiction of sex and violence in the comic books of Wertham's generation. As a regular media offering, gore was a given and Wertham had clearly missed his mark. Curbing the content of comic books did

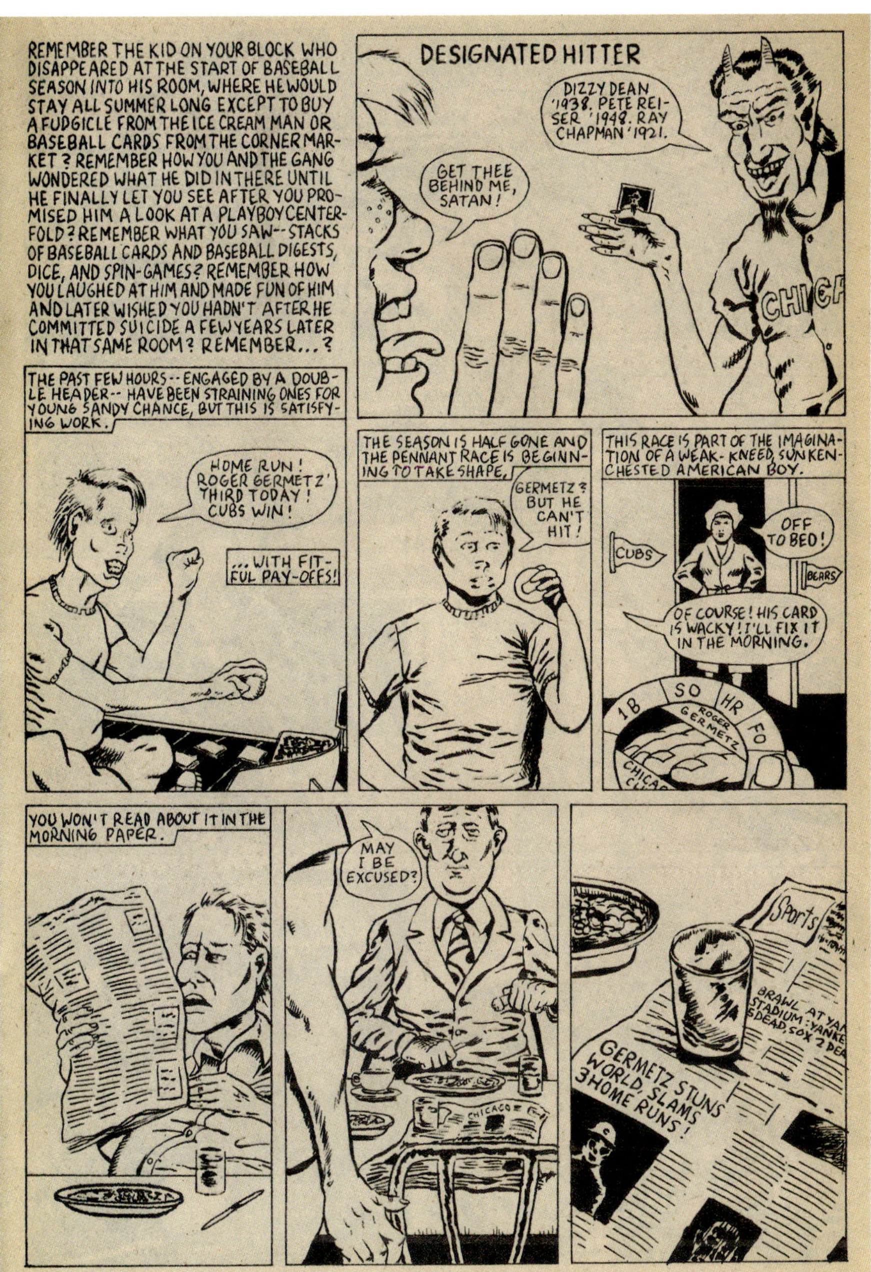

5 Raymond Pettibon, *Designated Hitter/ Captive Chains*, 1978, pen and ink on paper.

nothing to halt a series of events that would lead to a national mood shift from the post-war euphoria of the fifties to a fight over national values in the sixties and finally to a period of cynicism and profound uncertainty in the seventies. Photojournalist accounts of events such as the Kennedy assassinations, the Vietnam War, Charles Manson and the kidnapping of Patty/Tania Hearst, all of which were prominent subject matter in Pettibon's early works, make it hard to believe that comic books were worthy of national attention. Pettibon's decision, at the outset of his career, to adopt an aesthetic belonging to a disgruntled teenager of the 1970s, and later to adopt a more general aesthetic of Cold War deviancy marked by mushroom clouds, juvenile delinquents, organized crime, J. Edgar Hoover, Joan Crawford and film noir, clearly reflects this shift in ideals. The irony in Pettibon's earliest work underscores our collective resignation toward, yet inability at coming to grips with, the darker and often depraved undercurrents of our society, undercurrents that since the publication of *Seduction of the Innocent* have become both a national and a psychic fixture.

Pettibon's early career is well documented in promotional material for the

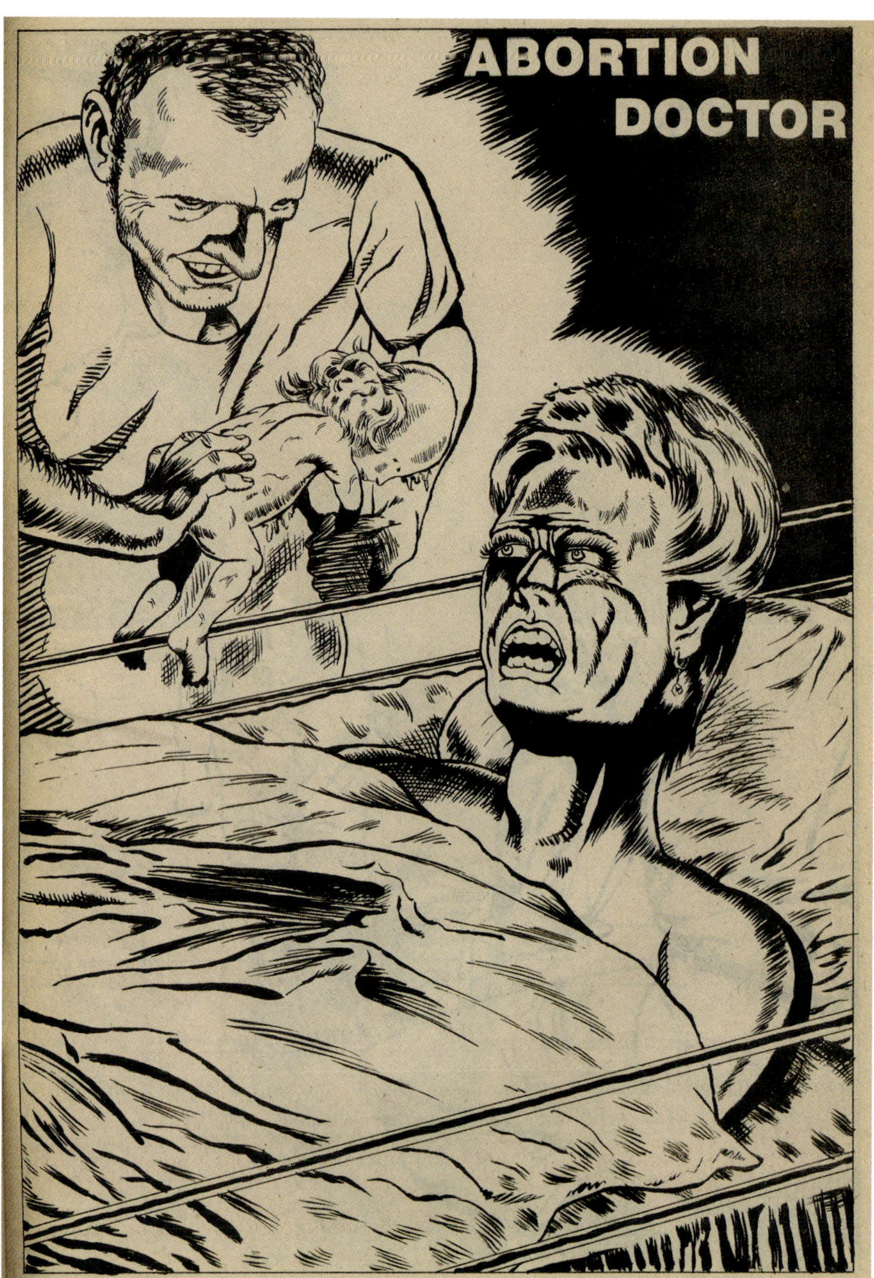

6 Raymond Pettibon, *Abortion Doctor /Captive Chains*, 1978, pen and ink on paper.

Los Angeles South Bay punk rock scene, most notably the flyers and record covers for the band Black Flag. If punk rock would pride itself on being louder, faster, angrier and, as far as production values concerned, crummier than its predecessors, then Pettibon had the graphics to match. As if one sign of deviant youth had finally found its long-lost sibling, between 1978 and 1985 Pettibon offered up his drawings for dozens of flyers and record covers. With album titles such as *Slip It In*, *Damaged*, *What Makes A Man Start Fires?* and *My War*, and concert flyers featuring drawings from *Captive Chains* and Pettibon's first fanzine, *Tripping Corpse*, these bands openly mocked any standards of decency. But the youth culture of the seventies was a far cry from the youth culture of the fifties. Prior to the sixties, youth culture and counterculture could be considered independent of one another. During the sixties, however, they would become inextricably linked as college campuses across the country became hotbeds of political protest. Rock and roll, the alternative press and their hybrid, the rock and roll fanzine, were the means by which youth and counterculture sanctioned themselves as critical social commentary. Although

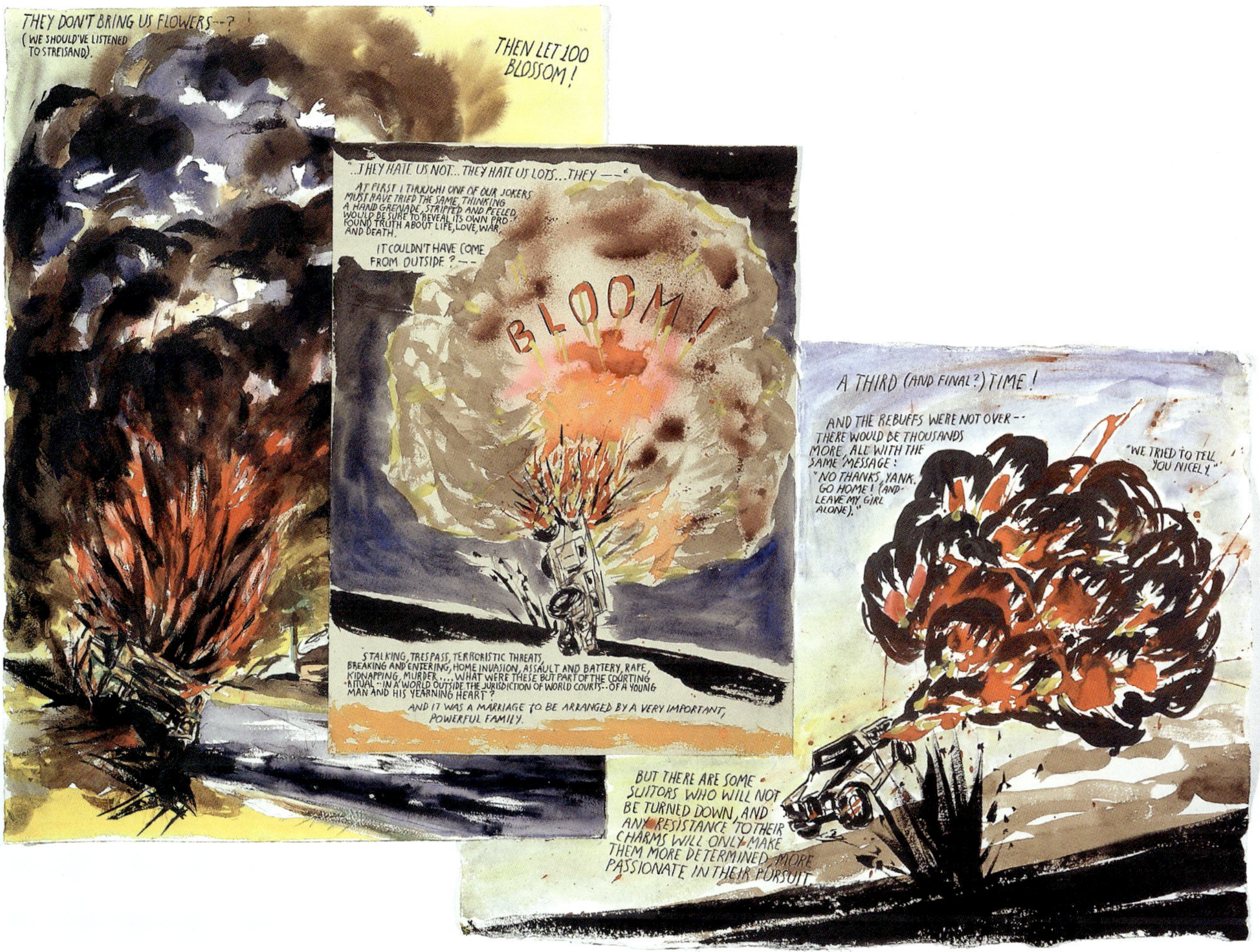

7 Raymond Pettibon, *No Title (They don't bring)*, 2008, pen, ink, gouache and collage on paper.

punks would try to distance themselves from the failed idealism associated with the sixties, after several years producing a graphic that would serve as a youth and countercultural aesthetic, Pettibon would be led to compare his efforts with those of his countercultural predecessors. A resentment for failed ideals aside, Pettibon understood that there were certain fundamental values from the previous counterculture that were indispensable to forging an audience for his endeavours and those of his punk rock colleagues. In the face of an unassailable rock music industry on the verge of declaring itself classic at the ripe old age of thirty, a do-it-yourself means of and attitude towards production, distribution and promotion of a genuine youth and countercultural product would prove invaluable. This could not be more the case than with the fanzine.

Pettibon published roughly 100 fanzines between 1978 and 1993, with the bulk of them produced between 1985 and 1992. These were the initial means by which he made his work available. Throughout the 1980s, Pettibon's publications were distributed by SST (Systematic Record Distribution), a label founded by members of Black Flag in 1978. If anything serves as proof that Pettibon considered his

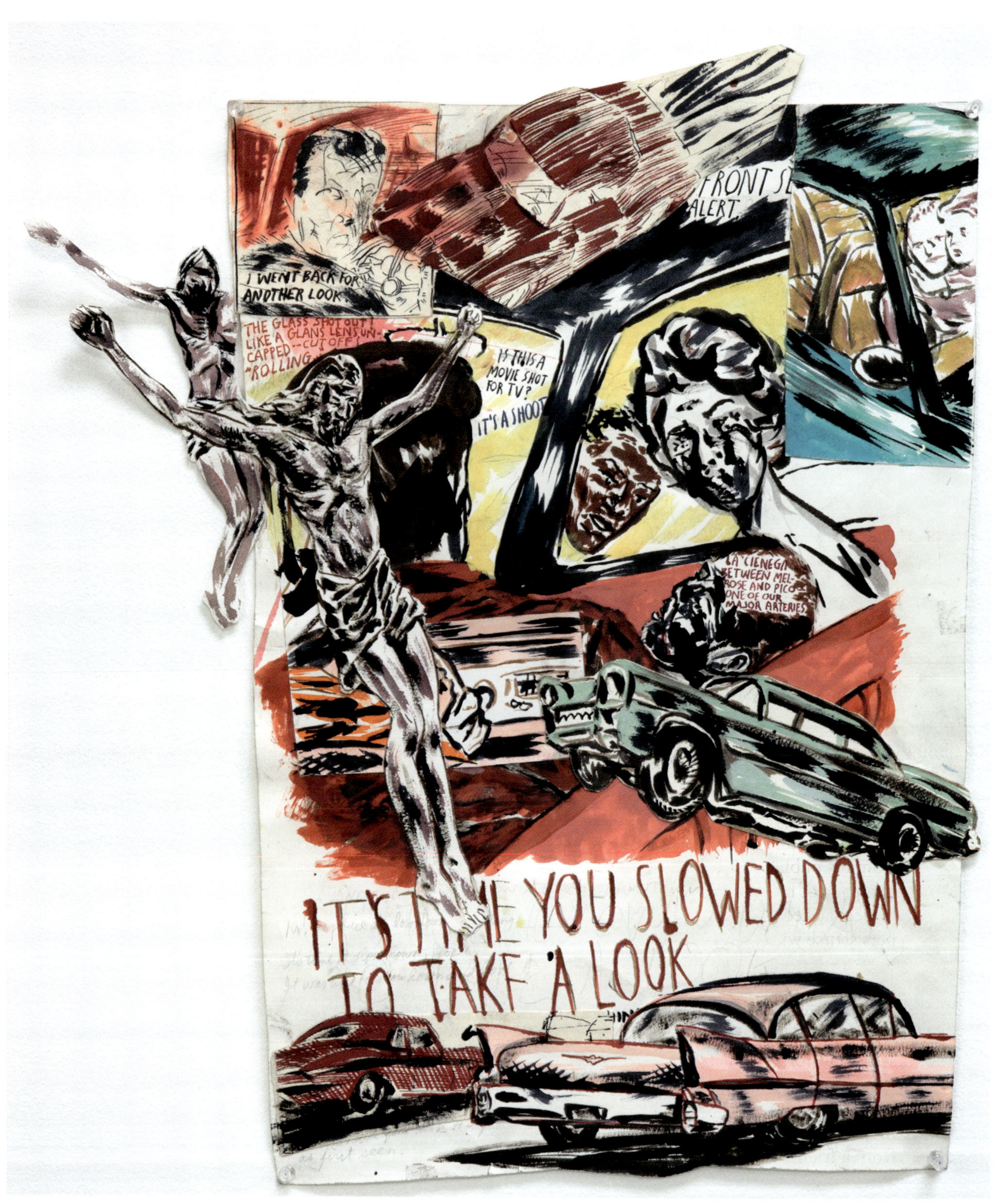

8 Raymond Pettibon, *No Title (I went back)*, 2008, pen, ink, gouache and collage on paper.

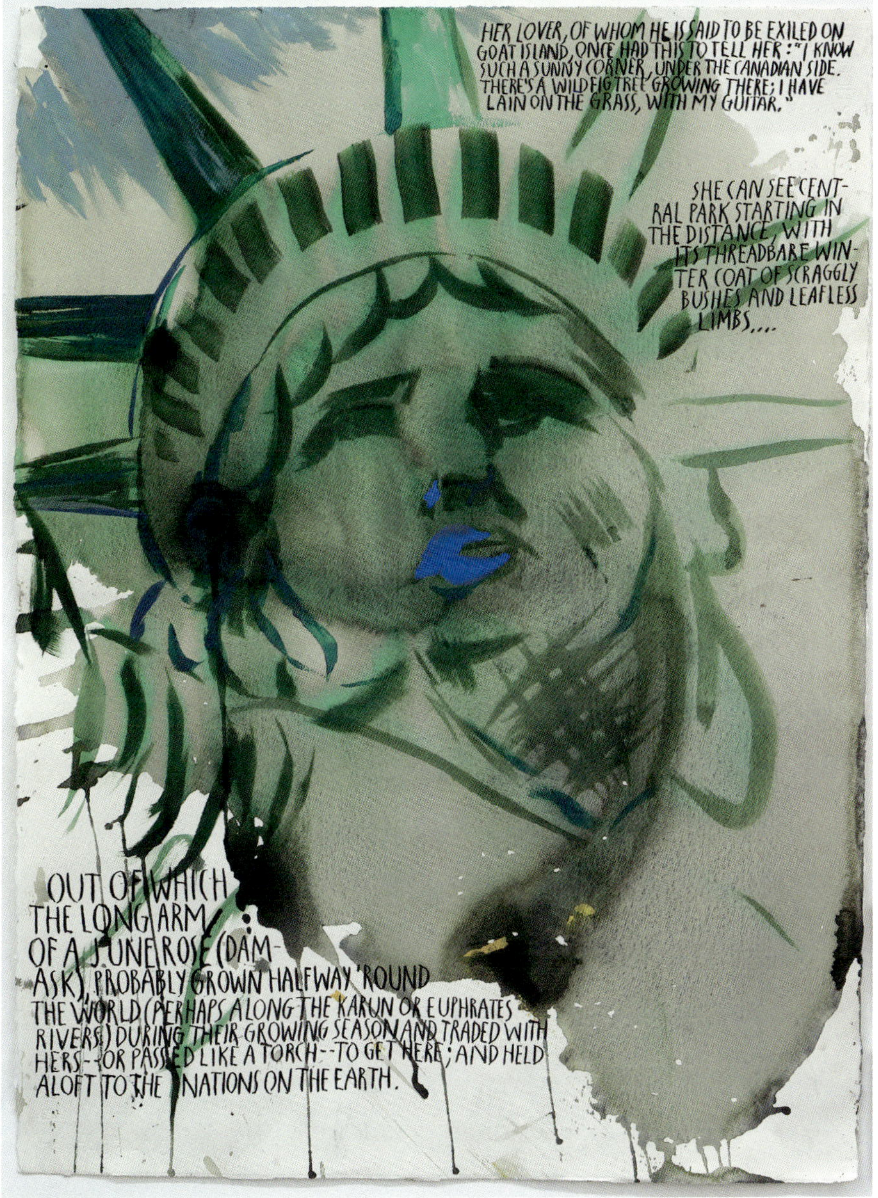

9 Raymond Pettibon, *No Title (Her lover, of)*, 2007, ink and watercolour on paper.

career trajectory that of a fine artist it would be the fact that he made no money from his publications, which were treated like the courtesy stick of chewing gum in a pack of baseball cards. Like most genuine punk endeavours, the fanzine project lacked a profit motive. But unlike most punk endeavours, Pettibon's persistence with the pen outlived his anger. It was the fanzine project that set the breakneck pace at which he was to work for the next several years, making it the means by which he would realize a body of work. Although he had collaboratively produced a couple of stray fanzines between 1978 and 1980 and a lone issue of *Tripping Corpse* in 1981, it was not until 1983 that Pettibon would secure his folded letter-size format. With the exception of *Tripping Corpse*, all fanzine titles would be different. By 1985 he was producing on average ten fanzines per year. Although they contain the occasional interview with band members from Black Flag, Sonic Youth and the Minutemen, poetry or fiction from a friend, or drawings from his nephew, whom he dubbed Master Nelson Tarpenny, the greater portion was given over to drawings. By 1985 Pettibon would expand his drawing practice, wedding a repertoire of graphic styles to recurring motifs capable of accommodating subjects from the socio-political to the idiosyncratic. Whereas his drawings were originally intended for

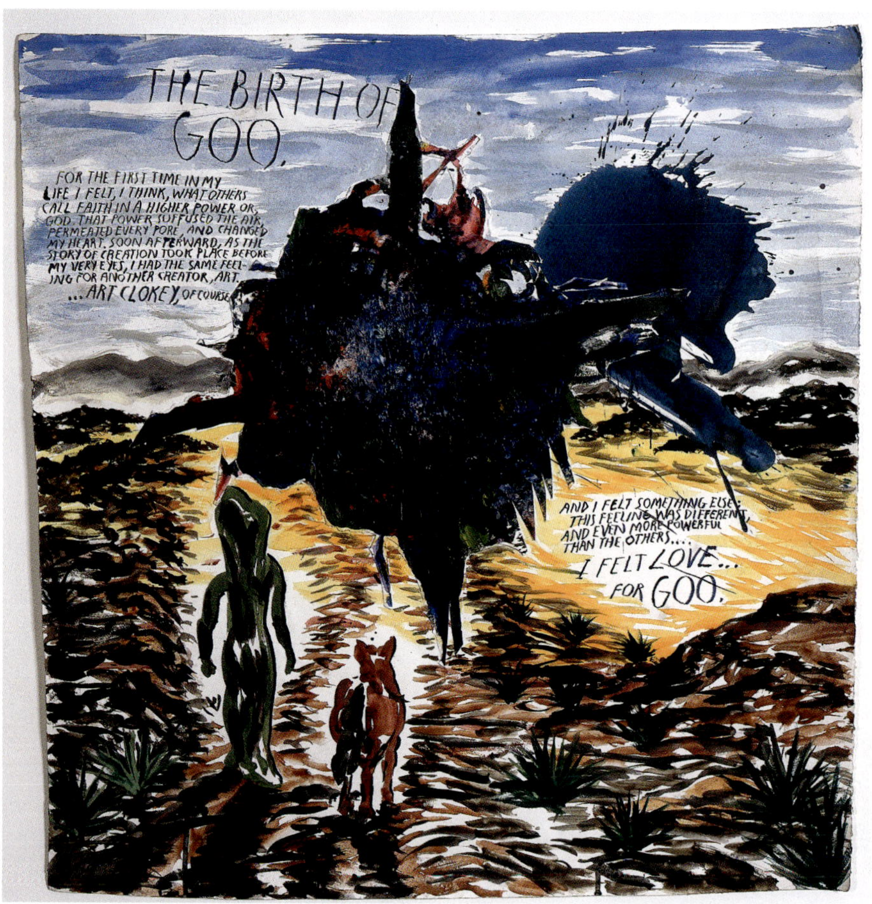

10 Raymond Pettibon, *No Title (The birth of)*, 2008, pen, ink, gouache, acrylic and collage on paper.

reproduction, by 1985 only a fraction of them were being published.

There are several clues by which to distinguish between Pettibon's late and early work – borders, blue cross-hairs in the corners, type of paper, the introduction of a particular subject and so on. Perhaps the most misleading characteristic by which to date his work is drafting skill, since he uses a variety of styles which require varying degrees of control. In general, however, establishing a chronological order for Pettibon's output is somewhat problematic due to the fact that there may be a substantial discrepancy between the date of a drawing and the addition of text. Although seriality and grouping by subject are possible ways to make sense of Pettibon's work, those are exercises he has reserved for several fanzines, artists' books and an occasional drawing in which he renders the same subject in a series of panels, changing the text in each panel. Since his first gallery exhibition in 1984, Pettibon has maintained the practice of displaying his drawings unframed, tacked directly to the wall in groupings that reflect their eclecticism. By and large, collectors of his work have adopted this method, obtaining a mix of drawings that consists of early and late works as well as a range of subjects. Exhibiting Pettibon's body of work in this manner tends to place emphasis on its eclecticism. But again, eclecticism is hardly a distinguishing characteristic. The quality that allows his

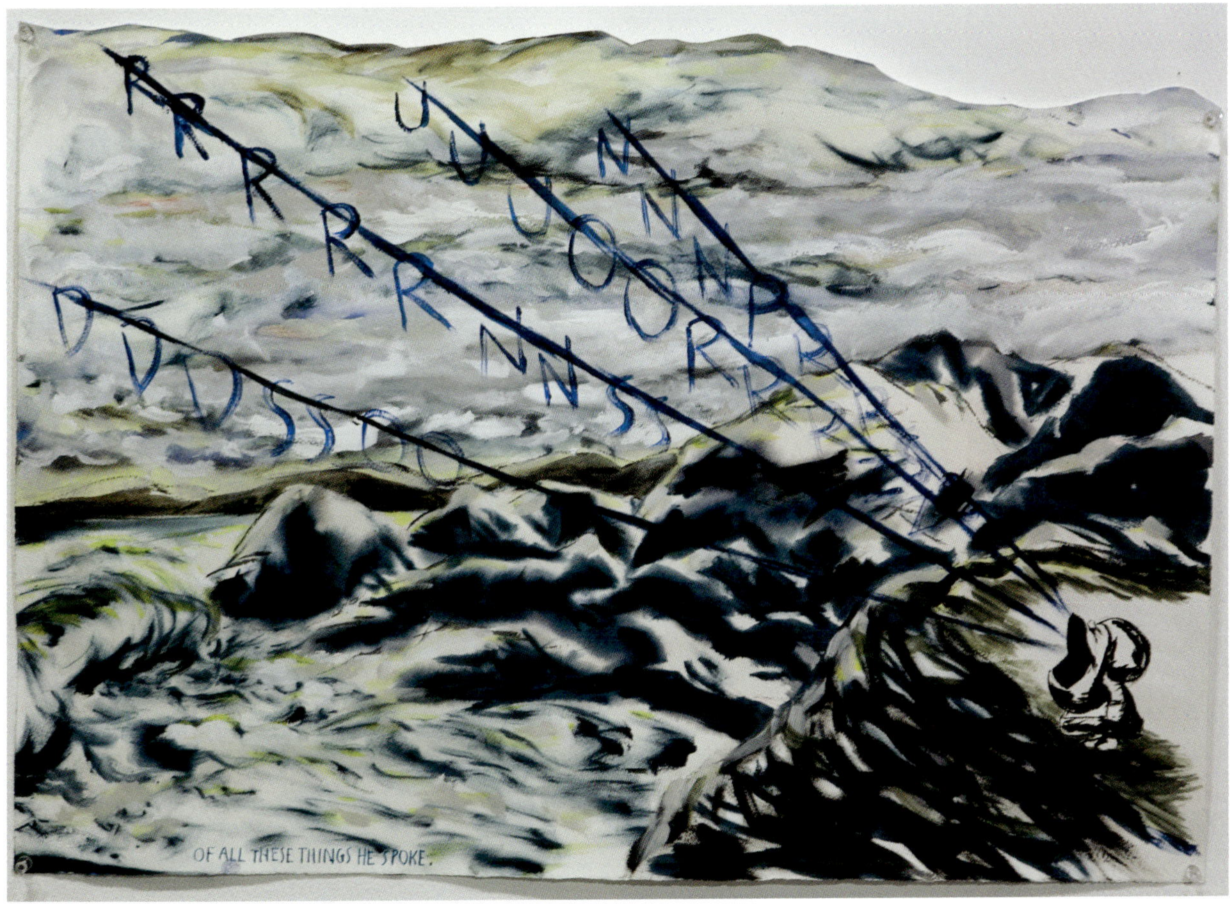

11 Raymond Pettibon, No *Title (Of all these)*, 2008, pen, ink and gouache on paper.

output to be called a body of work is also the one that would mark his development as a mature artist, and that is the introduction of multiple excerpts of text.

Pettibon's work has always been riddled with an ironic subtext or code and it is difficult to determine exactly when he introduced multiple excerpts into his work. The best approximation is provided by a 1985 fanzine in which he began Xeroxing fragments of texts cut directly from books onto drawings. Prior to incorporating multiple speaking subjects into his work, Pettibon's drawings functioned in a relatively straightforward manner. Like most comic books, the text is attributable to a subject. No matter how harrowing the thought or hardened the irony, the overall effect is similar to the union of text and image via the comic book's thought-bubble and dialogue balloon. Pettibon's early drawings are characterized by a double-edged, rock and hard place, teen angst irony, one that centres around the moral and social U-turn the country underwent from Eisenhower to Nixon. But their irony is a thin veneer not for angst but for anger. What comes across in the rape, racism and numerous electric chairs of Pettibon's early drawings is that by the mid-1970s the USA had become a country which knew how to hate, and hate is hardly ironic. Oscillating between unbridled sin and salvation lost, these drawings are not

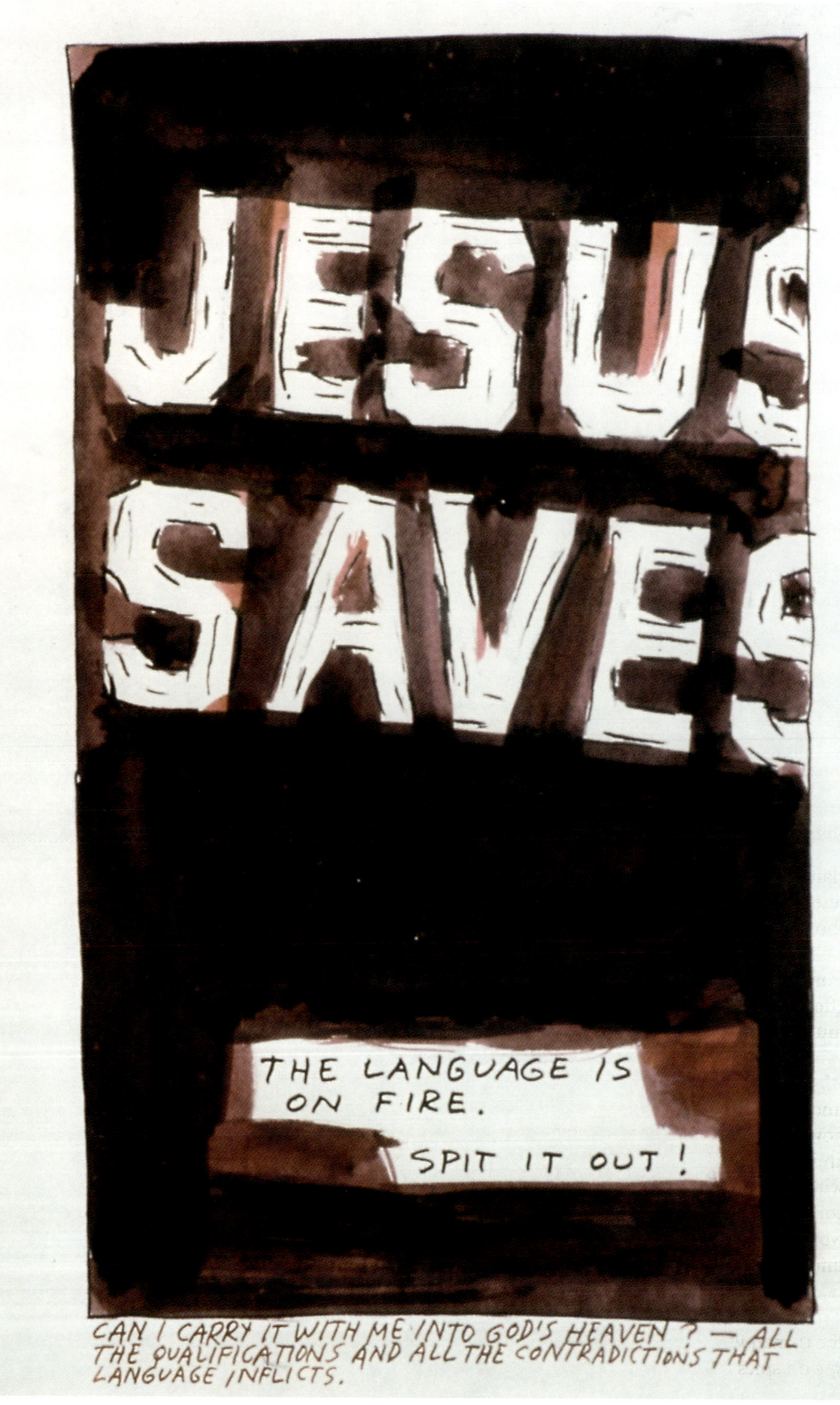

12 Raymond Pettibon, *No Title (Jesus Saves)*, 1986, pen and ink on paper.

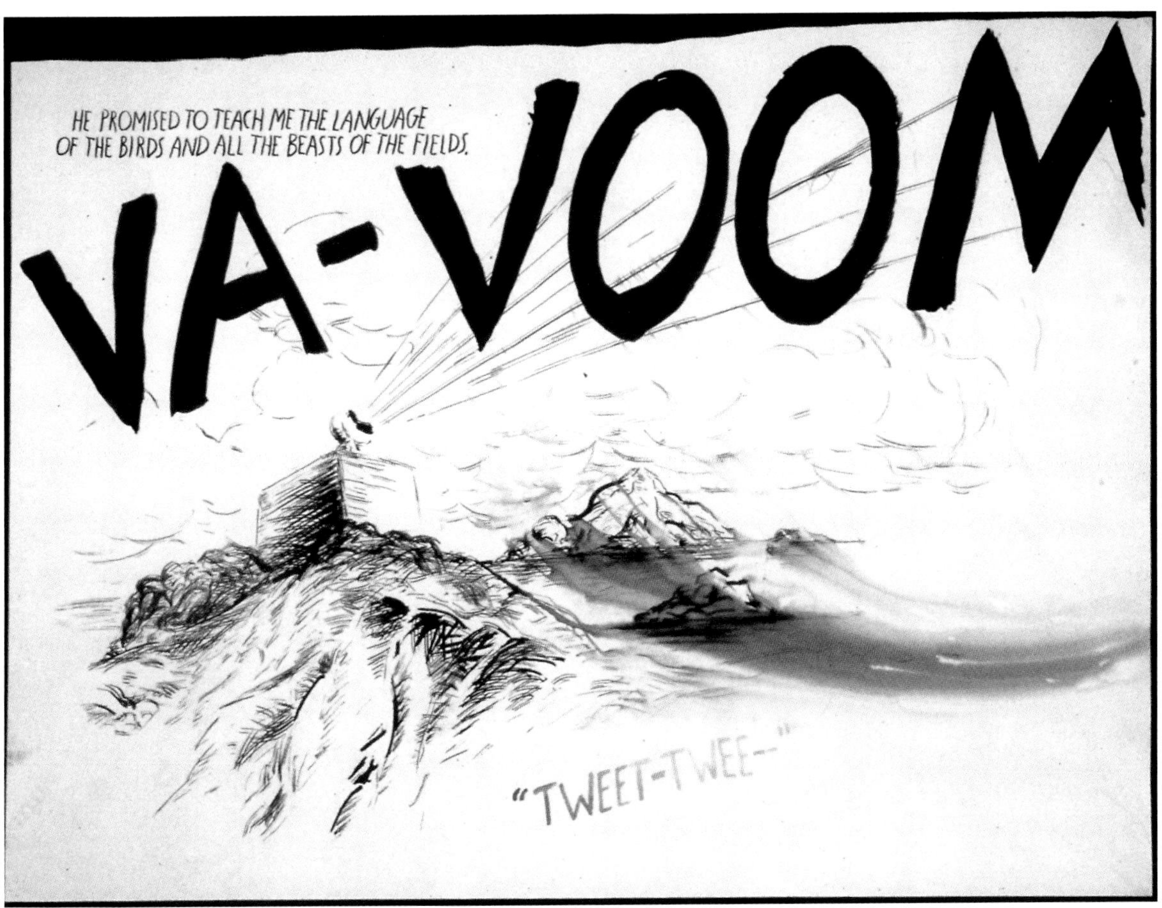

13 Raymond Pettibon, *No Title (He promised to)*, 1993, pen and ink on paper.

simply dark. They altogether lack redemption. These pictures hardly require a thousand words. With voices firmly fixed to a subject, they stand on cruelty alone. But Pettibon's narratives are far from new. What lends them their nasty resonance is the extent to which they are already known. Pettibon hardly need claim responsibility for his artistic intentions since they draw upon a standing reservoir of social, historical and personal narratives fueled by psychosis. In short, his irony need no longer be fabricated for it was in fact ready-made.

Although the goal of using ready-made texts was to fortify an already bitter irony, the mingling of various texts produced a more subtle and sophisticated effect that did not so much involve an inversion of meaning as it did a multiplication of meaning. The detection of an 'ironic code' in Pettibon's early work relies on references that derive their stability from a stark contrast of then versus now. The inversion if not perversion of values, rests upon a broad understanding of the turn of events from Hiroshima to Patty Hearst. Irony, however, is a code and as such the degree to which it is explicit, competing with an intentional surface meaning, can vary greatly. The multiplication of texts within a single drawing would destabilize these references, lessening the contrast, allowing Pettibon to exploit irony's more subtle gradations. The irony would be transformed from one of cruel certainty to one of profound uncertainty. Take, for example, drawings of J. Edgar Hoover (1895–1972) dating from 1985 and 1989, in which the difference in the kind of irony is due largely to a difference in degree of intensity. Both images are of a Cold War Hoover, not the G-man who made his reputation combating organized crime or the wartime spy on spies but the post-war surveillance hound who was invaluable to Senator

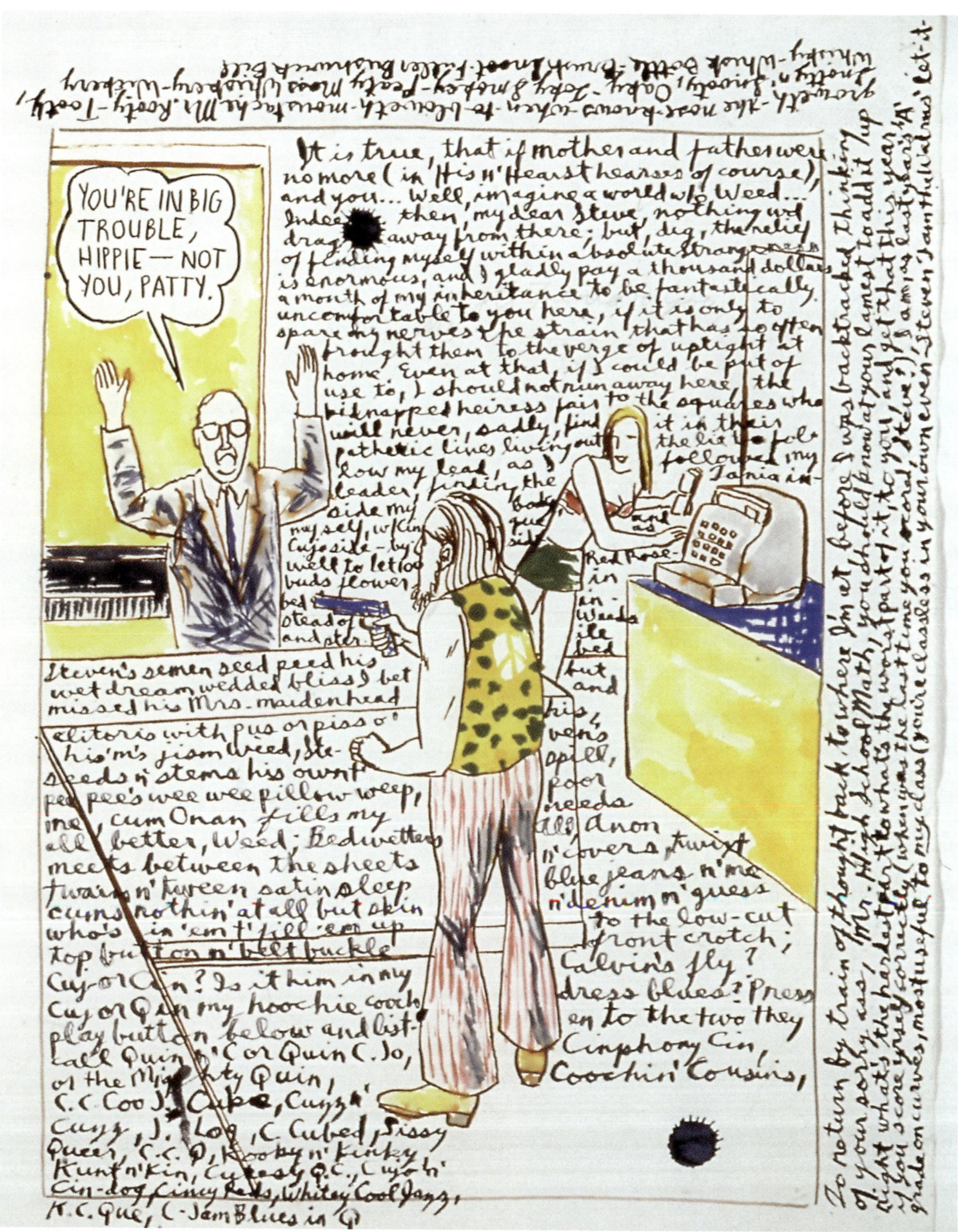

14 Raymond Pettibon, *No Title (You're in big)*, 2004, pen and ink on paper.

Joseph McCarthy and the House Committee on Un-American Activities in their crusade against Communism. This was a Hoover whose web of information was used to strategically leak information about the private lives of his political opponents; a Hoover whose desire to know many considered obscene. But the link between Hoover's unscrupulous gathering of intelligence and later speculation regarding his private life can only lead one to wonder exactly how deep the head G-man's thoughts were when the photographs upon which these drawing are based were taken. Whereas the single line of text in the 1985 drawing portrays a titillated Hoover, the 1989 drawing is an uneasy psychic portrait of a Hoover whose homosexual, misogynist proclivities actually fuelled his desire to undermine the right to privacy. Starting with a paranoia that developed from a 'sudden revelation' regarding genitalia, read pubescent trauma, leading to an obscenely vicarious investigation of human acts, and ending with homosexual eugenics, the logic of the drawing's punchline belongs to a convoluted sociopath. Hoover was certainly dark, but this is a Hoover whose psychological drives go way beyond titillation towards a deviancy that brings him full circle, face to face with the enemy of the previous decade, the Nazis. Unlike the 1985 drawing, this is an irony of psychoanalytic depth. But more important than explaining a maturation in the content of his work, Pettibon's skill at exploiting an ironic code also accounts for why and how production would become part of the work's meaning.

References

Preface *by* Michael R. Leaman

1 Joseph Leo Koerner, *The Reformation of the Image* (London, 2004), p. 282.

2 Stephen Roger Fischer, *A History of Language* (London, 1999), p. 95.

3 Jacques Ranciére, *The Future of the Image*, trans. Gregory Elliott (London, 2007), p. 73.

Introduction *by* John Dixon Hunt

I must acknowledge above all the innumerable authors whose work has been published in *Word & Image: A Journal of Verbal/Visual Enquiry*. I have edited this quarterly since its inception in 1987 and it would not have been possible to write both this introduction and the historical survey that follows without the endless stimulation and instruction I have garnered from that editorial work. I hope my debts are fully acknowledged to all the authors whose essays I have re-read for this particular project. Readers of this volume will, in their turn (I hope), be led to realize how rich and (yes) eclectic a conspectus of writing on the topics of word and image is contained within the volumes of *Word & Image*. That said, I hope not to have neglected and to have adequately acknowledged the considerable body of other scholarship that this topic of verbal/visual exchange has generated in other journals and publications. It is an inexhaustible subject, and in the last 30 years it has blossomed in the interstices of traditional disciplinary boundaries, and this volume is testimony to that. And my final word must be to acknowledge that I am not a specialist in many of the topics or periods at the centre of verbal/visual enquiries, trying here only to guide readers into a recognition of the extent and intricacies of their study. My debts to colleagues who have assisted me at various moments are recorded in the notes.

1 There are various diagrams available of the brain's function, some of which introduce, quite properly, a more complex set of activities than are needed for my argument here. Diagrams anyway are 'geographic' rather than mechanistic: that is, they do not show connections and modes of interaction, since we apparently lack the scientific understanding for such demonstrations (personal communication from Professor Martha J. Farah, Director of the University of Pennsylvania Center for Cognitive Neuroscience). Otherwise I have consulted online articles in the *Scientific American* for 24 March 2005, 24 May 2007 and 26 January 1998, for which references I am grateful to my research assistant, Charlie Nelson.

2 Gotthold Ephraim Lessing, *Laocoön: An Essay on the Limits of Painting and Poetry*, trans. with intro. and notes by Edward Allen McCormick (Baltimore, MD, 1962), p. 77.

3 A brief account by Christopher S. Wood of 'Iconoclasm and Iconophobia' is available in the *Encyclopedia of Aesthetics* (New York and Oxford, 1998), II, pp. 450–54. Liz James has noted that 'Byzantium is the only major world power to have undergone political upheaval on a vast scale as a result of an argument about art', *Art and Text in Byzantium Culture* (Cambridge, 2007), p. 1; see also in the historical essay below.

4 See Clement Greenberg, 'Modernist Painting', *The Collected Essays and Criticism: Modernism with a Vengeance, 1957–1969* (Chicago, 1993), IV, pp. 85–94.

5 A useful collection of these is *Speaking Pictures: A Gallery of Pictorial Poetry from the Sixteenth Century to the Present,* ed. Milton Klonsky (New York, 1975). There is also Nicholas Wade's sequence of 'Literal Pictures', published in *Word & Image*, I (1985), pp. 242ff.

6 The literature on *ekphrasis* is immense and over the years *Word & Image* has published a succession of essays on the topic. Otherwise, see Murray Krieger, *Ekphrasis: The Illusion of the Natural Sign* (Baltimore, MD, 1992), James A. W. Heffernan, *Museum of Words: The Poetics of Ekphrasis from Homer to Ashberry* (Chicago, 1993), and John Hollander, *The Gazer's Spirit: Poems Speaking to Silent Works of Art* (Chicago, 1995).

7 In the case of Wyeth, the artist has himself resorted to words to tell the story of this figure, Christina, and many of his studies and paintings of her have the thrust and aura of portraits. But his paintings are, nonetheless, typical of images that solicit our sentimental (because extra-visual) involvement in what is depicted beyond what the painting itself can communicate.

8 Two essays are useful here: Ernst Gombrich, 'Image and Word in Twentieth-century Art', and Stephen Bann, 'The Mythical Conception is the Name: Titles and Names in Modern and Post-modern Painting', respectively in *Word & Image*, I/2, pp. 176ff, and I/3, pp. 213ff. My two examples are taken from Gombrich's essay. Another provoking and witty use of a title-cum-caption came to hand during the writing of this piece: the *New Yorker* cover for 3 December 2006 by Christoph Niemann showed a US helicopter with armed soldiers hanging outside while Santa Claus and his sack of gifts rode inside. Turning to the contents list (as one always has to to find the title), the reader saw that it was 'Violent Night'. Both *The New Yorker* and *Punch* have occasionally run competitions where new captions are invited for existing cartoons.

9 A succinct overview of all these verbal responses to Poussin's painting is available in the Louvre exhibition catalogue of 1994, *Nicolas Poussin 1594–1665*, cat. 179, pp. 406–8. But see also Anthony Blunt, *Nicolas Poussin* (New York, 1967), p. 286. An exhibition of Poussin landscape in 2008, however, was distinguished by considerable emphasis on the unnecessary focus upon Poussin's learned references: see *Poussin and Nature: Arcadian Visions*, exh. cat. ed. Pierre Rosenberg and Keith Christiansen, Metropolitan Museum of Art, New York (New Haven, CT, 2008).

10 Michel Conan, 'The *Imagines* of Philostratus', *Word & Image*, III (1987), pp. 162–71, here p. 163.

11 See Lindsay Duguid's review of the 2007 show at Manchester Art Gallery that commemorated the earlier one: *Times Literary Supplement*, 9 November 2007 (p. 17).

12 For a much fuller analysis of how the frame's inscriptions could direct our response in this instance, see Linda Freedman, '*The Scapegoat* and the Story of Grace', forthcoming in *Word & Image*. It is actually quite astonishing how much this painting is reproduced in modern art history books without its frame, thereby denying the image its essential verbal accompaniment.

13 James Joyce, *Ulysses* (Paris and London, 1934), p. 38. Stephen Dedalus makes common cause here with other modernist writers, Ezra Pound or William Carlos Williams, in celebrating, against the grain of the literary, what the eye alone sees.

14 See Ian J. Lochhead, *The Spectator and the Landscape in the Art Criticism of Diderot and his Contemporaries* (Ann Arbor, MI, 1982), and

the exhibition catalogue, *Diderot et l'Art de Boucher à David. Les Salons 1759–1781*. Some of Diderot's texts are available in *Diderot. Essais sur la peinture [and]. Salons de 1759, 1761, 1763*, ed. Gita May and Jacques Chouillet (Paris, 1984). Diderot may be seen as picking up the strategy of Philostratus' *Imagines*.

15 Even a select bibliography is impossible: enter *Mona Lisa* in any major library electronic catalogue and stand back.

16 I am grateful to my colleague Robert Maxwell for help with understating this example.

17 These covers are collected, illustrated in full colour and discussed by Martijn F. Le Coultre, *Wendigen: A Journal for the Arts, 1918–1932*, with an intro. by Ellen Lupton and an essay by Alston W. Purvis (New York, 2001).

18 See Michael White's essay, 'Sense and Nonsense in Kurt Schwitters'.

19 Again, the literature is considerable, including the journal *Emblematica: An Interdisciplinary Journal for Emblem Studies*: but see John Manning, *The Emblem* (London, 2002), Michael Leslie, 'The Dialogue between Bodies and Souls: Pictures and Poesy in the English Renaissance', *Word & Image*, I (1985), pp. 16–30, and Mario Praz, *Studies in Seventeenth-century Imagery* (2nd edn, Rome, 1964).

20 I have discussed the emblematic work of Finlay's garden art in *Nature Over Again: The Garden Art of Ian Hamilton Finlay* (London, 2008).

21 'The Author as Producer' and 'One-Way Street (Selection)', *Reflections: Essays, Aphorisms, Autobiographical Writings*, ed. Peter Demetz (New York, 1978).

I THE FABRIC AND THE DANCE: WORD AND IMAGE TO 1900 *BY* JOHN DIXON HUNT

1 W.J.T. Mitchell, *Iconology: Image, Text, Ideology* (Chicago, IL, 1986), pp. 43 and 44 (for the following remark).

2 'Between word and image, between what is depicted by language and what is uttered by plastic form, the unity begins to dissolve; a single and identical meaning is not immediately common to them'. *Madness and Civilization*, trans. Richard Howard (New York, 1965), p. 18.

3 See note 6 in my Introduction, above, and Grant F. Scott, *The Scuptured Word: Keats, Ekphrasis, and the Visual Arts* (Hanover, NH, 1994).

4 See in Stelios Lydakis, *Ancient Greek Painting and its Echoes in Later Art* (Athens, 2002, and Los Angeles, 2004), the chapter on 'Vase Painting', p. 76. We are also frequently reminded that the Greek word *graphein* means both writing and engraving.

5 See Julian Reade, *Assyrian Sculpture* (London, 1983), figs 62–3, 95, 98, 101, all of imagery in the British Museum's collections. The author warns that 'some of the words used are rare and we do not know their exact connotations'.

6 For commentary on the tomb painting I am indebted to E. H. Gombrich, *The Story of Art* (London, 1950), pp. 38–9.

7 The literature is substantial: not being an expert I have benefited most from Stéphanie Rossini, *Hieroglyphs: Read and Write* [also in French and German] (Tubingen, 1987), and David Sandison, *The Art of Egyptian Hierogliphics* (London, 1997).

8 See under 'inscriptions' in index of Thomas Edmund, *Monumentality and the Roman Empire* (Oxford, 2007). Also John Sparrow, *Visible Words: A Study of Inscriptions in and as Books and Works of Art* (Cambridge, 1969), and the essay by Amy Papalexandrou, 'Echoes of Orality in the Monumental Inscriptions of Byzantium', in *Art and Text in Byzantine Culture*, ed. Liz James (Cambridge, 2007).

9 I am indebted for this section to Richard Marks, *Stained Glass in England during the Middle Ages* (London, 1993), particularly chapter Three. He points to the symbolism of light in the Christian experience and therefore the prominence of church windows; to which one might also add the centrality of the 'Word'.

10 Ibid, p. 64. He notes that the glazing of Canterbury Cathedral is an exception,

probably because they were planned by Prior Benedict.

11 Ibid, p. 61.

12 To leaf through the famous book by Millard Meiss, *Painting in Florence and Siena after the Black Death* (Princeton, NJ, 1951), is to observe images where saints are named (illus. 1) or hold relevant texts, including those of which they were the authors (illus. 4, 59 or 69), where subject matter is announced (illus. 36), or characters like the vicesare labelled (illus. 71).

13 I draw upon Erwin Panofsky, *Early Netherlandish Painting* (New York, 1953), pp. 144–8 and Millard Meiss, *The Painter's Choice: Problems in the Interpretation of Renaissance Art (*New York, 1976), pp. 3–18.

14 On early work see Richard Brilliant, *Visual Narratives: Storytelling in Etruscan and Roman Art* (Ithaca, NY, 1984).

15 Meyer Schapiro, *Late Antique, Early Christian and Mediaeval Art* (New York, 1979), pp. 249–65.

16 See Nancy P. Sevcenko, 'The *Vita* Icon and the Painter as Hagiographer', *Dumbarton Oaks Papers*, LIII (1999), pp. 149–65.

17 They have, accordingly, produced a large critical literature, for which James, ed., *Art and Text in Byzantine Culture*, provides an introduction and many suggestions for further reading.

18 A rich but not extreme example is the church of the Panagia Arakiotissa in Lagoudera, Cyprus, for which see D. and J. Winfield, *The Church of the Panaghia tou Arakos at Lagoudhera, Cyprus: The Paintings and their Painterly Significance* (Washington, DC, 2003).

19 An incident of 1438 is discussed by Robert S. Nelson, 'Image and Inscription', in *Art and Text in Byzantine Culture*, ed. James, p. 102.

20 I am again indebted to Meyer Schapiro, 'The Religious Meaning of the Ruthwell Cross', in *Late Antique, Early Christian and Mediaeval Art* (New York, 1979), pp. 150–95.

21 See Georges Ritter, *Les Vitraux de la Cathédrale de Rouen* (Cognac, 1926). I am indebted here to Michael J. Call's essay, 'From Glass to Paper: Flaubert's Expropriation and Transcription of the Legend of Saint Julian', *Word & Image*, XXV (2008), pp. 85–95.

22 Benjamin Bart and Robert Francis Cook, *The Legendary Sources of Flaubert's 'Saint Julian'* (Toronto, 1977), p. 30.

23 Interestingly, as Call observes (see note 21), when Flaubert's friend provided him with an explanation of the window's narrative, he included a scene derived from his reading of a Latin manuscript that nowhere appears in the window.

24 Ludwig Wittgenstein, *Philosophical Investigations* (Oxford, 1958), #139.

25 The complex composition of medieval codices has been much studied, as well as how they would have been 'read'. See Mary Carruthers, *The Craft of Thought: Meditation, Rhetoric, and the Making of Images* 400–1200 (Cambridge, 1998), and Michael Camille, *Image on the Edge: The Margins of Medieval Art* (London, 1992). See also note 30.

26 See Maria Evangelatou, 'The Exegetical Initials of CODEX PARISINUS GRAECUS 41', *Word & Image*, XXIV (2008).

27 This manuscript tradition of close liaison continued into the early printing of illustrated books: see *The Painted Page: Italian Renaissance Book Illumination* 1450–1550 (Munich and New York, 1994) for examples.

28 The literature is huge, so fascinating are its images: see Debra M. Hassig, *Medieval Bestaries: Text, Image, Ideology* (Cambridge, 1995); Ann Payne, *Medieval Beasts* (London, 1990); and for a case study of one such collection see Willene B. Clark, *The Medieval Book of Birds: Hugh of Fouilloy's 'Aviarum'* (Binghampton, NY, 1992).

29 I am grateful to Peter Parshall for this item: see his 'Imago Contrafacta: Images and Facts in the Northern Renaissance', *Art History*, XVI (1993), pp. 554–79, especially p. 564.

30 I would only indicate as examples of this complex, erudite and often speculative exegesis of how a medieval reader read, the following: Jessica Brantley, *Reading in the Wilderness: Private Devotion and Public Performance in Late Medieval England* (Chicago, IL, 2007); the essays edited by Nancy P. Sevcenko in a special issue ('The

Word on the Page') of *Word & Image*, XII (1996); Anne Rudloff Stanton, 'The Psalter of Isabelle Queen of England 1308–1330: Isabelle as the Audience', *Word & Image*, XVIII (2002), pp. 1–27; Gerald Guest, 'Authorizing the Toledo Moralized Bible: Exegesis and the Gothic Matrix', *Word & Image*, XVIII (2002), pp. 231–51; Natalie Crohn Schmitt, 'Continuous Narration in the *Holkham Bible Picture Book* and *Queen Mary's Psalter*', *Word & Image*, XX (2004), pp. 123–37; Morgan Powell, 'The Visual, the Visionary and her Viewer: Media and Presence in the Psalter of Christina of Markyate (St Albans Psalter)', *Word & Image*, XXII (2006), pp. 340–62; and Bronwyn Stocks, 'Text, Image and a Sequential 'Sacra Conversazione' in Early Italian Books of Hours, *Word & Image*, XXIII (2007), pp. 16–24.

31 Herbert L. Kessler, 'Turning a Blind Eye: Mediaeval Art and the Dynamics of Contemplation', *The Mind's Eye: Art and Theological Insight in the Middle Ages*, ed. Jeffrey Hamburger (Princeton, NJ, 2006), p. 417.

32 Alexa Sand, 'Vision, Devotion, and Difficulty in the Psalter Hours "of Yolande of Soissons"', *Art Bulletin*, LXXXVII (2005), p. 6.

33 Marguerite Debae, 'Le "Chemin de Paradis" de Jean Germain', *Les Dossiers de l'archéologie*, XVI (1976), pp. 130–37, and J. Vanessa Lyon, '"The wheel inside the wheel": Reading Margaret of York's Burgundian Miniatures According to the Fourfold Sense of Scripture', *Word & Image*, XXIV (2008).

34 I simplify excessively; for detailed commentary see Ulrich Rehm, '"Accende lumen sensibus": Illustrations of the Sherborne Missal Interpreting Pentecost', *Word & Image*, X (1994), pp. 230–61.

35 Of fundamental importance for its commentary on verbal apprehensions of painted images is Michael Baxandall, *Giotto and the Orators: Humanist Observers of Painting in Italy and the Discovery of Pictorial Composition* 1350–1450 (Oxford, 1971); see also his *Patterns of Intention: On the Historical Explanation of Pictures* (New York, 1985).

36 Pierre Rosenberg and Keith Christiansen, ed., *Poussin and Nature: Arcadian Visions* (New Haven, CT, 2008). I am also indebted to the review of this exhibition by Andrew Butterfield in *The New York Review of Books* (LV/6: 17 April 2008).

37 This section is particularly helped by the three-volume monograph on this very topic: *Boccaccio visualizzato. Narrare per parole e per immagini fra medioevo e rinascimento*, ed. Vittore Branca (Turin, 1999).

38 See two articles by Paul J. Papillo, 'Sandro Botticelli: Morgan M676 and Pictorial Narrative', *Word & Image*, XXIII (2007), pp. 89–115, and 'Rogue Images in Manuscripts of the *Divine Comedy*', *Word & Image*, XXIII (2007), pp. 421–38.

39 See in particular *Boccaccio visualizzato*, I, pp. 168ff.

40 *Hypnerotomachia Poliphili: The Strife of Love in a Dream*, trans. Joscelyn Godwin (London, 1999), p. 73.

41 Richard Krautheimer and Trude Krautheimer-Hess, *Lorenzo Ghiberti* [1956] (Princeton, NJ, 1982) and *Journal of the Warburg and Courtauld Institutes*, XLIV (1982), and Jack Greenstein, '"Visual Invention": The Angels at Eve's Side in Ghiberti's *Genesis* Panel', *Word & Image*, XXIV (2008).

42 The Italian phrase (a bigger sea) is Tintoretto's, applied to the art of the painter, but here invoked for the wide opportunities of textual interpretation available today.

43 Jean H. Hagstrum, *The Sister Arts* (Chicago, IL, 1958), pp. 9–10.

44 See Claire J. Farago, *Leonardo da Vinci's 'Paragone': A Critical Interpretation with a New Edition of the Text . . .* (Leiden, 1992), and Leah Mendelsohn, *Paragoni: Benedetto Varchi's due Lezzioni and Cinquecento Art Theory* (Ann Arbor, MI, 1982).

45 I am indebted to Daniel Unger, 'The Yearning for the Holy Land: Agucchi's Program for *Erminia and the Shepherds*', *Word & Image*, XXIV (2008), pp. 367–77.

46 See, for example, François Garnier, *Le Language de l'image au moyen age* (Paris, 1989). Such visual signs continued to be a

familiar and comprehensible repertoire in the theatre: see Bert Joseph, *Elizabethan Acting* (Oxford, 1951).

47 It seems a useful parallel here to invoke the idea of 'paratext', words hovering around the main 'text' or image, from Gérard Genette, *Palimpsestes* (Paris, 1981), p. 9.

48 For a full repertoire of verbally inscribed portraits see Roy Strong, *The English Icon: Elizabethan and Jacobean Portraiture* (London and New York, 1969).

49 However, the extent to which such northern art needs these extra-pictorial handles has been effectively challenged, most strenuously by Svetlana Alpers in *The Art of Describing* (Chicago, 1983). Her insistence that Dutch artists were concerned more with describing the world than imbuing it with significances ('the recent rash of emblematic interpretations') is based upon what she emphasizes as the contemporary emphasis in Dutch culture on new mechanisms for looking, like the telescope and microscope. But beyond such scholarly invocations her book also speaks both for a modernist prejudice against paintings that appeal to non-visual media, narrative or emblematic works, and for an art-historical concern to counter an excessive emphasis on Italian art where the word was always a crucial – if anterior – presence. Alpers's book is interesting in this context for her strenuous rebuttal of commentary that relies upon the implicit or supplementary word.

50 Humphrey Wise, *Claude: The Poetic Landscape* (London, 1994).

51 See W. Moelwyn Merchant, *Shakespeare and the Artist* (London, 1959), and Marcia Pointon, *Milton and English Art* (Manchester, 1970). Also Richard D. Altick, *Paintings from Books: Art and Literature in Britain, 1760–1900* (Columbus, OH, 1985).

52 Philip Brockbank, 'The Measure of *Comus*', *Essays and Studies*, XXII (1968), p. 54.

53 Indeed, John Barrell's interpretations in *The Dark Side of the Landscape: The Rural Poor in English Painting* 1730–1840 (Cambridge, 1980) are focused on these anecdotal inferences, albeit to expose their sentimentality.

54 Robert Southey, *Letters from England,* ed. Jack Simmonds (London, 1951), p. 165.

55 Quoted in W. D. Templeton, *The Life and Works of William Gilpin* (Urbana, IL, 1939), p. 228.

56 Apart from the example used here, other such visual-verbal ensembles were W. Watts, *The Seats of the Nobility and Gentry in a Collection of the most Interesting Picturesque Views* (1779) and W. Angus, *Seats of the Nobility and Gentry in Great Britain and Wales* (1787).

57 I must thank my colleague Catriona MacLeod for transcribing Goethe's verses.

58 See André Rogger, *Landscapes of Taste: The Art of Humphry Repton's Red Books* (London, 2007).

59 For my paragraphs on Turner, a frustrating exercise on the margins of this great painter, I have as always had recourse to Andrew Wilton's *The Life and Work of J.M.W. Turner* (London, 1979) and the Tate catalogue for the 1974 exhibition. See also my 'Ruskin, "Turnerian Topography" and *genius loci*', *Gardens and the Picturesque* (Cambridge, MA, 1992), pp. 215–39.

60 W. Holman Hunt, *Pre-Raphaelitism and the Pre-Raphaelite Brotherhood,* 2 vols (London, 1905), I, p. 90. There are some nice 'Hogarthian' touches in several Pre-Raphaelite paintings: the music abandoned on the carpet of Hunt's *The Awakening Conscience* is a setting of Tennyson's 'Tears, Idle Tears' lyric from *The Princess*, or the titles of books piled up before the young Mary Virgin in Rossetti's painting.

61 Here the reader is directed to the extremely detailed survey by Altick, *Paintings from Books*. See also a similar survey by Martin Meisel, *Realizations: Narrative, Pictorial and Theatrical Arts in Nineteenth-Century England* (Princeton, NJ, 1983).

62 Illustrations are not the subject of this book, but the extent to which an artist's career as illustrator conditioned him and the audience for his paintings proper in their search or need for extra-pictorial references may be explored through the work of Millais: see Paul Goldman, *John Everett Millais: Illustrator and*

Narrator (Aldershot, 2004) and *Beyond Decoration: The Illustrations of John Everett Millais* (London, 2005).

63 There is, of course, an enormous amount more to say about Pre-Raphaelite painting than the topic of this book allows; for those interested in understanding some of the complexities of their work beyond the merely verbal associations, the Tate Gallery catalogue *The Pre-Raphaelites* (London, 1984) is still invaluable. Scholarship on the Pre-Raphaelites has flourished hugely in the last 40 years and their literary sources, with the incidence of display on frames or in catalogues, are well established; what is missing, though, is some attention to how viewers of all sorts *used* those verbal adjuncts in their responses. And it does not help that so few modern reproductions include the all-important frames with their engraved words.

64 Many examples are illustrated in Martin Harrison and Bill Waters, *Burne-Jones* (London, 1973).

65 Quoted by George Wesley Whiting, *The Artist and Tennyson*, Rice University Studies, L (1964), p. 2.

66 Garrett Stewart, *The Look of Reading: Book, Painting, Text* (Chicago, 2006) reviews this whole chapter of paintings showing people reading.

67 *The Pre-Raphaelites*, pp. 106–8.

68 John Ruskin, *The Collected Works*, The Library Edition (London, 1903–12), XXXIII, pp. 272–3.

69 Henry Mas, J. L. Duncan and W. G. Good, ed., *The Letters of Aubrey Beardsley* (Rutherford, NJ, 1970), p. 61. The second part of Beardsley's remark does not concern us, but the exchange between poetry and painting was considerable and in both directions: see my '"Story Painters and Picture Writers": Tennyson's *Idylls* and Victorian Painting', in *Tennyson*, ed. D. J. Palmer (London, 1973), pp. 180–202, and '"The Poetry of Distance": Tennyson's *Idylls of the King*', in *Victorian Poetry*, ed. M. Bradbury and D. J. Palmer (London, 1973).

70 *The Painter's Eye: Notes and Essays on the Pictorial Arts*, selected and with an intro. by John L. Sweeney (London, 1965), p. 148.

1 Blake's Illuminated Word *by* Joseph Viscomi

1 For more information about Blake's life as a graphic artist and printing techniques, see my *Blake and the Idea of the Book* (Princeton, NJ, 1993), Robert N. Essick's *William Blake, Printmaker* (Princeton, NJ, 1980), and *The William Blake Archive* at www.blakearchive.org, ed. Morris Eaves, Robert N. Essick and Joseph Viscomi. All quotations from Blake are drawn from *The Complete Poetry and Prose of William Blake*, newly revd edn, ed. David V. Erdman (New York, 1988); facts from Blake's life are also drawn from Alexander Gilchrist's *Life of Blake* (London, 1863) and G. E. Bentley's *Blake Records* (Oxford, 1969). These works are cited throughout this essay as 'E', 'G' and 'BR' followed by a page number.

2 Robert N. Essick, *William Blake and the Language of Adam* (Oxford, 1989), p. 170.

3 Northrop Frye, 'Poetry and Design in William Blake', in *Blake, A Collection of Critical Essays*, ed. Northrop Frye (Englewood Cliffs, NJ, 1966), p. 120. W.J.T. Mitchell, *Blake's Composite Art* (Princeton, NJ, 1978), p. 42.

4 In *Blake and the Idea of the Book*, I estimate Blake's production costs per book by focusing primarily on the amount of paper and metal used per edition and their costs. What emerged was a pricing formula that was roughly the same as that used by conventional publishers: retail price about five times the cost of production (see chap. 24).

5 Blake received £80 from Macklin to engrave *The Fall of Rosamond* after Stothard in 1783 (BR 569). In 1799 Blake told Trusler that his rate for engravings was thirty guineas (E 703). The idea that £22 pounds was equal to about three months' income is based on *The Book of Trades* (London, 1804), which notes that a copperplate printer earned 40 shillings a week (116). An engraver's income would fluctuate more than a printer's, compositor's or most others in the trade because the work was commissioned freelance.

11 'NEW IN ART... ': WORD AND IMAGE 1900–1945 *BY* DAVID LOMAS

1 Judi Freeman and John Welchman, *The Dada & Surrealist Word-Image*, exh. cat., Los Angeles County Museum of Art (1989).

2 On Apollinaire, see *Picasso and Apollinaire: The Persistence of Memory* (Berkeley, CA, 2008).

3 F. T. Marinetti, 'Destruction of Syntax – Imagination without Strings – Words-in-Freedom' (1913), in *Futurist Manifestos*, ed. Umbro Apollonio (Boston, MA, 2001), pp. 104–5.

4 Alan Bartram, *Futurist Typography and the Liberated Text* (London, 2005).

5 Gotthold Ephraim Lessing, *Laocoön: An Essay on the Limits of Painting and Poetry* [1766], trans. Edward Allen McCormick (Baltimore and London, 1962), pp. 77–8.

6 Cited in Yve-Alain Bois, 'Kahnweiler's Lesson', *Representations*, XVIII (Spring 1987), pp. 33–68.

7 See Rosalind Krauss's seminal essay, 'In the Name of Picasso', *October*, 16 (Spring 1981) pp. 5–22.

8 Roman Jakobson, 'The Metaphoric and Metonymic Poles', in *Fundamentals of Language* (Mouton, 1956), pp. 76–82.

9 Bernard-Paul Robert, 'André Breton et la parole intérieure', *Revue de l'Université de l'Ottawa,* XLIV, July–September 1974, pp. 281–301.

10 Roland Barthes, 'The Death of the Author', *Image, Music, Text*, trans. Stephen Heath (London, 1982), p. 146.

11 Cited in Filiz Eda Burhan, 'Vision and Visionaries: Nineteenth Century Psychological Theory, the Occult Sciences and the Formation of the Symbolist Aesthetic in France', PhD dissertation, Princeton University, 1979, p. 75.

12 André Breton, *Surrealism and Painting*, trans. Simon Watson Taylor (New York, 1972), p. 117.

13 Guillaume Apollinaire, *The Cubist Painters* (1913), *Theories of Modern Art: A Source Book by Artists and Critics*, ed. Herschel B. Chipp (Berkeley, CA, 1969), p. 231.

14 Jeffrey Weiss, 'Picasso, Collage and the Music Hall', in *Modern Art and Popular Culture: Readings in High and Low*, ed. Kirk Varnedoe and Adam Gopnik (New York, 1990), pp. 83–115.

15 Sophie Bowness, 'Braque and Music', in *Braque: Still Lifes and Interiors*, exh. cat., The South Bank Centre London, (1990), pp. 57–67.

16 Molly Nesbit, 'Ready-Made Originals: The Duchamp Model', *October*, 37 (Summer 1986), pp. 53–64.

17 Christine Poggi, 'Frames of Reference: "Table" and "Tableau" in Picasso's Collages and Constructions', *Art Journal*, XLVII/4 (Winter 1988), pp. 311–22.

18 Robert Rosenblum, 'Picasso and the Typography of Cubism', in *Pablo Picasso 1881–1973*, ed. Roland Penrose and John Golding (London, 1973), pp. 49–75.

19 Walter Benjamin, 'On Some Motifs in Baudelaire', *Illuminations*, trans. Harry Zohn (New York, 1969), pp. 155–200.

20 David Walker, *Outrage and Insight: Modern French Writers and the 'Fait Divers'* (Oxford, 1995).

21 Christine Poggi, 'Mallarmé, Picasso, and the Newspaper as Commodity', *Yale Journal of Criticism*, I/1 (Fall 1987), pp. 133–51.

22 Patricia Leighten, 'Picasso's Collages and the Threat of War', *Art Bulletin*, LXVII/4 (December 1985), pp. 653–72.

23 These issues of interpretation are judiciously assessed in David Cottington, 'What the Papers Say: Politics and Ideology in Picasso's Collages of 1912', *Art Journal*, XLVII/4 (Winter 1988), pp. 350–59.

24 For a detailed presentation of this argument, see Yve-Alain Bois, 'Kahnweiler's Lesson', *Representations*, XVIII (Spring 1987), pp. 33–68.

25 Charles Baudelaire, *Art in Paris 1845–62: Salons and Other Exhibitions* (London, 1965), pp. 119 and 32.

26 Charles Baudelaire, *The Painter of Modern Life and Other Essays* (New York and London, 1986), p. 130.

27 Guillaume Apollinaire, *Zone*, trans. Samuel Beckett (Dublin, 1972).

28 Cited in Marianne W. Martin, 'Futurism, Unanimism and Apollinaire', *Art Journal*,

XXVIII/3 (Spring 1969), pp. 260–61.
29 Umberto Boccioni et al., 'The Exhibitors to the Public' (1912), in *Futurist Manifestos*, ed. Apollonio, p. 47.
30 Stephen Kern, *The Culture of Time and Space, 1880–1918* (Cambridge, MA, 1983).
31 Roland Barthes, 'The Eiffel Tower', *A Barthes Reader*, ed. Susan Sontag (London, 1982), p. 237.
32 See Virginia Spate, *Orphism: The Evolution of Non-Figurative Painting in Paris, 1910–1914* (Oxford, 1979).
33 Marjorie Perloff, *The Futurist Moment: Avant-Garde, Avant-Guerre, and the Language of Rupture* (Chicago and London, 1986).
34 Quoted by Walter Benjamin as an epigraph to his essay 'The Work of Art in the Age of Mechanical Reproduction', in Benjamin, *Illuminations*, p. 217.
35 Peter Bürger, *Theory of the Avant-Garde* (Minneapolis, 1984).
36 Jeffrey Weiss, *The Popular Culture of Modern Art: Picasso, Duchamp, and Avant-Gardism* (New Haven and London, 1994).
37 Cited in Katia Samaltanos, *Apollinaire: Catalyst for Primitivism, Picabia and Duchamp* (Ann Arbor, MI, 1984).
38 Picabia's reliance on *Le Petit Larousse* was first documented in the exhibition catalogue *Francis Picabia*, Galeries nationales du Grand Palais (Paris, 1976).
39 Salvador Dalí, 'The King and Queen Traversed by Swift Nudes' [1959], in *The Collected Writings of Salvador Dalí*, ed. Haim Finkelstein (Cambridge, 1998), p. 368.
40 Seeing the work *en masse* at the recent exhibition, *Duchamp, Man Ray and Picabia*, Tate Modern (London, 2008), confirmed this impression.
41 Charlotte Stokes, 'Dadamax: Ernst in the Context of Cologne Dada', in *Dada/Dimensions*, ed. Stephen Foster (Ann Arbor, MI, 1985), pp. 111–30.
42 On the matter of titles, see John Welchman, *Invisible Colors: A Visual History of Titles* (New Haven and London, 1997).
43 See Robert Rainwater et al., *Max Ernst: Beyond Surrealism: A Retrospective of the Artist's Books and Prints* (New York and Oxford, 1986).
44 Dawn Ades, *Photomontage* (London, 1976).
45 Benjamin, *Illuminations*, p. 242.
46 Bürger, *Theory of the Avant-Garde*, p. 75.
47 Maud Lavin, *Cut With the Kitchen Knife: The Weimar Photomontages of Hannah Höch* (New Haven and London, 1993).
48 'Die Merzmalerei', *Der Sturm*, X/4, July 1919. Quoted in John Elderfield, *Kurt Schwitters* (London, 1985), p. 50.
49 Christina Lodder makes this argument in *Russian Constructivism* (New Haven and London, 1983).
50 Bertold Brecht, 'Popularity and Realism' [1938], in *Aesthetics and Politics* (London, 1977), p. 82.
51 See *'Degenerate Art': The Fate of the Avant-Garde in Nazi Germany*, ed. Stephanie Barron, exh. cat., Los Angeles County Museum of Art (1991).
52 André Breton, *Manifestoes of Surrealism* (Ann Arbor, MI, 1972), p. 26.
53 Breton, *Surrealism and Painting*, p. 36.
54 Margit Rowell, 'Magnetic Fields: The Poetics', in *Joan Miró: Magnetic Fields*, exh. cat., The Solomon R. Guggenheim Foundation (1972).
55 Interviewed in 1937, Miró remarked: 'I make no distinction between painting and poetry. I have sometimes illustrated my canvases with poetic phrases, and vice versa. The Chinese, those great lords of the spirit – isn't that what they did?' Joan Miró, *Selected Writings and Interviews* ed. Margit Rowell (London, 1986), p. 151.
56 Michel Leiris, 'Glossaire: J'y serre mes gloses', *La Révolution surréaliste*, III, 15 April 1925, p. 7.
57 André Breton, *What is Surrealism? Selected Writings*, ed. Franklin Rosemount (New York, 1978), p. 7.
58 Miró, *Selected Writings and Interviews*, p. 116.
59 See Sidra Stich, *Joan Miró: The Development of a Sign Language*, exh. cat., Washington University Gallery of Art (St Louis, MI, 1980).
60 Roland Barthes, 'André Masson's Semiography', in *The Responsibility of Forms*, trans. Richard Howard (Berkeley, Los Angeles, London, 1991).

61 Jennifer Mundy, 'Tanguy, Titles and Mediums', *Art History*, VI/2 (June 1983), pp. 199–213.
62 Pierre Naville, 'Beaux-Arts', *La Révolution surréaliste*, III (15 April 1925), p. 27.
63 Walter Benjamin, 'Surrealism: The Last Snapshot of the European Intelligentsia', in *Reflections*, trans. Edmund Jephcott (New York, 1986), pp. 177–92.
64 Miró, *Selected Writings and Interviews*, p. 103.
65 See Caroline Levitt, 'Screening Poetry: Guillaume Apollinaire, André Breton and Experimental Cinema', *Immediations*, II/1 (2008), pp. 61–78.
66 This sequence of works is reproduced in David Lomas, *The Haunted Self: Surrealism, Psychoanalysis, Subjectivity* (New Haven, CT, 2000), p. 204.
67 André Breton, *Manifestoes of Surrealism*, trans. Richard Seaver and Helen R. Lance (Ann Arbor, MI, 1972), p. 20.
68 René Magritte, 'Les mots et les images', *La Révolution surréaliste*, XII (December 1929), pp. 32–3.
69 Michel Foucault, *This is Not a Pipe*, trans. James Harkness (Berkeley and Los Angeles, 1982).
70 Though the topic is beyond the scope of the present essay, Renée Riese Hubert argues that the illustrated book can be regarded as 'the most representative surrealist art form'. In *Surrealism and the Book* (Berkeley, CA, 1988).
71 Breton, *Surrealism and Painting*, p. 284.
72 Hans Bellmer, *Little Anatomy of the Physical Unconscious, or The Anatomy of the Image*, trans. Jon Graham (Waterbury Center, VT, 2004).
73 André Breton, *Anthology of Black Humor*, trans. Mark Polizzotti (San Francisco, CA, 1997).
74 Salvador Dalí, *The Secret Life of Salvador Dalí*, trans. Haakon M. Chevalier (London, 1948), p. 24.
75 Christopher Maurer, ed., *Sebastian's Arrows: Letters and Mementos of Salvador Dalí and Federico García Lorca* (Chicago, IL, 2004).
76 Salvador Dalí, *Metamorphosis of Narcissus*, trans. Francis Scarpe (New York, 1937).
77 See the lineage traced by Stephen Bann in *The True Vine: On Visual Representation and the Western Tradition* (Cambridge, 1989).
78 Claude Cahun, *Disavowals*, trans. Susan De Muth (London, 2007).
79 The verbal-visual collages of Georges Hugnet's *La Septième face du dé* [*The Seventh Face of the Dice*], 1936 present a strong visual resemblance to Jess's aesthetic. Concerning the literary ambiance in which Jess operated, see Ingrid Schaffner, *Jess: To and From the Printed Page*, exh. cat., Independent Curators International (New York, 2007).
80 Heidegger defines truth in painting as an unconcealedness (*Unverborgenheit*) that emerges within an opposition of clearing and concealing. The role of the word-image nexus, particularly as found in collage, in enabling an unconcealment of Being for queer Surrealist artists, as well as an ensuing generation influenced by Surrealism, has yet to be fully charted.
81 Geoffrey Hinton, 'Max Ernst: "Les Hommes n'en Sauront Rien"', *The Burlington Magazine*, CXVII/866 (May 1975), p. 292.
82 Clement Greenberg, 'Towards a Newer Laocoön', *Partisan Review*, VII (July–August 1940), pp. 296–310. In *Pollock and After: The Critical Debate*, ed. Francis Frascina (London, 1985), pp. 44–5.
83 Greenberg, 'Towards a Newer Laocoön', p. 42.
84 Michel Foucault, '"Ceci n'est pas une pipe"', *October*, I (Spring 1976), p. 16.

2 Paul Klee as 'Poet-Painter' *by* Jeremy Adler

1 Marc Le Bot, *Paul Klee* (Paris, 1992), p. 85.
2 Paul Klee, *Tagebücher*, ed. Felix Klee (Cologne, 1957), Entry No, 812, p. 232. Hereafter references to the diaries are given in the main text by entry number.
3 Paul Klee, *Gedichte*, ed. Felix Klee (Frankfurt, 1992), p. 107.
4 Ibid., p. 105.
5 Klee's poetry, his pictorial use of language and the semiotic content of his painting has

attracted increasing attention in recent years. The most systematic account of this aspect of the paintings is K. Porter Aichele, *Paul Klee's Pictorial Writing* (Cambridge and New York, 2002). See also Rainer Crone and Joseph Leo Koerner, *Paul Klee: Legends of the Sign* (New York, 1991); Paul Bauschatz: 'Paul Klee's "Speaking Images"', *Word & Image*, VII (1991), pp. 149–64 and 'Paul Klee's Anna Wenne and the Work of Art', *Art History*, XIX (1996), pp. 74–101. On Klee's poetry, see the invaluable monograph by K. Porter Aichele, *Paul Klee Poet / Painter* (Rochester, NY, and Woodbridge, 2006). Porter Aichele here takes a largely synchronic tack, albeit with some important comments on tradition, arguing that Klee's poetry and painting are embedded in the aesthetics of modernism; in what follows, I aim to stress the diachronic links to tradition, both to German Classicism and to the Orient. The latter I believe provides the most important inspiration for Klee's merging of language, poetry and painting.

6 Although the painting is lost, as Aichele has observed, the drawings survive: *Paul Klee Poet / Painter*, p. 1. See the invaluable catalogue *Paul Klee. Das Fruehwerk 1883–1922* (Munich, 1980).

7 Music, like poetry, also provided a further dimension to Klee's art. See Hajo Düchting, *Paul Klee: Painting Music* (Munich, London, New York, 1997).

8 Klee, *Gedichte*, p. 33.

9 Ibid., p. 40.

10 Ibid., p. 10.

11 Ibid., p. 79.

12 See Christian Geelhaar, 'Journal in time oder Autobiographie? Paul Klee's Tagebücher', in *Paul Klee. Das Fruehwerk*, pp. 246–60.

13 Ibid., p. 252.

14 See especially John J. White, *Literary Futurism: Aspects of the First Avant-Garde* (Oxford, 1990).

3 Sense and Nonsense in Kurt Schwitters *by* Michael White

1 For an account of the reaction to 'An Anna Blume' see Hans-Jürgen Hereth, *Die Rezeptions- und Wirkungsgeschichte von Kurt Schwitters dargestellt anhand seines Gedichts 'An Anna Blume'* (Frankfurt am Main, 1996). Various English translations have been made of 'An Anna Blume', including one apparently by Schwitters himself, giving it titles such as 'To Eve Blossom' and 'Eve Blossom Has Wheels', each attempting to capture something of the flavour of the original by departing quite far from it. For the purposes of this discussion, I have stuck to fairly literal translations of the title and quoted extracts.

2 'Das Material ist so unwesentlich, wie ich selbst.' Kurt Schwitters, 'Merz', *Der Ararat*, II (1 January 1921), p. 5.

3 'Das Wort "Merz" hatte keine Bedeutung, als ich es formte. Jetzt hat es die Bedeutung, die ich ihm beigelegt habe.' Ibid., p. 5.

4 'Der Sinn ist nur wesentlich, wenn er auch als Faktor gewertet wird. Ich werte Sinn gegen Unsinn. Den Unsinn bevorzuge ich, aber das ist eine rein persönliche Angelegenheit. Mir tut der Unsinn leid, daß er bislang so selten künstlerisch geformt wurde, deshalb liebe ich den Unsinn.' Ibid., p. 5.

5 Werner Schmalenbach, *Kurt Schwitters* (New York, 1967), p. 116.

6 Gwendolen Webster, *Kurt Merz Schwitters: A Biographical Study* (Cardiff, 1997), p. 97.

7 Annegreth Nill, 'Rethinking Kurt Schwitters, Part One: An interpretation of "Hansi"' *Arts Magazine*, LV/1 (1981), pp. 112–17. There has been some dispute over the proper title of the collage based on the difficulty of deciphering Schwitters's handwriting. The catalogue raisonné lists it as 'Zeichnung A2 Haus. [Hansi]' (Karin Orchard and Isabel Schulz, *Kurt Schwitters. Catalogue raisonné. Band* 1, *1905–1922* (Ostfildern-Ruit, 2000), p. 136). I am following the Museum of Modern Art's preference for Hansi over Haus, given Schwitters's predilection for titling his collages after fragments contained in them.

8 For a thorough overview of this aspect of Schwitters's career see Dietrich Helms et al., *'Typografie kann unter Umständen Kunst sein': Kurt Schwitters Typographie und Werbegestaltung* (Wiesbaden, 1990)

9 'Ich nannte meine neue Gestaltung mit prinzipiell jedem Material MERZ. Das ist die 2te Silbe von Kommerz. Es entstand beim Merzbilde, einem Bilde, auf dem unter abstrakten Formen das Wort MERZ, aufgeklebt und ausgeschnitten aus einer Anzeige der KOMMERZ UND PRIVATBANK, zu lessen war.' Kurt Schwitters in *Merz*, XX (1927) reprinted in *Das Literarische Werk*, ed. Friedhelm Lach (Cologne, 1981), V, p. 252.

10 In a longer account of the collage in her PhD thesis, Nill does make more of the non-textual elements in the collage but very much from the point of view of their representational qualities, suggesting that they stand in for a crucifixion scene. See Annegreth Nill, 'Decoding Merz: An Interpretive Study of Kurt Schwitters' Early Work, 1918–1922', PhD thesis, University of Texas at Austin, 1990, pp. 25–53.

11 Ibid., p. 114.

12 This observation is made by Joachim Pissarro in unpublished object files on 'Drawing A2: Hansi' (acquisition no. 96.1936, MoMA, New York), and is related to Arp's bilingualism in French and German. Many thanks to Adrian Sudhalter, Assistant Curator, Department of Painting and Sculpture, MoMA, for helping me with queries relating to the collage and its title.

13 Schwitters wrote many 'number' poems made entirely of digits rather than letters. As regards pattern-making with numbers, we might compare the sequencing effect of 200.11.20 to his poem 'Gedicht 25' (Poem 25), first published in Kurt Schwitters, *Elementar. Die Blume Anna* (Berlin, 1922) repr. in Kurt Schwitters, *Anna Blume und Ich* (Zurich, 1965), p. 182, which begins with the number 25 and ends with the fraction 1/24.

14 Nancy Perloff, 'Two Visions of the Universal: The Collaboration of Kurt Schwitters and El Lissitzky' in *Dada Cologne Hanover*, ed. Charlotte Stokes and Stephen C. Foster (New York, 1997), *Crisis and the Arts: The History of Dada*, III, (Cologne and Hanover, 1998) p. 179.

15 Perloff's quoted commentary extends to another collage, *The Holy Saddlers' Portfolio*, but there do not appear to be any lips there either.

16 John Elderfield, *Kurt Schwitters* (London, 1985), p. 68.

17 'Man kann nicht den Ausdruck eines Bildes in Worte fassen, wie man den Ausdruck eines Wortes, etwa des Wortes "und" nicht malen kann.' Schwitters, 'Merz', p. 5.

18 Schwitters played on this effect deliberately in his collage *Mz336. Threeone* (1921), which features a large fragment with the digits 31 on it, disrupting the natural tendency to read them as thirty-one (einunddreizig in German).

19 For a useful discussion of Schwitters's terminology see Elderfield, *Kurt Schwitters*, p. 237.

III WORD AND IMAGE IN ART, SINCE 1945 *BY* MICHAEL CORRIS

1 Ian Burn, *Looking at Seeing and Reading* (Sydney, 1993), n.p.

2 The overlay of image with text has a history that predates Conceptual art. Asger Jorn's 'Modifications' – or 'peinture détournée' – are paintings based on the overpainting and addition of text to amateur canvases. The first public exhibition of this work took place at Gallerie Rive Gauche, Paris, May 1959. Gérard Berréby, ed., *Textes et documents Situationists, 1957–1960* (Paris, 2004) and Claire Gilman, 'Asger Jorn's Avant-Garde Archives', *October*, LXXXIX (Winter 1997), pp. 32–48.

3 See W.J.T. Mitchell, *What Do Pictures Want? The Lives and Loves of Images* (Chicago, IL, 2005), especially chap. 16.

4 W.J.T. Mitchell, *Picture Theory* (Chicago, 1994), p. 16.

5 See Alison and Peter Smithson, 'But Today We Collect Ads', *Ark*, XVIII (November 1956), reprinted in Brian Wallis and Thomas Finkelpearl, *This is Tomorrow Today: The*

Independent Group and British Pop Art (New York, 1987), pp. 52–5.

6 A remark by the author Ring Lardner, cited by Nelson Goodman to illustrate the problem of the exemplification of predicates: 'What startles and amuses us in Ring Lardner's remark that one of his stories "is an example of what can be done with a stub pen" is that the story, although it may have the property that is manuscript was written with a stub pen, does not in the context, or in any usual context, exemplify that property.' See Nelson Goodman, *Languages of Art: An Approach to a Theory of Symbols* (Indianapolis, IN, 1976), p. 54.

7 W.J.T. Mitchell, 'The Family of Images', in *Images: A Reader*, ed. Sunil Manghani, Arthur Piper and Jon Simons (London, 2006), p. 297.

8 Stuart Davis, *Notebook:* 1920–22, entry for 4 December 1920, cited in *Stuart Davis: American Painter*, ed. Lowery Stokes Sims (New York, 1991), p. 151.

9 Ad Reinhardt, 'Abstraction vs. Illustration' (1943), in *Art as Art: The Selected Writings of Ad Reinhardt* (New York, 1975), p. 49.

10 Meyer Schapiro in conversation with Martica Sawin cited in Martica Sawin, *Surrealism in Exile and the Beginning of the New York School* (Cambridge, MA, 1997), p. ix.

11 Jean-Paul Sartre, 'Qu'est-ce que la littérature?', May 1947, cited in ibid., p. 384.

12 Lawrence Alloway, 'The Long Front of Culture', *Cambridge Opinion*, XVII (1959), reprinted in *This is Tomorrow Today*, ed. Wallis and Finkelpearl, pp. 30–33.

13 Thomas Crow, *The Rise of the Sixties: American and European Art in the Era of Dissent* 1955–69 (London, 1996), pp. 44–6.

14 Guy-Ernest Debord, 'Why *Lettrism*?', *Potlatch*, XXII (1955), author's translation, retrieved on 15 December 2008 at: http://library.nothingness.org/articles/SI.

15 *Détournement* was first used in the 1950s by the Belgian surrealist Marcel Marien, a contributor to the journal *Les Lèvres Nues*.

16 Debord, 'Why *Lettrism*?'.

17 Roland Barthes, 'The Wisdom of Art', in *The Responsibility of Forms: Critical Essays on Music, Art and Representation*, trans. Richard Howard (Berkeley, CA, 1992), p. 178.

18 Rosalind Krauss, 'Cy was here; Cy's up – Cy Twombly', *Artforum*, 33, no. 1 (September 1994), p. 118.

19 See James Panero, 'Gallery Chronicle', *The New Criterion*, XXIII (March 2005), p. 46.

20 Ann Hindry, 'Conversation with Roy Lichtenstein', and David Shapiro, 'The Unbearable Lightness of Roy Lichtenstein', *Artstudio*, XX (Spring 1991), p. 13, 136.

21 See David Carrier, 'Comics and the Art of Moving Pictures: Piero della Francesca, Hergé and George Herriman', *Word & Image*, XIII/4 (October–December 1997), pp. 317–32.

22 Vivien Raynor, 'Jasper Johns: "I have attempted to develop my thinking in such a way that the work I've done is not me"', *Artnews*, LXXII/3 (March 1973), cited in *Jasper Johns: Writings, Sketchbook Notes, Interviews*, ed. Kirk Varnedoe (New York, 1996), p. 145.

23 Philip Fisher, *Making and Effacing Art: Modern American Art in a Culture of Museums* (Cambridge, MA, 1991), pp. 81–2.

24 Thomas McEvilley, 'Arakawa and Gins at the Guggenheim SoHo', *Art in America* (January 1998).

25 The identity of the artists constituting Art and Language varies over time; from 1972 through 1974 the group included: Terry Atkinson, Michael Baldwin, David Bainbridge, Harold Hurrell, Graham Howard, Ian Burn, Mel Ramsden, Joseph Kosuth, Michael Corris, Andrew Menard, Terry Smith and Preston Heller.

26 Boris Groys, 'Communist Conceptual Art', in *Die Totale Aufklärung Moskauer Konzeptkunst* 1960–1990 (Frankfurt, 2007), p. 2.

27 For a discussion of Ed Ruscha's *Twentysix Gasoline Stations*, see Melanie Mariño, 'Almost Not Photography', in *Conceptual Art: Theory, Myth, and Practice*, ed. Michael Corris (Cambridge, 2004), pp. 63–79.

28 The full task is: 'Holding a camera, aimed away from me and ready to shoot, while walking a continuous line down a city street. Try not to blink. Each time I blink: snap a photo.'

29 Andrew Benjamin, 'Kiefer's Approaches' in *Thinking Art: Beyond Traditional Aesthetics*, ed. Andrew Benjamin and Peter Osborne (London, 1991), pp. 96–7.
30 Jeffrey Thompson, 'Spray Paint, Vandalism, and Reclamation: Gordon Matta-Clark's Graffiti Truck and the Urban Ritual of Art-Making', lecture delivered at College Art Association, 21 February 2008, Dallas, Texas.
31 Lucy R. Lippard, 'Real Estate and Real Art', *Seven Days* (April 1980), pp. 32–4.
32 The participants of Group Material included Julie Ault, Doug Ashford, Patrick Brennan, Beth Jaker, Mundy McLaughlin, Marybeth Nelson, Tim Rollins and Peter Szypula. See 'Group Material Talks to Dan Cameron: '80s Then', *Artforum*, 41, no. 8 (April 2003) pp. 198–9, 253.
33 Goodman, *Languages of Art*, p. 31.
34 Edward R. Tufte, *The Cognitive Style of PowerPoint* (Cheshire, CT, 2003), pp. 3–4.
35 Ibid., p. 13.
36 Ibid., p. 13.
37 See Mitchell, *Picture Theory*, chap. 2. One of the artists instanced by Mitchell in this chapter is Saul Steinberg.
38 Frances Stark, cited in Mary Leclère, 'For Some Perverts the Sentence is a Body: On the Work of Frances Stark' (Houston, TX, 2007), p. 4.
39 Alan Liu, *The Laws of Cool: Knowledge Work and the Culture of Information* (Chicago, IL, 2004), p. 278.
40 Jonathan Jones, 'A Man for All Seasons', *The Guardian*, 13 January 2003; retrieved on 1 December 2008 at www.guardian.co.uk/artanddesign/2003/jan/14/artsfeatures.

4 August Walla: Devil/God, Image/Text *by* Stephen Barber

1 Leo Navratil, *August Walla: Sein Leben und seine Kunst* (Nördlingen, 1988), p. 27.
2 Ibid, p. 17.

5 'The Sound of Painting': Colin McCahon *by* Rex Butler and Laurence Simmons

1 'Spreading the Word: Colin McCahon: Thomas Crow Talks with Marja Bloem', *Artforum International*, XLII/1 (2003), p. 198.
2 See Francis Pound, 'ENDLESS YET NEVER: Death, Prophecy and McCahon's Last Painting', in *Colin McCahon, The Last Painting*, exh. cat., Peter Webb Galleries (Auckland, 1993), pp. 3–16; Laurence Simmons, 'I AM: Colin McCahon Genius or Apostle?', *Interstices: Journal of Architecture and Related Arts*, VII (2006), pp. 85–94; and Stephen Zepke, 'McCahon's Promised Land: The Politics and Aesthetics of Bicultural Mistranslation', *Landfall*, CCXI (2006), pp. 73–83.
3 'Spreading the Word: Colin McCahon', p. 254.
4 Colin McCahon to John Caselberg, 10 August 1961, quoted in Peter Simpson, *Answering Hark: McCahon/Caselberg: Painter/ Poet* (Nelson, 2001), p. 87.
5 Colin McCahon, *Colin McCahon/ A Survey Exhibition* (Auckland, 1972), p. 31.
6 Marja Bloem and Martin Browne, eds, *Colin McCahon: A Question of Faith* (Nelson and Amsterdam, 2002), p. 9.
7 'Spreading the Word: Colin McCahon', p. 254.
8 See Gordon H. Brown, *Elements of Modernism in Colin McCahon's Early Work* (Wellington, 2003), p. 43, n. 33.
9 Colin McCahon, 'Beginnings', *Landfall*, LXXX (1966), p. 360.
10 'Spreading the Word: Colin McCahon', p. 203.
11 Gordon H. Brown, 'With my Left Hand, I Write: A Consideration of Colin McCahon's Word Paintings', *Ascent*, I (1969), pp. 16–28.
12 Wystan Curnow, catalogue essay in *I WILL NEED WORDS: Colin McCahon's Word and Number Paintings* (Wellington, 1984), np.
13 Francis Pound, 'Colin McCahon and the Language of Practical Religion,' *Art Monthly Australia*, XXXII (July 1990), pp. 9–13; 'McCahon, Skies, Stars, Writing', *Scripsi*, VI/3 (November 1990), pp. 153–64; 'Painting and *Landfall*: Painting as Literature's Death',

Landfall, CLXXXV (April 1993), pp. 78–85; and 'ENDLESS YET NEVER'.

14 Brown, 'With my Left Hand, I Write', p. 20.

15 Curnow, essay in *I WILL NEED WORDS*, np.

16 Pound, 'McCahon, Skies, Stars, Writing', p. 158.

17 Pound, 'ENDLESS YET NEVER', p. 3.

18 Ibid, p. 9.

19 Ibid, p. 9.

20 Stephen Zepke also suggests that it is mistranslation that 'forms the basis of McCahon's later negotiation with Maori over the use of their language and cultural artefacts', 'McCahon's Promised Land', p. 74.

21 McCahon, *Colin McCahon/ A Survey Exhibition*, p. 36. Gordon Brown notes that Matire Kereama – whose book *The Tail of the Fish* was the source for McCahon's 'song' – at a later date sang the song in the gallery where the painting was being shown; *Colin McCahon: Artist*, revd edn (Wellington, 1993), p. 230, n. 12.

22 See, for example, his *The Angel of the Annunciation* (1947) and *Annunciation* (1949).

6 Revelation in Image and Word: The Apocalypse according to Horst Haack *by* Barbara Weyandt

1 Jorge Luis Borges, 'Das Aleph', in *Die zwei Labyrinthe* (München, 1986), pp. 112–28 (p. 124).

2 Max Imdahl, 'Ikonik, Bilder und ihre Anschauung', in *Was ist ein Bild?*, ed. Gottfried Boehm (Munich, 1995), pp. 300–24. On the organization of senses, p. 310.

3 Alois M. Haas, 'Religions- und Kulturgeschichtliche Bemerkungen zum Weltuntergangsthema', in *Der Weltuntergang*, ed. Martin Müller und Ernst Halter (Zurich, 1999), pp. 17–28 (p. 23).

4 Here we need to stress the interpretative statement of Jürgen Roloff that the network of thematic axes, compositional references and motif connections need working out. Jürgen Roloff, *Die Offenbarung des Johannes* (Zurich, 1983), p. 24. Roloff directs our gaze to the situation that accords with the contents of the Seven Cycles.

5 Cf. Felicitas Goodman, *Trance, der uralte Weg zum religiösen Erleben* (Gütersloh, 1992).

6 With reference to Hartmut Böhme's informative statements. Hartmut Böhme, *Past and Present of the Apocalypse in 'Natur und Subjekt'*, ed. Hartmut Böhme (Frankfurt, 1988), pp. 380–98. On the paratactish sequence see esp. p. 380.

7 Quoted from Walter Scherer, 'The Revelation of John' in *Kindlers Neuem Literaturlexikon*, XVIII, ed. Walter Jens (Munich, 1998), pp. 303–4.

8 Michel Covin, 'The Passion of the Words', in *Bildlichkeit*, ed. Volker Bohn (Frankfurt, 1990), pp. 357–83. See p. 362.

9 Leo Perutz, *Der Meister des Jüngsten Gerichts* [1923] (Munich, 2006). This quote from p. 177.

10 Ernst Benz, *Die Vision. Erfahrungsformen und Bilderwelt* (Stuttgart, 1969) p. 73.

11 Gottfried Boehm, 'Die Wiederkehr der Bilder', in *Was ist ein Bild?*, ed. G. Boehm (Munich, 1995), pp. 11–38. Quoted from p. 28.

12 Christoph Eggenberger, 'Das apokalyptische Weib – das Schwert im Munde Christi – Himmlisches Jerusalem. Der mittelalterliche Blick auf die Endzeit in *Apokalypse oder Goldenes Zeitalter? Zeitenwenden aus historischer Sicht*, ed. Walter Koller (Zurich, 1999), pp. 49–70, quote from p. 66.

13 Benz, *Die Vision*, p. 416.

14 Brigitte Weingart, 'In/Out. Text-Bild-Strategien in Pop-Texten der Sechziger Jahre', in *Sichtbares und Sagbares. Text-Bild-Verhältnisse*, ed. Wilhelm Vosskamp and Brigitte Weingart (Cologne, 2005), pp. 216–47. Quoted from p. 227.

15 Johann Wolfgang Goethe, 'Maximen und Reflexionen', in *Werke*, Hamburg Edition, vol. XII (Hamburg, 1953), p. 493. The complete quotation is: 'Word and Image are correlates, which continually seek each other out as we beome sufficiently aware of tropes and allegories.'

16 Ernst Benz, *Die Vision*, p. 415.

17 Sibylle Krämer, 'Schriftbildlichkeit. Oder: über eine fast vergessene Dimension der Schrift', in

Bild – Schrift – Zahl, ed. Sibylle Krämer und Horst Bredekamp (Munich, 2003), pp. 157–76. Quoted from p. 160.

18 Ibid., p. 161.

19 Böhme, 'Vergangenheit und Gegenwart der Apokalypse', in *Past and Present of the Apocalypse*, p. 385. 'Visions are the "film" of Writing.'

20 Max Peter Maass, *Das Apokalyptische in der modernen Kunst. Endzeit oder Neuzeit? Versuch einer Deutung* (Munich, 1965). The quotes are from p. 168 and p. 27.

7 Raymond Pettibon: Words and Images *by* Hamza Walker

1 Raymond Pettibon, *The Books, 1978–1998* (New York, 2000).

Contributors

JEREMY ADLER is Professor Emeritus and Senior Research Fellow in the Department of German, King's College London. He is especially interested in the borderline areas between literature and art, science and anthropology. His publications include a study of Goethe's novel *Elective Affinities* (1987), a catalogue of visual poetry, with Ulrich Ernst (third edition, 1990), and a pictorial biography of Franz Kafka (2002). His most recent publication is a translation of Hölderlin's philosophical essays (2009).

STEPHEN BARBER is Professor in the Visual and Material Culture Research Centre, Faculty of Art, Design and Architecture, Kingston University London. He is the author of five books for Reaktion, including *Fragments of the European City* (1995), *Projected Cities* (2002) and *Abandoned Images* (forthcoming, 2010).

REX BUTLER is Associate Professor in the School of English, Media Studies and Art History at the University of Queensland, Australia. He has written a number of books on Australian art and a number on theoretical figures (*Jean Baudrillard: The Defence of the Real*, 1999; and *Slavoj Žižek: Live Theory*, 2005). He is currently writing a history of 'UnAustralian' art.

MICHAEL CORRIS is an artist and Professor of Art and Chair of the Division of Art, Meadows School of the Arts, Southern Methodist University, Dallas, Texas. His recent books are *Conceptual Art: Theory, Myth and Practice* (2004) and *Ad Reinhardt* (Reaktion, 2008). He is currently working on a study of philosophy in relation to the practice of late-modern and contemporary art.

JOHN DIXON HUNT is Professor Emeritus of the History and Theory of Landscape Architecture at the University of Pennsylvania. He is editor of the journals *Word and Image* and *Studies in the History of Gardens and Designed Landscapes*, and the author of many books, most recently *Nature Over Again: The Garden Art of Ian Hamilton Finlay* (Reaktion, 2008).

MICHAEL R. LEAMAN is Publisher at Reaktion Books and the initiator of this volume – *Art, Word & Image: Two Thousand years of Visual/Textual Interaction*. He has contributed several essays in the area of cultural history to magazines, journals and anthologies.

DAVID LOMAS is Reader in Art History at the School of Arts, Histories and Cultures, University of Manchester. Prior to taking up postgraduate research in the history of art at the Courtauld Institute in London he had studied medicine in Australia. He has published widely on twentieth-century art and culture, and his books include *The Haunted Self: Surrealism, Psychoanalysis and Subjectivity* (2000).

LAURENCE SIMMONS is Associate Professor in the Department of Film, Television and Media Studies at the University of Auckland, New Zealand. He has written a book on New Zealand art (*The Image Always Has the Last Word*, 2002) and edited books on Jean Baudrillard, Jacques Derrida and Slavoj Žižek. He is currently writing a book on the connection between Žižek and Hitchcock, entitled *Everything You Wanted to Know About Slavoj Žižek (But Were Afraid to Ask Alfred Hitchcock)*.

JOSEPH VISCOMI is the James G. Kenan Distinguished Professor of English and Comparative Literature at the University of North Carolina at Chapel Hill. He is a co-editor with Morris Eaves and Robert N. Essick of the William Blake Archive, with whom he also co-edited volumes 3 and 5 (1993) of The William Blake Trust's *William Blake's Illuminated Books*. He is the author of *Prints by Blake and his Followers* (1983), *Blake and the Idea of the Book* (1993), and numerous essays on Blake's illuminated printing, colour printing, mid-nineteenth-century market and reputation.

HAMZA WALKER is a curator and Director of Education for The Renaissance Society at the University of Chicago, a non-collecting museum devoted to contemporary art. He has written articles and reviews for numerous publications, including *Trans*, *New Art Examiner*, *Parkett* and *Artforum*.

BARBARA WEYANDT is Lecturer in Modern and Contemporary Art at the University of Koblenz-Landau and a freelance collaborator with the Institut für aktuelle Kunst Saarlouis in Germany. She has written extensively on a range of twentieth- and twenty-first-century artists, including August Macke, Daniel Depoutot and Katharina Fritsch, and her books include *'Maschinerie des Todes. Der Mengele Totentanz' von Jean Tinguely* (2002).

MICHAEL WHITE is a Senior Lecturer in History of Art at the University of York. He has published widely on the interwar European avant-gardes, particularly Dada and Constructivism, including his recently reprinted book *De Stijl and Dutch Modernism* (2003, 2009). He is currently putting together a new study of the Berlin Dadaists that will consider the full range of their activities, artistic, literary and performative.

Select Bibliography

Abse, D., and J. Abse, ed., *Voices in the Gallery: Poems and Pictures* (London, 1986)

Austin, J. L., *How To Do Things With Words* (Cambridge, MA, 1962)

Bann, S., 'The Mythical Conception Is the Name: Titles and Names in Modern and Post-Modern Painting, *Word & Image*, 1/2 (April–June 1985)

Barthes, R., *Elements of Semiology*, trans. A. Lavers and C. Smith (New York, 1967)

—, *Mythologies*, trans. A. Lavers (New York, 1972)

—, *S/Z*, trans. R. Howard (New York, 1974)

—, *The Responsibility of Forms*, trans. R. Howard (Berkeley and Los Angeles, 1991)

Belting, H., *Likeness and Presence: A History of the Image before the Era of Art*, trans. E. Jephcott (Chicago, IL, 1994)

Benjamin, W., 'The Work of the Art in the Age of Mechanical Reproduction', in *Illuminations*, trans. H. Zorn, ed. H. Arendt (London, 1973)

Billeter, J.-F., *The Chinese Art of Writing* (New York, 1990)

Blackwell, L., *Twentieth Century Type: Remix* (London, 1998)

Bologna, G., *Illuminated Manuscripts: The Book before Gutenberg* (London, 1988)

Bolter, J. D., *Writing Space: The Computer, Hypertext, and the History of Writing* (Hillside, NJ, 1991)

Brand, J., N. Gast and R.-J. Muller, eds, *Der Woorden en de Beelden: Texte en beeld in de kunst van de twintigiste eeuq/ The Words and the Images: Text and Image in the Art of the Twentieth Century*, exh. cat. (Central Museum, Utrecht, 1991)

Bringhurst, R., *The Elements of Typographic Style* (Vancouver, 1992 and 1996)

Bryson, N., *Word and Image: French Painting of the Ancien Régime* (Cambridge, 1981)

Butor, M., *Les Mots dans la peinture* (Geneva, 1969)

Camille, M., *Image on the Edge: The Margins of Medieval Art* (London, 2004)

Chomsky, N., *New Horizons in the Study of Language and Mind* (Cambridge, 2000)

Christin, A.-M., *A History of Writing: From Hieroglyphics to Multimedia* (Paris, 2002)

Davis, E., *TechGnosis: Myth, Magic and Mysticism in the Age of Information* (London, 1999)

Derrida, J., *Of Grammatology*, trans. G. C. Spivak (Baltimore and London, 1981)

Drucker, J., *The Alphabetic Labyrinth: The Letters in History and Imagination* (London, 1995)

—, *The Visible Word: Experimental Typography and Modern Art, 1909–1923* (Chicago, IL, 1994)

—, *The Century of Artists' Books* (New York, 1995)

Eco, U., *Semiotics and the Philosophy of Language* (Bloomington, IN, 1984)

—, 'The Future of the Book', in *The Future of the Book*, ed. G. Numberg (Berkeley and Los Angeles, 1997)

Eisenstein, E., *The Printing Press as an Agent of Change: Communications and Cultural*

Transformations in Early-Modern Europe, vol. I–II (Cambridge, 1979)
Elkins, J., *Our Beautiful, Dry, and Distant Texts: Art History as Writing* (University Park, 1997)
Evers, B., et al., eds, *Die Lesbarkeit der Kunst* (Berlin, 1999)
Fisher, S. R., *A History of Language* (London, 1999)
—, *A History of Writing* (London, 2001)
Flusser, V., *Writings*, trans. E. Eisel, ed. A. Ströll (Minneapolis and London, 2002)
Fowler, A., *Renaissance Realism: Narrative Images in Literature and Art* (Oxford, 2003)
Freedberg, D., *The Power of Images: Studies in the History and Theory Response* (Chicago, IL, 1989)
Freeman, J., *The Dada and Surealist Word-Image* (Cambridge, MA, 1989)
Friedl, F., N. Ott and B. Stein, eds, *Typographie: Wann Wer Wie* (Cologne, 1998)
Gandelman, C., ed., 'Inscriptions in Painting', *Visible Language*, XXIII/2–3 (1989)
Gauer, A., *A History of Calligraphy* (London, 1994)
Gombrich, E., 'Image and Word in Twentieth-Century Art', *Word & Image*, I/3 (July–September 1986)
Goodman, N., *Languages of Art: An Approach to a Theory of Symbol* (Indianapolis and Cambridge, 1976)
Gray, N., *A History of Lettering* (Oxford, 1986)
Hagstrum, J., *The Sister Arts: The Tradition of Literary Pictorialism and English Poetry from Dryden to Gray* (Chicago, IL, 1958)
Harrison, C., *Essays on Art and Language* (Oxford, 1991)
Hartman, J., *The History of the Illustrated Book* (London, 1981)
Hayakawa, S. I., *Language in Thought and Action* [1939] (3rd edn London, 1974)
Heusser, M., ed., *Word & Image Interactions* (Basel, 1993)
Hollander, J., *The Gazer's Spirit: Poems Speaking to Silent Works of Art* (Chicago, IL, 1995)
Homem, R. C., and M. de Fatima Lambert, ed., *Writing and Seeing: Essays on Word and Image* (Amsterdam, 2006)
Jay, M., *Downcast Eyes: The Denigration of Vision in Twentieth Century French Thought* (Berkeley and Los Angeles, 1993)
Jean, G., *Writing: The Story of Alphabets and Scripts* (London, 1992)
Kern, S., *The Culture of Time and Space: 1880–1918* (Cambridge, MA, 1983)
Khalfa, J., ed., *The Dialogue between Painting and Poetry: Livres d'artistes, 1874–1999)*, exh. cat. (Cambridge, 2001)
Kinross, R., *Modern Typography: An Essay in Critical History* (London, 1992)
Kostelanetz, R., ed., *Esthetics Contemporary* (Buffalo, NY, 1989)
Kress, G., and T. van Leeuwen, *Reading Images: The Grammar of Visual Design* (London, 1996)
Kristeva, J., *Language: The Unknown*, trans. A. M. Menke (New York, 1989)
Lewis, J., *The Twentieth Century Book* (London, 1967)
Loizeaux, E. B., *Twentieth-Century Poetry and the Visual Arts* (Cambridge, 2008)
McGann, J. T., *The Textual Condition* (Princeton, NJ, 1991)
McLean, R., *Typography* (London, 1980)
Manning, J., *The Emblem* (London, 2002)
Merleau-Ponty, M., *Phenomenology of Perception*, trans. C. Smith (London, 1989)
Miller, J. Hillis, *Illustration* (London, 1992)
Mitchell, S., *The Rise of the Image, The Fall of the Word* (Oxford and New York, 1998)
Mitchell, W.J.T., *Iconology: Image, Text, Ideology* (Chicago, IL, 1986)
—, *Picture Theory: Essays on Verbal and Visual Representation* (Chicago, IL, 1994)
—, *What Do Pictures Want?* (Chicago, IL, 2005)
Morley, S., *Writing on the Wall: Word and Image in Modern Art* (London, 2003)
Neef, S., *Abdruck und Spur: Handschrift im Zeitalter ihrer technischen Reproduzierbarkeit* (Berlin, 2008)
Ong, W., *Orality and Literacy: The Technologising of the Word* (London, 1982)
Oosterling, H., 'Intermediality, Art Between Images, Words and Actions', in *Think Art: Theory and Practice in Art Today*, ed. J.-M. Shaeffer (Witte de With, Center for Contemporary Art, Rotterdam, 1998)
Packer, R., and K. Jordan, eds, *Multimedia: From Wagner to Virtual Reality* (New York and London, 2001)
Peirce, C. S., 'What is a Sign?', in *Essential Peirce*, ed. The Peirce Editorial Project (Bloomington, IN, 1998)

Perloff, M., *Twentieth Century Modernism: The 'New' Poetics* (Oxford, 2002)
Pinker, S., *The Language Instinct: The New Science of Language and Mind* (London, 1995)
Rancière, J., *The Future of the Image*, trans. G. Elliott (London, 2007)
Reisner, R., *Graffiti: Two Thousand Years of Wall Writing* (New York, 1971)
Rice, A., and A. Reid, ed., *A Conversation Piece: Poetry and Art* (Newry, 2002)
Rothenberg, J., *Technicians of the Sacred* (New York, 1968)
Saussure, F. de, *Course in General Linguistics*, trans. W. Baskin (New York, 1966)
Scobie, S., *Earthquakes and Explorations: Language and Poetry from Cubism to Concrete Poetry* (Toronto, Buffalo and London, 1997)
Seitz, W., *The Art of Assemblage*, exh. cat. (Museum of Modern Art, New York, 1961)
Shlain, L., *The Alphabet Versus the Goddess: The Conflict Between Word and Image* (London, 1998)
Sparrow, J., *Visible Words: A Study of Inscriptions in and as Books and Works of Art* (Cambridge, 1969)
Spencer, H., *The Liberated Page: A Typographica Anthology* (London, 1987)
Die Sprache der Kunst: Die Bezeihung von Bild und Text in der Kunst des 20. Jarhunderts, exh. cat. (Stuttgart, 1993)
Steiner, G., *Language and Silence* (London, 1967)
—, *After Babel: Aspects of Language and Translation* (Oxford, 1975)
—, 'After the Book' in *On Difficulty and Other Essays* (Oxford, 1980)
—, 'The Retreat from the Word', *George Steiner: A Reader* (Harmondsworth, 1984)
Steiner, W., *The Colors of Rhetoric: Problems in the Relation between Modern Literature and Painting* (Chicago, IL, 1982)
Stiles, K., and P. Selz, eds, *Theories and Documents of Contemporary Art: Sourcebook of Artists' Writings* (Berkeley and Los Angeles, 1996)
Timms, E., and D. Kelly, eds, *Unreal City: Urban Experience in Modern EuropeanLiterature and Art* (Manchester, 1985)
Ulmer, G. L., *Applied Grammatology: Post(e) Pedagogy from Jacques Derrida to Joseph Beuys* (Baltimore and London, 1985)
Welchman, J. C., *Invisible Colours: A Visual History of Titles* (New Haven and London,1997)
Wittgenstein, L., *Philosophical Investigations*, trans. G.E.M. Anscombe (3rd edn, London, 1953)
Wollheim, R., 'Pictures and Language' in *The Mind and Its Depths* (Cambridge, MA, 1983)
Words: Works from the Arts Council Collection, exh. cat. (Hayward Gallery, South Bank Centre, London, 2002)

Photo Acknowledgements

The illustrations in this book were published with the assistance of the British Academy.

'PREFACE': Getty Images: p. 6 bottom; Petteri Löppönen Photography: p. 6 top.

'INTRODUCTION': Ashmolean Museum, Oxford: p. 24 right; The British Library, London: pp: 18, 30; Courtesy of Peter Blum Gallery, New York: p. 31 bottom; Guggenheim Museum, New York 2009: p. 29 (© Hattula Moholy-Nagy/DACS 2009); Photo Scala, Florence: p. 22 (© 2009. Digital Image, The Museum of Modern Art, New York); 28 (courtesy of the Ministero per i Beni e le Attività Culturali); © Tate, London 2009: p. 27.

'WORD AND IMAGE TO 1900': AKG Images: pp. 39 (Bildarchiv Steffens), 70 (British Library), 38 (British Museum), 62 (Erich Lessing), 80 bottom (Erich Lessing); All Soul's Chapel, Oxford: p. 41 (left); Bodleian Library, Oxford (MS Douce 308): p. 52; The British Library, London: pp. 54, 56 top left; Emily T. Cooperman: p. 40 bottom; Fitzwilliam Museum, Cambridge: p. 71; The J. Paul Getty Museum, Los Angeles: p. 64; Fondation Martin Bodmer, Cologne: p. 73; Photo Scala, Florence: pp. 41 right (© 2001, courtesy of the Ministero per i Beni e le Attività Culturali), 43, 50, 57 (© 2009, courtesy of the Ministero per i Beni e le Attività Culturali), 60 (© 2009, courtesy of the Ministero per i Beni e le Attività Culturali); Dr Nancy Sevcenko: p. 48; By permission of the Master and Fellows of St John's College, Cambridge: p. 46 bottom right; © Tate, London 2009: pp. 66 bottom, 75, 76, 80 top; Yale Center for British Art, New Haven, Conn., Paul Mellon Fund (B1976.1.2): p. 67; University of California, San Diego: pp. 36, 37 right, 46 top left, 63 bottom left; Warburg Institute, University of London, London: p. 40 top; West Yorkshire Archive Service, Leeds: p. 74 bottom left.

'BLAKE'S ILLUMINATED WORD': © Trustees of the British Museum, London: p. 94, 101; The Huntington Library and Art Gallery, San Marino, California: pp. 102, 103; Collection of Robert N. Essick. Copyright © 2009 The William Blake Archive. Used with permission: p. 107; Lessing J. Rosenwald Collection, Library of Congress, Washington, DC. Copyright © 2009 The William Blake Archive. Used with permission: pp. 86, 92, 95, 97, 99, 100, 104; Metropolitan Museum of Art, New York: pp. 90, 91; Morgan Library and Museum, New York: p. 93; Yale Center for British Art, New Haven, Conn.: p. 105.

'WORD AND IMAGE 1900–1945': © ADAGP, Paris and DACS, London 2009: p. 113 bottom right, 122 bottom, 126 bottom, 136 bottom, 137, 140, 141, 142 top left, 145, 152, 153 bottom, 156, 157, 159, 160, 161, 164, 165, 167, 169, 170, 177; Art Resource, New York: 166 top left (Erich Lessing Culture and Fine Arts

Archives/ © ADAGP, Paris and DACS, London 2009); © The Joseph and Robert Cornell Memorial Foundation / DACS, London / VAGA, New York 2009: p. 168; © DACS 2009: pp. 143, 144, 146 top right, 147 top left and bottom right, 151 left (Rodchenko & Stepanova Archive), 154 top left; © Salvador Dalí, Gala-Salvador Dalí Foundation, DACS, London 2009: pp. 172, 173, 174; © Estate of Stuart Davis / DACS, London / VAGA, New York 2009: p. 127; Courtesy of the Frances Loeb Library, Harvard Graduate School of Design, Cambridge, Mass.: p. 151 top right; © The Heartfield Community of Heirs / VG Bild-Kunst, Bonn and DACS, London 2009: p. 146 top left; © 2009 C. Herscovici, London /© ADAGP, Paris and DACS, London 2009: p. 166 top right; The Minneapolis Institute of Arts, Minneapolis, Minn., Gift of Daniela Mrazkova (93.36.2): p.114 (© DACS 2009); © Sucession Marcel Duchamp / ADAGP, Paris and DACS, London 2009: p. 135, 136 top, 138 top and bottom, 142 top right; © Succession Miro / ADAGP, Paris and DACS, London 2009: pp. 110, 153 top, 154 bottom right, 155, 163; © Succession Picasso / DACS 2009: pp. 118, 119, 120, 122 top, 123 top, 124, 126 top; Photo Scala, Florence: p. 130 (courtesy of the Ministero per i Beni e le Attività Culturali © ADAGP, Paris and DACS, London 2009), 139 (© Man Ray Trust / ADAGP, Paris and DACS, London 2009), 148 (2009 Digital Image, The Museum of Modern Art, New York / © DACS 2009), 171 (© Man Ray Trust / ADAGP, Paris and DACS, London 2009); © Tate, London 2009: p. 131; University of California, San Diego: p. 149 (© DACS 2009).

'PAUL KLEE': © DACS 2009: p. 191, 200 top right; Solomon R. Guggenheim Museum, New York: p. 195 (© DACS 2009); The Frances Lehman Loeb Art Center, Poughkeepsie, Gift of Mrs. John D. Rockefeller III: p. 200 top left (© DACS 2009); Private collection, Germany: p. 193 (© DACS 2009); Rosengart Foundation, Lucerne: p. 200 bottom centre (© DACS 2009); Photo: Scala, Florence: pp. 196 (Collection of Etta and Otto Stangl, Kunstmuseum, Stuttgart / © DACS 2009), 198 (The Metropolitan Museum of Art, New York, The Berggruen Klee Collection / © DACS 2009); Stiftung Sammlung Dieter Scharf zur Erinnerung an Otto Gerstenberg, Berlin: p. 190 (© DACS 2009); Technische Universität, Berlin: p.179; Zentrum Paul Klee, Bern: pp. 180, 181, 186, 192, 194, 201 (© DACS 2009).

'KURT SCHWITTERS': © DACS 2009 : pp. 207, 212; Stella and Joe Kattan: p. 213 top right (© DACS 2009), Museum of Modern Art, New York: pp. 206, 208 (© DACS 2009); Sprengel Museum, Hanover: p. 202, 211 top right, 211 bottom right, 213 top left (© DACS 2009); Staatsgalerie Stuttgart: p. 210 (© DACS 2009).

'WORD AND IMAGE IN ART SINCE 1945': Courtesy Vito Acconci: p. 277; © ADAGP, Paris and DACS, London 2009: pp. 268, 269 top, 273; Anko Photography/ ADAGP, Paris and DACS, London 2009: p. 269 centre left; © The Estate of Jean-Michel Basquiat: p. 249 (© ADAGP, Paris and DACS, London 2009); Photos courtesy: Mary Boone Gallery, New York: pp. 228, 229 (Copyright Barbara Kruger); *If Nancy Was an Ashtray* by Joe Brainard is used by permission of the Estate of Joe Brainard: p. 216 bottom right; Courtesy of The Broodthaers Estate: p. 286 (© DACS 2009); Courtesy of Victor Burgin: p. 287; Courtesy of Avril Burn: p.223; Martha Cooper: p. 248 (© The Estate of Jean-Michel Basquiat / ADAGP, Paris and DACS, London 2009); Courtesy of the Peter Blum Edition, New York: p. 246; The Bridgeman Art Library: pp. 254–5 top (Musée National d'Art Moderne, Centre Pompidou, Paris / Giraudon © ADAGP, Paris and DACS, London 2009), 253 (Kunsthalle, Tübingen / © Richard Hamilton. All Rights Reserved, DACS 2009); Courtesy of the Leo Castelli Gallery, New York: p. 260 (© Jasper Johns / VAGA, New York / DACS, London 2009); Paula Cooper Gallery, New York: pp. 291 (© Sophie Calle. Photo: Ellen Page Wilson / © ADAGP, Paris and DACS, London 2009), 297 (© DACS 2009); Michael Corris: p. 247 bottom; © DACS 2009: p. 232; Courtesy of Annabel Daou: p. 306; Courtesy of the artist, Free Agent Media, and Elizabeth Dee, New York: p. 290 centre left (Photo credit: Tom Warren); Photograph courtesy the artist; © 2006 Madeline Djerejian: p. 233; © Estate of Stuart Davis / DACS, London / VAGA, New York 2009: pp. 238, 242; Courtesy Edlin Gallery, New York: p. 250 bottom (Copyright Kiyoko Lerner/ © ARS, New York and DACS, London 2009; Courtesy of Marc Foxx, Los Angeles: p. 301; Courtesy Gagosian

Gallery, New York: pp. 283 (© Anselm Kiefer), 214, 274, 275 (© Ed Ruscha); Galerie Maurice Garnier: p. 257 (©ADAGP, Paris and DACS, London 2009); Courtesy of Arakawa and Madeline Gins: p. 262; Courtesy of Vilma Gold: p. 231 top; Courtesy of the artist and Marion Goodman Gallery, New York: p. 278; Image courtesy the artist and Greengrassi, London: p. 302; © 2009 Jenny Holzer, member Artists Rights Society (ARS): P.226 (© 1983 Lisa Kahane , New York City / © ARS, NY and DACS, London 2009), 227 (Text: "To the Forty-third President," from Blackbird and Wolf by Henri Cole, copyright (c) 2007 by the author. Used by/reprinted with permission from Farrar, Straus & Giroux, LLC, New York. Photo: Attilio Maranzano/© ARS, New York and DACS, London 2009); Courtesy of Alfredo Jaar: p. 219, 229; © Jasper Johns / VAGA, New York / DACS, London 2009: p. 264; JWT, London: p. 234 top and centre; © The Estate of Roy Lichtenstein / DACS 2009: p. 26; Los Angeles County Museum of Art, Purchased with funds provided by the Ansley I. Graham Trust / Photograph © 2009 Museum Associates / LACMA: p. 294; Courtesy of the artist and Sean Kelly Gallery, New York: p. 267 top (Joseph Kosuth. Information Room – Special Investigation), 1970. Photography by Jason Wyche, installed at the Sean Kelly Gallery, 25 October–6 December 2008/ © ARS, New York and DACS, London 2009); Courtesy of Brian Kennon: p. 295 top; Courtesy of the Artist and Kent Gallery, New York: p. 245 top; Courtesy of Sharon Kivland: p. 295 bottom; Courtesy Galerie Lelong, New York: p. 300 (© Nancy Spero / © DACS, London/VAGA, New York 2009); Courtesy of the artists and Lisson Gallery: pp. 222, 266, 267 bottom; Courtesy the Estate of Gordon Matta-Clark and David Zwirner, New York: p. 284 (© 2009 Estate of Gordon Matta-Clark / Artists Rights Society (ARS), New York and DACS, London 2009); Courtesy Mitchell-Innes and Nash: p. 289; The Museum of Contemporary Art, Los Angeles, The Panza Collection (86.15): p. 240 (© DACS, London / VAGA, New York 2009); National Gallery of Art, Washington, DC: pp. 224 (© Jasper Johns / VAGA, New York / DACS, London 2009), 263 (© The Andy Warhol Foundation for the Visual Arts / Artists Rights Society (ARS), New York / DACS, London 2009); Images courtesy the artists and Pierogi: pp. 231 bottom, 296; Courtesy of Postmasters Gallery: p. 293 bottom; © Richard Prince: pp. 236, 237; Courtesy of the Royal Art Lodge: p. 250 top; Royal College of Art, London: p. 217; Photo Scala, Florence: pp. 254 bottom (© ADAGP, Paris and DACS, London 2009), 218 (Copyright © 1965, the Estate of Brion Gysin and the William S. Burroughs Trust / © 2009. Digital Image Museum Associates / LAMA / Art Resource, New York), 225, 241, 247 top (digital image, The Museum of Modern Art, New York / © DACS, London / VAGA, New York 2009), 259, 285, 312, 313, 314, 315 (2009 Digital Image, The Museum of Modern Art, New York); Courtesy of Carolee Schneemann: p. 276 (Photo: Anthony McCall); Hirshhorn Museum and Sculpture Garden, Smithsonian Institution: p. 216 top left (© 2009 Morgan Art Foundation Ltd / Artists Rights Society (ARS), New York, DACS, London); Silkeborg Kunstmuseum: pp. 255 bottom, 265 (Work of joint ©. DACS only reps Asger Jorn. © Donation Jorn, Silkeborg / DACS 2009); Courtesy of Joe Scanlan: pp. 308, 309; Courtesy of Lorna Simpson: p. 293 top; Courtesy of the artist and Smith-Stewart Gallery, New York: p. 307 (artwork: Copyright 2008 Brian Lund / Photo: Cathy Carver); Saul Steinberg, *Large Document*, 1951, ink, rubber stamp, and collage on paper, 29 x 23 in. (73.7 x 58.4 cm) / Private collection © The Saul Steinberg Foundation/ Artists Rights Society (ARS), New York / DACS, London 2009: p. 251 top; Saul Steinberg, *Group Photo*, 1953, ink, thumbprints, and rubber stamp on paper, 14 x 11 in. (35.6 x 27.9 cm) / Collection of Richard and Ronay Menschel © The Saul Steinberg Foundation/Artists Rights Society (ARS), New York/ DACS, London 2009: p. 251 bottom; © Tate, London 2009: p. 282; © Tate, London 2009: pp. 304, 305 (© DACS 2009); Berkeley Art Museum and Pacific Film Archive, University of California: p. 290 top; Courtesy of Kara Walker: p. 311; White Cube, London: p. 303 (© Tracey Emin. All rights reserved, DACS 2009).

'AUGUST WALLA': P.Art Brut KG: pp. 318, 319, 320, 322, 324 top.

'COLIN MCCAHON': Auckland Art Gallery Toi o Tamaki, Auckland, New Zealand / © Courtesy of Colin McCahon Research and Publication Trust: pp. 337, 338, 340; Jennifer Gibbs Trust, Auckland,

New Zealand / © Courtesy of Colin McCahon Research and Publication Trust: p. 334 bottom; Govett-Brewster Art Gallery, New Plymouth, New Zealand / © Courtesy of Colin McCahon Research and Publication Trust: p. 341; Museum of New Zealand Te Papa Tongarewa, Wellington (1983–0049-1)/ © Courtesy of Colin McCahon Research and Publication Trust: p. 331; National Gallery of Australia, Canberra / © Courtesy of Colin McCahon Research and Publication Trust: pp. 333 (1983-0049-1), 334–5 top (1985-0022-1); Private collection, Auckland, New Zealand / © Courtesy of Colin McCahon Research and Publication Trust: p.343; Hocken Library, University of Otago, Dunedin, New Zealand (Acc. No.73–171) / © Courtesy of Colin McCahon Research and Publication Trust: p. 332.

'HORST HAACK': Courtesy of Horst Haack: pp. 348, 349, 351, 352, 353, 355, 356, 357, 359, 361, 362.

'RAYMOND PETTIBON': Courtesy Regen Projects, Los Angeles, © Raymond Pettibon: pp. 366, 367, 368, 369, 370, 371, 372, 373, 374, 375, 376, 377, 378.

Index

Numbers in *italics* indicate the page numbers of illustrations.

Acconci, Vito *277*, 279
Adams, Dennis 244, *245*
Adorno, Theodor 215, 364
Al Diaz *248*, 285
Alciato, Andrea *32*
All Saints Church, York 41
All Souls College Chapel, Oxford 39, *41*
Alÿs, Francis 258
American Artists Congress 239
Andrew, John *33*
Apollinaire, Guillaume 111, 112, 116, 121, 124, 125, 128, 129, 134, 135, 136, 151, 160, 162, 166, 192
Arakawa, Shusaku *262*, 265–6, 269
Arnatt, Keith 279
Arp, Hans 170, 203, 205
Art & Language *222*, *267*, 270
Artaud, Antonin 155, 159
Atget, Eugène 125
Austin, John L. 279

Bacher, Lutz 244, *245*
Bailly, David 62
Baldessari, John *278*, 279
Bann, Stephen 32
Barnes Foundation, The 26
Barry, James 67, 88
Barthes, Roland 115, 128, 155, 233
Basire, James 87
Basquiat, Jean-Michel *248*, *249*, 285
Baudelaire, Charles 124, 158, 306
Bellmer, Hans 168–9, 170
Benjamin, Walter 33, 121, 143, 158, 329
Bernheim-Jeune Gallery, Paris 128
Bernstein, Michèle 256
Beth-Alpha Synagogue, Israel 36, *37*
Beuys, Joseph 216, 332
Beveridge, Karl 220, *232*
Birch, William *72*
Blake, Robert 91
Blake, William 31, 32, 86–109, *86*, *90*, *91*, *92*, *93*, *94*, *95*, *97*, *99*, 100, 101, 102, 103, *104*, 105, *107*
Boccaccio, Giovanni 57–9, 74, 78
Boccioni, Umberto 128, *129*
Boiffard, Jacques-André *162*
Boucher, Catherine 89
Boydell, John 67, 69, 108
Brainard, Joe 216, *216*
Braithwaite, Fred 285
Braque, Georges 116–17, 119, 120, 124–5, 179, 190, 191
Brauner, Victor 165, *167*
Breton, André 8, 111, 114, 115, 116, 121, 139, 149, 151, 154, 156, 157, *157*, 158, 162, *162*, 164, 165, 166, 168, 169, *169*, 170, 175, 243
Breughel, Pieter 64–5
Brisset, Jean-Pierre 134
Broodthaers, Marcel *286*, 287
Brouwn, Stanley 258
Brown, Gordon 335–6, 339
Browning, Robert 25

Bruskin, Grisha 273
Buffet, Bernard 257–8, *257*
Bulatov, Erik *273*, 275
Burgin, Victor 220, 287, *287*
Burn, Ian 220–22, *223*, 269
Burne-Jones, Edward 57, 78, *79*
Burroughs, William S. 155, *218*, 354
Bushmiller, Ernie 216

Cahun, Claude 173–4, *176*
Callcott, John 82
Calle, Sophie 258, 288, 290–92, *291*
Campos, Augusto de 8
Cappelle, Jan van de *63*
Carpaccio, Vittore 42, *42*, *43*
Carrà, Carlo 189, 191
Carracci, Ludovico 61
Carrington, Leonora 170
Cendrars, Blaise 8, 13, 114, 128–9, 130, *133*, 189
Chagall, Marc 24
Chinese script 11, 15, *16*, 23, 155, 192
Chuikov, Ivan 275
Claude (le) Lorrain 59, 64, *64*
Cocteau, Jean 8, 257–8
Condé, Carole 220, *232*
Constable, John 70
Coptic-Sahidic *14*
Cornell, Joseph 165–6, *168*
Costley, Ron 32, *33*
Crow, Thomas 253, 329, 330, 332–3, 335
Cruikshank, George 8
Cumberland, George 106
Curnow, Wystan 335, 336, 339

Dalí, Salvador 137, 160, 164, 169, 170, 172, *172*, 173, *173*, *174*
Dante Alighieri 17, 58, 69
Daou, Annabel 301, *303*, *306*
Darger, Henry *250*
Davis, Stuart 125, *127*, 238–9, *238*, *242*
Dawson, Shannon *248*, 285
Dean, Tacita 244, *246*
Debord, Guy 216, 244, *255*, 256–8, *256*
Delaunay, Robert 128, 129, *131*, 132, 189
Delaunay, Sonia 13, 114, 130, *134*, 189
Derain, André 121, *122*
Desnos, Robert 140, 152, *153*
Deverell, Walter Howell 82, *83*
Diao, David *293*, 296
Diderot, Denis 26–7
Djerejian, Madeline *233*
Doesburg, Theo van 146
Dubuffet, Jean 246, *247*, 319
Duchamp, Marcel 134–7, *135*, 138, 140, *142*, 165, 172, 278
Dufrêne, François 244, 256
Dürer, Albrecht 64, 87, 350
Durham, Jimmie 13

Egger, Victor 115
Eluard, Paul 139, 169
Emin, Tracey 301, *303*
Ernst, Max 139–40, *142*, 149, 152, 154, 158, 161, 170, 175, *177*
Exter, Alexandra 129
Eyck, Jan van 42, *45*

Fahlström, Öyvind *304*, *305*
Fashion Moda, New York 286
Fend, Peter 288
Finlay, Ian Hamilton 9, 32, 33, *33*, 39
Fiore, Jacobello del 50–51, 50
Flaubert, Gustave 49, 50
Flynt, Henry 285
Foucault, Michel 35, 163, 164, 177
Fournival, Richard of *52*
Foxe, John 20
Freud, Sigmund 8, 139, 160, 164, 166, 170, 172–3, *174*, 175, 178, 295
Friedrich, Caspar David 20, *22*
Fromentin, Eugène 17
Fulton, Hamish 258, *258*
Fuseli, Henry 67, *68*, 69

Gabriel, the Archangel 50, 51, 341
Gainsborough, Thomas 70
Galerie Nächst St Stephan (Vienna) 319, 320
Gautier, Théophile 17
Germain, Jean *53*, 55
Gheeraerts, Marcus, the Younger 63, *63*
Ghiberti, Lorenzo 60, *60*
Gilbert and George 279, *280*, *281*
Gillray, James 8, *21*, 59, *59*
Gilpin, William *71*
Ginn, Raymond *see* Pettibon, Raymond
Gins, Madeline *262*, 265–6, 269
Giorgione 27, *28*, 62
Glazier Psalter 46, *46*

Gloucester cathedral 41
Goethe, Johann Wolfgang von 73, *73*, 182, 183–4
Goldstein, Jean-Isidore (known as Isou) 243, 244, 246, 257
Gomringer, Eugen 9
Green, Renée 288, *290*
Greenberg, Clement 121, 175
Gregori, Giovanni and Gregorio de *56*
Gris, Juan 125, 239
Grosz, George 142, *143*, *144*
Group Material 287, *290*
Guilbaut, Serge 243
Gysin, Brion *218*

Haack, Horst 346–64, *348*, *349*, *351*, *352*, *353*, *355*, *356*, *357*, *359*, *361*, *362*
Haacke, Hans *297*, 298
Hains, Raymond 9, 253, *254*, 256
Hakuin, Ekaku 12
Hamilton, Richard 252–3, *253*
Hausmann, Raoul 112, 113, 142, 143, *145*
Heartfield, John122, 143, *146*
hieroglyphs (Egyptian) 7, 11, 37
Höch, Hannah 143, 145, *146*, *147*
Hoffmann, Josef 31, 197
Hogarth, William *65*, *66*, 67, 69, 70
Holman Hunt, William 26, *27*, 77, *77*, *78*, 82, *84*
Holzer, Jenny 226, *226*, *227*, 236, 236, 286
Hoover, J. Edgar 369, *377*, *379*
HSBC (Hong Kong & Shanghai Banking Corporation) 232, 233, *234*, 236
Hughes, Arthur *81*, 82
Hugnet, Georges 165
Hugo, Victor 17, 252, *252*

Independent Group, the 252, 253, 287
Indiana, Robert 216, *216*
Isou *see* Goldstein, Jean-Isidore

Jaar, Alfredo *219*, 220, 228, *230*, 236, 287
Jahan, Pierre 8
Jakobson, Roman 115, 186, 187
James, Henry 83–4
Jenson, Nicolaus *34*
Jess (Collins) 175
Jin Nong 12
Johns, Jasper 221, *224*, 225, *260*, 262, *264*, 265, 284, 310, 316
Jorn, Asger 246, *255*, 256, *256*, 257, 258, 332

Kabakov, Ilya *273*, 275
Kahnweiler, Daniel-Henri 114–15, 116
Kandinsky, Wassily 27, 183, 188
Kauffman, Angelica 59, *59*
Keats, John 36, *36*, 37, 57, 77–8
Kiefer, Anselm 279, *283*, 284
Kivland, Sharon *295*, 296
Klein, Yves 9, 256
Klosterneuberg, Austria 319, 320, 322
Klutsis, Gustav 148
Kolář, Jiří 270, *271*, 273
Komar, Vitaly 275
Kosuth, Joseph 236, *267*, 270
Kruger, Barbara 226, *228*, *229*

Léger, Fernand 117, 125, *126*, 128, 140
Leiris, Michel 152
Lemaître, Maurice 244, 246
Leonardo da Vinci 27
Lessing, Gotthold Ephraim 15, 62, 114, 175, 181, 182, 190, 192
Levner, Bill 239
Lewis, Wyndham 17
Lichtenstein, Roy *261*, 262–3, 265
Lippi, Filippino 23, *23*
Lissitzky, El 146, 148, *149*
Liu Maoshan 23–4, *24*
Lombardi, Mark 296–8, *296*
London Underground map 29
London Heathrow Airport 232, 233
Lorenzo Veneziano 41, *41*
Lower Austria Psychiatric Hospital 317, 320, 326
Lund, Brian 303, 305, *307*

Magritte, René 163, 164, *164*, 165, 166, *166*, 167
Mallarmé, Stéphane 8, 112, 114, 121, 122, *123*, 154
Man Ray 137, *139*, 140, 169, *171*
Manchester 382
Mantegna, Andrea 42, 44
Marcoussis, Louis 162
Marinetti, Filippo Tommaso 111, 112, *113*, 114, 121, 125, 129, 188, 191, *191*
Martin, John 69–70, *70*
Masson, André 155
Matta-Clark, Gordon 284–5, *284*
McCahon, Colin 329–45, *331*, *332*, *333*, *334*, *335*, *337*, *338*, *340*, *341*, *343*
Melamid, Alexander 275
Metropolitan Museum of Art, New York 57

Michaux, Henri 9, 17, 155, *158*
Michelangelo 87, 181–2
Millais, Sir John Everett 59, 78, *79*
Milton, John 65, 67, 69, 103, 104
Miró, Joan 24, 110, 149, 151–2, 153, 154, *154*, 155, 160, 162, 163
Mitchell, W.J.T. 35–6, 62, 106, 226, 238
Moholy-Nagy, László *29*, 213
Morland, George 70, *71*
Morris, Robert 16, 225, *225*
Morris, William 31, *31*
Mulready, William *81*, 82
Murphy, Dudley 140
Murray, Fairfax 31

Nauman, Bruce 137
Naville, Pierre 158
Navratil, Leo 319–20, 321
New York 148, 239, 243, 260, 285
New York Times see The Yes Men
Nill, Annegreth 205, 207

Opalka, Roman *268*, 269, *269*
Ordnance Survey maps 29

Palm, Gustaf Wilhelm 19, 20
Palma (il) Vecchio *58*, 59
Paolozzi, Eduardo 252, 253
Paris 121, 124, 128, 158, 188–90
Pettibon, Raymond 332, 365–79, *366*, *367*, *368*, *369*, *370*, *371*, *372*, *373*, *374*, *375*, *376*, *377*, *378*
Picabia, Francis 130, 134, 135–6, *136*, 137–8, *137*, 139, 140, 141, 172
Picasso, Pablo 116–17, *118*, 119, 120, 121, 122–4, *122*, *124*, 125, 126, 149, 170, 190, 191
Pino, Francisco 9
Pittman, Lari *294*
Pivovarov, Viktor *272*, 273
Pollock, Jackson 9, 329, 332
Pomerand, Gabriel 244, *244*
Pound, Francis 335, 336–7, 339
Poussin, Nicolas 24–5, *25*, 57
Prince, Richard 236, *236*, *237*
Psalter of Henry the Lion *18*

Queen Mary Psalter 30, *30*
Quills (film) *8*
Quinones, Lee 285

Ramsay, Allan *74*
Ramsden, Mel 266, *269*
Raphael 181–2, *182*
Rauschenberg, Robert *240*, *241*, 243
Reinhardt, Ad 239, 243, 269
Repton, Humphry 73, *74*
Rodchenko, Alexander 112, *114*, 121–2, 125, 148, 149, 151
Romains, Jules 128
Rosenblum, Robert 117, 121
Rosler, Martha 220, 287, *289*
Rossetti, Dante Gabriel 17, *80*, 81
Rossetti, William Michael 78
Rouen Cathedral, St Hubert 49, *49*
Royal Academy of Arts, London 26, 74, 78, 88
Rozanova, Olga 130, *134*
Rumney, Ralph 216, *217*, 258
runes 7
Ruscha, Ed *214*, *274*, *275*, 276, 278, 296
Rushton, Dave *220*
Ruskin, John 75, 82–3
Ruthwell Cross, Bewcastle 48, *49*

Sade, Marquis de *8*, 169, *171*, 244
Saltram, Devon *72*
Samokhvalov, Alexander 150
San Marco, Venice 19, 20
Sant, James 82
Sartre, Jean-Paul 243
Saussure, Ferdinand de 115
Scanlan, Joe 219, 307, *308*, *309*, 310
Schneeman, Carolee 220, 231, *276*, 278–9
Schwitters, Kurt 139, 145–6, *148*, 203–13, *204*, *206*, *207*, *208*, *210*, *211*, *212*, *213*
Severini, Gino 128, 130
Shakespeare, William 65, 67
Shelley, Ward *231*
Sherborne Missal *54*, 55
Simpson, Lorna 287, 292, *293*
Smithson, Robert 252, 288
Solomon R. Guggenheim Museum, New York 24, 27, 298
Sotheby's (auction house) 275
Spero, Nancy 155, 300
sst (Systematic Record Distribution) 371
Stark, Frances 219–20, 299, 301, *301*, 302
Steinberg, Saul 249–50, *251*, 252
Stothard, Thomas *67*, 88
Sturtevant, Elaine 216

Swedenborg, Emanuel 92, 93

Tanguy, Yves 155, 157, 160
Tennyson, Alfred, Lord 65, 81–2
The Royal Art Lodge 250
The Yes Men 233, *234*, *235*, 236
Titchner, Mark *231*
Tobey, Mark 9
Tufte, Edward R. 299
Turner, J. M. W. 26, 73–5, *75*, *76*, *77*
Twombly, Cy 9, *259*, 260, 262, 310, *312*, *313*, *314*, *315*, 316

Vikings *see* runes
Villeglé, Jacques 253, *254*, *255*, 256
Villeneuve, engraver *9*
Vogtherr, Heinrich *53*

Walker, Kara 296, 310, *311*, 316
Walla, August 317–28, *318*, *319*, *320*, *322*, *323*, *324*, *325*
Wang Hui 23, *24*
Warhol, Andy 216, 262–3, *263*, 276, 287
Wearing, Gillian 279, *282*
Webster, Thomas 82
Weiner, Lawrence 9, 287
Wölfli, Adolf 10, 246
Wolman, Gil J. 256
World's Fair, Paris (1937) 149, 151
Wright, Joseph, of Derby 69, *69*
Wyeth, Andrew 20, *22*

Yeats, W. B. 35
York Minster 39–41

Zuccarelli, Francesco 67